THE ARMED VISION

Stanley Edgar Hyman

The
ARMED VISION

*A Study in the Methods of Modern
Literary Criticism*

"The razor's edge becomes a saw to the armed vision."
SAMUEL TAYLOR COLERIDGE: *Biographia Literaria*

ALFRED A. KNOPF: NEW YORK
1952

PUBLISHED MAY 24, 1948
SECOND PRINTING, AUGUST 1952

To Shirley Jackson

A CRITIC OF CRITICS OF CRITICS

BUT IN REALITY there is another light in which these modern critics may, with great justice and propriety, be seen; and this is that of a common slanderer. If a person who pries into the characters of others, with no other design but to discover their faults and to publish them to the world, deserves the title of a slanderer of the reputation of men, why should not a critic, who reads with the same malevolent view, be as properly styled the slanderer of the reputation of books? Vice hath not, I believe, a more abject slave; society produces not a more odious vermin; nor can the devil receive a guest more worthy of him, nor possibly more welcome to him.

—*Henry Fielding*

I TAKE UPON ME absolutely to condemn the fashionable and prevailing custom of inveighing against critics as the common enemies, the pests and incendiaries of the commonwealth of Wit and Letters. I assert, on the contrary, that they are the props and pillars of this building; and that without the encouragement and propagation of such a race, we should remain as Gothic architects as ever.

—*Anthony, Earl of Shaftesbury*

AS TO THE HERD OF CRITICS, it is impossible for me to pay much attention to them, for, as they do not understand what I call poetry, we talk in a foreign language to each other. Indeed, many of these gentlemen appear to me to be a sort of tinkers, who, unable to *make* pots and pans, set up for *menders* of them, and, God knows, often make two holes in patching one.

—*Sir Walter Scott*

FIRST-RATE CRITICISM has a permanent value greater than that of any but first-rate works of poetry and art.

—*Matthew Arnold*

KILL THE DOG, he is a reviewer.

—*Johann Wolfgang von Goethe*

FOR IT IS CRITICISM which removes mountains.

—*Georg Brandes*

THE REALLY COMPETENT CRITIC must be an empiricist. He must conduct his exploration with whatever means lie within the bounds of his personal limitation. He must product his effects with whatever tools will work. If pills fail, he gets out his saw. If the saw won't cut, he seizes a club.

—*H. L. Mencken*

THE MAIN IDEAL of criticism, as I conceive it, is to use all that there is to use.

—*Kenneth Burke*

AH, IF WE only had decent critics!

—*Anton Chekhov*

FOR I AM nothing, if not Criticall.

—*Iago*

PREFACE

THE AIMS of this book are comparatively simple: first, to study the nature of modern critical method as exemplified by selected contemporary literary critics; second, to note the ancestry of their techniques and procedures, both as disciplines in themselves and as gradual developments in the history of criticism; third, to suggest some possibilities for an integrated and practical methodology that would combine and consolidate the best procedures of modern criticism. ("Integrative" is the good word, Kenneth Burke remarks in one of his books, for a method that the reader who preferred a bad word could call "eclectic.") The third aim, which is the least fully treated in this book, is probably the most important, in so far as modern criticism, as it has become increasingly specialized and efficient, has become increasingly partial and fragmentary. A number of contemporary critical methods in actual fact require the critic to know only one thing well, his own discipline, and to have read only one book, the one under discussion. An integrated method would require the knowing and reading of "all," or at least a good deal more. To each contemporary critic's limited "efficiency," an integrated method would thus oppose a "counter-efficiency" in a wider context, so that the Freudian, the Marxist, the scholar, the folklorist, etc., would have to become a Freudian *plus*, a Marxist *plus*, etc. The possibilities for such an integrated method, however, can only be sketched out here in the most tentative fashion.

The things it is *not* the intention of this book to do can be demarcated with equal sharpness. It is not a study of æsthetic or philosophic theory, of critical theory or definitions, or of specific literary judgments by critics. The important question, for this book at least, is not what the critic *says* but what he *does*, and chiefly the principal thing he does, the "essence" of his work. Thus where previous commentators on Edmund Wilson's work, including Wilson, have identified it as psychological or historical criticism, its core would seem to be neither of these, but criticism by "translation" or paraphrase; where some writers on Yvor Winters have emphasized his activities as a moralist, and others his activities as a technical or logical critic, these seem clearly secondary to

ix

his function as an evaluator; and so forth. At the same time, except incidentally, this book is not a study of critics, but of method as exemplified in the practice of critics, the only place it can be exemplified or discussed at all. In the attempt to take the emphasis off the man and put it on the method as far as possible, most of the following chapters contain a section on the development of some aspects of the method in the past, and a section discussing a few other contemporary critics who use a comparable method with greater or lesser success.

There is no claim that the twelve critics here discussed are the only modern critics, or the best, or the best using their respective methods, or that their methods are the only ones, or the best. They are all, however, serious men and women doing something of significance, and among them are a number of our finest practitioners of the art. Beyond that, they have been selected simply for their usefulness as illustrating techniques and procedures that seem fruitful. It is thus a matter of deep regret that a number of important American critics, among them F. O. Matthiessen, John Crowe Ransom, Allen Tate, Cleanth Brooks, Ezra Pound, and others, have been omitted, because their work either does not illustrate a significant method, or does not illustrate it as clearly as the work of someone else; and the same thing is true of valuable British critics like John Middleton Murry, Herbert Read, G. Wilson Knight, the *Scrutiny* group, and others. Some attempt has been made to discuss the work of these men briefly in the relevant chapters. In addition, it has proved impractical to devote chapters to the work of men who have not published a body of criticism available in book form, thus entailing the neglect of several very significant critics, like Francis Fergusson and William Troy, who have not so far published volumes of criticism, as well as of a number of greatly promising younger men. In addition, no chapters are devoted to contemporary critics writing in any but the English language (although a number of European critics are treated briefly in the relevant chapters). This is due in part to my inadequate familiarity with contemporary European criticism, in greater part to the fact that, on the basis of that inadequate examination, the phenomenon discussed in this book as "modern" criticism does not seem to exist to any degree at this time anywhere but in England and America, although its sources are to be found in almost every European literature.

Finally, this book makes no attempt to be stylistically impressive: it is written in as simple a style and vocabulary as possible, as befits an explanatory work; it makes no attempt to be impartial, but is frankly both biased and opinionated, with my own bias and opinions; and although it attempts to explain what a number of contemporary critics are doing, neither its information nor its opinions are authorized in any fashion: it makes no claim to speak officially for the critics it examines, or even that they would agree with its contentions, and no chapters were

submitted for the approval of their subjects or result from any con-
sultation with them on other than a few purely factual matters.

I hope in the future to be able to illuminate and document some of
my contentions and provide an accompanying volume of examples, by
compiling an anthology or symposium of critical essays to illustrate the
methods here discussed. I additionally hope that some attempt will be
made by others to examine the applicability of some of the methods and
principles treated in this book to other fields of criticism besides the
literary—among them music, the graphic and plastic arts, the theater,
and the dance—since that ability is at the moment, and will perhaps
always be, beyond my competence.

ACKNOWLEDGMENTS

PARTS OF THIS BOOK have appeared in *Accent, The Antioch Review, The Kenyon Review, The New Mexico Quarterly Review, Poetry: a Magazine of Verse,* and *The Western Review,* and are reprinted through the kindness of the editors. Two passages from T. S. Eliot's "East Coker" are printed with the kind permission of Harcourt, Brace and Company. I have drawn freely and gratefully on a number of reference and survey works for some of the information in my background sections, especially on George Saintsbury's *History of Criticism,* J. E. Spingarn's *A History of Literary Criticism in the Renaissance,* and Herbert J. Muller's *Science and Criticism.* Throughout I have tried to acknowledge the source of any observation not original with me, but one of the special problems of dealing with literary critics is the li̶k̶e̶l̶i̶h̶ood that in a number of cases I have remembered th   heir phrasing as my own, and for all such neglecte   by apologize.

My pe   is extensive. I am grateful to my former students a   both in my Criticism class and elsewhere, for teachii   than I taught them; as well as to Mrs. Gladys Le   ns, and the staff of the Bennington College Li   every sort. Bernard Smith, formerly with Alfrec   bert Weinstock and members of the present staf   elpful. My friends and various colleagues hav   ossible fashion: providing me with information or   nformation, lending or giving me books and other m   on matters of every sort, helping me to read copy   and to transfer corrections, toning me down or stirring me up as the occasion warranted, criticizing and suggesting, and in many cases even telling me what to say and how to say it—although they are far too many to list by name, I would like each of them to know my gratitude. Without The Seven Bookhunters, who seemed at times to suspend every other activity in order to find me needed books, this work would have been far more difficult; and without June Mirken, who kindly typed it for me and made the index, it would have been impossible.

Three of my debts are so great that no expression of gratitude can do them justice. One is to Harold Ross and William Shawn of *The New Yorker*, whose unparalleled kindness allowed me to combine working for them with writing this book. To Leonard Brown, who is, as Ascham said of Sir John Cheke, "teacher of all the litle poore learning I haue," I am obligated, quite literally, for anything of value the book may contain. Finally, the book's indebtedness to my family is as great as such things can possibly be: to my children, who somehow bore with it over the years; to my parents, who facilitated it in every way possible; and most particularly to my wife, Shirley Jackson, who did everything for me that one writer can conceivably do for another and whose patience and kindness in regard to it are worthy of a far better work.

S.E.H.

North Bennington, Vermont
January 1948

CONTENTS

THE ARMED VISION

INTRODUCTION

MODERN LITERARY CRITICISM

1. *Its Nature*

THE LITERARY CRITICISM written in English over the past quarter of a century is qualitatively different from any previous criticism. Whether you call it the "new" criticism, as many have, or "scientific criticism," or "working criticism," or, as this book does, "modern criticism," its only relation to the great criticism of the past seems to be one of descent. Its practitioners are not more brilliant or alert to literature than their predecessors; in fact they are clearly less so than giants like Aristotle and Coleridge, but they are doing something radically different with literature, and they are getting something radically different from literature in return. What modern criticism is could be defined crudely and somewhat inaccurately as *the organized use of non-literary techniques and bodies of knowledge to obtain insights into literature.* The tools are these methods or "techniques," the nuggets are "insights," the occupation is mining, digging, or just plain grubbing. The non-literary techniques are things like psychoanalytic associations or semantic translations, the non-literary bodies of knowledge range from the ritual patterns of savages to the nature of capitalist society. And all of these result in a kind of close reading and detailed attention to the text that can only be understood on the analogy of microscopic analysis.

The key word of this definition is "organized." Traditional criticism used most of these techniques and disciplines, but in a spasmodic and haphazard fashion. The relevant sciences were not developed enough to be used methodically and not informed enough to have much to contribute. The bodies of knowledge of most usefulness to criticism are the social sciences, which study man functioning in the group (since literature is, after all, one of man's social functions), rather than the physical or biological sciences (since literature is not a function of the human structure in the sense that walking or eating is, but a part of the cultural or societal accretion). Although Aristotle clearly aimed to turn what we now call the social sciences on drama and poetry, to study them in terms of what he knew of the human mind, the nature of society, and primitive survivals, he had few data to apply beyond his own empiric observations, brilliant as they are, and unverified traditions. The miracle Aristotle

3

performed, the essential rightness of his criticism, based almost entirely on private observation and keen sensibility, is a triumph of critical insight hitting largely by intuition on a good deal later discovered and developed. Even by Coleridge's time, two thousand years later, not much more was known accurately about the nature of the human mind and society than Aristotle knew.

A good deal of criticism, of course, is contemporary without being modern in the sense defined above; that is, it makes no organized critical use of any of this material (it is surprising, however, how much unconscious use it makes). Although such criticism has a place, and frequently an important one, it is by definition another kind of thing and not our concern here. At the same time, besides its special functions or the special degree to which it does things done only haphazardly and informally before, modern criticism does a number of things that criticism has always done: interpreting the work, relating it to a literary tradition, evaluating it, and so on. These are relatively permanent features of any criticism (evaluation, we might note, has largely atrophied in the serious criticism of our time), but even where a modern critic tends to specialize in one of these more traditional functions, he does so along with other less traditional things, or in a fashion profoundly modified by the characteristic developments of the modern mind.

John Crowe Ransom, who has been chiefly influential in popularizing the term "the new criticism" with his book of that name, insisting on its qualitative difference from earlier criticism (on the basis of the modern detailed reading in "the structural properties of poetry"), has claimed that ours is an age of more than usual critical distinction, and that in depth and precision contemporary critical writing is "beyond all earlier criticism in our language." There is, I think, little doubt of this, but we cannot flatter ourselves that the superiority lies in the caliber of our critics as opposed to their predecessors. Clearly, it lies in their methods. Modern criticism has vast organized bodies of knowledge about human behavior at its disposal, and new and fruitful techniques in its bag of tricks. To the extent that some of this can be consolidated and the erratic, sometimes unbalanced and incomplete, if brilliant work of a number of isolated critics co-ordinated and integrated, vistas for the immediate future of criticism should be even greater, and a body of serious literary analysis turned out in English of a quality to distinguish our age.

Among the methods and disciplines that have been established as useful for literary criticism, the social sciences come to mind first, a reservoir so vast that it has hardly yet been tapped. From psychoanalysis critics have borrowed the basic assumptions of the operations of the subconscious mind, demonstrating its deeper "wishes" through associations and "clusters" of images; the basic mechanisms of dream-distortion, such as condensation, displacement, and splitting, which are also the basic mechanisms of poetic-formation; the Jungian concept of archetypes, and much else. They have taken the concept of "configurations" from the gestalt-ists; basic experimental data about animal and child behavior from the laboratory psychologists; information about the pathological expressions of the human mind from the clinical psychologists; discoveries about the behavior of man in groups and social patterns from the social psycholo-gists; and a great deal more, from Jaensch's "eidetic images" and similar purely subjective material to the most objective physical and chemical data reported by neurological and endocrinological psychologies. From competing sociologies criticism has borrowed theories and data regarding the nature of society, social change, and social conflicts, and their relation to literature and other cultural phenomena; and from anthropological schools, theories and data regarding primitive and savage societies and social behavior, from the sweeping evolutionary generalizations of theorists like Tylor to the meticulously observed detail of the Boas school. An offshoot of anthropology, the field of folklore, has also been of particular fruitfulness to criticism as a source of information about the traditional popular rituals, tales, and beliefs that underlie the patterns and themes of both folk art and sophisticated art.

In addition to the social sciences, a number of other modern disciplines have been very fruitful, or are potentially so. Literary scholarship, al-though hardly a new field, has by our century accumulated so great a body of accurate information and so exact a body of procedures that with the addition of critical imagination it has been made to produce a type of scholarly criticism completely "modern" in the sense used above. The traditional scholarly areas of linguistics and philology, with the addition of the modern field of semantics, have opened up to criticism enormous vistas, only slightly explored. The physical and biological sciences have provided criticism with such basic ingredients as the experimental method itself, as well as theories of great metaphoric usefulness, like "evolution" and modern physical "relativity," "field," and "indeterminacy" concepts. Philosophy, although traditionally concerned with literature only in the guise of æsthetics, has proved of use to criticism, particularly in ethical and metaphysical formulations with which it can confront questions of ultimate value and belief; and a number of critics have even turned the doctrines and insights of religion and mysticism on literature. Besides these bodies of theory and knowledge, modern criticism has developed a number of specialized procedures of its own and methodized them, some-times on the analogy of scientific procedure. Such are the pursuit of biographical information, the exploration of ambiguities, the study of symbolic action and communication in literary works, and close reading, hard work, and detailed exploration of texts in general.

For the most part these new critical techniques and lines of investiga-tion depend on a small number of assumptions that are basic to the modern mind and characteristic of it, assumptions that are principally the contributions of four great nineteenth- and early twentieth-century thinkers—Darwin, Marx, Frazer, and Freud. A few of those key assumptions, relatively new to literary criticism in our century, can be noted here at random, with the reservation that probably no single modern critic would accept them all. From Darwin, the view of literature as an evolutionary development, within the work of a single author and in larger patterns outside him, changing and developing (although not necessarily "improving") in orderly sequence. From Marx, the concept of literature as reflecting, in however complex and indirect a fashion, the social patterns and conflicts of its time. From Freud, the concept of literature as the disguised expression and fulfillment of repressed wishes, or the analogy of dreams, with these disguises operating in accord with known principles; and underlying that, the even more basic assumptions of mental levels beneath consciousness and some conflict between an expressive and a censorship principle. From Frazer, the view of primitive magic, myth, and ritual underlying the most transcendent literary patterns and themes. Other basic assumptions would include Dewey's doctrine of "continuity," the view that the reading and writing of literature are a form of human activity comparable to any other, answerable to the same laws and capable of being studied by the same objective procedures; the behaviorist addition that literature is in fact a man writing and a man reading or it is nothing; and the rationalist view that literature *is* ultimately analyzable. Negatively modern criticism is equally distinguished by the absence of the two principal assumptions about literature in the past: that it is essentially a type of moral instruction, and that it is essentially a type of entertainment or amusement.

Operating on these assumptions, modern criticism asks a number of questions that have, for the most part, not been asked of literature before. What is the significance of the work in relation to the artist's life, his childhood, his family, his deepest needs and desires? What is its relation to his social group, his class, his economic livelihood, the larger pattern of his society? What precisely does it do for him, and how? What does it do for the reader, and how? What is the connection between those two functions? What is the relation of the work to the archetypal primitive patterns of ritual, to the inherited corpus of literature, to the philosophic world views of its time and of all time? What is the organization of its images, its diction, its larger formal pattern? What are the ambiguous possibilities of its key words, and how much of its content consists of meaningful and provable statements? Finally, then, modern criticism can get to the older questions: what are the work's intentions, how valid are they, and how completely are they fulfilled; what are its meanings (plural rather than singular); and how good or bad is it and why?

All of these, obviously, are questions asked about literature, either in general or of a specific work. Nevertheless, modern criticism for the most part no longer accepts its traditional status as an adjunct to "creative" or "imaginative" literature. If we define art as the creation of meaningful patterns of experience, or the manipulation of human experience into meaningful patterns, a definition that would probably get some degree of general acceptance, it is obvious that both imaginative and critical writing are art as defined. Imaginative literature organizes its experiences out of life at first hand (in most cases); criticism organizes its experiences out of imaginative literature, life at second hand, or once-removed. Both are, if you wish, kinds of poetry, and one is precisely as independent as the other, or as dependent. "No exponent of criticism . . . has, I presume, ever made the preposterous assumption that criticism is an autotelic art," T. S. Eliot wrote in 1923, in "The Function of Criticism." Whether or not anyone had made that "preposterous assumption" by 1923, modern criticism, which began more or less formally the following year with the publication of I. A. Richards's *Principles of Literary Criticism*, has been acting on it since.

As R. P. Blackmur has pointed out, however, criticism "is a self-sufficient but by no means an isolated art," and in actual practice modern criticism has been at once completely autotelic and inextricably tied to poetry. That is, like any criticism, it guides, nourishes, and lives off art and is thus, from another point of view, a handmaiden to art, parasitic at worst and symbiotic at best. The critic requires works of art for his raw material, subject, and theme, and in return for them performs such invaluable secondary functions on occasion as helping the reader understand and appreciate works of art; helping the artist understand and evaluate his own work; and helping the general progress and development of art by popularizing, "placing," and providing standards. The critic also, in special cases, calls up a generation of poets, as Emerson or the early Van Wyck Brooks did; assigns subjects for writers as Gorky or Bernard DeVoto do; changes the course of art or attempts to, with Tolstoy and the moralists in the latter category, and Boileau and perhaps the romantic critics in England in the former; or even furnishes the artist (sometimes himself) with specific themes, techniques, and usable formulations, as do a number of contemporary critics of poetry.

In one direction literary criticism is bounded by reviewing, in the other by æsthetics. The reviewer, more or less, is interested in books as commodities; the critic in books as literature or, in modern terms, as literary action or behavior; the æsthetician in literature in the abstract, not in specific books at all. These are thus functional rather than formal categories, and they are constantly shifting, so that the reviewer who ignores the commodity aspects of the book under discussion to treat of its significance as a work of literature becomes, for that review at least, a critic; the critic who generalizes about the abstract nature of art or the beautiful becomes, temporarily, an æsthetician; and the æsthetician who criticizes specific works of literature in terms of their unique properties is at that time a critic. One of the most remarkable features of our time is the number of ostensible critics, like Henry Seidel Canby or the brothers Van Doren, who on examination turn out to be disguised reviewers.

Another feature of contemporary criticism worth remarking is that each critic tends to have a master metaphor or series of metaphors in terms of which he sees the critical function, and that this metaphor then shapes, informs, and sometimes limits his work. Thus for R. P. Blackmur the critic is a kind of magical surgeon, who operates without ever cutting living tissue; for George Saintsbury he is a winebibber; for Constance Rourke he is a manure-spreader, fertilizing the ground for a good crop; for Waldo Frank he is an obstetrician, bringing new life to birth; for Kenneth Burke, after a number of other images, he has emerged as a wealthy impresario, staging dramatic performances of any work that catches his fancy; for Ezra Pound he is a patient man showing a friend through his library; and so forth.

The methods and techniques of modern criticism noted above filter through these master metaphors and also filter through something even more intangible, the critic's personal apparatus of intelligence, knowledge, skill, sensibility, and ability to write. No method, however ingenious, is foolproof, and almost every technique of modern criticism is used brilliantly by brilliant critics and poorly by stupid, ignorant, incompetent, or dull ones (as the succeeding chapters of this book will attempt to demonstrate). On the other hand, a good man possessed of the critic's virtues may operate well or brilliantly, today as at any time, with no method but the application of his own intelligence and sensibility. He would not be a modern critic in our sense of the term, however, and is not our concern here. Any critic, no matter what his method, needs the intelligence to adapt it specifically to the work with which he is dealing; the knowledge, both literary and otherwise, to be aware of the implications of what he is doing; the skill to keep from being picked up and carried away by his method to one or another barren and mechanical monism; the sensibility to remain constantly aware of the special values of the work he is criticizing as a unique æsthetic experience; and the literary ability to express what he has to say. There is no test for these personal characteristics. Even Shakespeare, the traditional touchstone, is not much help: the two men who have most distinguished themselves in contemporary criticism by disrespect for Shakespeare have been Waldo Frank, a professional exhorter to piety only slightly concerned with literature of any sort, and John Crowe Ransom, one of the subtlest and most acute critical minds of our day. In the last analysis, these personal capacities are incalculable, and in a discussion of critical method objectified and abstracted from the living critic they can only be presumed or, more honestly, prayed for.

One of the principal implications of modern criticism is its development toward a science. In the foreseeable future, literary criticism will not become a science (we may be either resigned to this or grateful for it), but increasingly we can expect it to move in a scientific direction; that is, toward a formal methodology and system of procedures that can be objectively transmitted. As an experiment can be copied and checked from the report, at any time and place by anyone capable of the necessary manipulations, so will critical procedures be capable of repetition by anyone with the requisite interest and ability. The private sensibility is unique with the critic and dies with him; his methods will increasingly be capable of objective transmission. The reproducer, it goes without saying, will need a sensibility and other qualifications roughly comparable to the originator's, in a sense that has not been true of physical science since the beginnings of the experimental method. (That is, a fool and a boor, granted elementary competence, by repeating Boyle's experiments will get the same results that Boyle did.) Furthermore, no matter to what extent the method of critical analysis becomes a body of objective procedures, with the words "evaluation" or "appreciation" the critic will always be entering a purely subjective area: whether the good man's reasonable superstructure built on objective analysis or the bad man's indefensible whim or whimsy.

The other principal implication of modern criticism is its development in the direction of a democratic criticism, Edmund Burke's hopeful doctrine of "every man his own critic." Burke writes in his essay on *The Sublime and Beautiful*: "The true standard of the arts is in every man's power; and an easy observation of the most common, sometimes of the meanest things, in nature will give the truest lights, where the greatest sagacity and industry that slights such observation must leave us in the dark, or, what is worse, amuse and mislead us by false lights." This is, piously, the view that the unaided powers of any man make him a critic. The directly contrary view is Francis Bacon's in *Novum Organum*, that the adoption of his method would equalize all minds, as a compass or a rule equalizes all hands. Somewhere between the two lie the democratic possibilities for modern criticism: by extending method, *more* men can be capable critics, in most cases not professionally, but in their private reading and their lives. And the vested interests *that* possibility menaces are much bigger game than the priesthood of literary criticism.

II. *Its Ancestry*

MODERN LITERARY CRITICISM, we might say, begins with Plato and is continued and extended by Aristotle. Actually, of course, they were its great forerunners, anticipating, as they anticipated so many things, much of contemporary critical practice. Plato turned his dialectical philosophic method, as expounded in Books V and VII of *The Republic*, on poetry, as well as psychological and social assumptions about its origin and functions. If his conclusion was to reject it philosophically as too far removed from the true Platonic reality, and socio-psychologically as harmful to the good society, his method was nevertheless the modern method of bringing to bear on it all the organized knowledge he had. In Aristotle's case there has been a recent effort, by the neo-Aristotelian school of criticism at the University of Chicago, to insist that he applied no deductive knowledge or principles whatsoever to poetry, but merely examined poems inductively as formal organizations unique in themselves. This view has been demolished by, among others, John Crowe Ransom (in "The Bases of Criticism," in the *Sewanee Review*, Autumn 1944) and Kenneth Burke (in "The Problem of the Intrinsic," reprinted as an appendix to *A Grammar of Motives*). Burke in addition demonstrated that not only was Aristotle thoroughly "Platonic" in his practice, but that so are the neo-Aristotelians, surreptitiously, precisely at their most successful. It takes no more than a reading of the *Poetics* to establish that, although Aristotle worked as inductively and close to the specific text as the neo-Aristotelians would have him, at the same time he continued much of Plato's approach, deepening Plato's charge of *mimesis* or imitation to give poetry philosophic validity, and substituting a sounder socio-psychological concept, *catharsis*, for Plato's inadequate concept of poetic function as harmful stimulation of the passions. In addition to analyzing poetry by means of these remarkably explicit philosophic, social, and psychological *a priori* assumptions, Aristotle also turned on it an embryonic anthropology, traditions of the primitive origins of Greek drama, that has turned out to be surprisingly accurate to later anthropological, archæological, and philological research (despite such inevitable flaws as his concept of the choric song as a mere "embellishment" to tragedy). Aristotle thus anticipated the chief features and techniques of the literary criticism we have come to call "modern."

Later classical and medieval critics continued one or another of these modern strains, from Aristarchus and the scholiasts in the second century before Christ, writing an embryonic social criticism, to Dante, Petrarch, and Boccaccio in the fourteenth century, furnishing allegorical interpretations of literature very close to what we would now call "symbolic" readings. The modern environmental criticism of literature began with Vico's *New Science* in 1725, which includes a social and psychological interpretation of Homer; it developed more fully (apparently independently of Vico) in Montesquieu's work, particularly *The Spirit of Laws* in 1748. After this Italian and French origin, the movement spread principally in Germany through the latter half of the eighteenth century, shifting its focus from history and law to literature and art. In the work of Winckelmann, Lessing, and Herder it became an aspect of burgeoning German nationalism. Winckelmann began it in 1764 with his *History of Ancient Art*, which studies Greek plastic art in terms of its political, social, and philosophic background; Lessing continued it, principally in his *Laocoön* two years later, with particular emphasis on the relativity of forms in historical usage and the importance of Aristotle's principles; Herder developed the environmentalist approach still further, increasing the method's relativism by opposing folk art and Gothic to the classic-worship of Winckelmann and Lessing, extending Vico's dynamic historical concepts in his own *Philosophy of History* and emphasizing a comparative method in all the fields he touched (making him the ancestor of our modern fields of comparative philology, comparative religion and mythology, and comparative literary study).

All of this flowered in the next century in the work of the first really great modern critic, Coleridge, in England, and in a substantial school in France. The *Biographia Literaria*, published in 1817, is almost the bible of modern criticism, and contemporary critics have tended to see it, with Arthur Symons, as "the greatest book of criticism in English," and, with Herbert Read, as "the most considerable." On its first page it announces the manifesto for modern criticism: the application of Coleridge's political, philosophic (including psychological), and religious principles to poetry and criticism. The *Biographia* was thus a century in advance of its time, and only the inadequacy of the knowledge available to him kept Coleridge from founding modern criticism then and there. He is, however, with the exception of Aristotle, certainly its most important progenitor. His work found no one to carry it on, unfortunately, and when the doctrines of environmentalist criticism reappeared in England, in H. T. Buckle's *History of Civilization in England* in 1857, they were derived not from Coleridge but from his German predecessors and his French successors.

Meanwhile, the German doctrine of literature as an expression of society was brought to France by Madame de Staël in *Literature in Relation to Social Institutions* (1800), which was responsible in part for such diverse progeny as the rationalist history of Guizot, the populist history of Michelet, and the skeptical history of Renan, as well as for the biographical literary criticism of Sainte-Beuve and the sociological literary criticism of Taine. Sainte-Beuve was the point at which the whole earlier tradition split in two. On the one hand, he saw criticism as a social science, "the natural history of literature," with a methodical procedure that studies the author, in the words of MacClintock in *Sainte-Beuve's Critical Theory*, in relation to "his race, his native country, his epoch, his family, his education and early environment, his group of associates, his first success, his first moment of disintegration, his peculiarities of body and mind, especially his weaknesses," and much else. This is the tradition that continues in Taine, Brandes, Brunetière. On the other hand, Sainte-Beuve insists, in his criticism of Taine, in "M. Taine's History of English Literature," that the critic must also "continue to respect and inhale the scent of that sober, delicately perfumed flower which is Pope's, Boileau's, Fontanes'." This second tradition has been continued in the line through Arnold, Babbitt, and Eliot, equally indebted to him. Sainte-Beuve defines the combination of the two schools as the formula for the perfect critic, but admits that the hope of this reconciliation in one man is "an impossibility," "a dream." So it has proved to be for most of a century, at least, although in our time we might express the same hope with somewhat more reason.

Taine himself claimed the historical imagination of Lessing and Michelet as part of his ancestry, and in the incidental literary analyses in the latter's *History of France*, some of them sharp class-anglings (like the reading of *Manon Lescaut* as an expression of the small landed gentry before the Revolution), the resemblance to Taine is obviously more than a matter of historical imagination. At the same time Taine's three principal criteria for criticism—*race, moment, milieu*—had all been anticipated by Sainte-Beuve, who got them from Hegel's *Zeit, Volke, Umgebung*, which were in turn derived from Herder. Taine thus brought to a focus most of the earlier tendencies toward a scientific criticism, and his work logically enough became the target for all attacks on these tendencies. The Goncourts, for example, wrote very superciliously on meeting him: "This was Taine, the incarnation in flesh and blood of modern criticism, a criticism at once very learned, very ingenious, and very often erroneous beyond imagining." Perhaps the sharpest and most perceptive recognition of his weaknesses and the weaknesses of a good deal of modern criticism, more perceptive than Sainte-Beuve's strictures, came from Flaubert, who wrote in one of his letters, on the *History of English Literature:*

There is something else in art besides the milieu in which it is practiced and the physiological antecedents of the worker. On this system you can explain the series, the group, but never the individuality, the special fact that makes him this person and not another. This method results inevitably in leaving *talent* out of consideration. The masterpiece has no longer any significance except as a historical document. It is the old critical method of La Harpe exactly turned around. People used to believe that literature was an altogether personal thing and that books fell out of the sky like meteors. Today they deny that the will and the absolute have any reality at all. The truth, I believe, lies between the two extremes.

In 1869 Flaubert wrote to George Sand on the subject of critics: "At the time of La Harpe they were grammarians; at the time of Sainte-Beuve and Taine they were historians. When will they be artists—really artists?" It was a question not to be answered for half a century.

The next major development in modern criticism came in 1912 and the years immediately following. That year Jane Ellen Harrison, a professor of Greek studies at Newnham College, Cambridge, published *Themis: A Study of the Social Origins of Greek Religion*. The book includes "An Excursus on the Ritual Forms Preserved in Greek Tragedy" by Gilbert Murray, to whom the book is dedicated, and "A Chapter on the Origin of the Olympic Games" by F. M. Cornford, one of Miss Harrison's colleagues at Cambridge. Although most of it is Miss Harrison's independent work, *Themis* thus constituted a kind of collective manifesto of what is known as the Cambridge school of classical scholarship, which completely revolutionized the study of Greek art and thought by turning on it the anthropological knowledge and theories of Sir James G. Frazer and his followers.[1] Both Murray and Miss Harrison had published before, the latter in fact for more than a quarter of a century, but *Themis* is the first full statement of their ritual view of origins and the first really detailed application of anthropology to the analysis of literature, here the Greek drama. Since in addition to printing and using Murray and Cornford, Miss Harrison drew heavily on unpublished work by another colleague, A. B. Cook, and by others, it also constitutes a genuinely collective production by the group. Shortly afterwards, the same year, Cornford published *From Religion to Philosophy*, a similar anthropological tracing of the ritual origins of Greek philosophic thought.[2] In 1913 Murray published *Euripides and His Age*, a study of Euripides and his drama against the background of the ritual origin of tragedy, and Miss Harrison published *Ancient Art and Ritual*. The following year Cornford published *The Origin of Attic Comedy*, which analyzes Greek comedy in the same terms, and Cook published *Zeus*, an application of anthropological material to still another area. Finally, in 1920, Miss Jessie Weston, with great success, tried the method of the Cambridge school on non-Greek material in her *From Ritual to Romance*, an anthropological exploration of the origins of the grail romances in ritual terms.

[1] In fairness to indignant Oxonians, it should be pointed out that Oxford scholars, among them Murray and Andrew Lang, had sketched out the techniques for applying not only Frazer's disreputable Cantabrigian anthropology, but Sir E. B. Tylor's authentic Oxonian anthropology to literature as early as 1907, in the symposium *Anthropology and the Classics*, edited by R. R. Marett, and that Murray had published *The Rise of the Greek Epic* the same year.

[2] 1912 was a watershed year for more than this. It also saw the publication of F. C. Prescott's "Poetry and Dreams" in the *Journal of Abnormal Psychology*, the first detailed and authentic application of psychoanalysis to poetry by a literary man.

Although these books, for all practical purposes, are modern literary
criticism, as the work of scholars writing in fairly specialized fields they
failed to attract the attention of literary men sufficiently to inaugurate
the new movement. In America in 1919 Conrad Aiken turned Freudian
and other psychologies on poetry in *Scepticisms* and clearly formulated
the basic assumption of modern criticism, that poetry is "a natural,
organic product, with discoverable functions, clearly open to analysis."
Like the Cambridge group, however, he lacked the literary influence to
set criticism following out his assumption. It remained for I. A. Richards's
Principles of Literary Criticism in 1924 to constitute the formal beginnings
of modern criticism with a variant of the same statement: that æsthetic
experiences are "not in the least a new and different kind of thing" from
other human experiences, and can be studied in the same fashion. It was,
as we have noted, no new doctrine (not only had Aiken specifically
anticipated it five years before, but John Dewey had stated substantially
the same thing as his doctrine of the "continuity" of experience as early
as his *Studies in Logical Theory* in 1903, and Aristotle had clearly operated
on that assumption), but this time it was supported by the tremendous
prestige of Ogden and Richards's *The Meaning of Meaning*, published the
year before, it carried general conviction, and it bore fruit in a quarter
of a century of modern literary criticism.

The battle, of course, is not yet won. The past century has seen critic
after critic quarrel with every assumption or method of modern criticism,
including every type of knowledge that might be brought to bear on
literature, and even the basic assumption of continuity. At one end of the
scale these attacks are the simple pettishness of James Russell Lowell in
a review of Longfellow, mocking the modern critical view that "the form
of an author's work is entirely determined by the shape of his skull, and
that in turn by the peculiar configuration of his native territory," and
Ludwig Lewisohn, in his Preface to Rank's *Art and the Artist*, dismissing
all modern criticism since Taine offhand for leaving Hamlet out of the
play. At the other end of the scale they include the reasoned skepticism
of Chekhov, writing to Suvorin in November 1888, noting the amount
of "rubbish" by "blockheads" that scientific criticism, working from ir-
reproachable principles, has produced; or of Anatole France, in a criticism
of Brunetière in *La Vie littéraire*, proposing the same balance and reservations Sainte-Beuve had earlier proposed:

As a matter of pure theory a critical method is conceivable that,
proceeding from science, might share the latter's certainty. . . .
All things in the universe are inextricably intertwined. In reality,
however, the links of the chain are, in any given spot, so jumbled
that the devil himself could not disentangle them, even if he were a
logician. . . . One cannot foresee today, whatever one may say,

a time when criticism will have the rigorousness of a positive science. One may even believe, reasonably enough, that that time will never come. Nevertheless the great philosophers of antiquity crowned their cosmic systems with a poetics. And they did wisely. For it is better to speak of beautiful thoughts and forms with incertitude than to be forever silent. Few things in the world are so absolutely subject to science that they will let science reproduce or predict them. And one may be sure that a poem or a poet will never be among those few. . . . If these things sustain a relation to science, it is to one that is blended with art, that is intuitive, restless, forever unfinished. That science or, rather, that art exists. It is philosophy, ethics, history, criticism—in a word, the whole beautiful romance of man.

A number of critics have found themselves sharply split on the matter. Thus John Middleton Murry, in *The Problem of Style*, attacks "the fantastic dream" that criticism "might be reduced to the firm precision of a science," and "the vain hope" of giving its language "a constant and invariable significance," but later in the same book proposes an equally scientific (or mechanistic) social and economic criticism, including a one-to-one correlation between economic and social conditions and artistic and literary forms, and even *An Economic History of English Literature*. Allen Tate, an outstanding product of the assumptions of modern criticism and practicer of its methods, in *Reason in Madness* attacks the social sciences as the fundamental menace, as well as modern criticism itself, which he calls "the historical method," and in which he lumps, along with history, the use of the physical, biological, social, and political sciences in criticism. Similarly, John Crowe Ransom has at one time or another attacked the use of science in criticism, been violently opposed to social sciences like anthropology, and announced that he does not share Max Eastman's "sanguine expectations" for psychology, while himself drawing brilliantly on all three in his own criticism.

Probably more damaging to modern criticism than the attacks by good men and the ambivalence in some of its practitioners has been its enthusiastic defense by men whose own practice ranges from weak to execrable. Thus Louis MacNeice, in *Modern Poetry*, announces a watered-down form of Richards's continuity doctrine, that poetry is a normal activity, the poet being "a specialist in something which every one practices," but then fails to follow up that assumption in the book by turning any knowledge whatsoever on poetry. It would be hard to find two more violent enthusiasts for scientific criticism in recent times than Max Eastman, writing a manifesto in *The Literary Mind* for "a department of science which will have literature as its object of study," and V. F. Calverton, in *The New Ground of Criticism*, eloquently advocating a

criticism that will synthesize psychology, sociology, and anthropology—
and it would be equally hard to find two worse or more infuriating critics
in our time. A comparable mistrust is inspired by Henri Peyre. He makes
the very shrewd statement in *Writers and Their Critics:* "Modern criticism is still groping for its method and enthusiastically experimenting
with several techniques. It has not yet outgrown the primitive stage in
which physics similarly fumbled before Bacon and Descartes, chemistry
before Lavoisier, sociology before Auguste Comte, and physiology before
Claude Bernard." Then in the book Peyre reserves his sharpest attack for
precisely those methods—of social, psychological, textual, and other
analysis—and precisely those critics—Richards, Empson, Burke, and
Blackmur—who most clearly represent the attempt of criticism to outgrow the primitive stage he describes.

At the same time modern criticism has been regularly under attack by
the invested enemy, the reviewers and the professional obscurantists. A
characteristic illustration of the first, worth quoting for its typicality, is
a review by Orville Prescott that appeared in the *New York Times,*
March 28, 1945. The book under discussion is Florence Becker Lennon's
study of Lewis Carroll, *Victoria through the Looking-Glass*. Prescott
writes:

> Miss Lennon has performed prodigies of research, but in spite of
> her conscientious labors her book is disappointing and tedious. The
> enchanting magic of the Alice books defies analysis. To seek its
> source in Freudian probings into Carroll's complexes and repres-
> sions is as fruitless as to attempt to find explanations for a butter-
> fly's flight or the lightning's choice of a target. Genius mysteriously
> exists; and flowers into enduring treasures as inexplicably.
>
> That Carroll lived a blameless bachelor life is true; but then
> some men are bachelors from choice and quite content with their
> lot, in spite of Miss Lennon's Freudian suspicions. That Carroll
> liked the company of little girls better than that of boys or adults
> is also true, and rather odd of him. But all Miss Lennon's solemn
> pryings into his psyche, into the sexual symbols of his books, just
> don't seem to get anywhere.
>
> . . . But Lewis Carroll, to whom "hardly anything ever hap-
> pened," led a singularly blank life. . . .
>
> But Lewis Carroll led a life without exterior conflict of any
> kind, and with few inner ones (just those vague religious hesita-
> tions). He knew neither love nor close friendships. He was a good
> man and a good Christian. He tried to get his own salary reduced
> and he insisted on a publishing contract that insured that he himself
> would bear any possible loss. But his life was dull and colorless. . . .

As these quotations should make clear, in the course of attacking Miss Lennon's psychoanalytic study Prescott gives all the reasons why a psychoanalytic study seems very much to the point, and in the course of insisting that Carroll's life was uneventful fills it full of the most remarkable events. Like many contemporary reviewers, Prescott attacks modern criticism seemingly not so much out of malice as out of simple ignorance. In other cases, such as J. Donald Adams's weekly column in the *Sunday Times* and his book *The Shape of Books to Come*, malice and a kind of shrill venom are added, and the picture clearly is of the happily superficial reviewer fighting to preserve his status and investment in what he thinks is criticism against a mob of sans-culottes.

The attack by the professional obscurantists is a more complicated matter. Perhaps the best example is Mark Van Doren, whose approach to criticism, consistent with his St. John's College approach to education, is opposed to the inroads of any modern knowledge whatsoever. In the Preface to *The Private Reader* Van Doren has written the most complete and eloquent attack on modern criticism with which I am familiar. He describes it as "deserts of ingenuity and plateaus of learning," reproaches it with "doing all it can to arrest the lyric in its flight," concludes that "it is at best a faulty science . . . not an art." To it Van Doren opposes a pure obscurantism: "Arnold was wrong in the emphasis he placed upon ideas"; "We do not know that much about poetry, and we never shall"; "undiscussable," "the mystery," and so on. The piece is remarkable for its tone of bitter elegy, beginning on a theme of exile ("contemporary criticism, a house in which I no longer feel at home"), rising to a wail of keening ("Our literary age is sick"), and ending on the imagery of self-extinction ("My only ambition as a critic is henceforth to be one of those nameless strangers with whom writers dream that they communicate. Poetry itself can do with silence for a while"). The final comment on Van Doren's slogan of "private reading," the bringing of nothing to bear on literature but the reader's attention, was made accidentally by I. A. Richards. He writes in *Interpretation in Teaching*:

> The remedy, I suppose, is growth, which will occur if testing occasions enough force the adolescent survivals of the child's dreamworld habit to withdraw into their proper place. Unluckily, private reading—when it is only a partially controlled form of dreaming—is a protection from such tests. It too often becomes a romantic preserve for mental processes which are relatively extinct in fully waking life.

Contemporary with modern criticism, along with embattled reviewers and obscurantists, are the violently controversial schools of æsthetic and philosophic doctrine that have enlivened the literary magazines in the past: impressionists and expressionists, neo-humanists and naturalists, classicists and romanticists, positivists and anti-positivists, etc. Their current successor seems to be the largely pointless quarrel between the neo-Aristotelians and the neo-Platonists or neo-Coleridgeans. All of these schools and controversies have their function, but it tends to be one of debating large generalities and saying little so far as actual method is concerned. In one way or another they are all contemporary blind alleys for the man really concerned with the analysis of literature. While the bricks are flying overhead, the serious modern critic will tend to be down in the mine, digging away. He gets his hands dirtier, but he may also turn up a nugget now and then.

CHAPTER 1

EDMUND WILSON

and Translation in Criticism

IN A DAY when a wide gap exists between serious literature and the reading taste of the public, that part of the critic's function which requires him to serve as a conduit between the obscure or difficult work and the reader attains a great importance. Edmund Wilson is probably our foremost practitioner in this field of interpreting or "translating" the content of literature, and it is no accident that with the exception of Van Wyck Brooks (a special case of merchandising) he is probably the most widely known of our critics. The great translators of the Tudor period made the resources of other literatures available by rendering them into English from other languages, and it is ironic and perhaps significant that in our own day a comparable need exists for translation *within* the language.

Wilson has phrased his work as providing "scenarios" for poems, and there is no doubt that many of his "scenarios" have been invaluable. There must be any number of people who owe to Wilson their first intimation that Joyce or Eliot can be understood and is worth reading for pleasure (just as there are probably many others who are indebted to him for synopses that permit the display of literary knowledge without any reading whatsoever). His first work, *Axel's Castle* (1931), probably had an effect in our time, in opening up a whole new area of literature to a wide audience, second only to that of T. S. Eliot's *The Sacred Wood*. *Axel's Castle* is memorable for Wilson's dogged pages of detailed interpretation of the symbolisms of Eliot's *Waste Land*, for the amazing thirty pages that summarize Proust's giant novel almost scene by scene, for the lengthy recital of the incidents of Joyce's *Ulysses* and their significance, and for similar labors. No one is so well equipped as Wilson to tell the novice reader why Eliot's nightingale calls "Jug Jug," or what Stephen Dedalus's mother means to the story, or that the noonday in Valéry's *Le Cimetière marin* is at once inorganic nature, the absolute in the poet's mind, his twenty years of inaction, and the noonday itself.

Sometimes Wilson's exegesis is subtle symbolic analysis; sometimes, as in the long synopses of *Yevgeni Onyegin* and *The Turn of the Screw* contained in the Pushkin and James chapters in *The Triple Thinkers*

19

(1938), it is straight plot-summary, incident by incident, like an under-graduate précis. Sometimes it is remarkably ingenious, as where he translates Shaw's *The Apple Cart* into musical terminology, and some-times merely overambitious, like the attempt to compress the theoretical heart of Marxist thought into two paragraphs in *To the Finland Station* (1940). At all times, to the relatively uninformed reader at least, it continues to be stimulating, and sometimes it is essential.

Wilson is at his best as an "introductory critic," a term that John Macy defined as "one who by his own skill and charm summons strangers to make the acquaintance of a great man." The introductory critic suffers the handicap, however, that his value decreases in direct proportion to the literacy of his audience and its familiarity with the work he is dis-cussing, until it becomes almost nil for the relatively informed reader. Wilson is fully aware of this, has always consciously slanted his writing at the uninformed reader, and has always thought of himself as primarily a "popularizer." In an autobiographical essay, "Thoughts on Being Bibliographed," in the February 1944 issue of the *Princeton University Library Chronicle*, devoted to a bibliography and discussion of his work, he wrote:

> There remained for the young journalist, however, two roads that had still to be broken: the road to the understanding of the most recent literary events in the larger international world—Joyce, Eliot, Proust, etc.—which were already out of the range of readers the limits of whose tastes had been fixed by *Egoists* and *The Quintes-sence of Ibsenism;*[1] and to bring home to the "bourgeois" intellec-tual world the most recent developments of Marxism in connection with the Russian revolution. I was of course far from being either alone or first in popularizing either of these subjects; but they were the matters with which I was mostly concerned, and I felt that what I was doing had some logical connection with the work of the older men I admired.

(The "older men" referred to, incidentally, are Shaw, Mencken, and Huneker, perhaps the three most eminent "popularizers" of the gen-eration before Wilson's own.) Wilson has sometimes spoken slightingly of his summaries, paraphrases, and synopses. Reviewing Lionel Trilling's *Matthew Arnold* in the *New Republic*, he remarked that Trilling's sum-maries of Arnold's poems and essays "become occasionally a little dull," and added parenthetically: "Anyone who has ever tried it, however, knows how hard it is to make this kind of thing readable." He is thor-oughly aware, nevertheless, that as a writer of epistles to the philistines, his summaries are as essential as they would be in an opera program.

[1] Note that Wilson is apparently still writing for precisely that group of readers, long after it has disappeared.

Wilson has many abilities that make him an excellent popularizer. He writes clearly and readably and is able to work the most recondite material into simple and comprehensible English sentences. He has a wide reading, or at least a competent lay background, in a number of the primary fields that filter into literature, including history, philosophy, and psychology, particularly those two chief conditioners of the contemporary literary mind, Marxism and psychoanalysis. He has, for an American literary critic, an unusual command of languages, including Latin and Greek (Wilson is sometimes given to printing untranslated passages of Sophocles in his essays, and he once had the temerity to correct a Greek rendering of Irving Babbitt's), French, and (learned in middle age for the purpose of aiding his researches into Marxism) German and Russian.

Another attribute of Wilson's, perhaps less admirable, that makes him an excellent interpreter of literature is his skillful use of other men's researches and insights, sometimes without credit. In his Joyce material in *Axel's Castle* and *The Wound and the Bow* (1941), for example, Wilson relied on data from such miscellaneous sources as Stuart Gilbert's authorized interpretation, Herbert Gorman's biography, Max Eastman's dubious interview, the collection of *transition* articles by a dozen writers published in Paris as *Our Exagmination round his Factification for Incamination of Work in Progress*, and several others. For information on Marxism, Wilson acknowledged the aid of at least a dozen contemporaries, including such "authorities" as Max Eastman, Sidney Hook, Mark Starr, Max Nomad, Herbert Solow, and Mary McCarthy, besides a number of more official sources. On Russian literature Wilson used D. S. Mirsky's two histories and his study of Pushkin, de Vogüé's *Le Roman russe*, and many of the specific insights of Vladimir Nabokov, whose translations he has been working with for several years. (Wilson is quite possibly indebted to Nabokov for the remarkable, and quite uncharacteristic, detailed analysis of musicality in a poem by Pushkin he printed in his Pushkin article in the *Atlantic Monthly*, an analysis that seems to represent a remarkable acquaintance with the Russian language on Wilson's part and seems at the same time very characteristic of Nabokov.) In fact, almost all of Wilson's pieces show this skillful use of primary analysis, sometimes amplified or revised, sometimes merely rendered into more popular terminology. In addition Wilson has drawn on almost every creative modern critic, frequently again without credit, for theory, as well as on a wide variety of other sources for various specialized and technical information.[2]

---

[2] The direct charge of critical cribbing, or straight dishonesty, is a risky one to make in print, and a difficult one to prove. I have been many times informed, for example, by people in a position to know, that at least three full-length theses covering much of the material in *Axel's Castle* appeared in France in the decade before the book's publication, but no one has ever attempted to trace in print Wilson's unacknowledged

In addition to his knowledge and his ability to draw on the knowledge of others, Wilson is excellently qualified for the kind of translation and interpretation he does by a genuine critical shrewdness, an ability to perceive relationships and generalize from them. The evidences of this ability in his books are far too many to list, but in so far as prediction is the test of analysis, it is worth noting that Wilson has made a number of literary predictions that have panned out, not the least of them the judgment in *Axel's Castle* (1931) that Eliot's talent is essentially dramatic and that he would inevitably move in the direction of verse drama.[3]

Along with these formidable qualifications for exegesis, Wilson suffers from a number of limitations and inadequacies. The most basic of these (undoubtedly both the chief source of his success as a popularizer and the greatest threat to his seriousness as a critic) is his fundamental view of literature, which he sees in terms of a completely separate form and content, the content being the work itself and the form merely a device for presenting it. In his excellent study "The Writing of Edmund Wilson," in *Accent* for Spring 1942, Delmore Schwartz expressed this (which is almost the first thing a reader of Wilson notices) in a valuable metaphor. For Wilson, Schwartz writes, literary form is "the wrapping-paper which covers the gift; it is necessary to spend some time taking off the wrapping-paper and undoing the difficult knots of the cord tied around it, but the main thing is the gift inside, the subject matter."

From this point of view, poetry would be no more than prose statements forced into an unnecessarily complex form, and that is precisely what poetry is for Wilson, who is at his worst in dealing with it and seems generally to dislike it. Wilson himself renounced the career of poet formally in 1929, in a series of five elegiac poems called *Poets, Farewell!* ("I leave that speech to you who have the tongue"), and although he has written verse since, it is now obviously casual and avocational.

Wilson has been announcing the obsolescence or death of poetry at least since *Axel's Castle*, when he wrote that the poetic personality seemed to be becoming extinct, that poetry is a "more primitive and more barbarous" technique than prose, and that, as Valéry said, poetry or imaginative literature is based on the *abuse* of language and will even-

indebtedness to these works, if it exists.

William Troy, who has a special interest in Joyce criticism, where such borrowings are particularly flagrant, has come close to making the charge against other critics, delicately, in a review in *Partisan Review*, July–August 1947, identifying a "neo-academic group of scholars," including Harry Levin, Richard M. Kain, and others, who seem "unconcerned about sources."

[3] In noting, in his discussion of John Steinbeck in *The Boys in the Back Room* (1941), Steinbeck's tendency to present human life "in animal terms," Wilson shrewdly anticipated a development that has become much more obvious in Steinbeck's subsequent works. This is perhaps a special case of prediction, however, because the same tendency is so strong in Wilson's own fiction and reporting as to make him something of an authority on the phenomenon.

tually be replaced by the proper use of language, scientific communication. Since then he has carried on a constant sniping at poetry in his reviews, articles, and books, particularly in the chapter of *The Triple Thinkers* entitled "Is Verse a Dying Technique?"

There is little point in discussing the arguments involved in Wilson's obituary for poetry, except to say that they are based on a series of redefinitions of the terms "poetry," "prose," and "science" so drastic that once the definitions are granted, further arguments are unnecessary, and poetry could be immediately relegated to the status of filigree work or frosting. In fact, Wilson claims that the best modern prose *is* poetry, or what used to be called poetry, and that Flaubert "marks the self-conscious taking-over by prose of the delicacy, precision and intensity which had formerly been applied to large human subjects almost exclusively through the medium of verse."

Wilson analyzes and judges poetry badly and tends to avoid the job whenever he can. It is worth noting that in his critical introduction to Mallarmé's highly obscure sonnet *"Le Tombeau d'Edgar Poe,"* in his anthology *The Shock of Recognition* (1943), instead of discussing the poem, Wilson reprinted Roger Fry's commentary, surely an unequaled job of shirking in a professional critic. This inability to handle poetry is particularly noticeable in an estimate of the American writers of the time, which Wilson published in the *New Republic* in 1926. Although the evaluations of prose hold up exceptionally well after two decades (just as we do now, he felt "more interest" in Dos Passos and Fitzgerald than in such contemporary giants as Lewis, Hergesheimer, Cabell, and Cather), the judgments of poetry are flatly absurd (Marianne Moore's work is "rarely precipitated out as poems," Wallace Stevens "has a fascinating nonsense gift of words . . . and he is a charming decorative artist," William Carlos Williams "I have never been able to believe in," and so forth).

A number of other factors limit Wilson's potentiality as a popularizer. He has never been able to work his plot-summaries and synopses into his articles architecturally, and his work is full of such awkward transitions and interpolations as: "In that part of the book which we are discussing," "In the section which I have just been discussing," "First, however, we may pause a moment to examine" (these three all in one page), "To return, however, to the story where we left it" (that classic of the synopsizer), "Let us go through the story from the beginning," and so on. Wilson's simplifications frequently become oversimplifications, and his popularizations entirely *too* popular. As Malcolm Cowley has pointed out, *Axel's Castle* loses a great deal of its point because Wilson merges symbolism as a literary technique and symbolism as a way of life as though they were the same thing. This has the disastrous result of leading him, in his conclusion, into such absurdity as the statement that the writers he has been discussing have in general taken Axel's course, the cultivation of private fantasy, instead of living in the real world, when all he can properly say is that their writing is obscure, as the example of Yeats at least should make clear. (This too efficient popularization and constant either-or fallacy are particularly obvious in *To the Finland Station*, which sometimes reads enough like *Crucibles* or *Microbe Hunters* to suggest that it might have been called *Men Who Made Our Marxism* and sold to the Junior Literary Guild.) It is probably a fundamental criticism of *Axel's Castle*, for example, that although it was meant as an attack on the post-symbolist writers as a literary dead end and dismisses them all in the last chapter in favor of a new socially responsible writing, its tone throughout is so sweetly appreciative that it achieved success as a *vade mecum* to the writers, a job of sympathetic introductory criticism. Surely this is an efficiency in being for and against at the same time that few critics have ever achieved.

Along with this tendency to be overwhelmed by the responsibilities of popularization, Wilson seems to have a genuine weakness of taste. "An enthusiasm for Poe is the mark of a decidedly primitive stage of reflection," Henry James wrote with great accuracy of perception, and Wilson long ago put himself in the forefront of the Poe claque in our time. He has been booming Poe in print at least since his novel *I Thought of Daisy* in 1929, and in a review of Van Wyck Brooks's *The World of Washington Irving* he made Brooks's enthusiasm for Poe one of the chief evidences of the book's value. For him Poe has a first-rate mind "like a bright vivid shaft," and belongs, "not with O. Henry and S. S. Van Dine," but with "the great inquiring and versatile minds like Goethe." Furthermore, Poe's criticism is "the most remarkable body of criticism ever produced in the United States" (in the favorable sense of "remarkable"), and Poe himself is "a prince."

Wilson's great respect for Poe would be a pardonable eccentricity, perhaps even some form of personal identification, were it alone, but it becomes more significant accompanied as it is by an equally great respect for such writers as Mencken (whom he has confessedly imitated) and Edna St. Vincent Millay (who is "one of the sole surviving masters of English verse" and, with Robinson and Eliot, one of the three contemporary poets most likely to survive as "first-rate poets of the full stature"). As Delmore Schwartz has pointed out, Wilson's "tenderness" toward such authors as Millay, Thornton Wilder, the later Van Wyck Brooks, Max Eastman, and Henry Miller is chiefly significant because of a contrasting "indifference or aversion to" men like Gide, Kafka, Mann, and Rilke, and both lists could be much further prolonged. Schwartz calls this, charitably, a "lack of critical pioneering," but it seems to be a basic superficiality. The man who can write that "Kubla Khan" is a nonsense poem like "Jabberwocky," "The Jumblies," and

"The Owl and the Pussycat" is simply a man who suffers from a defect of sensibility.

As a corollary, Wilson either cannot or will not follow things through, and his typical evasion is the passage from *Axel's Castle:*

> This discussion would, of course, lead us, if we pursued it, to the nature of language itself and hence to the mysteries of human psychology and what we mean when we talk about such things as "reason," "emotion," "sensation" and "imagination." And this must be left to the philosophers. . . .

These things are, oddly enough, the very things which the critic in our time *cannot* leave to the philosophers, but must concern himself with to the best of his ability. They constitute the cornerstone of any serious discussion of literature. The fact that Wilson has never permitted himself to go into them is merely another evidence that the attempt to interpret, "translate," and promote major literature on no more solid a basis than sharp reading and eclecticism cannot result in more than flashes of insight at its best and in the shoddy popularization of "100 Great Books Digested" at its worst.

2

The Wound and the Bow is neither Wilson's best book nor his most typical, but it is the most profitable to study from the point of view of method because it represents the extreme to date of his "translating." Moreover, it is the most consistently organized about a theory of literature (whereas *Axel's Castle* was organized only around the faulty analogies of Axel and Rimbaud, *The Triple Thinkers* around Flaubert's conception of the artist's godlike function, *To the Finland Station* around the nature of history, and *The Boys in the Back Room* around the geography of California). In *The Wound and the Bow* all of Wilson's tendencies reach a kind of fruition. Of the seven essays in the book, four deal with novelists—Dickens, Kipling, Edith Wharton, and Hemingway—one with the author of a memoir, Casanova; and two with specific works of art, James Joyce's *Finnegans Wake* and Sophocles' *Philoctetes*. Thus from *Axel's Castle*, at least half of which dealt with poets and poetry, through *The Triple Thinkers*, where the proportion of poetry to total content was something less than a third, to *The Wound and the Bow*, which slights poetry almost entirely, a definite progression is evident. Moreover, Dickens and Kipling, the subjects of the first two long chapters that together make up about two thirds of the book, are probably the two best choices conceivable for a man who specializes in plot-synopsis and summary.

Wilson's principal aim in these chapters, going beyond his plot summaries, is to establish both Dickens and Kipling as serious and tortured artists: Dickens as "incomparably the greatest English writer of his time" and Kipling as "among the few genuine masters of his day." His technique for achieving this aim is a remarkably canny one. In the Dickens chapter he has a preliminary discussion of Dickens's literary importance ("Dostoyevsky's master," etc.), then a section of biography with emphasis on Dickens's traumatic experience with his family's poverty and his work in the blacking-factory, then a detailed study of the novels with constant biographical reference, and finally, by way of conclusion, a long section summarizing and interpreting *The Mystery of Edwin Drood*, which Wilson uses as a dramatization of Dickens's dual personality, the "two Scrooges" displayed in John Jasper. Thus exegesis serves to make Dickens's work seem both obscure (that is, "deep") and revelatory of basic psychological truth (that is, "profound"), and demonstrates his importance as a major writer without actually affecting his easy readability. *Edwin Drood*, an unfinished and rather mysterious work, is an excellent choice for this complex function, but there is no doubt that by taking proportionately greater pains something comparable could be done with any of Dickens's works, or in fact with any work at all.

It is worth noting that Wilson still pays attention to psychology and sociology to the extent of using isolated insights—Scrooge is "the victim of a manic-depressive cycle," and the final implication of *Our Mutual Friend* ("to state it in the Marxist language") is that "the declassed representatives of the old professional upper classes may unite with the proletariat against the commercial middle class"—but his method seems increasingly to be straight translation. (It is at least possible, in this connection, that Wilson's rather surprising praise for T. A. Jackson's straight Marxist critique of Dickens in the book is not so much respect for the political point of view as one synopsizer's courtesy to another, since Jackson's little book spends 143 pages on straight plot summary, including a 40-page synopsis of *Our Mutual Friend*.)

The Kipling article is similar. Wilson analyzes the eclipse of Kipling's reputation; discusses his early life with particular emphasis on his childhood traumatic experience, desertion by his parents and consequent breakdown; discusses *Stalky & Co.* and *Kim* in some detail; and then spends the rest of the chapter interrelating Kipling's mature life, ideas, and writing, particularly emphasizing the frustration of his American experience as the key to his later bitter imperialism. The Kipling study is more directly psychological than that of Dickens, and Wilson's prime interest is in displaying Kipling's neurosis, the weakling's memory of the bully that resulted in Kipling's vicious counter-bullying and hatred of foreigners, Negroes, Jews, and democracy itself. Again, Wilson tries to exhibit his subject as an author of great power and importance, and if sometimes this leads him into unconscious comedy, as where he proposes

Kipling's stories as the ancestry of material as disparate as Ring Lardner's baseball stories and the Cyclops episode of *Ulysses*, it also leads him into perhaps the best interrelationship of life and works he has yet achieved. The books are here the direct key to the man, instead of vice versa (so that actually, in the end, we are left with case history rather than literary criticism), but the man himself, as an extreme of literary warp, is undeniably of great interest.

The shorter pieces in the book follow a similar pattern, with less necessity for overestimation. The Casanova chapter is a short appreciation, similar to those of Virginia Woolf but less expertly done, retelling some of the anecdotes in the *Memoirs* and proposing Casanova as a more attractive Rousseau. The "Justice to Edith Wharton" chapter is another short appreciation, with summaries and moderately overfavorable estimates of a number of her books, and a hint that her work originated in the mental troubles that afflicted both her husband and herself. The Hemingway chapter is a series of brief paraphrases of the stories and books one by one, rather superficial, with again no more than the suggestion of a "wound," the growing antagonism to women in the work, plus a postscript vastly overestimating *For Whom the Bell Tolls*, in which Hemingway has fully "sloughed off his Stalinism." The chapter called "The Dream of H. C. Earwicker" is an interpretative précis of *Finnegans Wake*, very detailed for the time it was written (immediately after the publication of the book), but naturally incomplete in terms of the revelations since. Wilson relies heavily on the *transition* articles for his material (acknowledging that without them he doubts whether "it would be possible to get the hang of the book at all"); for his most detailed analysis, of a complicated passage on Swift's blindness (which seems to have been excluded from the final draft of the book!), he has simply taken over Robert McAlmon's explanation, "which I take to be more or less authoritative."

The final chapter, on the *Philoctetes* of Sophocles, is meant to be the integration of the book as well as the statement of Wilson's most recent literary theory and emphasis. "The bees of our English criticism do not often roam so far afield for their honey," Matthew Arnold wrote on a similar occasion, in words that may be applied to Wilson's use of Sophocles, "and this critic deserves thanks for having flitted in his quest of blossom to foreign parts, and for having settled upon a beautiful flower found there." Wilson discusses Sophocles' play and other works on the subject of the Philoctetes legend, and through them the legend itself and its possibilities as a fable on the nature of art, in which superior strength is always inseparable from some disability. (It is worth noting that Wilson finds that Sophocles projected himself into Philoctetes, and further points out that the figure of Philoctetes has always interested the psychologically disordered, including Gide, John Jay Chapman,

Lamb—and presumably Wilson himself, who has apparently been fascinated by the character for many years.)

What *The Wound and the Bow* needs badly is a final chapter of explanation and integration, generalizing the wound-and-bow metaphor and summarizing and relating the various "wounds" and "bows" of the authors discussed. Without such a chapter the book is to a certain extent a cheat, since Wilson in a number of cases only hints at the wound and leaves the reader to make the deductions and conclusions. The trouble with this procedure is that every writer (and non-writer) has a "wound" of some sort, and Johnson's *Lives of the Poets*, for example, could be called *The Wound and the Bow* just as efficiently, in that the reader can supply "wounds" to each of Johnson's subjects, sometimes from his data, and then interpret their "bows" or art in terms of them. The necessity is to show how and why this *specific* wound results in this *specific* art. Wilson does this crucial job of relating in the cases of Dickens and Kipling, but leaves the reader to fill out from the evidence in the chapter or even from his own knowledge the implications of Casanova's "heritage of moral squalor," Mrs. Wharton's breakdown, Hemingway's "men without women" problem, Joyce's blindness and exile, and Sophocles' amorous torture (which Wilson has, incidentally, only on the basis of the one celebrated reference in Plato's *Republic*).

The significance and possibilities of this theory and the metaphor for it will have to be discussed in a later section, but it should be pointed out here that the theory itself is not new for Wilson. Schwartz finds it to be the central theme of *I Thought of Daisy*, an acceptance of the personal unseemliness of artists as inseparable from their art, and there is no doubt that it figures implicitly in the criticism as early as *Axel's Castle*, where Joyce's magnificent verbal music is seen as the other side of his poor sight and Proust's novel as a function of his physical and psychological ailments (although Proust's chief "wound," his homosexuality, Wilson slides over euphemistically). *To the Finland Station*, in fact, is almost a parody of the doctrine, and there are times when Marxism seems to be no more for Wilson than the sum total of Marx's insomnia, carbuncles, boils, influenza, rheumatism, ophthalmia, toothache, headache, enlarged liver, and excremental obsession, not to speak of Lassalle's syphilis and Bakunin's impotence. ("I hope that the bourgeoisie as long as they live will have cause to remember my carbuncles," Marx once wrote to Engels, and one bourgeois at least has never forgotten them.)

3

Wilson's work is traditional in a sense that most contemporary criticism is not. Next to evaluation, interpretation or "translation" has probably been the chief function of criticism since antiquity. The Greeks recognized and named hermeneutics, the science of interpretation, of which the exegesis of texts is the practical application. Anaxagoras, more than a century before Aristotle, displayed interpretative, even symbolist, criticism very similar to Wilson's in his analysis of the imagery of Homer, translating the arrows of Apollo as the rays of the sun and Penelope's web as the processes of the syllogism, and Saintsbury lists other early Greeks who have come down to us as interpreters of Homer, among them Anaximander, Stesimbrotus, and Glaucus or Glaucon. The interpretation of such mythical Greek figures as Hercules and Theseus as symbols of virtue was developed by the Sophists and thoroughly exploited by the later Stoics, and with the spread of Christianity the same techniques were naturally turned on the Bible, which succeeded Homer and mythology as the chief subject of exegesis. Philo Judæus did the first allegorical translation of the Old Testament, and on the strength of St. Augustine's defense of the method the Biblical figures and stories gradually became accepted symbols for types of human virtue and moral struggle.

Fulgentius, in the sixth century, translated the _Æneid_ as an allegory on the human soul, and this tradition of interpreting both sacred and profane literature continued through the Middle Ages. Gregory the Great ascribed three levels of meaning to the Bible: the literal or historical, the allegorical or typical, and the tropological or moral, and later theologians added a fourth, the anagogical or mystical (all four of which Dante claimed for his _Divine Comedy_). Allegorical exegesis continued undiminished until almost the end of the Renaissance, with Petrarch still reading the _Æneid_ as a moral fable, Tasso interpreting his own romantic epics allegorically, and Sir John Harington, in the preface to his translation of the _Orlando Furioso_, attempting to Anglicize Gregory's medieval three levels of meaning. Allegorical moral interpretation in England received its death-wound with Bacon's statement in _The Advancement of Learning_ that works tended to be written first and the meaning added later, and Jonson buried the corpse with his revival of the Aristotelian concept of art as an imitation of life, and thus relatively an end in itself.

Naturally, allegorical interpretation in other forms and plural interpretation continued, and survive to this day in Biblical criticism and Dante scholarship, among others, but the main line of interpretative criticism became the essentially modern work of paraphrasing the obscure into the more easily comprehensible. Every critic since the Renaissance has done this to an extent, and almost no critic to the exclusion of other activity. When Dryden translated Chaucer into the English of his own time, with the defense that "the first aim of a writer is to be understood," he was engaging in a form of criticism that Wilson was to use, less formally, on Joyce; and when Balzac, a century and a half later, devoted more than half his long study of _The Charterhouse of Parma_ to an incredibly detailed summary of the plot, he was doing almost exactly what Wilson was to do later with Proust. Shakespeare criticism has been largely interpretive from the beginning, in part because of special problems of meaning arising out of the confusion of the texts. With the development of the Industrial Revolution, the rise of the romantic movement, and the progressive alienation of the artist from his public, with consequent maladjustment and "cultism," the necessity for interpretative criticism grew, and the criticism itself flowered.

By the nineteenth century, poets were spending as much time interpreting to the public their own work and the work of members of their circle as they spent writing poetry, and by the last quarter of the century, with the symbolist movement, the exegetical works themselves were written for a literary elite, and they too required elucidation. With our own century, and the shift in the status of writing from profession to trade and of book-publishing from trade to large-scale business, interpretative criticism and "translation" flowered at both ends of the literary scale. At the top, under the influence of Pound and Eliot, critics specialized in the most obscure authors available—Dante, Donne, Blake, Hopkins—by way of reaction (perhaps unconscious) to the commercialization of letters; and at the bottom, that commercialization itself created the mechanical popularization as a money-maker.

4

There are almost as many forms of translation and interpretation in contemporary criticism as there are critics. One of the most distinguished, almost too much a matter of personal attribute to be discussed as a method, is William Empson's exceedingly close reading for subtleties and ambiguities of meaning. A typical example is his amazing twelve-page analysis in *Some Versions of Pastoral* of a few of what he facetiously calls the "4,096 possible movements of thought" in Shakespeare's Sonnet 94, "They that haue powre to hurt, and will doe none." This is translation on the highest and most intricate level, with all the possibilities spread out on the page for consideration, and although it is certainly not popularization, being always a good deal more complex than the original, as a display of "reading" at its most intelligent it has markedly broadened literary communication in our time. Another contemporary form of translation, of equal intricacy though much greater singleness of line, is Kenneth Burke's symbolic analysis, which is exegesis and even paraphrase, like Wilson's, but on a deeper level of meaning. Where Wilson, for example, treats Joyce's puns simply as a complication of the meaning and translates them into intelligible statements, Burke translates the punning-form itself as a symbolic criminality, a rejection of Catholic pieties extended into rejection of the congruities of language, and thus reinforces the literal with a symbolic "content."

It is not surprising that many contemporary forms of translation have been exercised on the works of James Joyce, perhaps the richest field for it in modern literature. (Kafka runs a close second, as the anthology *The Kafka Problem* shows.) Almost all the books on Joyce and his work have been primarily exegetical. There have been a number of so-called "keys" to *Ulysses*, the only important one Stuart Gilbert's authorized commentary, an amazingly elaborate interpretative work; the collected *transition* articles and the *Skeleton Key to Finnegans Wake* by Joseph Campbell and Henry Morton Robinson have performed the same work on Joyce's last book. A vast number of articles, Wilson's two among them, have attempted partial translations of *Ulysses* or *Finnegans Wake*, and two young writers, Richard Levin and Charles Shattuck, in the Winter 1944 *Accent*, have even attempted an interpretation of Joyce's *Dubliners* on the basis of a Homeric parallel similar to that of *Ulysses*. Some sense of the problems of interpretative criticism today can be obtained from the realization that an "adequate" translation of either *Finnegans Wake* or *Ulysses* would have to embody all the individual insights of these books and articles, plus a great many more not yet obtained, would require at least a monumental knowledge of history, mythology, the geography of Dublin, philology, psychology, literary history, and the details of Joyce's own life, and would probably take, as Joyce remarked, perhaps jokingly, in his interview with Eastman, the critic's lifetime.

The source of serious interpretative criticism in our time (ignoring such historically important but artistically uninteresting jobs as William Lyon Phelps's on Russian literature) is probably Ezra Pound. By comparison with their megalomaniac originator, Pound's theories of criticism have always been curiously modest. He believes that the critic is no more than a man showing his library to a friend, pointing out books that the friend would probably like to read. However, as Pound said of Fenollosa and meant of himself, "the exotic is always a fructification," and frequently the items pointed out need translation in both the figurative and the literal sense. In *The Spirit of Romance*, published in 1910, Pound introduced the medieval literature of Latin Europe to ordinary literate readers in England and America for almost the first time. Patterning his book after Rossetti's *Early Italian Poets*, Pound discussed the literature of Italy, France, Provence, Spain, and Portugal and furnished innumerable examples of the poetry, with English translation, exegesis, and appreciation. The book is almost the perfect pattern for adult introductory criticism, popularization at a level of genuine literacy and good taste; and although Pound has done remarkable individual translations and interpretations since, including his exegetical studies of Arnaut Daniel, Cavalcanti, and Henry James, he never again achieved the solid usefulness of his first book.

While Pound went off into pigheadedness of various sorts, T. S. Eliot continued his friend's method of introductory criticism. The appearance of Eliot's *The Sacred Wood* in 1920 was a literary bombshell of major proportions, doing for the Elizabethans and other favorites what Pound had done for Cavalcanti and Daniel, but doing it, by audience standards, a good deal more successfully, so that Jonson and Marlowe almost rivaled Mencken and Cabell as literary hits of the twenties. Eliot assumed as much intelligence and taste in his readers as Pound did, but made much slighter demands on their education, and it is obvious, particularly in pieces like his studies of Dante and Seneca, that he presumes no previous familiarity with his subjects' work on the part of his public, and is undoubtedly right. Eliot wrote much shorter pieces than Pound did, almost always on individual writers, and lacking his preceptor's linguistic ability, specialized in temporarily neglected English writers (principally of the sixteenth and seventeenth centuries) and, when he did tackle a foreign writer, rarely did his own translating. Otherwise his method is very similar, relying chiefly on copious quotation, comparison, exegesis, and appreciative comment. Although he is almost as little interested in prose as Wilson is in verse, Eliot is almost the perfect serious introductory critic for our time, and he handles the popularizer's elaborate paraphernalia of foreground and background material with a balance and sureness that Wilson has never achieved.

Two recent special forms of translative or introductory criticism that might be called "non-popularization" deserve mention here, those of Cleanth Brooks and Vladimir Nabokov. Brooks, after a first book, *Modern Poetry and the Tradition* (1939), that attempted conventional translation or exegesis of difficult poetry, particularly that of Eliot and Yeats, and a series of collaborative textbooks, *Understanding Poetry*, *Understanding Fiction*, and *Understanding Drama*, that made things perhaps a little too simple for college students, has reversed the technique in his latest book, *The Well Wrought Urn* (1947). In it, in the course of analyzing the "structure" of ten poems, he attempts, with some success, to demonstrate that poems traditionally thought simple and readable, like Gray's "Elegy Written in a Country Churchyard" and Tennyson's "Tears, Idle Tears," are actually ambiguous, paradoxical, and almost "metaphysical." He thus "introduces" and "popularizes" familiar poems in new terms and "translates" them from simple to complex. Vladimir Nabokov, in his odd study *Nikolai Gogol* (1944), does a comparable job of reinterpreting Gogol, generally thought to be a readable and humorous social satirist, by insisting that he is difficult, serious, and unconcerned with society; an irrational and almost surrealist *avant-garde* writer. In this translation-in-reverse Nabokov (who has apparently known Wilson for a number of years, and whose work has received Wilson's highest praise) even uses Wilson's favorite technique, the plot summary, although, as he explains, he gives only "the real plots" that Gogol wrote "behind the obvious ones." (Nabokov also, it might be noted, uses the technique of literal translation, in Pound's fashion, making new English translations of the passages and works he discusses, out of a frankly expressed conviction that the old ones are wholly inadequate to style and tone—his *do* seem far superior, it must be admitted—and even elaborately translating the plays of suggestion and meaning in Gogol's proper names.)

There is obviously no point to devoting any space to a discussion of the other extreme of popularization, the commercial attempt to cash in on the public's desire for the prestige of literary acquaintance. These books are all of a pattern: a biography, preferably of an author known for sexual irregularity, like Byron or Wilde, written with as much emphasis on the scandal as possible, plus enough summary to enable the reader to pretend he has read the man. The names of these books can be found on old best-seller lists, where they are, we can note gratefully, more the province of the social psychologist than our concern here.

5

There are many aspects of Wilson's work requiring discussion besides his function as a translator. He seems to regard himself as primarily a historical critic, and in *Axel's Castle* describes his work as "literary history." The three historical critics Wilson sees as his chief "ancestors" are Vico, Herder, and Taine, and in claiming these three men for his tradition of social criticism Wilson seems curiously oblivious of the dubious implications of the doctrines of at least the first two. One would get no idea from Wilson's account that Vico was an enemy of science, modern thought, and the democratization of culture so fanatic that even De Sanctis, who greatly respects his achievement, refers to him as "an out-and-out reactionary"; or that Herder's emphasis on the national nature of thought and art, the irrational intuition of genius, and the "folkish" were a basic source of Nazi blood-and-race thinking. Wilson's use of the "historical" slogan frequently tends to abstract it from its social implications, so that, for example, he charges that Eliot uses a Spenglerian comparative criticism that is "fundamentally non-historical" without any seeming awareness that the literary periods slighted in, or omitted from, Eliot's "tradition" constitute a negative historical criticism of sharp awareness, and that the "timeless" can be a historical period too.

As Wilson sees the historical method, it embraces biography, and thus, by extension, psychological data and psychoanalysis, so that Johnson,

Sainte-Beuve, Coleridge, and Freud are equally in the line of historical criticism. Wilson's own method has always embraced both sociological and psychological factors, with greater emphasis on the sociological in his early criticism and the proportion gradually shifting in favor of the psychological as he developed. Wilson's analyses have been perhaps most successful where he used both criteria at once, translating back and forth between Marx and Freud, as when he discusses Proust's giant novel not only as the expression of Proust's abnormal dependence on his mother and consequent "impulses toward a sterile and infantile perversity," but also as the "Heart-break House of capitalist culture."

The history of Wilson's attitude toward Marxism is a curious record. In the early thirties he seems to have considered himself a Marxist, as *The American Jitters* and more directly political writings about the same time (1932) testify, and he apparently began *To the Finland Station* in 1932 as a tribute to Marxism, a demonstration of its ability to convert historical theory into action. During the seven years of writing the book Wilson lost faith in Marxism, and the book changed in midstream,[4] finally appearing with the thesis that if Marxism inevitably meant Stalin, as he thought it might, Wilson would have none of it. Moreover, he tried to accept Marxism while rejecting two of its principal pillars, dialectical materialism and the labor theory of value, as mystic nonsense. For Wilson, influenced by Sidney Hook and Max Eastman, the dialectic is an unconscious survival of the Christian Trinity and the magical triangle of Pythagoras (as well as probably symbolic of "the male sexual organs"), while the labor theory of value is simply Marx's metaphysics. Since these two theories are, respectively, the philosophic and the economic bases of the Marxist theoretical structure, Wilson was hacking at the roots of his own belief, and it inevitably toppled.

The corollary to Wilson's gradual rejection of Marxism, and perhaps its deeper cause, were his disillusionment with Russian Communism. His books are a fascinating record of this transition. In *Axel's Castle* (1931) Russia is "a country where a central social-political idealism has been able to use and to inspire the artist," and is the hope for both art and (secondarily) society. By *The American Jitters* (1932) Wilson had begun to worry about the Soviet artist; perhaps "a rigid political creed which is always demanding fables to point its morals may have its irksome side." In his next book, *Travels in Two Democracies* (1936), he reports on a rather strained visit to the Soviet Union, has measured praise for Stalin and his government (Russia is still "the moral top of the world"), but bitterly attacks the American "Stalinist Communists." By his next book, *The Triple Thinkers* (1938), he is frankly attacking Stalin

[4] We might conjecture a similar change in midstream during the writing of *Axel's Castle*, to explain why a book that starts as a castigation of writers Wilson believed socially irresponsible ends as a bouquet to them.

and "the prisons of the GPU," although he still feels that the Soviet government is an improvement over czarism. By *To the Finland Station* (1940) the Soviet government combines "the butcheries of the Robespierre Terror with the corruption and reaction of the Directory," and "the despotism of Stalin" has "uprooted Russian Marxism." Since then his hatred of Stalin, Communism, and the Soviet Union has become obsessive and hysterical, and bitter and apparently uncontrollable references to them turn up in almost everything he writes.

Besides the general assumptions of social and psychological criticism and the necessities of "translation," Wilson has chiefly based his work on two theories of art. The first, and more important, is expressed in the metaphor of Philoctetes' wound and bow, the theory that artistic talent is the obverse side of some unpleasant disability. As a general statement that the artist will naturally express what chiefly concerns him, his own suffering, or that art is a product of suffering, this is a cliché of critical thought. In its more direct phrasing, the idea that the art is simply another form of the sickness, the reverse side of it, the chief modern sources of the theory have been Mann and Gide, both of whom seem to have derived it from Schopenhauer through Nietzsche. In discussing this concept in *Dostoevsky*, Gide relates it to the theory held by Lombroso that genius is a neurosis, and it is also obviously related to Freud's theory that the artist is an immature personality in whom the childhood pleasure principle never gives way to the adult reality principle, Adler's theory that the artist is the victim of an inferiority feeling, and other psychoanalytic variants. There is no doubt that in any of these phrasings the theory is substantially true, but it is part of the truth only. What its defenders have never satisfactorily explained, and must explain before it can be of any great use to literary criticism, is why only a small number of the sick, neurotic, regressive, or inferior-feeling personalities become artists; that is, why the wound is only accompanied by the bow in some cases, and why in *those* cases, and why *that* specific bow.[5]

Apart from the diagnostic side of the wound-and-bow theory, its specific formulation in the Philoctetes myth is worth discussing.[6] Some

[5] One of the most plausible statements of the theory, which fails, however, to answer these questions satisfactorily, is contained in W. H. Auden's essay "Psychology and Art To-day," in Geoffrey Grigson's symposium *The Arts To-day*" (1935). The general problem of art and neurosis, as well as Wilson's specific wound-and-bow theory, was exhaustively discussed in a controversy between Dr. Saul Rosenzweig and Lionel Trilling in *Partisan Review*, Fall 1944 and Winter 1945, and was reduced to its proper scale in the larger framework of psychoanalytic criticism by Robert Gorham Davis in the Summer 1945 issue.

[6] The story of Philoctetes is summarized thus by Wilson:
   The demigod Heracles had been given by Apollo a bow that never missed its mark. When, poisoned by Deianeira's robe, he had had himself burned on Mount Œta, he had persuaded Philoctetes to light the pyre and had rewarded him by

time before Wilson published *The Wound and the Bow,* Kenneth Burke suggested in one of his essays the usability of the Orpheus and Perseus myths as allegories on the nature of art, and after the book appeared, possibly picking up Burke's idea, Delmore Schwartz proposed in his article on Wilson that a number of other classical myths, among them the stories of Pegasus, Orpheus, and Œdipus, could express aspects of the creative situation just as well as the Philoctetes story, and the Œdipus myth rather better. Undoubtedly, all of these classical myths, in fact any archetypal story, could be developed as a theory of the nature of art with comparable fruitfulness. Just as the artist combines his magic powers with a repellent disability, so does he go down into hell to regain from oblivion that which he loves; so is he unable to face the serpent-headed monster without being turned into stone, but is safe if he observes its reflection in a mirror, and so on. Not only are these legends and others equally usable, but as Schwartz and Granville Hicks[7] point out, the Philoctetes story is not quite satisfactory for its job, because Philoctetes has his bow before he suffers the wound, making the wound actually accidental and unrelated to the power of the bow, and because it does not show the use of the bow exacerbating the wound.

A theory is always to some extent the projection of its creator's special problems and situations (so that—to mechanize the bow image—

bequeathing to him this weapon. Philoctetes had thus been formidably equipped when he had later set forth against Troy with Agamemnon and Menelaus. But on the way they had to stop off at the tiny island of Chrysè to sacrifice to the local deity. Philoctetes approached the shrine first, and he was bitten in the foot by a snake. The infection became peculiarly virulent; and the groans of Philoctetes made it impossible to perform the sacrifice, which would be spoiled by ill-omened sounds; the bite began to suppurate with so horrible a smell that his companions could not bear to have him near them. They removed him to Lemnos, a neighboring island which was much larger than Chrysè and inhabited, and sailed away to Troy without him.

Philoctetes remained there ten years. The mysterious wound never healed. In the meantime, the Greeks, hard put to it at Troy after the deaths of Achilles and Ajax and baffled by the confession of their soothsayer that he was unable to advise them further, had kidnaped the soothsayer of the Trojans and had forced him to reveal to them that they could never win till they had sent for Neoptolemus, the son of Achilles, and given him his father's armor, and till they had brought Philoctetes and his bow.

Both of these things were done. Philoctetes was healed at Troy by the son of the physician Asclepius; and he fought Paris in single combat and killed him. Philoctetes and Neoptolemus became the heroes of the taking of Troy.

[7] In his essay "The Intransigence of Edmund Wilson" in the *Antioch Review,* Winter 1946–7, to which I am indebted for a number of facts and insights. Hicks's essay is in my opinion the best study of Wilson's career so far printed. It is marred only by an enormous overvaluation of his abilities, finding him "the country's best critic," "a first-rate critical intelligence," etc., and a curious blindness that permits Hicks to see Wilson's stubborn commercialism as "integrity."

any specific bullet from the artist's gun carries the marks of all the im-
perfections in the gun-barrel, which are themselves the record of previous
usage) and for that reason is always worth turning on its creator, where
it ought to function best. It would be a very valuable service to turn the
wound-and-bow theory on Wilson, examining the nature of *his* "wound"
and relating it to his powers, but such a detailed personal analysis is far
beyond the scope of this essay. A few notes for such a study, however,
might be worth recording. They come, almost without exception, from
his imaginative or non-critical writing, which, perhaps because of inadequate artistic fusing, seems always to be markedly autobiographical
and sometimes to be embarrassingly personal. Wilson's ten volumes of
non-critical writings—a novel, a volume of stories, three books of reporting, a volume of poetry, a book of plays, and three volumes of
miscellaneous verse, prose, and drama—when combed out, seem remarkably revealing. Going over them in sequence, we may note some "wound"
clues, without at all attempting to analyze the works in literary terms.

The first book is *The Undertaker's Garland* (1922), a volume of mixed
prose and verse on the theme of death, a "Dance of Death," by John
Peale Bishop and "Edmund Wilson Jr.," with pseudo-Beardsley illustrations by Boris Artzybasheff. The respective contributions of the two
writers are identified in a prefatory note, and the contrast between those
of the late John Peale Bishop and Wilson's ingenious, literary-derived,
and frigid works is perhaps the most significant thing in the book.
(Searching for an impulse that could lead Wilson to print his verse in
conjunction with that of a natural poet of great talent, we might note
that Wilson has spent three decades reacting to the mild joke of his class
at Princeton's having elected him "Worst Poet.")

Wilson's next book, a solo performance, was *Discordant Encounters*
(1926), a series of four dialogues and two plays. The plays are chiefly
dream fantasy and not particularly significant, but the "discordant encounters" themselves are fascinating. In each of them Wilson dissociates
his own personality into two contending antagonists: Paul Rosenfeld and
Matthew Josephson, Van Wyck Brooks and Scott Fitzgerald, a professor
of fifty and a journalist of twenty-five (presumably Christian Gauss, his
teacher at Princeton, and himself), and William Beebe and a Marine
Iguana. In these disguises he argues out four of the basic problems he
faces as an artist and critic—traditional culture vs. modernism, integrity
vs. artistic commercialism, moral vs. environmental criteria, and science
vs. instinct—and, taking advantage of the dialogue form, leaves each of
them unresolved.

I Thought of Daisy, the novel, appeared in 1929. It is told in the first
person, seems markedly autobiographical, and centers in the two protagonists almost all of Wilson's fiction and drama was to center in: the
priggish young writer of good family, and the dominant, rather eman-

cipated girl from a lower social background who says "the trouble withum." It also includes a long monologue on Sophocles, Philoctetes, and the relationship of art to disability (almost formulating the wound-and-bow theory), and ends in a real frenzy of phallic imagery, a sequence on the last page running from lipstick to mouth-organ to pistol to snake.

Poets Farewell (1929), a collection of poetry (and some prose) written from the time Wilson got out of college, is principally distinguished for a good deal of obsessive sexuality unfused into poetry ("Crowd wide your thighs with steady knee"), what Randall Jarrell has called, in connection with another poet, "real gardens with real toads in them." It also includes a very funny parody of Edwin Arlington Robinson, a poem rather curiously comparing Henry James to President Wilson, and Wilson's series of poems constituting his elegiac farewell to the art.

The next two books were social reporting: *"The American Jitters: A Year of the Slump* (1932) and *Travels in Two Democracies* (1936). From the standpoint of Wilson's "wound" they seem particularly revealing. The strongest impression they make is of an interest in "social conditions" combined with a disinterest in people as individual human beings, almost a positive dislike of them. Wilson uses the clichés of chauvinism, "nigger," "nigger wench," and "darky song," as well as vaudeville Yiddish dialect; he refers constantly to people in the imagery of beetles, moths, starfish, frogs, "fat bass or logy groupers"; he seems entirely lacking in either humor or human warmth. The part of *Travels in Two Democracies* dealing with his personal experiences (as distinguished from his objective reporting) in Russia is nightmarish, from the first terrible foretaste of Russian slatternliness, when he boarded the Soviet boat and found the stewardesses working in run-down high heels, with cigarettes dangling from their mouths,[8] and in the course of trying to get a bath, fell against a hot pipe and "burned his elbow severely"; through a mounting series of irritations with Russian crowds, Russian unpunctuality, Russian slovenliness, Russian unkept promises; to the final horror of his sickness in Odessa, with a mounting tempo of hysteria about the dirt, the smell, the bugs, the lack of sanitation, the lack of privacy, and so forth. The most effective statement (frank and ironic enough, certainly) of Wilson's quality of fussiness, bitter snobbishness, and dislike of human contact, comes in the piece in the book called "The Old Stone House":

> So here, it seems, is where I live: in an old, cramped, sour frame house, having failed even worse than my relatives at getting out of

[8] It is interesting to see the same imagery turn up for postwar Britain in *Europe without Baedeker:* "Down below in the dining-room, the clothless tables seemed never to have been wiped, for they were soiled with innumerable spillings of soup, gravy, eggs, jam and tea; and you were waited on by slovenly skivvies so pallidly unappetizing that they made the meager food seem more tasteless."

the American big business era the luxuries and the prestige which I should unquestionably very much have enjoyed. Here is where I end by living—among the worst instead of the best of this society—the sordid and unhealthy children of my sordid and unhealthy neighbors, who howl outside my windows night and day. It is this, in the last analysis—there is no doubt about it now!—which has been rankling and causing my gloom: to have left that early world behind, yet never to have made myself comfortable in what was till yesterday the new.

The three plays published as *This Room and This Gin and These Sandwiches* in 1937, three "variations" on the theme of "the artistic and moral revolt which had its headquarters in New York after the war," all center on the rather dull and priggish literary hero and the aggressive lower-class "meetum" heroine, and all, in addition, end with the same happy wish-fulfillment. *Notebooks of Night* (1942) is a collection of poetry and prose divided into three sections: short lyrics, serious and comic, with the new obsessive theme of Stalin added to the old obsessive theme of sex: longer poems, including the remarkable parody-criticism of MacLeish; and prose, including parody and reminiscences of his childhood. Some of the parodies and satires in the book are brutal and quite successful, others are merely in quiet bad taste. (Incidentally, one of the love poems in the book, "Home to Town: Two Highballs"—"The little cunning shadow between the narrow thighs"—seems clearly addressed to the "Anna" of *Hecate County*.)

Finally, in 1946, *Memoirs of Hecate County* itself appeared and, after selling fifty thousand copies in about four months, was declared "obscene" by the Court of Special Sessions and banned from further sale (both greater triumphs than Mary McCarthy's *The Company She Keeps* had achieved). The book includes six stories told in the first person, unified in that they deal with life in the same fictitious "county," of which the one long story taking up about half the book, "The Princess with the Golden Hair," was the principal offender against public morals. (It deals, as the prosecution gleefully pointed out, with twenty separate acts of sexual intercourse, involving four women, and described with a certain precision of anatomic detail, as well as "assorted acts of sexual debauchery" and "disgusting embellishments.") The reviewers and critics generally agreed that the story was substantially autobiographic—Ralph Bates remarking: "I am convinced every word of it is true," Granville Hicks referring to "its exposure of his sex habits" and announcing: "internal evidence indicates that it is autobiographical, and there are traces of 'Anna' in Wilson's writings of the middle '30's." The attempts to throw off this autobiographic identification are of the flimsiest: the narrator is an *art* critic whose field is the social basis of *painting*, he went to Yale rather than Princeton, he is "tall and thin" rather than short and fat, and the like.

"The Princess with the Golden Hair" is written with what seems to be Wilson's substitute for literary talent, a devastating, painful, embarrassing (and rather admirable) honesty, and for that reason, in terms of our present inquiry, warrants somewhat more space than Wilson's other works. The story is social irony, perhaps allegory, expressed in terms principally sexual: the narrator's conflicting and simultaneous relations with Anna, a working girl, and Imogen, a remarkably beautiful, crippled (we learn later, hysterically) married woman of his own class. The narrator is frankly shown with all the mechanical, plotted, and one-way sexuality of adolescence, carried over into adult life: "I finally persuaded her," "she is now willing," "went a good deal further," "but I never got beyond," etc. He sees people constantly in the imagery of dogs, cats, monkeys, even sea anemones (Anna is "a beast or bird picked up in the fields"), as well as in the imagery of food, which is an obsessive theme in the story (he remarks casually of a dinner party: "I remember the courses better than the conversation"). The narrator exposes his own snobbery relentlessly: explains frankly that his interest in working people began with the Crash, calmly discusses the precariousness of "one's relations with persons of an inferior class," expresses his fears that he may very well be ashamed of Anna ("I wouldn't quite dare to bring her out to Hecate County"), etc. His unconscious revelations are even more significant: he is a Babbitt (when he begins to be successful, "I bought a black derby"); a timid prig ("I was careful to take no risks," "though of course I was taking the proper precautions"); a junior Don Juan ("my ardent and expert induction," "I had applied such variety and delicacy"); a sentimental vulgarian ("my tongue in her soft little mouth"); a plain vulgarian ("the mossy damp underparts," "the prime human oven of heat and juice"); and even what used to be called "a cad" (rejecting the idea of "making love to" Imogen while she is wearing her brace, "I was afraid it would be impracticable or unchivalrous"). The narrator additionally reveals a curious kind of eroticism toward the clothed female form ("appetite, on these hurried occasions, increased by dress, stockings and shoes," "by a sudden revival of appetite after she had put on her clothes to go"), which at times resembles the sadism of an aging roué in Krafft-Ebing ("the brace did not discourage desire; on the contrary, it stimulated me oddly"). The most revealing thing in the story, however, is not directly sexual at all, but is an unconscious pun: he realizes that Anna is not "common" on the same page that he mentions his growing attraction to "communism."

The other stories, and the book as a whole, confirm and extend some of these insights, as well as earlier clues in Wilson's work. "The Man

Who Shot Snapping Turtles" burlesques the world of commerce, again with animal imagery for human beings; "Ellen Terhune" attempts a Jamesian ghost story to illustrate the wound-and-bow thesis; "Glimpses of Wilbur Flick" merges the irony of the useless rich man flirting with causes and an odd allegory of art as "conjuring," again with frequent imagery of human beings in animal terms; "The Milhollands and Their Damned Soul" manages to be a scathing satire on the big-business aspects of publishing, full of some of Wilson's most murderous parodies and burlesques, without ever displaying a trace of real humor; "Mr. and Mrs. Blackburn at Home," is a long, dull demonological nightmare, merging the imagery of politics and sex, again with the bitter satire unrelieved by humor (with the exception of what is probably the funniest single line in all of Wilson's writing: "I said nothing, for the kiss said all").

Wilson's latest book, *Europe without Baedeker*, published in 1947, is a collection of his reports on postwar Europe, about half of which appeared in the *New Yorker*. Aside from the fury of its hatred against all things British, which at times comes close to rivaling Wilson's Russophobia, the book's most interesting feature is its naked reliance on the popularizer's (or Gunther) syndrome, the idea that Wilson can make news of anything by discovering it (as his earlier *Atlantic* pieces on Russian literature held the literary world tense with the revelation that the Russian language has all sorts of interesting words and sounds). The book furnishes further documentation for familiar themes, rather than adding anything new. There is the same fundamental disinterest in human beings, so that in Greece all the people he meets are types, abstract political attitudes, rather than individuals; in Milan he avoids the crowds; and in London he notes, not people, but "the greasy marks of heads" they leave in hotel rooms. The tone of megalomania has increased, and Wilson not only projects into Santayana's less attractive aspects and defends them, but in one place, suggesting that British intellectuals have infuriated him by praising only his early work, projects himself as Shakespeare. There is still the obsessive interest in sex: Wilson notes the "remarkably good looking" and "marvelous" girls with their "tempting" and "provocative" appearances wherever he goes (even the bas-reliefs in Crete have "pert breasts"); he remarks on the attractiveness of disproportion and perversity of shape; and he displays exhaustive interest in prostitutes, with interminable accounts of encounters with them, comparative essays on their living-conditions, and even a hierarchy of prostitution, crowned by "a really good-looking girl who accosted me in French" in London, and an exotic Polish-German girl, "very pretty," in Naples. Food is equally obsessive, with meals and service in various parts of shattered Europe greedily compared; Wilson sees Delhi as "gobs of mutton on a shashlik skewer"; and his most memorable experience in Crete seems to have been "an Homeric banquet." Perhaps the most revealing note in the pieces is Wilson's account of the trick he uses to amuse children, making a jumping mouse out of his pocket handkerchief, "with which I have usually had great success." He tries it on the children in Athens, "but it did not go over very well. The boy, at any rate, seemed much more interested in listening to the political discussion."

A number of other miscellaneous notes could be compiled toward a study of Wilson's "wound": some obsessive quality to his experiences at Princeton and the Hill School, which he is still writing about in endless reminiscence and which gives his work a Peter Pan quality (Malcolm Cowley noted in a review of *To the Finland Station* that Wilson describes Lenin as having the sure dignity of a "respected headmaster"), with old college friends still turning up in all of his writing; an obsessive interest in stage magic and conjuring (which, as Wilson himself has pointed out, seems always to represent some compulsive symbolism, like Houdini's death-and-burial ritual); and much else. Granville Hicks's essay contributes some items of value: the story of Hicks's one encounter with Wilson, when his remarks about friends in common were "almost without exception bitter and destructive," and he "was so much more emphatic and overbearing than there seemed any need of being at a dinner table"; the phrase "his basic incapacity for co-operation with any group of human beings"; and particularly the form Wilson had printed to use on suitable occasions, which I reprint from Hicks's study:

Edmund Wilson regrets that it is impossible for him

	read manuscripts,
	contribute to books or periodicals,
	do editorial work,
	judge literary contests,
without compensation to	give educational courses,
	deliver lectures,
	address meetings,
	make after-dinner speeches,
	broadcast;
	contribute to or take part in symposiums, take part in chain poems or other collective compositions,
	contribute manuscripts for sales,
under any circumstances to	donate copies of his books to libraries,
	autograph books for strangers,
	supply personal information about himself,

"   "   "   "   supply photographs of himself,
                                  allow his name to be used on letter-
                                      heads,
                                  receive unknown persons who have
                                      no apparent business with him.

All of this material seems to boil down to a series of basic paradoxes
or dilemmas, which, since we cannot, without a good deal more personal
evidence, identify in Edmund Wilson himself, we are forced to say seem
the distinguishing characteristic of all his fictional protagonists, particularly his first-person narrator. This fictional man is coldhearted and
repelled by human contact, yet exacerbated by a rampant sensuality;
lacking in creative talent, yet impelled to produce imaginative work;
committed to commercialism and admiring only integrity; "democratic"
and "socialist" while bitterly chauvinistic, snobbish, and contemptuous
of people; almost without humor and addicted to parody and satire; aware
of the complex and oversimplifying everything, from literature to human
relations, in a series of false "either-ors"; hating all ties, yet unable to
cut the umbilical cord binding him to school; desperate for adulation,
yet repelling admirers; skeptically minded and dogmatically mannered;
yearning to be Flaubert and ending up as Emma Bovary.[9] If any of this
applies to Wilson himself, and if the wound-and-bow theory makes any
correlation between the extent of the wound and the power of the bow,
we are reduced to wondering why Edmund Wilson is not the foremost artist of our time.

Wilson's other theoretical contribution to criticism, admittedly a
secondary one, is his shock-of-recognition theory, the basis of selection
in his 1943 anthology, which he defines with the epigraph from Melville:
"For genius, all over the world, stands hand in hand, and one shock of
recognition runs the whole world round." Silly as this sounds in any
literal sense, Wilson seems to believe it to the extent that he compiled
1,290 pages of critical estimates of American writers, not by critics, but
by other writers. Obviously, many great writers have recognized the
genius of their contemporaries and predecessors with a heart-warming
"shock of recognition," including some of those in Wilson's anthology.
Literature is full of such examples and anyone could compile a long list
of them: Balzac on Beyle, Beyle on Scott and Byron, Symonds on Whitman, Tolstoy on Chekhov, and Chekhov on Gorky (the warm and
immediate reactions of these two great Russian authors to younger men
was particularly memorable), Boileau (of all people) on Molière, Keats

---

[9] I am aware that Flaubert said "*Madame Bovary, c'est moi!*" He meant something
very different, however.

on Shakespeare, and Arnold on Keats (with reservations), Racine on La Fontaine, Dryden on Milton, and so on.

However, a list of shocks of non-recognition or unrecognition ten times as long would be just as easy to compile. Byron disliked the work of Keats, Emerson scorned Poe, Ronsard insulted Rabelais, Whitman was detested by Lowell, Longfellow, Holmes, Lanier, and Whittier (Whittier threw *Leaves of Grass* into the fire) as well as by Swinburne and innumerable others, Lamartine despised La Fontaine, Sophocles could see nothing of value in either Æschylus or Euripides, Wordsworth could not read Keats, Corneille preferred Boursault to Racine, Emerson liked Hawthorne but pitied his lack of talent, Whitman disliked Melville; as readers for publishing houses, Gide rejected Proust's novel and Meredith rejected Butler's *The Way of All Flesh*; Milton had a low opinion of Shakespeare, and Johnson of Milton; Wordsworth had unbelievably little understanding of the work of his friend Coleridge; George Moore detested Hardy; Sainte-Beuve slighted Beyle, Baudelaire, Balzac, and Flaubert; and so on indefinitely.

The worst of the shock-of-recognition theory is that the writers who are most mistreated by their contemporaries, like Whitman, tend to be no better in judging others in their turn, and that many writers, among them Wordsworth, Hardy, James, and Melville himself (despite his quotation) were so badgered by non-recognition that they either retreated into silence for a period or for the rest of their creative lives, or gave up a literary form that may have been their natural one. Turning *this* theory on Wilson, it is amusing to note his failure to appreciate a vast number of distinguished contemporary writers (some of them listed above), as well as the general failure to appreciate *his* creative work.[10] Obviously, such a theory, having no relationship to the reality of the situation, is chiefly useful on the wholly personal levels of consolation and self-vindication. It would seem to be a perfect heads-I-win, tails-you-lose structure, since a writer who believes it, if a failure, can feel that at least other men of talent appreciate him, and if a success, can feel

---

[10] This is perhaps the place to point out that Wilson's critical work still has what seems to me an abnormally inflated reputation. In this country he has been praised and acknowledged by men immeasurably his superiors, like F. O. Matthiessen and R. P. Blackmur. In Britain he seems generally accepted as America's foremost critic; *Axel's Castle* appears to be considered the very model of psychological and social criticism, and a whole poetic generation from Spender, MacNeice, and Day Lewis to Francis Scarfe and Philip Toynbee, as well as such critics as F. R. Leavis, has praised and acknowledged his work (even Eliot has referred to it). This is due, obviously, to the fact that almost all his books of criticism have been published in England, making him practically the only modern American critic so honored, but that phenomenon in its turn then requires explanation. Whatever the reason, it is to be hoped that a state of affairs wherein Edmund Wilson is the living American critic whose work is familiar to English writers, while that of say Kenneth Burke and Blackmur is largely not, will not continue indefinitely.

that the magic circle of hand-holding genius has established his claim
to immortality.

Wilson's current status, now that he has turned fifty (he was born in
1895), is somewhat puzzling. His taking a job as regular book reviewer
for the *New Yorker* was a reversal of the traditional pattern of the
serious critic, who tends to outgrow the ability to do weekly or biweekly
reviewing, with its compulsion to waste time on trash and write superficially within a limited space, and go on to longer and more ambitious
projects with an increasingly narrow specialization. In general his
column has proved disappointing to those readers who had hoped for
serious criticism in the *New Yorker* (which has always specialized in
breezy reviewing) and who found Wilson superficial; without gratifying
that group of readers who wanted a light and readable column like
Clifton Fadiman's and who found Wilson merely dull. Wilson has spent
a good deal of his space breaking on the wheel such butterflies as Louis
Bromfield, a Kay Boyle potboiler, Lloyd Douglas's *The Robe*, and Anya
Seaton's *The Turquoise*, while ignoring a good deal of the serious writing
appearing at the same time. His opinions have been for the most part
conventional, with a few aberrations like wild praise for Isabel Bolton
and qualified disprase for Kafka. A few good pieces, or pieces with good
things in them, have emerged from the general gloom: a sharp and
cogent (if humorless) attack on the detective story; a study of the relation of Wilde's art to his syphilis; an excellent long review of books
by Malraux and Silone (Wilson, as he has also shown in pieces on
Koestler and others, has a special insight into the minds and work of
disillusioned radicals); a study of the symbolic action underlying stage
magic and conjuring; and a brilliant social analysis, in dramatic terms,
of Emily Post's *Etiquette*.

Wilson seems to be at some turning-point in his life. In his above-
mentioned article in the *Princeton University Library Chronicle*, Wilson,
at the age of forty-nine, confessed that he had arrived at middle-age
"under the illusion that I had not really yet begun to write." He has
made no secret of the fact that he is disillusioned with criticism, that he
regards his *New Yorker* reviewing and his 1943 *Atlantic* series on Russian literature as no more than journalistic projects, and that his volume
of war reporting and *Hecate County* represent his permanent return to
creative writing as a profession. Even more serious than this contempt
for his own reputation as a critic seems to be his new contempt for the
art of criticism itself, and a shocking willingness to abdicate the critical
function. There seems no other way to read his statement in a *New
Yorker* review of Katherine Anne Porter: "I am spoiling Miss Porter's
stories by attempting to find a formula for them when I ought simply to
be telling you to read them."

Here Wilson may have been victimized by his professional method, which has perhaps finally caught up with him. In the same *Library Chronicle* article Wilson called himself a "journalist" and described "how a journalist works," a description well worth quoting:

> My own strategy—to make an anticlimax—has usually been, first to get books for review or reporting assignments to cover on subjects in which I happened to be interested; then, later, to use the scattered articles for writing general studies of these subjects; and finally to bring out a book in which groups of these essays were revised and combined.

This has the ring of accuracy, and it is unquestionably the explanation of something that makes any serious reader of Wilson's volumes uneasy, the fact that he has not actually written any critical books (or, with the exception of *I Thought of Daisy* and *To the Finland Station*, any organic books at all), but merely collections of magazine articles and studies, given some semblance of unity by a title or an organizing principle. Attractive as this scheme seems in terms of the writer's economy, it has undoubtedly limited Wilson to the extent of forcing his criticism into commercial channels, requiring short pieces of no frightening profundity, and leaving him, in his fifties, with less concretely achieved than a critic who has written only one book, but that organic and large-scale. This sense of a sudden need to do something that posterity will remember may be one of the causes of Wilson's present disillusionment with criticism.

One aspect of Wilson's creative writing requires discussion in connection with his criticism—his real talent for parody or burlesque. This is obviously the reverse side of his emphasis on translation and exegesis in the criticism, perhaps even a compensation for it, as though so much emphasis on the "matter" alone required an area where he had to emphasize "manner" alone. Wilson has done some remarkably successful parodies, from the poem in the style of Edwin Arlington Robinson first published in 1923, through his high point, "The Omelet of A. MacLeish" in 1938, to some of the good things in *Hecate County*. His most ambitious effort, an imitation of Joyce's style in *Finnegans Wake*, is an impressive performance, although it does not quite come off in either its earlier published form or its rewritten form as "The Three Limperary Cripples" —it lacks the *rightness* of Joyce (the three names, Carl Van Doren, Herbert Gorman, and Gorham B. Munson, have no basic connection and seem to have been chosen only because of phonetic similarity) as well as the *meaningfulness* of Joyce's word-distortions (Wilson has to rely on both the baby-talk lisp of "motht theriouth" and the primitive American humor of "abstrack" and "konckrete").

These parodies and burlesques are most interesting in the light of

Wilson's statement in *The Triple Thinkers:* "The impulse to satirize romanticism implies, as in the case of Flaubert, a strong predisposition toward it," which would presumably generalize into the statement that the impulse to satirize *anything* implies a strong predisposition toward it. Since Wilson's three obsessive subjects for parody and satire are the vanity and commercialization of Hollywood, the abject mental slavery of Stalinism, and poetic style, anyone who accepted Wilson's doctrine could draw some interesting deductions. (Presuming a "strong predisposition" toward poetry in Wilson, combined with his obituaries for it, might be put down as a further note for a "wound" study.) Many reviewers who were puzzled by the extravagant amount of space Wilson allotted in his *Shock of Recognition* to such tedious trash as James Russell Lowell's *A Fable for Critics*, Bayard Taylor's *Diversions of the Echo Club*, and Amy Lowell's *A Critical Fable* (a total of 246 pages, or almost a quarter of the book) might have had their problem solved for them had they considered the possibility of the satirist's or parodist's loyalty to other practitioners of the art.

Finally, no estimate of Wilson would be complete without a consideration of his present elegiac mood. Wilson's tone has been funereal when he talked of poetry ever since *Axel's Castle*, and when he talked of Marxism at least since the sad little essay called "Marxism and Literature" in *The Triple Thinkers*. Recently, however, all his writing has been taking on that tone. He has been writing memoirs of his childhood and youth (including several scenes in the Hecate County book) very nostalgic for vanished glories; his memoir to T. K. Whipple, a fellow undergraduate at Princeton who died in 1939, was full of such phrases as "one has already seen so many gifted friends fail to do any of the things one had hoped of them"; his "Thoughts on Being Bibliographed" article is entirely elegiac, for his Princeton friends who are dead or who failed,[11] for his generation of writers who are dead or who failed, and for writing itself, which he sees as having reached another period of sterility; and his *New Yorker* reviews constantly bury the present and yearn after the past, particularly the twenties, when *transition* and *This Quarter* flowered, when Scott Fitzgerald and John Bishop were still alive, when our literary movements had not "spent themselves," when people were freer "in their emotions, in their ideas and in expressing themselves," and when Edmund Wilson was a young writer fresh out of college and full of promise. Wilson has,

[11] F. Scott Fitzgerald and James Joyce died within a month of each other, in December 1940 and January 1941 respectively, at a time when Wilson was filling in as literary editor of the *New Republic*. It is amusing to note that Fitzgerald, who had been a fellow student of Wilson's at Princeton, and in his letters (since published by Wilson as part of *The Crack-Up*) had called him his "intellectual conscience," received an elaborate series of obituary tributes in the magazine, extending over two issues, while Joyce received a three-paragraph editorial.

in fact, written his own obituary so effectively that it would be presumptuous for anyone else to kill him off. He feels that he is part of something that is lost to literature, and perhaps he is. Even the children seem to have grown tired of seeing that pocket handkerchief turn into a mouse.

CHAPTER 2

YVOR WINTERS

and Evaluation in Criticism

To THE extent that the evaluation of works of art has not become an extinct critical function in our time, credit must be largely due to the redoubtable labors of Yvor Winters, poet, professor of English at Leland Stanford University, and the author of four remarkable volumes of literary criticism: *Primitivism and Decadence* (1937), *Maule's Curse* (1938), *The Anatomy of Nonsense* (1943), and *Edwin Arlington Robinson* (1946).[1] Winters is a serious man, and in some respects quite a useful one, and it is regrettable that to a generation of writers younger than himself he has become largely a comic figure, the man who thinks that Elizabeth Daryush is our foremost living poet and that Edith Wharton is a better writer than Henry James. Winters has made these statements, and others more extreme, but he is our foremost and perhaps sole representative of a vanishing art, Johnsonian criticism, and he is well worth careful study.

Winters is very much in earnest about the act of evaluation, which he sees as the crowning glory, the ultimate reason for being, of critical analysis. He has listed in detail the processes, culminating in evaluation, that constitute literary criticism as he sees it. He writes:

> It will consist (1) of the statement of such historical or biographical knowledge as may be necessary in order to understand the mind and method of the writer; (2) of such analysis of his literary theories as we may need to understand and evaluate what he is doing; (3) of a rational critique of the paraphrasable content (roughly, the motive) of the poem; (4) of a rational critique of the feeling motivated—that is, of the details of style, as seen in language and technique; and (5) of the final act of judgment, a unique act, the general nature of which can be indicated, but which cannot be communicated precisely, since it consists in receiving from the poet his own final and unique judgment of his matter and in judging that judgment. It should be noted that the purpose of the first four

[1] The first three of these were republished in one volume in 1947, along with an essay on Hart Crane's "The Bridge," as *In Defense of Reason.*

CEDAR CREST COLLEGE
LIBRARY

processes is to limit as narrowly as possible the region in which the final unique act is to occur.[2]

For "poem," of course, we read "any work of art," and we observe that inasmuch as art itself is the act of evaluating experience for Winters, he sees criticism as a remarkably complicated double judgment, secondary in evaluating the poet's evaluation of his experience (the "subject" of the poem) and primary in evaluating the critic's own experience (the poem itself).

To this difficult and subtle task Winters brings a set of persuasive principles. The critic should display "reasonable humility and caution" in evaluating, and even at that, "it is only fair to add that few men possess either the talent or the education to justify their being taken very seriously, even of those who are nominally professional students of these matters." However, "every literary critic has a right to a good many errors of judgment." Whether or not Winters actually displays "reasonable humility and caution" in evaluating, and whether he has not, as he charges against Poe, far exceeded his generous quota of errors, are another question.

Winters's dogmatic evaluations are most striking in the case of the half-dozen writers he admires almost to the point of worship. One of those is Edith Wharton. He has written that Mrs. Wharton, at her best, is nearly the perfect example of an effectiveness in the novel that Jane Austen, Melville, Hawthorne, Henry James, Fielding, and Defoe can only exemplify after making allowances for "limitations of scope and defects of procedure." In terms of the celebrated comparison with James, he believes that Mrs. Wharton gives a greater precision to her moral issues than James was ever able to achieve, and that the prose of at least *The Age of Innocence* and *The Valley of Decision* is certainly superior to the prose of James. *The Age of Innocence*, because of its superior prose and because it "corrects a defect" in James's conception of the novel, is undoubtedly "the finest single flower of the Jamesian art." Not to slight *The Valley of Decision*, however, it also "might be defended as superior to any single work by James."

Perhaps the highest praise in Winters's vocabulary has been reserved for the work of Robert Bridges. Bridges's poetry is superior to that of T. S. Eliot, Hart Crane, William Carlos Williams, Marianne Moore, and practically every other modern poet, "incomparably" superior to that of Ezra Pound, and superior to and more original than that of Gerard Manley Hopkins in every respect. Moreover, Bridges is a "more civi-

---

[2] We might note that Winters himself seldom does any of these fine things, in most cases merely announcing the evaluation itself, as a flat obiter dictum, with no evidence for it given and in terms so semantically meaningless as to preclude discussion. This failure in practice should not, however, detract from the relevance of his statement of intentions.

lized" and a "saner" man than any of his contemporaries. To bring him
into comparison with his equals, he has written a number of poems that
"will stand the most scrutinizing comparison with any of Shakespeare's
sonnets," he is "probably the most finished and original master of blank
verse since Milton," and he has written at least two fine occasional
sonnets that "would cast no discredit on Milton" and a formal ode "no
whit inferior" to Dryden's "Ode on the Death of Mistress Anne Killi-
grew." "It seems to me beyond all question," Winters writes, "that
Bridges' two plays on Nero are the greatest tragedy since *The Cenci* and
(if we except that furious and appalling composition, *Samson Agonistes*,
which, though a tragedy, is no play) are quite possibly superior to any
English tragedy outside of Shakespeare." Furthermore, Winters has
classified Bridges's poetry, for the convenience of lazy readers, into
"short lyrics, first level" (ten poems), "short lyrics, second level"
(twelve poems), "longer lyrics at a slow tempo, first level" (three
poems), "second level" (one poem), plus two fine epigrams, two admirable didactic poems of some length, "of which the second is nearly
on the first level," and the above-mentioned two fine occasional sonnets
and formal ode.

"The nearest rival to Bridges since Shelley," in Winters's belief, is
T. Sturge Moore. Moore has written poetry "that has been equalled by
not more than two or three living writers, and more great poetry than
any living writer has composed." He is a far greater poet than William
Butler Yeats without Yeats's "talent for self-dramatization," and he has
"revised and greatly improved two of the most confused poems of
Gerard M. Hopkins."[3] Moreover, he is a "perfectly lucid mind," he has
written at least one poem of which each line is "a masterpiece in itself,"

---

[3] It might be instructive here to look at what Sturge Moore did to Hopkins.
Winters is referring to an essay, "Style and Beauty in Literature," in the *Criterion*,
July 1930. Moore takes the opening lines of Hopkins's "The Leaden Echo and the
Golden Echo":

> How to kéep—is there ány any, is there none such,
>   nowhere known some, bow or brooch or braid
>   or brace, láce, latch or catch or key to keep
> Back beauty, keep it, beauty, beauty, beauty, . . .
>   from vanishing away?

and rewrites them as:

> How to keep beauty? is there any way?
> Is there nowhere any means to have it stay?
> Will no bow or brooch or braid,
> Brace or lace
> Latch or catch
> Or key to lock the door lend aid
> Before beauty vanishes away?

Moore explained that he had retained most of Hopkins's felicities while discarding
"his most ludicrous redundancies."

and "he has more to teach us of our present literary difficulties than has any other writer of our century."

To conclude Winters's trinity, "the finest British poet since T. Sturge Moore" is Mrs. Elizabeth Daryush, who, as Robert Bridges's daughter raises at least the possibility that the quality Winters has isolated as greatness is transmissible genetically. (It is worth noting, perhaps, that I had never heard of her until I encountered her name in Winters's first book, and have never seen her mentioned elsewhere except in reference to Winters's critical opinions.) "She is one of the few great poets living," he writes, and to clinch the argument, with the comment that "the medium could not be used with greater beauty than in this poem," he reprints a sonnet of hers entitled "Still-Life," of which the most charitable opinion possible is that it is a gentle, rather pedestrian piece of rhymed prose.[4]

In 1946, without much previous warning, Winters added a fourth deity to his trinity, in his *Edwin Arlington Robinson*, written for New Directions' Makers of Modern Literature series. Robinson is a "great and austere poet," who has written, in "The Wandering Jew," "one of the great poems not only of our time but of our language," "perhaps as great as one can easily find," as well as ten other short poems that can be equaled "in the work of only four or five English and American poets of the past century and a half"; one long poem, *Lancelot*, which is "one of the few deeply impressive narrative poems written in English in more than two hundred years"; and some poems of medium length, of which two "rank among the greatest of their kind in English," two others are simply "great," two others are "successful," and a few more are "memorable." In general, Robinson is "on certain occasions one of the most remarkable poets in our language," and his best work ranks with the greatest work of Wordsworth, Tennyson, Browning, Hardy, and Bridges, among whom Robinson "seems at moments to find his closest relatives and quite possibly his closest rivals on this side of Milton and Dryden; and his position in relation to these poets is not that of the lowest."

Where a new reputation for an obscure or inferior poet cannot be stimulated by this kind of pressure, Winters is perfectly willing to pretend that one already exists, as where he remarks that Adelaide Crapsey is not only "certainly an immortal poet," but "has long been one of the most famous poets of our century."

Probably the highest single point of Winters's praise for his favorites, however, is found in Post Scriptum V of *The Anatomy of Nonsense*, where he lists the seventeen American poets of his own and the subsequent generation he chiefly respects, and names their forty-eight best poems

---

[4] One of the worst features of Winters's violent dogmatism is that it inevitably provokes an equally violent counterdogmatism. Mrs. Daryush would probably not seem as bad as that, encountered elsewhere.

(two of them modified by "perhaps"). His own name is omitted, as is that of his wife, Janet Lewis (he explains in a footnote that although he believes her to be "one of the best poets of her generation, as well as one of the best fictionists," he endeavors, "on general principles, not to discuss her work"). Nevertheless almost half the names on the list are of his friends, disciples, or students; almost all the generally accepted major poets of our day are omitted; and the choice of poems seems whimsical or worse. All in all, the list is one of the most curious documents of contemporary critical writing.[5]

Winters is fully as dogmatic in evaluating the poets he detests. High on that list are Eliot, Yeats, and Ezra Pound. Eliot is the author of "purely derivative poetry," he does everything Pound does "with less skill," he is markedly inferior to William Carlos Williams, among others, and at least one passage of his, from "The Hollow Men," is dismissed with the charitable sentence: "There are few attempts more pathetic than this in modern literature to keep on going, line by line, in spite of everything." Pound is simply "a barbarian loose in a museum." Yeats is a poet full of "melodramatic emotionalism," and in another place, with no great straining after consistency, a poet with sensibilities so chilled as to be benumbing. All three of them, naturally, are vastly inferior to Bridges, Sturge Moore, and Winters's other favorites.

For all his passion and dogmatism, Winters's opinions are something less than stable. In *The Anatomy of Nonsense*, published in 1943, Winters describes Wallace Stevens as the corruption and degradation of a great poetic talent, a man who has written nothing first-rate since the publication of *Harmonium* in 1923. Yet in *Primitivism and Decadence*, published in 1937, or after Stevens had been on the downgrade for fourteen years, according to Winters, Stevens was simply "probably the greatest poet of his generation," and in 1939, in a review, Winters predicted that the year 2000 would see Stevens and Williams established as the "two best poets" of their generation. It is interesting to compare Winters's literary opinions in an early essay, "The Extension and Reintegration of the Human Spirit through the Poetry Mainly French and American since Poe and Baudelaire," published in *The New American Caravan* in 1929, with his later opinions, published during this decade. In 1929 Allen Tate was "without the skill" of Archibald MacLeish, the novels of Elizabeth Madox Roberts ranked above those of Henry James, a chapter of Dr. Williams's *In the American Grain* was superior "to any other prose of our time and most of the verse," the trio of living Americans who excited

---

[5] This sort of claque operation works both ways, of course. Alan Swallow, his current publisher, has identified Winters as "the greatest critic of the recent critical renaissance," and Lincoln Fitzell, one of Winters's seventeen elect poets, has called him "the fine poet and critic," who, "although not a native of the West, likes the country and at least some of the people."

Winters most were Williams, Crane, and Tate (unskilled as he was), and Lawrence was the only major poet in England since Hardy. By 1943 Tate was "surely" one of the major talents of our time, MacLeish "wears thinner and thinner with time," Williams and Crane were victims of the "Whitmanian fallacy" of national expression, pantheism, and so forth, and Lawrence is nowhere mentioned, having been succeeded by Bridges, Moore, and Mrs. Daryush. Miss Roberts's novels also go unmentioned, Winters having killed them off as early as 1933 with the charge of "mannerism."

Winters tends to make his obiter dicta in extreme detail, isolating one poem or even a few lines for special evaluation. Wallace Stevens may be afflicted with a "hedonist degeneracy," for example, but his "Sunday Morning" is "probably the greatest American poem of the twentieth century and is certainly one of the greatest contemplative poems in English"; Tate's "Shadow and Shade" and "The Cross" are "two of the great lyrics of our time"; and Herrick's "Gather Ye Rosebuds" is "clearly superior" to Marvell's "To His Coy Mistress." The passage of nine lines in Eliot's "Gerontion" beginning: "I that was near your heart was removed therefrom" is Eliot's "one passage of major poetry"; a poem of Robinson Jeffers's has no quotable lines "save perhaps three," and those "heavy with dross"; and a poem by Bridges is described as having all its power concentrated in the middle paragraph (*sic*), while another by Williams is chiefly carried by eight good lines. A poem by Robinson has six stanzas that "show less strength" than seven others, and another is turned into "perfect tragedy" by two fine lines.

Winters's comparative evaluations, like Eliot's, have the capacity for cutting across barriers of time as well as wide differences of type in the quest for similarity. "My own preference for Pope and Blake remains unshakable," he writes typically. Winters's pose is that of a mind flashing across the whole corpus of poetry in English in the search for a comparison, and he is perfectly capable, in one passage, of placing Byron by comparisons with aspects of Jonson, Campion, Googe, Turberville, Lawrence, and Poe, or, in another, of discussing the difference between Hart Crane and William Carlos Williams in terms of the Petrarchan rhetoric of the sixteenth century, the metaphysical verse of the seventeenth century, the sonnets of Shakespeare and Donne, and the poetry of Fulke Greville, Vaux, Googe, Gascoigne, Turberville, Daniel, and Drayton.

In all this welter of comparison, dictum, evaluation, and posturing Winters retains one constant point of view, that of "morality." Art is moral, he has written, and criticism must necessarily be the same. Precisely what he means by "moral" in this connection is vastly complicated and contradictory, and will be discussed later in more detail, but some sense at least of how he sees the process of moral evaluation operating in

art can be obtained from a key passage in *The Anatomy of Nonsense.*
Winters writes:

> According to my view, the artistic process is one of moral eval-
> uation of human experience, by means of a technique which renders
> possible an evaluation more precise than any other. The poet tries
> to understand his experience in rational terms, to state his under-
> standing, and simultaneously to state, by means of the feelings
> which we attach to words, the kind and degree of emotion that
> should properly be motivated by this understanding. The artistic
> result differs from the crude experience mainly in its refinement of
> judgment: the difference in really good art is enormous, but the
> difference is of degree rather than of kind.

Implicit in this view of the moral nature of art and criticism is the
obligation on the critic to "correct" traditional opinion in so far as he
believes it to be wrong. Without question, this wearying ethical burden
is in part responsible for some of Winters's wilder evaluations. His
attempt in *Maule's Curse* to establish Jones Very as the superior in every
way of Emerson—an attempt doomed to failure when he printed twenty-
two of Very's poems as an appendix to the volume—is only a small part
of the vast plan Winters defines with unusual humility in the Foreword
to the book. "My ultimate hope," he wrote, "is to establish a critical
basis for a fairly complete revision of the history of American literature,
a plan which may require a good many years of labor." Inasmuch as
Winters in another place refers to Churchill, Gascoigne, and Johnson as
"great masters obscured by history," and has for years been carrying on
a running campaign to ensure Gascoigne, as well as Barnabe Googe and
Turberville, their "rightful" place in the literary hierarchy, there is at
least a possibility that after disposing of American literature he looks
forward to rearranging the history of English literature or even of world
literature.

Into this giant project in the correction of opinion only now beginning
to emerge, all of Winters's critical writing is designed to fit. *Primitivism
and Decadence*, he has explained, is a study of the moral significance of
forms, with writers discussed merely to illustrate them; *Maule's Curse*
complements it, as a study of the moral significance of individual writers;
The Anatomy of Nonsense is a study of what Winters believes to be the
four "most influential tendencies in the literary practice of our time, and
as far as may be the most influential minds themselves." (That this is a
shaky eminence for John Crowe Ransom and Wallace Stevens at least,
if not for T. S. Eliot and Henry Adams, goes without saying.) Alan
Swallow, an admirer of Winters, in an appreciation in the *Rocky Mountain
Review* for Fall 1944, has added to this list what he considers to be a
fourth major work, Winters's long article "The Sixteenth Century Lyric

in England" in *Poetry: A Magazine of Verse* for February, March, and April of 1939. Mr. Swallow puts this forward as Winters's chief essay in construction rather than destruction, "a study of the history of what he considers the wiser tradition of method and idea." Since then Winters has added what would seem to be a similar essay in construction, the study of Robinson.

Winters is nothing if not a patient and far-sighted worker, as is demonstrated (according to his account) by the seventeen years he spent working on the five long essays that make up *Primitivism and Decadence:* revising them constantly, working most of his periodical writing into them, conferring on them with everyone available, and even changing his attitude toward modern poetry completely and carrying on. Opposite the title page of *Maule's Curse* Winters listed two further volumes of literary criticism "in preparation": *Studies of the American Historians and Critics* and *A Brief Outline History of the Rhetoric of the Short Poem in English. The Anatomy of Nonsense* is presumably a thin slice of the first, but what has become of the rest of it and of the entire second project in the year since 1937, only Winters knows. Significantly, perhaps, *The Anatomy of Nonsense*, issued by the same publisher five years later, carries no listing of works in preparation. If Winters has discarded them, there is no doubt that it is only because some other part of the literary canon seems in more desperate need of reconditioning and overhaul at the moment.

2

For detailed study of the evaluative method at work, Winters's second book, *Maule's Curse*, is probably best, since it is his only book concerned primarily with writers, the first having dealt with forms, the third with ideas, and the fourth with a single poet. It is also probably his most substantial, although certainly not his flashiest, piece of work. The "curse" of the title is the prophecy in Hawthorne's *The House of the Seven Gables:* "God will give him blood to drink!" predicted for Colonel Pyncheon by a man he had wronged. Winters believes that our great writers of the last century, from Cooper to James, suffered from this figurative curse; specifically, that having been cut off from their true literary heritage, they were "abnormally sensitive to the influence of European romanticism," and thus drank blood—their own. To an extent, the book's unity around this curse is factitious, since in one sense every writer, even the most severe classicist, drinks his own blood, and in another sense our major nineteenth-century writers, who produced a line of genuinely great works from *The Scarlet Letter* through *Moby Dick* to *The Ambassadors*, can hardly be considered to have been cursed at all, at least not unless Winters is prepared to ask still greater work of them or establish it as within their potentialities.

(This, incidentally, is the stumbling-block that largely shattered the early work of Van Wyck Brooks, as well as a good deal of sociological criticism by other writers: the fact that before you can show James or Twain, Hawthorne or Melville to have been the victims of a hostile environment, you have to establish that they were capable of finer work than they achieved; that is, you have to demand a better book than *Moby Dick* or *Huckleberry Finn*. It is obvious that in a more favorable social environment they would have produced vastly different works, and probably, in the case of James particularly, works for a much broader public, but that is about as far as environmental criticism alone can go.)

Take Winters's book, then, merely as a series of critical essays on nineteenth-century American writers, or, as it is subtitled, *Seven Studies in the History of American Obscurantism*. The seven essays deal with Hawthorne, Cooper, Melville, Poe, Emerson and Jones Very, Emily Dickinson, and Henry James. Winters's procedure in each chapter, roughly, is to discuss the writer's mind, analyze examples of his work with specific evaluations and extensive quotation, and, finally, summarize the values of his work and ideas.

Hawthorne comes through as fundamentally a failure, a man who produced "one of the chief masterpieces of English prose," *The Scarlet Letter*, then sank into inane romanticism; Cooper as a man who embodied a great social ideal, but was corroded by romantic sentiment and can hope to survive only in isolated great fragments; Melville as "the greatest man of his era and of his nation," a man who faced down the fruition of Maule's curse in the character of Ahab, comprehended and mastered it; Poe as a man of remarkable consistency in his criticism and creative writing and of exceptional worthlessness in both; Emerson as vastly inferior to Jones Very (who had "moral intelligence"), and the source of much of our literature's confusion;[6] Emily Dickinson as "a poetic genius of the highest order" and "one of the greatest lyric poets of all time," nevertheless impoverished by tastelessness and crudity; and Henry James as a monstrous failure whose aims and incidental abilities were so vast as to make him a phenomenon of unequaled interest. To me, at least, these judgments (which have been presented as fairly as possible, but always with the reservation that the total judgments inherent in Winters's long and ambiguous essays cannot be summarized in a sentence) seem beautifully and exactly right in the cases of Melville and Poe, vastly unfair to Emerson and James, far too kind to Cooper, and in the cases of Hawthorne and Miss Dickinson at least debatable.

[6] By *Edwin Arlington Robinson* (1946), Emerson has emerged as the great enemy, and almost everything bad in Robinson is "Emersonian."

The good things in *Maule's Curse* are valuable critical work. The fine surgical job on Poe, for example, was long overdue, and should have given our contemporary Poe-worshippers, among them Edmund Wilson and Van Wyck Brooks, the literary equivalent of cauliflower ears. Winters displays Poe's ignorance and pretension to learning as a critic; explores the vulgar sentimentality of his mind; registers reasonable shock at the corrupt and mechanical nature of his poetics, which reduce poetry to "triviality and charlatanism" and constitute a formal æsthetics of obscurantism; exposes the absurdity of his metrical theories and the crudity of his ear; lists his fantastic evaluations of writers; and finally demolishes his poems and tales, with particular attention to the puerility of his style. All together, it is a remarkable job of deserved butchery, and the possibility that it was all done for the wrong reasons, the suggestion on almost every page that Winters's chief objection to Poe is Poe's opposition to the concept of art and criticism as acts of moral evaluation, cannot detract from it. (Even the reader's awareness that there is more than a little kinship between Poe and Winters, that Winters's evaluations of writers are equally fantastic and his metrical theories almost as absurd, besides pointing up the familiar irony of the pot and the kettle, do nothing to vitiate a solid critical achievement.)

Whenever he is able to take time off from the responsibilities of moral evaluation, Winters is impressive as a close and imaginative reader, and several critical readings in the book, particularly a detailed analysis of the allegorical symbolism in the scene from *The Scarlet Letter* where Hester and Pearl wait in Governor Bellingham's mansion and see themselves distorted in a mirror, are quite penetrating. Despite Winters's dubious theories of metrics, particularly his theory of the metrical basis of free verse (discussed below), he sometimes produces remarkably stimulating metrical analyses, of which one in *Maule's Curse*, of three of Emily Dickinson's poems, is a fine example. The book is also useful for sharp analyses of various aspects of American cultural history, the best example being Winters's discussion of the "Puritan Paradox," the belief in predestination combined with action on the basis of a belief in free will. For the details of this idea Winters seems to be indebted to Henry Bamford Parkes, to whom he acknowledges a wide debt on many aspects of American thought, but his specific application of it to the strain of allegorizing in New England writers from Cotton Mather to Henry Adams is a genuine achievement.

Just as his treatment of Poe is probably the most convincing thing in the book, Winters's vast overestimation of Fenimore Cooper is easily the least convincing. Winters attempts to establish Cooper as a realistic writer, defending the factual accuracy of such things as the feats in the Leatherstocking Tales, when it is obvious (as D. H. Lawrence, John Macy, and others have pointed out) that the only possible basis for treating

Cooper with any seriousness is as a mythmaker. He quotes most of a scene from *The Deerslayer*, paragraph after paragraph of Cooper's stilted and heavy-handed prose, with such commendations as: "probably as great an achievement of its length as one will find in American fiction outside of Melville," or "the prose suddenly takes on a quality of universality and of grandeur such as to prepare one for the metaphysical quality of the action shortly to follow." Winters's chief praise, however, is for Cooper's novel *The Water-Witch*, which he evaluates moderately as "certainly one of the most brilliant, if scarcely one of the most profound, masterpieces of American prose." There seems little doubt that the actual basis of Winters's praise for Cooper lies in Cooper's undemocratic and aristocratic political ideas, and his cognate "rhetorical grandeur"; Winters devotes the first section of his essay to praising and defending Cooper's "public morality" in detail, and concludes his estimate with what must be surely one of the most plaintive rallying-cries for reaction ever uttered: "He embodies a social ideal that in his own lifetime was so far gone in decay that his defense of it cost him his reputation, and that it may scarcely be said to have survived him to the extent of two decades."

Winters's evaluations in the book are possibly most offensive in his offhand dismissals of major figures. He sees Thoreau and Alcott only as two harmless Emersonian eccentrics, referring to "the pastoral idiosyncracies of Thoreau" and "the mild idiocy of Alcott," and if the word "madness," used repeatedly, means anything at all, he thinks Henry James was as insane as his characters. However, every chapter of *Maule's Curse* contains Winters's usual quota of flat evaluative dicta about individual works, passages, or even lines, all of them highly subjective and few of them documented. To choose a few examples at random, he dismisses everything of Hawthorne's except *The Scarlet Letter* as either "failures" or "slight performances"; chooses the seventh chapter of *The Deerslayer* as probably "the best single passage of prose in Cooper," and the first and last chapters of *The Prairie* as "the next best" prose; lists "the greatest works of Melville, aside from *Moby Dick*," as *Benito Cereno*, *The Encantadas*, and *Billy Budd*; enumerates the only passages of Poe's verse that are "fairly well executed," a total of fewer than a hundred lines scattered over five poems; prints the three poems of Emily Dickinson's that combine "her greatest power with her finest execution"; and points out that a man named Frederick Goddard Tuckerman is "much like the Hawthorne of the last romances, except that he writes better," and that the poems of Jones Very, "an impressive writer," are as excellent, "within their limits," as those of Traherne, Herbert, or Blake.

Winters deserves particular praise for his treatment of Herman Melville, to whom (almost alone of contemporary critics, with the honorable exception of F. O. Matthiessen) he has at last given his rightful due as America's greatest writer and one of the world's supreme novelists. Winters is weak, or at least too limited, in interpreting the deeper meanings of *Moby Dick*, but in detailed symbolic interpretation of passages he is invaluable. He seems to be totally unaware, for example, of the elaborate homosexual imagery running through Melville, especially concentrated in his favorite short novel, *Billy Budd* (a particularly surprising limitation in view of the fact that Winters is one of the few critics who have commented on homosexuality in print, and he has even noticed a possibly homosexual theme in a Robinson poem). Winters's study of Melville is nevertheless a remarkable piece, if only for its full and excellently chosen quotations, and despite the possibility, as in the case of his Poe study, that Winters is actually evaluating the man accurately for the wrong reasons, for a "morality" that seems to be his chief interest in all of the works of Melville's he praises.

A few additional points about *Maule's Curse* deserve mention. First, the matter of "obscurantism," the key word of his subtitle and a charge at least as frequent in the book as "romanticism," to which Winters closely relates it. By "obscurantism" Winters means "the development of feeling in excess of the motive," which is more or less what the Greeks thought of as "hysteria" and regarded as a specifically female complaint, seated in the womb. On the basis of this definition, Winters sees all his seven writers as afflicted with obscurantism in some form, and in fact sees it as the chief phenomenon of what he calls "the romantic period," from 1750 to the present. Needless to say, the "obscurantism" phrasing of Maule's curse holds no more water than does the blood-drinking phrasing of it, and the position of a man indicting two centuries of literature *in toto*, except for such anachronisms as Bridges and Sturge Moore, is at best precarious. Secondly, it should be remarked that the treatment of Henry James in the book, quite apart from Winters's tortured and contradictory evaluation of him as both a monstrous failure and the greatest novelist in English after Melville, is one of the most completely inadequate in critical writing of our time.

3

The systematic æsthetic evaluation of works of art as the principal aim of criticism did not come into literary history until after the Renaissance, but in the modern period, until the present century, it has been the dominant tradition. The Greek and Roman critics were chiefly interested in poetics and analysis of the social nature and effects of art; medieval critics devoted their principal attention to moral and allegorical interpretation; and Renaissance criticism, particularly in England, centered on the moral justification of imaginative literature. By Jacobean times in

England, however, criticism began to assume the concentration on evaluation it was to display for three centuries, as it did throughout Europe after the Renaissance and in America, following a natural lag, about the time of the Revolution.

During the seventeenth and eighteenth centuries in England evaluative criticism flowered, and figures like Thomas Rymer, John Dennis, and Samuel Johnson reached heights of dogmatic statement that even Winters has never equaled. Rymer, whom Macaulay called with some justice "the worst critic that ever lived," has come down to us as a complete joke, his name a synonym for abysmal critical stupidity, but in his day he was remarkably influential. Readers were impressed when he dismissed Chaucer with the statement that "our language was not then capable of any heroic character," rewrote Beaumont and Fletcher according to his idea of classical correctness, or tore *Othello* apart as a tissue of nonsense, "a bloody farce without salt or savor," written by a man who thought a noble-born Venetian woman could love a blackamoor. In tragedy, Rymer wrote, Shakespeare "appears quite out of his element; his brains are turned; he raves and rambles without any coherence, any spark of reason, or any rule to control him, and set bounds to his frenzy." As for his poetry, "the neighing of a horse or the howling of a mastiff possesses more meaning."

John Dennis, who considered Rymer's censures of Shakespeare, despite some disagreement, "in most of the particulars very sensible and very just," and who "improved" *The Merry Wives of Windsor* into *The Comical Gallant*, was a somewhat more moralistic critic, convinced that the principal aim of poetry is the reformation of the sinful human mind. His dogmatic evaluations, particularly of his bête noire, Alexander Pope, or the remarkable going-over he gave Addison's *Cato*, were just as arbitrary, and his general dicta on literature somewhat more detailed.

Dr. Johnson's vigorous evaluations of writers, in conversation with Boswell and in his *Lives of the Poets*, should be too well known to need retelling, but some of his lesser-known statements may be worth noting. In an essay in the *Rambler*, Johnson flayed Spenser's "vicious style" and the "difficult, unpleasing, and tiresome" Spenserian stanza, and even in his reverential *Preface* to Shakespeare he listed such defects as "in his comick scenes he is seldom very successful" and "his declamations or set speeches are commonly cold or weak," and added that, considering the condition of Shakespeare's life and the barbarity of his age, readers should "make some allowance for his ignorance."

The great dogmatic evaluator of the nineteenth century, the successor to Rymer, Dennis and Johnson, was Walter Savage Landor. Landor was capable of slapping Vergil for a phrase "scarcely Latin," announcing that of Politian's poems "one only has merit," attacking Coleridge viciously, dismissing French literature *in toto*, particularly French tragedy and

Voltaire, and slaughtering Pope and Byron. Explicitly carrying dogmatic evaluation to its logical conclusion, as Winters only has by implication, Landor stated of his own work that his ten worst *Imaginary Conversations* could not be equaled by the most talented of their attackers in ten years of labor, and that the two fingers that held his own pen had more power than the two houses of Parliament.

It is obvious that Yvor Winters is directly in the line of these men— that, like Landor, he is a throwback to the violent oracular tradition of an earlier century. Like all of these men Winters bases his evaluations in classicism and traditionalism, and like most of them he enlists his evaluations in the cause of political reaction. Some of these comparisons have been made in print before. Cleanth Brooks compared Winters with Rymer in the *Kenyon Review* for Spring 1944, for "sheer guts and blindsides," and many reviewers, perhaps following Winters's own lead in calling Johnson the only critic in English who deserves the epithet "great," have noted the parallel with Johnson. No one, however, seems to have noticed the more startling parallel with Dennis. When Dennis attacks the poets he finds bad, not only as faulty artists but as wicked men, enemies of morality, or remarks: "And when a man is sure, 'tis only his duty to speak with a modest assurance," he might almost be an earlier incarnation of Winters, so little have two centuries and a half altered the manner of literary evaluation. The vocabulary and examples of Winters's criticism are contemporary, but his heart and mind seem firmly back in the London of 1700.

Winters himself has furnished another genealogy for his criticism. "This view of poetry in its general outline is not original," he writes in *Primitivism and Decadence*, "but is a restatement of ideas that have been current in English criticism since the time of Sidney, that have appeared again in most of the famous apologists for poetry since Sidney, especially in Arnold and Newman." He means, of course, the line of moral critics of literature which began with the earliest Greek writers, a tradition sometimes coinciding with that of dogmatic evaluation, sometimes veering away. Obviously, Winters is in this tradition as well, although it comes as something of a shock to find him identifying his violent and uncharitable dogmatism with the gentleness of Sidney or Newman. The identity with Arnold is much closer, and, although Winters might deny it indignantly, his central doctrine, the concept of art as "the permeation of human experience by a consistent moral understanding," seems to be no more than a rephrasing of Arnold's concept of art as "the criticism of life" through the application of moral ideas.

There are, of course, other moral criticisms of literature that Winters tactfully does not mention. There is Macaulay's stuffy and utilitarian Whig morality, Tolstoy's fanatical hatred of any art obscure to a nineteenth-century Russian serf, the timid prudishness of William Dean

Howells proposing that fiction include nothing a novelist would not say to a young girl, and many others as bad. It would be unfair to put Winters's aloof morality in a class with these. Nevertheless, all of them are implicit in the tradition of moral criticism, just as Rymer's worst excesses are implicit in the tradition of dogmatic evaluation, and a man who merges within his work both traditions, like Dennis or Winters, can be saved from falling into either priggishness or pontifical foolishness only by being invariably right. There should be no need to point out that Winters is hardly that.

4

In our own time there are other types of critical evaluation, most of them somewhat less moral than Winters's, if fully as dogmatic. On the level of journalism there is (or was, since he seems to have given up literary criticism permanently) that redoubtable foe of the booboisie H. L. Mencken. His dogmatic evaluations seem almost always the product of simple ignorance, yet, in a curious fashion, they parody Winters's. Mencken has described Poe and Mark Twain as "the two undoubted world figures that we have contributed to letters," has announced that Lizette Woodworth Reese "has written more sound poetry, more genuinely eloquent and beautiful poetry, than all the new poets put together," has claimed that in Henry James America achieved its own "Horace Walpole," and has immortalized one of the two or three creative thinkers of undoubted genius in America, Thorstein Veblen, as "a geyser of pishposh." The basis for Mencken's evaluations, in presumable contrast to Winters's, is probably only his honest inability to comprehend serious writing, and he is the lifelong enemy of any form of morality, but it is remarkable how close his statement about Poe and Twain is to Winters's about Cooper, or how much his estimate of Lizette Reese resembles that of Winters on Elizabeth Daryush.

The other principal fount of dogmatic evaluation in our criticism is Mencken's long-time friend Ezra Pound. Long before his stage of Fascism-cum-paranoia Pound was printing obiter dicta beside which Winters's best look pale. Pound has described *Paradise Lost* as a conventional melodrama written by a "coarse-minded," "asinine," "disgusting," and "beastly" man; dismissed the literature of the nineteenth century *in toto*; announced his preference for Whistler's drawing of young Miss Alexander to all the "Judaic drawings" of Blake; consigned Tasso, Ariosto, and Spenser "to the scrap heap"; discarded Dryden as a "lunkhead" and his work as "outstanding aridity"; announced that Herodotus is literature and Thucydides "journalism"; and attacked the "hedging, backing and filling" of a man he calls sometimes Aristotle and sometimes "Arry Stotl."

It is at least possible, however, that Pound himself doesn't believe these judgments. Referring to a statement he had made to the effect that Catullus was in some ways a better writer than Sappho, Pound once explained: "I don't in the least know whether this is true. One should start with an open mind," and he has put on record both a fine and detailed study of James's genius and the statement: "for sheer dreariness one reads Henry James."

One of the most curious aspects of Pound's evaluations is that almost every time he praises a good writer or work he has managed to couple him with a poor writer as equally good. He has discussed Wyndham Lewis's *Tarr* and Joyce's *Portrait of the Artist as a Young Man* in the same terms, spoken of "Mina Loy and Marianne Moore," and referred to Joseph Gould and William Carlos Williams as two fine modern poets. (Incidentally, Waldo Frank, another passionate evaluator, has had the same unhappy result with such pairs as "Sherwood Anderson and Manuel Komroff," "D. H. Lawrence and J. D. Beresford," and those two "comedic talents" Dorothy Richardson and James Joyce.) Probably this yoking of a great writer and an inferior one, hack or fool, in the same adulatory sentence displays a more fundamental, and certainly more dangerous, want of taste than would praising only fools and hacks.

Another leading type of critical evaluation in our time is what might be called "the correction of opinion." On the Mencken level one of the most distasteful examples of this is Ernest Boyd's book *Literary Blasphemies*, an attempt to revise downward the traditional estimates of a number of authors from Shakespeare to Hardy, by such expedients as describing Milton as a paranoid albino whose blindness was undoubtedly the result of hereditary syphilis, or Henry James as an Anglomaniac social climber who spent all his time inventing euphemisms for the word "typewriter." On a more scholarly level, practically every professor of literature who has ever written a book has tried his hand, either directly or indirectly, at suggesting writers he believes should be ranked higher and lower. This is a more or less pointless form of activity, since the critic rarely, and the professor never, succeeds in altering literary taste, but except for the arbitrary venom the corrector of opinion seems almost always to feel toward the holder of any established reputation (Winters's own activities here are unfortunately typical), it is harmless enough, a mild professorial form of goldfish-eating.

5

Probably the most important single question to consider about Winters's evaluations is precisely what he means by the word "moral." He has defined or used it to mean almost a dozen different things, some of them completely inconsistent with others and some of them simply meaningless. He has equated it with "striving toward an ideal of poetic form," with classical as opposed to romantic, with traditional as opposed to experimental, with "just feeling, properly motivated," with "personal form and controlled direction," and, in at least one place, with "human." Sometimes it seems to be a technical literary term, very close to Arnold's "grand style" or "high seriousness," sometimes it means didactic, sometimes it is ordinary ethics or good taste, sometimes it means simply "reactionary," and in many cases it seems to mean nothing more than that Winters liked the work and thought it good. The only conceivable thread on which all these usages can be strung is the theory that originally "moral" meant one clear thing to Winters, perhaps some personal, artistic discipline equivalent to the neo-humanist's "inner check," and then gradually extended in usage until it applied to the results of this control and finally to any work or attitude where the control could be presumed, that is, to any work Winters likes or any attitude he respects.[7]

Another way of getting at what Winters actually means by moral is noting what he regards as immoral. First, of course, the opposite of all his synonyms for morality: formlessness, romanticism, experimentalism; extravagant, hysterical, or "improperly motivated" feeling, "obscurantism," and so on. Principally, he detests two things he calls "primitivism" and "decadence." "Primitive" poets, as Winters defines them, are "those who utilize all the means necessary to the most vigorous form, but whose range of material is limited," while "decadents" are "those who display a fine sensitivity to language and who may have a very wide scope, but whose work is incomplete formally . . . or is somewhat but not too seriously weakened by a vice of feeling." The primitive poet, Winters explains, is thus the major poet on a smaller scale, while the decadent poet is the major poet with some important faculty absent. He regards William Carlos Williams as an example of the former, Wallace Stevens as an example of the latter.

These distinctions are valid, and although his use of the terms, like his use of "obscurantism," is almost wholly arbitrary, bearing no particular relation to the etymological origins of the words or their traditional usages, there is probably no reason why he shouldn't call "primitive" and "decadent" what another writer might call "minor" and "defective" or a third "X" and "Y." However, Winters creates confusion by also using "decadent" in a more traditional sense, as where he says that

---

[7] In Winters's recent work, "moral" seems to have become almost entirely a matter of the attitudes expressed in the paraphrasable prose content of the poem. Thus Robinson's "choice of matter," "subjects," and "themes" frequently constitute his morality, and a poem like "Hillcrest" appears to be moral and "counter-romantic" largely because "it tells us that life is a very trying experience, to be endured only with pain and to be understood only with difficulty." In other words, a stoic poem dealing with "the endurance of suffering" and taking an approved attitude toward it is a "moral" poem.

Sidney and Spenser are decadents "for they are concerned with relatively meaningless fabrications of procedure," or attacks Henry Adams as the decadence of Puritanism and Swinburne as "the decadence of a literary tradition." Finally, the particular enemy of Winters's morality is something he calls "hedonism," which led Cleanth Brooks to tag him a Stoic, and which he finds in its purest form in Stevens (on the very flimsy basis, incidentally, of reading "Sunday Morning" on the level of paraphrasable content alone, as he has come increasingly to read poetry, although elsewhere he explicitly condemns the method). The end-product of hedonism, he says, is "ennui," just as the end-product of Adams's decadence is "confusion," and in one or the other of those pits, Winters believes, any literature not firmly based in morality must inevitably fall.

For his moral emphasis, the core of his critical position, Winters seems chiefly indebted to the neo-humanists, particularly to Irving Babbitt (from whom he also inherits the example of dogmatic and intemperate judgments). Winters has confessed to admiring Babbitt and having "learned a good deal from him," as well as acknowledged specific indebtedness to a number of Babbitt's ideas and analyses, but he seems to have little use for any of the other neo-humanists, and he has announced that he does not consider himself to be one of them. Moreover, in an essay in C. Hartley Grattan's symposium, *The Critique of Humanism*, Winters bitterly attacked the neo-humanist movement and many of its spokesmen for "bastard impressionism" and "moral mechanism," not to speak of bad writing, intemperate violence (an amusing charge), illbreeding and "spiritual bankruptcy." Nevertheless, Winters's central opposition to romanticism as seeking to "free" the emotions rather than "control" them is the key doctrine of the movement, and Winters is certainly closer to the neo-humanist position than he is to any other.

Next to Winters's "morality," his metrical theories probably most need clarifying. Winters pays a good deal of attention to scansion, particularly in *Primitivism and Decadence*, and many of his metrical analyses, like his above-mentioned work on three of Emily Dickinson's poems, are genuinely valuable. However, two serious errors vitiate much of his metrical theory and some of his metrical practice. The first is what might be called the fallacy of imitative rhythm, the idea that meters and metrical variations alone serve to suggest (rather than to reinforce) meaning or mood. This theory has been exploded so often and so efficiently (by Richards, among others), by the simple substitution of other words or nonsense syllables in the same rhythm, in which form the rhythm produces none of the suggestion that was claimed for it, that it is surprising to see Winters apparently still believing it. His second error is the theory that free verse is regular and scannable in terms of a long foot containing one heavy accent and any number of light accents and unaccented syllables; that is, that it is not free verse at all but accentual verse. To the establishment of this theory Winters has devoted a long section of *Primitivism and Decadence* and has created a vast and elaborate rationale, permitting so many types of exceptions and irregular lines that they cover anything that does not fit into his scansion. Winters takes up the inevitable, and utterly damning, question of why any passage of prose, including his own, could not be scanned in the same fashion, but except for the arguments that the syllabic arrangement of prose is accidental, while the same syllabic arrangement in free verse would presumably be intentional, and that some sense of the rhythm he describes is *felt* in free verse and not in prose, he has no answer to it.

The "science" of metrics has always been, to the extent that most of it exists in the scanner's mind and not on the page, a form of sleight-of-hand (so that, for example, Hopkins could scan anything in a falling rhythm by the simple expedient of beginning each foot with the accented syllable—he could have scanned everything in a rising rhythm just as easily by beginning the feet a syllable later), and on that basis Winters's scansion of free verse is probably no more illegitimate than most arbitrary scansions. When he writes free verse, however, on the basis of his own system of scansion, Winters is roughly in the position of a magician off the stage whose pocket handkerchief still stubbornly keeps turning into the American flag.[8]

Any general estimate of Yvor Winters must take account of his failings and limitations. One of the most apparent is the narrowness of his knowledge. Winters is fairly well read, but seemingly only within a very restricted compass, specifically the English and American novel and English, American, and modern French poetry. He seems to be totally unfamiliar with any Continental literature other than the French, and except for Dante I can recall no mention in all his critical writing of any imaginative author who did not write in English or French, and the French references are limited. To choose a few names at random, Winters has never mentioned Dostoyevsky or Pushkin, Boccaccio or Petrarch, Goethe or Heine, Cervantes or Lope de Vega, or even Stendhal or Villon. This is not to insist that he discuss foreign writers, particularly since he seems to be scrupulous about not referring to a man he is unable to read in the original, but simply to make the point that it is absurd to list the great novelists or poets, as Winters has done endlessly, and make them all English and American.

Even in his own specialties there are curious gaps in Winters's knowledge. He did a long and detailed chapter on Hawthorne without seeming

---

[8] It is not within the province of this essay to examine Winters's poetry, but it may be in order here to note that what of it I have read seems always remarkably consistent with his critical principles: that is, traditional in form, moral, heavily classical, and somewhat old-fashioned. Much of it is occasional or dedicatory in nature, all of it is restrained, and it simply depends on one's personal preference whether it seems graceful and quietly moving or academic and deadly dull.

to know of the existence of Hawthorne's extremely realistic and repor-
torial Journals, let alone having read them. He makes a number of highly
debatable statements about the history of English poetry without offering
any evidence or documentation for them, as Ransom has pointed out, and,
as Horace Gregory has charged, seems not to know the difference between Elizabethan and early Tudor verse.

Along with his limitations of knowledge, Winters frequently suffers
from a refusal to use his mind. There are enough real contradictions in
Eliot's critical thought, for example, to make it unnecessary for Winters
to invent others, as he has done by the simple process of finding two
superficially contradictory passages and refusing to resolve them by
reading them on any level except the literal. Taking an apparent pride
in ignorance, Winters has cited a sonnet of Edwin Arlington Robinson's,
"En Passant," "for which I am unable to offer an explanation," and has
boasted that the significance of the title of Stevens's poem "The Comedian
as the Letter C," "I regret to say, escapes both my learning and my
ingenuity." It did not, however, escape the learning and ingenuity of
R. P. Blackmur, who published, in the *Hound & Horn* in 1932 and on
page 101 of *The Double Agent* in 1935, a remarkable and completely
satisfying interpretation of the title. One might wish that where Winters
refuses to think he would at least consent to draw on the thought of
others, particularly when it has been available to him for a decade.[9]

The products of this occasional ignorance and mental rigidity are a
number of opinions that are not so much overdogmatic or eccentric as
simply ridiculous. Winters has described Shakespeare as having written
Macbeth and *Othello* in order to put a moral evaluation of sin on record.
He has announced that Henry Adams's *History of the United States* is
"the greatest historical work in English," with the exception of Gibbon,
not by way of praising Adams, whom he detests, but in order to club
Adams's other books with it. (Adams himself, incidentally, although
Winters does not mention and may not know it, wrote that he preferred
a dozen pages of his novel *Esther* to the whole history, "including maps
and indices.") Winters has identified Matthew Arnold as "one of the
great poets of the nineteenth century" and "one of the worst poets in
English" in the same sentence. He finds Carlyle so literally unmentionable that the only reference to him in Winters's work is a footnote: "I
am simply taking it for granted that my reader feels, as I do, that the less
said about Carlyle the better," reinforced by omission from the book's

[9] T. Weiss, in his brilliant analysis of Winter's critical failings in "The Nonsense
of Winters' Anatomy," in the *Quarterly Review of Literature*, Spring 1944 and Summer
1944, comes to a conclusion somewhat more extreme than mine, that Winters's
troubles stem from a fundamental "inability to read," "inability to write," and
"inability to understand poetry." I am indebted to Weiss's excellent study for a
number of insights, I am in general agreement with almost everything it says, and
I am not at all certain that Weiss is not right on this point too.

index. Finally, he has found the "tone" of Yeats and Robinson Jeffers similar, and has traced T. S. Eliot's theories of poetry back to those of Edgar Allan Poe.

Winters's political and social ideas also seem to have a bearing on his critical opinions. "Winters' position is that of the Christian," Alan Swallow writes of him in the *Rocky Mountain Review*, but although advocating "the discipline fostered by the Catholic and Anglo-Catholic Churches," Winters has identified himself as "one of the unregenerate; I am not a Christian," and he prefers Irving Babbitt's label "reactionary," used as a term of highest praise. Winters would probably deny making literary judgments on the basis of political prejudice, but, to choose two obvious examples, it is hard to interpret his bitter attack on Parrington's *Main Currents in American Thought* and Bernard Smith's *Forces in American Criticism*, in Post Scripta II and III of *Anatomy of Nonsense*, as made on any but that basis.

Like Babbitt, his mentor (who once wrote: "there are tastes that deserve the cudgel"), Winters is neither the gentlest nor the best-bred controversialist imaginable. Some of his worst invective is reserved for Henry Adams, who occupies approximately the same position in Winters's cosmos that Rousseau does in Babbitt's or that Satan does in that of the Fundamentalist Christian. He has described Adams as "the radical disintegration of a mind," and has attacked him with such moralist name-calling as "hedonist," "nihilist," "neurotic," "childish," and "insolent," and, a little below the belt, charged that the suicide of his wife was the logical outcome of Adams's position. Suicide for an opponent is a favorite suggestion of Winters's, whose taste is perhaps not quite all that a moralist's should be, and he has proposed "the suicide of a gentleman" at least twice in print, once for Robinson Jeffers and once for Eugene Jolas. When Winters warms up to a controversy he runs to bitter sarcasm, and tends to make remarks on the order of "my acquaintance with the minds of my literary contemporaries is extensive . . . and to my regret I have found that many of the most brilliant of them understand simple matters only with the greatest of difficulty," or "in failure to note my criticism of these lines [his opponent] adhered rigidly to a convention of contemporary literary controversy against which it would ill become a very young writer like myself to protest."

Winters is, in fact, a wicked man to tangle with in print, and at one time or another he has quarreled with a good percentage of contemporary critics and reviewers. He seems to read every scrap of print that mentions his name, and replies to reviews with counter-reviews of the reviewer, articles with counter-articles, and chapters in books with counter-chapters in *his* books. He never forgets an attack, although he may wait years to reply, but sometimes he manages to forget details of what he originally wrote. His controversy with Theodore Spencer is instructive. In *Hound*

& Horn, April 1933, in a review of T. Sturge Moore's poetry, Winters claimed that Moore was a greater poet than Yeats. In *Hound & Horn*, October 1933, Spencer picked up Winters's remark and quietly demolished it by the simple expedient of printing the first quatrain of Moore's "Apuleius Meditates," which Winters had praised very highly, along with the first four lines of Yeats's "Leda and the Swan." In *The Anatomy of Nonsense*, in 1943, Winters continued the controversy, charged Spencer with misquoting him, and *completely misstated his original contentions!* (Any reader who doubts this statement is invited to check what Winters actually said about Yeats and Moore against his account of his remarks a decade later.) When tactics like this will not work, Winters descends to simple abuse. He answered one reviewer, who had been neither harsh nor personal, with "This is merely illiterate foolishness," and charges of "careless examination, amateur thinking, pretentious pedantry, and aimless innuendo." His reply, in Volume II, Number 2, of the *Quarterly Review of Literature*, to T. Weiss's review (which, it must be admitted, *was* both harsh and personal) rose to a real height of hysteria, shrieking "ignorance," "low-grade abuse," "he cannot understand a sentence," "misrepresentation and abuse," "deliberate dishonesty," and concluding gently: "Weiss is an ignoramus, a fool, and a liar." One sentence of Winters's reply is so revealing as to require quotation:

> The reasons for answering him are threefold: I believe that what I have written in my book is important, and I do not wish to see issues confused; I earn my living as a scholar, and my professional reputation is impugned by this kind of thing, and there are unfortunately a few persons in my profession, and occasionally in places of power, who believe everything they see in print—I speak from experience, not as a theorist; and finally there is too much of this kind of reviewing going on at present and it ought to be labelled for what it is.

Here, perhaps, in a patent and rather frightening insecurity, lies the basic clue to both Winters's personality and his criticism. It seems to be this insecurity that underlies his grandiose and pretentious projects announced and never pursued; his sweeping judgments given without a shred of evidence, and altered from one year to the next; his need to impress by any means; his private hierarchies of merit and minute authoritative gradings; his desperate need for a claque as well as his extreme susceptibility to any criticism; his insistence on such external props and rigidities as "moral," "logical," "rational," "discipline," "control," "reactionary"; his feeling that his poetry has been unappreciated and the consequent resentment, bitterness, and projection into obscure and unappreciated figures like Jones Very and Elizabeth Daryush; his vaunting of ignorance and his posturings in general; his bad manners and abusive snarlings. It adds up to what might be called the "baroque personality," [10] which occurs, like baroque in general, at the end of a line, when all functional possibilities seem exhausted, and the only way to counteract consequent insecurity and sense of failure is through more and more massive and grandiose ornamentation. Many of the dogmatic evaluators preceding Winters, from Rymer and Dennis to Mencken and Pound, seem baroque and insecure in precisely this fashion, as does a good part of the neo-humanist contingent Winters so much resembles, Irving Babbitt in particular.

In terms of this baroque personality, many of Winters's concepts and ideas become more readily comprehensible. For example, one of his contributions to modern criticism (inherited from Babbitt, but chiefly developed and propagated by Winters) is the concept of "the heresy of expressive form," which he defines as the belief that disintegration can best be expressed by a disintegrated or chaotic form, rather than by an ordered or disciplined form. He sees it as the outstanding characteristic of modern literature, particularly evident in Eliot, Pound, and Joyce, and traces it to Coleridge's doctrine of "organic form." As Weiss and a number of others have pointed out, Eliot, Pound, Joyce, and similar modern writers are *not* using a disintegrated or chaotic form, but a disintegrated-*seeming* and chaotic-*seeming* form that arises organically out of the nature of their subject-matter, but which is nevertheless carefully contrived, disciplined, and ordered (*Finnegans Wake* has so much order we don't know what to make of it, Weiss points out) in a sense and to an extent that a good deal of contemporary literature in traditional forms, including Winters's own verse, is not. Winters's problem here would seem to be that, himself requiring an externally imposed form and discipline to support his own self-doubts and the weight of his baroque ornamentation, he cannot conceive of an internally imposed form arising naturally and organically out of the artist's material.

Winters has contributed a number of things of value to contemporary criticism: some good metrical analyses; some brilliant close reading and studies of poetic structure (particularly in *The Anatomy of Nonsense*: of Stevens's "Anecdote of the Jar," Tate's "Death of Little Boys," and two lines from Browning's "Serenade at the Villa"); a salutary insistence on "the intellectual and moral significance of literary forms," and the relationship between beliefs and forms (although most of the specific relationships and significances he points out are foolish). Most important, he has, almost single-handedly, kept an important critical function, evaluation, alive for us. His evaluations tend to be made in terms that are semantically meaningless, contradictory, purely subjective, and never defined: "great," "superior," "major," "masterpiece," "sane," "flawed,"

[10] For this concept of the "baroque personality" and many of the ingredients that constitute it I am indebted, as for so much else in this book, to Leonard Brown.

"defects," "limitations," "civilized," "lucid," "first level," "second level." He gives only his conclusions, almost never with any evidence approaching adequacy, and in a form in which it is impossible to argue with him or even understand what he is trying to say. Nevertheless, he does evaluate, does compare, contrast, grade, rate, and rank, at a time when most serious criticism only analyzes and interprets, and when the reader of a critical article has to go to the newspaper reviewer to find out whether the work is any good or not (and then is misinformed more often than not). What criticism can adopt from Winters is his vigor and bold-ness of evaluation, while making sounder evaluations than his, making them on a basis of more significance to literature than his concepts of "rationality" and "morality," and with them giving the reader the whole structure of analysis, to serve as a basis for the reader's checking the evaluation or making his own on the evidence. Winters's own five-stage process culminating in evaluation (see above) is a fairly good basis for such a process. Winters himself has seldom taken advantage of it. Testing it first by turning it on him, as this essay has attempted to do, it works out pretty well. We find Yvor Winters, in a "unique act of judgment" dogmatic and impolite enough to flatter his methods, an excessively irritating and bad critic of some importance.

CHAPTER 3

T. S. ELIOT

and Tradition in Criticism

T. S. ELIOT's contribution to the new criticism has been chiefly, as John Crowe Ransom once phrased it, "the recovery of old criticism." His influence in this direction has been very great, and although it is hard to tell how much of this is the influence of the criticism itself and how much is respect for his authority as one of the foremost living poets, Eliot is undoubtedly our chief spokesman for a critical viewpoint that can be roughly called "traditional." He is a critic after the fashion of the poet-critics of earlier centuries, not so much a professional analyst of literature as a professional poet with a public function to perform. All his volumes of criticism are arrangements and rearrangements of the seventy-odd essays, reviews, prefaces, and lectures he has thought worth preserving, of the several hundred he has written, and almost none of his criticism has not first either appeared in a periodical, prefaced someone else's work in a book, or been delivered from a platform.

Eliot believes that criticism functions as a service to the reader of poetry and has spoken of the "preposterous assumption" that it is an autotelic activity. He sees this reader-service as dual, one function "the elucidation of art and the correction of taste," the other "to bring the poet back to life." The "tools" of the critic, with which he performs these functions, are "comparison and analysis," and the end of criticism is to establish a "tradition," a continuity, between present literature and taste and the literature of the past.

The word "tradition" is undoubtedly the key term in Eliot's critical writing, and what he means by it is at least as shifting and complex as what Winters means by "moral" or what Empson means by "ambiguity" (though Empson, unlike Eliot and Winters, recognizes the ambiguity of "ambiguity"). Sometimes, like Winters's "moral," Eliot's "traditional" means no more than "good," that he likes the work; and sometimes, as Ransom has pointed out, the concept of "tradition" is simply a metaphorical way of telling a writer not to be "too new." Actually Eliot's "tradition" is a utilitarian concept, and he constantly emphasizes the *using* of the tradition. He writes, for example, of Jonson: "We can even apply him, be aware of him as a part of our literary inheritance craving

73

further expression." The best way to find out what Eliot means by tradition, then, would be to watch it operating in his work.

Perhaps Eliot's most detailed use of tradition in a relatively pure literary sense is the second half, entitled "The Hawthorne Aspect," of his essay "Henry James," written for the James number of the *Little Review* in 1918 and not included in the *Selected Essays* in 1932. He exhibits James against the background of Hawthorne; thus illuminating the fiction of both of them by the comparison, asserting James's basic Americanism, and showing in detail what permanencies and what modifications are revealed in a literary tradition when it carries over a period of time.

A different and more characteristic use of tradition, this time for essentially nonliterary ends, is found in such essays of Eliot's as the ones on Bishop Andrewes and Archbishop Bramhall in *For Lancelot Andrewes* (1928), where he attempts to refurbish, amplify, and even artificially provide an Anglican literary tradition. He claims that Andrewes's sermons "rank with the finest English prose of their time, of any time," and are superior to Donne's because Donne's motives were "impure" and he lacked "spiritual discipline," a deficiency that has had the effect of making Donne's sermons more widely known. Thus, at one blow, Eliot establishes a literary tradition on the basis of criteria that are wholly ethical, attacks a great writer, *as writer*, with a whispered hint of apostasy or at least careerism in his clerical profession, and exalts a right relation to the English Church as the fount not only of salvation in a future life but of the best prose here and now. Eliot does a similar job with Bramhall, beginning with his philosophic usefulness as the scourge of Hobbes's materialism ("so similar to that of contemporary Russia") and ending with Bramhall somehow secure on a pinnacle of prose excellence.

Even at its broadest (that is, in the earlier essays), Eliot's tradition is highly exclusive. It seeks out the classic and excludes the romantic, and by "romantic" Eliot means a great many writers he does not like: the classic is "complete," "adult," and "orderly" where the romantic is "fragmentary," "immature," and "chaotic." This is not quite the same as dismissing the nineteenth century *in toto*, as Pound did (contrary to popular opinion, and unlike the much more consistent classicist Pound, Eliot tends to praise the poetry of Milton, Blake, Keats, and Tennyson and dislikes that of Pope), but Eliot in general sees his task as the substitution of his "tradition" for theirs: rescuing the Elizabethan dramatists from Lamb and Swinburne, combating the verdict of Hazlitt and Pater on Dryden, and in general reversing the nineteenth century's hierarchy.

Eliot carries a good share of the weight of tradition in his criticism by his prose style. It is formal, reserved, eloquent without ever becoming shrill, and at once highly stylized and transparently clear; an eighteenth-century style larded with twentieth-century terminology. It gives the

effect, frequently delusive, of being far removed from the tawdry concerns of the present in a concentration on the timeless. In part, of course,
this effect is obtained by Eliot's resolute refusal to print in book form
(with a very few exceptions) his criticism of contemporaries. His Harvard
lectures in 1933 on James, Pound, Joyce, and Lawrence, for example,
still languish unprinted, and he has never collected his six appreciations
of Pound, his pieces on other modern writers, or the various introductions he has written for contemporary books.[1] The sense Eliot's prose
gives of being non-temporal is so sharp, in fact, that coming on footnote
references to contemporary literary controversies in his work is always
a shock. This emeritus quality, incidentally, has not developed with time.
The first essays Eliot published, in his twenties, gave the same courtly-
old-gentleman effect, and in fact the work of the past few years is relatively mellow and informal by comparison.

The chief fault of Eliot's tradition lies in its omissions. Not only has
he paid almost no attention to contemporaries (which might be excusable
in a critic like Sainte-Beuve, since biographical data is never rounded out
until the subject's death, but is certainly inexcusable on the basis of any
method that claims to judge the new against a background of literary
tradition), but he has dealt with few Americans of any period (Poe is
perhaps the only one he mentions with any frequency). Except for a few
prefaces to books by such authors as Pound, Marianne Moore, and Djuna
Barnes (in some cases, I believe, *Criterion* reviews reprinted) he seems
never to have devoted an essay to any American creative writer but Henry
James, and never reprinted that after its first publication. Despite
F. O. Matthiessen's noble effort, in *The Achievement of T. S. Eliot*, to
place him in the American tradition—Puritanism, Dante scholarship at
Harvard, similarity of theme and manner to Hawthorne, Emily Dickinson, and James—Eliot seems almost entirely blind to the American
tradition, if not in flight from it.

Just as the Americans are omitted, a noble literary roster could be
compiled of the authors who do not seem to be in Eliot's tradition. As

---

[1] Some of Eliot's published pieces on his more distinguished contemporaries warrant
listing, for those who might be interested in looking them up. He has done at least six
on Pound: *Ezra Pound: His Metric and Poetry*, a pamphlet published in 1917; "A Note
on Ezra Pound" in *Today*, September 1918; "The Method of Mr. Pound" in the
Athenæum, October 24, 1919; the Introduction to Pound's *Selected Poems* in 1928,
which he edited; an article in the *Dial*, January 1928, entitled "Isolated Superiority";
and "Ezra Pound," in *Poetry: A Magazine of Verse*, September 1946. He has written
on Joyce in "Ulysses, Order and Myth," in the *Dial*, November 1923, and an Introductory Note to his selection of Joyce's prose, *Introducing James Joyce*, in 1942; on
Proust in the *Criterion*, October 1926; on Yeats in the *Southern Review*, Winter 1942
(a published lecture); and on Valéry in an Introduction to an English edition of *Le
Serpent* in 1924, and in the *Quarterly Review of Literature*, Volume III, No. 3 (a brief
obituary tribute reprinted from *Cahiers du Sud*).

Matthiessen has pointed out, "there is a conspicuous lack of comment on Chaucer in Eliot's criticism," as there is on Skelton and almost all pre-Elizabethan English poets. He has written on no Italians but Dante and Machiavelli, no Romans but Seneca, no Greeks but Euripides, no French authors (curiously enough, since French poetry has greatly influenced his own work) but Baudelaire and Pascal, and on little imaginative prose of any sort. In Eliot's tradition there is seemingly no room for Homer, Villon, Goethe, Cervantes, or any of the great masters of the novel except James.

The two chief personal faults that limit Eliot's criticism are a fuzzy and contradictory thinking that results in key terms that are meaningless or nebulous (or a nebulous terminology that results in fuzzy and contra-dictory writing, depending on how you look at it), and an extra-literary irritation, grown more frequent of late, with his subjects. The first is central to his thought and it is impossible to read Eliot's criticism for very long without beginning to feel that he is making statements in a language in which it is impossible to discuss the matter with him. In one of his finest essays, "Experiment in Criticism," which appeared in the *Bookman* for November 1929 and which he has never reprinted, Eliot states: "There is an urgent need for experiment in criticism of a new kind, which will consist largely in a logical and dialectic study of the terms used." Despite this excellent avowal, which he may not have meant for himself, Eliot has constantly refused to study or even define the terms he uses, resorting to such evasions as: "In making this statement I refuse to be drawn into any discussion of the definitions of 'personality' and 'character,'" or "But if any one complains that I have not defined truth, or fact, or reality, I can only say apologetically that it was no part of my purpose to do so, but only to find a scheme into which, whatever they are, they will fit, if they exist." Sometimes Eliot writes passages that appear to be entirely meaningless manipulations of terms cloudy enough to give the semblance of conveying a critical judgment, like the following, of Rostand:

> Not only as a dramatist, but as a poet, he is superior to Maeter-linck, whose drama, in failing to be dramatic, fails also to be poetic. Maeterlinck has a literary perception of the dramatic and a literary perception of the poetic, and he joins the two; the two are not, as sometimes they are in the work of Rostand, fused; his characters take no conscious delight in their role—they are sentimental. With Rostand the centre of gravity is in the expression of the emotion, not as with Maeterlinck in the emotion which cannot be expressed.

Principally as a result of Eliot's use of terms like these, almost every writer who has ever discussed his criticism has caught him in contradic-tions. Lionel Trilling, for example, found Eliot making a distinction

between "poetry" and "verse," for Kipling's benefit, in his introduction
to *A Choice of Kipling's Verse,* which Eliot had himself demolished in his
Dryden essay many years before, as made by Arnold against Dryden.
Yvor Winters, in a chapter in *The Anatomy of Nonsense* that charges
contradiction after contradiction in Eliot's critical thinking (many of
them, it must be admitted, based on no more than Winters's own refusal
to read clearly, in context), has noted at least one actual howler, Eliot's
damning as "heretical" in *After Strange Gods* (1934) a statement of
Herbert Read's that poetry is the product of our personality, which we
should not attempt to remake, and then in the same book defending himself against charges of inconsistency between his poetry and prose with a
variant of Read's heretical argument.[2]

One of the reasons for these contradictions is a trick Eliot undoubtedly
learned from Pound, of proposing theories he doesn't himself believe,
just to hear the roar. In at least one place he has been explicit about this.
He writes in "Shakespeare and the Stoicism of Seneca":

> I propose a Shakespeare under the influence of the stoicism of
> Seneca. But I do not believe that Shakespeare was under the influ-
> ence of Seneca. I propose it largely because I believe that after the
> Montaigne Shakespeare (not that Montaigne had any philosophy
> whatever) and after the Machiavelli Shakespeare, a stoical or Sene-
> can Shakespeare is almost certain to be produced. I wish merely to

---

[2] The most incisive criticism of Eliot's critical manner with which I am familiar is
Alick West's in *Crisis and Criticism.* He quotes the following passage from *The Use
of Poetry and the Use of Criticism:*

> This is the sort of remark, which, when made by a man so young as was Keats,
> can only be called the result of genius. There is hardly one statement of Keats
> about poetry, which, when considered carefully and with due allowance for the
> difficulties of communication, will not be found to be true; and what is more, true
> for greater and more mature poetry than anything that Keats ever wrote.

West comments:

> That first sentence is characteristic of Mr. Eliot's style. It is not a statement
> about Keats: together with the rest of the paragraph it conveys no idea of what is
> the excellence of Keats' remarks on poetry. It depends for its effect on the dogmatic
> use of the word "genius"; on the implied possession of such discrimination that
> one knows at what age what remark may be regarded as the result of genius; and
> on the typically Philistine trick of hinting at a criticism of great men and refraining
> from stating it. For the limiting clause of the first sentence suggests that if the
> remark had been made by Keats when he was older, it would not have to be called
> the result of genius; there is something lacking in the remark, which, if it had been
> made at the age when statements are judged without allowances for the youth of
> the writer, would have disqualified it from the rank of genius. What is that want?
> Mr. Eliot does not say; but he suggests that he could, if he wanted to. The sentence
> is not about Keats; it is about Mr. Eliot's insight. The style subordinates Keats
> to Mr. Eliot. Mr. Eliot does indeed extinguish his personality in dogmatic appeals
> to received ideas; but it is Keats, not himself, who is sacrificed.

disinfect the Senecan Shakespeare before he appears. My ambitions
would be realized if I could prevent him, in so doing, from appearing
at all.

After which, naturally, he goes on to demonstrate the influence of the
stoicism of Seneca on Shakespeare, which he returns to again and again
in his work.

Another reason for the contradictions Eliot has explained himself. "I
can never reread any of my own prose writings without acute embarrass-
ment," he writes in "The Music of Poetry." "I shirk the task, and
consequently may not take account of all the assertions to which I have
at one time or another committed myself; I may often repeat what I have
said before, and I may equally well contradict myself." This could conceivably be a joke, except that it would be a quite uncharacteristic joke
(Eliot is addicted to being deprecatory about his own work, but not
comic), and that Eliot has repeated it at various times, among them a
particularly solemn occasion, his Memorial Lecture for Yeats. It is
almost certain that Eliot is using it as a perfectly serious apology for
contradictions, with no sense of its pettishness compared even to Whitman's silly but rather grand: "Do I contradict myself? Very well then, I
contradict myself, (I am large, I contain multitudes)."

Eliot's peculiar irritation with the subjects he is criticizing results in
another rather untraditional trick, his pretense of not understanding
simple poetry. He has protested that he is able to make no sense whatsoever of the fifth stanza of Shelley's "To a Skylark," the messy but
certainly understandable:

> Keen as are the arrows
> Of that silver sphere,
> Whose intense lamp narrows
> In the white dawn clear
> Until we hardly see—we feel that it is there.

He has maintained that Keats's line: "Beauty is truth, truth beauty,"
"means nothing to me," and so on. It is obvious that this sudden pose of
dull-wittedness is meant as Socratic irony, both from the examples he
chooses (always the fuzzier sentiments of romantic poets), and from the
fact that he has praised F. H. Bradley for "his habit of discomfiting an
opponent with a sudden profession of ignorance." It is ironic that one
of his bitterest critics, Yvor Winters, should have attacked him almost
exclusively in that fashion.

The other form Eliot's growing irritation with writers takes is his
habit of reproaching them for not being something else he would have
found more satisfactory. Blake and Shakespeare *should* have had a better
philosophy, the Victorian poets *shouldn't* have written so much, Goethe

shouldn't have written poetry at all ("his true role was that of a man of the world and sage—a La Rochefoucauld, a La Bruyère, a Vauvenargues"), Shakespeare *should* have written *Othello* so Rymer couldn't have raised his objections, Shelley *should* have been a better man, and so on.

2

A rewarding way to study Eliot's work in detail is to annotate his essay "Tradition and the Individual Talent," which was first printed in 1917 and which after more than a quarter of a century is still his most important essay and the key to all his later work. Implicit within it are all the later developments, and some attempt will be made in this section to note a few of those implications.

(1) Yet if the only form of tradition, of handing down, consisted in following the ways of the immediate generation before us in a blind or timid adherence to its successes, "tradition" should positively be discouraged.

Eliot seems to hold a curious doctrine that tradition always skips the preceding generation. In the essay "Baudelaire in Our Time" in *For Lancelot Andrewes* he had documented this with an arbitrary and rather foolish listing of the last five literary generations: (1) Baudelaire, (2) Huxley, Tyndall, George Eliot, and Gladstone, (3) Symons, Dowson, and Wilde, (4) Shaw, Wells, and Lytton Strachey, (5) Eliot and his school. Eliot claims that his continuity embraces (1), (3), and (5), and he leaves (2) and (4) to embrace each other.

(2) It [tradition] involves, in the first place, the historical sense, which we may call nearly indispensable to anyone who would continue to be a poet beyond his twenty-fifth year; and the historical sense involves a perception, not only of the pastness of the past, but of its presence; the historical sense compels a man to write not merely with his own generation in his bones, but with a feeling that the whole of the literature of Europe from Homer and within it the whole of the literature of his own country has a simultaneous existence and composes a simultaneous order. This historical sense, which is a sense of the timeless as well as the temporal and of the timeless and of the temporal together, is what makes a writer traditional.

Eliot is using "historical" here in a curious sense, and the ambiguity of the word has made for something of a critical controversy over whether or not Eliot's critical method is "historical." Edmund Wilson, in *Axel's Castle* and in an essay on "The Historical Interpretation of Literature," has discussed Eliot as the very type of the unhistorical critic, one who treats all literature as though it coexisted simultaneously, comparing and judging it by absolute standards, in a temporal vacuum. John Crowe Ransom, on the other hand, chose Eliot as his example of "The Historical Critic" in *The New Criticism*, pointing out that Eliot "uses his historical studies for the sake of literary understanding." Obviously, the parties in the controversy are using "historical" in two different senses: Wilson meaning the use of contextual or relative criteria, Ransom (and apparently Eliot himself) meaning historical knowledge or awareness of the past. Even in Wilson's sense, Eliot is sometimes a historical critic, in a Spenglerian fashion, as when, in "Shakespeare and the Stoicism of Seneca," he finds a common factor of social dissolution in Elizabethan England and imperial Rome and then proceeds to show its reflection in their literatures. Generally, however, he is laughably non-historical in this sense, and when he writes: "Whether the arts flourish best in a period of growth and expansion, or in one of decay, is a question that I cannot answer," the word "best" is almost the ultimate in non-historicity. Considering Eliot's additional statement that he cannot understand why poetic drama seems to have died, it might be suggested as a tentative resolution of the controversy that Eliot does not know enough history, in Ransom's sense, to be a consistent historical critic in Wilson's sense.

(3) Whoever has approved this idea of order, of the form of European, of English literature, will not find it preposterous that the past should be altered by the present as much as the present is directed by the past.

Here are a number of Eliot's key ideas. "Order" later became "orthodoxy," just as "disorder" became "heterodoxy" or "heresy"; the idea of "altering" past literature became a whole body of critical work aimed at revising the history of literature to emphasize his "tradition"; and the concept of "directing" the present by the past flowered in his religious, social, and political reaction.

(4) To proceed to a more intelligible exposition of the relation of the poet to the past: he can neither take the past as a lump, an indiscriminate bolus, nor can he form himself wholly on one or two private admirations, nor can he form himself wholly upon one preferred period. . . . The poet must be very conscious of the main current, which does not at all flow invariably through the most distinguished reputations.

However true this may be of his poetry (which has always been rather more catholic), it has certainly not been true of the tradition Eliot has created in his criticism. His tradition has sometimes been an indiscriminate bolus, the dead writers en masse; it has always been one or two private admirations, principally Dante and Dryden; it has always been a preferred period or two, principally the Elizabethan dramatists and the Metaphysicals; and although it has not been the most distinguished reputations, it has not been the main current, either, or at best only fragments of it.

(5) I am alive to a usual objection to what is clearly part of my program for the *métier* of poetry. The objection is that the doctrine requires a ridiculous amount of erudition (pedantry), a claim which can be rejected by appeal to the lives of poets in any pantheon. . . . Shakespeare acquired more essential history from Plutarch than most men could from the whole British Museum.

Eliot sometimes plays a little game of pretending that he is the simple uneducated poet or critic awed by scholarship and writes such modest demurrers as: "It is not fitting that a literary critic should retrace all this labor of scholarship, where either his dissent or his approval would be an impertinence." Nevertheless, Eliot's ideal has always been the one he inherited from Pound (who once described himself as a philological instrument "of the utmost refinement"), the scholar-critic. By the standards of contemporary criticism, particularly in America, Eliot's learning is remarkable, although naturally nowhere near as comprehensive as that of critics like George Saintsbury, who are primarily scholars. Eliot studied under Babbitt and Santayana at Harvard, did graduate work there in philosophy, read French literature and philosophy at the Sorbonne, read Greek philosophy at Oxford, and spent two years studying Sanscrit and Indic philology and one year studying Indian metaphysics. Although he is not polylingual to the extent Pound is, he reads five languages besides English: Greek, Latin, Italian, French, and Sanscrit, with greater or lesser facility, and in them his reading is undoubtedly both broader and deeper than Pound's, just as his philosophic and scientific background is undoubtedly superior.

(6) What happens is a continual surrender of himself as he is at the moment to something which is more valuable. The progress of an artist is a continual self-sacrifice, a continual extinction of personality.

This is another of Eliot's key ideas, his theory of the impersonal nature of art. Poetry, he writes in another place in the essay, "is not a turning loose of emotion, but an escape from emotion; it is not the expression of personality, but an escape from personality." The poet struggles "to transmute his personal and private agonies into something rich and strange, something universal and impersonal"; the dramatist's effort is "the process of transfusion of the personality, or, in a deeper sense, the life, of the author into the character." Although this has a general metaphoric truth, on the literal level it is obviously the æsthetic of a suffering man, one that would be incomprehensible to a Victor Hugo or a Jane Austen. Eliot has a positive terror of personality, including his own, and the overpowering discipline of a literary tradition is his refuge from it. For many years the literary romantics' glorification of personality seemed to be the menace, but eventually he realized that basically the enemy was Protestantism. He writes in *After Strange Gods:*

> What I have been leading up to is the following assertion: that when morals cease to be a matter of tradition and orthodoxy—that is, of the habits of the community formulated, corrected and elevated by the continuous thought and direction of the Church—and when each man is to elaborate his own, then *personality* becomes a thing of alarming importance.

Obviously, it is Eliot, rather than society, that is "alarmed."

> (7) . . . the more perfect the artist, the more completely separate in him will be the man who suffers and the mind which creates; the more perfectly will the mind digest and transmute the passions which are its material.

Not only is art a "transmutation" of suffering and passion, Eliot suggests, but the better the art, the more complete the transmutation. This is an artist's catharsis to match Aristotle's audience-catharsis and is actually, although Eliot seems never to have noticed it, the very quintessence of romantic individualism and Protestantism, a utilitarianism that finds the value of art in its services to one superior individual, the artist, and thus the farthest extreme from the tradition and from Catholic criteria of "communion."

> (8) The experience, you will notice, the elements which enter the presence of the transforming catalyst, are of two kinds: emotions and feelings.

Eliot's distinction between "emotion" and "feeling" is both very important and very obscure. It seems to be that emotion exists in the poet, while feeling inheres for the writer "in particular words or phrases or images." The doctrine of the "objective correlative," which Eliot developed later in his essay "Hamlet and His Problems," is related to this theory, in that the objective correlative is a situation, containing inherent "feelings," that expresses the poet's "emotion" and evokes a similar "emotion" in the reader. Thus the emotion-feeling distinction is a way of barring "emotion" from poetry, in keeping with the im-impersonal and traditional theories, and then sneaking it back under another name and (perhaps) another form.

> (9) And emotions which he has never experienced will serve his turn as well as those familiar to him.

This is a hint of another basic belief of Eliot's, closely related to "impersonalism," the belief that art is fundamentally a closed system, and that criteria of belief or correspondence to reality are irrelevant to it. The fact that Dante had a coherent system of thought behind him and that Shakespeare did not (as Eliot believes) is "an irrelevant accident"; the poet "makes" poetry organically and without belief, the way the bee makes honey or the spider secretes a filament; "genuine poetry can communicate before it is understood," or in fact if it is never understood; the poet may express the mood of his generation "by some strange accident while at the same time expressing a mood of his own quite different" (here Eliot implies his own experience with *The Waste Land*), and so on. Eliot has formulated these beliefs in a theory, closely related to that of I. A. Richards, that poetic "assent" at the moment of reading is quite apart from questions of "belief," and has gone Richards one better by adding that anything the poet chooses to believe is automatically "established," "for its truth or falsity in one sense ceases to matter, and its truth in another sense is proved." It is thus perfectly satisfactory if the poet believes nothing whatsoever but merely "uses" any handy belief.

Here, then, are all the themes that were to develop into Eliot's critical theory and practice: the "tradition" that later became "orthodoxy," and the "order" that later became "the idea of a Christian society"; the emphasis on certain preferable literatures in the past; the necessity for erudition and historical knowledge; and the four key concepts: impersonalism, irrelevancy of belief, emotion versus feelings, and the objective correlative. Apparently these key concepts arose out of the necessities involved in abstracting a tradition from its historical context and throwing it into ours, but in actual fact the process may have been reversed, and the concept of "tradition" itself have been developed to legitimize a personal necessity for an art that "extinguishes" the personality, "transmutes" suffering, and can "use" beliefs without believing them. The driving necessity in Eliot's criticism would then seem to be the need to erect a scaffolding of objective, traditional, unemotional, and formal elements he could use to sustain himself, much the way Hopkins confessed that in the final period of his creative life only the rigidity of the sonnet form permitted him to write at all.

All of Eliot's essays can be regarded as illustrations of the ideas and traditional method sketched out in "Tradition and the Individual Talent," a kind of vast appendix of applications and examples. We can see Eliot's tradition in action as early as *The Sacred Wood* (1920), his first collection of critical essays, in which "Tradition and the Individual Talent" appears. F. O. Matthiessen, in *The Achievement of T. S. Eliot*, begins the modern "detailed intensive re-examination of the quality and function of poetry" with *The Sacred Wood*, and the book had a historical effect far greater than the effect it produces on a present-day reader. One of the book's virtues was the constant quotation of poetic texts, so that the essays are practically copious quotations from a writer, larded with comparison, exegesis, and evaluation. Eliot believed then that poetry is "a superior amusement," its chief purpose "to give a peculiar kind of pleasure," and that the chief function of criticism is to increase the enjoyment of poetry. "If we seek not Blue-book knowledge but the enjoyment of poetry, and ask for a poem, we shall seldom find it," he wrote, pettishly but accurately, of the criticism of the time. Looking backward on *The Sacred Wood* from the distance of his 1928 preface, Eliot observed:

> It is an artificial simplification, and to be taken only with caution, when I say that the problem appearing in these essays, which gives them what coherence they have, is the problem of the integrity of poetry, with the repeated assertion that when we are considering poetry we must consider it primarily as poetry and not another thing. At that time I was much stimulated and much helped by the critical writings of Remy de Gourmont. I acknowledge that influence, and am grateful for it; and I by no means disown it by having passed on to another problem not touched upon in this book: that of the relation of poetry to the spiritual and social life of its time and of other times.

This is not precisely accurate, since *The Sacred Wood* clearly defines the tradition that later flowered as Eliot's religious and social ideas, but the quotation does hint at one significant change: that with the later shift in interest from "poetry as poetry," the quotation of texts diminished almost to the vanishing-point. *The Use of Poetry and the Use of Criticism*, Eliot's last book dealing principally with literature, quotes fewer than a hundred lines of poetry, or less than he would have quoted in any one essay in *The Sacred Wood*.

"It is part of the business of the critic to preserve tradition—where a good tradition exists," Eliot wrote in the Introduction of the original volume, and later in the book he makes it clear that a good one did exist, that it was "the literature of the great ages, the sixteenth and seventeenth centuries." All the threads of his tradition appear in *The Sacred Wood* in detail except the Metaphysicals, who turned up a year later (1921) in a review of Grierson's anthology of metaphysical poetry, and Dryden, whom Eliot first wrote about in 1922. Besides "Tradition and the Individual Talent," a general discussion, Eliot devotes specific essays to Dante, four Elizabethan dramatists (Marlowe, Shakespeare, Jonson, and Massinger), critics who have attempted to use a tradition similar to Eliot's (including Charles Whibley, Irving Babbitt, Paul Elmer More, and Julien Benda), and various aspects of poetic drama, a major preoccupation of Eliot's and a major element in his tradition. Two essays and a part of a third in the book sketch out what Eliot regards as the opposing tradition, Swinburne and Blake. Blake is treated with moderation and a great deal of admiration, as a "poet of genius" who missed being a "classic" like Dante by being born into the wrong environment, but Swinburne, as poet and critic, is slaughtered, and in general the "romantic" tradition is opposed and overturned throughout.

3

The source of Eliot's tradition may be a literary need, but its ends are social and religious, and the social and religious application and extension of his tradition is worth examining. One of the chief of these, of course, was his conversion to the Anglo-Catholic Church. Harry M. Campbell, in a study of Eliot in the *Rocky Mountain Review* for Summer 1944, claims, on what evidence I do not know, that Eliot's conversion occurred as early as 1922, the year he published *The Waste Land* and became editor of the *Criterion*. In any case, the first public statement on his conversion with which I am familiar occurred in 1928, when Eliot wrote a new preface to *The Sacred Wood*, renouncing "poetry as poetry," and published *For Lancelot Andrewes*, with its famous Preface announcement that he was a classicist in literature, an Anglo-Catholic in religion, and a royalist in politics. The royalism has hardly been heard from again, the classicism, in so far as it meant anything at all, was not news, but the Anglo-Catholicism gradually asserted itself as his major preoccupation and flowered into a broad social position.

When Eliot republished *For Lancelot Andrewes* as *Essays Ancient and Modern* in 1936, he omitted the Preface, "which has more than served its turn." This was far from a repudiation of the beliefs. He later explained in *After Strange Gods* that his objection had been to the injudicious phrasing of the statement, which permitted the inferences that the three subjects were of equal importance to him, that he accepted them all on the same grounds, or that they all hang or fall together. On reconsideration, one is "the Faith" while the other two are merely a "political principle" and a "literary fashion." The particular danger is in putting these things forward as "a dramatic posture."

That last phrase gives some sense of the difficulties Eliot seems to have encountered in his conversion. A man's religious beliefs and his relations with his Maker (if he believes he has one) are his private concern, but when they become a point of view and a source of propaganda in literary criticism, they warrant discussion. Eliot has never chosen to explain his conversion in writing, but some sense of difficulty is obvious in his later poetry and in such nettled and patently self-referent statements as the one on Hopkins's conversion: "To be converted, in any case, while it is sufficient for entertaining the hope of individual salvation, is not going to do for a man, as a writer, what his ancestry and his country for some generations have failed to do." Writing as far back as 1927, in *The American Caravan*, Francis Fergusson pointed out some of the contradictions in Eliot's make-up: "a romantic individualism in morals and a strict discipline in art; of a passionate faith and an equally passionate agnosticism, and of a profound comprehension of the creative act and an inability to escape the personal in his own poetry."

R. P. Blackmur has also described the contradictions between Eliot's nature and his conversion. Speaking of Eliot's mind, he writes: "It is the last mind which, in this century, one would have expected to enter the Church in a lay capacity. The worldliness of its prose weapons, its security of posture, its wit, its eye for startling fact and talent for nailing it down in flight, hardly go with what we think of today as English or American religious feeling."

Eliot's conversion has led him into some strange positions. Unlike Ransom, who admits being chiefly attracted by the ritual in religion, Eliot, like Hulme before him, is chiefly attracted by the dogma, the letter that "giveth life" while "the spirit killeth." He is, however, greatly interested in the liturgy, which seems chiefly important to him as the origin and basis of the drama (a scale of values with a faint Alice in Wonderland air). On the one hand, Eliot is powerfully drawn to Rome, and occasionally his Church is so High you can't get over it, as when in "Thoughts after Lambeth" he "regrets" that the Anglican bishops "have placed so much reliance on the Individual Conscience" in their birth-control position. On the other hand, Eliot has powerful survivals of the Puritan Protestantism of his early life, he is constantly resisting authority in favor of his own revelation, and he has even enunciated a doctrine of "every man his own critic" (amusingly, in the same address on "Religion and Literature") that seems almost the essence of Protestantism ("and we should all try to be critics, and not leave criticism to the fellows who write reviews in the papers").

Eliot's religion has social implications for him ranging from the feudal to the directly fascist.[3] He has sketched out an ecclesiastical authoritarian state with education by monastic teaching orders, birth control in the

---

[3] Forced to choose between them, it must be admitted, Eliot sometimes chooses the social implications rather than the religion itself. For a number of years in the twenties he supported Charles Maurras and his *Action française* in the *Criterion*, printing an article by Maurras himself in the January 1928 issue, and generally praising him as a better example than Mussolini for British fascists to follow. When Maurras and the *Action française* were condemned by the Roman Catholic Church for advancing a doctrine that Catholicism is "useful" to a monarchical or authoritarian state, Eliot defended him with the statement that Maurras "simply is concerned with the aspect of the Roman Church which is not necessarily Christian, because his point of view is that of an agnostic philosopher." As Delmore Schwartz has pointed out, the possibility that a man may be a Catholic and "not necessarily Christian" (but satisfactory if he is a royalist) is rather an interesting one.

hands of the Church, censorship at Lambeth Palace, and so on. This pattern seems markedly like that of such states as Spain and Vichy France, and it is a matter of some amusement that in a Letter to the Editors in *Partisan Review* for March–April 1942 Eliot took great pleasure in announcing a rumor that his writings had been condemned by the Vichy government, a rumor that seems not to have been substantiated since. His ideal state, in fact, is explicitly feudal, and his lectures on *The Idea of a Christian Society*, as well as more recent essays, sketch out at some length an idealized feudal community (words like "ideal" and "idealized" are essential, since Eliot confesses that his title uses "Idea" in the Platonic sense), "a small and mostly self-contained group attached to the soil and having its interests centred in a particular place."

In all of this, aristocracy has a definite part. Eliot believes literally in "royal blood," which produces "kingly and steadfast behaviour," in an "aristocracy of birth," in an "elite," and so on. He certainly believes in imperialism, even of the naked Kipling variety. He is "instinctively in sympathy" with such reactionary economic panaceas as distributism, credit reform, American Southern agrarianism; and what is worse, "for I have no gift whatever for abstruse thinking," is perfectly willing to blend the doctrines of Chesterton, Major Douglas, Donald Davidson, and "several Scottish nationalists" in one giant pot and simmer to taste. Eliot certainly believes in a variety of racism, and his Christian society would not permit "an influx of foreign populations" and "foreign races" that have ruined parts of the United States, particularly New York; it would find "any large number of free-thinking Jews undesirable," and so on.

All of this adds up, not quite to fascism, but to a kind of tentative and embarrassed flirting with it. The morality of fascism, he writes, "is capable of great good within limits"; there "is" a fallacy in democracy while there only "may be" a fallacy in dictatorship; fascism offers immediate, "though perhaps illusory," relief; General J. F. C. Fuller, a self-identified "British Fascist," "has as good a title to call himself a 'believer in democracy' as anyone else"; the Nazis were right in relegating women to kitchen, children, and church; Eliot favors "the corporative state" if it is not "pagan" (that is, presumably, he favored Franco's, Salazar's, Mussolini's, Pétain's, and rejected Hitler's), and, in any case, fascism is only "the extreme degradation of democracy."

The doctrine of tradition in Eliot's criticism seems primarily a weapon for achieving this unattractive society. The function of traditional criticism, he writes, is the establishment of order, and the enemy is disorder. In purely literary terms, this makes the critic the scourge of the "romantic," the "hysteric," and so on; in Eliot's later usage it makes him a heresy-hunter, a witch-finder. He issues general jeremiads—"The whole of modern literature is corrupted by what I call Secularism"; it is doubtful

whether the reader of modern literature "would be made a better man"—
and announces his role frankly as that of the "moralist." He hunts out
specific "heretics," and in fact his series of lectures *After Strange Gods*,
subtitled, *A Primer of Modern Heresy*, is a discussion of modern literary
heterodoxy supplemented with a rather amusing appendix of four "heretical" passages drawn from such diabolical sources as Herbert Read
and the London *Times*. The aim of literature, he proclaims, is to fight
liberalism, and when Eliot's niggling criticisms of Gerard Manley Hopkins, a Jesuit priest and thus theoretically estimable, finally reduce to the
statement that in this struggle "Hopkins has very little aid to offer us,"
Eliot signalizes the absence of any dispassionate æsthetic concern whatsoever.

It is interesting to conjecture how much of Eliot's concern with a more
popular poetry is purely propagandistic—that is, how much he wants
merely to have a larger audience for his social and religious ideas. There
is no doubt that Eliot is obsessed with the question of a larger public for
poetry. "I believe that the poet naturally prefers to write for as large and
miscellaneous an audience as possible," he writes, and "it is the half-
educated and ill-educated, rather than the uneducated, who stand in his
way: I myself should like an audience which could neither read nor
write." He modified and developed this later into the theory that the
writer needs three concentric publics: "a small public of substantially the
same education as himself, as well as the same tastes; a larger public
with some common background with him; and finally he should have
something in common with everyone who has intelligence and sensibility
and can read his language."

One of the chief forms this obsession with a larger audience for poetry
takes is Eliot's interest in poetic drama. His own verse dramas serve a
complex of functions. As Eliot has recognized, the characters in a drama
"are somehow dramatizing, but in no obvious form, an action or struggle
for harmony in the soul of the poet," and thus writers torn by conflict
tend to work it out in the dialectical form of drama. Eliot's verse dramas
obviously do this, with *Murder in the Cathedral* a patent example. Also,
as F. O. Matthiessen has pointed out in a review of *Four Quartets*, Eliot
has made his later poetry, particularly the *Quartets*, less dramatic, more
meditative (that is, more "resolved") than his earlier poetry by concentrating his dramatic impulses into purely dramatic poems.

But more important than these private functions is the public function
of drama for Eliot, the fact that it can cross poetry and propaganda in
the guise of popular entertainment. He asks for the theater a verse medium "in which we shall be able to hear the speech of contemporary
human beings, in which dramatic characters can express the purest poetry
without high-falutin and in which they can convey the most commonplace
message without absurdity." As a basis for this hope, Eliot has a theory,

obviously related to his theory of the poet's three concentric audiences, that a mature play, say one of Shakespeare's, has several "levels of significance": "For the simplest auditors there is the plot, for the more thoughtful the character, for the more literary the words and phrasing, for the more musically sensitive the rhythm, and for auditors of greater sensitiveness and understanding a meaning which reveals itself gradually." In line with this he has elsewhere written that *Hamlet*, *Macbeth*, and *Othello*, not to speak of *Œdipus Tyrannus*, have "thriller interest" akin to that of our contemporary detective drama.

One of Eliot's most significant essays is "Marie Lloyd," in which, in the guise of writing about a distinguished English music-hall performer and the loss occasioned by her death, he defines his ideal relationship between artist and audience, the audience a cohesive social class to whose life and aspirations the artist gives voice, raising them to the level of art and giving them dignity; the artist appreciated, loved, and always understood; the two, artist and audience, collaborators in the creation of art. Not far beneath the surface here is the writer of complex and obscure poetry yearning to be widely read and appreciated in large areas of society that tend never to hear of him, but there is also an element of conscious propagandistic design. Some years before Eliot had written in *The Sacred Wood*:

> The Elizabethan drama was aimed at a public which wanted *entertainment* of a crude sort, but would *stand* a good deal of poetry; our problem should be to take a form of entertainment and subject it to the process which would leave it a form of art. Perhaps the music-hall comedian is the best material.[4]

To an extent, Eliot has attempted to follow this in his practice. Parts of *Murder in the Cathedral* are popularly written, although not quite on the music-hall level; the two fragments of his Aristophanic melodrama, *Sweeney Agonistes* (perhaps significantly unfinished), are very definitely

[4] A much more remarkable document is a fragment from a letter to Ezra Pound which was published in the *Townsman*, July 1938. Its far greater frankness on the subject, combined with its unusual style, makes it a fascinating sample of the published Eliot-Pound correspondence we may eventually get:

Opinion about the writing of a play is simply this:

1. You got to keep the audience's attention all the time.
2. If you lose it you got to get it back QUICK.
3. Everything about plot and charactyar and all else what Aristotle and others say is secondary to the forgoin.
4. But IF you can keep the bloody audience's attention engaged, then you can perform any monkey tricks you like when they ain't looking, and it's what you do behind the audience's back so to speak that makes your play IMMORTAL for a while. If the audience gets its strip tease it will swallow the poetry.
5. If you write a play in verse, then the verse ought to be a medium to look THROUGH, and not a pretty decoration to look AT!

music-hall writing, with some of the song lyrics exceeding in corniness anything Tin Pan Alley ever managed to turn out; and most significant, Lionel Trilling, who seems to have heard a record of Eliot reading *The Waste Land*, reports in the *Nation* being "struck by how much that poem is publicly intended, shaped not so much for the study as for the theater— or at least the pulpit and the altar—by how much, in the full dialect rendition of the cockney passages, it is even shaped for the music hall, by how open the poet's voice makes the music we are inclined to think secretive."[5]

Another of Eliot's formulas for a more popular poetry, closely related to music-hall appeal, is Rudyard Kipling. Many readers were surprised that Eliot, in his fifties, should suddenly seem to depart from the whole pattern of his poetic taste and edit a selection of Kipling's verse prefaced by an exceptionally flowery tribute that speaks of such poetry as "Recessional" as having "the true prophetic inspiration" and, through the use of a dubious distinction between "verse" and "poetry," classifies Kipling as a writer of "great verse," perhaps the greatest. These readers (including critics and reviewers) would not have been half so surprised

[5] An even more fascinating possibility is raised of musical influence on Eliot. As far back as 1935, before any of the *Quartets* were written except "Burnt Norton" (and that not identified with a musical form), Stephen Spender noted, in *The Destructive Element*, the parallel between Eliot's work and Beethoven's last quartets (written at a time when Beethoven, in accordance with Eliot's ideal, was "divested of the love of created beings"), specifically identifying the structure of the second section of "Ash Wednesday" with the second movement of Beethoven's Quartet Opus 130 (presumably Spender means the third movement of Opus 132) in A Minor, and remarking the similar shifts in mood in the poem and the quartet. In 1942, in "The Music of Poetry," his Ker Memorial Lecture at the University of Glasgow (printed in *Partisan Review*, November–December 1942), Eliot proposed a relationship between music and poetry, despite his confessed lack of "technical knowledge of music forms." He said:

> The use of recurrent themes is as natural to poetry as to music. There are possibilities for verse which bear some analogy to the development of a theme by different groups of instruments; there are possibilities of transitions in a poem comparable to the different movements of a symphony or a quartet; there are possibilities of contrapuntal arrangement of subject matter. It is in the concert room, rather than in the opera house, that the germ of a poem may be quickened.

When *Four Quartets* appeared, critics immediately pointed out all the superficial parallels between them and Beethoven's last quartets: the fact that Eliot finished them at fifty-four, the age at which Beethoven began his, the fact that both reached a relatively placid formal haven after earlier tortured work, and so on. No one seems to have noticed the possibility of a formal parallel to the musical structure of the Beethoven works, particularly to the quartet Spender mentioned, (presumably Opus 132), which, unlike most quartets, has five movements, the fourth of them a short transitional movement (as have *The Waste Land* and all four *Quartets*). Lacking the requisite musical knowledge, I can only propose, on the basis of Eliot's statement, that a detailed comparison of themes, voices, transitions, and counterpoint in the Eliot poems and the Beethoven quartets by some musically informed reader of poetry might prove very rewarding.

had they been aware of Eliot's tribute to the greatness of Dickens in his preface to *Bubu of Montparnasse*, or of one of the chief themes in Eliot's criticism, the "nonliterary" standard of evaluation. "The 'greatness' of literature cannot be determined solely by literary standards," Eliot has written, and he has spoken elsewhere of the fact that most people judge poetry in terms of their own sentimental memories, and:

. . . when any poet conquers a really large public in his lifetime, an increasing proportion of his admirers will admire him for extraneous reasons. Not necessarily for bad reasons, but because he becomes known merely as a symbol, in giving a kind of stimulation, or con- solation, to his readers, which is a function of his peculiar relation to them in time. Such effect upon contemporary readers may be a legitimate and proper result of some great poetry. . . .

Kipling is thus a poet (or versifier) achieving both greatness and a wide audience for nonliterary reasons, and far from condemning this fact, Eliot admires and would, if he could, do likewise. Obviously, for many reasons (all to his credit), he cannot, but he can put Kipling forward as the area where poetry, political reaction, and wide appeal meet in almost the perfect amalgam. The fact that, as W. H. Auden pointed out in the *New Republic*, Kipling is profoundly non-Christian, even anti-Christian, in all his basic attitudes, only shows how much religion Eliot is prepared to sacrifice for an *effectively* functioning tradition, a mass audience for reac- tion. Eliot has sometimes written longingly of writing for a theatre audience in terms very reminiscent of Henry James's. Considering the purity of James's motives in comparison with those of Eliot, the extent of Eliot's success compared with James's total failure is something of an ironic comment on how the pure in heart fare in this wicked world.

4

Few critics have been so conscious as Eliot of the fact that they were creating and using a tradition. But every critic, in his explorations into the past, abstracts those writers and writings that have meaning for him in the present, and to that extent creates a functioning tradition or part of one for himself and other writers. In our day a number of critics, some of them as consciously "traditional" as Eliot, have reinterpreted our literary past, and the wide variations in their results make it obvious that Eliot has furnished *a* tradition rather than *the* tradition. (Eliot's assistant editor on the *Criterion*, Herbert Read, has, in fact, attempted to balance Eliot's with a precisely opposed "romantic" tradition, omitting almost everyone between Shakespeare and Wordsworth, in *Phases of English Poetry* and other books.) The chief grouping of these traditions seems to be political, with one large body of them organizing a usable past for the Right and another for the Left, but there is a third body of traditional reinterpretations that seems non-political or only remotely political, designed chiefly to create a usable, politically neutral past for the artist.

Besides Eliot's, the chief contemporary traditional criticism for the Right has been the work of the Southern school of John Crowe Ransom and Allen Tate, a loose group that roughly includes Cleanth Brooks and Robert Penn Warren, as well as several other younger critics of distinction. At one time, when it had a more or less concrete political program of Southern regionalism and agrarianism, the group looked to Donald Davidson as its leader. The advantages that this group has over such isolated reactionary traditionalists as Winters, Pound, Wyndham Lewis, and Eliot himself are that it has a number of co-operating talents; that it has had a base to work from, in two or three Southern universities, as well as what amount to "colonies" in Northern universities; that it has always had one or two excellent literary organs, first the *Southern Review* under Brooks and Warren, from 1935 to 1942, then the *Kenyon Review* under Ransom, begun in 1939 and still continuing, then the *Sewanee Review*, taken over by Tate in 1944 and continued by J. E. Palmer, all of which have made a practice (like Eliot's own *Criterion*) of giving space to the widest latitude of opinion and variety of point of view, along with their own people.

The leader of the group at present is probably John Crowe Ransom, who taught Tate at Vanderbilt College, and who, on the basis of a scientific training, a philosophic bent, a wide learning, and a first-rate mind, has been the group's outstanding theoretician. Ransom has written a book in defense of orthodox religion, *God without Thunder* (1930), which despite odd gaps in knowledge (he is perhaps the only writer on theology, for example, who ever confused the Immaculate Conception with the Virgin Birth) is an excellently reasoned and dramatistic attack on the enemy: Comte, naturalism, science (particularly anthropology), and liberalism. He defines his purpose in the book as "to win back by new tactics," and this Jesuit principle seems to have carried over into his two subsequent volumes of literary criticism, *The World's Body* (1938) and *The New Criticism* (1941). Ransom's literary tradition shares with Eliot's a vast respect for Donne, and differs from it chiefly in an equally great respect for Milton and an unusual scorn for Shakespeare (who, lacking the "university discipline" and learning of Milton and Donne, is an "amateur," a writer of "ill-constructed" sonnets, and generally an inferior poet). Ransom's key word for criticism is "ontological," by which he seems to mean the critical study of poetic structure, or the logic of the poem, and its relationship to what he calls poetic "texture," or the local detail of the poem. As a result of this concern with structure and structure-texture relations Ransom has been a leading advocate of the closer reading of poetic texts (having a position somewhat analogous to that of F. R. Leavis in England). Although he himself has produced a disproportionately small amount of it, devoting much of his attention to poetics and philosophic problems of belief and cognition in poetry, his influence has been pervasive, and what close reading he himself has produced has been generally excellent. Although Ransom's tradition involves a religious and political orientation, he has insisted, in opposition to Eliot, that moralistic criteria in criticism are an intrusion (as are scholarly, linguistic, historical, impressionist, and other criteria) and that the critic's only concern must be æsthetic, technical. (It is amusing to note in this connection that his two favorite poets, Donne and Milton, were respectively the one a divine and the other a religious and political propagandist, whereas the poet he so much undervalues, Shakespeare, was about as close to a narrowly "æsthetic" writer as we have.)

Allen Tate has continued a number of Ransom's tendencies (some of which, Ransom has acknowledged, he helped to originate) as well as developed some of his own. Working from Ransom's "æsthetic of regionalism," Tate has attempted some specifically regional criticism, interpreting, say, Emily Dickinson's work as primarily a product of New England. He has not, however, developed the tradition much in a specifically literary direction, and a large proportion of his two collections of essays and reviews, *Reactionary Essays on Poetry and Ideas* (1936) and *Reason in Madness* (1941), is devoted to social, political, and educational problems. He has developed a program calling for "reaction" and "violence" (although in fairness it must be admitted that his "violence" seems to be less machine guns in the streets than a verbal violence) and he has announced his opposition to science, positivism, and scientific criticism in even sharper terms than Ransom's. Again like Ransom, the comparatively small amount of close technical reading of poetry he has done has been on a high level.

The member of this group who has most consistently applied its ideas to literature is Cleanth Brooks, who more than any of his associates shows the influence of Eliot. In his first book of criticism, *Modern Poetry and the Tradition* (1939), Brooks attempted, like Winters, to "revise" the history of English poetry, along lines similar to Eliot's less explicit attempt and Leavis's *Revaluation*. Brooks is a confessedly eclectic critic of real acuteness, and with the help of almost every important modern critic he constructed a tradition of "wit" embracing principally the seventeenth century: Donne and the Metaphysicals, Jonson, Herrick, and others; and the twentieth century: Hardy, Yeats, Eliot, and a number of other contemporaries. Unlike Eliot's, Brooks's tradition in his first book would skip most of the late seventeenth century and the entire eighteenth as well as the nineteenth (with the exception of a few isolated figures like Swift, Gay, Blake, Emily Dickinson, and Hopkins) would slight Dryden and Pope, and would accept only the metaphysical or "witty" fragments of such poets as Milton. While creating this tradition, the book illustrates its nature by detailed close reading, fairly eclectic and acknowledging insights from a great number of other critics, of poetic texts, especially Eliot's *Waste Land* and some of Yeats's lyrics. In 1947 Brooks published a second book, *The Well Wrought Urn*, continuing both these directions. Subtitled *Studies in the Structure of Poetry*, the book includes readings of ten important poems, from Donne's "Canonization" to Yeats's "Among School Children," displaying varying degrees of elaborateness. At the same time it extends Brooks's earlier tradition and modifies it substantially in the direction of greater catholicity, so that Pope's "Rape of the Lock," Gray's "Elegy," Wordsworth's "Ode," Keats's "Ode on a Grecian Urn," and even Tennyson's "Tears, Idle Tears," are "now poems which most of us will feel are close to the central stream of the tradition." The earlier Eliot-inspired emphasis on "wit" has been broadened to include "irony," "paradox," "symbolism," "ambiguity," and "dramatic structure," so that almost any poem can now be treated as a kind of metaphysical poem. Nevertheless, as might be expected, the studies of poets like Donne, Shakespeare, and Pope are much fuller and better examples of close reading than the studies of poets like Milton (a particularly dull and pointless essay) and Tennyson. The book is by definition an application of Ransom's ideas, in its technical exploration of poetic structure, its concentration on the elaborate reading of texts, and its emphasis on Donne and the Metaphysicals, so that it is amusing to see Ransom moderately attacked, in one of the book's appendices devoted to general critical questions, for inelasticity of ideas and over-admiration for Donne.

In 1938 Brooks and Robert Penn Warren compiled an anthology for college students entitled *Understanding Poetry*, which sponsors a certain amount of close reading and structural analysis as well as Brooks's "tradition" (frequently the latter, incidentally, by choosing the examples, loading the questions, and generally stacking the cards on behalf of Donne and metaphysical poetry against Shelley and romantic poetry). Warren's own criticism, which has not been large in bulk and has not yet been collected in book form, has been less concerned with a literary than with a moral tradition. This has ranged consistently from his essay "The Briar Patch" in the agrarian symposium *I'll Take My Stand* in 1930, where he argued from impeccable moral principles that equality, higher education, and such luxuries are wrong for the Negro, to his introduction to an illustrated edition of Coleridge's *Rime of the Ancient Mariner* in 1946, which reads the work as a complicated moral allegory and introduces criteria of "truth" into Coleridge's concept of "pure imagination."

Undoubtedly the chief contemporary creator of a tradition for the Left was Vernon L. Parrington, whose giant three-volume work, *Main Cur-*

rents in American Thought, cut short by his untimely death, is one of the monumental creations of an American tradition. Subtitled *An Interpretation of American Literature from the Beginning to 1920,* it is not so much that as a history of American social and economic ideas, reflected in that literature, with "literature" used in the broadest sense. Parrington rescued the vital American tradition of radicalism and democracy running from Roger Williams, Franklin, Sam Adams, Tom Paine, Jefferson, through Whitman and the Abolitionists, to the progressive writers of our century. Parrington wrote as a confessed liberal and Jeffersonian, a defender of the Declaration of Independence and the Bill of Rights against the Constitution, his point of view an economic determinism derived more from Taine and an obscure professor named J. Allen Smith (whose *The Spirit of American Government* appeared in 1907) than from Marx's semi-deterministic "historical materialism."

His book is weak and deficient æsthetically: Parrington ignores Poe (consigning him to the psychoanalyst and the "belletrist"), distorts Melville by following Weaver's absurd biography, sees Thoreau chiefly important as an economic experimenter, fails to do justice to Hawthorne, and slaughters Henry James. This might all be by design, since Parrington is concerned with ideas and admits "with aesthetic judgments I have not been greatly concerned," except that in the same book one can read the twenty-five pages he devoted to James Branch Cabell, "the supreme comic spirit thus far granted us," "as whimsical as Shaw, as provocative as Chesterton," a man to be compared with Carlyle and Twain.

Furthermore, even on his own terms, Parrington's book is full of faults: he ignores the Negro contribution to American history and literature, slights John Brown, drops economic determinism to praise Cooper (an obvious spokesman for the landed tories) because he happens to like his work, is capable of writing of Bryant: "He may not have been a great poet, but he was a great American," and finds Bancroft a greater historian than Prescott, Motley, or Parkman because they were "Brahmins," "aloof," and Bancroft was "the only militant Democrat among them." Nevertheless, Parrington's book is a fine and important job, with a vast influence on his own and the subsequent generation of literary critics, and it created perhaps the first rounded progressive-democratic-social tradition for American writers to match the reactionary-aristocratic-religious tradition of Eliot, Ransom, Winters, et al.

Another important tradition for the Left has been that of Van Wyck Brooks and his school. All the works of the Brooks school, even those of Lewis Mumford, whose concept of culture is broad enough to embrace architecture and invention, were more belletristic (to use his word) than Parrington's, with less interest in social ideas and more in literature, but their emphasis was similar. Since the views of Brooks and his disciples will be discussed in a later chapter, it is only necessary to note here that whatever tradition they produced was seriously vitiated by ignorance and distortion: the typical example is Waldo Frank glorifying Fanny Brice and attacking Shakespeare as a "charming," rather than great, writer who created "the most fetching of melodramas." The Marxist and near-Marxist critics, most of whom have created a tradition utilizing other varieties of ignorance and distortion, will also be discussed in a later chapter.

A third group of tradition-creators, more or less ignoring political purposes, have been chiefly interested in erecting a usable past for the creative writer, sometimes themselves. Two of the best books in this category have been D. H. Lawrence's *Studies in Classic American Literature*, a highly personal reinterpretation along the lines of Lawrence's mythic, "blood-knowing" ideas, and a book much influenced by Lawrence's, William Carlos Williams's *In the American Grain*. The Williams book is actually a reinterpretation of American history rather than literature, with only one professional writer, Poe, discussed, but it is explicitly designed to erect a tradition for the American writer. "Because the fools do not believe they spring from anything," Williams writes, and although his judgments are generally unorthodox, glorifying such figures as Morton of Merrymount and Aaron Burr, Williams's book has been recognizably influential on writers, outstanding among them Hart Crane and an impressive novelist named John Sanford. Williams polarizes American history into the groupings Indian-French-Catholic and white-English-Protestant, identifying freedom, gaiety, and artistic creation with the former, and Puritan dourness, repression, and prudery with the latter. His view of Puritanism is oversimple and falsified, a characteristic of the twenties, when Puritanism was the artist's enemy and meant Anthony Comstock rather than John Brown, but the book itself is not only one of the finest prose works of our time but a stimulating and invigorating reappraisal.

A final and somewhat limited group of traditional critics is the group that might crudely be called "literary genealogists," the critics interested in showing the specific literary descents of writers. This has always been one of the ways critics found to occupy their time, at least since Dryden, who not only found Spenser the poetical son of Chaucer, and Milton the poetical son of Spenser, but with great éclat traced Waller back to Edward Fairfax. Probably the foremost contemporary tracer of literary genealogies was the French critic Ferdinand Brunetière, who attempted to apply a literal evolutionism derived from Darwinian biology, and whose work shows forms and influences growing, proliferating, evolving, and becoming extinct like so many animal species. A number of English and American critics, however, have developed genealogy-tracing as a method without carrying it to that extent. Horace Gregory, for example, will spend two pages tracing the influence of Byron's Don Juan into Beyle's Julien Sorel, Ibsen's Gregers Werle, Shaw's Juan, Robinson's Miniver Cheevy, and Eliot's Prufrock. Cecil Day Lewis's essay *A Hope for Poetry* is an elaborate study in literary genealogy, using Auden's concept of "my uncle, my ancestor," and rooting the poetic movement that included Auden, Spender, and himself in such various "ancestors" as Gerard Manley Hopkins, Wilfred Owen, and Eliot. For Day Lewis the "ancestor" expresses "the only possible patriotism, the one necessary link with the past, and the meaning of tradition." Another young English poet and critic, Francis Scarfe, is constantly genealogical, tracing Dylan Thomas to Joyce, Freud, and the Bible; literary surrealism to Rimbaud, Nerval, and Lautréamont, and so on. The specialists in comparative literature, like Mario Praz, are consistently genealogical, but more as a matter of scholarship than criticism.

Almost the parody of literary genealogy is found in the work of an American critic, Joseph Warren Beach. As influences on Dos Passos in *Manhattan Transfer* he suggests *Ulysses*, Dorothy Richardson, Virginia Woolf, *The Waste Land*, Sandburg, Jules Romains, Gertrude Stein, the French cubists and post-impressionists, modern music, the Russian ballet, and the moving picture. Beach particularly likes the influence of *Ulysses*, which (along with Proust) he also finds in Thomas Wolfe and in James T. Farrell's *Gas-House McGinty*. Beach's method really goes mad when he hits a genuinely eclectic writer like John Steinbeck. In Steinbeck he finds the influence (or recall) of James Branch Cabell, Arthur Machen, W. H. Hudson, *Don Quixote*, *Gil Blas*, Charles Lamb, Anatole France, the *Morte d'Arthur*, the *Little Flowers* of Saint Francis, and so on. By this point traditionalism has come a long way.

5

Eliot has digested his influences so smoothly and with such little apparent effort that he seems almost a primary source, yet his work is highly derivative, and a number of contemporaries have affected his criticism greatly. Chief on the list, of course, is Ezra Pound. From Pound, Eliot inherited his translative method, his method of comparative study, and the concept of the scholar-critic, and it is worth noting that Eliot's call, in one of his earliest essays, "Euripides and Professor Murray," for a timeless scholarship "which can assimilate both Homer and Flaubert" is almost a paraphrase of Pound's earlier demand for "a literary scholarship to weigh Theocritus and Mr. Yeats with one balance." Moreover, Eliot is indebted to Pound for a number of his specific doctrines, among them the concept of impersonalism and, according to Mario Praz, the doctrine of the objective correlative. Praz finds its origin in Pound's statement in *The Spirit of Romance* that poetry is "a sort of inspired mathematics which gives us equations, not for abstract figures, triangles, spheres, and the like, but for the human emotions."

Eliot has had a respect amounting to veneration for Pound, despite a basic religious disagreement and other quarrels, and regards him as not only one of the greatest of contemporary critics but "probably the most important living poet in our language."[6] Nevertheless, it is ironic that Eliot's most famous tribute, his dedication of *The Waste Land* to Pound, *"il miglior fabbro,"* should be so generally misunderstood. *"Il miglior fabbro,"* "the better craftsman," is Dante's description of Arnaut Daniel in the *Purgatorio* (put in the mouth of Guido Guinicelli), but it carries a sense of ironic, courteous overpraise now (if it did not then), since even if Dante did not know he was a better, greater craftsman than Arnaut, we know it. Thus used by Eliot in speaking of Pound, it is at once a polite tribute and an implied boast of superior potentiality.

An influence on Eliot probably second only to Pound was T. E. Hulme, who was killed in the war in 1917 at the age of thirty-four and whose work was not published until 1924, when Herbert Read edited a collection of his papers as *Speculations*. Hulme was a translator of Bergson and Sorel, a rationalist Catholic, classicist, militarist, and premature fascist. His notebooks circulated among friends in manuscript, and it is certain that Eliot, Pound, and a number of other critics were familiar with them long before their publication. From Hulme, Eliot to some extent derived his classical tradition, his concept of dogma as being the vital element in religion, for the sake of which it is possible to "swallow" sentiment and ritual, and his principal example of art and criticism in the service of religious orthodoxy and political reaction. Hulme was possibly the only contemporary critic who could have wholly agreed with Eliot's perverted doctrine that the spirit killeth but the letter giveth life. Hulme, in the quarter-century since his death, has acquired a reputation as the standard-bearer for traditional criticism. Besides Eliot, his influence is marked on Pound (who has put on record an offensive conversation with Hulme where he is the teacher and Hulme the awed student), Allen Tate and others of the Southern school, the neo-humanists, T. Sturge Moore, and, in the other camp, Richards and Herbert Read.

Despite their basic opposition, I. A. Richards has been a third major influence on Eliot's critical thought. Eliot has frequently acknowledged

---

[6] One factor at least in this seemingly excessive respect was finally explained in Eliot's essay "Ezra Pound" in *Poetry*, September 1946. Eliot writes: "It was in 1922 that I placed before him in Paris the manuscript of a sprawling, chaotic poem called *The Waste Land* which left his hands, reduced to about half its size, in the form in which it appears in print." When, later in the piece, he says of the *Cantos:* "There is nobody living who can write like this: how many can be named, who can write half so well?" the statement makes no more objective sense than variants of it did before, but now at least it makes a good deal of subjective sense.

indebtedness to Richards and similarity in their ideas, has found his work "of cardinal importance in the history of literary criticism," and has undoubtedly derived from the early Richards one of his basic concepts, the theory of the irrelevancy of belief to poetic appreciation, both in the reader and (with reservations) in the poet. Eliot has resisted Richards's basic scientific orientation, frequently with sharp attack, while at the same time borrowing many of its concepts and a good deal of its vocabulary.

One of the chief problems raised by T. S. Eliot's criticism is the problem of the critic who also happens to be a creative writer of importance. Of the dozen critics studied in this book, several seem to do no writing other than critical or scholarly, among them Brooks, Richards, Caroline Spurgeon, and Maud Bodkin; a number, such as Wilson, Winters, Caudwell, Blackmur, Empson, and Burke, are poets or novelists of varying degrees of importance and literary excellence, but only Eliot is a first-rate creative writer of major importance. As Matthiessen has reminded us, Eliot is in "the main line of poet-critics that runs from Ben Jonson and Dryden through Samuel Johnson, Coleridge, and Arnold," and it is this quality of being a craftsman talking of what he knows at first hand that has given Eliot his authority.

In our day, characteristically, the chief glorifier of the poet-critic has been Pound, who remarks in one place: "Pay no attention to the criticism of men who have never themselves written a notable work," and in another: "If you wanted to know something about an automobile, would you go to a man who had made one and driven it, or to a man who had merely heard about it? And of the two men who had made automobiles, would you go to one who had made a good one, or one who had made a botch?" Nevertheless, all argument is not on the side of the poet-critic. Winckelmann's argument, that the artist criticizing art tends to make difficulty overcome the test of achievement, has never been satisfactorily answered, and the current practice of literary periodicals, particularly the liberal weeklies, in giving poetry automatically to poets for review has revealed that Winckelmann's objection only applies to the best examples, while in the worst examples the poet-critic is only concerned with matters of private squabbling, log-rolling, jealousies, and revenge.

A glance at some types of criticism indulged in by creative writers of importance may cast some light on the matter. The most notable example of such criticism in our time, by general agreement, is the Critical Prefaces of Henry James. James combined insight into his own creative processes, detailed self-revelation, and remarkable generalizing ability to furnish us with one of the most valuable records of the creative mind ever penned. He lacked that insight, however, into the creative processes of other writers, and despite a sensitivity to craft perhaps greater than any in our time, he never achieved, in discussing any other writer, the same results he got in self-analysis.

The James tradition of critical self-revelation has been continued in a number of poet-critics of our day. Outstanding among them are Allen Tate and John Crowe Ransom. (Curiously enough, Eliot himself, despite such statements as: "I maintain even that the criticism employed by a trained and skilled writer on his own work is the most vital, the highest kind of criticism," has put very little of this on record, and almost never discusses his own work openly, preferring to write of "the poet" in general). In a remarkable article called "Narcissus as Narcissus" in *Reason in Madness* Allen Tate has analyzed his own poem "Ode to the Confederate Dead" in twenty pages of detailed commentary. It is a tremendously useful analysis, fit to rank with Hart Crane's letter interpreting his poem "At Melville's Tomb" as a study of the contemporary poetic mind, but it is almost impossible to discuss as criticism, if only because the poet dealing with his own work has a monopoly on any facts he cares to furnish.

John Crowe Ransom, a different case, deals in critical self-revelation somewhat more subtly. As a critic he has created a poetics that seems chiefly based on his own procedure in writing poetry. It involves his distinction between the "structure" and the "texture" of a poem, and a further opposition between meter and meaning. The poem is thus a compromise between structure and texture, and a further compromise is achieved when the intended meaning has to be altered to fit the meter, and the intended meter to fit the meaning. These distinctions are undoubtedly valid in the case of Ransom's own writing or the work of a man like Yeats (who wrote first in prose and then hammered the work into verse), but in the case of a poet whose composition flows freely, say Shakespeare or the early Keats, they would be extremely inappropriate. What Ransom has done, in creating a poetics in his own pattern, is what any poet-critic must inevitably do, but his pattern seems somewhat too specialized to be of much help.

In these few examples of the poet-critic, among the best our age has to offer, some of the problems involved emerge. The creative writer is (under certain circumstances) best equipped to discuss his own work, but in that case no one else is equipped to discuss it with him, and criticism becomes as isolated an art as autobiography. If, instead of discussing his work, he erects a theory of composition on it, that theory may suffer from his own atypicality, since to some extent and in one way or another all writers are atypical. If he discusses the work of others, from the inevitable specialization of his work he is very likely to lack the knowledge and theoretical background of the professional critic, as does E. M. Forster in his literary pieces, or to be disqualified as an ordinary reader by greater craft awareness while unable to speak purely as a critic or craftsman, as was the case with Virginia Woolf in *The Common Readers*. He may be debarred by personal taboos from frankly discussing his own work, like Eliot, or unable to bring the same insight to bear on anyone else's, like James. He may be, finally, too obsessed with his own formula, jealous, or afflicted with any of the other vices of the poet-critic suggested above. In view of these objections and others, it might be suggested that first-rate objective criticism may accidentally arise from a first-rate creative writer, as in the case of Eliot, but that as a general rule the best criticism, like the best of anything else, will be the work of professionals. (This is not to deny one of the basic principles of criticism, which is that the critic requires some experience as a creative writer or he cannot possibly understand the problems involved, or to attack the great importance as literary documents of such pieces as James's Prefaces or the Tate article.)

"His essays are his conscious thoughts about the kinds of work he was doing," Eliot has written of Dryden, and in introducing the concept of the poet writing criticism as the *conscious* poet, he has proposed the view from which he would like to be considered. Eliot plainly considers some critical quality, which he sometimes speaks of as "the historical sense," to be indispensable to the survival of a poet "beyond his twenty-fifth year." Having himself continued to write past that crucial year (the statement was made at twenty-nine), Eliot can be presumed to find it in himself. Nevertheless, he would draw a definite line between the content of a poet's poetry and his criticism. "I would say that in one's prose reflexions one may be legitimately occupied with ideals," he writes, "whereas in the writing of verse one can only deal with actuality." This was, so far as I know, Eliot's first reply to the constant charge of inconsistency between his poetry and his criticism. This attack ranges from Ernest Boyd's pigheaded "his aesthetic theory bears no relation whatever to his practice" to Ransom's sympathetic:

> And the poet clashed with the critic. The critical Eliot was Jekyll, the poetical Eliot was Hyde; and it was wonderful to imagine that somewhere in Jekyll's pervasive wisdom was the word which justified the Hyde; both the Jekyll and the Hyde were studied the harder in the effort to harmonize them. I think it cannot be done, and the word was not there. The drift of the criticism was heavily against the drift of the poetry.

F. O. Matthiessen, almost alone, has been moved to defend Eliot's consistency. Beginning by conceding "Eliot's preference for a very different kind of poetry from that which he is capable of writing," Matthiessen has maintained that "his criticism steadily illuminates the aims of his verse, while his verse illustrates many aspects of his critical theory." By the time *Four Quartets* appeared, Matthiessen had come to believe that the best understanding of Eliot's poetry was derived from the criticism, and pointed out that Eliot's essay "The Music of Poetry" "throws the most relevant light upon his poetic intentions, and is thus a further piece of refutation to those who persist in the fallacy that there is no harmony between his 'revolutionary' creative work and his 'traditionalist' criticism."[7]

Despite a good deal of nonsense from all parties, there is a serious point involved, the organic unity of a human personality. The critics who find no such consistency in Eliot's work are inevitably dissociating a man out of all semblance of meaning, if not of life, while on the other side Matthiessen errs in making the relationship too simple, the criticism a handy guidebook or trot for the poetry. Eliot's own position is soundest on some of the possible ways a poet's criticism can complement his verse. "The poetic critic is criticizing poetry in order to create poetry," he wrote in an early essay, noting the most obvious relationship. He has also recognized the poet projecting and defending in the critic: "Arnold was, perhaps, not altogether the detached critic when he wrote this line; he may have been stirred to a defense of his own poetry." By 1942 Eliot had stopped implying detachment in his own work and wrote: "But I believe that the critical writings of poets, of which in the past there have been some very distinguished examples, owe a great deal of their interest to the fact that at the back of the poet's mind, if not as his ostensible purpose, he is always trying to defend the kind of poetry he is writing, or to formulate the kind that he wants to write." That is, the criticism does a number of jobs for the man, just as the poetry does, is in fact another kind of poetry, and these two poetries may overlap to varying degrees without ever being wholly dissociated or wholly identical.

In recent years, however, they seem to have been growing more and more dissociated. Eliot's latest essays, done in the forties, have tended to confront the religious, educational, social, and political aspects of his tradition frankly rather than through the medium of poetic texts. *The Classics and the Man of Letters*, his presidential address to the Classical Association, published as a pamphlet in 1942, centers on problems of "Christian culture"; and his introduction to *A Choice of Kipling's Verse*, published the same year, is chiefly a political defense of Kipling's "im-

---

[7] The *Quartets* seem to have won many more people to Matthiessen's view. Since this chapter was written, several statements of it have appeared, among them Miss M. C. Bradbrook's in *T. S. Eliot: A Study of His Writing by Several Hands* (1947), which argued that "the criticism is often the best commentary on the poetry" with persuasive documentation, and William York Tindall's in the *American Scholar*, Autumn 1947, which insisted that Eliot's criticism is "whatever its ostensible subject, a criticism of his own practice."

perial patriotism" and racism (Eliot "cannot believe he held a doctrine of race superiority").[8] "Notes toward a Definition of Culture," published in the *New English Weekly* in 1943 and reprinted in *Partisan Review*, Spring 1944, continues the tendencies in *The Idea of a Christian Society*, with more emphasis on the cultural and educational aspects of Eliot's ideal ecclesiastical totalitarianism. "The Man of Letters and the Future of Europe," reprinted in the *Sewanee Review*, Summer 1945, from the Norwegian *Norseman*, is a proposal that men of letters as a class agree on such public matters as culture and education; and "What Is Minor Poetry," an address to an association of Welsh Bookmen, published in the *Sewanee Review*, Winter 1946, taking an educational rather than a critical approach and patronizing in tone, devotes a good part of its space to classifying the functions performed by anthologies and little magazines. The recent essay on Pound and the obituary for Valéry are concerned, respectively, with what of Pound and what of Valéry's Europe will survive (Valéry had said "*L'Europe est finie*"), and here we can imagine a certain amount of projection. Finally, a number of Eliot's recent writings are directly religious or political: a pamphlet on Church union, an introduction to an anonymous book, *Dark of the Moon*, about the Russian mistreatment of Poland, and so on. Since "The Music of Poetry" in 1942, I am not aware of any criticism by Eliot that focuses on literature *as* literature (except perhaps for a recent lecture in New York on Milton, which revised upward his former estimate). The pattern of all Eliot's recent work seems to be one of the tradition gradually overcoming the literary concern from which it sprang, just as the political reaction (in cases like that of Maurras) sometimes overcomes the religious view it was once designed to support.

Despite all Eliot's protest to the contrary, the *man* Eliot is of course the clue to both the poetry and the criticism, just as in the last analysis the "tradition" seems to be reducible to a personal need. Another literary controversy, quite as bitter and fruitless as the debate over his prose versus his verse, is the question of the degree to which Eliot's poetry is autobiographic. Matthiessen has legitimately slapped critics like Granville Hicks and C. Day Lewis, who have had Eliot writing his social autobiography respectively in "Gerontion" and "Prufrock," and it is obvious that Eliot as an Aged Eagle in his early forties is a little ridiculous. Nevertheless, it is impossible to read certain passages, notably in the *Quartets*, as anything but direct personal statements from the poet, written in the tone of almost conversational prose. He writes in "East Coker":

[8] Under pressure from a review by Lionel Trilling, Eliot explained in the *Nation*, January 15, 1944: "I am not aware that he cherished any *particularly* anti-Semitic feelings" (italics mine).

> That was a way of putting it—not very satisfactory;
> A periphrastic study in a worn-out poetical fashion,
> Leaving one still with the intolerable wrestle
> With words and meanings. The poetry does not matter.
> It was not (to start again) what one had expected.
> What was to be the value of the long looked forward to,
> Long hoped for calm, the autumnal serenity
> And the wisdom of age?*

And a few pages later:

> So here I am, in the middle way, having had twenty years—
> Twenty years largely wasted, the years of *l'entre deux guerres*—
> Trying to learn to use words, and every attempt
> Is a wholly new start, and a different kind of failure
> Because one has only learnt to get the better of words
> For the thing one no longer has to say, or the way in which
> One is no longer disposed to say it. And so each venture
> Is a new beginning, a raid on the inarticulate
> With shabby equipment always deteriorating
> In the general mess of imprecision of feeling,
> Undisciplined squads of emotion.*

The chief emphasis here, even to the "feeling" and "emotion" banished from poetry a quarter of a century ago, is on suffering, the suffering Eliot once proclaimed, in his book on Dante, as not only the source of poetry but its only material. He has confessed that after writing poetry he feels "a sudden relief from an intolerable burden, and remarked in another place: "We all have to choose whatever subject-matter affords us the deepest and most secret release." It is easy enough, certainly, to see the suffering man in the famous statement: "We fight rather to keep something alive than in the expectation that anything will triumph," or in Eliot's "Last Words" for the *Criterion* in 1939, on giving up the magazine after sixteen years:

> In the present state of public affairs—which has induced in myself a depression of spirits so different from any other experience of fifty years as to be a new emotion—I no longer feel the enthusiasm necessary to make a literary review what it should be.

The personality that emerges finally is not, as we should expect, that of the triumphant great artist who has achieved, in the *Quartets*, one of the authentic masterpieces of our time, but that of a sick, defeated, and suffer-

* From "East Coker" in *Four Quartets* by T. S. Eliot, copyright, 1943, by T. S. Eliot. Reprinted by permission of Harcourt, Brace and Company, Inc.

ing man; the discipline and impersonality of the poetry, the "tradition" of the criticism, chiefly props to sustain him. "Traditional" criticism can yet be, unlike Eliot's, turned with hope toward the future, but it will want different things of literature and it will have to choose a different tradition.

CHAPTER 4

VAN WYCK BROOKS
and Biographical Criticism

IN THE case of Van Wyck Brooks it is particularly difficult to abstract a usable critical method from the rest of the man and his work. It has been at least a decade since anyone concerned with literature took him very seriously, and in that decade he has at once achieved an enormous popular success (*The Flowering of New England* "headed best-seller lists for fifty-nine consecutive weeks") and become a narrow and embittered old gentleman with a white mustache. He has entered the lists against "coterie literature"—that is, James, Joyce, Eliot, and the rest of the serious moderns, who represent the "death-drive"—opposing to them "primary literature"—that is, Sandburg, Frost, and Lewis Mumford, who represent life and health. "Literature has been out on a branch. We must return to the trunk," he remarked pontifically, and, spurred on by Archibald MacLeish's wartime *Kulturkampf*, suggested burning German books and announced that writers in the democratic countries had poisoned the minds of their readers and sapped France's will to resist Hitler. He has emerged as increasingly xenophobic, his early resentment of immigrants, particularly "young East Siders," with their "alien wants" bewildering "hereditary Americans," hardening in the later books to a kind of Yankee racism, so that New England declined when "alien races pressed on the native race," and in the last books "race" and "racial" are scattered thick as nuts in fudge. At the same time he has become increasingly preoccupied with genealogy, with the pursuit of "one's forbears," with "the burgher-aristocracy, the Van Wycks" (Brooks wrote of Alcott: "He was much concerned with his genealogy. At fifty-four, why not?"), and the footnotes of *New England: Indian Summer* are chiefly long lists of the family lines of writers, or which writers went to Harvard and which to Yale. He was now "convinced" by Spengler, devoted to "the great Hans Zinsser" and Dr. Alexis Carrell.

Brooks has made so many switches in his forty years of writing and his nineteen books that it is difficult to perceive any consistent pattern. He has been an æsthete, a socialist, a Freudian, a manifesto-writer, a Jungian, a Tolstoyan book-burner, and finally a compiler of literary pastiche and travelogue for the Book-of-the-Month Club. He has moved from total arty rejection of America and its culture to total uncritical acceptance. He has occupied almost every political and philosophic position of our time, and called them all "socialism." Nevertheless, there is a consistent pattern in his work, from his first book to his last, but it is a method rather than a viewpoint, the method of biographical criticism.

The basic assumption of biographical criticism is that the chief clues to a man's work can be found in the study of his life, personality, and character. "The only fruitful approach is the personal approach," Brooks wrote in *America's Coming-of-Age*, and a quarter of a century later, in *The Opinions of Oliver Allston*, he defined what he meant by the personal approach in biography and distinguished it from the scientific approach:

> But these facts [of psychoanalysis] are no more useful than other facts, and all his facts are useless until the biographer has reconceived them in the light of his intuitive faculty, with its feeling for reality and proportion. This is a different mental organ from the intelligence, which actually paralyzes its operation. It is not the causes that matter in biography, it is the character itself, which belongs to the moral and aesthetic sphere, a sphere that is quite apart from the sphere of causation. The attempt to turn biography into a science is as futile as it is with history.

This intuition of character or personality, with brief forays into using the intelligence, that paralyzing organ, has been the central feature of all Brooks's work. It is a thread of consistency running through bewildering heterogeneity, and to follow its permutations the order and dates of his books are important.

His first critical book was *Wine of the Puritans*, published in London in 1908, while Brooks was living in England. (Before that, as Harvard undergraduates in 1905, he and John Hall Wheelock had published a pamphlet of their verse anonymously.) Subtitled "A Study of Present-Day America," *Wine of the Puritans* is in the form of a dialogue between Brooks and a young man called "Graeling" at Baja in Italy, and it is one of the most purely precious, artiness for artiness' sake, documents of the twentieth century, lacking only the Beardsley illustrations. "Another shipload of Italians going to take our places at home," one of the young men murmurs, pointing a languid ivory finger. "American history is so unlovable," Brooks assures us, writing a little manifesto for expatriation: Barnum is the typical American; socialism is "a dazzling dream of impossible Utopias." Nevertheless, amid all the absurdity, the book contains two serious points. One is a distinction between the wine of the Puritans, the emphasis on the real in America, which became commercialism, and the aroma of the wine, the emphasis on the ideal, which became transcendentalism. Here, in embryo, is the distinction between "highbrow" and "lowbrow" of which Brooks was later to make so much.

The other significant thing in the booklet is the germ of the later bio-graphical method. Brooks is able to place American culture only by seeing it in terms of personalities ("personality was always to be his key word")—Barnum, Brigham Young, Rockefeller—and he confesses that he had tried to write a book called *The American Humorists*, but was forced to give it up when he couldn't "recreate the personalities" behind their pseudonyms.

Brooks's next little book, published in London in 1913 and just pub-lished in this country for the first time in 1947, was *The Malady of the Ideal*, a melancholy discussion of Maurice de Guérin, Amiel, and Sé-nancour's *Obermann*. Along with some extravagant pastoral lyricism about "deep-bosomed milkmaids" a pæan to Catholic pantheism, and some high-flown racial nonsense about the French soul and the Teu-tonic soul, Brooks furnishes three intelligent biographical studies of souls sick with longing for the Absolute, the de Guérin piece almost straight factual biography, the other two tinged with critical analysis, particularly the shrewd comparisons of Sénancour with Arnold and Gissing.

The next two works were short critical biographies, *John Addington Symonds* in 1914 and *The World of H. G. Wells* in 1915. The Symonds is a rather evasive study, ignoring Symonds's nervous disease and alter-nately hinting at and denying his homosexuality. It opposes "social order" and "muses" as the two conflicting poles and sees Symonds as torn between the respective claims of "man" and "artist." The book also announces one of Brooks's most interesting and valuable theories: that a writer's "choice of themes is never accidental," that a critic deals with writers with whom he has "special affinities," and that critical works are thus "slips," "half-confessions." The study of Wells goes through five chapters of critical analysis before Brooks gets down to biography, but the one biographical chapter is the core of the book. Wells was the child of a shopkeeper and a lady's maid; like Dickens and Defoe he rose out of this class by his own intellectual efforts, and all his views and all his books are thus projections of the opportunism of his own life. Points of view, Brooks writes, "are determined very largely by the characters and modes of living of the men who hold them." The book is one of Brooks's best, and the view of Wells as characteristic shopkeeper furnishes an amazing insight into the fluid and changeable world of his philosophy.

The next works were *America's Coming-of-Age*, published in 1915, and *Letters and Leadership*, published in 1918, both of them collected in one volume, along with an essay on *The Literary Life in America*, as *Three Essays on America* in 1934, with a preface apologizing for their "impu-dence" and "levity." All three are manifestoes and calls for action, and all three were tremendously influential on a literary generation, although precisely what action they called for never quite became clear. *America's*

Coming-of-Age announced that "One cannot have personality . . . so long as the end of society is an impersonal end like the accumulation of money"; castigated the warped division of our thinkers, beginning with Edwards and Franklin, into "Highbrow" and "Lowbrow"; and proposed as the hope "personality on a middle plane," self-fullfillment, and socialism. Exalting Whitman, it got in some good cracks at Emerson's "imperfect interest in human life," "the grotesque, pathetic and charming futility of men like Bronson Alcott," and the deficiencies of the rest of "Our Poets." *Letters and Leadership* attacked the blighting effect of pioneering utilitarianism, or Puritanism, on American culture, announced that poetry, art, and Wells's "science" would finally save society from its own spiritual corruption, and discussed in rather sharp terms some of the critical and artistic personalities the times had produced. *The Literary Life in America* announced that the American artist is an exile and a criminal, and called for a "school" of writers with a sense of "free will" and "genuine, full-blooded egoism" to "reforestate our spiritual territory."

The Ordeal of Mark Twain, published in 1920, was Brooks's first major book. It is discussed in some detail below, but it is worth noting here that it represents the best balance of the biographical method he ever achieved, the use of social and psychological insights to deepen the "intuitions of personality" without ever pushing any of them far enough to take him out of the frame of biography into science or pseudo-science. The work is partially straight biographical criticism; partially a social study, Twain seen against an oppressive social background; and partially amateur psychiatry, with Brooks drawing on Freud for concepts like repression, sublimation, and projection, techniques of dream-analysis, and a theory of the function of humor, drawing on Adler for terms like "masculine protest" and drawing on any other psychoanalysis for anything he can pick up.

Some time between 1914, when it appeared in French, and 1924, when he translated it for an American edition, Brooks read Léon Bazalgette's *Henry Thoreau, sauvage*, and was apparently fascinated by the method, which consisted in using the writer's words without quotation marks or any indication of their source to give his thoughts. Even used on a writer like Thoreau, who wrote little not directly autobiographical, the method was a wrench, but when Brooks used it in his book on James, *The Pilgrimage of Henry James*, which appeared in 1925, it produced an utter botch. The method resulted in a series of increasingly offensive interior monologues, reducing James's first-rate mind to the stature of his simplest characters, culminating, in the chapter called "The Altar of the Dead," in an almost incredible vulgarization: James as a sniveling old woman complaining of how lonely he is in an England of bad manners, usurpers, nest-foulers, monsters, upstarts, vulgarians, gamins, and cads.

Apart from the absurdity of the method, *The Pilgrimage of Henry James* is a poor book because Brooks, a critic of extremely limited imagination and æsthetic sensibility, had chosen to write about a writer he neither liked nor understood. He particularly disliked James's later works, what F. O. Matthiessen has aptly called "the major phase," and revealed very little understanding or appreciation of any of them. Even if this had not been an inevitable result of an æsthetic deficiency, it would have been an inevitable result of the assumption underlying the book, that James killed his talent by cutting his native roots, which required Brooks to find James's work progressively deteriorating, just as a comparable assumption about the social destruction of Twain required him to overestimate Twain's potential enormously. The method is still biographical, but it is less social, less psychoanalytic, less productive of insights into the work, and, in the last analysis, relatively pointless.

Brooks's next full-length study was *The Life of Emerson*, published in 1932. It was his first work that made no pretense of being a critical study, was admittedly a biography, and, unlike the *Symonds*, the *Wells*, the *Twain*, and the *James*, had no point of view. (The title is an interesting confirmation of this: instead of being an *Ordeal of*, a *Pilgrimage of*, or some similar slanting, it is simply *The Life of*.) Not by coincidence, it became a Literary Guild selection, was Brooks's first book to have a wide popular sale, and marked the end of his serious work and the beginning of his total uncritical acceptance. Studies of Whitman and Melville he had projected after the *James* had been postponed or given up (Brooks's announcement of failure on Melville was the remark in "Notes on Herman Melville," never since reprinted: "We cannot penetrate the mystery of a personality"), and Emerson was now, as Whitman had once been, his "personality on a middle plane," Franklin *plus* Edwards, Twain *plus* James.

Meanwhile, in 1927, Brooks had published a collection of short pieces, *Emerson and Others*, including "Emerson: Six Episodes," chiefly notes for the 1932 life, the "Notes on Melville," and a half-dozen other essays. In 1932 he published *Sketches in Criticism*, an extensive collection of his critical essays, some of them going back before 1920, from the *Seven Arts*, the *Freeman*, and other sources. In these the biographical method is frequently a simple, pat formula almost parodying itself: Barnum, for instance, was fooled by his family as a child, therefore he grew up to fool others. The new developments were: a shift from Freud and Adler to Jung's glossier terminology, particularly those tempting simplifications, the latest pairing for his highbrow-lowbrow dichotomy, "introvert" and "extrovert," which he was to continue through the following books; plus a new tone of pettishness, in pieces like "The Parvenu Intellectuals" and "The Doctrine of Self-Expression," toward modern literature (Henry James, Eliot, etc.), never named, but always attacked as "expressionism," or literature of "psychology" and "experiment." Many of the pieces are frankly biographical, like a short one simply called "From the Life of Stephen Crane" and a memoir of John Butler Yeats, and very few of them deal with the living, since, like Sainte-Beuve, Brooks found himself confronted with the problem that a biographical method cannot really begin to function until all the facts are in. What little criticism is essayed is generally the marshaling of giant cannon to blast such gnats as Hamilton Wright Mabie and Joaquin Miller.

In 1936 Brooks published the first volume in his magnum opus, a literary history of the United States, calling it *The Flowering of New England*. Poor as it is in comparison with the work of such serious literary historians as Taine, Brandes, de Sanctis, and Parrington, the three volumes that have so far followed it at intervals of about four years are a good deal worse. *The Flowering* at least has a subject, the cultural climate of New England before the Civil War, the interstices *between* the writers; whereas *New England: Indian Summer* tried to create a comparable cultural climate by flat for New England writers after the Civil War, even if it meant kidnapping Henry Adams from Washington and Cummings from Greenwich Village; and *The World of Washington Irving* and *The Times of Melville and Whitman* abandoned even this fiat unity and have no organizing principle other than two dates and the idea that any writer not already treated ought to be included somewhere. All four books are mosaics of quotations, scraps from old letters and documents, records of remarks made, lists of works written. They have no point of view, no standards, no depth, no ideas, and boundless love for everyone without distinction: in the first, Bancroft, Prescott, Motley, and Parkman are four comparable historians; in the second, Howells and James are two equally important writers; in the third, Jefferson, Hamilton, and Aaron Burr are three equally valuable statesmen; in the fourth, Walt Whitman and James Whitcomb Riley are two American poets.

The method is still pastiche; quote and paraphrase, quote and paraphrase. Brooks is aware of Brandes and Taine, quotes them approvingly, and regards his book as in their tradition, but the actual literary world he sees is an undetermined anarchy where accident and coincidence rule: Lowell had a period of radicalism because his wife was fervent and he was suggestible; it ended because she died and he stopped being suggestible; Melville "acquired in the forecastle the tragic sense of life" (why didn't Dana?). Most annoying, since the Brooks of the *Wells* and *Twain* volumes had been at least a writer of real clarity, is a new mistiness and obscurity of style, a failure to come out of the fog and say anything definite, a doubt as to whether any given phrase is quoted, paraphrased, or Brooks's own, an infuriating inability to find out *which* Boston Abolitionist received a slave's ear in the mail ("One might receive . . ."). The primary interest is still biographical, but increasingly biography that fails to lead to any conclusions, or brings forth a stillborn mouse: that Adams was inevitably a dilettante, that Poe's work must have had its source in the insecurity of his life, that Motley's politics determined his histories.

Meanwhile, before the appearance of *The World of Washington Irving*, a slim volume called *On Literature Today* and *The Opinions of Oliver Allston* had both appeared in 1941. *On Literature Today*, a brief address delivered at Hunter College, is an affirmation that the mood of "health, will, courage, faith in human nature" found in Robert Frost and Lewis Mumford is "the dominant mood in the history of literature," and can most charitably be dismissed as an honest hysterical reaction to what looked like defeat for the democratic nations in the early years of the war. *The Opinions of Oliver Allston* is a much deeper and more pernicious book. An autobiography thinly disguised as a memoir to "my friend Oliver Allston, who died last year in his early fifties," the book offers a channel for filtering off all the venom accumulated in Brooks by the sugary literary-history volumes. The device itself was undoubtedly borrowed from Randolph Bourne's *History of a Literary Radical*, an autobiography that purported to be about "my friend Miro." It serves a number of excellent purposes: allowing him to be as frank as he wants and use his journals directly without violating his formidable reserve; allowing him to change the record where he wants, since this is not his life, but Allston's; allowing him to be as effusive about himself and his value as he wants, "objectively"; and, finally, allowing him to kill Allston off, and with him the last vestiges of his literary conscience, in a complicated rebirth ritual. Brooks plays all sorts of ironic tricks with the personality of Allston and gets some fairly subtle effects: "If Allston had read" a book Brooks has, he might have felt differently; one of Allston's comments "strikes me as intemperate, to say the least"; Allston agreed with a view of Brooks's and his informed agreement confirmed Brooks in it, and so forth. (The name, incidentally, would seem to be a weighting in favor of Brooks's Puritan qualities—Oliver [Cromwell?] All-stone.)

The Opinions of Oliver Allston repudiated the early works for "ignorance" and "brashness" and went on to achieve an ignorance and brashness the early works had never even approximated. The new criteria, explicitly applied, are the moral strait-jackets of Tolstoy's *What Is Art*: our literature is sick, off-center, and reflects the death-drive, it must be "rebuked" (a key word);[1] writers are no longer the voices of the people; "true literature transmits sound feeling"; it is time to restore the American classics; Henry James was "fatuous," a "guilty child disloyal to his mother," Rimbaud "a little neurasthenic wretch," Joyce a "sick Irish Jesuit," his works "trivial," "salacious," "bad-smelling," "the ash of a burnt-out cigar"; Laforgue was "a naughty brat," Proust "a spoiled

---

[1] After almost forty years Irving Babbitt, who had had Brooks in his first class at Harvard, was having his revenge.

child," and so on. "What made Proust an authority on love?" he asks, and we might answer: the same thing that made Brooks, who mentions in the book Allston's breakdown, his neurosis, his time in an English sanitarium, an authority on mental health—its absence. As Brooks gets more and more worked up about the state of contemporary literature, the Allston pose drops away and he speaks with his own voice, by now a remarkably shrill one.

Brooks had finally worked his biographical method through to its logical implication: if criticism is the capturing of personality, if the critic writes only of authors for whom he has an affinity, and if writing is determined by the author's life, Brooks can encompass all of value in criticism by exploring the roots of his writings in his own life, by intuiting his own personality. "A man who has the courage of his platitudes is always a successful man," Allston noted in his journal, reversing the procedure and doing an obituary for Van Wyck Brooks.

2

Although flawed, *The Ordeal of Mark Twain* is Brooks's best book, if not his only one in which the biographical method succeeds, and it is worth examining in some detail. Its thesis is that Twain's bitterness "was the effect of a certain miscarriage in his creative life, a balked personality, an arrested development of which he himself was almost wholly unaware, but which for him destroyed the meaning of life." The two related factors that arrested Twain's creative development were: on the personal level, the excessive influence of his mother and her passionate attachment to him, later succeeded by his wife and daughter as mother-symbols; and on the social level, the Gilded Age in America with its false standards of gentility, and its demand on the writer that he help the tired businessman to relax or be broken by it. There is probably a substantial portion of truth in both factors, but to fit Twain perfectly into the Procrustean bed of his thesis, Brooks is forced to stretch and lop off, that is, to underestimate Twain's accomplishments vastly, calling him the author of works "of inferior quality" appealing to "rudimentary minds," while at the same time vastly overrating his potential, insisting that he could have been a Voltaire, Swift, or Cervantes.[2] It is true that only a few of Twain's books still warrant reading, and the rest now tend to seem both tedious and puerile, but it is equally true that those few, particularly *Huckleberry Finn* and *Life on the Mississippi*, are first-

[2] Some time after the completion of this essay I encountered F. W. Dupee's excellent study "The Americanism of Van Wyck Brooks," reprinted in *The Partisan Reader*, (1946) from *Partisan Review* in 1939. I observe that Dupee anticipates me on this point (his phrase is "to assume in happier conditions your writer would have been a Tolstoy") as well as on a number of others.

rate literature. When Brooks assumes that Twain, under other circumstances, would have been capable of writing *Gulliver's Travels* or *Don Quixote* he is wrong, and when he assumes that what he was capable of writing, *Huck Finn*, is not worth bothering about, he is foolish. But the central insight of the book, its contrast between the potential of Twain's sensibility and the tawdriness of most of what he accomplished, is sound, although certainly exaggerated.

Much of the book is very perceptive: among other things, Brooks's recognition that the symbol of the Mississippi pilot was the archetype of freedom and creative satisfaction, even of art, for Twain (just as it satisfies Brooks by being on a middle plane between idealist and practical man, highbrow and lowbrow, Edwards and Franklin); his awareness that Twain's later receiving in bed was a regressive pattern, like Proust's cork-lined room; his identification of Twain's concern with dual personality in such stores as "Those Extraordinary Twins" as essentially cycloid; his observation that *The Gilded Age* is essentially a discussion of business in religious imagery. The book also contains a good measure of foolishness, distortion, an oversimplified use of Marx, Veblen, Freud, and whatever theoretical club comes to hand, even a rather corny moral to the effect that since the system did this to Twain, writers, revolt! But the total effect is overwhelmingly useful, and the book is at once a tribute to the effectiveness of biographical criticism within its limits and an indictment of the later Brooks for making so little of it.

Perhaps the greatest weakness of the book is Brooks's absolute and lifelong humorlessness (he once suggested that Adams should have called his autobiography not *The Education* but *The Betrayal* of Henry Adams), and his characteristic device is analyzing as a serious statement a Twain joke of which he has missed the point. He prints Twain's comic announcement, on taking over an editorship of the *Buffalo Express*, that "I am not going to hurt the paper deliberately and intentionally at any time" with the comment: "Never, surely, was a creative will more innocently, more painlessly surrendered than in those words"; he quotes Twain's introduction to *Huck Finn:* "Persons attempting to find a motive in this narrative will be prosecuted; persons attempting to find a moral in it will be banished; persons attempting to find a plot in it will be shot" with the comment: "He feels so secure of himself that he can actually challenge the censor to accuse him of having a motive!"

One of the most interesting features of *The Ordeal of Mark Twain* is the revised and reset edition of it that Brooks published in 1933, without any introduction or comment. For the thirteen years between he had been under fire for the book, from Bernard De Voto in particular, and when De Voto's book *Mark Twain's America*, largely an attempt to demolish Brooks's book, was in galley, a revision of Brooks's book was announced. I have not read the book through word by word for alterations, but the changes and rewritings that emerge from even a random comparison are almost unbelievable. On page 58 Brooks inserts a parenthetical remark, before telling a story, explaining away Twain's later contradiction of it on the grounds of Twain's treacherous memory. On page 61 he omits some sob stuff about Twain breaking his mother's heart. On page 63 he drops some strong statements about Twain's being inhibited. On page 92 he omits: "New England, in short, and with New England the whole spiritual life of the nation, had passed into the condition of a neurotic anæmia in which it has remained so largely to this day." On page 95 he changes "a vast unconscious conspiracy actuated all America against the creative life" to "a sort of unconscious conspiracy."

On page 96 Brooks goes to town: he omits a half-page attack on American writers as spineless, dependent, and avocational; changes "Essentially, America was not happy" to "Was America really happier, during the Gilded Age, than any other nation?" he drops the two following major statements:

> it was a nation like other nations, and one that had no folk-music, no folk-art, no folk-poetry, or next to none, to express it, to console it;

> it was a horde-life, a herd-life, an epoch without sun or stars, the twilight of a human spirit that had nothing upon which to feed but the living waters of Camden and the dried manna of Concord:

and, after a reference to the American joy of action, omits "that left them old and worn at fifty-five." On page 98 he omits a "moral judgment" that the devil had already marked Twain out for destruction. On page 104 he changes "he always yielded in the end" to "he always yielded goodnaturedly in the end." On page 109 he hedges on two statements, toning them down with modifiers like "a suggestion of," "whether he was conscious of them or not," etc. On page 131 he changes "the recognized American game" and "the recognized American rules" to "the recognized game" and "the recognized rules." On page 143 he changes "this moral surrender—shall we call it?" to "this capitulation" (obviously, we shall not call it). On page 151 he inserts new evidence to reinforce a dubious case for Twain's cringing servility. On page 154 he omits a metaphor about Twain as a sleeping Samson, "yielding his locks to that simple Delilah his wife." On page 161 he omits an anecdote about Twain sneaking a smoke, the point of which is that Twain is an "Incorrigible naughty boy!"

On page 180 Brooks omits a crack Twain made about Mr. Rockefeller, Jr., and Joseph's Egyptian policy. On page 182 he omits a page and a half of material sharply critical of Twain as a self-recognized failed writer and a businessman of letters. On page 190 he omits two sentences, obviously unpatriotic, invidiously comparing Twain's mind to that of any "French or English writer of rank." On page 192 he changes "I should like to point out" to "One might almost say." On page 196 patience and conscience, formerly "of the essence of all art," now "belong to the creative life also." On page 261 he inserts a defense of one of his statements against Ludwig Lewisohn's contrary view. On page 278, he omits a crack at New England snobbery and the suggestion that he might be exaggerating the significance of an anecdote. On page 284 "the wiles of simple folk" become, not "the most successful of all," but "the most complicated of all." On page 292 the sentence "It is perhaps the most pitifully abject confession ever written by a famous writer" becomes "It is a very sad confession, surely, to have come from a famous author." On page 315 he omits the sentences: "Do we ask, then, why Mark Twain 'detested' novels? It was because he had been able to produce only one himself, and that a failure."

These are only a few of the innumerable major changes, not counting those that merely corrected grammar, eliminated some of the repetition, or substituted a better word. The pattern they compose is one of wild statements having to be toned down by the more cautious older writer, hedging, backing out of misstatements, weaseling on contradictions, a new servility and pseudo-patriotism that omits slights to America, New England, and John D. Rockefeller, Jr., and a new caution prepared to discard a good part of his thesis under attack. It is not a pretty picture.

It is obvious that Bernard De Voto had caught him far off base. De Voto's book, when it appeared, cast grave doubts on what he correctly identified as the cornerstone of Brooks's theory, the deathbed scene of Twain's father; recognized accurately that Brooks thought Twain wanted to be Shelley; charged Brooks fairly with "parlor" psychoanalysis based on inadequate knowledge, with hasty, unscientific procedures, and with shifting offhand from Freud to Adler to Jung as each of them served his purpose; hit on the basic fault of the book, that "Mr. Brooks dislikes humor"; and, finally, found Brooks guilty of contradictions, distortions, misrepresentations, and unwarranted assumptions on page after page (only some of them corrected or modified in the revision). De Voto's *Mark Twain's America* itself is a stupid and ignorant book, full of the most incredible howlers, its literary judgments alternately provincial and silly (*Moby Dick* is "chaotic," "structureless"), its positive theories of Twain childish (Twain's neurosis was due to the frightening Negro stories he heard as a child), its bias all-pervasive (De Voto takes out his venom against Brooks impartially on Emerson, Alcott, Holmes, Whittier, and any Abolitionist foolish enough to want to free "the childlike race of slaves"), and its style the smart-aleck cantankerousness of Mencken and Thomas Beer, diluted with water. Nevertheless, in regard to Brooks's book De Voto is more often right than wrong, and his book serves as an irritating but valuable corrective.

The controversy had a comic sequel in 1944, when De Voto, a decade crustier, wrote a book called *The Literary Fallacy*, a study of the sins of contemporary writers, which devoted almost half its one hundred and seventy-five pages to attacking Van Wyck Brooks. The attack boiled down to the charge that Brooks hadn't begun to hate modern literature until 1940, whereas De Voto had been hating it at least since 1920. As usual, it made a number of accurate criticisms of Brooks, documenting his early ignorance of American literature at a time when he was most eloquent about it, and polishing off the New England books with a rare perception: "These writers seldom fall in love, and one feels that only those have children whose children also became writers." The rest of the book is brash and ignorant: De Voto invents a writer named "Falkner" (after the third appearance of the name, it is obviously no misprint), finds Farrell "the most considerable American novelist developed during the 1930's," finds Alfred Kazin's *On Native Grounds* "the best study of modern American literature so far written," dismisses Eliot as an "epistemologist," and finally ends up by reproaching our writers for convincing Hitler that America was decadent, and for never mentioning in their work the man who founded the National Park Service or the work American medicine did on the problem of burns, both of which he regards as more important aspects of American culture than all this literary nonsense. The "literary fallacy" De Voto accuses our writers of holding is the belief: "that a culture may be understood and judged solely by means of its literature, that literature embodies truly and completely both the values and the content of a culture, that literature is the highest expression of a culture, that literature is the measure of life, and finally that life is subordinate to literature." (As usual, De Voto has the goods on Brooks, who once wrote: "And so if we really care for the conservation of our natural resources, those that essentially matter, we shall have a more than ordinary concern for the welfare of American literature, in which largely lies whatever hope our civilization has.") Applied generally to American writers, however, the charge has little point and makes little sense, and De Voto's book assumes a number of logical fallacies much more substantial than the one he called "literary." A few of them are:

That writers can freely decide what they want to do and what they want to write about.

That the aim of writing is to portray reality, especially democratic, American reality.

That the best writers are those who make the most realistic portraits.

That an entire body of literature can be "wrong."
That writers freely produce their own cultural climate.
That the literary term "culture" and the anthropological term "culture" are the same term.
That writers or critics can "escape" if they wish.
That the more a critic "knows," the better a critic he is.

I do not believe that Brooks ever replied to *The Literary Fallacy*, but Sinclair Lewis, who had also been attacked, rushed to Brooks's defense in an article entitled "Fools, Liars and Mr. De Voto" in the April 15, 1944, issue of the *Saturday Review of Literature*, writing with his usual bad temper. Seeing De Voto, with a bad-tempered, stupid, and largely erroneous book clubbing Brooks for a bad-tempered, stupid, and largely erroneous book with which he was in substantial agreement, and Lewis rushing into the fray with a bad-tempered, stupid, and largely erroneous article, all the person seriously concerned with literature could do was say with the pioneer woman whose husband was attacked by a bear: "Go it, husband; go it, bear."

3

The tradition of biographical criticism Brooks inherits is a substantial one. Almost any literary biography must be to some extent critical (although too few critical studies, perhaps, are adequately biographical). The first real English literary biography, Izaak Walton's *Lives of Donne, Herbert*, and others is not much concerned with their poetry, "honest Izaak" not having much of a taste for metaphysical verse, but a century later, in Dr. Johnson's *Lives of the Poets*, the contribution the life makes to an understanding of the work is neatly assayed, and in such places as the discussion of the relation between Rochester's moral character and his verse in the "Life of Rochester," actual biographical criticism emerges. In Scott's *Lives of the Novelists* half a century later the tradition is further developed, and the fine bourgeois character of Richardson's novels, say, is fully explored in terms of his rather prim middle-class life. A few years later, with Carlyle (who saw history as "the essence of innumerable Biographies") and Macaulay, it is a fully developed form (although Macaulay's finest essay, the merciless dissection of Francis Bacon, in the last analysis does not succeed in finding the relation, which seems rather obvious to us, between Bacon as a trimmer and Bacon as a utilitarian philosopher). The method even works out to a *reductio ad absurdum*, at about the same time, in De Quincey's study of Coleridge, which sees the poetry almost entirely in terms of kleptomania, an unfortunate marriage, overindulgence in narcotics, and any other personal factors De Quincey is able to find or invent.

The great development of biographical criticism, however, came not in England but in France, with Sainte-Beuve's *Causeries du lundi*, beginning in the middle of the last century. He almost perfectly defined the method with his statement:

> Real criticism, as I define it, consists in studying each person, that is, each author, each talent, according to the conditions of his nature, in order to make a vivid and pregnant description of him so that he can later be classified and put in his proper place in the hierarchy of art.

This principle of the identity of the man and his work led Sainte-Beuve into a rather elaborate study of the private lives of the literary, from their physical appearance to the elaborate trivia of their daily routine. From this jumble he produced what few of the literary gossips who have followed his method since ever produced: real insights into the man and his work. On occasion, as in his essay on Gibbon, he pushed the realm of biography into an exhaustive study of the relationship between the author and his time and environment, anticipating the direction the method would later take with his chief disciple, Taine. Taine began as a biographical critic like Sainte-Beuve (and his treatment of Pope largely in terms of his physical infirmities in the *History of English Literature* shows that he never wholly renounced it), but he soon converted the method into an emphasis on *race, moment, milieu,* and thus became chiefly a social determinist critic of literature, in the tradition largely represented by Marxist criticism in our time.

A line of thought essentially German was added to the brew. Goethe had announced that art springs from disease, is a kind of blood-letting. Schopenhauer turned this into an emphasis on the artist's suffering, and Nietzsche added the modification that the art is not only the product of the disease, but a kind of record of it, that every philosophy is a confession, "a species of involuntary and unconscious autobiography." Max Nordau made news of the doctrine that genius is a form of neurosis in his book *Degeneration*, and recently Thomas Mann has been frequently identified with a view of art as produced out of sickness and neurosis, the way the pearl is produced from the oyster, with that art then at once the product of that sickness, its record, and its transcendence. This is, of course, more or less the "wound and the bow" theory that Edmund Wilson has made his own; but with the emphasis taken off disease and neurosis, reduced to a simple determinism of the nature of the life over the works, it is the characteristic assumption of present-day biographical criticism.

Of this criticism, there are a number of special contemporary forms. Henry James had one almost exclusive with him, the private history of a work of art; what he was doing, what he heard, what he said, what he thought of, during its genesis. Following Lytton Strachey, who dealt chiefly with historical figures, Virginia Woolf has developed a method of her own in *The Common Reader* and *The Second Common Reader* for making literary figures, schools, and periods come alive by vivid portraits and vignettes. She summons up their atmosphere, their quality of life, their very aroma. It is not analysis, not quite biography, not quite criticism, perhaps it is a kind of closet-drama, but whatever it is, it is charming and invaluable. Herbert Read in his biography of Wordsworth reversed the method ironically and set out to analyze Wordsworth's poetry "to explain his life," the way social critics like Taine, implicitly, and T. K. Whipple in this country, explicitly, have studied society using literature as a clue in their literary history, rather than vice versa. Other contemporary critics who have relied heavily on the biographical method are Mark Schorer in his *William Blake*, F. O. Matthiessen in his *Sarah Orne Jewett* and *American Renaissance*, and Peter Quennell in his *Baudelaire and the Symbolists*, *The Profane Virtues*, and several books on Byron. We have also had a number of literary biographies that are valuable critical studies, including Georg Brandes's books on Goethe, Voltaire, Shakespeare, and Nietzsche, Gissing's and Chesterton's studies of Dickens, Newton Arvin's *Hawthorne* and *Whitman*, Joseph Wood Krutch's *Samuel Johnson*, Lionel Trilling's *Matthew Arnold*, Max Brod's *Franz Kafka*, Wallace Fowlie's *Rimbaud* and Philip Horton's *Hart Crane*. Biographical studies that have been chiefly psychoanalytic will be treated elsewhere.

One of the great problems of the biographical method has been the problem of frankness, when personal information stops being relevant and becomes simply prying into the private life of the author. If an important modern poet has an insane wife, is that information relevant? If the decision is that it is relevant and is intimately bound up with his work, is it ethical or even possible to print it? The decision usually made is that scandalous revelations can be printed about authors safely dead, so that Wilde's syphilis, de Gourmont's leprosy, and Dostoyevsky's epilepsy can now be discussed critically, but that similar information about living authors can only be used if they have themselves publicized it, as Gide did his homosexuality. Homosexuality is, as a matter of fact, the chief problem, since it is widespread in contemporary letters, almost unmentionable in print, usually obsessive in a writer's work, and a very important critical consideration in relation to that work. Brooks's problem with John Addington Symonds, who is unmistakably homosexual in his writings and confessedly homosexual in his letter to Whitman, is a case in point, but perhaps most typical is the case of Whitman himself.

Whitman's homosexuality was first asserted by Europeans—Eduard Bertz in Germany, Jean Catel in France, the physician W. C. Rivers in

England—and was picked up most enthusiastically in America, for the purpose of discounting Whitman as a democratic symbol, by Mark Van Doren in 1935. Biographers sympathetic to Whitman, like Newton Arvin and Henry Seidel Canby, have been forced to admit the charge, although still disputing the possibility of overt practice, and in the *New Republic* in 1946 Malcolm Cowley published a fully documented and absolutely convincing case for Whitman as a practicing homosexual. In all his writing on Whitman, to my knowledge, Brooks has not so much as mentioned the suspicion of homosexuality, and it is fascinating to see him skirt around the problem in *The Times of Melville and Whitman*, and to speculate on why the projected earlier study of Whitman was suddenly dropped.

The amazing thing about these few recent and embattled recognitions of Whitman's homosexuality, which have hardly penetrated even to the colleges and certainly not to the book-club public, is how unmistakable the thing is to anyone bothering to read the poetry, and how vital its recognition is to the study of the poetry. If the Whitman battle has barely been won, the other battles on American writers have not yet begun. Almost every major American writer has been a sexual problem of one sort or another: the extreme homoeroticism of Melville, the frigidity or repression or prolonged virginity of Emerson, Thoreau, and Hawthorne; the probable impotence of Henry James, and so on. The pattern of major American literature has involved a related pattern of sexual maladjustment, and every attempt to study the literature and blink the problem has been inevitably foredoomed to failure.

There is a sign of hope in the recent increase in critical frankness, typified by the Cowley article on Whitman, particularly in regard to homosexuality. Gide's frank confession in his autobiography and Philip Horton's frank handling of the problem in his biography of Hart Crane are excellent signs. As far back as 1929, in an essay in *The New American Caravan*, Yvor Winters had the courage, combined with his usual faculty for drawing the wrong conclusions, to write of "the depressing but steady increase of sexual perversion, not only in our 'art centers,' but in nearly all our universities, large and small, with the ultimate spiritual dishonesty and sterility that it seems in nearly all cases to entail." In the thirties, in an essay called "Writers and Morals," C. Day Lewis drew a much more sensible conclusion, speaking of the contemporary English writer and the factors that tend to "drive him to homosexualism as a refuge from responsibilities. This also results in his written work in a certain evasion —a leading up to a dramatic climax or a moral judgment and then shying away from it." Eric Bentley, in his book *A Century of Hero Worship*, is remarkably frank about the importance of such sexual factors as Carlyle's impotence, Stefan George's homosexuality, and D. H. Lawrence's extreme homoeroticism; and Wallace Fowlie, in *Rimbaud*, discusses homosexuality at some length. Perhaps most significant, a relatively old-school French professor at Yale, Henri Peyre, in his book *Writers and Their Critics* in 1944, felt the climate of opinion was strong enough for him to venture a list of writers and artists who have been insane (Tasso, Nerval, Holderlin, Lenau, Nietzsche, Hugo Wolf), epileptic or otherwise seriously diseased (Pascal, Flaubert, Dostoyevsky), either homosexual or preoccupied in their work with homosexuality (Socrates, Plato, Sophocles, and many other Greeks, Catullus, Virgil, Michelangelo, Leonardo, Shakespeare, Winckelmann, Platen, Wilde, Verlaine, Rimbaud, George, Whitman, Proust, Gide, Hart Crane), and so on. When other critics are willing to face these lists (with a few additions, Poe and Rousseau among the insane, Hopkins and Samuel Butler among the homosexuals, Swift in all the categories he turns out to fit, and so forth) and their implications, biographical criticism can come out of the fog of suggestion and innuendo and get to work. One of the things it will have to renounce is any moral implication in this information. Despite Winters and others of his view, the fact that a writer is homosexual does not mean that his writing will be dishonest and sterile, or so the example of Shakespeare and Sophocles should argue. All it does mean, as does the information that he is insane, diseased, alcoholic, impotent, or otherwise abnormal, is that this abnormality will be a major factor in determining the form and character of his work. It is quite possible that a new debunking, Procrustean, or other nut critical school could arise on the basis of a new frankness about the private lives of writers, but since it is almost impossible for it to do any worse than similar schools that already exist without the frankness, the attempt is certainly worth making. It is not likely that Van Wyck Brooks will be in the vanguard.

4

A number of other matters not directly related to the biographical method are worth discussing in connection with Brooks. The first is his debt to his close friend Randolph Bourne, the brilliant and promising young radical critic who died in 1918 at the age of thirty-two. Both *America's Coming of Age* and *Letters and Leadership* were to a large extent inspired by Bourne's crusading fury, and with Bourne's untimely death Brooks's ardor quickly lessened. He persuaded Brooks of the reality of a class struggle in America, helped to turn him from dilute European æstheticism to a preoccupation with American literature (he was not responsible for the provincialism this finally developed into), and, had he lived, would almost certainly have been a major American critic, just as Brooks would have been a better one.

Brooks has been influential enough almost to have had a school. His chief disciples were Waldo Frank and Lewis Mumford, but he had a substantial influence on Paul Rosenfeld and Matthew Josephson, and for a while on T. K. Whipple and F. O. Matthiessen (although the former eventually broke away to become a Marxist critic and the latter broke away early, after *Sarah Orne Jewett*, to substitute serious æsthetic analysis for biographical and social oversimplification). Frank was chiefly a critical moralist, writing sermons and exhortations from literary springboards. Lewis Mumford, on the other hand, was in many respects a better critic than Brooks—his *The Golden Day* is a better-informed, more perceptive, and more critical book than the New England volumes of Brooks that it parallels—and Brooks in recent years has become increasingly *his* disciple, adopting his mystic ideas of "organicism" and celebrating his genius and "health." Matthew Josephson, except for one survey of American literature in *Portrait of the Artist as American*, confined his work to French literary figures, where his basic good sense kept him from many of the Brooksian excesses. Paul Rosenfeld, perhaps the most independent of the group, wrote only two volumes of literary portraits, *Port of New York* and *Men Seen*, like Brooks's centering chiefly on personality, but much more sharply perceptive; much more interested, like his other master, Huneker, in popularizing unknown moderns; and much more sensitive to æsthetic values. The most curious thing about the Brooks school, while it held together, was how aware all of them were of Brooks's failings and limitations (although a certain amount of projection must be assumed here). The most incisive criticism of Brooks yet written can be found in the works of Mumford, Frank, Josephson, and Rosenfeld, particularly the last, written at the period of their most passionate discipleship.

The principal view that Brooks succeeded in imposing on his school was the idea that America after the Civil War had been a retarding cultural environment which crippled its victims the artists in various ways. With the substitution of "altered" for "crippled," and "products" for "victims," this would have been a sound and usable doctrine of the intimate relationship between an artist and his society; in Brooks's form it was a crude generalization that led to inevitable distortion in every literary judgment. Not only was this half-truth imposed on Brooks's school, but it influenced the mechanical Marxists like Granville Hicks and V. F. Calverton, who added Brooks's excesses to their own and simply parroted his oversimplifications of men like James and Twain; it took in almost a whole critical generation to some extent, including Parrington (on James) and a number of Soviet critics (on Twain); and it influenced a number of creative writers who should have known better, among them Dreiser and Anderson.

One of the most curious aspects of Van Wyck Brooks's work is the way he has written all his literary studies as elaborate footnotes to his manifestoes. Both the *Twain*, published in 1920, and the *James*, published in 1925, are documentation for a single sentence published in *America's Coming-of-Age* in 1915, with all their distortions implicit in it:

In effect, an examination of American literature will show, I think, that those of our writers who have possessed a vivid personal genius have been paralyzed by the want of a social background, while those who have possessed a vivid social genius have been equally unable to develop their personalities.

James is the first half of that coin, Twain the other. The affirmation of the next period, beginning with *The Life of Emerson* and continuing through the New England books, is all contained in a question asked in *The Literary Life in America* in 1921:

How can one explain why, at a time when America, in every other department of life, was more distinctly colonial than it is now, American literature commanded the full respect of Americans, while today, when the colonial tradition is vanishing all about us, it so little commands their respect that they go after any strange god from England?

(It is thoroughly characteristic of Brooks's prissiness, incidentally, to omit the verb from "whoring after strange gods.") The last manifesto was *On Literature Today* in 1941, and allowing for the normal Brooks lag of anything up to a decade, we can expect at least another book or two to stem from one or another of its oracular sentences.

Brooks has a number of limitations on which he has to some extent capitalized. One of the most obvious is that, like Edmund Wilson, he is a critic who fundamentally doesn't like poetry, but, unlike Edmund Wilson, he has never been at all interested in writing about it and has never published any verse of his own since college (and that quite poor). "Could Wells write a poem?" he asks rhetorically in his book on Wells, and the question might just as easily be phrased: "Could Brooks write a poem?" with the same sad negative answer. Another related limitation is the lack of a broad enough general culture to permit him to handle European literature (although he and his wife have translated at least thirty works from the French). Since *The Malady of the Ideal* in 1913 he has written nothing on any European writer, except a few brief uncollected introductions; and since the *Symonds* and *Wells* books in 1914 and 1915, with the exception of introductions and short pieces on Swinburne, whom he met in London, and John Butler Yeats, whom he knew in New York, he has written nothing on any British writer or artist. In *The Opinions of Oliver Allston* Brooks defends this limitation of Allston's, first with a quotation from Sainte-Beuve (who wrote a good deal about foreign writers): "literary criticism has its full worth and originality only when it applies itself to subjects of which it possesses, through immediate contact and from a long way back, the source, the surrounding facts and all the circumstances"; and then with a misunderstood quotation from Yeats: "One can only reach out to the universe with a gloved hand— that hand is one's nation, the only thing that one knows even a little about." He comments:

> This was a principle that Allston followed in all his work. He wrote, I might say, exclusively of American subjects; for, although he had written of foreign subjects, he had begun with American subjects—and how could he ever cease to be interested in them?

Another limitation that Brooks has converted into something meritorious is his great dependence on his own notebooks, journals, recorded phrases, anecdotes, and aphorisms. He is constantly living off accumulated fat: some of his Emerson material was used in "Emerson: Six Episodes," *The Life of Emerson*, *The Flowering of New England* and its successors, and in random essays; all his old anecdotes turn up again and again, sometimes in the same words, sometimes altered because Brooks has thrown away the note and forgotten to whom Greeley said: "You can be fixing me some." He is probably the most repetitious American author since Thomas Wolfe died, and a book like *The Ordeal of Mark Twain* has almost every anecdote or quotation repeated at least twice, and one of them, a line from Herbert Croly, used four times by page 143. (Some of these repetitions were eliminated in the revised edition.) Brooks has converted this remarkable economy of material into a virtue, praising Allston for his habit of keeping and using journals like such New England worthies as Emerson and Thoreau, and in fact in his utilization-of-by-products economy *The Opinions of Oliver Allston* was a major factor, since it gave him an opportunity to print, without alteration, any scraps from the journals he had not been able to use anywhere else, thus getting good fat sausage out of the last scrap of hide, hair, horn, tail, and tripe.

Brooks's attitude toward two of the principal intellectual developments of our time, Marxism and psychoanalysis, has been more or less one of throwing out the baby and keeping the bath. He has used Marx at every opportunity, generally in the oversimplified and vulgarized form of seeing the artist's function as direct social service: Twain was useful to the businessman by relaxing his mind, was thus an aid to efficiency; Longfellow sped the pioneer on his way; Barnum fooled the public and thus sharpened commercial instincts, and so on. He has always attacked Marx, however, identifying Marxism as mechanical economic determinism and calling himself an *idealist* socialist. (His most impassioned political statement in the Allston book—"communism cannot go far in this country because Americans are *naturally* free. We have a great deal more to lose than chains"—has a little of the tone of the old lady's rejoinder to the revivalist that no one who was born in Boston need be born again.) On psychoanalysis, after a lifetime of filching, for his biographies, half-understood insights from Freud, Adler, Jung, and others, he announced in *Allston:* "The method of psychoanalysis, in the writing of biographies, has a very limited value, and I believe that, once having passed, it will not be used again."

It would be interesting to see Brooks's biographical method applied to Van Wyck Brooks: growing up, of old New England and New York Dutch stock, in exile in Plainfield, New Jersey; the influence of Harvard and the two stories and the poor poetry he wrote there; the oppression of working on the staff of *The Standard Dictionary* and the magazine *World's Work;* the exile in England, lecturing for the Workers' Educational Association; the neurosis, breakdown, and sanitarium his friend Allston experienced; the friendship with the terribly crippled Bourne, and Bourne's death; his first Literary Guild success, followed by a popular triumph no American literary critic had ever known when *The Flowering of New England* won the Limited Editions Club's gold medal "for the book most likely to attain the stature of a classic" in addition to the Pulitzer Prize, and the Book-of-the-Month Club took *New England: Indian Summer. The Ordeal of Van Wyck Brooks*, it might be called, or *The Pilgrimage*, or *The Betrayal*. Meanwhile, until this is done, anyone who wants an epitaph for Brooks might do worse than take as his model the one that Brooks wrote for Lowell, certainly with himself in mind:

> If the fresh and courageous note of the *Fable for Critics* has died out of the picture, the note of the young man who spoke his mind, regardless of what anyone thought or said, the critic hitting and missing, with the rashness of the young, often hitting well and always trusting his own opinions—if this note has vanished, another note has taken its place. This later Lowell has abandoned a role for which he was ill-fitted by nature and training. He has stooped to conquer, but he conquers. Take him on his own ground! Do not remind him of his old pretensions. Do not embarrass him with questions. Forget the radical views of his earlier days. Let him rejoice in royalists and churchmen, lovers of good ale and seasoned pipes who would have had small use for Abolition. Do not trip him up with insinuations about his inconsistencies and his timid aversions.

With the substitution of a few words, and perhaps with less charity, it would do.

CHAPTER 5

CONSTANCE ROURKE

and Folk Criticism

WHEN CONSTANCE ROURKE died in 1941, at the age of fifty-six, she had only begun to find her direction. She had published six books and was at work on a monumental three-volume *History of American Culture*, for which all the other books were merely preliminary exploration. A few years before, in *Charles Sheeler*, she had hit on what will probably emerge as her chief contribution to contemporary criticism, a method of analyzing formal art in terms of its roots in folk tradition. At the same time she was engaged in finding, organizing, interpreting, and popularizing an American folk tradition that would be available to future artists. Her work was thus both analytic and synthetic, and the two strands together constitute one of the most promising activities in American criticism, unfortunately carried on since her death by no one.

Her first book, *Trumpets of Jubilee*, published in 1927,[1] is a study of five persons of wide popular appeal in America in the middle years of the last century: Lyman Beecher, Harriet Beecher Stowe, Henry Ward Beecher, Horace Greeley, and P. T. Barnum. It is to some extent biography, to some extent social history, and to some extent, in the section on Mrs. Stowe, the only literary figure in the group, genuine criticism (including a shrewd analysis of why *Uncle Tom's Cabin* had a power none of her other novels achieved, and a very perceptive comparison with Hawthorne). Some of the social history gets down to underlying causal factors, but a good deal of it is simply a skimming of the surface, a reporting on vagaries of furniture and costume, and the folk material in the book—an interpolated fragment of "Old Dan Tucker," some fine tall tales—is of the latter order, a kind of superior local color. The book is least satisfactory in regard to the Beecher clan, since Miss Rourke never quite manages to define their appeal; most generally satisfactory in the Barnum section, a brilliant study of the man as a focus for an age's giantism; and perhaps most dramatically effective in the portrait of Horace Greeley, a deeply moving story sharpened into tragedy by the only editorializing Miss Rourke permitted herself in the

---

[1] I am informed that Miss Rourke published magazine pieces over a pseudonym before this, but so far I have been unable even to learn the pseudonym.

book, an ironic picture of the social pretensions of the Greeley children after their father's death. As a book it is rather a mixed performance, but all the strains of the later work are in it, struggling to break through the crust of traditional social history.

The next book, *Troupers of the Gold Coast*, published a year later, is Miss Rourke's least ambitious work. It is an undistinguished, pleasant, and superficial attempt to create the atmosphere of old-time theatrical trouping, and it has something of the tone of a scrapbook full of faded theater programs, a button off Edwin Booth's jacket, and a garter worn by Adah Menken. It is not a book that anyone without golden childhood memories of Lotta Crabtree or Lola Montez would bother reading. The book has nothing that could fairly be called either social or cultural history, and of folk material only a dozen fragments of folksongs and popular songs of the period, and a few brief pages on the "characters" of early San Francisco: the Great Unknown, "George Washington," the Fat Boy, Guttersnipe, Rosie, two dogs named Bummer and Lazarus, and the Emperor Norton. It has no critical method, and in fact no criticism.

American Humor, subtitled *A Study of the National Character*, appeared in 1931, an ambitious unraveling of one strand in the cultural history of the United States. The book divides American folk-related culture into a number of separate studies (frequently obtaining what Kenneth Burke calls "perspective by incongruity" through the use of shrewd juxtapositions): the Yankee and backwoodsmen as American types; the minstrel show; trouping performers and religious cultists as two types of American "strollers"; Lincoln and the comic writers; the classic American writers; the Western humorists; James and Howells as facets of the American artist; contemporary writers through the twenties. The formal literary figures are treated as outgrowths of the folk culture, sometimes with a certain distortion—Hawthorne becomes a teller of folk tales, *Moby Dick*, with its comic Biblical names and nautical puns, a cousin to the joke-books of the day—but sometimes the distortion is a brilliant restoration, like the recognition of Lincoln as a literary figure. Miss Rourke is constantly hovering on the verge of a deeper concept of folk culture, a matter of archetypal myth and ritual, which she learned from Jane Harrison's *Ancient Art and Ritual* but never quite manages to apply. She notes that Mike Fink was "a Mississippi river-god, one of those minor deities whom men create in their own image and magnify to magnify themselves," and that Crockett "became a myth even in his own lifetime," and after his death assumed "an even bolder legendary stature than before." She sees the process, though, as essentially a euhemerizing one, a fairly civilized folk somehow "mythologizing" a historical character within a few years, instead of recognizing the dynamic development implicit in Miss Harrison's view, whereby historical char-

acters with what might be called "myth-attracting" features acquire
older mythic attributes and stories.

Miss Rourke notes that a "legendary assumption of wisdom" has
"appeared persistently among American comic characters," but is unable
to go on and interpret it as a complex transference from ancient oracles
to Old Zip Coon (if not directly from an African prototype). She mentions
"the primary stuffs of literature": "the theatre that lies behind the drama,
the primitive religious ceremony that has been anterior to both, the tale
that has preceded both the drama and the novel, the monologue that has
been a rudimentary source for many forms." She is able to recognize
these ancient patterns underlying American pseudo-folk-poetry, but the
understanding of processes of the "folk work" like transmission, independent origin, accretion, continuity, and alteration that would have
enabled her to define the relationship is beyond her. The closest she
comes to it is a kind of negative (and somewhat erroneous) definition:

> As by a concerted impulse the American had cut himself off from
> the older traditions; the natural heritage of England and the conti-
> nent had been cast away so far as a gesture could accomplish this
> feat. Perhaps the romanticism of the pioneer in relation to the
> Indian was part of that instinct by which new peoples attempt to
> enrich themselves from old; the Indian possessed established tribal
> unities which the American lacked. Even the American absorption
> of Negro lore may have been an effort in the same direction. But
> the Negro would offer only the faint and distorted reflection of a
> primal culture; and the quest for that of the Indian had been abor-
> tive.

What Miss Rourke manages to do in the book is define the "primitive
base," consisting of "songs and primitive ballads and a folk-theater and
rude chronicles," often "full of coarse and fragmentary elements, full of
grotesquerie or brutality," on which our literature, like any other, rests,
and insist on that relationship as her central theme and concern:

> Through the interweaving of the popular strain with that of a
> new expression on other levels a literature has been produced
> which, like other literatures, is related to an anterior popular lore
> that must for lack of a better word be called folk-lore.

The conclusion of the book formulates the synthetic function: few artists
have worked without a rich traditional store, the task of criticism is
"discovering and diffusing the materials of the American tradition" in
which the artist may steep himself.

Miss Rourke's next two books were attempts at diffusing that traditional store. The first was *Davy Crockett*, in 1934, and the second *Audubon*

in 1936. The *Crockett* is Miss Rourke's only thorough failure. Written in the condescending popular style of a juvenile for teen-age readers, the book is a jumble of the real Crockett and the legend; a sequence of dramatized anecdotes, including Crockett's children speaking "tall talk" around the house, strung-together Crockett fables from the *Almanacs*, with little interest in the real man and his significance. The sort of thing Miss Rourke is reduced to is sneaking in Crockett's vote in defense of Biddle and the Bank, buried in a sentence about something else with no attempt made to explain it. *Davy Crockett* is unscholarly, unanalytic, "folksy" in the worst sense of the word, and generally an unreadable and poor book. *Audubon* two years later somewhat redeemed the record. Although straight biography with no attempt at criticism or analysis, the book is at least, unlike the *Crockett*, interesting and well written, and Miss Rourke confined her gullibility to accepting as a strong possibility the legend that Audubon was the little lost Dauphin, and telling an extremely dubious etiological myth of his inventing the combination of pastel and water-color technique he used by a lucky movie accident one day. Both books made available to American writers aspects of American frontier tradition, the pioneering man of action and the pioneering artist, but unfortunately made them available in a form any serious writer could be pardoned for ignoring.

Constance Rourke's first book of genuine folk criticism was *Charles Sheeler*, published in 1938. In Sheeler she found a serious artist (although not so good a one as she believed) who had discovered an American folk tradition for himself, the functional form of the Shaker artisans, and who had consciously grounded his work in it, to the work's great benefit. Looking at Sheeler's paintings and photographs (many of them reproduced as evidence in the book), she discovered the basic principle that had eluded previous popularizers of the folk tradition, that a tradition is not in subject but in *form*, that the secret does not lie in painting a hillbilly building a silo, but in painting *as* a hillbilly builds a silo. (This was the key realization that helped her to such later insights as that the writers who said we had no native theatrical tradition were wrong. They hadn't known where to look. She looked in the public ceremonial of the Indian treaty, in the dialectic play of the Calvinist sermon, and found it.) On the strength of this discovery in Sheeler, she affirmed her principles with a new certainty. "Possibly our soil has not been too shallow for a full creative expression," she wrote; and she showed Sheeler studying architectural and handicraft form in Bucks County, discovering Shaker buildings and furniture and the Shaker motto "Every force has its form," and finally emerging as a "pathfinder in the use of American traditions in art," American without being provincial, modern and still rooted in the past, responsive at once to Shaker barns and primitive Negro sculpture.

A further level of abstraction that would have found the formal relation between Shaker barns and African sculpture was beyond Miss Rourke's power. She was always on the verge of relating her American material to the great stream of world folk culture (she noted, without further exploration, that behind a graveyard tall story in *Life on the Mississippi* is the Osiris myth, that the legends of Crockett's birth are taken over from Hercules, his fire-bringing from Prometheus, his silver bullet from the Scandinavian, other features from Celtic and American Indian lore), but she lacked the background, the learning, perhaps the imagination, to do that job successfully. What she settled for was the narrower ambition of creating a specifically American and democratic folk tradition to oppose to the sophisticated and undemocratic European formal tradition defined by men like Eliot. She explained the difficulty of the job: "we sometimes seem to be hunting for a tradition . . . but traditions are often hard to discover, requiring a long and equable scrutiny; they are hard to build, consuming an expanse of time which may pass beyond a few generations." Even a few more years of life might have enabled her to do a good part of that building.

2

The Roots of American Culture, Constance Rourke's last book, published posthumously in 1942, consists of brief sections from the manuscript of her *History of American Culture*, several of which had previously appeared in magazines, salvaged and edited with a preface by Van Wyck Brooks. The material is very fragmentary: an essay on "The Roots of American Culture," a long study of early American theatricals, a piece on early American music, one on the Shakers, a "note" on folklore, a study of an obscure naturalistic artist named Voltaire Combe, a survey of the extent of genuine Negro folk culture in the minstrel shows, and a piece on a possible future direction for American painting. The art and music criticism, by dealing with the relatively obscure, avoids the necessity of having to be technical with a somewhat untrained eye and ear, but the theatrical study reveals a real sense of the theater, and she has a sureness about folk forms that must have distinguished her work on the Index of American Design.

By far the best essay, and one that shows most fully her developed critical method, is the short piece on the minstrel shows called "Traditions for a Negro Literature." Against the opposition of writers like S. Foster Damon, who claimed that no legitimate Negro material exists in the minstrel show (and the presumable opposition of the George Pullen Jackson, Guy Johnson, Newman Ivey White school, who claim that no Negro art exists anyway not stolen from white art), Miss Rourke opposed fact. She demonstrated that all the classic white minstrel compositions were borrowings: that Dan Emmett's "Old Dan Tucker" was either

Negro-derived or wholly of Negro origin, with a Negro-type tune, a Negro shouting choral effect, and a content of cryptic Negro animal fables about the jaybird and the bulldog; that "Turkey in the Straw" is certainly a Negro dance song; that "Dixie" begins with a characteristically Negro Biblical legend; that Dan Rice's "Clar de Kitchen" is an animal fable in which the Negro triumphs, and so on. She further showed that the ritual forms and conventions of the minstrel show, its dance routines, its cries, in addition to its musical and anecdotal material, were all Negro or Negro-derived. Having performed that analytic job, using the first part of her method, the tracing of formal art to its folk roots, Miss Rourke went on to do the synthetic half of the job, the organization of a folk tradition for artists to use, by showing that much of the Negro material preserved in a distorted and offensive form in the minstrel shows has been preserved nowhere else, and that it could be lifted from the minstrel setting, cleansed and refurbished, to furnish a vital tradition for American Negro literature. (Miss Rourke does not make use of, or perhaps was not familiar with, one of the best illustrations of her case, the minstrel song "De Blue-Tail Fly," which under the accretions of cheap minstrel dialect is a serious and very fine song of slave protest and rebellion.)

Because of the specialized nature of her subject, Miss Rourke did not take up what is probably the basic question about American Negro folk material, its complicated relationship to primitive African myth and ritual, and by extension the basic problem of her field, the general relationship of art to rite. In another part of the book, however, the section, "The Indian Background" in the long essay "The Rise of American Theatricals," Miss Rourke found the problem precisely at the heart of her topic and manages in a few pages to be remarkably suggestive. She claims that the Indian treaties are the earliest American drama, and one of the sources, along with the European tradition, of later American drama. She describes their nature:

> These treaties were essentially plays—chronicle plays—recording what was said in the parleys, including bits of actions, the exchange of gifts, of wampum, the smoking of pipes, the many ceremonials with dances, cries and choral songs. Even the printed form of the treaties was dramatic: the participants were listed like a cast of characters, and precise notations were made as to ceremonial action. Symbolic phrases were used to seal promises, even to raise questions.

Not only were the treaties drama, but like the Greek dramas they were based on the patterns of primitive ritual. The Iroquois treaties used traditional forms from the Iroquois book of rites, and all the ceremonial arrangements were based on "deeply rooted communal experience." The fifty Indian treaties known to have been printed, Miss Rourke points out, form a cycle with "epic proportions as well as an epic theme," and are "poetry of a high order." These are not only our first plays, she insists, but also inevitably our best early plays: "That the treaties could be matched in poetic or imaginative values by individual effort in their own time was hardly to be expected: they were traditional, communal, they expressed values that had long been accumulated."

Here she is very close to the same discovery about which she hovered in *American Humor*: that the important relationship of art literature to folk literature lies, not in the surface texture of folk speech, but in the archetypal patterns of primitive ritual, the great myths. Again, in "A Note on Folklore" in the book, she recognizes that something basic is lacking in her subject, the use by American writers of folk material, that it tends to be a "placing of quaint bits end to end," but she fails to perceive what it is that is lacking, and the piece falls off into inconsequence.

The thing Miss Rourke *did* discover in the book, a basic critical concept continuing her discovery in *Charles Sheeler* that a tradition lies not in content but in form, is her recognition that the American folk tradition is not primarily naturalistic but abstract: the abstraction of a Jonathan Edwards sermon, a Navajo blanket, a John Henry feat, and a Vermont hooked rug; and that it is Marin who is painting in it, not Norman Rockwell. A number of other fragmentary elements of promise are buried in the book: a recognition (borrowed from Ruth Benedict) of the importance of Gestalt "configurations" in studying cultures; a plan for the serious teaching of American folk literature in the colleges; a study of how a people like the Shakers can acquire something like the communality of a "folk" in one generation. But these were promises she did not live to fulfill.

3

In her last two books Constance Rourke left the field of folk collecting and retelling and entered the tradition of serious folk criticism. Folk criticism is not, like a number of types of contemporary criticism, a single method, but rather a number of possible approaches having in common a body of material. Miss Rourke's school is that of Herder, and she gives an excellent one-sided tracing of it as an aspect of the romantic movement in her essay "The Roots of American Culture": beginning with Montaigne's theory of *poésie populaire*, or primitive song springing from idyllic communal life; going through Vico's folk-wisdom of the primitive; continued in Rousseau's Natural Man; fully developed in Herder's theory of the folk arts as the basis and shaping force of the fine arts in form, spirit, and expression; and going to seed in the "antiquarianism" of Schlegel and the Grimms. (The other side of the Vico-Herder tradition, its flowering in Nazi *Kultur*, Miss Rourke ignores.)

A much more important tradition of folk criticism, of which Miss Rourke seems hardly to have been aware, is the English anthropological school of the nineteenth century, beginning with Sir E. B. Tylor and Sir James G. Frazer and continued by Andrew Lang, E. S. Hartland, A. E. Crawley, and others. Although all were men of enormous reading, and Frazer and Lang were first-rate classical scholars in addition, their chief work lay in studying, not literature, but the patterns of primitive behavior on which our literature is based. There is space here to note only a few of their many books. Tylor in his chief work, *Primitive Culture*, studied the evolutionary process whereby cultural factors transcend their function, from the witch doctor's rattle in the baby's hand to the survival of animism in philosophy; Frazer's monumental twelve-volume *Golden Bough*, as well as his other books, are poetically organized, compendious collections of lore, beliefs, and customs underlying almost every aspect of our culture; Lang covered almost the entire breadth of the field, from Australian totemism to Homer and fairy tales; Hartland studied primitive myth and belief in his great works *Primitive Paternity* and *The Legend of Perseus*; Crawley, in *The Mystic Rose*, *The Tree of Life*, and *The Idea of the Soul*, dealt respectively with primitive origins of marriage, religion, and a philosophic idea.

Their work has been continued, chiefly in the field of classical studies, by what is known as "the Cambridge school," (although Gilbert Murray of Oxford is probably its leading spirit, and other Oxford scholars like Tylor and Lang have greatly influenced it), consisting of Murray, F. M. Cornford, A. B. Cook, and Jane Harrison. All of the group, in books that overlap and supplement one another, has dealt with the ritual base behind Greek art, drama, epic, religion, and philosophy: Murray has shown the ritual conflicts underlying the form of Greek tragedy and the stories of Homer; Cornford did a similar analysis of Greek comedy and traced Greek philosophy from its beginnings in religious ritual; Cook studied the Greek god-king exhaustively as a ritual figure; and Miss Harrison, in a series of books going back as far as 1882, traced an underlying pattern of ritual conflict through almost every aspect of Greek art and religion.

Of the four, Jane Harrison is perhaps most important to mention in connection with Constance Rourke, both because she is the only one with whose work Miss Rourke seems to have been familiar (she quotes her once in *American Humor*) and because she is an excellent example of the sort of work Miss Rourke might have done with another background and a great deal more learning. Miss Harrison's most important book is *Themis*, a tremendously valuable study of "the social origins of Greek

religion" as it is reflected in drama, poetry, visual art, and even the
Olympic Games, a product of both enormous learning and creative imagination. Her other well-known book, *Ancient Art and Ritual*, is a short,
popularly written summary of the position of the group on the relationship between primitive Greek fertility rites and such highly sophisticated
productions as drama and sculpture. Both books, like Miss Rourke's,
analyze art forms in terms of their folk roots and document a living
popular tradition on which the artist bases himself, but Miss Harrison's
recognition of ritual as central (in Kenneth Burke's phrasing, "ritual
drama as the hub"), as well as her greater learning and the richer field
she has chosen to harvest, have made her books basic to folk criticism,
rather than, like Miss Rourke's, merely peripheral and suggestive.

Of solitary workers along similar lines, Jessie Weston and Lord
Raglan are probably the most important. Miss Weston, a scholar in the
field of medieval romance, particularly the Arthurian cycle, came under
the influence of Frazer, Murray, and Miss Harrison fairly late in her
career and decided to try applying their ritual view to the origins of
romance. *From Ritual to Romance*, a greatly influential book on which
T. S. Eliot based *The Waste Land*, is a witness to the success with which
she made the grail legend finally intelligible in terms of its genesis in a
fertility cult. Lord Raglan, a rather crusty and independent English
baron, has written two books dealing with folklore, *Jocasta's Crime* and
The Hero.[2] *Jocasta's Crime* is a study of the incest taboo, invaluable in its
general picture and its destruction of other theories, but rather absurd
in the theory Raglan himself finally posits. *The Hero*, one of the most
important and little-appreciated books of our time, is a study of traditional heroes and religious figures in the cultures of various peoples—
Robin Hood, Siegfried, Arthur, Cuchulainn, Œdipus, Romulus, Moses,
and others (although Raglan avoids Christ, who obviously falls into his
pattern)—as one archetypal hero, never historical, but always derived
through a myth from a ritual drama. The method is Galton's, fixing an
archetypal hero through twenty-two key points and checking each figure
against them. (Earlier writers, among them Alfred Nutt, in *The Legends
of the Holy Grail*, and Otto Rank, in *The Myth of the Birth of the Hero*, had
done part of the job before without the same success.) It is a cheeky,
snobbish, and frequently irritating book, but its general contentions are
so sound, so unquestionable, and so revolutionary (although implicit in
the Frazer-Harrison-Weston line) that, more widely read, it could
single-handedly end a good deal of the nonsense that currently passes
for folk criticism.

A somewhat comparable tracing of underlying ritual patterns, but with
a heavily mystic emphasis, has been turned on Shakespeare by Colin

---

[2] Since this was written, a third book in the field, *Death and Rebirth*, has been
published in England, but I have not yet been able to see a copy.

Still, in *Shakespeare's Mystery Play: A Study of the Tempest* and its later revision, *The Timeless Theme*, and continued, following Still's lead, by G. Wilson Knight in several of his works. The most recent inheritor of the method is George Thomson (a Greek professor and former Cambridge fellow), who has combined it with Marxism to produce a remarkable book, *Æschylus and Athens*, subtitled *A Study in the Social Origins of Drama*. In addition to drawing heavily on all the Cambridge people, Thomson utilizes a more scientific field anthropology of the type represented by Malinowski and Bateson. The greatest influence, on him, however, is Caudwell's Marxist *Illusion and Reality* (also, incidentally, somewhat influenced by the ritual theory) and although he constantly reads Æschylus and Greek drama in terms of ritual origins (with touches of euhemerism), his emphasis is on ritual origins themselves as an aspect of productive labor, with the chief function of magic or incantation that of making the crops grow. Another English critic, Walter Allen, although not much concerned with ritual, has made brilliant use of myth (along with theological concepts) in studying the fiction of such writers as Kafka, Malraux, Graham Greene, and Henry Green, in recent periodical and anthology pieces.

All the above are British scholars and critics, and there has been little comparable in America. Perhaps the most exciting folk method in this country is that of William Troy, a fully developed literary criticism working from a basis of myth and ritual, but since the dozen or so articles and reviews in which he has displayed his ideas have never been collected in book form, his work has had nothing like the recognition it deserves. He has analyzed a Zola novel in terms of the basic mythic pattern of Orpheus and Eurydice; interpreted Lawrence against the patterns of his chosen role as the Dying God or Sacrificial King; read Mann's works in terms of a number of basic myths and rites, from the initiation ritual underlying *Death in Venice* to the advanced social myth of the Joseph novels; seen Stendhal's heroes as scapegoats and his works as the ritual sequence of Greek tragedy; read some of Henry James's novels in terms of the Eden myth; identified Fitzgerald's Gatsby with the grail heroes, and Stahr with Icarus; and been more successful than any other contemporary critic (if Joyce's own testimony means anything) in placing the patterns of myth and ritual underlying Joyce's work and analyzing their significance. Although he calls his method "mythic" and relies particularly on Frazer for the archetypal patterns he finds at the heart of literary meaning, Troy also draws heavily on both Marx and Freud (as well as on such relatively abstruse matters as field physics). His method is generally so consistently pluralist it might better be called "Dantean" (Troy being perhaps the only modern critic to insist on the need for reviving Dante's medieval concept of the four levels of meaning). Under whatever name, it seems to be the closest thing in America, on a smaller scale, to the triumphs of the Cambridge group in England.

Francis Fergusson, who has been the only important American critic centrally concerned with the drama, has consistently read it in terms of the ancient sacrificial pattern exemplified in Sophocles' *Œdipus the King*. He has attempted to read poets and novelists like Dante, James, and Lawrence in the same fashion in a number of periodical pieces, like Troy's, not yet collected in book form. Aside from Fergusson and Troy, there has been little serious attempt in America at a folk criticism of art literature. Randall Jarrell has been heavily influenced by myth and ritual in his poetry, but his excellent criticism has used them only sporadically. Joseph Campbell, a scholar and critic of folk literature and mythology, has applied his material with some success (as well as some reductive simplification) to that twentieth-century touchstone *Finnegans Wake* in the *Skeleton Key* he wrote in collaboration with Henry Morton Robinson. His work in this direction is handicapped, however, by a slighting of ritual factors that tends to break the ties of myth to the real earth and send it floating off into the thin air of metaphysics, comparative theology, or worse. Mary Austin, in several books, has worked profitably in an area all her own, the relationship between the forms and rhythms of American Indian poetry and those of modern American verse. Within the past year or two there has been a sudden flood of criticism concerned with "mythic" patterns: some of it, like Charles Olson's *Call Me Ishmael* and Parker Tyler's books on the movies, also drawing on psychoanalysis and very much to the point; some of it, like the studies of Gide and Henry Miller that Wallace Fowlie has published in England and Richard Chase's periodical pieces, muddled or superficial; some of it, like the *Chimera* symposium on Myth, a mixture of both. It is hard to say how lasting this movement will be, or how much it simply represents a new obscurantism or reflects the current cult of the "folksy."

Far more numerous than the folk critics are the collectors, a group frequently scholarly but rarely critical. The list of men from the days of Bishop Percy (if not from the days of Herodotus and Ovid) to the present and the types of work they have done are endless and fortunately do not lie within our province here, but it must be noted that one of the reasons for the thinness of Constance Rourke's work in comparison with that of comparable figures in England is the poor quality of American collecting, which is now largely in the hands of men of little learning or imaginative breadth. The gap between Professor Francis James Child, the learned and polylingual scholar who organized the study of the ancient ballad, and a man like John Lomax, the late dean of American folksong-collectors, represents a steady deterioration of personnel in the field over the past half-century.

Miss Rourke goes out of her way in her "Note on Folklore" in *The Roots of American Culture* to praise the work of such men as Lloyd Lewis, George Pullen Jackson, Roark Bradford, and B. A. Botkin in American folk study, but her list exposes the poverty of the field. Lewis is a journalist whose *Myths after Lincoln* is the embryo of the book someone could have written who knew more about the subject than can be obtained from a quick reading of the one-volume condensation of *The Golden Bough*; Jackson is a Southern white chauvinist who has tricked out with trappings of pseudo-musicology his conviction that the Negro, as an inferior human, could hardly produce a first-rate art like the spirituals; Bradford's achievement was watering down the magnificent John Henry legend in his book of that name until it had the consistency of sugar water taken for a hiccup; and Botkin, easily the best of the lot, has been seduced away from genuine folk material by an interest in the texture of folk speech, the anecdotal or picturesque, what he calls "folk-say," to the point where his *Treasury of American Folklore* is an absolutely undiscriminating jumble of everything from first-rate Child ballad texts to long dull stretches of the *Congressional Record*. Most current American study has been preoccupied either with the aimless collection of folksongs, children's rhymes, and so forth, without any comprehension of their significance or ability to sort them out, or with the retelling of such phony legends as the Paul Bunyan material for an audience on the juvenile level (or even, as in the case of Paul Beath, the cool manufacture of a legendary hero, Febold Feboldson, of one's own, and the attempt to treat him as traditional).

Besides the danger of simple devotion to inanity, there are two other and more serious dangers in the folklore position, both of which Miss Rourke had the good sense to avoid. At one extreme is the "folksy," drawing on the folk for cuteness or using the presumed pastoral virtues of some primitive performance as a club with which to beat formal art. The classic example of this is the incredible passage in Tolstoy's *What Is Art?* where he expresses his preference for the Vogul pantomime deer hunt ("a true work of art") to *Hamlet* ("a false imitation of a work of art"). At the other extreme is the Nazi *"volkisch,"* the blood-and-soil mysticism of irrationality, best represented in reputable literature by D. H. Lawrence's cult of the primitive, with its insistence on "blood-thinking" and the mystic "knowing" of peasants, Indians, and miscellaneous savages. Miss Rourke has made it clear that she is aware of the dangers of the first in her suggested contrast between Grant Wood's phony use of folksy subject-matter and Sheeler's serious use of a folk formal tradition, and although she has never been explicit about the second (particularly in relation to Herder), she has attacked embryonic forms of it in terms of social "regression."

Another type of criticism closely related to folk criticism is cultural history, which deals with folklore and myth in the other sense of the words, the sense of Thurman Arnold's *Folklore of Capitalism*, as fallacious popular beliefs, which it tends to "debunk." Vernon L. Parrington, one of our few serious cultural historians, furnishes an interesting contrast in method to Constance Rourke on Crockett. While she is chiefly interested in the charm of the legends themselves and anxious to deny any evidence she thinks might detract from them, his effort is to place the Crockett legends in terms of political genesis and function. In a withering analysis in *Main Currents of American Thought* he strips the legendary hero down to the real Crockett: a rather pathetic figure, ignorant, boastful, and ambitious; built up as an American symbol by skilled Whig publicists who wanted a coonskin hero to oppose to Jackson; used by the Whigs as long as he was usable; and then when his backwoods constituents repudiated his voting record of uninterrupted support for Eastern banking interests, tossed aside by his Whig friends. Parrington shows how the legend was built step by step, conjectures shrewdly as to who ghosted each of the books, shows the constant anti-Jackson propaganda smuggled into their comedy, and at the end shows Crockett, like so many mythologized real heroes, coming to believe the legends himself.

Miss Rourke simply affirms, against the weight of the evidence, that Crockett created the legend himself by his character and racy talk, although the Whigs "probably added momentum to his fame"; that he wrote all or nearly all of the books himself, and that he was an honest democratic figure who honestly opposed Jackson in his constituents' interest. What a more reasoned view than Miss Rourke's would have done was accept Parrington's account of the political genesis of Crockett as folk hero and then go on to study the way in which this artificial figure later became genuine folk legend, or at least folk-transmitted legend, in the *Crockett Almanacs* after Crockett's death (which Parrington apparently either didn't know or didn't care about, and in which, as Miss Rourke rightly says, "few traces of a political bias appear").

A lowbrow form of American cultural history is the running picture of the American folk mind that H. L. Mencken furnished in his series of *Prejudices* and a number of other books (in which the popularity of Brieux and paper-bag cookery are equally important cultural phenomena of the twenties) and Thomas Beer in his *Mauve Decade* and the studies of Mark Hanna and Stephen Crane. A very specialized and useful type of it is the area Malcolm Cowley has staked out for himself, the cultural climate of writers, in *Exile's Return* and his *New Republic* pieces: elaborate Menckenian lists of books people were reading any given year, samples of what writers were thinking about and talking about, discussions of the effect events like the suicides of Hart Crane and Harry Crosby and the Depression had on a literary generation. In addition, there are a number of specialized ways of handling folk material that will be discussed in later chapters: the psychoanalytic in the chapter on Maud

Bodkin, the sociological in the chapter on Christopher Caudwell, and Kenneth Burke's treatment of it as symbolic action, as strategies for doing various types of job, in the chapter on Burke.

4

A few other aspects of Constance Rourke's work need discussion. One is a curious conflict, a division of focus, between the titles and the subtitles of her earlier works. *Troupers of the Gold Coast* is subtitled *or the Rise of Lotta Crabtree*, and the actual book is a good deal less than the first and a good deal more than the second. *American Humor*, subtitled *A Study of the American Character*, fits the subtitle a good deal better than the title, since little of it has anything to do with humor (except in the other, or Jonsonian sense of "humor"; if the title is an unconscious pun it is beautifully applicable, although perhaps *The American Humor* or *American Humors* would be more precise). Only with *Charles Sheeler*, subtitled *Artist in the American Tradition*, do Miss Rourke's titles and subtitles stop working at cross-purposes and finally get together, just as that was the first book in which she found a valid relationship between the individual artist and the larger American picture.

Miss Rourke's work was unquestionably limited. She lacked Jane Harrison's learning and her focus on the ritual drama as hub; Raglan's familiarity with the breadth of the material; the pluralism and integrative ability of Thomson and Troy; the acquaintance with a relatively primitive people, or true "folk," of Mary Austin; even Parrington's basic toughmindedness. She began with every handicap: a concept of folklore as local color and sentimental theatrical memories; an unexplored field in the hands of ignoramuses specializing in the guitar and the ten-gallon hat; a country whose true folk tradition lacks all homogeneity, consisting of Indian and Negro survivals and European imports, all modified beyond recognition to fit their new contexts. Despite all these handicaps, her work represents a steady development toward more and more significant criticism: discovering her analytic and synthetic functions in *American Humor*, as well as the relationship between folk and art literature; synthesizing a tradition of folksy content in *Crockett* and *Audubon;* discovering that a tradition lies in form rather than content in *Sheeler*, and that her true method was the folk analysis of formal art; realizing that the American folk tradition is abstract and has basic ritual elements in her unfinished *History of American Culture*, and on that basis doing her most significant jobs of analysis (the Indian roots of American drama) and synthesis (the minstrel tradition reconstructed for a Negro literature).

Miss Rourke's relationship to Van Wyck Brooks may be worth mention here. The only book of his she has ever quoted specifically is *The Pilgrimage of Henry James*, in her James chapter in *American Humor*, and that to accept some of its incidental judgments and demolish its basic conclusion, that James broke with the American tradition by concentrating on the international scene rather than the meal in the firkin. She has attacked Brooks by indirection in her discussion of Twain in *American Humor* ("It is a mistake to look for the social critic—even manqué—in Mark Twain"), and attacked his manifestoes in the *Freeman* at some length in *Charles Sheeler* for calling for the mechanical creation of a hierarchical school of American artists rather than the free use of American materials arising out of concrete needs and situations. Even *The Roots of American Culture*, which Brooks assembled and introduced with a respectful and proprietary preface, contains in the title essay a sharp attack on Brooks's central position (although Brooks is not named), what De Voto has tagged "the literary fallacy," when she writes: "The governing idea that ours is a literary culture, or any similar preconception, may throw our judgments awry." Brooks, on the other hand, has unquestionably learned from her. It is probable that the much-commented-on statement in the first version of *The Ordeal of Mark Twain* that America has no folk art of its own disappeared after he became acquainted with Miss Rourke's works, and by way of recompense the recent volumes of the literary history contain great gobs of folk material, some of it lifted directly from Rourke's books, none of it credited.

Much of Constance Rourke's special approach and significance is typified by the basic quarrel with Brooks over Henry James. As one endeavoring to create a valid and usable American tradition, she felt it absurd to throw James to the enemy, and she worked passionately to renaturalize him. The point of her James chapter in *American Humor* is that James is, as Howells said, basically and fundamentally in the American tradition, never more so than when he lived abroad and concerned himself with the international scene. In the last analysis she was not only the isolater of folk sources and roots in formal art, the synthesizer of a living folk tradition for other artists to come, the educator of provincial critics like Van Wyck Brooks, the popularizer of obscure and misapprehended figures and cultural phenomena in our past—Audubon, Voltaire Combe, the minstrel show, Horace Greeley; she was also a democrat and a patriot, in a deeper and better-informed sense than the ranters and the book-burners. Her own folk roots were substantial. Had she lived, she would have helped the American folk and the individual artists it has formed and inspired to earn their places in the cultural history of the world. She knew the secret that the true artist has two homes: his native land and the globe.

CHAPTER 6

MAUD BODKIN

and Psychological Criticism

IT IS Maud Bodkin's distinction to have made what is probably the best use to date of psychoanalysis in literary criticism. Her book *Archetypal Patterns in Poetry*, subtitled *Psychological Studies of Imagination*, was published by Oxford in England in 1934 and attracted almost no attention whatsoever. It was reviewed in a handful of periodicals, getting what enthusiastic comment it got in magazines devoted to folklore and psychology and receiving rather condescending treatment from the general literary press. It has had no appreciable influence on any English criticism I have encountered (although Knight, Day Lewis, and Auden have acknowledged it, and Leavis has attacked it in *Scrutiny*). In this country Miss Bodkin is even less known. For some reason her book was not published by Oxford in America, and has been almost impossible to obtain here. She has never, to my knowledge, been reviewed or discussed in an American periodical. (Again, a few critics, among them Burke and Warren, have managed to discover and utilize her work.) She is not listed in any American or British work of reference I have ever managed to find in a library, including *Who's Who*, and she seems never to have published in any periodical other than the *British Journal of Psychology* (and, if she is the A. M. Bodkin she cites in a footnote, the *British Journal of Medical Psychology*) until the war, when she contributed one essay to the *Wind and the Rain*, a new English review with a religious and moral emphasis.

There are a number of reasons for this obscurity. First Miss Bodkin is not a professional psychoanalyst, which would have lent her work professional authority, nor does she seem to be a professional critic. She is apparently an amateur student of literature (at one time she was a publisher's reader) who happens to have a wide acquaintance with both psychology and imaginative literature, as well as genuine literary sensitivity, sense of proportion, and taste that effectively keep her from all the familiar excesses of psychoanalytic criticism. As far as I have been able to learn, Miss Bodkin became interested in the literary possibilities of psychoanalysis in middle age, and attended a group of seminars for lay students held by Dr. Carl G. Jung in Zurich in the twenties on his analytical psychology and some of its implications. Her work is chiefly dependent on Jungian theories and insights, although it is obviously her own, and it is unlikely that Dr. Jung is familiar with it and questionable whether he would approve of it if he were.

I am not competent to discuss the ideas of Dr. Jung (or any psychologist) technically, but a brief summary of those which apply to art is essential for any consideration of Miss Bodkin's work. The most important of them from a literary viewpoint is the concept of "archetypes." Jung defines these most fully in the article "On the Relation of Analytical Psychology to Poetic Art" in *Contributions to Analytical Psychology*. They are unconscious primordial images, the "psychic residua of numberless experiences of the same type" shared by ancestors going back to primitive times, which are somehow inherited in the structure of the brain. They are thus basic, age-old patterns of central human experience, and Jung's hypothesis, which Miss Bodkin devoted her book to investigating, is these archetypes lie at the root of any poetry (or any other art) possessing special emotional significance.

For Jung, these archetypal patterns exist all along the chain of communication: as configurations in the poet's unconscious, as recurring themes or image sequences in poetry, and as configurations in the reader's or audience's unconscious. This is based on the concept of a "collective unconscious" bearing the racial past, which generated mythic heroes for the primitive and still generates similar individual fantasies for the civilized man, and which finds its chief expression in a relatively familiar and timeless symbolism, endlessly recurring. (It should be obvious how close this idea is to cyclic theories of history like Vico's, as well as to Stekel's modification of Freud's free and experiential dream symbolism in favor of a fixed, gypsy-dream-book symbolism, and how captivating it would be to a writer like Joyce, already influenced by Vico, seeking a psychology he could use in creating H. C. Everybody.)

For Jung, the artist as well as the neurotic reproduces in detail the myths derived from the ritual experience of primitive man, sometimes consciously, sometimes by a "visionary" process. The artist, however, is *not* a neurotic; is, in fact, as artist, of far greater significance than the neurotic. In his article "Psychology and Poetry" in *transition*, Jung dignifies the poet as "the collective *man*, the carrier and former of the unconsciously active soul of mankind." With this goes the idea that in the last analysis art is an autonomous complex of whose origin we know nothing, an expression baffling the ingenuity of science, and that all psychoanalysis can do is study the antecedent materials and describe the creative process without explaining it.[1]

[1] In keeping with this view, Jung has written very little on specific artists and works of art. The only literary studies I know of are a brief discussion of Goethe's *Faust* in *Psychology of the Unconscious*, and an analysis of Joyce's *Ulysses* in *Wirklichkeit der Seele*.

Jung's other concepts—his primary quarrel with Freud over "libido," which he defines as "psychic instinctive energy in general," a kind of Bergsonian *élan vital,* rather than simply "sexual energy"; his basic personality types, introvert and extravert, the results of inward and outward turning of the libido; and his other terms like "anima," the ideal or soul-image, and "persona," the complementary outer character—are of less significance in Miss Bodkin's work and to literary criticism in general. For literary analysis, as she recognized, the basic concepts are the collective unconscious and its archetypal patterns.

In a number of respects Jung's analytical psychology might seem to be more fruitful for literary criticism than Freudian psychoanalysis. Miss Bodkin has expressed two of its advantages as she sees them:

> Freud's terminology cannot do justice to it (the interaction between the individual mind and the social heritage in a poem) because the postulates within which he works require that later and higher products of the life process be explained in terms of elements present in the beginning. Also, the concentration of Freudian writers upon the physical relation of parent and child cuts off that other equally valid viewpoint, from which the parent's magic for the child, and overpowering influence, appear due to his acting as the first channel of the wider influence of the community and its stored achievement.

The major advantage over Freud, however, that Jungian psychology has in terms of literary criticism is that, unlike Jung, Freud *did* at one time tend to see art largely as a neurotic expression, specifically the product of a narcissistic stage of development, a fantasy wish-fulfillment or substitute gratification resulting from unsatisfied longings in the real world. He writes typically in *Civilization and Its Discontents* of "beauty": "Its derivation from the realms of sexual sensation is all that seems certain; the love of beauty is a perfect example of a feeling with an inhibited aim," which is not mitigated by the admission that psychoanalysis "has less to say about beauty than about most other things."

At the same time the fact remains that it is Freud, rather than any of his dissenting disciples, who has tremendously influenced almost every modern writer and critic. Adler has had relatively little literary influence, aside from the ubiquitous term "inferiority complex" (although it should be admitted that almost every contemporary novel that has been concerned with ego or power drives or compensations, from *The Great Gatsby* to *What Makes Sammy Run* has unwittingly absorbed something of Adler's individual psychology).[2] Outside of Zurich, where Joyce came

[2] *William Ernest Henley,* a biographical study by Jerome Hamilton Buckley, which appeared in 1946, is an Adler-influenced work that treats Henley's character as a "masculine protest" against his crippling bone-tuberculosis, and may finally herald an Adlerian literary trend.

somewhat under Jung's influence, even Jung has had few literary followers, chiefly Eugene Jolas and the *transition* crowd in Paris for a brief period, and a group of Socialist poets and critics around James Oppenheim in this country.[3] Stekel, Rank, and the other Freudian dissenters have been even less important outside their own fields.

The collective and affirmative nature of Jung's psychology is its greatest advantage for literary criticism, but it also constitutes its greatest danger, a tendency to turn into a glorification of irrationality, mysticism, and "racial memory," the sort of thing that made Jung so attractive to Nazi and Fascist thinkers.[4] Miss Bodkin has largely avoided this pitfall

[3] W. P. Witcutt, in *Blake: A Psychological Study*, published in England in 1946, attempted to use Jungian psychology "to indicate a path through the Blakean jungle" of the Prophetic Books. His book seems to me a maddening and almost pointless one, and makes an interesting contrast to Miss Bodkin's. Witcutt employs Jung's most mystic and theosophical concepts to turn on Blake's metaphysical muddles, and the result is confusion worse confounded.

[4] In a three-part series in the *Protestant*, June–July 1946, August–September 1946, and February–March 1947, Albert D. Parelhoff proved, it seems to me pretty conclusively, and with exhaustive documentation, that Nazi and Fascist thinking in turn were attractive enough to Jung to have made him a bitter anti-Semite and Nazi collaborationist. Parelhoff shows Freud recognizing Jung's "racial prejudices" and careerism as far back as 1914; Jung identifying Freud's as "a Jewish psychology" in 1927, and boasting that in 1930 he wrote anti-Semitism "officially on my banner—a necessary reform in psychology." When Hitler came to power in 1933, Jung, who as a resident of Zurich in Switzerland was under no necessity whatsoever to collaborate, took over the editorship of the *Zentralblatt für Psychotherapie*, published at Leipzig (which had suspended for six months, following the resignation of Kretschmer as editor!), and immediately announced the magazine's new editorial line: "the definite distinctions between Germanic and Jewish psychology long apparent to sensible people shall no longer be obscured." In the next issue, in a long article entitled "The Present Status of Psychotherapy," he attacked the Jewish "nomad" menacing the creative Aryan, identified Freud's "Jewish psychology" and "dirty imagination" as a menace to the "creative unconscious" of "Christian Germans and Slavs," and announced that the true Germanic soul had only been revealed by National Socialism. In 1934, in a Zurich newspaper, Jung defended his collaboration on the basis of the necessity "to come to terms with the powers that be in Germany" in defense of "our common German culture," described the Jewish problem as "a festering wound," and even got in an oblique defense of the concentration camps. Through the thirties Jung wrote a number of comparable articles, culminating in an interview in the January 1939 issue of Hearst's *Cosmopolitan*, suggesting appeasement of Germany ("let her go into Russia") and defending Hitler's dictatorship. According to Parelhoff, Jung got off the public bandwagon in 1939, with the declaration of war, and did not turn up again as a political expert until 1945, when in an interview with a Swiss newspaper he announced that *all* Germans are equally guilty, including the regime's opponents. He said nothing about Swiss.

As far as I know, the case against Jung was first stated authoritatively in an article by Dr. Feldman in the *American Journal of Psychiatry*, September 1945. Since then it has received wide acceptance in this country and abroad, and Jung himself, in his defense, has never denied the essential facts, but their interpretation. It is only fair to state, however, that there is apparently still controversy about the matter, that a number of psychiatrists are not convinced, and that at least one of them, Dr. Harms, in Jung's thought, but at least once in the book she calls for the continual endeavor to render underlying psychological patterns "in terms of feeling rather than intellect" with the same ambiguous possibility of glorifying irrationality that has endeared Jung to the blood-and-soil contingent. For the most part, though, she uses the scientific-analytic aspects of Jung's work rather than the metaphysical-mystic, and it is significant that her epigraph for *Archetypal Patterns in Poetry* should be Jung at his least world-shaking and most honestly humble:

> Philosophical criticism has helped me to see that every psychology —my own included—has the character of a subjective confession . . . it is only by accepting this as inevitable that I can serve the cause of man's knowledge of man.

2

Archetypal Patterns in Poetry is one of the few books that perform precisely the action its title denotes; it discusses archetypal patterns in poetry. The book consists of six chapters, the first raising the general problem of archetypes as illustrated by tragic drama, and discussing Ernest Jones's exploration of the Œdipus complex in *Hamlet*; the other five dealing respectively with the rebirth archetype in *The Ancient Mariner*; the heaven-hell archetype in Coleridge, Milton, and Dante; some archetypal women in poetry; the archetypal devil, hero, and god; and some archetypes in contemporary literature. Methodologically her work divides into two sorts: the detailed exploration of an archetype in a single work, like rebirth in *The Ancient Mariner*; and the comparison of variants of an archetype in a number of works, like the chapter on the archetypal women of great poets. Both methods warrant examination.

In *The Ancient Mariner* Miss Bodkin begins by noting the passages describing the becalming of the ship and its later miraculous motion and finds that they introduce the problem of death and rebirth in a specific symbolization of Coleridge's experience of futile mental effort followed by a sudden creative inspiration. For this reading she relies, first on her own associations and memories inspired by the lines, then on available records of Coleridge's private associations, and finally on the general relationship, illustrated by Biblical quotations, between the rising of the wind and the quickening of the human spirit. Then Miss Bodkin goes on to consider the climax of the poem, the blessing of the snakes and its consequence, which she relates to Jung's archetypal myth of "the night journey under the sea" as illustrated by the Jonah story—the basic Re-

---

rushed into print with a defense of Jung (which claimed that Jung was being quoted out of context, and, to me at least, made the case more damning by giving more context for the quotations).

birth ritual, organized around guilt and expiation. Here her method includes her own associations and dreams again, Lowes's exploration of Coleridge's sources, Baudouin's analysis of similar imagery in Verhaeren, Hamlet's predicament, other types of the "guilt-haunted wanderer" like Cain and the Wandering Jew, and the general problem of the craving for death or re-entry into the womb, as reflected in dreams, poetry, and psychoanalytic theory. When she concludes, she not only has used the poem to illustrate her archetypal pattern, but has made the pattern illuminate the poem and its effects, fix it in the corpus of major poetry, and greatly heighten and inform enjoyment.

Miss Bodkin's comparative method operates in a similar fashion. In the chapter on the archetypal image of woman, she considers Milton's muse-mother in *Paradise Lost*, relates it to the goddess-mothers in Homer, and identifies them both with the wife-mother mourning for Tammuz and the other slain vegetation gods. She then takes up the ambiguous balance, in Milton's Eve, of Proserpine, the figure of doomed youth, and Delilah, the betrayer; finds the same ambiguity of betrayed-betrayer in Euripides' Phædra; notes the idealization of these two archetypes in Dante's Beatrice, the mother-imago, with all their earthly elements gone to make Helen, Dido, Cleopatra, and Francesca (particularly Francesca); observes that Vergil's variants of the archetypes, Eurydice and Dido, bear ambiguously within each both the Beatrice and the Francesca elements; and concludes with these elements as stages in the dramatic development of Goethe's Gretchen, Francesca *becoming* Beatrice. In dealing with the shifting interrelationship of these archetypal women, Miss Bodkin is able to discuss their temporal aspects in the differing views of the poets' historical periods, as well as their timelessly archetypal aspect in the central poetic vision.

When Miss Bodkin turns to contemporary literature, finding the Rebirth archetype represented in opposing bodily and spiritual terms by Lawrence's *Plumed Serpent* and Charles Morgan's *The Fountain*, the archetypal poet-figure as a father-imago in Virginia Woolf's *Orlando* and the phantasmagoric fragments of rebirth rites in Eliot's *Waste Land*, she establishes, although almost as an afterthought, the persistence of these patterns, not only in great literature of the past but as the organizing principle of any serious work of art to our own day.

In noting the persistence of these archetypes, Miss Bodkin tangles willy-nilly with the problem of *how* they are transmitted. If, as Jung (following Freud) claims, they are primal experience somehow recorded in the structure of the brain, then they require a belief in the inheritance of acquired characteristics and a demolition of Weismann's monumental hypothesis of the continuity of the germ plasm (whereby germ plasm is never created out of somatic plasm and consequently cannot reproduce its experiential alterations). Freud was prepared to accept this responsibility and, as late as 1939, in *Moses and Monotheism*, affirmed his belief in the inheritance of acquired characteristics despite the views of contemporary biological science. On the other hand, if, as many contemporary psychoanalysts believe, they are inherited not in the physical organism but in the cultural context and are reproduced in each generation by similar infantile experience, then they would disappear automatically in any society, generation or single child with radically different infantile experience (as Malinowski found the matrilinear Trobrianders had no Œdipus complexes). Miss Bodkin attempts to get around this problem by leaving the matter moot, and suggests her reservations toward the Jungian position in the first few pages of the book:

> In Jung's formulation of the hypothesis . . . it is asserted that these patterns are . . . "inherited in the structure of the brain"; but of this statement no evidence can be considered here. Jung believes himself to have evidence of the spontaneous production of ancient patterns in the dreams and fantasies of individuals who had no discoverable access to cultural material in which the patterns were embodied. This evidence is, however, hard to evaluate; especially in view of the way in which certain surprising reproductions, in trance states, of old material, have been subsequently traced to forgotten impressions of sense in the lifetime of the individual.

By page 257, however, she has so far forgotten her reservations as to concede that: "No doubt both an inherited and an individually acquired factor are present" in the superego, the inheritance "that of the tribe throughout the racial past."

Miss Bodkin is saved from the excesses of psychoanalytic criticism by a constant wariness about overemphasizing the psychological factors in poetry. She writes:

> Enjoyment of the beauty of poetry is spoiled only if certain of these psycho-physiological echoes are emphasized, as though they were somehow more real than all the other elements with which in a mature mind they are fused—as though these other elements that contribute to the actually experienced response were a mere evasion or disguise of those few primitive elements newly identified by the analyst.

Her psychological factors never cause a poetic effect except "in part." In her central defense of the psychological method, printed as an appendix entitled "Psychological Criticism and Dramatic Conventions," Miss Bodkin answers the objections of E. E. Stoll and others to psychological analysis with the moderate statements that we cannot and should not "cancel the psychological awareness that our own age has conferred on us," that genuine appreciation must be "with the complete resources of our minds," and that psychological insights as well as anything Stoll or other critics can teach us are all valuable components of this enriched apprehension.

One of her most valuable concepts in this judicious use of psychology is Jung's description of the fallacy of "nothing but" thinking, the idea that a poem is "nothing but" an example of some category (a type of thinking now sometimes called "thalamic" from the thalamus, the part of the brain capable of only crude distinctions). Miss Bodkin insists that poetry, instead of being *nothing but* her psychology, is that *and also* a good many other things.

Unlike the professional psychoanalysts, who rely as much as possible on case histories and clinical records, Miss Bodkin relies chiefly on introspection, analyzing and reporting to the best of her ability her own psychological reactions. "Our analysis is of the experience communicated to ourselves," she writes. She describes the sensations of her own mind on reading poetry, what images she becomes aware of, what significance or tension she feels, what associations are evoked, what reactions of empathy or projection arise, what transitions are made, even what dreams she dreams. She attempted to objectify these introspections, or at least widen their base, only once, in the essay on *The Ancient Mariner*. For this she adapted I. A. Richards's laboratory method, described at length in *Practical Criticism*, of giving poems to readers for their reactions, with the modifications that in her case poem and author were identified and she asked only emotional response, the result of "absorbed musing, or reverie" (Galton's "free association"), rather than evaluative opinion. Although the material obtained resulted in a shrewd series of questions aimed at the reader, she announced regretfully in her preface to the book that she had abandoned the attempt, "since it was not found practicable to secure from those with whom the writer was in touch the prolonged, concentrated effort required." She expressed the conviction, however, that eventually "intensive work on the poetic experience of individuals must replace more extensive methods of research."

In addition to her basic indebtedness to Jung, and modifications of the experimental psychology of Galton and Richards, Miss Bodkin has drawn on almost every available psychology. Her indebtedness to Freud is particularly heavy, and not only in areas where Jung accepts him. She questions Freud's assertion that Œdipal attitudes underly all guilt-sense in dreams, but concedes that "some form of failure in relation to the parents" does—to the extent of merging with any other factors that may be operative. She accepts Freud's concept of the superego and attempts to mediate between Freud and Jung as to whether it is primarily the influence of the parents in infancy or of the tribe, proposing a compromise. She also accepts, sometimes with a degree of reservation, such miscellaneous Freudian concepts, with their implications, as the death instinct or Nirvana principle, the ego and id, the pleasure principle, the father-imago, and items ranging from flight in dreams to the serpent and the apple in the story of the Fall, as varieties of sex symbol.

In addition, Miss Bodkin is indebted to a number of Freud's disciples who have analyzed literature. She acknowledges Ernest Jones's study of *Hamlet* for a good deal of her method, particularly such basic devices in the psychological genesis of literature as dissociation and decomposition. She also uses Charles Baudouin's modified Freudian study of Verhaeren, *Psychoanalysis and Æsthetics;* the Freudian anthropology of Geza Róheim, and others. At the same time, she is able to draw on non-psychoanalytic psychologies. From Gestalt psychology, through such anthropologists as Goldenweiser, she adopts the term "configuration" for a cultural pattern, and is directly familiar with at least Köhler's work on *The Mentality of Apes,* from which she borrows the concept of an interval of suspension before the resolution of a problem.

Besides her eclectic psychology, Miss Bodkin uses philosophers, theologians, anthropologists, and sociologists, as well as a number of modern literary critics, among them William Empson on ambiguity, G. Wilson Knight's work on *Othello,* and John Livingston Lowes's exhaustive study of Coleridge. (It is ironic that Miss Bodkin, the obvious person to extend Lowes's observations on the sources of Coleridge's images in the only area in which they can bear extension, the psychoanalytic, should resolutely refuse to do so. She is as oblivious as he is, for example, of the obvious sex symbolism of the caverns and mountains in *Kubla Khan.*)

With the aid of this eclectic bundle of theories and concepts, Miss Bodkin has made literary criticism, not pseudo-science. Despite all the apparatus, she is insistently a lover of poetry and a sensitive reader. *Archetypal Patterns in Poetry* is noteworthy for its brilliant insight into the emotional structure of *King Lear,* its explanation (perhaps the first satisfactory one for our time) of the power Shelley's poetry had on its readers, its sensitive and perceptive analysis of Virginia Woolf's techniques, and much else. To borrow a distinction from Kenneth Burke, she is primarily interested not in *patterns* in poetry, but in patterns in *poetry.*

3

The psychological criticism of literature, much more than any other critical method here discussed, is a development in our own century, since the science of psychology as an organized body of knowledge began within the lifetime of men now living. Informally, criticism has been psychological from its beginnings, in the sense that any critic has obviously attempted to apply what he knew or believed about the operations of the human mind. With the recognition of the unconscious by Freud just before the turn of the century, psychology acquired a dimension from which it could contribute insights otherwise unobtainable into the origins and structure of works of literature. Of psychological critics before Freud, only a few require mention. The most important of these, of course, is Aristotle, the principal source of both psychology and the psychological criticism of literature. Aristotle's empirical psychology is all through his work, and is the central topic of *De Anima* and of the *Parva Naturalia*, the short physical treatises on memory and reminiscence, on dreams, and on prophesying by dreams. He applied his psychology to poetry in *The Poetics*, answering Plato's psychological fallacy in *The Republic*, that poetry *feeds* the passions and is thus socially harmful, with the much sounder psychological theory of catharsis, that poetry arouses the passions of pity and terror in a controllable symbolic form and then purges them through its operations. The *Poetics* is almost a textbook in the psychology of art; and such concepts as *hamartia*, the tragic flaw that comes from the hero's imperfect insight into his situation; *peripateia*, the shock of change; the preference of the probable impossible over the improbable possible; and many others are anticipations of basic psychological truths. For Plato in *Ion* the poet is an inspired madman, a neurotic. For Aristotle he is closer to an inspired psychologist.

Aristotle's psychological insights into art were extended and developed by later classical writers like Longinus and Horace, but the next major step in psychological criticism came only with Coleridge's *Biographia Literaria*. Coleridge took Aristotle's psychology, as modified by Aquinas, Descartes, Hobbes, and Hartley, none of whom made any significant advances on it, and turned it on poetry. The only thing that kept Coleridge from achieving full-blown psychological criticism was the same thing that had prevented Aristotle, the quantitative and qualitative inadequacy of the psychology. Coleridge actually anticipated the unconscious, referring to "those flights of lawless speculation which, abandoned by *all* distinct consciousness, because transgressing the bounds and purposes of our intellectual faculties, are justly condemned as *transcendent*," but he was so far in advance of his time as to be unable to do anything with the discovery. Other anticipations of modern psychological criticism in the *Biographia* include a proposal for reader experiments similar to those Richards made in our century, a distinction in terms of reader-affect between poetry and science, and an invaluable concept of Imagination (which Richards spent an entire volume, *Coleridge on Imagination*, developing into modern psychological terminology).

A contemporary of Coleridge's who requires mention in this chapter, although nowise near as important, is Charles Lamb. Although Lamb never had a formal psychology, his sister's tragic insanity and his own disturbed mental states made him particularly sensitive to the relationship between psychology and art. In "The Sanity of Genius" he wrote one of the best distinctions between art and neurosis we have, and in

"Witches and Other Night Fears" he actually anticipated Jung's archetypes. He wrote:

> Gorgons, and Hydras, and Chimæras—dire stories of Celæno
> and the Harpies—may reproduce themselves in the brain of super-
> stition—but they were there before. They are transcripts, types—
> *the archetypes are in us, and eternal.*—These terrors—date beyond
> body—or, without the body, they would have been the same.

(Walter Whiter, who preceded Coleridge and Lamb by a generation
with an astounding anticipation of modern psychological criticism, is
discussed below in the chapter on Caroline Spurgeon.)

4

With the publication of Freud's *The Interpretation of Dreams* in 1900,
the psychoanalytic criticism of literature began. Freud's contribution has
a number of aspects. Perhaps the most important is the body of writing
about nonliterary problems, particularly dreams, wit, and neurotic symp-
toms, that contains principles that can profitably be applied to literature. This includes *The Interpretation of Dreams* itself, with its dream
mechanisms like condensation, displacement, secondary elaboration, and
splitting that appear to be the basic mechanisms of literary creation, its
basic concept of wish-fulfillment, equally applicable to art, and its invaluable explorations into the nature of symbolism; as well as other
works like *Wit and Its Relation to the Unconscious* and *Three Contributions
to the Theory of Sex.*

Of next importance, perhaps, are Freud's specific comments on the
nature of art and the artist. The earlier ones, in "The Relation of the
Poet to Day-Dreaming," "Contributions to the Psychology of Love,"
"Formulations Regarding the Two Principles in Mental Functioning,"
and even Lecture 23 of *A General Introduction to Psychoanalysis*, as late
as 1920, tend to establish the artist as an infantile neurotic, as discussed
above. Later discussions, particularly in *New Introductory Lectures* and
Beyond the Pleasure Principle, tend to see through this easy formulation to
a recognition of the artist as a neurotic *plus* his art, through which he
can understand and alter reality; and in an address at his seventieth
birthday celebration Freud refused credit for having discovered the
subconscious, claiming that that credit properly belonged to the writers.

The final category of Freud's contributions to psychoanalytic literary
criticism is his specific discussions of artists and works of art. These are
scattered all through the works in brief comments, some of them very
perceptive, like the mention of Hamlet in *The Interpretation of Dreams*
(on which Jones based his reading), the analysis of *King Lear*, and the

discussion of Greek tragedy in *Totem and Taboo*. He did only three long studies: *Leonardo da Vinci: A Psychosexual Study of Infantile Reminiscence*, an article on "Dostoyevsky and Parricide," and a study of an obscure German novel called *Gradiva* by Wilhelm Jensen. With these three works Freud established both types of analysis with which his followers were to concern themselves: the pathography, or the study of a neurotic or psychotic personality using his works for clues; and actual psychoanalytic literary criticism, or the study of a work of literature using psychoanalytic mechanisms and clinical conjectures as clues.

Leonardo da Vinci is largely pathography (although Freud insists that Leonardo was not in any sense a neurotic). It is an attempt, relying heavily on a remarkable analysis of a fantasy-memory of Leonardo's about a vulture, to reconstruct the artist's biography and psychic development by way of understanding his later sexual and artistic inhibitions. Freud calls his work "a biographical effort," insists that it is tentative, and devotes most of his space to conjecturing infantile roots for what he diagnoses as Leonardo's ideal, or incipient, homosexuality. Freud's only concern with Leonardo's works is to explore them for further evidence of the artist's psychic life, with the reservation that "when one considers what profound transformations an impression of an artist has to experience before it can add its contribution to the work of art, one is obliged to moderate considerably one's expectation of demonstrating something definite." He disregards other aspects of the works and at one place seems to suggest that he has no choice, that "the nature of artistic attainment is psychoanalytically inaccessible to us." Nevertheless, within its own terms, the book is one of Freud's finest works and an almost miraculous reconstruction of the life and mind of a complex artist four hundred years dead.

"Dostoyevsky and Parricide" is about halfway between the two, chiefly interested in getting at Dostoyevsky's hysterical epilepsy, Œdipal wish for his father's death, and latent homosexuality. Nevertheless, despite his statement that "before the problem of the creative artist, analysis must lay down its arms," Freud is highly appreciative of Dostoyevsky's novels as remarkable works of art and very much concerned with contributing what he can to their comprehension, both in their symbolic relationship to the author's neurosis and in their purely formal relations.

Delusion and Dream in Wilhelm Jensen's Gradiva is pure literary analysis. With the curt "we have not access to the psychic life of the author," Freud renounces any attempt to explore Jensen's complexes or neuroses, and confines himself to interpreting the psychological and dream structure of the book, analyzing its symbolic techniques of condensation and displacement, and in general deepening and strengthening its meaning. His conclusion is that Jensen was generally aware of psychoanalytic truths, not from any knowledge of formal psychoanalysis, but from the exploration of his own psyche. The artist is another kind of psychoanalyst. In fact, Freud's treatment of the book is so delicate and respectful that it is not really Freudian enough, and he misses or ignores a fine Œdipus complex in the hero (and presumably the author) and some first-class sex symbolism having to do with lizard-catching. Part of Freud's respect for the book is obviously that it neatly coincides with psychoanalytic theory, thus to some extent "confirming" it in its early years ("Story-tellers are valuable allies and their testimony is to be rated high, for they usually know many things between heaven and earth that our academic wisdom does not even dream of"), but there is not much doubt that *Gradiva* is a poor and silly little novel well deserving its obscurity, and that Freud in overrating it and analyzing it at length has written his own very much better novel.

Actually the pathography tradition was not new with Freud, but merely continued, in long-range unscientific psychiatric diagnosis, a nineteenth-century tradition of long-range unscientific medical diagnosis, in which a learned physician deduced for the eager literary world that from his poetry Byron must have had gallstones, or Pope high blood pressure. This is the tone not so much of Freud as of many of his disciples, including some of the rebels. It is the tone, for example, of Brill's discussion of the love of poetry as simply an expression of oral eroticism, "a chewing and sucking of beautiful words."

The only psychoanalyst who has devoted himself to art with any thoroughness is Otto Rank. Before he broke with Freud in the early twenties, Rank wrote a number of valuable psychoanalytic literary studies: *The Artist* in 1907, *The Myth of the Birth of the Hero* in 1909, a study of the *Lohengrin* story in 1911, *The Incest-Motive in Poetry and Legend* in 1912, and two essays in 1914 and 1922 later published as *Don Juan and the Double* (most of these available in English). Of these, *The Myth of the Birth of the Hero* is perhaps most important. Picking up a suggestion of Freud's that he try Galton's method of creating an archetype of the mythic birth (and apparently ignorant of the fact that a similar job had been done, along very fragmentary lines, for the whole life of the hero by Alfred Nutt), Rank achieved an impressive psychoanalytic study in comparative mythology, very important to literature and probably the genesis of Lord Raglan's invaluable *The Hero* in 1935.

The Incest-Motive included a number of stimulating Œdipal analyses, among them one of Shakespeare's *Julius Cæsar* (pointing out that Brutus, Cassius, and Antony are three splittings of Cæsar's "son"—the first representing his rebelliousness, the second his remorsefulness, and the third his natural piety) and one of Baudelaire's sonnet "The Giantess." After Rank broke with Freud, he wrote little of any value about art,[5] and his major book on the subject, *Art and the Artist*, published in English in 1932, is a dull and very Germanic treatise on æsthetics, drawing chiefly on warmed-over anthropology, centering the art-urge in a desire to immortalize the self, warning that increasing consciousness will be the death of art, and resisting psychoanalytic interpretations at a number of points where they would prove valuable, while in other places vulgarizing psychoanalysis overzealously, particularly in a reading of *Hamlet* as direct autobiography.

Of full-length psychoanalytic literary studies by professional analysts or psychologists, the best and most influential is probably Ernest Jones's study of *Hamlet* in his *Essays in Applied Psychoanalysis*. In a hundred informed and closely reasoned pages, revealing a real Shakespeare scholarship and general literacy, Jones demolishes every Hamlet theory that had been previously maintained; elaborates and sustains his own, an Œdipal structure unconscious in Hamlet, unconscious in Shakespeare, and unconscious in the audience; and substantially increases appreciation of the play by showing what no one had yet succeeded in showing, the reasonableness and inevitability of its action, although still leaving a number of questions unanswered. Jones has done no other comparable literary analysis, but his book contains a number of other essays suggestively applying psychoanalysis to such disparate fields as art, folklore, history, politics, religion, and even journalism.

A book as sensitive to literary values and far from the pathography as Jones's *Hamlet* essay, if not as intrinsically exciting, is Charles Baudouin's *Psychoanalysis and Æsthetics*, a lengthy study of poetic symbolism in Verhaeren by a man who is himself a poet. Baudouin's psychoanalysis is extremely eclectic, drawing impartially on Freud, Jung, Adler, Rank, and Ribot. Although it rarely goes all out in psychoanalytic readings, Baudouin's book is a remarkable job of detailed symbolic analysis with significant incidental forays anticipating a number of new critical techniques: multiple translation of meaning into several different terminologies; polarization of obsessive imagery into paired terms in parallel columns; and discussion of the significance of sounds and auditory symbolism. Baudouin insists early in the book that analysis of the works of genius will show genius, not neurosis, but then he falls into error at the other extreme, and insists at the end that because a poem is "an admirable illustration of the psychology of sublimation," therefore "true," it is a "beautiful" poem, and that because the poems generally accepted as Verhaeren's masterpieces are those "most fraught with symbolical meaning," other poems as fraught with psychological meaning are probably also masterpieces.

---

[5] The relationship here is not necessarily causal, although it is not necessarily irrelevant either.

At the other pole from Baudouin's analysis of Verhaeren is the work of his countryman the French psychoanalyst René Laforgue, on Baudelaire. *The Defeat of Baudelaire* is pure pathography, subtitled *A Psychoanalytic Study of the Neurosis of Charles Baudelaire*, and announces its intention frankly on the first page:

> It is not my purpose to consider Baudelaire's position in literature; neither do I wish to undertake an analysis of his art. For me, Baudelaire is simply a man, a sick man among many others, a victim of life. He is a representative of an army of the misunderstood. My only reason for discussing him first before considering the others is that thanks to his art he is more accessible to study and within easier reach of comprehension.

Frankly using Baudelaire's poems, journals, and records, along with Porché's biography, as no more than clinical records, Laforgue finds that Baudelaire had an Œdipus complex, a masochistic complex with whipping and masturbation fantasies, latent homosexuality, penis-inferiority, probably impotence and voyeurism (the last based on an absolutely conjectural childhood experience), and constipation. For Laforgue, who continually insists that his aims in writing the book included warning educators not to frighten children and reforming the treatment of criminals, the artist is a "privileged" neurotic who can create art, and poetic form is a device for making the poet's neurosis unrecognizable except by clinicians. Nothing more need be said about it in a discussion of literary criticism.

Among the great number of literary discussions by psychoanalytic psychiatrists,[6] only two more can be touched on, as examples of current American practice. Lawrence S. Kubie, under the title *The Literature of Horror*, wrote an article on Faulkner's *Sanctuary* and one on Caldwell's *God's Little Acre* for the *Saturday Review of Literature* in 1934 (along with one on Hemingway that seems never to have appeared). Kubie makes some good points, particularly in the Faulkner piece, among them: a discussion of the erotization of horror and anxiety in contemporary American literature; the insistence that he is not psychoanalyzing authors, that the statement that *Sanctuary* is a series of male impotence fantasies is *not* the statement that Faulkner is impotent, but merely that he is imaginative; and the much-needed rejection of Faulkner's claim that the book is a piece of meaningless hack work. He ends up, however, with

[6] I have not yet been able to locate the psychoanalytic literary criticism of Wulf Sachs, either the studies of works by authors ranging from Shakespeare to Sarah Gertrude Millen in *Pyschoanalysis; Its Meaning and Practical Applications*, or the uncollected pieces on Proust, Steinbeck, and others, except for a pathography of Dostoyevsky, an extension of Freud's essay, which Dr. Sachs has kindly allowed me to read in manuscript. From its combination of orthodox Freudianism with a social emphasis and genuine respect for literature, I should expect Sachs's work to be of real value.

the rather oversimple formulation of Popeye as id, Benbow as ego, and the mob as superego, an example of where terminology can lead with no checkrein on it. The Caldwell piece continues some of these topics, but is less concerned with the work itself than with exploring the nature of obscenity and the implications of reader-reactions to it.

A more literate work, but limited to the pathography, is Saul Rosenzweig's essay "The Ghost of Henry James" in *Character and Personality* for December 1943, reprinted in the Fall 1944 *Partisan Review*. Rosenzweig uses some of James's short stories to establish James as suffering from castration anxiety and inferiority complex, with constitutional bisexuality "a speculative possibility." Despite this narrow clinical formulation, and liberal salting with terms like "repression," "frustration," "sublimation," and "overcompensation," Rosenzweig's actual readings of the stories are extremely shrewd and sensitive to literary values, an example of how valuable he and men like him could be if they turned their method to analyzing the work and its *form* rather than the man (or, in Rosenzweig's case, if he had even attempted, for example, to discuss the concealment-evasion aspects of James's late baroque style).

The professional literary men who have used Freud and psychoanalysis are almost innumerable. The first orthodox use came as early as 1912, in Frederick Clarke Prescott's article "Poetry and Dreams" in the *Journal of Abnormal Psychology*, reprinted in book form in 1919. Prescott took Freud's *The Interpretation of Dreams*, not then translated into English, and applied it systematically to the interpretation of poetry, finding poetry to be, like dreams, the disguised fulfillment of repressed wishes, and suggesting that the mechanisms Freud found in the "dream work" might also be the mechanisms of the "poetic work." At the same time he attempted to support and document many of Freud's new and shocking contentions with quotations from literary men through the ages. Despite a somewhat mechanical application, a concept of poetry as "escape from reality," and a contempt for Coleridge's "obfuscations" on fancy and imagination, Prescott's book is an important beginning, and later work has been heavily dependent on it. In 1922 he published *The Poetic Mind*, a fuller treatment, which despite a number of things of value, among them an anticipation of Empson's "ambiguity" and an insistence on plural meaning, represents a considerable falling-off, with the Freudian psychoanalysis watered down to fit a new romantic mysticism and Shelley-worship.

One of the first lay attempts to use psychoanalytic concepts in criticizing specific works of literature came in 1919, in Conrad Aiken's *Scepticisms: Notes on Contemporary Poetry*. Aiken not only utilized Freud's view of art, but attempted to reconcile it with Kostyleff's theory of poetry as a verbo-motor discharge, Pavlov's concept of the conditioned reflex, and other scraps of assorted psychology. Not much insight came from this jumble, but Aiken got from Freud the basic attitude of contemporary criticism, anticipating Richards's influential statement of it by a few years: that poetry is a human product, satisfying human needs like any other, and that it has discoverable origins and functions, open to analysis.

One of the earliest English exponents of psychoanalytic criticism was Robert Graves, in a series of books including *On English Poetry* (1922), *The Meaning of Dreams* (1924), and *Poetic Unreason* (1925). Graves attempted detailed psychoanalytic readings of specific poems, particularly in *The Meaning of Dreams*, where he analyzed Keats's "La Belle Dame sans merci," Coleridge's "Kubla Khan," and a poem of his own. Perhaps because Graves largely rejected Freud and Jung in favor of the psychoanalytic theories of W. H. R. Rivers, emphasizing dissociation of unconscious personalities and traumatic experiences; perhaps because he attempted to correlate the best poetry with the best unconscious personality conflicts; more likely because he combined ignorance with brashness to an amazing degree, the results were atrocious and may have discouraged later British efforts. (The one completely successful application by an English critic of psychoanalytic concepts to a work of art, William Empson's essay on *Alice in Wonderland*, will be discussed in the chapter on Empson.)

A special and rather confusing English case is Herbert Read. No one has written so enthusiastically on the importance of psychoanalysis, and in fact of all psychology, for literature and literary criticism. He writes that the critic must pick from psychology, particularly psychoanalysis, "his brightest weapons," that in some areas the critic can only ask questions for psychology to answer, that psychology has finally been able to explain æsthetic mysteries like *catharsis*, and so on. In an article on "Psychoanalysis and Criticism" in *Reason and Romanticism* (later expanded as "The Nature of Criticism" in *Collected Essays in Literary Criticism*) Read has written a remarkably reasoned and persuasive argument for psychoanalytic criticism, emphasizing eclecticism, moderation, and the limitations and dangers of psychoanalysis as well as its enormous possibilities. The only trouble with this is that Read has practiced very little of what he preaches. Aside from his book on Wordsworth, a long essay on Shelley, and a study of the Brontës, none of them very deep or very perceptive, and the frequent use of some Freudian terms and Jung's "introversion-extraversion," Read's own work seems to have been almost untouched by psychoanalysis. Like Moses, he saw the Promised Land, but somehow never managed to enter it. W. H. Auden, similarly has done a brilliant analysis of Freud's significance for art in "Psychology and Art To-day" in the symposium *The Arts Today*, without ever making much use of the method in his criticism.

Lionel Trilling's case in America is somewhat comparable. He wrote a remarkably good estimate of Freud's literary and æsthetic significance, reflecting wide familiarity with Freud's work, in the *Kenyon Review* for Spring 1940, pointing out that in one respect Freud actually sees the human mind as a poetry-making organ, and that psychoanalysis is thus a science of tropes. However, he so hedged this around with limitations based on a contrary tendency he saw in Freud, a contemptuous attitude toward art, that it ended up more or less on the fence. Trilling's critical practice, in his studies of Matthew Arnold and E. M. Forster, reflects this divided mind, and although his use of psychoanalytic insights is fairly extensive, they tend to be always tentative, half-hearted, and sometimes stillborn.

Other American critics who have attempted to utilize psychoanalysis include Edmund Wilson and Van Wyck Brooks (discussed in earlier chapters), the former moving increasingly toward it as he discarded Marxism, the latter sampling tasty bits of every psychoanalysis eventually to discard them all. William Troy has done at least one psycho-analytic piece, on Stendhal's Œdipus complex. Of the men influenced by Brooks, Frank went head-over-heels for the mistier areas of psycho-analysis, to repudiate them all later, psychoanalysts being "philosophi-cally shallow men," for his private mysticism—holism, the good life, and the athletic soul; and Mumford picked up Raymond Weaver's silly and lyric biography of Melville, *Herman Melville, Mariner and Mystic*, and based on it a sillier and even more lyric one of his own, *Herman Melville*, full of undigested Freud and plain bad taste ("it may be" that Melville's wife "was timid and irresponsive as a lover"). A few other psychoanalytic biographies of the twenties and thirties seem better and more perceptive, like Katharine Anthony's of Margaret Fuller and Louisa May Alcott, Rosamond Langbridge's study of Charlotte Brontë, and Joseph Wood Krutch's biography of Poe, although they could all have ended on a variant of the ultimate "nothing but" fallacy with which Krutch ended his: "We have, then, traced Poe's art to an abnormal condition of the nerves."

Much contemporary American critical use of psychoanalysis has in fact been a good deal worse. The chief sinners are the amateur sexologists and Peeping Toms of criticism, typified by Ludwig Lewisohn's *Expres-sion in America* (Thoreau, for example, is a clammy prig, the result of being hopelessly inhibited to the point of psychical impotence, or else hopelessly undersexed; and almost every American writer is similarly debunked). Only a few steps above this are such readings as Thomas Beer's straight sexual interpretation of Henry Adams in *The Mauve Decade*, Mark Van Doren's debunking of Whitman's poetry and ideas on the basis of his homosexuality, and Edward Dahlberg's sexual readings of all literature in *Do These Bones Live*, in the name of anti-psycho-analysis and Tolstoy's statement that man's deepest suffering is always the tragedy of the bedroom.

Other psychologies besides psychoanalysis have been turned on art with a good deal of success in our time. Perhaps the most influential is the integrated psychology of I. A. Richards, drawing on neurological psychology, behaviorism, psychoanalysis, and Gestalt, as well as his own empirical observations (discussed below in the chapter on Richards). Kenneth Burke, who has used Freud extensively, and has written the most penetrating analysis I know of the implications and necessary modifications of psychoanalysis for criticism in "Freud—and the Analysis of Poetry" in *The Philosophy of Literary Form*, has also drawn on every modern psychological school to achieve an integrated psychology which he calls "phenomenological," based chiefly on Gestalt, which would avoid "the tenuousness of the purely introspective" as well as "the impoverish-ment of the purely behavioristic" (also discussed below).

A psychology that seems at least as promising for literary criticism as psychoanalysis is the Gestalt school, which as far as I know has had little direct professional application to literature.[7] This seems due in part to the laboratory-science emphasis given it by its founders, Max Wer-theimer, Kurt Koffka, and Wolfgang Köhler, in favor of phenomena objectively ascertainable in a controlled experiment. So far the concern of the school has chiefly been with the conscious surface of the mind, with processes like "perception" and "learning," which comes clear in Wer-theimer's book *Productive Thinking*, where the examples tend inevitably to come from the reasonable processes of geometric theorems and Ein-stein's discovery of relativity rather than from less reasonable and ascertainable phenomena, like poetic images or Shakespeare's discovery of Lear. Nevertheless, the basic conception of the school, that reaction is to the total configuration or *Gestalt* of an experience, rather than to any single "stimulus," and that in this respect the whole is greater than the sum of the parts and determines their character, seems to be one of central relevance to problems of literature and art. Genetically, in fact, the Gestalt conception of total configuration was inspired by the formal nature of art, in von Ehrenfels's recognition that when a musical melody

[7] A few Gestalt works on the general subject of art have been produced, among them H. E. Reese's *A Psychology of Artistic Creation*, Werner Wolff's *The Expression of Personality* (which, although it deals largely with such self-expressions as walking and talking, has obvious relevance to æsthetic expression), and Rudolf Arnheim's article "Gestalt and Art," in the *Journal of Æsthetics*, Fall 1943. Arnheim is also currently teaching a Gestalt course in the Psychology of Art at the New School for Social Research, and contributed an essay, "Psychological Notes on the Poetical Process," to *Poets at Work*, Charles D. Abbott's symposium on the collection of poets' worksheets in the University of Buffalo library.

is transposed, and all the component notes changed, its *Gestaltqualität* remains the same, because the relations of the notes are preserved. The artist's problem of communicating the essential pattern of his experience, through a medium in which he did not have the experience, and often one utilizing a different sense (a landscape in a poem, a bird-song in a sculpture, etc.) would seem to be precisely a matter of this *Gestaltqualität*, and thus an area in which Gestalt psychology could be particularly fruitful. Its theoretical framework, emphasizing "field" concepts, makes full provision for the behavioral patterns of the unconscious mind, which are just as configurative, and recognizes in theory that the incongruous relationships of poetic metaphor are as "productive" perceptions for poetry as the more traditional relationships of mathematics are for science. There is not much doubt that when the younger integrative gestaltists, followers of the late Kurt Levin (who wrote in *Principles of Topological Psychology:* "the only approach to deeper problems was the brilliant work of Freud"), and social gestaltists like S. E. Asch and J. F. Brown finally turn their attention to the structural relations, configurations, "fields," and "topology" of works of literature, and professional critics pick up and extend their insights, a new area of tremendous value will open up to literary criticism.

Another greatly promising school that has done little specific literary analysis is the loose band of social Freudian analysts and psychiatrists, including Erich Fromm, Karen Horney, Alexander Martin, Abram Kardiner, Franz Alexander, Sandor Rado, Harry Stack Sullivan, and a number of other figures in America and England. They are frequently at each other's throats, but in general all are working along similar lines, to preserve the best of Freud's insights while substituting dynamic social and cultural determinants, frequently Marxist, for his changeless biologic determinants, and to substitute the Gestalt concept of pattern or configuration of personality for his autonomous instincts. Of them, only Fromm seems to have devoted much attention to literature. His only books available in English, *Escape from Freedom* and *Man for Himself*, make only glancing references to writers, but in his teaching he has dealt exhaustively with literary works (typified by a multiple-level reading of Kafka's *Trial* in political, psychoanalytic, and religious terms), as well as philosophy and folk material, and it is to be hoped that his future books will make some of that work available.

The work of Fromm and the Freudian revisionists raises the problem, a source of great controversy during the thirties, of the possibility of integrating Freud and Marx. Fromm not only believes that it can be done, but has made the formulation in a public lecture that Marx functions as a kind of collective psychoanalyst, breaking down society's ideologies and exposing repellent social reality to it in precisely the fashion that the analyst breaks down the individual's rationalizations and forces him to face repellent psychic reality. In the twenties Wilhelm Reich was the most enthusiastic psychoanalytic spokesman for a Freud-Marx integration (he is said to have been a member of both the International Psychoanalytic Association and the Communist Party and to have been expelled from both in the same week), with a theory of sex repression as a capitalist device to break the revolutionary spirits of the working classes. He and his followers engaged in a good deal of polemic on the subject in Marxist circles (discussed below, in the chapter on Caudwell), but the integration had been more or less defeated in Freudian circles as far back as 1911, when Adler and nine followers, all of them Socialists, were expelled from the Freudian movement (for other reasons as well, it must be said). Nevertheless, a number of orthodox Freudians, like Wulf Sachs, have continued to draw on Marx in much the same fashion as Freudian revisionists like Fromm.

The Freudian probably doing most to integrate Freud and Marx today is a clinical psychiatrist with an interest in literature, Frederick Wertham of the New York City Department of Hospitals. Wertham has used the resulting social psychology, which is to be defined in his forthcoming book on Freud and Marx, not only in his psychiatric and criminological practice, but as a literary point of view in a series of impressive reviews of psychological books in the *New Republic* and in psychological critiques prefacing each story in the anthology *The World Within*. He has also developed two new and significant techniques of literary criticism. The first, represented by a book called *Dark Legend*, the study of a young Italian boy who killed his mother, he calls the "bioliterary" method. It is the comparison of literary figures with living persons studied in the clinic, in the hope of casting light upon both. *Dark Legend* is an elaborate comparison of Gino, his young matricide, with Hamlet and Orestes, and from it Wertham deduced what he calls the Orestes complex, a modification of Freud's Œdipus complex, which he used at once in the diagnosis and cure of his patient, and in modifying and extending Ernest Jones's reading of *Hamlet*.

Wertham's second literary technique is a method he invented of psychoanalytic sessions with a writer, by way of revealing the subconscious sources of his work through traditional techniques of free association. The first of these, a series of conversations with Richard Wright about the sources of *Native Son*, resulted in some valuable discoveries, first reported before the American Psychopathological Association and later printed in the *Journal of Criminal Psychopathology* for July 1944. Although very much restricted by professional ethics in what he could reveal, Wertham succeeded in establishing pretty definitely the source of the name "Dalton" in the book, the author's forgotten experience underlying its crucial scene, and finally the fact that Wright's article, "How

Bigger Was Born," in the *Saturday Review of Literature,* like almost all similar explanations by authors, was a clear rationalization to obscure the book's actual roots.

The hope of the future is for a unified social psychology, probably founded on Gestalt "field" concepts, utilizing the valid insights and concepts of psychoanalysis and other psychologies, conditioned by the insights and concepts of Marxism and other sociologies, and organized in a body of generally accepted laws, data, and laboratory experimental techniques that would make the field a mature science. In such a field, which might eventually absorb anthropology and the other social sciences into one unified science of man, the integrative work of Lewin, Fromm, Wertham, Sachs, and the rest, as well as that of critics like Richards and Burke, will eventually find a place. From it literary criticism can expect the greatest invigoration it has had since Coleridge first attempted to turn formal scientific knowledge on poetry. Until then, the work of psychological critics like Maud Bodkin and her fellows can make only a small clearing, valuable as it is, in a jungle that must eventually give way entirely to the plowed fields of knowledge.

5

A few problems raised by Miss Bodkin's work and psychological criticism in general remain to be discussed. The first of them is her moral and religious emphasis, present in *Archetypal Patterns in Poetry* but not obtrusive; very obtrusive in her only other book, a rather disappointing pamphlet published in 1941 called *The Quest for Salvation in an Ancient and a Modern Play.* In it Miss Bodkin compares the *Eumenides* of Æschylus and T. S. Eliot's *Family Reunion,* principally in terms of their different salvations. Salvation in the *Eumenides,* she finds, is collective and historical, with Athena's conversion of the Erinyes, or Furies, into the Eumenides, or Fair-Minded Ones, and a consequent better order of justice for the community. Although Eliot's predicament is as collective as Æschylus', Miss Bodkin maintains, his hero's salvation at the end is entirely individual and spiritual, in terms of new personal relations and psychological insight, by which his private "Furies" are pacified. On the strength of this comparison, Miss Bodkin explores the contrast between the Athenian age and our own in terms of morality, justice, and peace. She writes:

> Certainly we know beforehand that the poet of today cannot write in such mood of exultation as seems to have possessed Athenians of the time of Æschylus. Their poet could shape his drama to reveal to his fellow citizens and celebrate with them the greatness of their city's achievement. The advance of the human spirit accomplished

by Athens leads our thought forward today to the greater advance—conceived by us but still far from achievement—of some tribunal, or centre of government, that should replace violence by equity between nations throughout the world. Had we succeeded in founding an institution that could tame national resentments, as resentments have been tamed between fellow citizens, some myth of divine intervention might take shape for us in poetry reflecting our collective triumph. But at this dark hour of the world's fortunes, if poet of ours fashions a myth of achieved deliverance, it is individual and spiritual triumph only his symbol can reflect.

In *The Quest for Salvation* Miss Bodkin is still to some extent concerned with psychoanalytic readings; she still quotes Freud and Jung and even suggests a Furies archetype, the energy of passion fixed in an evil relationship but capable of transformation into a good one. In line with her new emphasis, however, her chief quoting is of assorted mystic doctrine, including that of John Macmurray's *The Structure of Religious Experience*, Nicolai Hartman's *Ethics*, and Whitehead's concept of "causal efficacy" in *Process and Reality*. From Hartman she picks up the view of the "super-æsthetic function of poetry in giving concrete unity and shape to 'prospective ethos'—ideals dawning in the moral consciousness of the community," and on the strength of it confesses that her pamphlet is not æsthetic study but super-æsthetic study, an attempt to explore "certain realities of our common life through the medium of the poetry of these plays." Valuable as this may prove to be for ethics, religion, or international law, it seems largely the abnegation of the literary critic's function.

A major problem raised by Miss Bodkin's use of Jungian archetypes in criticism is their relation to folklore and anthropology. Her debt to Frazer is, of course, obvious, and an unsigned brief review of *Archetypal Patterns* in the *London Mercury* began "Under the pleasant shadow of Frazer's *Golden Bough* . . ." Miss Bodkin draws heavily not only on Frazer and on such later anthropologists as Emile Durkheim, G. Elliot Smith, Robert Briffault, and Alexander Goldenweiser, but specifically on the anthropological students of ancient art and religion: Gilbert Murray, Francis Cornford, Jane Harrison, R. R. Marett, and Jessie Weston. She makes particular use of Cornford, whose "spiritual power," derived from "the collective emotion and activity of the group," she finds an anticipation of Jung's collective unconscious, just as she finds Murray anticipating Jung's archetypes in his "situations deeply implanted in the memory of the race, stamped as it were upon our physical organism."

Miss Bodkin's central point of view is the ritual genesis of art associated with the Cambridge group, and when she is writing most rationally and farthest from Jung's mystic concept of biological memory, she recognizes that the transmission of her archetypes is actually a ritual one, writing: "It may be that an influence of this kind can pass, embodied only in tradition—in the emotion communicated, first through ritual with accompanying myth and legend, then on through poetry preserving, as Virgil's poem preserves, the influence of a ritual." In an appendix to *Archetypal Patterns*, "Criticism and Primitive Ritual," Miss Bodkin makes explicit her belief in the ritual origins of art and religion and defends Eliot's references to ancient ritual in *The Waste Land* against criticism by Alec Brown, finding them an enhancement of the magic and beauty of the poem rather than scraps of pseudo-learning.

There is a necessary and inevitable relationship between the genetic study of folk literature in terms of ritual origins and the functional analysis of it in terms of psychological and social needs that makes Jung's or some collective psychology as essential to folk criticism as Frazer's anthropology. Such a folk critic would have to go beyond Miss Bodkin, however, in rejecting Freud's and Jung's concept of inherited memory and treating the psychological need for these ritual patterns as having been re-created afresh in each generation by cultural conditioning, as she suggests in the quotation above. Not only are the archetypal patterns the basis of literature, as Miss Bodkin so excellently shows, but at least for our own time literature is one of the great disseminators of the archetypal patterns.

Two general questions raised by psychological criticism remain. The first is the problem, new to our own day, of criticizing the writer who has himself had serious acquaintance with psychoanalytic literature. Frederick J. Hoffman, in *Freudianism and the Literary Mind*, raises this problem in his discussion of the influence of Freud on writers like Joyce, Lawrence, Mann, and Kafka; William York Tindall, in *Forces in Modern British Literature*, discusses it in connection with Dylan Thomas and his followers; and Wertham would have run into it in connection with Richard Wright had he chosen to analyze a later work consciously using psychoanalytic discoveries, like *The Man Who Lived Underground*. When Ernest Jones analyzed the Œdipus pattern in *Hamlet*, he could safely assume that Shakespeare had not read about the Œdipus complex in Freud and decided to organize his work around it for greater effectiveness, but the same assumption is no longer possible about writers like Joyce and Mann. In his two essays on Freud, "Freud's Position in the History of Modern Thought" and the eightieth-birthday tribute "Freud and the Future," Mann makes it clear not only that he has consciously written formal psychoanalytic insights into his novels, but also that the *Joseph* tetralogy was specifically inspired by Freudian writings. In the case of such writers (and there is every reason to assume that the situation is now permanently with us) the critic happily dredging up a psychoanalytic insight from a work is somewhat in the position of a man finding buried treasure at Fort Knox. The psychoanalytic critic can still assume that the pattern taken over is personally meaningful, since a writer expresses his basic needs as clearly in formal material consciously chosen as in unconscious material, but he can no longer assume that in revealing it he is making any substantial critical contribution. Some of the effect of sad inadequacy in such Freudian criticisms of D. H. Lawrence as Horace Gregory's *Pilgrim of the Apocalypse* undoubtedly comes from the reader's feeling that Lawrence himself could do a much deeper and more perceptive psychoanalytical criticism of either his own work or anyone else's.

Finally, there is the general problem of the possibilities and future of psychoanalytic criticism. The disappointing feature of the *Partisan Review* controversy on the subject, inspired by Dr. Rosenzweig's pathography of Henry James, is that it was centered almost exclusively on the problem of art and neurosis, one of the questions least needing exploration these days. Only Robert Gorham Davis's contribution, "Art and Anxiety," in the Summer 1945 issue, faced the major problem of suggesting what psychoanalysis *can* do rather than defining what it cannot do. In a few suggestive hints analyzing the Red Ridinghood story; in a call for joint Freudian and Marxist analyses, unsimplified and unvulgarized; and particularly in a formulation of the field for psychoanalytic criticism in the study of *how* a work of art satisfies unconscious emotional needs (that is, a psychoanalytic study of *form*), Davis sketched out the hopeful direction.

The obvious limitation of traditional Freudian literary analysis is that only one study can be written, since every additional one would turn out to say the same thing. Ernest Jones could do a beautiful job finding the underlying Œdipus complex in *Hamlet*, but had he gone on to analyze *Lear* or *A Midsummer Night's Dream* or the *Sonnets* he would have found to his surprise that they reflected Shakespeare's Œdipus complex too, and, in fact, granting his theories, he would have made the same discovery about any other work of art. A criticism that can only say, however ingeniously, that this work is a result of the author's repressed Œdipal desires, and that everybody has repressed Œdipal desires, turns out not to be saying very much.

Here Maud Bodkin's *Archetypal Patterns in Poetry* is the hope. By focusing, not on the neurosis of the artist, not on the complexes concealed beneath the work, not on the art as a disguised fulfillment of repressed wishes, but on *how* a work of art is emotionally satisfying, what relationship its formal structure bears to the basic patterns and symbols of our psyches, she has furnished psychological criticism with endless vistas. What does this poem do, she asks, and how does it do it? These are the traditional questions of criticism, psychologies—psychoanalysis perhaps more than any other—offer great resources in answering them, and the answers will be as different as the poems. Let it be said to the credit of this all but unknown woman and her book that in one sense she performed as essential a job for literary criticism as Sigmund Freud did. He turned the blinding light of science on the depths of the human unconscious; she showed that in that fierce glare even the most delicate poem need not wither away.

CHAPTER 7

CHRISTOPHER CAUDWELL

and Marxist Criticism

IN THE century since *The Communist Manifesto*, it is more than a little ironic that the foremost work of Marxist literary criticism, if not the only large-scale work, should have been written by a young Englishman of twenty-eight, who had become a Marxist the year before, and was dead the following year. The book is *Illusion and Reality: A Study of the Sources of Poetry*, and the author is Christopher St. John Sprigg, who signed his serious work "Christopher Caudwell." He died in Spain, fighting with the British Battalion of the International Brigade in defense of the Republic. On his first day of action, as a machine-gunner holding a hill above Jarama to cover a retreat, he was killed by the Moors. His body was never found.

The life of Christopher Caudwell was something of a miracle of precosity. He was born in London in 1907, of well-off middle-class parents, and grew up in Yorkshire. Before he was fifteen he left school, the Roman Catholic college of St. Benet's Ealing, to become a journalist. He edited *British Malaya*, founded an aeronautical publishing house and edited one of its technical periodicals, and designed for automobiles an infinitely variable gear that attracted a good deal of attention until it was discovered that its inventor was seventeen years old.

His work on the dirigible, written at the age of eighteen, became a standard text in the field, and he learned to fly. At the age of twenty-one he turned to writing detective novels, popular books on aviation, and newspaper serials, supporting himself as a free-lance writer while he wrote verse and studied science.

In 1934, at the age of twenty-seven, he became interested in Marxism and spent the next summer in Cornwall reading Marx, Engels, and Lenin. That fall he came back to London, moved to the dockside working-class district of Poplar, and joined the Communist Party. He spent a year in Poplar, during which time he wrote *Illusion and Reality*, two other serious books published after his death, and probably the mystery stories that supported him, besides working exhaustively at Communist activities. The pattern of guilt about his class that presumably inspired his moving to a proletarian neighborhood also led to his insistence on performing only the most menial Communist duties (like drawing up and distributing leaflets, chalking up slogans, selling literature, and bill-sticking) as well as to his absolute avoidance of Communist intellectuals. He attended classes on Marxism and literature at Marx House for a brief period, but quit to go back to selling *Daily Workers* at the tube station. He did not write for the Communist press. He also gave up writing poetry from the time he joined the Communist Party. In December 1936, having tried to persuade his party to send him to Spain and having failed,[1] he left England to drive an ambulance across France into Spain, promising to return. Instead, apparently impelled by the same class guilt and contempt for intellectual activity, he joined the republican army, was transferred to the International Brigade, and learned the number-one job on a machine gun so well that in a few months he was instructing others. When his training was over, in February 1937, he went into battle and was immediately killed.

Aside from *Illusion and Reality* (discussed below) Caudwell published only one other book in his lifetime over the pseudonym he reserved for his serious work. (His reversal of the pattern, in using his real name for hack work and a pseudonym for serious, makes an interesting corollary to the guilt, the renunciation of poetry, and so on.) It is *This My Hand*, his novel, said to be extremely psychoanalytic, which exists in America in so few copies (the Library of Congress lacks one) that I have been unable to locate a copy. John Strachey announced in his introduction to one of Caudwell's posthumous books that he has read it, and that it is a failure (considering Strachey's frequent defects of taste, that need not carry very much weight). Over the name of Sprigg, Caudwell published seven thrillers (the titles may be of interest to posterity): *The Death of an Airman, The Perfect Alibi, The Corpse with the Sunburned Face, Six Queer Things, Crime in Kensington, Death of a Queen,* and *Fatality in Fleet Street*. They were more successful in America than in England, and four of them were dignified with the imprint of Doubleday Doran's Crime Club. Also over the name of Sprigg he published five books on aviation: *The Airship: Its Design, History, Operation and Future; Fly with Me* (with a collaborator), *British Airways, Great Flights,* and a fifth book of which I have been unable to learn the name.

After Caudwell's death the two other serious works he wrote in 1936 were published, over the name of Caudwell. The first was *Studies in a Dying Culture*, published in 1938 with an introduction by Strachey. It is a series of eight related essays, studying four writers, Shaw, T. E. Lawrence, D. H. Lawrence, and Wells, and four conceptual problems, Pacifism, Love, Freud and psychoanalysis, and Liberty. The theme relating these eight essays is the idea that the crisis in bourgeois culture

---

[1] Caudwell's brother, Mr. S. Stanhope Sprigg, has denied categorically in a newspaper letter that his brother went to Spain without his party's full consent.

is caused by the survival of Rousseau's fallacy (heresy would be more accurate) that "man is born free and everywhere he is in chains." Caudwell writes: "This illustion is that man is naturally free—'naturally' in this sense, that all the organisations of society are held to limit and cripple his free instincts, and furnish restraints which he must endure and minimise as best he may. From which it follows that man is at his best and noblest when freely working out his own desires." In terms of this central illusion Caudwell analyzes: T. E. Lawrence's failure as a leader (opposed to Lenin, the successful leader); the inadequate art and ideas of Shaw, Wells, and D. H. Lawrence; the weaknesses of psychoanalysis, pacifism, and the bourgeois concepts of love and liberty. To it he opposes the rigor of the Marxist view of freedom *in* society rather than *from* society, of man born in chains but *attaining* to freedom. Essentially it is Engels's "Freedom is the recognition of necessity" opposed to Rousseau's freedom as the *ignorance* of necessity, and the Engels line runs like a red thread through the book as well as through all of Caudwell's work.

Studies of a Dying Culture has a good many flaws, some of them derived from the tradition of Marxist criticism, some of them Caudwell's own contribution. Some of the political reasoning, for example, is childish, like the following *non sequitur:* "Only when the bourgeois begins to see the inevitability of Communism does he begin to regard Russia as a greater danger than any other bourgeois State. But this realisation is just what causes the capitalist class to resort to Fascism and therefore the Fascist States constitute the main danger to Russia today." Some of the political predictions do little to sustain the claim of Marxism to being a basis for social prediction and control, like the following denial, ironic in its inadequacy to later Nazi reality: "Consequently England need have no fear that a victorious Germany would have raped all Englishwomen and beheaded all Englishmen and transported the Elgin marbles to Berlin. Bourgeois States do not do such things." Some of the judgments are simple class-indictment, the constant surprised refrain against a contemporary thinker "but he is also a bourgeois," as though that were a charge or a dismissal, as though bourgeois art were bad by definition because it is bourgeois by definition. Nevertheless, the level of insight is generally very high, the irony is mordant, a number of the special treatments are first-rate analyses in the social conditioning of ideas (particularly the last half of the book, where Caudwell gets away from sticking pins in personalities and deals with movements), and the criticism of psychoanalysis in particular, from the viewpoint of neurology as well as materialism, is brilliantly penetrating.

Caudwell's other serious work, *The Crisis in Physics*, was published in 1939, edited with an introduction by Professor Hyman Levy. It was left in an unfinished state, and was apparently never intended for publication, Caudwell having written it to straighten the problem out in his own mind.

It is a discussion of new trends in physical thought, beyond relativity and quantum physics, particularly the challenge to causality by the younger men. Caudwell attacks these manifestations of "positivism" and "empiricism," charges that they lead to the abdication of science by substituting theory for experiment, and dismisses them finally as bourgeois idealism, the physical universe imaging bourgeois society. In this Caudwell seems to be echoing Lenin's similar attack, in *Materialism and Empirio-Criticism*, on relativity physics, and it may be that he is as wrong as Lenin proved to be in that case. I am not competent to judge, and in fact am able to follow the latter half of the book only with difficulty. The book seems extraordinarily well-informed, and Levy, who is professor of mathematics at the Imperial College of Science and Technology in London, praises it highly in the introduction and credits Caudwell with "a combined social and scientific understanding that would be rare in a scientist of mature experience; to find them in this young man is almost phenomenal." How the book impresses non-Marxist physicists I do not know.

The third volume published posthumously was *Poems*, brought out in 1939 with an unsigned biographical introduction. It seems to contain only a small selection of the poems Caudwell left in manuscript, but from it it is easy to see why Caudwell permitted only one poem to be published in his lifetime. The poetry is satiric, ideational, markedly informed by psychoanalysis, very derivative in style (particularly from the Metaphysicals), and although often lyric and always extremely talented, obviously the work of a poet not yet formed. There is not much doubt, however, that Caudwell would have lived to become a serious poet, assuming that like Hopkins, who also gave up writing poetry at his conversion, he would eventually have repudiated the decision and returned to poetry in his new terms.

Caudwell's short stories, of which he seems to have written a great many, "in the manner of Kafka," have never been published, and one can only conjecture from that fascinating description in the biographical notes what they are like.

When *Illusion and Reality* appeared, it went almost entirely unnoticed not only in America but in England. Horace Gregory and W. H. Auden reviewed it favorably, Gregory rather pointlessly comparing it to T. E. Hulme's *Speculations* on the strength of the fact that both Hulme and Caudwell died prematurely in wars. John Gould Fletcher reviewed it with high praise in *Poetry*, October 1938, calling it "the most considerable attempt to equate the production of poetry to the forms of society" that he had read, "in a far higher sphere" than such journalism as Granville Hicks's *Great Tradition*, and found it clear-thinking, original, and honest, with the chapter relating science and art particularly brilliant. A year later Arthur Mizener reviewed it unfavorably in an omnibus review with other criticism in the *Southern Review*, attacking the book sharply on a number of general theoretical points and dismissing all its specific judgments of poetry. That was all. I am informed that the English reviews, which I did not follow, were neither fuller nor more adequate. The only one I have seen, H. A. Mason's in *Scrutiny*, March 1938, is a bitter categorical attack, completely imperceptive.

The first Marxist use of the book in England came in 1941, when George Thomson's *Æschylus and Athens* appeared, very much influenced by Caudwell, and acknowledging indebtedness for his general theoretical framework to Lewis Morgan's *Ancient Society*, Engels's *Origin of the Family*, and *Illusion and Reality*. Later an article by Douglas Garman, which I have not seen, appeared in the *Left Review*. No American Marxist periodical mentioned Caudwell or the book, for what reason I cannot imagine, until 1945, when *New Masses* printed an article by Louis Harap, entitled "Christopher Caudwell, Critic," in the issue of November 20. Harap more or less confined himself to giving a précis of *Illusion and Reality* and tentatively suggesting its great importance. He followed it up with an article "Christopher Caudwell: Marxist Critic, Poet and Soldier" in the *Worker*, November 24, 1946, giving a biographical account (to which I am indebted for almost all of my factual information)[2] and discussing Caudwell's other books and writings. Both pieces succeeded in stimulating and channeling a rapidly growing interest in Caudwell. At the same time George Thomson's pamphlet *Marxism and Poetry*, which appeared in England in 1945 and in America in 1946, attempted to popularize Caudwell, and the resulting discussion in the Marxist press revealed that by then it was largely an unnecessary labor.

Except for Thomson, however, no critic has yet shown the influence of Caudwell on his own work, or continued his most fruitful line, the study of the social relations of literary *forms*, and I am aware of only a handful of mentions of *Illusion and Reality* in works of criticism in the decade since its publication. Of these, only William York Tindall's in *Forces in Modern British Literature* approaches adequacy, only Tindall seems to be aware that Caudwell wrote any other books than *Illusion and Reality*, and even he seems to think of him as an interesting minor figure, as his bracketing of "Caudwell and Orwell" makes clear. Early in 1946, with the revival of the British Marxist magazine the *Modern Quarterly* under new editorship, the Caudwell movement found an outlet in England. Almost every contributor to the magazine uses and quotes *Illusion and Reality* and *Studies in a Dying Culture*, attempts to apply Caudwell's concepts, and praises his "uniquely acute analytical mind" or his "sensitive, penetrating and constructive analysis of contemporary literary and art problems." Even the Communist political paper *World News and Views*, in the issue of February 15, 1947, devoted a good-sized article

[2] Mr. Harap is not responsible, however, for my opinions.

by Hyman Frankel to celebrating the tenth anniversary of Caudwell's death, calling him a "genius" and discussing his theoretical works in some detail. As a result of this wave of recognition, finally past the word-of-mouth stage, *Illusion and Reality* (which, like all of Caudwell's books, had been extremely scarce and fetched a prohibitive price in second-hand bookshops when it could be found at all) has been reissued by Lawrence & Wishart, London, and International Publishers, New York, with a biographical note by George Thomson and, finally, an index, and *Studies in a Dying Culture* has been announced for reissue. Assuming that *The Crisis in Physics* will also be back in print in England soon, and that some of the tentative plans to reprint these books in America materialize, it is to be hoped that the movement will not stop there. The interest should inevitably broaden enough to warrant reprinting *This My Hand* and the *Poems* and compiling a sixth volume of the remaining unprinted poetry, the short stories, and any fugitive critical or political pieces Caudwell may have left. If Caudwell is finally to receive belated recognition as the most genuinely important Marxist cultural thinker of our time, it is essential that his work be available, even that part of it which antedates his conversion to Marxism. If, on the other hand, he is to remain the cult of the relative few who have so far discovered him, even a cult needs more ikons than currently circulate.

2

Illusion and Reality, which is significantly subtitled, not "A Study of Poetry," but *A Study of* the Sources *of Poetry*, sets out to be a Marxist work by definition, an exploration of the roots of poetry in the social life of man. The first three chapters are introductory, a discussion of the relations of poetry in general to production, beginning with a conjecture as to its ancient origins in the collective poem-song-dance of primitive harvest ritual. The next three chapters are a detailed study of the specific relationship of English poets, from Tudor times to the present, to economic and social development. This analysis is summed up and made graphic in what is probably the best single thing in the book, a remarkable six-page chart entitled "The Movement of Bourgeois Poetry." In one column Caudwell lists the economic stage and its dates, in another the general characteristics of the accompanying literature, and in the third the specific formal characteristics of that literature. Thus a typical entry, for "Primitive Accumulation, 1550–1600," is:

General Characteristics

The Elizabethan Age.—Marlowe, Shakespeare. The dynamic force of individuality, realizing itself by smashing all outward forms, is expressed in poetry. Its characteristic hero is the absolute prince, with his splendid public life, which is collective and through which other individualities can therefore realise themselves without negating his.

Technical Characteristics

(a) The iambic rhythm, expressing the heroic nature of the bourgeois illusion in terms of the ancient world, is allowed to flow luxuriantly and naturally; it indicates the free and boundless development of the personal will. It is collective—adapted for declamation; noble—suitable to princely diction; flexible—because the whole life of the prince, even to its intimacies, is lived in easy openness.
(b) The lyrics are suitable for group singing (simple metres) but courtly (ornamental stanzas) and polished (bright conceits).

Caudwell does a comparable job of relating the verse of Milton to the Bourgeois Revolt, Pope to the Era of Mercantilism and Manufacture, the Victorians to the Decline of British Capitalism, and so on. The chart alone seems somewhat overschematic and arbitrary, but as amplified in the text, with separate studies of the principal writers of each period, its society-style correlations come through as more than persuasive.

The second half of the book is a discussion of poetry in general; its nature, characteristics, relation to science and other arts, and its future. The last chapter is a manifesto for the revolution that will free poetry from its bourgeois fetters and restore its earlier glory. The central emphasis of this section, as of the whole book, is naturally Marxism, but in the course of his discussion of poetry Caudwell draws upon almost every science, discipline, or body of theory. The theoretical justification for this is his belief, shared by Marx and Engels and taken seriously by only a few contemporary Marxists, that Marxism is a framework able to accommodate and utilize in dialectic interplay the most advanced thought in any field. He writes in the Introduction:

> But physics, anthropology, history, biology, philosophy and psychology are also products of society, and therefore a sound sociology would enable the art critic to employ criteria drawn from these fields without falling into eclecticism or confusing art with psychology or politics. There is only one sound sociology which lays bare the general active relation of the ideological products of society with each other and with concrete living—historical materialism.

Some idea of the encyclopedic range of the mind and learning of this young man can be obtained from the book's bibliography of three hundred and fifty titles. It is one of the most remarkable bibliographies of recent times and, unlike many, seems to represent only books utilized directly or indirectly in the text, although it was difficult to check on this because of the absence of an index. A glance at the bibliography, which is almost a catalogue of the best of twentieth-century thought, is instructive. In his own area Caudwell uses not only classics like Marx and Engels, but a wide miscellany of Marxist writers from Plekhanov to T. A. Jackson and Emile Burns. Even more extensive are his readings in psychology and anthropology. His psychologists include: Freud, Jung, Adler, and great masses of their followers; Koffka and Köhler; pre-Freudian classics like William James and Morton Prince; Jaensch, Kretschmer, Sherrington, Watson, Pavlov, MacCurdy, Wundt, Ribot, Piaget, McDougall, Rivers, and innumerable others (the only gaps would seem to be lesser Freudian rebels like Stekel and Rank, and the Freudian social revisionists). His readings in anthropology are equally extensive: Morgan and Frazer; field workers like Seligman, Malinowski, Skeat, Codrington, Mead, Fortune, and Wissler; theoreticians and compilers like Crawley, Van Gennep, Lévy-Bruhl, Westermarck, Benedict, Kroeber, Lowie, Atkinson, and Marett; psychoanalytic anthropologists like Róheim and Money-Kyrle, and any number of others (Tylor and Boas are curious omissions). In addition, tirelessly, he draws on philosophers like Dewey, Russell, Bergson, Wittgenstein, Whitehead, and Cassirer; physical scientists like Bridgman, Planck, Eddington, and Jeans; historians like Breasted, Mommsen, and Spengler; aestheticians like Bell, Hirn, and Croce; students of language like Sapir, Jesperson, Sayce, and Paget; and innumerable biologists, geneticists, Egyptologists, community-planners, theologians, industrial historians, Orientalists, economists, mathematicians, and specialists in almost every other branch of knowledge known to man. The only omission, understandable (rather than defensible) in terms of his faith in Marxism as "the only sound sociology," is of other modern sociologies; Durkheim, Tawney, and minor figures like Hobhouse and the Webbs are represented, but no Pareto, no Mannheim, no Weber, no Sombart, no Park, Ward, or Lynd; not even Herbert Spencer is included (although Darwin is). Adam Smith is listed, but not Veblen.

The purely literary figures in Caudwell's bibliography are not numerous, since he has not included the volumes of poetry he deals with as his subject. There is not much besides Plato and Aristotle; a few poets writing on their art, like Sidney, Coleridge, Wordsworth, and Shelley; and a few contemporary scholars and critics, like Gosse and Saintsbury, Praz and de Gourmont, Eliot and Hulme, Richards and Empson. He has relied heavily, however, on the ritual scholars and folklorists: Lang and Hartland, Murray, Cornford, Miss Harrison, and Miss Weston.

Caudwell is much less respectful toward critics and literary thinkers than he is toward his scientists of various sorts, and all his theorists on literature, including Plato ("such reactionary or Fascist philosophies as Plato's are always accompanied by a denial of culture"), are treated very cavalierly, with the exception of Aristotle. Caudwell affirms the greatness of Aristotle's views of literature, correctly centers them on the basic conceptions of *mimesis* and *catharsis*, and claims Aristotle as the ancestor of his study of the social functions of poetry, (although insisting that terms extending *mimesis* are necessary in order to distinguish forms of literature that have arisen since Aristotle, like the novel and the prose play).

As the easy dismissal of Plato reveals, Caudwell frequently falls into the common Marxist foolishness of using Marx or political criteria as clubs with which to beat literature rather than as tools with which to understand it. What saves him in most cases is a genuine love for poetry and concern for æsthetic values rather than anything in his method. His introduction confesses this fondness in about as backhanded a fashion as can be imagined. He writes:

> Although the other arts are discussed in their general relation to society, it was thought better to concentrate primarily on one particular art, that of poetry, because its ancient history and somewhat obsolescent appearance today raises [*sic*] crucial problems for the student of æsthetics, while, in addition, the fact that it was the art most attractive to the writer gave him a special interest in the task.

The combination of Caudwell's Marxist method and his genuine concern with poetry leads him to a number of insights that are genuine contributions to critical knowledge. He knows, for example, as Eliot does not, why the great poetic drama died with Webster and Tourneur and is not revivable as a living art form in our day: that it was a collective form depending on a collective feudal institution, the court, and died with it (just as Shakespeare could not write plays at Stratford, apart from it). Recognizing that his general picture of the poetic situation at any given time does not cover all the cases, for special cases he introduces the concept of the poetic "pocket," or area sheltered from contemporary social development, like Hardy's "country" and Housman's Cambridge. Caudwell is best at correcting the oversimplifications and reductions of non-Marxist thinkers, noting that the Œdipus complex explains everything about *Hamlet* but its greatness, or that Frazer's god-king acts as though he had worked out the idea of god-kings for himself in the act of seizing power.

Caudwell produces his own oversimplifications, reductions, and distortions, however. He is apt at any time to make a parody Marxist reading unintentionally, like Caliban "the bestial serf" and Ariel "the free wage-labourer," or to build a pyramid of jargon, like the statement about Pope (whom he happens to like) that he "perfectly expresses the ideals of the bourgeois class in alliance with a bourgeoisified aristocracy in the epoch of manufacture." Imagining this as a description of any of Pope's poems exposes its essential pomposity. The great fault of the book, in fact, is that it talks about specific poems so little. Very few lines of poetry are quoted; one or two on an occasional page, and the shock of five full lines of Apollinaire on page 294. Despite Caudwell's reasonable disclaimer that he is writing a study of the sources of poetry—that is, men in society—rather than a study of poetic texts, all his points would have been much improved with specific poetic examples.

Despite Caudwell's contempt for Plato, the whole of *Illusion and Reality* is organized around a central Platonic "myth." Plato's account of the origin of the sexes given in *The Symposium* is the myth of their being splittings of an original whole, thus explaining love as a yearning to be reunited in the original unity, or, as Aristophanes explains it to the company, "so ancient is the desire of one another that is implanted in us, reuniting our original nature, making one of two, and healing the state of man." Caudwell's "myth" for the origin of poetry is almost identical, except that his is the original unity of poetry and production, with each now wandering around lost without the other. He begins with the concept of a common primitive origin of the arts in a unity of dance, poetry, and music, admitting that it is too sweeping a hypothesis "to be capable of rigorous proof." The function of this ancestral art was to make the crops grow in the most literal sense, to persuade the primitive to sow (a procedure otherwise senseless to him—throwing away good food in the ground) by dramatizing the harvest to him. Poetry thus bridges the time-lag between cause and effect that is beyond primitive comprehension, promotes the sowing with a "phantasy" of the harvest, and thus eventually produces the real harvest, bringing Reality out of Illusion (it is only fair to point out that this paraphrase considerably vulgarizes Caudwell's careful and persuasive theory).

For Caudwell, poetry is thus born out of economics; springing into being indissolvably tied to production, in which it finds its function and its justification. He then interprets the whole history of bourgeois poetry in terms of this mythic primitive relation, its rupture, and the consequent alienation and sense of being functionless in the poet, to be solved when socialism shall have reunited poetry and production. The mind of any poet, as well as the characteristics of his poetry, will thus be primarily the results of the distance from productive function in which his art stands in his time, modified by the false social relationships that arise to fill the lack. (He does not go so far as to say, as Alick West does in *Crisis and Criticism:* "The basis of the value of literature is the relation of the writer to this productive activity.") Although the primitive unity of the myth, in which the individual is both worker and poet, singing the harvest and digging for it, is no longer recoverable because of the division of labor, Caudwell sees socialism as the force that will reunite the broken halves, bringing the poet, if not back into the worker's body, at least into a vital functional relationship with him. (This would be something like the status of the medieval craftsman, or the early Soviet doctrine of the "social command," as described by Mayakovsky in "How One Writes a Poem," in which the community simply tells the poet what it needs written, like a satiric quatrain to help the Red Guards drive Yudenich out of Petrograd.)

The myth of the poet severed from productive function is only one of the two central themes of *Illusion and Reality*. The other is Spinoza's deterministic doctrine of freedom as the acceptance of necessity, paraphrased and made less pessimistic by Engels as "Freedom is the recognition of necessity," which Caudwell uses as the epigraph for the book. Kenneth Burke has claimed that a book is one sentence indefinitely expanded (a good book, that is; a poor book would be *nothing* indefinitely expanded, and a great or important book a *new* sentence indefinitely expanded). If so, that epigraph is Caudwell's sentence. It is the core of his philosophic view and the theoretical basis of all his literary evaluations. His criticism of surrealism, for example, is that its free associations, far from being really free, are more compulsive than ordinary rational associations, as psychoanalysis has shown. He writes:

> In rational association images are controlled by a social experience of reality—the consciousness of necessity. In free association the images are controlled by the iron hand of the unconscious instincts—and it is therefore no more free than the "thinking" of the ant. Man becomes free not by realising himself in opposition to society but by realising himself through society, and the character of the association itself imposes certain common forms and conventions which are the badge of his freedom. But because the *surréaliste* is a bourgeois and has lost control of his social relationships, he believes freedom to consist in revolting against these forms whereby freedom has been realised in the past.

Caudwell defines this conviction as "the classic bourgeois illusion that freedom is the ignorance of necessity" and, after making it and the Marxist counter-view the theme of the book, devotes *Studies in a Dying Culture* to an even more extensive exploration of the problem. Each of the studies is a restatement of these opposed concepts of freedom, and the chapter on T. E. Lawrence illustrates them with Caudwell's classic analogy of chicken-carving:

> But, just as a man can only carve a chicken properly if he knows where the joints are, and follows them, so a hero dominates events only because he conforms closely with the law that produces them. The man masterfully carving a chicken therefore corresponds also to the Tolstoyan conception of the hero as a man who is really a slave to circumstances. There is only one way of carving a chicken perfectly, and therefore the man who completely dominates the chicken by carving it perfectly is also completely dominated by it in that he has to follow its anatomy slavishly. But all the same it ends by being carved up.

To this Marxist carver Caudwell would oppose the Rousseauesque carver, perfectly free to hack at the chicken anywhere, fruitlessly. In his introduction John Strachey describes the book as "the analysis, from every angle, of the concept of human liberty," and in it Caudwell affirms liberty as "the most important of all generalized goods—such as justice, beauty, truth—that come so easily to our lips." In that deterministic sense *Illusion and Reality* might be described as the analysis of poetic liberty (as distinguished from poetic license, which would be the Rousseauesque opposite), arising out of the recognition of external necessity in society and internal necessity in form.

3

The sociological criticism of literature originated, like so much else, with the Greeks. Plato's *Republic* includes an exhaustive application of sociological criteria to literature, in terms of both its genesis and its function. Not only is poetry propaganda, he proclaimed, but the greater the poetic charm, the greater the propaganda danger, and he fittingly banned all but types of art he considered useful or harmless from his ideal state. Aristotle's concept of the social origins and function of art was, like Plato's, based on psychology, but since it was a different psychology, the catharsis of passion versus the stimulation of passion, it resulted in a very different social view. Horace continued Aristotle's functional view, but made it ethical and legal rather than psychological and reduced form to no more than a sugar-coating for functional content, so that it was originally the function of the poet to "set the bounds of public and private property, and the limits of the sacred and the secular, to prohibit promiscuous concubinage, and found the rite of marriage; to establish the civic order and record the laws: it was in these performances that the honor and renown of the divine bards and poems came into being." In the Renaissance the classical view of the social origin and function of poetry was revived. Lodge, in his *Defence of Poetry* against Gosson's *School of Abuse*, quotes approvingly the theory of "Donate the gramarian" that tragedy and comedy were invented as ways of praising God for a good harvest or a fruitful year. The Puritans, represented by Gosson, were as eager to establish the social function of poetry, but, like Plato, to establish it as harmful. The classical view survived as late as Shelley's *Defense of Poetry* in 1824, which not only defines the poet as the "unacknowledged legislator" of mankind, but gives a rather dubious anthropological theory for the origin of poetry in savage attempts at social communication.

Modern sociological criticism of literature more or less begins in the eighteenth century with Vico, who explains authors in terms of their historical conditions in the *New Science*, and continues in Herder's view of literature as primarily the product of national and temporal conditions. In England at about the same time relative social criteria began to be applied to literature, particularly to the "barbarous" work of Shakespeare, by critics like Pope and Dr. Johnson, and Warburton and Bishop Hurd came out for a complete historical relativism, the latter arguing that Gothic architecture must be judged by Gothic standards and no other and analyzing romance literature in terms of feudal society and chivalric life. The great line of sociological criticism, however, developed in France, from Montesquieu, through Madame de Staël's *Literature in Relation to Social Institutions,* to the historical criticism of Michelet and Renan. In Sainte-Beuve it became an important literary criticism, but with personal and biographical elements emphasized more than the social, and in Sainte-Beuve's disciple, H. A. Taine, finally emerged as full-fledged modern sociological criticism.

Taine's *History of English Literature,* published in 1864, is still the best history of English literature we have, an almost miraculous feat for a foreign critic. It studies English literature as the result of changing English society, the product of race, epoch, and environment. At times it is almost a class analysis, with Robin Hood a poetry of the yeoman class, Burke a literary representative of the "natural landed interests," Addison a spokesman for the new bourgeoisie, and so on. The literary judgments are sometimes off, particularly in the sort of English author difficult for foreigners to handle, like Skelton and Donne (the latter "of terrible crudeness"), and Taine doesn't understand Shakespeare very well, vastly underrates Coleridge, and dismisses out of hand the whole English classical tradition. His picture generally, however, is so learned, so sensitive to poetic nuance, and so full of insights and sharp perceptions (he sees Tudor architecture, for example, as the giving up of fortresses) that it more than outweighs the deficiencies. Taine's *History of English Literature* remains to this day the great triumph of sociological criticism, and he showed in his *Balzac* that the method is just as valuable used intensively on one writer as it is in literary history, reading the *Human Comedy* as the bourgeois heroic epic with a complete sensitivity to both its social implications and its literary values.

The great continuers of Taine's tradition of socio-æsthetic literary history were Francesco de Sanctis, whose *History of Italian Literature* appeared in 1870, and Georg Brandes, the Danish critic, whose monumental *Main Currents in Nineteenth-Century Literature* began appearing in 1872. Both, like Taine, were liberal or radical in sympathy, romantic, class-conscious, rationalistic, deterministic, and enamored of science; and both had, in addition, Taine's deep sensitivity to literature, which enabled them to avoid mechanical pigeonholing and evade the rigid determinism of their own concepts. De Sanctis's book (although difficult for anyone substantially ignorant of Italian literature to judge) is a large-scale picture of Italian literature as an expression of the Italian people, and its insistence on the importance of æsthetic form and the relation between form, rather than content, and social conditions make it a very important work. Brandes's great book is an intensive coverage of the first half of the nineteenth century in French, German, and English literature. Although Brandes's class analysis is sharper than either Taine's or de Sanctis's and he quotes specific texts a good deal less than Taine, his æsthetic and formal perception is fully as deep as that of either. Like Taine, Brandes carried the method into full-length individual studies, including books on Goethe, Shakespeare, Nietzsche, Voltaire, and a number of others, in each case exhaustively relating the man to his society without losing either him or the work as individual and unique values.

Non-Marxist sociological criticism in America has not been a very substantial movement. Its only major work is Parrington's *Main Currents in American Thought*, which drew largely on Taine, Brandes, and the economic determinism of J. Allen Smith, but also made liberal use of Marxist insights (most of them unidentified). Besides Parrington and Van Wyck Brooks and his school (both discussed above) the most important American sociological criticism is probably that of John Macy. Macy's first book, *The Spirit of American Literature*, published as long ago as 1908, is the application of social criteria, including a good deal of direct propaganda for socialism, to the major figures of American literature, but in terms of economic and social debunking (literature is "the expression of outworn states of society") rather than Marxist analysis. Macy made little or no use of Marxist concepts, and his second book, *The Critical Game*, made it clear that he was a Socialist whose critical mentors were Poe, Tolstoy, and Remy de Gourmont (the last "the greatest critic that has been born"). His only other book, *The Story of the World's Literature*, is a tasteless and ignorant hack job in the Van Loon tradition, requiring no discussion.

Randolph Bourne continued the Macy tradition of independent radical criticism, drawing on native sources like Veblen, but his work was much more aware of Marx; and *The History of a Literary Radical* and essays in *Untimely Papers* (particularly a class analysis of morals) make it pretty certain that he would have emerged as a Marxist critic had he lived. His revival of the nineteenth-century theory of the book review as "an independent inquiry," in which the reviewer turns up his own information and develops his own views on the subject, restored one of the most fruitful methods possible for sociological criticism (Marx and Engels had jointly used it), but it faded out again as an idea after Bourne's death for the good reason that it demanded more of the critic than almost any of our contemporary sociological or Marxist critics have.

Another American sociological critic who did not live long enough to fulfill his promise was T. K. Whipple, who died in 1939 in his forties. He had lived long enough, however, to progress from a marked indebtedness to Brooks in his first non-academic book, *Spokesmen*, in 1928, to a clear-headed and independent Marxism in his second, *Study Out the Land*, published posthumously in 1943. *Spokesmen* deals with contemporary American writers in terms of the Brooks thesis of the artist truncated by society, but the pieces in *Study Out the Land* are a genuine attempt, not to assign truncations *a priori* to writers, but to study calmly and analytically the complex web of relationship between a work of art and society. (Even when using a wholly pejorative term like Michael Gold's "fascist unconscious," Whipple remakes it as a term of objective social description.) With the conversion of Whipple some time in the thirties, with Bourne and Parrington dead and Macy retired, the last possibility of a non-Marxist American sociological criticism disappeared. From then on, either American sociological criticism was Marxist or it was nothing. In the case of Brooks and his school it was nothing.

Little contemporary literary criticism has attempted to use any formal sociology other than Marxism. L. C. Knights (discussed below) has drawn heavily on Tawney, as well as on Weber, Sombart, and others, in *Drama and Society in the Age of Jonson*. The contemporary German critic Levin L. Schücking published *The Sociology of Literary Taste* in 1931, apparently influenced by both Mannheim and Weber, but rather than an actual sociology it is only the barest sketch for a proposed science. Although it asks some of the questions about the determinants of literary popularity, it has none of the answers. *Toward a Critique of the Popular* would be a much more apt title, and what warrant the book has to discussion is in connection with I. A. Richards's critical analysis of reader-reaction (discussed below).

The Marxist criticism of literature begins, naturally enough, with Karl Marx, although he himself wrote comparatively little specifically on literature.[3] Its theoretical basis is the relationship of literature to society defined by Marx in the Introduction to the *Critique of Political Economy:*

> In the social production of their means of existence men enter into definite, necessary relations that are independent of their will, productive relationships that correspond to a definite stage of development of their material productive forces. The aggregate of these productive relationships constitutes the economic structure of so-

[3] All but a few of the writings of Marx and Engels referred to below, as well as much additional material, are now available, in better and smoother translation, in *Literature and Art*, an anthology of selections from the writings of Marx and Engels, published by International Publishers in 1947. Although it contains many of the important documents, the book is much skimpier than such equivalents as Lifschitz's 800-page job in Russian, and the publishers announce an additional volume in preparation.

ciety, the real basis on which a juridical and political superstructure arises, and to which definite forms of social consciousness correspond. The mode of production of the material means of existence conditions the whole process of social, political, and intellectual life. It is not the consciousness of men that determines their existence, but, on the contrary, it is their social existence that determines their consciousness.

Literature, then, like the rest of culture, is a superstructure of social consciousness erected on productive relationships. However, as Marx points out elsewhere, like the rest of culture, through dialectical interaction it then modifies and conditions productive relationships.

Little of Marx's writing directly discusses literature. He quotes Sophocles (in Greek), Balzac, Dante, and *Timon of Athens* in *Capital*, but only their attacks on the evils of money. He discusses "literature" in Section III of the *Communist Manifesto*, but it turns out to be the "literature" of Socialist pamphleteering. The Introduction to the *Critique of Political Economy* discusses Greek art, literature, and mythology, but in no real detail. Marx's most detailed critical writing is probably *The Holy Family*, a discussion of speculative æsthetics, including lengthy analysis of Eugène Sue's *The Mysteries of Paris*. In it Marx defines the worst feature of bourgeois writing as tendentiousness ("Romanticism is always tendentious poetry," he had written in an article), resulting from an idealistic attitude toward reality, which transforms living characters into automata designed to prove the author's abstract ideas. In an unfinished manuscript, *Political Economy and Philosophy* (written in 1844, when Marx was just on the verge of Communism; not published until 1932, and not yet translated into English), Marx quotes passages from *Timon* and analyzes them at great length and with remarkable subtlety, but again only as insights into the power of money. Marx wrote a number of lengthy book reviews in collaboration with Engels, including a scorching study of Carlyle ("the whip imagines that it has become full of genius") that shows a real sense of literary craft in its comments on his style. It is hard to say how much of these productions is Marx's, however, and except that the sarcasm is more bitter, they very much resemble Engels's independent reviews. Most of Marx's direct references to literature are asides in books or articles on other subjects, or come in personal letters, mostly to Engels. He sent Engels a copy of Diderot's *Rameau's Nephew*, describing it as a "unique masterpiece" (Freud, incidentally, also thought very highly of it); wrote him about "good old Heine," about his furious dislike of Chateaubriand's work, about a Russian writer named Flerowsky he had discovered; advised him to read "two little masterpieces" by Balzac; and so forth. One of Marx's most detailed criticisms of literary technique occurs in a letter to Ferdinand

Lassalle, commenting on the latter's play *Franz von Sickingen*; and one of Marx's most brilliant literary observations, that the French classical dramatists did not so much misunderstand the Aristotelian unities as understand them "in accordance with their own art needs," also occurs in a letter to Lassalle. With the addition of a comment to his daughter on Shelley as a truer revolutionary than Byron, a few brief remarks in his work on the subjects of style, beauty, and literary movements in England and Germany, these constitute just about all of Marx's writing directly concerned with literature.

Marx was tremendously well read (although he and Engels were hardly, as Earl Browder once announced, "the two most cultured men of history"), and his taste was surprising for that of an active politician. Paul Lafargue, his son-in-law, reports that he considered Æschylus and Shakespeare "the two greatest dramatic geniuses of all time," that he read Æschylus every year in the Greek and had studied Shakespeare exhaustively and seen to it that his three daughters knew him by heart, and that he was a great reader of novels. "He liked above all those of the eighteenth century, and especially Fielding's *Tom Jones*. The modern authors who tempted him most were Paul de Kock, Charles Lever, Alexandre Dumas, and Walter Scott. . . . His favorite novelists were Cervantes and Balzac." Franz Mehring, his biographer, adds: "In his literary judgments he was completely free of all political and social prejudices." He also thought highly of Goethe, Lessing, Homer, and Dante; learned Russian in order to be able to read Russian literature in the original, particularly Pushkin; and learned Spanish in order to be able to read Calderon and other classics. In his youth he had been a romantic poet (not a very good one), and when he and Engels, who both loved Heine's work, were disturbed by Heine's political foibles, he reminded Engels that we could not demand of poets what we demand of ordinary people.

Nevertheless, in his youth as a disciple of Hegel he had acquired the Hegelian doctrine of the inevitable decadence of art in modern times, as an inferior way of freeing the spirit, better suited to the childhood of mankind. This idea stayed with him, unconsciously transformed into a concept of the inevitable decadence of art under capitalism. "Capitalist production is hostile to certain branches of spiritual production, such as art and poetry," he wrote, and his bitterest fury was reserved for the bourgeois view of art as a commodity. One of the charges against the bourgeoisie in the *Communist Manifesto* is that it has converted poets into "paid wage laborers," and Marx writes in an ironic article: "even the highest forms of spiritual production are recognized and forgiven by the bourgeoisie" because they represent wealth. As bourgeois civilization progresses, Marx felt, art must inevitably decay, and the artist comes to think of his work as a means, or a trade, rather than a sacred end. Nevertheless, in the classless society, with the disparity between social and artistic development removed, and the emphasis taken off specialization, art could again flower naturally as it had in the primitive past. "In a communist organization of society there are no painters," he and Engels wrote in *The German Ideology*; "at most there are people who, among other things, also paint."

At the same time Marx carefully avoided the suggestion of a too simple correspondence between art and social relations. Along with his statement of the relations between the two in the Introduction to the *Critique of Political Economy*, he includes a number of important demurrers, writing:

> It is well known that certain periods of highest development of art stand in no direct connection with the general development of society, or with the material basis and the skeleton structure of its organization. Witness the example of the Greeks as compared with the modern nations or even Shakespeare.

And this art then goes beyond its social relations. Marx adds:

> The difficulty is not in grasping the idea that Greek art and epos are bound up with certain forms of social development. It rather lies in understanding why they still constitute with us a source of æsthetic enjoyment and in certain respects prevail as the standard and model beyond attainment.

It was in this sense of great art transcending both the limitations of its social origins and the artist's views that Marx thought so highly of Balzac, who in terms of the decadence of bourgeois art and his own monarchical-Catholic-reactionary beliefs should have been detestable to Marx. In *Capital* and in his correspondence enthusiastic references to Balzac are frequent, and Lafargue reports that "he proposed to write a critical work on *La Comédie Humaine* when he had finished his economic work." His economic work was never finished, and this book on Balzac, which might have been the Marxist æsthetic to prevent, if only by authority, nine tenths of the idiocy of later Marxists, was never written.

Marx's co-worker, Frederick Engels, not only wrote more specifically on the dangers of oversimple sociological analyses, but devoted the most famous of these warnings, the 1888 letter in English to Margaret Harkness, to the topic of Balzac. He wrote:

> Balzac, whom I consider a far greater master of realism than all the Zolas, past, present or future, gives us in his *Comédie Humaine*, a most wonderfully realistic history of French "society," describing, chronicle-fashion, almost year by year from 1816 to 1848, the ever-increasing pressure of the rising bourgeoisie upon the society of nobles that established itself after 1815 and that set up again, as far

as it could (*tant bien que mal*), the standard of the *vieille politique française*. He describes how the last remnants of this, to him, model society gradually succumbed before the intrusion of the vulgar money upstart or was corrupted by him. How the *grande dame*, whose conjugal infidelities were but a mode of asserting herself, in perfect accord with the way she had been disposed of in marriage, gave way to the bourgeois, who acquired her husband for cash or costumes; and around this central picture he groups a complete history of French society from which, even in economic details (for instance, the rearrangement of real and private property after the French Revolution) I have learnt more than from all the professional historians, economists and statisticians of the period together. Well, Balzac was politically a legitimist; his great work is a constant elegy on the irreparable decay of good society; his sympathies are with the class that is doomed to extinction. But for all that his satire is never keener, his irony never bitterer, than when he sets in motion the very men and women with whom he sympathizes most deeply— the nobles. And the only men of whom he speaks with undisguised admiration are his bitterest political antagonists, the republican heroes of the Cloître Saint-Merri, the men who at that time (1830– 1836) were indeed the representatives of the popular masses. That Balzac was thus compelled to go against his own class sympathies and political prejudices, that he saw the necessity of the downfall of his favorite nobles and described them as people deserving no better fate; that he saw the real men of the future where, for the time being, they alone were to be found—that I consider one of the greatest triumphs of realism, and one of the greatest features in old Balzac.

As violently as Marx, Engels opposed mechanical tendentiousness in literature. "The more the opinions of a writer remain hidden, the better for the work of art," he wrote in the Harkness letter, and in a letter to Minna Kautsky:

> I am by no means an opponent of tendentious poetry as such. The father of tragedy, Æschylus, and the father of comedy, Aristophanes, were both very clearly poets with a thesis, as were Dante and Cervantes. . . . But I believe that the thesis must inhere in the situation and action, without being explicitly formulated, and it is not the poet's duty to supply the reader in advance with the future historical solution of the conflict he describes.

Most of Engels's writings on literature are attacks against "vulgar sociology," in defense of æsthetic values.[4] His *Anti-Dühring* includes

---

[4] Engels illustrated this admirably in his own work on such occasions as his acceptance, in *The Origin of the Family*, of Bachofen's brilliant reading of the *Oresteia*

violent sarcastic abuse of Dühring's project for a "people's school of the future" purified of the humanities. He writes:

> As for the æsthetic side of education, Herr Dühring will have to fashion it all anew. The poetry of the past is worthless. Where all religion is prohibited, it goes without saying that the "mythological or other religious trimmings" characteristic of poets in the past cannot be tolerated in this school. "Poetic mysticism," too, "such as, for example, Goethe practiced so extensively" is to be condemned. Well, Herr Dühring will have to make up his mind to produce for us those poetic masterpieces which "are in accord with the higher claims of an imagination reconciled to reason," and which represent the pure ideal that "denotes the perfection of the world." Let him lose no time about it! The conquest of the world will be achieved by the economic commune only on that day when the latter, reconciled with reason, comes in at double time in Alexandrines.

His commentary on Goethe's ambivalence, his letter to Paul Ernst on Ibsen, his letter to Schlüter explaining that revolutionary poetry and song do not tend to be lasting art because they reflect "the momentary prejudices of the people," are all warnings against the easy politicalizing of literature. The Ibsen letter, chiding Ernst for his oversimple dismissal of Ibsen as a typical petty-bourgeois writer, is particularly interesting. First Engels warns that "the materialist method is converted into its direct opposite if instead of being used as a guiding thread in historical research it is made to serve as a ready-cut pattern on which to tailor historical facts." He then goes on to define the difference between the Norwegian petty bourgeoisie and the German; to point out that, petty-bourgeois or not, the Norwegian literary renaissance is important; and to conclude with the statement that whatever the weakness of Ibsen, his dramas reflect a real world of human beings "possessed of character and initiative and the capacity for independent action."

Engels proposed to Miss Harkness the depiction of "typical characters in typical circumstances," but it was characteristic of the skeptical and elastic-minded man who had written in the *Theses on Feuerbach* "that which is recognized now as true has also its latent false side which will later manifest itself, just as that which is now regarded as false has also its true side," not to believe that any rigid principle could be imposed on art. His final warning was the letter to J. Bloch in 1890. He wrote:

> According to the materialist conception of history the determining element in history is *ultimately* the production and reproduction in

---

of Æschylus as a conflict between "mother-right" and "father-right." Engels calls it "this new and undoubtedly correct interpretation" and "one of the best and finest passages in the whole book," despite his fundamental quarrel with it and Bachofen's work in general as philosophic idealism.

88 THE ARMED VISION

real life. More than this neither Marx nor I have ever asserted. If
therefore somebody twists this into the statement that the economic
element is the *only* determining one, he transforms it into a meaningless, abstract and absurd phrase. . . . Marx and I are partly to
blame for the fact that younger writers sometimes lay more stress
on the economic side than is due to it. We had to emphasize this
main principle in opposition to our adversaries, who denied it, and
we had not always the time, the place or the opportunity to allow the
other elements involved in the interaction to come into their rights.
But when it was a case of presenting a section of history, that is, of
a practical application, the thing was different and there no error was
possible. Unfortunately, however, it happens only too often that
people think they have fully understood a theory and can apply it
without more ado from the moment they have mastered its main
principles, and those even not always correctly. And I cannot exempt
many of the more recent "Marxists" from this reproach, for the
most wonderful rubbish has been produced from this quarter too.

After Marx and Engels the great theoretician of Marxist criticism is
George V. Plekhanov, the Russian. A typical and very influential
work is the essay *Art and Society*, written at the end of the last century,
in which he attacks the shifting relationship between art and society from
the viewpoint of historical relativism. He shows with abundant evidence
that art is always conceived of as utilitarian when "a mutual bond of
sympathy exists between a considerable section of society and those more
or less actively interested in artistic creation." The doctrine of art for
art's sake, on the other hand, with its consequent obscure and esoteric
forms, arises "when a hopeless contradiction exists between the artists
and their social environment." The most important feature of this historical relativism, and Plekhanov's major contribution to Marxist criticism, is the basic recognition that artists reflect their class and time, not
another class and time that Marxists would like them to reflect. He
writes:

I do not say that contemporary artists *must* seek inspiration in the
emancipatory movement of the proletariat. Not at all. Just as apple-
trees must give forth apples and pear-trees pears, so must artists
who share the bourgeois point of view struggle against this movement. The art of a decadent epoch *must* be decadent. This is inevitable and it would be futile to become indignant about it.

Plekhanov wrote a number of other works on literature and art, in-
cluding *French Drama and Painting of the Eighteenth Century*, *Historical
Materialism and the Arts*, his brilliant long essay "Ibsen, Petty Bourgeois
Revolutionist" in *Die Neue Zeit* (which perfectly illustrates his relativist

theories in *Art and Society*), and others. In addition, a number of his political writings deal extensively with the arts, particularly *The Role of the Individual in History*. In all of them, the depth of his historical and æsthetic knowledge, the relativism of his point of view, the unblinking honesty of his observation, and the power and flexibility of his mind gave Marxist criticism the soundest documentation and extension it had yet had. He was the first Marxist critic to study the relationship between social relations and artistic *form*, as in his discussion of Ibsen's abstract and symbolist forms in relation to the class basis of Scandinavian society. Plekhanov drew enthusiastically on the best of non-Marxist sociological criticism, Taine and Brandes, just as he anticipated the best of later Marxist criticism, particularly Caudwell, in his use of the most advanced scientific knowledge (in his day, chiefly anthropology), in his undogmatic relativism, in his insistence on the importance of the artist's *sense* of social function at any given time, and particularly in his vast love and respect for literature and art.

The other Marxist theoreticians, outside of Soviet Russia, have added little to Plekhanov in the application of Marxism to literature. Franz Mehring, Marx's biographer, has been called "the originator of historical materialist criticism" and of Marxist æsthetics, but the only critical works of his with which I am familiar, *The Lessing Legend* (1892), an article on Ibsen (written in 1900), and "A Note on Taste" (1898), which appeared in *Dialectics* 4, abstracted from a review of an obscure book, seem much more interested in literature as a reflection of political history than in political history as a clue to literature. One of the most important of Mehring's ideas, and one that he shared with Plekhanov, is the concept in "A Note on Taste" that there is an objective basis of taste, and that it lies in historical relativism. Rosa Luxemburg, another great German radical who was deeply sensitive to æsthetic values ("In a novel I don't look for the point of view, but primarily for its value as art"), wrote a good deal in her letters and articles about literature (including a wonderful criticism of the style of Marx's *Capital*, "overloaded with rococo ornaments"), but as far as I know contributed little of a theoretical nature. Of Georg Lukacs, the Hungarian, whom Slochower has called "possibly the keenest and most learned Marxist critic since Franz Mehring," I am familiar with too little work to be able to venture an opinion.

4

"The philosophers have only interpreted the world," Marx wrote in the *Theses on Feuerbach*; "our business is to change it." This turned out to be not quite so sound a principle when applied to literature by contemporary Marxist critics (only a few of whom, for lack of space, can be touched on here). In America it led chiefly to the straight political distortion represented by men like V. F. Calverton, Granville Hicks, and Michael Gold. Calverton, the first and worst of the local Marxist literary historians, published in 1932 *The Liberation of American Literature*, which tears through our literature slaughtering Emerson, Thoreau, Melville, and Hawthorne, to announce that Whitman was our first poet and Twain our first important prose writer, and the only important contemporary writers are the "exponents of the proletarian outlook": John Dos Passos, Michael Gold, and Charles Yale Harrison. Granville Hicks's *The Great Tradition*, published a year later, is the same sort of thing, mechanical class-anglings based on the political criteria of the 1930's rather than on those of his subjects' own time, culminating in the same pæan to writers like Dos Passos and Gold. If better informed and less nervy than Calverton's book, it is more given to cheap cracks like calling Faulkner "the Sax Rohmer of the sophisticated." Hicks's second book, *Figures of Transition*, a study of British literature at the end of the last century, is more modest and sensible but even less concerned with æsthetic values, and generally no improvement. Michael Gold has never written a book on literature, but the collections of his *Daily Worker* pieces, *Change the World* and *The Hollow Men*, make it clear that not only is he the most ignorant and provincial of all the Marxist critics, a heroic warrior against Gilbert and Sullivan, but probably the least adequate Marxist. He is rather a sentimental and idealistic bourgeois radical of an earlier century, and the picture of Marx's reaction to his passionate love for Rousseau, "the father of Democracy," or Eugène Sue's "epic melodrama to strengthen the heart and hand of the revolutionary workers" (which Marx put across the barrel in *The Holy Family* as cheap bourgeois romanticism) is interesting to contemplate. Other contemporary American Marxist log-rollers and strait-jacketers of literature include Joshua Kunitz and Joseph Freeman, prominent in the thirties, and Samuel Sillen and Samuel Putnam, prominent in the forties.

A much more important group of American critics, either Marxist or much influenced by Marxism, have combined sociological criteria with an appreciation of æsthetic values. The most distinguished work produced by this group, and probably the best book yet written about American literature, is F. O. Matthiessen's *American Renaissance*. Matthiessen deals with the work of only five writers—Emerson, Thoreau, Melville, Hawthorne, and Whitman—over a period of only five years, from 1850 to 1855. Nevertheless, his book is on so monumental a scale, with so much concern both for ideas in a social context (drawing on Marxist insights) and for detailed formal analysis (drawing on his own great literary learning, sensitivity, and fine taste) as to represent perfectly the amplification of Parrington he visualized. (It is amusing that Matthiessen, an admirer of the dialectic, should come to the method as a synthesis of his thesis—a sociologic, Brooksian study of Sarah Orne Jewett—and his antithesis—a relatively pure æsthetic study of T. S. Eliot. Matthiessen's subsequent book, a study of Henry James's last period tending to slight social criteria, would presumably be the new antithesis his new thesis provoked.) Newton Arvin's *Whitman* represents a similar combination of Marxist insights and æsthetic awareness, on a smaller scale, but almost as successful. Conceived frankly as a job of "scanning the . . . past for whatever resources there may be in it on which a socialist culture may draw," Arvin's book studies the political, social, and economic ideas in Whitman's poetry with honesty, literary awareness, and keen sensibility. A third critic, who combines æsthetic concern not only with Marxism but with psychoanalysis and a substantial philosophic background, is Harry Slochower. In his first book in English, *Three Ways of Modern Man*, Slochower explores the literary ramifications of three modern ideologies, Undset's "Feudal Socialism," Mann's "Bourgeois Liberalism," and Nexö's "Socialist Humanism," finding, as Marx did in the case of Balzac, that great art transcends its ideological bias, and proposing at the end a "tragic" synthesis of elements from all three. His next book, *Thomas Mann's Joseph Story*, is a more detailed study of a single text, with Slochower able to utilize his whole pluralist critical frame, with significant success; whereas his most recent work, *No Voice is Wholly Lost* . . . is a complementary attempt to cover almost the whole of contemporary literature, and the resulting tempo is so fast that, despite isolated brilliant insights, Slochower's integrative method never quite gets going.

Other critics who have at one time or another attempted to combine Marxist insights and some concern with literary form include: Edwin Berry Burgum in *The Novel and the World's Dilemma*; Bernard Smith in *Forces in American Criticism*; David Daiches in *New Literary Values, Literature and Society, The Novel and the Modern World*, and *Poetry and the Modern World*; Malcolm Cowley in *Exile's Return* and a number of uncollected articles and reviews; Isidor Schneider in a number of uncollected articles and reviews. A very few examples of Marxist or near-Marxist criticism of this sort by other writers can be found in *Science and Society* and *New Masses*.

Except under Communist auspices or influence, not much Marxist literary criticism has been written in America. *Partisan Review*, the chief literary organ of the anti-Stalin Left, has printed almost no Marxist or sociological criticism of literature since its first years, although it has printed a good deal of criticism otherwise useful (as well as a good deal of faddism, hobby-horse-riding, and simple spite). Meyer Schapiro and Harold Rosenberg have perhaps some closest to traditional Marxist historical criticism, although always on the verge of veering off into philosophy; William Troy has made brilliant use of Marxist insights within a larger integration; William Phillips and Philip Rahv, the principal editors, still retain occasional traces of Marxist analysis, although in recent years their critical work has become largely a kind of ethical nail-biting; and a number of the younger men, among them Delmore Schwartz, Randall Jarrell, and Robert Gorham Davis, have written excellent criticism in the magazine, making some use of political criteria (in Davis's case, effectively combined with psychoanalytic). The only *Partisan Review* critic who has so far published a Marxist æsthetic is James T. Farrell, in *A Note on Literary Criticism* in 1936. It begins with the apology that Farrell is an amateur critic and amateur Marxist, and then goes on to demonstrate it at some length, with Farrell demolishing the oversimplifications of critics like Hicks and Gold, to set up his own oversimplifications in their place. His volumes of collected pieces, *The League of Frightened Philistines* (1945) and *Literature and Morality* (1947), make it clear, in pieces like the study of Dreiser, that his deficiencies include an absolute want of ear (explaining his own execrable style) and a sentimentalism and naïveté vast enough to insulate him from most literature almost completely.

The picture of British Marxist criticism, with the exception of Caudwell, is about as bad as that of America. None of the straight political critics is as egregious as Calverton or Gold, and they are all much better read, but, on the other hand, none of the men combining Marxist insights with æsthetic concern has produced books of the caliber of *American Renaissance*. Of the first group, typical examples are John Strachey, Ralph Fox, and T. A. Jackson. Strachey, the first of them, in the "Decay of Capitalist Culture" section of *The Coming Struggle for Power* in 1933, showed instead only the decay of Marxist sensibility, misreading *The Waste Land*, reducing Proust to simple snobbery, fantastically overestimating Huxley and his "tragic view of life"; and in *Literature and Dialectical Materialism* in 1934 he projected his own sins of distortion and oversimplification on Granville Hicks as a scapegoat and killed them off (as Hicks was later to do, in his turn, with Parrington). Fox, in *The Novel and the People* in 1937, bent the history of English fiction to the slogan of "socialist realism," and as De Voto does, from another point of view, assigned "epic" and "heroic" subjects for novelists. Like Caudwell, Fox was killed fighting for the Loyalists in Spain in 1937, and *A Writer in Arms*, an anthology of his work published posthumously in 1937, containing tributes, fragments of his books *Genghis Khan, Communism, Lenin,* and *Storming Heaven,* as well as letters and periodical pieces, shows an æsthetic sensibility capable of breaking through the fetters of his straight political criticism, had he lived. Jackson's study of Charles Dickens, subtitled *The Progress of a Radical,* is probably the worst of the lot, a ridiculous, ignorant, and sectarian book, mechanically presenting Dickens's development and mood in exact sequence with the development of Chartism, and noting each occasion on which Dickens shows the proletariat in an admirable light or comes close to recognizing the class struggle. Other British critics whose Marxism results in straight political distortion include: F. D. Klingender, an authority (fittingly!) on caricature, whose pamphlet *Marxism and Modern Art* in 1944 carried on the worst traditions of Marxist absolutism, ignorance, and parochialism of the thirties; Edward Upward, who achieved during his brief radicalism what may be the most stupid single piece of Marxist criticism ever written, an argument that the way to become a good writer is to become a Marxist, in his essay "Sketch for a Marxist Interpretation of Literature" in C. Day Lewis's symposium, *The Mind in Chains;* and Douglas Garman, a literary hatchet-man equivalent to Samuel Sillen in this country.

Typical of the British critics who have used Marxism, not as a distorting-glass, but as a sociology with which to understand and appreciate it more deeply, are Alick West, George Thomson, and Philip Henderson. West is far and away the best, similar to Caudwell in everything but scope, and his small book *Crisis and Criticism*, published in 1937, includes probably the most sensitive detailed reading of texts in Marxist criticism. The book surveys contemporary literary criticism from a dynamic and relativistic Marxist viewpoint similar to that of Caudwell, and with a comparable literacy, general soundness, and informed indebtedness to areas of knowledge like æsthetics and linguistics. The book exposes the critical limitations of men like Eliot, Richards, and Read with neatness and dispatch and concludes, like Caudwell, affirming the relationship of literature to production as its essential formal determinant. To illustrate his prescription for criticism, West makes brilliant incidental readings of *The Waste Land*, a Shakespeare sonnet, and *Paradise Lost* and concludes with an appendix constituting the toughest test of his method possible, a long and absolutely first-rate analysis of Joyce's *Ulysses*. Thomson, a professor of Greek at the University of Birmingham, admits his direct indebtedness to Caudwell in his chief work, *Æschylus and Athens*, a study of the social origins of Greek drama, utilizing a combination of Marxism and the Cambridge anthropological approach and avoiding oversimplification from both directions (his forthcoming book on early Greek society is to deal comparably with Greek epic). His pamphlet *Marxism and Poetry*, a study in the origin and evolution of poetry, amounts to a popularization of Caudwell, with the addition of Thomson's knowledge of Greek and primitive Irish literature. Thomson tends to go wrong when he veers from Caudwell, leaving the basic soundness of his theory of the origin of poetry in the collective ritual of primitive food-production to fall for Professor Chadwick's elaborate euhemerism and see Homer as the improvisation of the Homeric bards, or finding Elizabethan drama an expression of the rising bourgeoisie; but his work generally is informed, brilliant, and invaluable. Henderson, although extremely literate, as his edition of Skelton and scholarly introductions for Everyman's Library demonstrate, is frequently disappointing, and his books, *Literature and a Changing Civilisation*, *Poetry and Society*, and *The Novel Today*, tend to be somewhat mixed, capable of sensitive analysis and appreciation alongside blind dogmatism like the statement that *since* William Morris was a real Marxian socialist, he was able to write "the only really successful epic of the nineteenth century."

British critics more or less combining Marxist insights with æsthetic awareness include: Jack Lindsay, in *John Bunyan: Maker of Myths* and *A Short History of Culture* (in his case, along with Freudian insights); A. L. Morton, in *Language of Men*; Randall Swingler in a number of uncollected periodical pieces; and several members of the *Scrutiny* group (discussed below, in the chapter on Empson), particularly L. C. Knights. Two classics professors, Benjamin Farrington in *The Civilization of Greece and Rome, Science and Politics in the Ancient World*, and *Greek Science*, and C. M. Bowra, in *Sophoclean Tragedy, Tradition and Design in Homer*, and *Greek Lyric Poetry*, have, like Thomson, applied Marxist concepts (Bowra somewhat tentatively) in their scholarly fields. Other British Marxist criticism of value can occasionally be found in the *Modern Quarterly*, both the old and the new series, the *Left Review* (which came to an end in 1938) and *Our Time*.

A special category of English critics affected by Marxism is the group of poets that first came to notice in *New Signatures* in 1932, including W. H. Auden, Stephen Spender, Cecil Day Lewis, John Lehmann, and (a later affiliation) Louis MacNeice. Day Lewis, in *A Hope for Poetry* in 1934 and *The Revolution in Writing* in 1936, combined manifesto-writing, ancestor-chasing, and praise for himself and his friends with incidental sociological literary criticism, some of it quite shrewd.[5] Spender turned out some first-rate Marxist-æsthetic criticism in *The Destructive Element* in 1935, particularly his capture of Henry James for the Left, and has been working very hard since to unwrite it. MacNeice wrote *Modern Poetry* in 1938, largely an account of the genesis of his own taste, with stabs at social analysis, and a tepid study of Yeats's poetry in 1941 (both praised Caudwell but remained unpolluted by his ideas). Lehmann's work of criticism, a pamphlet on *New Writing in England*, is literary journalism of a high order. Auden, the most important poet of the group, has done the least criticism, chiefly fugitive pieces and reviews of a theological nature (he once attacked Joyce Kilmer's "Trees" as heretical),

---

[5] *The Poetic Image*, published in 1947, after this was written, is a charming and utterly superficial book. It goes all out for "that remarkable book *Illusion and Reality*," however, and makes a surprising and admirable attempt to integrate Caudwell's Marxist approach to poetry with Miss Bodkin's archetypal patterns and the scholarly methods of Miss Spurgeon and John Livingston Lowes.

untouched by Marxism and social criteria even when he called himself a radical. (Auden's real criticism appears in his poetry, in works like "The Sea and the Mirror: a Commentary on Shakespeare's *The Tempest*," and it is very good.)

Some account of Soviet Marxist literary criticism is essential, although any estimate on the basis of what little of it has been translated into English is bound to be both fragmentary and misleading. To understand it, in addition to its background of Marxist theory, the reader must know something of the work of a group, almost unknown to the English-reading public, that has influenced it tremendously, the nineteenth-century pre-Marxist Russian "enlighteners": Belinsky, Herzen, Cherny-shevsky, Dobrolyubov, and Pisarev. Vissarion G. Belinsky, whom Mirsky calls "the father of the Russian intelligentsia," in the 1830's and '40's propagated the concept of literature as a weapon in the social struggle, tracing democratic ideas in contemporary writers like Pushkin and Lermontov, and bitterly attacking reactionary ones in writers like Gogol and Dostoyevsky. Alexander Herzen, an idealistic socialist who spent most of his life in exile, was chiefly influential in the decade following Belinsky's death, calling in his works, particularly *From the Other Shore*, for realistic revolutionary thinking and writing. Nikolai Chernyshevsky, who inherited their influence, in 1853 published his doctoral thesis, *The Æsthetic Relations of Art to Reality* (reprinted in *International Literature* in 1935 as *Life and Æsthetics*), defining art as the reproduction and interpretation of life, and its function as the diffusion of knowledge. In *Studies in the Age of Gogol* in 1856 he applied his æsthetic to the valuation of literature in terms of social utility. His disciple, Nikolai Dobrolyubov, in a tremendously precocious literary career that ended with his death at twenty-four, extended the method further and did a very influential series of articles on literary works, using them only as texts for criticism of Russian life (Goncharov's *Oblomov* became "What is Oblomovism?" Turgenev's *On the Eve* became "When Will Real Day Dawn?" and so forth). He flatly ignored the literary aspects of the works he was discussing, making his only æsthetic criterion the quality of "being true to life." Dmitri Pisarev, an even more polemic radical journalist who also died in his twenties, pushed the method even further, rejected out of hand all art except that immediately useful for educational purposes, "uncrowning" writers like Pushkin, until ultimately, in the moderate words of Plekhanov, "he carried this concept to the point of caricature." (It should be obvious that the inheritor of this line of progressive hardening of the æsthetic arteries is Tolstoy, who from a different standard, religious morality, continued in his own criticism the narrow social functionalism and æsthetic unconcern of the "enlighteners.")

All these tendencies—the Marxist view of literature, the Russian critical tradition of social utilitarianism in art, even some of Tolstoy's moralism—came to a focus in Vladimir Ilyich Lenin, along with the characteristics of his own mind and the necessities of his life as a revolutionary leader and head of the new socialist state. Lenin's approach to art is vitally important, since so much of later Marxist criticism depends on it, and it is an incredibly complex approach in which at least six separate emphases (at different times and under different circumstances) can be distinguished. One is the attitude of simple functionalism that he takes in his 1905 article "Party Organization and Party Literature": that art is a weapon in the class struggle and must be recruited to help make a revolution. Lenin believed in an absolute objective truth, as his *Notes on Dialectics* and *Materialism and Empirio-Criticism* make clear, and he believed that he and his party had it, so that a writer could only find truth and freedom within or alongside of the party. Another attitude is the analytic Marxist view that art reflects social reality but in many respects transcends both it and the creator's views, shown in the six tributes to Leo Tolstoy—five of them available in English in *Dialectics 6* (1938)—that Lenin wrote in the years around Tolstoy's death, trying to reconcile the contradiction between Tolstoy's genius and his reactionary views. A third is a puritanic resistance to the "sinfulness" of art, related to that of the "enlighteners" and Tolstoy and very like Augustine's attraction-repulsion to Vergil. It is best shown in a statement Lenin made to Gorky, explaining why he loved the "miracle" of great music but couldn't listen to it very often:

> It acts on my nerves, makes me want to talk amiable stupidities and stroke the heads of these beings who, living in a filthy hell, can create such beauty. But today you can't stroke anybody on the head— they'll bite off your hand. You've got to pound them on the head, and pound them ruthlessly.

A fourth is the tired businessman's philistine conception of art as a soothing relaxation, shown in his generally academic taste (he wept at Bernhardt's Camille, liked Jack London and Upton Sinclair, saved the Great Theater after the Revolution because "a theater is necessary . . . to rest hard workers after their daily work," proposed that the Soviet state arrange mass distribution of reproductions of painters like Rubens and Murillo), combined with his strong dislike for the modern (he experienced "no joy" from modernist painting, wanted to know, like any philistine, whether the artist wasn't concealing his inability to draw, admitted that he couldn't understand Mayakovsky and always fell asleep after three lines of his poetry). A fifth is the social utilitarian view that art is a form of wealth, to be made accessible to the masses under socialism like any other form of wealth, typified by his statements to Clara

Zetkin that art must belong to the people and be comprehensible to them ("Must one offer cake to an infinitesimal minority at a time when the masses of workers and peasants are crying out for bread?"). A sixth is a number of reservations and hesitancies about the other five, compounded of his own rich personality, personal respect for the creative artist, devotion to tolerance and personal freedom, and sense of humor (typified by his marginal comments on someone's memo: "The creation of a new fundamental *class* culture is the fundamental goal of the Proletcult": "Ha, ha!" and "Bunk"). All six of these attitudes, despite their contradictions, were to be major features of Soviet criticism, marked by Lenin's strong personality, and were to be adopted as part of the inheritance by Marxist critics elsewhere.

Compared with Lenin's views, the criticism of other early Soviet leaders and literary thinkers is a fairly simple matter, merely picking up one or another strand of his thought. Leon Trotsky, in his collection of essays published in 1925 as *Literature and Revolution*, reveals an impressive sensitivity to æsthetic values, but is, nevertheless, chiefly concerned with criticizing Soviet writers in terms of the political needs of the Soviet state. As late as 1935, in the *Atlantic Monthly*, he was using an article ostensibly about Céline for a lengthy discussion of French governmental politics. Joseph Stalin, so far as I know, has never written on art and literature. He has been responsible for a number of slogans: that culture must be "proletarian in content and national in form," that "the writer is the engineer of the human soul"; and he is supposed to have named "socialist realism." His taste seems to be about as academic as Lenin's, with a particular interest in music; if newspaper reports can be trusted, he likes classical ballet and Russian opera of the Glinka-Borodin sort, he walked out on Shostakovich's *Lady Macbeth of Mzensk* with the comment that the music was difficult and unmelodic and that he didn't care for the story, and he directed Soviet composers to produce tunes that people can whistle on their way to work. In one respect at least Stalin has bettered Lenin: he seems to have a very high estimate of Mayakovsky, describing him as "the outstanding poet of the Soviet era" and writing in *Pravda* in 1935: "Indifference to the memory and works of Mayakovsky is a crime." Maxim Gorky, a major influence on Soviet criticism, reveals a tremendous critical sensitivity in brilliant snatches of his *Reminiscences* of Tolstoy, Chekhov, and others, but his formal criticism and literary pamphleteering, published in English in *On Guard for the Soviet Union* in 1933 and *Culture and the People* in 1939, is greatly disappointing—wholly political and unimaginative. Other Soviet criticism by the older generation ranges from the militant Leftism of Karl Radek, announcing that Joyce's work is "a heap of dung," to the moderation and good sense of Anatol Lunacharsky, cutting the Gordian knot of a Soviet controversy over whether Shakespeare was a spokesman for the feudal or the bourgeois class by announcing that he wasn't a spokesman for any class, but a great and conflict-ridden artist living in a great and conflict-ridden time.

For many years Soviet criticism was largely devoted to battles between Lefts and Rights, futurists and formalists, constructivists and Proletcultists, On-Guardites and At-Your-Postites, social-commanders and anti-social-commanders, a man announcing that *Yevgeny Onyegin* would have been written without Pushkin and another man countering that anyway no literary works could compare with revolutionary manifestoes, so that it was a rare literary critic who got a piece of criticism written. Within the thirties, however, Soviet criticism seems to have improved somewhat, and the recent controversies by the younger critics have at least been on issues of serious concern to Marxist criticism, definitely transcending Soviet literary politics. The chief of these was the campaign against "vulgar sociology" in 1936 and 1937 which soon turned into a much more fundamental controversy over relative versus absolute standards in Marxist criticism. It warrants some space.

The critics of "vulgar sociology" defended absolute criteria, under the ægis of Lenin, Chernyshevsky, and Dobrolyubov, proposing the evaluation of works of art in terms of timeless political values: that is, were they "for" or "against" the "people"? The group was more or less led by Mikhail Lifschitz of the Marx-Engels-Lenin Institute, the compiler of Marx's writings on art and author of a summary, *The Philosophy of Art of Karl Marx*, which, although generally useful, distorts Marx to make him an absolutist and enemy of "vulgar sociology" (neglecting even to mention, say, his views on Balzac). His camp included V. Grib, the author of an equally simplified study "capturing" Balzac; Mark Rosenthal, editor of the monthly *Literary Critic* and sponsor of the deathless syllogism that since great artists were anti-capitalist at any time, and Timon's speeches against gold show that Shakespeare was anti-capitalist, therefore Shakespeare is a great artist; and I. Satz and V. Kemenov, of similar views.

The "vulgar sociologists" defended relative criteria, under the ægis of Taine, Belinsky, Plekhanov, and Mehring; that is, the evaluation of works of art in terms of the writer's relation to the social forces and issues of his own day. They were more or less led by Professor I. Nusinov of the Institute of Red Professors, compiler of a Soviet edition of Hugo and comparable works, a sound man insisting in his articles on Plekhanov's point that in a decadent period the greatest writers (Proust and Joyce are his examples) are bound to be decadent; that wicked and anti-social ideas can produce great art; that truth is relative and subjective; that "the writer is no photographic camera, a work of art is no snapshot, and literature is no mirror." Despite Nusinov's ideas, his team included some fairly poor critics slanted toward "rejection": D. S. Mirsky, a czarist prince who had gone back to Russia in the early thirties an enthusiastic Communist and ran to such critical excesses as finding Joyce's exactitude of description a "class style" showing "an æsthetico-proprietary desire for 'things' " (just as an equally mechanical Freudian would find it "anal"); A. A. Smirnov, whose book on Shakespeare is the low point of Soviet criticism, analyzing *The Tempest* as a treatise on the colonial question; and Professor M. Kravchenko, whose studies of Gogol are similar, if not quite so extreme.

What muddled the controversy almost unbelievably was, first, that neither side would fly its proper banners; both sides claimed Lenin (and had proper Lenin quotes), disclaimed Plekhanov and Taine, and charged each other with the influence of Trotsky. In addition, a political issue was involved, in that the "vulgar sociologists" were "Leftist," "sectarian," in a Popular Front period when the aims were "moving in on," "broadening." It seems obvious that the "vulgar sociologists" were actually attempting to be Marxists, and their opponents only utilitarian politicians, capturing writers like Shakespeare and Pushkin for the working class. Nevertheless, the use the "vulgar sociologists" made of their social analyses (which were not terribly accurate as a rule) was generally to reject great writers indiscriminately, while their opponents had a framework, of no matter what validity, for accepting them. The solution here seems to be the approach of Feodor Levin, who took a median position between the two camps in the controversy. He slapped down the absolutists for renouncing Marxist analysis in terms of social classes and historical development, simplifying the past to the point where they could not conceive of a ruling class ever standing for anything but parasitism and exploitation, and "catapulting" present politics into the past. At the same time he slapped down the relativists for their actual vulgarizations and rejections. Quoting Marx on why we still enjoy Greek art and quoting Engels on Balzac (to flavor the ubiquitous Lenin quotations of the controversy), he concluded that both camps were actually vulgar sociologists and that a serious Marxist criticism would want to know what social reality a great work of literature arose from *and* why it was great. From Levin's articles it is possible to get a clear view of the controversy, to see both sides picking up aspects of Lenin's thought and using them in a vacuum, to see each side performing half the process of sociological criticism and coming out with absurd results. The hope would seem to lie in a Marxist criticism using the historically relativist standards of critics like Nusinov, applied with the discrimination and appreciation shown for artists by critics like Lifschitz. That is, Marxist analysis *without* consequent rejection; seeing greatness as best expressing class rather than contradicting it. Such a criticism would also, of course, stop using names, slogans, and Lenin quotations as arguments, discard its pieties, and start looking at literature.

A few examples of Soviet criticism of this sort give cause for hope. One is an essay called "Bacon in Shakespearian Surroundings," by Lunacharsky, part of an unfinished book on Bacon, which was published posthumously in *International Literature*, 1936, No. 1. It is a brilliant and imaginative study, very much in the tradition of modern criticism, defining two Shakespearian progressions, the "melancholy," Jaques to Hamlet to Prospero, and the "cynical," Richard III to Edmund to Iago, and then interpreting Bacon's mind and character against the pattern of those two movements. A piece even more impressive is J. Kashkeen's "Ernest Hemingway," in *International Literature*, 1935, No. 5. It is a really remarkable study of Hemingway's work, perhaps the best written to date, revealing a thorough knowledge and understanding of American literature (Kashkeen deals with the influence of writers from Thoreau to Gertrude Stein on Hemingway); a brilliant comparative method (he discusses Hemingway in terms of Dostoyevsky, Flaubert, Céline, Eliot, and innumerable others); great sensitivity to style; and a genuine understanding of the nature of Hemingway's power and depth as well as of his limitations.

In the decade since the "vulgar sociology" controversy, almost no Soviet criticism has been published in English. A volume of anniversary tributes to Pushkin published in English in Moscow in 1939, principally the work of Soviet professors, is as uninspired and academic as its equivalents elsewhere. During the war the few articles by Soviet critics that appeared in *International Literature* were almost entirely concerned with problems of war writing and morale, and of little general literary interest. Since the war the chief critical manifestation has been the depressing attack by Andrei Zhdanov on Anna Akhmatova and Mikhail Zoschenko, as well as on general aspects of Soviet culture. Zhdanov's attack appears to mark a return to the senseless tradition of the politician's laying down a literary "line" that so much inhibited Soviet criticism in the past, and seems an unhappy omen. He announced that the "great historical mission" of Soviet literature is "strengthening the moral and political unity of the people"; resurrected scapegoats dead for a quarter of a century, like the manifesto of the Serapion Brotherhood in 1922; and even revived the old turkey of scorn for the "outwardly beautiful form" of inwardly "rotten" bourgeois culture. Despite this setback, and with no particular evidence to go on, we can only hope that Soviet critics of the type of Levin and Kashkeen, the legitimate successors to Marx, Plekhanov, and Lunacharsky, have somehow continued over the last decade, and are continuing now, to build the valid Marxist criticism their work promises.

5

The faults of Marxist literary criticism, the fact that so much of it has been written in the last two decades and so little of it has come to anything, thus stem from a number of sources. Some of them are implicit in Marx and Engels; that is, in Marxist theory itself: the rosy nineteenth-century teleological evolutionism of Hegel, whereby the world would get progressively better and better, art dropping off somewhere along the line with other imperfect human expressions; the concentration on what men have in common at any given time, tending to slight their differences, which are the seeds of art; the constant confusion between interpreting the world and changing it, between the inevitability of socialism and the necessity of bringing it on by revolutionary action, between understanding the class nature of literature and making writers enlist in your class or party. Many of them come in with Lenin and to a lesser extent with other leaders: the revolutionist's unyielding absolutism; the busy politician's untrained philistine taste; the dedicated man's puritanic resentment of the temptations of art. Some of them are accidental Russian features that have been foolishly adopted by Marxists in other countries: the critical moralism and narrow functionalism of the "enlighteners" and Tolstoy, the special educational necessities of a new socialist country with a largely illiterate population. The principal faults, however, are none of these things, but the personal deficiencies of most of the Marxist critics. These are chiefly three. First, as Arnold said of the romantics, they do not know enough—either enough history or enough literature. As Plekhanov wrote, noting that Michelangelo said his teaching would procreate a great number of ignoramuses: "Nowadays it is Marx's teaching that is procreating ignoramuses." Second, most of them do not really like literature, or wide areas of it, and use Marxism as a weapon for killing it off. Third, they do not have enough imagination; their categories are too narrow, and their views too simple and mechanical. Examples could be obtained almost everywhere, but perhaps the clearest illustration is V. F. Calverton's *The Liberation of American Literature*. He didn't know American history, and he hadn't read, let alone understood, much American literature. He didn't much like it, either, particularly its great artists, its Hawthornes, Melvilles, and Thoreaus. Finally, his categories were far too narrow and his thinking childish. He announced that we had no Puritan art and that Franklin was opposed to art, thinking of the Greek arts, whereas Parrington and Constance Rourke, with a broader definition of art, recognized the "drama" in Indian treaties, the "lyric" in sermons, and the "art" of Franklin's fine printing. Finally, he was obsessed, as almost all the bad Marxist critics have been, with the term "escape" and "escapist."

It is about time someone polished off the term "escape" as a critical concept. As used as a Marxist term of abuse by such men as Michael Gold, it tends to mean that any writing about the past is a wicked avoidance of contemporary social reality. As F. O. Matthiessen sensibly pointed out in *The Achievement of T. S. Eliot*, "Only the narrowest conception of realism can hold that an author necessarily acquires any sovereign virtue by recording the surface details of a middle western city instead of those of eighteenth century Peru." As generally used, however, the charge smuggles in a much more absurd assumption, actually the height of flattery to the reviled author, that it really is possible for him to "escape" the problems of his life and time in his work if he wants to; rather than, as Kenneth Burke has devoted much of his criticism to pointing out, facing them inevitably on another level, in another form, generally one on which they are less capable of realistic solution. In *Permanence and Change* Burke writes:

> Properly used, the idea of escape should present no difficulties. If a situation is unsatisfactory, it is quite normal and natural that people should want to avoid it and should try any means at their disposal to do so. But the term escape has had a more restricted usage. Whereas it properly applies to *all* men, there was an attempt to restrict its application to *some* men. . . . In the end, the term came to be applied loosely, in literary criticism especially, to designate any writer or reader whose interests or aims did not closely coincide with those of the critic. While apparently defining a *trait of the person referred to*, the term hardly did more than convey the *attitude of the person making the reference*. It looked objective, as though the critic were saying "X is doing so-and-so"; but too often it became merely a strategic way of saying, "I personally don't like what X is doing."

Marxist criticism would discard meaningless battle-cries like "escape," "ivory tower," the pejorative use of "decadent,"[6] and the rest, if Marxist critics recognized that their sociological analysis is a tool for the understanding of literature, not the debunking of it, "unmasking its ideology," and so on. In a sense, this would violate the whole Marxist tradition, which, as a theory of interpreting society inextricably bound up with overthrowing it, sees all analysis in terms of present struggles and weapons. It would require making the "essence" of Marxism for literary criticism neutral, not polemic. Nevertheless, in a deeper sense, the sense in which the truth is always political, is always a revolutionary

---

[6] The all-time record here is held by Edwin Berry Burgum, who uses "decadence" five times, each time as a way of spanking writers, on a single page of *The Novel and the World's Dilemma* (p. 16). I have not counted his uses of "escape" and the others, but he would score high.

weapon, it would violate only short-sighted Marxism, the sacrifice of truth for immediate expediency. It was this that Marx and Engels saw in Balzac, as later Marxists have seen it in writers like Proust—that the *truthfulness* of great art results in a portrayal of social reality, whatever the class or views of the artist, more valuable to Marxism than all the pious slantings of propaganda artists.

Like Freud and psychoanalysis, Marx and Marxism can be of tremendous use to criticism if the critic has a clear delimitation of what the method can and cannot do. Psychoanalysis, Freud admitted, can deal with the personal origins and psycho-symbolic interrelations of the work, but not with its formal artistic techniques and its æsthetic value. Similarly, Marxism can deal with the social origins and socio-symbolic interrelations of the work, but it can, in addition, deal with its formal artistic techniques to some extent in social and historical terms, and in the same terms it can make rather limited statements of æsthetic value. What it *cannot* do is use its social analysis as a technique for debunking, erect reflection-of-social-reality as the major criterion of æsthetic value, or dismiss the author, his psyche, and his personal artistry as factors less important than social and historical factors. It is within these strict limits that the critics who have made the most effective use of Marxism in moderation—Burke, Empson, even Edmund Wilson to some extent (all discussed in other chapters), Matthiessen, Knights, and others—have operated. The best Marxist critics, from Plekhanov to Christopher Caudwell, have recognized similar limitations.

Finally we can return to Caudwell. In terms of the personal faults of Marxist critics discussed earlier in this section, he is blameless. He had, in one way or another, all the faults of the method; he even inherited Lenin's old-fashioned insistence on absolute objective truth, but he had none of the personal deficiencies. His taste was first-rate, his knowledge of history as well as of the advances of knowledge in almost every area substantial; he knew literature intimately and loved it thoroughly; and he was neither stupid, simple-minded, nor addicted to strait-jackets and pigeonholes. When he does use Marxism as a weapon for slugging poetry, we can put it down to the same adolescent guilt (his only adolescent feature) about being a middle-class intellectual of prosperous parentage that led him to renounce the writing of poetry, renounce his name and "identity," give up study for selling the *Daily Worker* in tube stations, and insist upon fighting in Spain instead of doing the work at which he could be most valuable. Had he lived, we can be sure he would have outgrown it, as those other bourgeois intellectuals Marx, Engels, and Lenin (if they ever felt the guilt) surely did.

A few general problems raised by Caudwell's work, illustrating some of these successful attributes or failings, remain to be discussed. One is

Caudwell's relation to science, on which I am particularly ill-equipped to write. In terms of background, a knowledge of theoretical physics and mathematics is invaluable equipment for the criticism of poetry, as Paul Valéry demonstrated, for example, in his discussion of Poe's "Eureka" in *Variété*. It is much less valuable when it is used, through faulty analogies, to simplify the complexities of human life or history, as Henry Adams demonstrated in his " The Rule of Phase Applied to History," based on the conviction that the Adams political fortunes had decayed in Washington because of the second law of thermodynamics, the sink of energy at zero potential, and the iron laws of mechanics. In these terms, in his literary criticism, Caudwell used his knowledge of physics as Valéry did, to cast light rather than, like Adams, to mechanize. In *The Crisis in Physics*, however, he used his Marxism not only to understand the thinking of the new physics, to place it socially, but to "class-angle" it as a way of rejecting it. In this he seems to have been following the cue of Lenin's *Materialism and Empirio-Criticism*, in which Lenin attacked the "crisis in science," the new relativity physics, as "idealism," an attempt to dissolve the material universe into energy. Assuming a relativism of perception, Lenin insisted, means "a denial of any objective measure or model existing independently of humanity to which our relative knowledge approximates." The modern view that scientific statements are "prescriptions for practice" rather than objective reproductions of reality he denounced as "capitulation to theism." Caudwell would seem to be in an analogous position in *The Crisis in Physics*.

The crisis to which Caudwell refers was a challenge by a number of the newer physicists, among them Schrödinger, Heisenberg, and Dirac, to the basic scientific conceptions of "causality" and "determinacy" still assumed by Einstein and Planck. In one sense, causality had been challenged as far back as 1760, when David Hume pointed out that the relationship between what we call "cause" and "effect" is put there by our own minds, as a convenience of discourse, based on customary perception; and the ultimate "determinacy" of the universe had always been challenged by idealistic philosophy. In the new scientific challenge, however, the challengers were men of important technical achievement who could claim to be proceeding from their own experimental results as well as accepting the implications of relativity and quantum physics (despite the opposition of Einstein and Planck), among them the basic dependence of causality on temporal sequence, which Einstein had exploded permanently with his revelation that at a speed greater than the speed of light, an "effect" would precede its "cause." What the new physics was asking for seems to be an alteration in ways of talking about phenomena, the substitution of "A is accompanied by B" for "A causes B" and "indeterminacy" under certain circumstances (as in locating electrons precisely) for inevitable "determinacy," but Caudwell, like Lenin, insisted that they wanted to alter the nature of reality, and he confronted them with the massed fire-power of dialectical materialism, determinism, and charges of "bourgeois idealism." Without being able to evaluate the correctness of the positions, the reader would nevertheless tend to find many of Caudwell's arguments, like Lenin's, appeals to authority and somewhat off the subject.

Another problem that needs discussion is the relation of Caudwell to Rousseau. To Caudwell, as to traditional Marxism based on the philosophic determinism of Spinoza, Rousseau is the ultimate heretic, and his doctrine that "man is born free and everywhere he is in chains" is the ultimate heresy. On the other hand, Rousseau is the founder of modern bourgeois democracy and liberty, the spiritual ancestor of Jefferson and Tom Paine, the theoretical source of the *Declaration of Independence* and the *Rights of Man*. Most contemporary Marxists are disguised Rousseauesque democrats like Michael Gold, and most of the Marxist thinking and sloganeering in a Popular Front period is in terms of Rousseauesque ideals. This is simple confusion. The logical inheritors of Rousseau are the anarchists, and the literary anarchists know it, as passionate tributes to Rousseau in the work of Herbert Read and Edward Dahlberg testify. In *Art and Social Nature* Paul Goodman insists that his private adolescent anarchist program is both "revolutionary" and "Rousseauian." The enemies of Rousseau in our day, on the other hand, have been loudly and fanatically the neo-humanists like Irving Babbitt, the reactionary classicists like Eliot and Hulme, the orthodox Christians, particularly Catholics like Maritain, and the anti-democratic and reactionary in general. When Caudwell organizes all his books on the thread of basic philosophic opposition to Rousseau and the bourgeois concept of freedom, and fulminates at length against Rousseau's inheritors (particularly in *Studies in a Dying Culture*), he is in the strange position of being in the camp of his enemies, opposing the friend of his friends. The ironic fact that he is right, that Marxism *is* fundamentally opposed to Rousseau's bourgeois views at every point, is a comment on the capacity of political exigency to confuse a philosophic issue, and on the difficulty of being a realist in the world of the sentimental.

The last problem is Marxism and psychoanalysis, which was considered from the viewpoint of psychoanalysis above (in the chapter on Maud Bodkin) and needs additional treatment from the viewpoint of Marxism. Caudwell has distinguished himself as perhaps the most violent of all Marxist opponents of psychoanalysis, using the same charge of "bourgeois idealism." Marxist writers on the subject have been very much split. In the early twenties, in the Soviet Union, Trotsky and Radek apparently first proposed reconciling Freud with Marxist materialism. In 1925 W. Jurinetz attacked Wilhelm Reich's group of "Freudo-Marxists" in an article in *Unter dem Banner des Marxismus*. In the same magazine in 1929 I. Sapir and Reich himself engaged in a polemic on the subject, with Reich taking a beating. In 1933 Audard's article "Du caractère matérialiste de la psychoanalyse" in *Cahiers du Sud* attempted another reconciliation, and George Politzer attacked it with an article in *Commune*. In England, Reuben Osborn proposed the same integration in 1937 in his book *Freud and Marx*, and was sharply attacked by J. D. Bernal in the *Labour Monthly* and T. A. Jackson in *Left Review*. A number of Marxists, among them Jack Lindsay and Arthur Calder-Marshall have argued that Freud and Marx are not in conflict, without engaging in polemic on the subject, and the most reasoned Marxist attacks on Freud, Alistaire Browne's "Psychology and Marxism" in *The Mind in Chains* and Francis H. Bartlett's *Sigmund Freud* and his article "The Limitations of Freud" in *Science and Society*, Winter 1939, actually turn out to be good outlines for a social psychoanalysis of the Fromm-Horney type (although Bartlett has since criticized Horney in *Science and Society*, Summer 1945). Meanwhile, psychoanalysts, psychiatrists, and psychologists like Fromm, Wertham, and J. F. Brown, who accept Marxism, have insisted on the necessity of integration, as have a number of enthusiastic Freud-Marx literary critics like Harry Slochower, Randall Swingler, and Robert Gorham Davis. In the Soviet Union, psychoanalysis, which was under sharp attack, more or less returned to favor, and Soviet practitioners renewed their membership in the Institute of Psychoanalysis, which had been dropped in 1929. Dr. Luria has been doing experimental laboratory work in psychoanalysis at the Psychological Institute in Moscow, including the production of artificial complexes and neuroses. To the current crop of Marxist reviewers, however, "psychoanalysis" is still a term of abuse, and it was amusing to see, in the Fall 1945 issue of *Science and Society*, on page 375, the charge of "too psychological" made against Eric Bentley's *Century of Hero-Worship* by one reviewer, and on page 377 the charge of "too Freudian" hurled against Harry Slochower's *No Voice is Wholly Lost . . .* by another.

As in the attack on Rousseau, Caudwell here finds himself in bad company, although in this case without the same justification. Many of his criticisms of psychoanalysis are sound and thoroughly reasoned. He exposes the solipsistic and religious aspects of psychoanalytic therapy; the Zoroastrian dualism and "mind-deities" of Freud, the regressive mysticism and epistomological metaphysics of Jung, the comic futility (which he refers to again and again) of Adler's proposal to solve all the problems of society through the establishment of "a chair of curative pedagogy." He grants the tremendous importance of Freud as the founder of scientific psychology and makes a brilliant attempt (on page 169 of *Studies in a Dying Culture*) to translate Freudian theory into physiological terms.

Nevertheless, Caudwell's attack is basically unfair, in several respects.

One of them is attacking psychoanalysis for faults he will allow to Marxism. He writes:

Therefore in analyzing a work of art, psycho-analysts seek just those symbols that are peculiarly private, i.e. neurotic, and hence psycho-analytic criticism of art finds its examples and material always either in third-rate artistic work or in accidental features of good work. In *Hamlet* they see an Œdipus-complex; but they do not see that this does not explain the universal power of the great speeches, or the equal greatness of *Antony and Cleopatra*, which cannot be analysed into an Œdipus complex.

Nor does Marxist criticism explain these things, as Caudwell himself concedes when he gives æsthetics, or "mere appreciation," as distinguished from Marxist criticism, the job "to rank Herrick below Milton, and Shakespeare above either, and explain in rich and complex detail why and how they differ." Also, he charges the Freudian movement with being rent by schisms, unlike other sciences, and announces that "Schism is the hall-mark of religion," without any recognition that the single movement in modern times that has been more rent by schism than even psychoanalysis is Marxism. (Here, as in so many critical problems, Kenneth Burke has the answer. In *Attitudes toward History*, in the discussion of "Bureaucratization of the Imaginative," he describes the "inevitable tendencies toward the negativistic, satanistic, sectarian, disintegrative, and 'splintering'" of any group alienated from the orthodoxy, until it succeeds in creating its equally strong counter-orthodoxy.) The other unfairness of Caudwell's attack on Freud is its essential reduction, going beyond accurate "placing," to the simple debunking dismissal of "bourgeois." Remembering Caudwell's exhaustive reading in psychoanalysis, his psychoanalytic novel and Kafkaesque short stories, and the general pattern of his post-conversion repudiation of everything most valuable to him (even writing poetry), projecting the sins of his class into it and killing it off, a Freudian might get revenge by seeing a yearning-guilt pattern in his attitude toward psychoanalysis.

In the last analysis, granting the essential brilliance and soundness of the man, all criticisms of Caudwell are probably based on things he would have outgrown, seen through, or otherwise sloughed off had he lived. Even dead in his twenties, with only two books of literary criticism written, he was probably the best Marxist critic we have ever had. Gregory's comparison of him with T. E. Hulme, the brilliant theoretician of reaction, also killed young in a war, is both absurd and insulting to Caudwell. A much more persuasive comparison is that with Randolph Bourne, whose tragic premature death snuffed out the closest thing America has had to Caudwell; but Caudwell was a thinker of vastly more power and ability than even Bourne. Had he lived, we cannot even limit by imagining it the work he might have done. The waste of his death, in intellectual terms, is tragic beyond belief. (In human terms, of course, it can easily be justified. The death of a man for his ideals, in this case for the heroic ideals of the Spanish Republic, is never in the deepest sense wasteful, no matter how many could have replaced him dying, and how few living. "A man can do no more than risk and perhaps lose his life," Caudwell himself wrote of T. E. Lawrence.)

It is always worth doing, as a kind of ultimate test, to turn a man's critical method on himself, his own life and work. The Marxist analysis of a man like Caudwell can be entirely summed up in a single famous paragraph from the *Communist Manifesto:*

> Finally, in times when the class-struggle nears the decisive hour, the process of dissolution going on within the ruling class—in fact, within the whole range of an old society—assumes such a violent, glaring character that a small section of the ruling class cuts itself adrift and joins the revolutionary class, the class that holds the future in its hands. Just as, therefore, at an earlier period, a section of the nobility went over to the bourgeoisie, so now a portion of the bourgeoisie goes over to the proletariat, and in particular, a portion of the bourgeois ideologists, who have raised themselves to the level of comprehending theoretically the historical movements as a whole.

Marx and Engels were thinking of their own lives when they wrote it, and Christopher Caudwell would ask no more than to be grouped with them. We can only mourn that he did not live to comprehend the phenomenon as objectively and, with the load of class guilt off his shoulders, sit down to do the work he could have done.

CHAPTER 8

CAROLINE SPURGEON
and Scholarship in Criticism

RELATIONS BETWEEN scholarship and criticism in literature have not been very good in our time. To the critic, the scholar is an academic fuddy-duddy whose only interest in great poetry lies in counting the semicolons it contains. To the scholar, the critic is a wild man who compounds his sweeping judgments about literature of equal parts of ignorance and brashness. Unfortunately for relations between the two fields, both charges are substantially true: the universities *are* full of fuddy-duddies and the magazines of wild men. Most of our scholars are extremely deficient in imagination, and most of our critics equally deficient in information. A few critics of our day, however, have managed, like Ezra Pound, to combine practice in their brash field with genuine scholarship, and a few scholars have managed to make a genuinely imaginative contribution to criticism. Prominent among the latter is Caroline F. E. Spurgeon, whose death in 1942 at the age of seventy-four brought to a close a distinguished career of Shakespeare and Chaucer study extending over half a century. The book for which she is chiefly noted, *Shakespeare's Imagery and What It Tells Us*, was published almost at the end of her career, in 1935, but in a sense it represents a culmination of all of her work.

Miss Spurgeon's first book was *Mysticism in English Literature*, published in 1913, when she was professor of English literature at the University of London. It is neither very scholarly nor very critical. In the guise of a survey of mystic thought in English poetry and prose, it is really a little tract for mysticism. Because of the book's fundamental bias, Miss Spurgeon displays a brisk unconcern with æsthetic standards, and is capable of writing: "it has ever been the habit of the English race to clothe their profoundest thought and their highest aspiration in poetic form. We do not possess a Plato, a Kant or a Descartes, but we have Shakespeare and Wordsworth and Browning." She seems to believe literally that the Song of Solomon was *written* as an allegory in erotic imagery of the wooing of the soul by God. She has no equipment for distinguishing the mystic experience from simple hysteria, and her account of the experience of Dame Julian, the famous mystic of the fourteenth century, who had visions after a seven days' sickness followed by six hours of what seem to be convulsions, approves the whole thing as just as reasonable a way as any other of getting near to God. At the end of the book she attempts to bolster up mysticism with evidence that "the last word in science and philosophy tends to reinforce and even to explain the mystic," but her evidence turns out to be largely Bergson. The book has some things of value, particularly a compact chronological sketch of mystical thought from Plato on, but for the most part it is a job of little intellectual interest, of value chiefly to literary occultists.

Miss Spurgeon's next book, *Five Hundred Years of Chaucer Criticism and Allusion*, published from 1908 to 1924 in six parts by the Chaucer Society, is entirely a work of scholarship and does not concern us here. In what will probably stand as the definitive compilation, needing only periodic supplementation, she summarized and noted every reference to Chaucer from 1357 to 1900.

Keats' Shakespeare in 1928 was apparently planned as a work of pure scholarship, like the Chaucer compilation, but the book actually points the way to a good deal more. In August 1927 Miss Spurgeon had been informed that Mr. Joseph Armour in Princeton owned Severn's copy of Shakespeare, which Keats had been reading in Rome and in which he had left some markings. On being permitted to inspect it, she discovered that it was Keats's own copy of Shakespeare's plays, which he had read and reread for the last three and a half years of his life, with extensive scorings, markings, and annotations, and that its existence was absolutely unknown to scholarship. With the two volumes of Shakespeare marked by Keats in the Dilke Collection at Hampstead (a reprint of the 1623 folio and a copy of the *Poems*) its seven volumes formed an invaluable record of the precise reaction of Keats to the greater poet who had so much influenced him. *Keats' Shakespeare*, subtitled *A Descriptive Study Based on New Material*, is her analysis of the remarkable find. It is a physically beautiful book, illustrated with a great many facsimiles, reprinting and discussing Keats's markings at length.

Miss Spurgeon arranges her book in three sections: the first a discussion of Keats's markings and their implications; the second a printing of passages from *The Tempest* and *A Midsummer Night's Dream* with parallel passages from *Endymion* to illustrate reminiscence of thought or verbal likeness; and the last a reprint of all the markings in the five most marked plays, *The Tempest*, *A Midsummer Night's Dream*, *Measure for Measure*, *Antony and Cleopatra*, and *Troilus and Cressida*. Thus five sevenths of the book is given over to reprint and only two sevenths, or about fifty pages, to commentary; but within that small confine the author makes a number of perceptive points. One of the first things she did, an idea so simple it would never have occurred to many scholars at all, was to calculate which plays Keats had read most, not only from the markings but from smudges and wear of the paper, ranging from *The Tempest*, which had apparently been lovingly read and reread, to *Troilus and Cressida*, which, having been read and marked in the folio reprint, apparently had not been read at all in the Princeton books.

Her subject-matter being the transmutation of what a poet reads into what he writes, Miss Spurgeon inevitably adopted the method John Livingston Lowes had used so successfully in his study of the same problem in Coleridge, *The Road to Xanadu*. After crediting Lowes with a "fascinating study" in his "great book," Miss Spurgeon goes on to use his method frankly, even to his theories of imaginative association, as when she notes that an image in Shakespeare that Keats marked and did not use was probably the connecting link in his mind between two passages, one from Shakespeare and one from Drayton, reminiscences of which ran together in one passage.

The chief limitation of *Keats' Shakespeare* is Miss Spurgeon's scholarly conservatism. Unwilling to go into the problem of Keats's own life and his identification with Shakespeare, she makes little or nothing of Keats's furious reaction, in his markings, to criticisms of Shakespeare by Dr. Johnson and Steevens, quoted as footnotes to the plays in his edition. He scratched them out with great scorings and curlicues, and wrote in comments like "Lo fool again" or "Wilt thou ever be a foul mouthed calumnising [*sic*] knave?" (which Miss Spurgeon refers to as his "humorous impatience and scorn of Dr. Johnson's measured and matter of fact criticism of the plays"). She fails to note that many of Keats's markings in *The Tempest* seem to focus on Prospero as a projection of Shakespeare's, a kind of magician-playwright, a theory of our own day very reasonable in Keats, considering his known theory that Hamlet was an expression of Shakespeare. She has no critical framework in the book for making a distinction between a Shakespeare line Keats marked as major poetry and a line he marked for personal, trivial, or even sententious reasons (he marked quite a number of old saws, as a matter of fact); both are markings in her system. Finally, a number of the Shakespeare reminiscences or similarities she finds in *Endymion* are, to put it simply, extremely dubious.

The major deficiency of the book comes clear from a comparison with John Middleton Murry's *Keats and Shakespeare, A Study of Keats' Poetic Life from 1816 to 1820*, which was published in 1925, before Miss Spurgeon discovered Keats's Shakespeare. She acknowledges herself "deeply" in his debt for a "moving and convincing narrative," but makes little or no use of his central insight, that Keats was not only overwhelmed by Shakespeare's genius emotionally and closer to him spiritually than any poet chronologically between them, but that he was also *consciously* studying Shakespeare with the craft eye of a prospective playwright, that, in fact, all of his poems after *Endymion* are *explicit* preparations for the dramas he did not live to write. Murry's book, on the other hand, is befogged with mysticism and metaphysical religiosity ("To know a work of literature is to know the soul of the man who created it"), with understanding through "soul-knowledge" that surpasses that obtained by the "logical mind," and it culminates in the rather odd idea that since pure poetry is a God-inspired revelation, and Keats found his revelation through Shakespeare, Shakespeare is literally an incarnation of God. Nevertheless, if Keats's Shakespeare had been available to Murry when he wrote his book, he would probably have made more of it than Miss Spurgeon did, since inevitably by his very wildness he sometimes hits on far-fetched truth. The ideal combination would be a critic possessing Murry's imagination without his looniness and Miss Spurgeon's scholarship without her timidity, but no such paragon has yet tackled the fascinating critical problem of Keats's relationship to Shakespeare.

Miss Spurgeon's final work, the study of Shakespeare's imagery, represents a much more definite bursting through of the narrow confines of scholarship, although still not to a full criticism in depth. Of it the book *Shakespeare's Imagery* is only a small part. From at least as far back as 1927 she was engaged in classifying and studying the seven thousand images (by which she meant metaphors and similes rather than simple visual pictures) in Shakespeare's plays, together with those from a large number of plays by his contemporaries. In 1930 she revealed some of her work in a lecture before the Shakespeare Association on "Leading Motives in the Imagery of Shakespeare's Tragedies," and in 1931 she delivered the annual Shakespeare Lecture before the British Academy on "Shakespeare's Iterative Imagery," both of which, with some revision, later appeared as chapters in the book. Her plan was to publish three books based on her study of the imagery: the first, *Shakespeare's Imagery*, concerned with Shakespeare's personality and the thematic imagery of the plays; the second to deal with questions of authorship considered in the light of her new evidence; and the third to investigate the background of Shakespeare's mind and the experiential sources of his imagery. She hoped in addition eventually to publish her tabulations themselves, for other students to check and extend. Her death cut off all of these books but the first, and any judgment of the limitations of her mind and method based on only the single volume she lived to finish is necessarily tentative, if not outright unfair.

2

Nevertheless, a close look at the achievements and inadequacies of *Shakespeare's Imagery and What It Tells Us* is essential. It does actually tell us a number of invaluable things. First, as to its method: Miss Spurgeon claimed, probably rightly, that the method of studying a writer by the classification and analysis of his images, as distinguished from his literal references, is new with her and "hitherto untried." Any reader, she points out, is aware of certain recurrent symbolic imagery in Shakespeare, but only a detailed classification and count reveals the extent of the imagery-patterns. Every critic who had studied Shakespeare previously had made haphazard observations about his imagery: Dryden had noted the extent of his images drawn from nature, Hazlitt had noted that *Romeo and Juliet* seems to center on images of vernal beauty, Bradley had tabulated thematic imagery in several of the plays, George Rylands and Wilson Knight had discussed a number of the associated images, Edmund Blunden had studied the imagery of *Lear*. Some of Shakespeare's related imagery is so obsessive that early editors noticed it. The most famous of Shakespeare's private "clusters," the dog-fawning-melting-candy association, was discovered as early as 1794 by Walter Whiter in his *Specimen of a Commentary on Shakespeare*. The basis of Whiter's method was Locke's doctrine of the "association of ideas" described in the *Essay on the Human Understanding*:

> Ideas, that in themselves are not at all of kin, come to be so united in some men's minds, that it is very hard to separate them; they always keep in company, and the one no sooner at any time comes into the understanding, but its associate appears with it; and if they are more than two which are thus united, the whole gang always inseparable shew themselves together.

Locke distinguishes this "association" of seemingly unrelated ideas from what he calls the "train" of naturally related ideas. Whiter's book takes over these concepts and applies them to Shakespeare. He writes:

> I define therefore the power of this association over the genius of the poet to consist in supplying him with words and ideas which have been suggested to the mind by a principle of union unperceived by himself, and independent of the subject to which they are applied.

Later Whiter refers to "the minute and even ridiculous combinations, which have been imposed on the mind of the poet, and which are able to deceive and control the most acute and powerful understanding." He notes the odd association between "love" and "books," among others, but his great triumph is the comment on the lines from *Antony and Cleopatra*, Act IV, Scene xii (as emended by Hanmer in 1744):

> *The hearts*
> *That spaniel'd me at heels, to whom I gave*
> *Their wishes, do discandy, melt their sweets*
> *On blossoming Cæsar.*

His remarks are so startling an anticipation of Miss Spurgeon's method
(as well as Lowes's) as to require reprinting. He writes:

> This passage and the succeeding quotations are well worthy of the
> reader's attention—"No, let the *candied* tongue *lick* absurd pomp,
> And crook the pregnant hinges of the knee Where thrift may follow
> *fawning.*"—*Hamlet*, III, ii, *55*; "Will these moss'd trees, That have
> outlived the eagle, *page* thy *heels*, And skip where thou point'st out?
> will the cold brook, *Candied* with ice, caudle thy morning taste,"
> etc.—*Timon*, IV, iii, *223*; "Why, what a *candy* deal of courtesy This
> *fawning greyhound* then did proffer!"—*I Hen. IV*: I, iii, 251. These
> passages are very singular. The curious reader will observe that
> the *fawning obsequiousness* of an animal, or an attendant, is connected
> with the word *candy*. The cause of this strange association I am un-
> able to discover; though the reader must know but little of the
> human mind—of Shakespeare—or even of the ordinary doctrine of
> *chances*, if he imagines that these matters were in *four* passages con-
> nected by *accident*. When the reader shall be convinced respecting the
> truth of this observation; his curiosity will be much gratified by
> the following lines from the *Tempest;* in which he will perceive that
> the same association still occupied the mind of the Poet, though a
> single *word* only is apparent, which relates to one portion of the
> preceding metaphor. "*Seb.* But, for your conscience? *Ant.* Ay, sir;
> where lies that? if 'twere a *kibe*, 'Twould put me to my slipper: but
> I feel not This deity in my bosom: twenty consciences, That stand
> 'twixt me and Milan, *candied* be they And *melt* ere they molest!"—
> *Tempest*, II, i, *275*. Surely the reader cannot doubt but that the intro-
> duction of the word *kybe* is to be referred to the former expressions,
> "page thy *heels*,"—"spaniel'd me at *heels*," though it is applied to a
> very different metaphor. Let me add, that the quaintness of the
> imagery is an argument for the remoteness of the original.

Miss Spurgeon does not credit Whiter nor mention any of the men who
followed his lead, remarking only that the association "has been noted
by others." She is able to make no improvements on his remarkable
anticipation of her work, however, other than adding some additional
examples from *Julius Cæsar* that had already been added by others, and
furnishing an explanation (equally unoriginal) that fails to explain anything: that Shakespeare, "who was unusually fastidious," hated the
Elizabethan habit of tossing sweets to dogs during meals and somehow
identified it with another thing he detested, the fawning of insincere
friends.

Although the superficiality of her explanation would seem to argue
against it, Miss Spurgeon's great debt in the book, one that she was
almost certainly unconscious of and that would probably have shocked

her had she been aware of it, is to the theories of Sigmund Freud. She describes her basic assumption about literary self-revelation:

In the case of a poet, I suggest it is chiefly through his images that he, to some extent unconsciously, "gives himself away." He may be, and in Shakespeare's case is, almost entirely objective in his dramatic characters and their views and opinions, yet, like the man who under stress of emotion will show no sign of it in eye or face, but will reveal it in some muscular tension, the poet unwittingly lays bare his own innermost likes and dislikes, observations and interests, associations of thought, attitudes of mind and beliefs, in and through the images, the verbal pictures he draws to illuminate something quite different in the speech and thought of his characters.

The imagery he instinctively uses is thus a revelation, largely unconscious, given at a moment of heightened feeling, of the furniture of his mind, the channels of his thought, the qualities of things, the objects and incidents he observes and remembers, and perhaps most significant of all, those which he does not observe or remember.

Although Miss Spurgeon seems much more at home with the term "unwittingly" than the term "unconsciously," which she uses in a popular sense, her statement is clearly post-Freudian. It must assume implicitly some such theory as his of mental areas below consciousness in which such material is stored, some structure of repression or censorship attempting to keep it there, and some dynamic energy in it that sends it forth, disguised and distorted, to emerge in works of art, dreams, and so on. One of Miss Spurgeon's limitations, in fact, is that she was not consciously enough Freudian, not able to recognize the suppression-expression conflict underlying the imagery she studied and carry her analysis further. Perhaps the third book was to be that project, but it is more likely that, to the extent that she recognized it, this problem was one of the ones she left for the "others" who were to use and extend her work.

Shakespeare's Imagery does a good many things of real value. For one thing, it puts in a clear, even visual form a number of fairly abstruse relationships. This is done by a series of seven invaluable charts on graph paper at the end of the book, showing respectively: the range and subject of images of five of Shakespeare's plays; the range and subject of Marlowe's images; the range and subject of Bacon's images; "Daily Life" images in Shakespeare and five contemporary dramatists; the range and subject of all of Shakespeare's images; the dominating images in *King John* and *Henry VIII*; and the dominating images in *Hamlet* and *Troilus and Cressida*. Charts I, II, III, IV, and V effectively demonstrate the uniqueness of Shakespeare's imagery and clearly differentiate it from the work of his contemporaries; and Charts III and V may actually succeed

in laying the Baconian theory finally to rest, with their clear visual
demonstration that the same man could not conceivably have written the
published work of Bacon and the body of plays and poems most of us call
Shakespeare's. The last two charts graph all the plays: the first for bodily
action and personification, with the historical plays, particularly *King
John* and *Henry VIII*, dominating overwhelmingly; the second for images
of food-drink-cooking and sickness-disease-medicine, with *Troilus and
Cressida* far ahead on the first, and *Hamlet* and *Coriolanus* leading on the
second.

In terms of scholarly problems, the book solves or points at a solution
to a good many Shakespeare controversies. Besides laying the ghost of
Bacon to rest with her charts, Miss Spurgeon polishes off Bacon as a
Shakespeare contender in the body of the book, while granting him his
due as a great imaginative writer. She compares his obsessive image, the
majesty of light, with Shakespeare's obsessive image, the garden, noting
the corollaries, Bacon's poverty of nature images, and Shakespeare's
general lack of concern with light, at least as a symbol of majesty. In
addition she is able to point toward the solutions to a number of specific
authorship problems in regard to which plays or parts of plays belong
in the canon (although this would certainly have been much amplified in
the next volume). On the strength of their extensive garden imagery,
for example, she argues that Shakespeare must have had a substantial
part in the authorship of *Henry VI*, *Parts 1, 2,* and *3,* and remarks:
"*Pericles* alone of the romances has no sign of any running 'motive' or
continuity of picture or thought in the imagery, a fact sufficient in itself
to throw grave doubts on its authorship." She is able to suggest a number
of reasonable biographical conjectures from the imagery: that some
personal experience with the plague in 1600 sharply changed Shakespeare's reactions to it from light unconcern before to horror and disgust
after; that although the frequency of Shakespeare's references to the chase
have led commentators to assume that he loved it ("a keen sportsman,"
is J. Dover Wilson's phrase), the *imagery* of the chase in his plays always
reveals Shakespeare's antagonism to and revulsion at the cruelty and
bloodshed. She is even able to confirm chronology from the imagery
(in the next book she might have gone ahead to correct it), and notes,
for example, that if we didn't know that *Troilus and Cressida* and *Hamlet*
were written within a short period of each other, it would be obvious
from the close similarity of their imagery.

Besides problems of pure scholarship *Shakespeare's Imagery* makes a
number of contributions to greater critical understanding and appreciation. The first part of the book, called "The Revelation of the Man," is
exactly that, a pursuit of Shakespeare's mind and personality, as distinguished from the objective details of his life, through his imagery.
The most exciting section is the chapter on "Association of Ideas,"

reinforcing Whiter's dog-fawning-candy cluster with others. The most fascinating of these, penetrating deeper into Shakespeare's psyche than scholarship would ever be likely to go, is a complicated association of death, cannon, eyeball, eye-socket of skull, tears, vault, mouth (sometimes teeth), womb, and back to death again. It appears all through the plays, it is obsessive, and any one of the terms is likely to key any other one, no matter how far-fetched the linkage, or stand surrogate for it. Miss Spurgeon does not attempt to explain this womb-death association or relate it to her earlier discussion of Shakespeare's *Liebestod* obsession with death as a lover or bride, but it is so evident from her explorations that the reader can easily make the linkage.

The second half of the book, "The Function of the Imagery as Background and Undertone in Shakespeare's Art," develops and establishes the important fact that almost every play of Shakespeare's is built around a series of recurrent images that constitute its special motif. Thus *Love's Labour's Lost* centers on war and weapons, *Hamlet* on images of sickness, disease, and corruption, *Lear* on the human body contorted in anguish. Miss Spurgeon makes it clear that these are not the surface references of the plays, but something much deeper. In *Timon of Athens*, for example, which *talks* excessively of gold (two hundred references), there is actually only one *image* drawn from gold; and the dominant *imagery* of the play is the fawning dog licking melting candy, the Whiter cluster. Miss Spurgeon believes, as anyone must from the evidence, that these dominant images in the plays were probably unconscious in Shakespeare. She reasonably enough excepts the motif of the human body in *Coriolanus* as a "preconceived design," since it is very much on the surface of the play and is equally the motif, as the metaphor of the body politic, in Shakespeare's source for the play, Plutarch's *Life of Coriolanus*.

Miss Spurgeon does not attempt to investigate the factors in Shakespeare himself that find expression in these leading motives, but that again may be something she left for a later volume. At the same time she recognizes that imagery can give a sense of approval or revulsion to a character apparently not accounted for by the text, actually reversing the surface attitude (the way Macbeth's grandeur is constantly built up in the references and belittled in the imagery); can give a cumulative effect of emotion or tension; and can reveal the temperament and character of the person using them when nothing else does. It would thus be both an unconscious device for expressing Shakespeare's deepest attitudes and a conscious device of high artistry for deepening, altering, or foreshadowing effects. Miss Spurgeon at one time or another analyzes both aspects of this duality of imagery, but it would need a work far deeper than hers to draw a definitive line between them in the plays as a whole or in any given image.

Shakespeare's Imagery contains a number of obvious errors and defi-

ciencies. Miss Spurgeon's chief fallacy, illustrated on page after page of
the book, is to make a too simple correspondence between imagery and
the playwright's nature or experience. If Shakespeare has more riding
images than Marlowe, and Dekker has more fishing images than Massinger, then Shakespeare and Dekker were outdoor types and Marlowe
and Massinger were not. It never occurs to her that a fishing or riding
image might be based, not on an obsessive love for sport, but on something fishing or riding in turn symbolizes. Since Shakespeare delights in
imagery of swift nimble body movements, he must have been "himself
as agile in body as in mind" (although, noting the example of Renoir's
lush healthy nudes and his arthritis, we might be just as apt to deduce
that Shakespeare was hopelessly crippled); because he uses frequent
images of the betrying change of color in the face, Miss Spurgeon "cannot
help surmising he himself, like Richard II, was fair and flushed easily";
"no one who was not himself very sensitive to the tone and timbre of
the human voice could have drawn so many characters who share this
peculiarity as Shakespeare has done"; he must have had a garden to draw
so many images from grafting and the killing effects of frost; and so forth.

The general assumptions are that Shakespeare must have done what
the images talk about, done well what the characters do well, and even
thought what they thought (so that despite her warning against crediting
Shakespeare with his protagonists' ideas, she slips into reading *Hamlet*
as Shakespeare torn between idealism and cynicism). The assumptions
parody themselves with the statement: "By 1599, when he was five and
thirty, Shakespeare has probably experienced heartburn as a result of
acidity"; and with the fanciful and absurd portrait of Shakespeare the
man Miss Spurgeon summarizes from the imagery:

> The figure of Shakespeare which emerges is of a compactly well-
> built man, probably on the slight side, extraordinarily well co-
> ordinated, lithe and nimble of body, quick and accurate of eye, de-
> lighting in swift muscular movement. I suggest that he was probably
> fair-skinned and of a fresh colour, which in youth came and went
> easily, revealing his feelings and emotions. All his senses were
> abnormally acute, especially—probably—those of hearing and taste.
>
> He was healthy in body as in mind, clean and fastidious in his
> habits, very sensitive to dirt and evil smells. Apart from many in-
> direct proofs of these facts in the plays, no man could have written
> his images on sickness, surfeit, gluttony, dirt and disease, who had
> not naturally a strong feeling for healthy living, a liking for fresh
> air and "honest water," and who was not himself clean, temperate
> and healthy.

And so on for six incredible pages about his quietness, love for the
country, interest in homely activities; "sensitiveness, balance, courage,

humour and wholesomeness"; "Christ-like; that is, gentle, kindly, honest, brave and true"; in short, the troop-leader of the Stratford boy scouts.

A number of the faults of Miss Spurgeon's book seem to be accidental neglects or omissions: she points out that Ben Jonson was apprenticed to his stepfather as a bricklayer, but neither notices nor explains that her chart of his imagery reveals that he and Chapman are the only playwrights who have no images drawn from buildings; she notes that Shakespeare has almost no images drawn from town life or scenes, but makes no attempt to explain why this should be so in a playwright who spent most of his adult life in London; and so on. Other faults seem to be definite weaknesses of her method. One obvious one is that her classification of images, being purely subjective, is bound to be arbitrary and inconsistent: on page 36 "alabaster arms" is an image drawn from the appearance of a substance, "not from its feel"; on page 82 Desdemona's skin, "smooth as monumental alabaster," is a touch image. A much deeper and more basic objection to her method, raised by I. A. Richards (without mentioning her by name) among others, is that "the metaphors are being sorted in respect to one only of the pair of 'ideas' which every metaphor, at its simplest, gives us"; that is, that all the other ambiguous possibilities of Shakespeare's "images" never get into her tabulation at all. Her comment on the "small number" of theatrical images, for example, as Sir E. K. Chambers points out in his *Shakespearean Gleanings*, is absurd, since they are plentiful; she merely indexed them under a reference she found more obvious. Miss Spurgeon admits the limitations and problems of her method in an appendix to the book entitled "Difficulties connected with the counting and classifying of images," explaining the complications she encountered in tabulating, classifying, and cross-referencing imagery. This may serve to explain specific errors, or even the general slovenliness of her classifications, but it is hardly an adequate answer to the charge, raised by many other scholars and critics as well as by Chambers and Richards, that her scheme is seriously vitiated from the start by too narrow a concept of the nature of metaphor.

The greatest limitation in Miss Spurgeon's method is not procedural at all, but her inability within its framework of assumptions to follow up psychological implications. When Shakespeare is obsessed with a river in a number of significant contexts, to Jung it would be a mythic pattern, to Freud it would probably symbolize a sex or birth flow, but to Miss Spurgeon it is simply "boyhood memories of the Avon at Stratford." When she points out that the running metaphor in the early historical plays is "the rash and untimely cutting or lopping of fine trees," any psychology would note its association with the figures of kings and interpret it as the destruction of authority or a father-symbol, if not specifically castration; Miss Spurgeon interprets it as an interest in orchards. Psychology would not deny her Avon or orchard readings; it would simply *begin* from there. A Freudian would interpret her leading motif in each play as a key experiential symbol in Shakespeare's own psyche, a Jungian would read it as an archetypal pattern, a gestaltist would see it as the essential configuration of the experience, and so on; but Miss Spurgeon is able to see it as nothing but a subject that Shakespeare just happened to be thinking about at the time.

Here we encounter the problem of what critics better equipped than Miss Spurgeon have done with her material, as an illustration of what she might have done or a sample of what still remains for criticism to do. The man who first showed the potentialities of her researches is the English critic G. Wilson Knight. Before the publication of any of Miss Spurgeon's material Knight had been working informally along closely similar lines, and *The Wheel of Fire*, published in 1930, notes the significance of a good deal of recurrent imagery, including such important clusters as love, jewels, and dangerous sea journeys, and traces parallel imageries through several plays. By *The Imperial Theme*, published in 1931, Knight was familiar with Miss Spurgeon's lecture on "Leading Motives in the Imagery of Shakespeare's Tragedies," which he acknowledges and uses extensively, although still continuing his own exhaustive imagery tabulations, particularly in his chapter on *Julius Cæsar*. By 1932, in *The Shakespearian Tempest*, Knight was familiar with Miss Spurgeon's lecture on "Shakespeare's Iterative Imagery," which he acknowledges for "extending and stimulating my general understanding," with the reservation that on one point, the imagery of overflowing water in "disorder" contexts, he claims independent origin. He still continues his own tabulation, and one of his appendices, "The Shakespeare Aviary," is a thirty-two-page summary of Shakespeare's bird imagery and references.

Knight had thus done his major work on Shakespeare before *Shakespeare's Imagery* appeared, utilizing no more of Miss Spurgeon's work than her two lectures revealed. After her book appeared, however, one brief chapter, on "The Shakespearian Integrity" in *The Burning Oracle*, makes it clear how much use he could have made of her detailed researches.[1] As Prof. Caroline Spurgeon has shown," he writes continually, "as Prof. Spurgeon observes," and so on. It is true that Knight is one of the most eclectic of modern critics, who has used and acknowledged almost every contemporary critic, and that in addition he and Miss Spurgeon had been working independently along similar lines (so that

[1] By 1947, when Knight returned to his Shakespeare study to discuss the final plays in *The Crown of Life*, he was too much preoccupied with "prophetic significance" and such matters to make more than perfunctory use of Miss Spurgeon's work, or any imagery study.

Shakespeare's Imagery returns the compliment by using a good deal of *his* work). Nevertheless, the way her exhaustive tabulations confirm some of Knight's old intuitions and suggest new ones to him is a tribute to her value for the critic, and his imaginative flights show by contrast how limiting she kept her aims. (Where Miss Spurgeon is able to correct Knight, as in his contention that "gold-symbolism" is dominant in *Timon*, it is not through superior insight but merely through her opening up a new area of information, the image-tabulation, as though she had discovered another lost book like Keats's Shakespeare.)

Almost all critical writing on Shakespeare since 1935 has taken advantage of Miss Spurgeon's researches, but very little of it besides Knight's used her work for the serious imaginative constructions it demands until the publication of Edward A. Armstrong's *Shakespeare's Imagination* in England in 1946. This amazing little book, subtitled *A Study of the Psychology of Association and Inspiration*, is not so much an extension of Miss Spurgeon's researches as an extension of her method itself, along with Knight's and Lowes's techniques (as well as a heavy reliance on E. M. W. Tillyard and his *Elizabethan World Picture*), to develop a "cluster criticism" as original as it is invaluable, and to test it on Shakespeare. Armstrong is apparently a Cambridge ornithologist (his three previous books have been *Birds of the Grey Wind*, *The Way Birds Live*, and *Bird Display: An Introduction to the Study of Bird Psychology*) as well as an entomologist, psychologist, folklorist, Shakespeare scholar, and skilled literary critic. This book focuses all his fields at once. Armstrong starts from Shakespeare's bird and insect imagery, follows their clusters of association through the plays, discovers the principles, polarities, and habits of mind underlying Shakespeare's association of images, along with a basis for predicting the development of associations; and concludes with (1) a new technique for solving problems of Shakespeare scholarship, (2) a theory of the workings of the creative process in general, and (3) one of the most stimulating and delightful surveys of Shakespeare's mind and work yet written.

Armstrong is greatly indebted to Miss Spurgeon for her basic concepts of "imagery" and "cluster," as well as for her specific discoveries of a number of relationships, associations, and clusters, and many of her tabulations and conclusions. In almost every case, however, he goes beyond her work, refuting her oversimple dichotomies, explaining what she fails to explain (like the death-eye-socket-mouth-vault-womb-etc. cluster, which he interprets convincingly as a chain of "hollow" symbols between birth and death), correcting her distortions, amplifying her illustrations and examples, extending her "dominant, running or reiterative" imagery with a more significant type he calls "thematic," criticizing the limitations of her system of classification in terms similar to Richards's strictures. (In only one case does he fall down significantly:

his only explanation for the Whiter cluster is "Probably Dr. Caroline Spurgeon was right.")

In the course of correcting Miss Spurgeon's faults or going beyond her, Armstrong does a number of invaluable things. He uses a great deal of formal psychology, from Freud and Jung (somewhat unhappily) to conclusions derived from prefrontal lobotomy, and insists on the modern psychological concept of the mind as an organic system, operating dynamically. He is aware of the ritual origins of drama and the significance for Shakespeare study of the researches of Jane Harrison and her group. He deals explicitly with the ambiguous and ambivalent possibilities of imagery and association, and insists that Shakespeare's images tend to derive from sound-correspondence and personal or traditional symbolism, rather than from observation and literal "experience." He is excellent on the applications of his "cluster criticism" to scholarly problems (here following Miss Spurgeon's leads), proving that Shakespeare had Hamlet say "handsaw" rather than "hernshaw" or any other bird, proving the authenticity of the disputed epilogue to *Troilus and Cressida*, and suggesting that more work with his method could check the chronology of the plays and, on his basic assumption that "no two poets employ the same image clusters," establish that the plays are the work of one man, refute all contenders other than Shakespeare, and determine the authorship of disputed passages or plays. Finally, Armstrong's four elaborate tables of key image clusters, the kite, the beetle, the drone and weasel, and the goose, are, if possible, even more exciting and useful than Miss Spurgeon's graphs.

These substantial achievements far outweigh the book's defects. Stylistically the defects include an awful archness in referring to the imagination ("an unrecognized sprite," "artful sublimal goblin," etc.) and an annoying, often comic, scientific pomposity ("I have used the term 'vermin' to include the various creatures which sting and bite, as 'insect' would not include the sheep tick"). Sometimes Armstrong falls down on his own principles and tries to use his clusters to answer questions about Shakespeare's private observation, experience, life, or personality (did some death-bed scene impress his mind, did he dislike dogs, did he ever steal deer or violets, did he suffer more from fleas or lice, did the Dark Lady use heavy make-up, did he ever catch the pox?), but generally Armstrong recovers and admits sadly that we cannot know, that personal investigation through clusters is at best "precarious" and that those who want evidence of "the poet's amours" or the characteristics of his mistress "must look elsewhere." Finally, the second half of the book, a generalized study of "The Psychology of Imagination" on the basis of the earlier exploration of Shakespeare's imagery, is very much inferior to the first half, chiefly as a result of inadequate psychology. Armstrong spends a good deal of his time quarreling pointlessly with

Freud, and positively seems unacquainted with the only psychology adequate to the picture of the mind his evidence constantly suggests (specifically, the Gestalt) and is consequently forced to rely on the fragmentary insights of MacCurdy, F. C. Bartlett, McDougall, Rivers, and others.

Although no one else has attempted the detailed extension of Miss Spurgeon's work it deserves, almost all the serious critics who have used it over the past decade have attempted to augment it or transcend its limitations in some fashion. In *Attitudes toward History* (1937) Kenneth Burke discusses, under "Clusters," the possibilities she raises of charting any author's clusters "to get our clues as to the important ingredients subsumed in 'symbolic mergers' "; and under "Imagery" (after praising the book as "usable" and discussing its suggestive possibilities at some length), attempts, from some of Miss Spurgeon's data, to plot the "curve" of Shakespeare's writings in relation to the curve of historical processes in his day. In *The Philosophy of Literary Form* (1941) Burke praises *Shakespeare's Imagery* as one of "the three most fertile works on literature since *The Sacred Wood*" (the other two are volumes by Richards and Empson), at the same time suggesting a further dimension her method lacks, the addition of *qualitative* criteria, based on significance, to her purely *quantitative* criteria for imagery; that is, special weighting for imagery that appears at such key spots in the work as opening, peripety, or closing.

In 1942, in *Shakespeare and the Nature of Man*, Theodore Spencer made frequent use of Miss Spurgeon's insights, while proposing another sort of extension, a dynamic rather than static treatment, which not only would note, as she does, that *Hamlet* contains more disease images than any other play, but would find it particularly significant that they build up to a climax, that eighty-five per cent of them occur after the middle of the play. In 1943, in "The Altar of Henry James" in the *New Republic*, William Troy proposed the use of her methods in another area, the later novels of Henry James; and in *Folktale, Fiction and Saga in the Homeric Epics* (1946), Rhys Carpenter paid tribute to her method and proposed its application to Greek epic. Miss Spurgeon's work has also been used and extended by Marxist critics. In the *Modern Quarterly Miscellany* No. 1 (1947), for example, in an article entitled "*Timon of Athens* and the Cash-Nexus," Kenneth Muir uses some of her material on *Timon*, while proposing a broadened concept of "image" to include such non-metaphoric symbolism as that of "gold" in the play. Finally, also in 1947, Cleanth Brooks, in *The Well Wrought Urn*, took her discovery and tabulation of the master-image of the "ill-fitting garment" in *Macbeth* as the starting-point for an analysis of the symbolic structure of the play of far greater depth and subtlety than anything in Miss Spurgeon's system. He continually acknowledges her discoveries and the material "which Miss Spurgeon has collected for us," while at the same time pushing beyond her, and his references all have that ambivalence: "one has to observe that Miss Spurgeon has hardly explored the full implications of her discovery," "she has realized only a part of the potentialities," "if we free ourselves of Miss Spurgeon's rather mechanical scheme of classification," "though Miss Spurgeon does not include the passage in her examples," "though Miss Spurgeon does not note it," "since the governing scheme of her book would have hardly allowed her to see it," and so on.

In all of these extensions and modifications of her work we can see both the limitations and the importance of Caroline Spurgeon. She herself did not venture very far, or cover even that distance very well. But with a wider concept of the nature of metaphor and symbolism, a better system of plural classification, a deeper psychological understanding of the workings of the mind, fuller and more careful evidence, new qualitative and dynamic dimensions, new works to explore, and far greater imaginative power, some of the subtlest and most important criticism of our day has been, and will increasingly be, enabled to venture far indeed because of her work.

3

The tradition of literary scholarship in which Miss Spurgeon works is both very extensive and not much to our purpose here. Its subdivisions are endless, and within any given sub-sub-subdivision a scholar can live out his years in productive content. It is the business of the scholar to produce an accurate text from a welter of corruptions, emendations, manuscript illegibilities, and even lacunæ; to annotate a text in reference to its sources, its obscure meanings, its analogues, available historical records, and any other criteria that seem important; to equip the reader with an accurate biography of the writer, literary history in which his work is related to a context, and comparative study in which his work and context are discussed in terms of other work and contexts; and finally to prepare the endless paraphernalia of learning, the bibliographies, chronologies, concordances, word-counts, studies or theses clearing up individual points, new editions, translations, compilations, variora or multiple-text editions, handbooks, anthologies, textbooks, and the rest.

The most distinguished and extensive scholarship, for obvious reasons, has been inspired by the most important works of literature, specifically the Bible, Homer, and Shakespeare. With the miracles of Biblical and Semitic scholarship, chiefly the so-called "higher criticism," which has largely succeeded in unraveling the innumerable documents, revisions, and editings that go to make up our Sacred Books, and the only slightly less miraculous feats of Homeric and Greek scholarship that have done a comparable job in identifying the medley of fragments and incrustations we know as Homer, we need not concern ourselves here. A very brief glance at a few aspects of Shakespeare scholarship, the specific tradition in which Miss Spurgeon worked, however, is in order, to place her work in context.

The special problems of Shakespeare scholarship arose from the absence of any of Shakespeare's manuscripts or any authoritative text known to be corrected by him. The plays were printed one by one in miscellaneous quartos, some of them "stolne, and surreptitious," some of them printed several times from different sources, before the plays thought to be by Shakespeare were officially collected in the first folio of 1623, so that in a number of cases, notably *Hamlet*, there are three ostensibly independent texts—two quartos and the folio—in which it is still possible for all three readings at any given point to be wrong. During the seventeenth century, along with more quartos, three more folios were issued, in 1632, 1664, and 1685, each one correcting some of the previous errors. In the eighteenth century the great Shakespeare editors, among them Rowe, Pope, Theobald, Hanmer, Warburton, and Dr. Johnson, issued critical editions culminating in the brilliant and learned texts of George Steevens and Edward Malone. These editors saw their function as correcting what they took to be misprints in previous texts (although frequently they merely altered them to new misprints), defending their corrections against opposition, and interpreting and annotating obscure or debated passages. The first variorum text, containing the readings of more than one authority, was issued in 1773, and through the next century, as scholars lost the conviction that all of the textual problems of Shakespeare were finally soluble and that there would eventually be one definitive text, variorum editions continued to be issued. The culmination of Shakespeare scholarship in our own century, as well as the history of it, can be found in the modern variorum editions, which for many years have been issued in America, almost as the private preserve of the elder and younger Horace Howard Furness. The contents of one is worth noting.

The Variorum Edition of *Antony and Cleopatra*, although substantially shorter than that of *Hamlet* or *The Sonnets* (because of the greater amount of comment they have elicited), is fairly typical. Edited by the elder Furness in 1907, the book includes an introductory preface about the play; the exact text as it appeared in the first folio, covering 375 pages, a few lines on a page; below the text, on each page, *all* later variant readings, and below that their authors' explanations and defenses of them, with interpretations of the passage. The Appendix, which covers more than two hundred additional pages, includes a compilation and discussion of all serious opinions on the play's date of composition; an account of the duration of action in the play; a transcript of every passage from North's *Plutarch* on which Shakespeare drew, keyed to the line of the play; the whole of Dryden's *All For Love*, a later play on the same theme, with a compilation of remarks on it; thirty pages of selected criticism of Shakespeare's play and its characters by English, German, and French commentators; seventy-five pages devoted to summarizing and quoting extensively from all other dramatic versions of the story; an account of the various acting versions, actors, and performances of Shakespeare's play; an account of all the costumes and settings it has had; a list of all the emendations of the folio adopted in the relatively definitive Cambridge Edition; a list of all the editions collated in the Variorum; a list of all the books quoted; and an extensive index. As can be seen, any student of a Shakespeare play armed with a modern variorum edition and a concordance to Shakespeare would be far better equipped than were two centuries of Shakespeare scholars.

The Variorum *Antony and Cleopatra* illustrates the best as well as the worst features of Shakespeare scholarship. At its best it is a brilliant flash of insight that is then unquestionable ever afterwards, like Hanmer's emendation in 1744 of "spaniel'd" for "pannelled" in "The hearts That pannelled me at heeles" (a reading almost as fine as the great classic of Shakespeare emendation, Theobald's substitution, in the description of Falstaff's death in *Henry V*, of "for his nose was as sharp as a pen, and a' babbled of green fields" for the meaningless "for his Nose was as sharpe as a Pen, and a Table of greene fields"). At its worst it is Heath explaining the mysterious lines "So many Mer-maides tended her i'th'eyes, And made their bends adornings" as "these seeming nereids were employed in adjusting Cleopatra's eye-brows, as often as they happened to be discomposed by the fanning of the boys, or any other accident." At its most pointless it is Theobald and all subsequent editors changing "For his Bounty, There was no winter in't. An Anthony it was" to "an autumn it was," when "an Anthony" is perfectly satisfactory, is supported by Cleopatra's earlier "Oh, my oblivion is a very Anthony!" and is far more expressive poetically.

In the last example we come to the gravest charge raised against Shakespeare scholars, that for the most part they do not tend to be very poetic men. William Empson has made this charge most effectively in *Seven Types of Ambiguity*, in the brilliant and ingenious theory that what Shakespeare editors tend to do is *unwrite* the play, working a Shakespearian ambiguity back to the simple one-meaning word with which he started and which he then enriched. He gives a number of examples, typical of which are the lines: "My way of life is falne into the Seare, the yellow Leafe," amended by Johnson (a very poetic man, but in a prosy century) to "May of life." Johnson's emendation, Empson writes ironically, "seems to me a valuable piece of retrospective analysis, because it shows how the poetry was constructed; first, there would be an orderly framework of metaphor, then any enrichment of the notion which kept to the same verbal framework and was suggested easily by similarity of sound." And so on, through a damning number of emendations Empson would re-emend back to the original.

W. W. Greg, in his brilliant "Principles of Emendation in Shake-speare," the Shakespeare Lecture of the British Academy for 1928, defines the nature of the problem and the rules it imposes, making them seem as fascinating and internally consistent as the rules of chess. He pleads for far greater conservatism in editing Shakespeare, using as one of his examples Dowden's charge that in amending Polonius's "I'll silence me even here" as he hides behind the arras, to "I'll sconce me here," Han-mer managed to deprive Shakespeare of one of his great dramatic ironies, Polonius's inability to keep silent under any circumstances except the death that inability brought on. Greg's lecture, which is the best concise and understandable statement I know of the whole problem of Shake-speare texts, is welcome evidence that the Shakespeare editors of our time may be in the process of coming around to Empson's view. After three centuries of turning Shakespeare's "Arme-gaunt Steede" into "arm-girt," "termagant," "arrogant," "merchant," "ardent," "arme-g'raunt," "barbed," and "arm-zoned," we shall perhaps have a breed of editors prepared to leave it "arm-gaunt."

Besides the history, textual scholarship and interpretation, compilation of sources and other material that have gone into the variora, Shakespeare scholars have devoted themselves to compiling concordances and chro-nologies, checking Elizabethan handwriting and legal papers, writing biographies of the master (almost entirely conjectural), and, a new emphasis in recent times, under the influence of the discoveries of Sir Edmund Chambers and others, analyzing him in terms of the theater and production problems now and then.[2] The greatest body of Shake-speare scholarship, however, has manifested itself in critical interpreta-tion of the plays and characters (the latter a great sport of the nineteenth century) and in theorizing about his views, ideas, topical references, and so on. At its best this scholarly criticism has resulted in the brilliant analytic work of men like Edward Dowden and A. C. Bradley; at its worst it is typified by the *Hamlet* theories: Mercade's that the play is an allegorical philosophy of history, with Hamlet as the Spirit of Truth-Seeking and Ophelia as the Church; Lilian Winstanley's that it is about the Scottish succession; John Dover Wilson's that it is about the con-spiracy of Essex; others that Hamlet was a woman in love with Horatio, or a wicked young man faking the ghost, and so on endlessly.

[2] An authoritative list of twenty-six major divisions of Shakespeare scholarship, for those whose interest may be stimulated by this superficial account, can be found on the first page of J. Isaacs's excellent essay on the subject in *A Companion to Shake-speare Studies*.

Dover Wilson is a typical case; an intelligent and conservative textual critic, one of the editors of the valuable (sometimes weird) new Cambridge edition, who has been one of those to make an exhaustive study of Elizabethan handwriting as a basis for reconstructing Shakespeare's manuscripts through compositors' misreadings, he frequently goes wild when he gets to critical interpretation, and relies on no evidence more objective than his own pipe dreams. Theories like the conjecture in *The Essential Shakespeare* that the great last poems Shakespeare undoubtedly wrote after his retirement were destroyed by his Puritan son-in-law, or the view in *What Happens in Hamlet* that Shakespeare chose Denmark as a setting because of its Lutheranism, make Greg's statement that Wilson's theories are the "careerings of a not too captive balloon in a high wind" seem surprisingly moderate.

4

Besides Caroline Spurgeon, a number of contemporary scholars have made real contributions to criticism. Perhaps the most important of them is the man whose method so much influenced Miss Spurgeon, Professor John Livingston Lowes of Harvard. Lowes is that rare scholarly combination, a man possessing both great learning and real imagination, and all his criticism is a utilization of scholarship, sometimes in fairly odd fashions. He is apt to make a point by counting the swoons in medieval French versions of classical epics (thirty swoons of heroes and heroines in the *Roman de Troie*, twenty-two in the *Thèbes*, "four or five times hand running during a single trying situation"); or to collect the constraining rhymes of poets, noting that Pope satirized the rhyme of "breeze" with "trees," but did it himself in four of the five occasions he ended a line with "breeze," and that the Alps in "Childe Harold" inevitably have scalps, since even *Walker's Lexicon* can suggest no alternatives, and so on.

Lowes's major critical-scholarly work is *The Road to Xanadu*, subtitled *A Study in the Ways of the Imagination*, a six-hundred-page tracing of the sources of Coleridge's two great poems, "The Ancient Mariner" and "Kubla Khan." It is a wholly fascinating and almost miraculous single-handed reconstruction of a poet's reading and precise state of mind after one hundred and twenty-five years. Relying on Coleridge's extensive habit of jotting and his curious trick of habitually passing from any given book he read to all the books to which that book referred, Lowes simply followed Coleridge through all his reading. As a result of his incredible doggedness (he read Priestley's *Opticks*, 807 quarto pages, on a hunch, and on the 807th page found what he was looking for, a proof that Coleridge had read and used the book) he was able to trace the conscious or unconscious source of almost every image in the poems, and in one stanza actually traced every word!

What started to be a simple pursuit of scholarly sources proliferated on Lowes the way *The Golden Bough* proliferated on Frazer and became a major study in the operations of the poetic imagination. Lowes was forced by the material to venture into the nature of memory and the imagination, and although he specifically disclaims a deeper psychological concern, writing: "I wish to state with emphasis that I am dealing in this study with what psychoanalysts call the material content of the dream, and with that alone. With its so-called latent content—its possible symbolism of wish-fulfillment or conflict or what not—I have nothing whatever to do"—he ends up with a wholly credible picture of Coleridge's subconscious mind, although presented in the odd psychological mechanism of Coleridge's "hooks-and-eyes of memory" and Poincaré's "hooked atoms." The book is actually a study in "the assimilating and incorporative power of the shaping spirit," or, in Baudelaire's words, "the labor by which a reverie becomes a work of art."

The Road to Xanadu does not exhaust Lowes's contribution. His studies of modern poetry were actually a sideline to his special field, which was Chaucer, and he has boiled down a quarter of a century of Chaucer study, in the great tradition of Skeat, Furnivall, and Kittredge, in one of the best popularizations written, *Geoffrey Chaucer and the Development of His Genius*, which studies the man, not as a dead text for scholars to nibble at, but as a first-rate poet living in a fascinating time. In addition, in the course of his Coleridge studies, Lowes made by-product discoveries into the unconscious sources of poets like Milton and Keats that suggest that books like *The Road to Xanadu* could develop a school capable of turning even the dull scholarly pursuit of sources into a critical activity.

The most obvious fact about *The Road to Xanadu*, as about *Shakespeare's Imagery*, is its enormous possibility for further extension, specifically in the psychoanalytic direction Lowes carefully disclaims. Lowes is legitimately scornful of Robert Graves's pseudo-psychoanalytic reading of "Kubla Khan" in *The Meaning of Dreams*, tagging its ignorance, brashness, specific inaccuracies, and general silliness, but he cannot deny the possibility of a sober and intelligent reading of the poem, which would in fact rely heavily on his work, taking over his deepest insights and deepening them further.[3] On the other hand, the scholars and their fellow traveler, Mark Van Doren, have reproached Lowes for doing too much, for venturing too far. Reviewing the book in the *Nation*, Van Doren complained that Lowes should have confined himself to the

[3] To some extent this was done by Robert Penn Warren in his long introduction to *The Ancient Mariner*, "A Poem of Pure Imagination," in 1946. Warren certainly deepens Lowes's reading, particularly through his use of Miss Bodkin's archetypal patterns, but a good deal of his effort is pointlessly expended, not in working from what Lowes did achieve, but in quarreling with what Lowes failed to do and with his limitations in general.

scholar's job of stating demonstrable facts, to the printing of a text with the poems on one side of the page and their sources on the other, "most of the time saying nothing," rather than daring to talk about processes and ways of the imagination.

The sharpest scholarly criticism of *The Road to Xanadu* came from Professor Lane Cooper of Cornell in the *Publications of the Modern Language Association* in 1928, and was reprinted in Cooper's *Aristotelian Papers* in 1939. Cooper, a self-styled "Aristotelian" critic and concordance-maker, who has liked little literature since Wordsworth, makes a very instructive contrast with Lowes. In 1910 Cooper had published a paper displaying remarkable insight, on "The Power of the Eye in Coleridge," showing the many variants of the fixing, magnetic eye in "The Ancient Mariner:" in persons, the sun, serpents, and so on. He seemed to be so displeased by finding something of interest in a poet he disliked that he spent most of the essay apologizing. When Lowes's book appeared, Cooper reviewed it in one of the pettiest, vainest, and most mean-spirited attacks ever committed in the name of scholarship. He announces: "I naturally tried to see how much use had been made of my study" (which Lowes had both used and acknowledged) and appears both to criticize Lowes's use of it and to complain of the fact that Lowes had found it necessary to say anything more. He suggests that Lowes's book contains little or no original work, but nevertheless protests its wildness, which he hints is a prostitution of scholarship for popularity. He attacks "Kubla Khan" for moral "blemishes," agrees with Wordsworth's "Aristotelian" criticism of "The Ancient Mariner" as not very good, and suggests that Wordsworth wrote what little there is of value in Coleridge. He raises endless minor quibbles with Lowes, triumphantly finds a dangling participle in his book, and counts his repetitions. Cooper's article is almost an anthology of the worst faults of scholarship, both in terms of the personal deficiencies of scholars and in the sterility of method and absence of vision. John Livingston Lowes and Lane Cooper make an interesting contrast as two types of scholar. It is needless to add that it is only with the first type that criticism need have any concern.

Scholarship by at least one man in a philosophic field has made a real contribution to literary criticism, and is potentially even more fruitful. That is the history of ideas, a philosophic field largely invented and pre-empted by Professor Arthur O. Lovejoy of Johns Hopkins. The history of ideas is the tracing of the unit ideas of philosophies through intellectual history, and just as it finds its chief clues in literary expression, literary criticism can draw on it for the philosophic background of literature. Lovejoy's chief book, *The Great Chain of Being*, is the tracing of the idea of that name, made up of the three related concepts of plenitude, continuity, and gradation, from its origin in Plato and Aristotle, through its temporalizing in the eighteenth century, into a Great Chain of Becoming, to its great flowering in Schelling and romanticism. In the course of the book Lovejoy actually writes a history of romantic thought, drawing on evidence not only from philosophy and literature, but also from theology, philology and semantics, science, politics, and gardening. The substance of *The Great Chain of Being*, which was delivered as the William James Lectures at Harvard, has been influential in the critical writings of a number of Harvard professors, among them F. O. Matthiessen and Theodore Spencer, but few critics besides Harvard and Johns Hopkins people (and, as usual, Kenneth Burke) seem to know of Lovejoy and his work, although the scholars have been tremendously influenced by it. Knowledge of it would have been of great value in such explorations of romanticism as Babbitt's *Rousseau and Romanticism*, Praz's *The Romantic Agony*, and Lucas's *The Decline and Fall of the Romantic Ideal* (the first two written before *The Great Chain of Being* appeared). For literary criticism, the great advantage of the history of ideas is its ability to reconstruct the "frame of reference," the context of thinking underlying great works of the past. Lovejoy has explored other ideas, in *The Revolt against Dualism* and in the documentary history, *Primitivism and Related Ideas*, which he collaborated in compiling, and he and his disciples have a magazine, the *Journal of the History of Ideas*, devoted to similar explorations, but no work comparable in importance to *The Great Chain of Being* has, to my knowledge, so far been produced.

A. C. Bradley is worth some discussion as illustrating a type of scholarship (E. E. Stoll's *Shakespeare Studies* is another example) that relies on no special method other than close reading and extreme familiarity. Aside from a few special and partial approaches, like Empson's, Knight's, Ernest Jones's, Miss Spurgeon's, and Armstrong's, Bradley has written the deepest and most perceptive Shakespeare criticism of our time. Regarding *Hamlet*, on the strength of nothing but careful reading and thinking, Bradley came to the threshold of Jones's conclusions, lacking only the psychoanalytic equipment that would have carried him farther. He recognized that all the major theories are untenable; that Hamlet's state is chiefly related to something about his mother, not his uncle; and in fact his term "melancholic paralysis" for Hamlet's inability to act is a remarkable anticipation of Jones's more scientific "aboulia." At the same time he foreshadows Miss Spurgeon, Knight, and Empson. Anticipating Miss Spurgeon, he tabulates Iago's use of nautical imagery, notices the abundance of animal images in *Timon* and *Lear*, lists imagery of darkness, light, blood, and violence in *Macbeth*, and so on. Anticipating Knight, he collects allusions to music in Shakespeare and notes that it seems to be Shakespeare's core symbol for peace and happiness, but misses going farther to the discovery that the tempest is its counter-symbol. He approximates Empson's theory of scholarly emenders unwriting Shakespeare, and illustrates with one of the emendations Empson based his case on, Johnson's "May of life" for "way of life."

The extent of Bradley's scholarship is not visible in the text of his chief book, *Shakespearian Tragedy*, a lengthy study of *Hamlet, Othello, Lear*, and *Macbeth*. He devotes two chapters to each play, the first chiefly a close discussion of structure, the second a discussion of the characters, almost as real people. The scholarship underlying the book's critical insights, however, comes through sharply in the thirty-two appended Notes, which embark on textual emendations, comparisons of quarto and folio texts, tabulations of word-usage, suggestions for staging, and chronology-determining through a number of technical tests. Much of the scholarship in itself comes to nothing—a note is just as apt to end with the conclusion that the matter may simply be an inconsistency in Shakespeare, or that there are two possible suppositions about the matter and that neither seems very likely—but it is the basis for the keen critical perceptions in the body of the book.

On literature other than Shakespeare Bradley has not been so successful. His discussions of English romantic poetry in *Oxford Lectures on Poetry* and *A Commentary on Tennyson's* In Memoriam tend to get involved in meaningless and rather musty controversies over whether one poet is more "sublime" than another, and the best part of the *Oxford Lectures* is the Shakespeare material on Falstaff, *Antony and Cleopatra*, and the Elizabethan theater and audience. Bradley's central interest in Shakespeare's characters, in which he is the logical heir of Coleridge, Hazlitt, and Brandes (a movement beautifully satirized by L. C. Knights in "How Many Children Had Lady Macbeth?") leads him to the traditional pitfall of Shakespeare investigation, the silly conjectures about Shakespeare's own character. He commits all the excesses Miss Spurgeon commits: tells us that Shakespeare's favorite flower was the violet, his favorite bird was the lark, and he didn't like spaniels; that such and such a passage seems "to have a personal ring," "came from the heart," or was "Shakespeare himself speaking."

For the most part, though, a basic good sense keeps Bradley sound. He is able to concentrate on minutiæ, like the number of lines in tense scenes, the occasions when Shakespeare shifts from prose to verse, or the number of combats and occasions for playing martial music in *Henry VI, Part 1*, but always uses them to get at a serious point and never bogs down in them. His chief deficiency, for his own purposes, is inadequate knowledge of classical drama and criticism. Although he makes frequent comparisons between Shakespeare and the Greek dramatists and relies heavily on Aristotle, in his central emphasis on "Character" as the essence of tragedy he is profoundly non-Aristotelian; a basic misconception of the nature of Greek drama leads him to find Macbeth an inadequate hero; and in phrasing the movement of a drama as "exposition," "conflict," and "catastrophe" he misses the central element of Greek and all later great drama, the final "acceptance" (compare, for example, Francis Fergusson's rounded series, "purpose, passion, and perception").

No one has better noted the limitations and deficiencies of scholarship than Bradley. He speaks scornfully of one type of scholar wearying himself with rival hypotheses and poring over minutiæ until he loses "the broad and deep impressions which vivid reading leaves," and writes:

> Research, though toilsome, is easy; imaginative vision, though delightful, is difficult; and we may be tempted to prefer the first. Or we note that in a given passage Shakespeare has used what he found in his authority; and we excuse ourselves from asking why he used it or what he made of it. Or we see that he has done something that would please his audience; and we dismiss it as accounted for, forgetting that it also pleased *him*, and that we have to account for *that*. Or knowledge of his stage shows us the stage convenience of a scene; and we say that the scene was due to stage convenience, as if the cause of a thing must needs be single and simple. Such errors provoke the man who reads his Shakespeare poetically, and make him blaspheme our knowledge. But we ought not to fall into them; and we cannot reject any knowledge that may help us into Shakespeare's mind because of the danger it brings.

Bradley himself was far from the sort of scholar he refers to; was in fact the successful combination of both scholar and "man who reads his Shakespeare poetically." The best description of his work is the phrase he used in reference to Maurice Morgann's remarkable "Essay on the Dramatic Character of Sir John Falstaff," that it interprets the process of Shakespeare's imagination "from within."

The contributions of only a few other scholars to criticism can be briefly summarized. Sometimes a scholar, through a loving and complete edition, can rescue a poet from obscurity and prepare the way for a critical revival, as the Reverend Alexander Dyce did with his magnificent edition of Skelton in 1843, a book that is a monument of erudition and appreciation and has required only slight correction in the century since. Professor Child did a similar job, even more comprehensive, in organizing the English and Scottish popular ballads, so that to this day all study and criticism begin with his edition. (The critical achievements of other scholars in the field of folk literature and the folk sources of formal literature, including the distinguished work of Gilbert Murray and the Cambridge group, have already been noted in another chapter.) Sometimes the scholar reinvigorates a traditional technique, as J. Leslie Hotson did with the familiar, dry-as-dust research into legal records. He produced two invaluable books, *The Death of Christopher Morlowe*, an account of who actually killed Marlowe and why, and *Shakespeare versus Shallow*, a proof that the original of Justice Shallow in *The Merry Wives of Windsor* is not Sir Thomas Lucy, but Shakespeare's old enemy Justice William Gardiner; both of which read like first-rate detective stories. Sometimes, on the other hand, the scholar develops a new technique or an extension of an old one, as Miss Spurgeon, Armstrong, Knight, and Lowes have done. George Ryland's study of Shakespeare's diction in *Words and Poetry* and L. C. Knights's explorations of the social and economic background of seventeenth-century literature (both discussed below) are other examples of these promising new techniques.

Margaret Schlauch, an American professor of English who has specialized in Chaucer, medieval saga and romance, as well as linguistics and philology, has made particularly valuable contributions to literary criticism in the last-named field. Her book *The Gift of Tongues*, although written as a popularization, represents a pioneer exercise in the organized application of philology to criticism. The chapter "Language and Poetic Creation" analyzes poetic effects in Shakespeare, Emily Dickinson, Joyce, Eliot, Auden, Hart Crane, Gertrude Stein, Hopkins, Cummings, and a number of other poets; discussing the poet's art in terms of such basic linguistic techniques as semantic rejuvenation, word-formation, punning, verbal and phrasal distortions, shifts of abstract and concrete, juxtaposition, evocation, and so on. Miss Schlauch disclaims any attempt at comprehensiveness with the statement: "I wish merely to indicate briefly the uses of some practical linguistic knowledge in studying literature, particularly the work of modern poets reputed to be 'difficult' for technical reasons," but a number of her insights, as well as a longer analysis of *Finnegans Wake*, "The Language of James Joyce" in *Science and Society* for Fall 1939, make it clear that she has a good deal to contribute to criticism.

Other scholars in the field—including phoneticists and linguists like Paget, Jesperson, and Sapir, semanticists like Korzybski, the logical positivists Carnap and Morris, and popularizers like Hayakawa, Hugh Walpole, and Stuart Chase—have dealt little with literature except by way of illustration, but the use critics like Richards, Empson, and Burke have made of their theories and discoveries, as well as Richards's own (and Ogden's), show how valuable the study of language in all its ramifications is and will be increasingly for literary analysis.

A contemporary work of scholarship that is not much to my taste, but which has received a good deal of approbation from qualified judges like R. P. Blackmur, is S. Foster Damon's *William Blake*. Using a method much like Lowes's, and fully as dogged, Damon worked out the endless ramifications of Blake's private system of mystic symbolism through a study of his reading, a reconstruction of his mind, a relentless tracing of almost every reference in the poems, and a study of mystic thought in general. His conclusion, in Blackmur's sympathetic phrasing, is that Blake was "exactly what he seemed least to be, perhaps the most intellectually consistent of the greater poets in English." Readers for whom the mystic meanings of Blake's *Prophetic Books* are the least interesting aspect of a great poet are likely to wish that Damon had devoted the same amount of hard labor and brilliantly imaginative scholarship to some more rewarding project.

A final scholarly project requires mention. Since 1935 Charles D. Abbott, librarian of the Lockwood Memorial Library at the University of Buffalo, has been collecting the worksheets of contemporary poets, with the idea of securing an objective exhibit of the actual process of poetic revision. He now has three thousand of them, including as many as eighty versions of a single poem. The first tentative study of some of this material has just been published. It is the volume *Poets at Work*, including essays by W. H. Auden, Karl Shapiro, Rudolf Arnheim, and Donald A. Stauffer, an introduction explaining the project by Abbott, and some reproductions of manuscripts. None of these essays, naturally, is able to do more than skim the material (Auden's never quite seems to come in contact with it at all), but it is to be hoped that they foreshadow an extensive and organized study, perhaps along the same symposium lines (of the contributors, two are poets, one a psychologist, and the fourth a teacher of literature). This is of course not a new idea in scholarship, and Lowes, for example, in *Convention and Revolt in Poetry*, examined poetic revisions by Tennyson, Coleridge, Keats, Wordsworth, and even Shakespeare (where, in the absence of a manuscript, he uses evidence from the *Hamlet* quarto generally thought to represent a Shakespeare revision). Doing the job in an organized and complete fashion, however, rather than haphazardly and partially, would probably produce as significant results as did Spurgeon's study of imagery, Lowes's quest for sources, and Lovejoy's tracing of an idea.

5

One other aspect of Miss Spurgeon's work remains to be considered, her interest in mysticism. *Mysticism in English Literature* shows her to be greatly concerned with mystic thought and revelation, to the extent of propagandizing for it, and very much influenced by such contemporary mystic tractarians as Evelyn Underhill. The preoccupation continued through *Shakespeare's Imagery*, perhaps even provoking the study, on the basis of Miss Spurgeon's conviction that images are of mystic significance. She writes:

> In the first place, metaphor is a subject of such deep import that it calls for an abler pen than mine to deal adequately with it. For I

incline to believe that analogy—likeness between dissimilar things—
which is the fact underlying the possibility and reality of metaphor,
holds within itself the very secret of the universe. The bare fact that
germinating seeds or falling leaves are actually another expression
of the processes we see in human life and death, thrills me, as it must
others, with a sense of being here in presence of a great mystery,
which, could we only understand it, would explain life and death
itself.

The portrait of Shakespeare's mind that emerges from the two chapters
on "Evidence in the Images of Shakespeare's Thought" is somewhat
more mystic than the plays would seem to suggest, emphasizing transcendent and Bergsonian elements, and concluding with Miss Spurgeon's
statement, on no particular evidence, that "Only once does Shakespeare
in his own person seem to tell us directly what he himself thinks about
death," and that is in "Sonnet 146," in which the soul annihilates death.
Her discussion of his philosophy in "Shakespeare the Man" concludes with
Shakespeare as a mystic humanitarian, like the Duke in *Measure for
Measure*, who believes that "we exist only just in so far as we touch our
fellows, and receive back from them the warmth or light we have ourselves sent out."
    Her scholarly objectivity, however, is nowise vitiated by her pre-
occupation, and it can be put down as one of the crotchets to which critics,
like other mortals, tend to be addicted. Many critics have crotchets that
merely run along harmlessly in their work, like Burke's war against
technology, without affecting its character essentially. Others, like T. S.
Eliot, have their work entirely biased by their preoccupation, but without
destroying its value or seriousness. A few, like Maud Bodkin and John
Middleton Murry, have renounced the critical method that gave them
distinction to indulge their crotchets, and others have given up criticism
entirely to sponsor a panacea, as I. A. Richards did with Basic English.
The most extreme and instructive case of a critic ridden by his crotchet,
and a particularly odd one, is G. Wilson Knight.
    Knight's work was riddled with mysticism from the beginning. His
first book, the pamphlet *Myth and Miracle*, explores the "spiritual quality" of Shakespeare's final plays. His subsequent books were serially
published in periodicals like the *Occult Review* and the *Quest*. Later in his
work he picked up a preoccupation with "Christian ethics," Bergson's
"naturalism," General Smuts's "holism," and D. H. Lawrence's "vital-
ism," adding them to the brew. With his two wartime books all his
mysticism combined with the influence of the war to produce some of the
most fantastic criticism, or rather non-criticism, ever written.
    The first, in 1942, was *Chariot of Wrath: The Message of John Milton to*

Democracy at War. It presents Milton as a lifelong royalist and conservative, the bitter enemy of the tyrant Cromwell (a contemporary Hitler),
a spokesman for twentieth-century constitutional monarchy, and a
prophet who predicted fifth-columnists in Delilah, aerial warfare in the
battle of the angels, Göring and Goebbels in Satan's followers, the tank
and the bomber in the Messiah's chariot, and even the recent war in
detail, complete to the line-up of the United Nations. Milton's doctrine,
according to Knight, is that the British Empire aims at power-goodness,
the Kingdom of Christ, a "service ideal," as opposed to the aims of
Machiavellian Europe; and Milton foresaw, with Knight's agreement,
that the only way Britain could establish this ideal world order would be
to assume world sovereignty, to follow Knight's doctrine of Christian
imperialism.

The second, in 1944, was *The Olive and the Sword: A Study of England's
Shakespeare,* an expansion of Knight's 1940 pamphlet on Shakespeare's
national message, *This Sceptred Isle.* Shakespeare, he reports, was a
national prophet concerned with the soul of England, opposed to appeasement and Hitler in the form of Richard and the Macbeths, his work
devoted to proclaiming Britain's Christian Imperial destiny. There are
the same military predictions, aerial combat forecast in *Julius Cæsar* and
so on, the same detailed parallel with contemporary events (so that not
only is Richard Hitler, but Buckingham is his Röhm; Hamlet is England,
Laertes and Fortinbras are Germany and Italy), and the same emphasis
on literature as "creative faith." "This is no twisting of great poetry
to serve contemporary propaganda," he writes. His point of view sobered
to some extent between the two books, and his plea for British world
domination in the second seems to consist more in moral leadership than
military rule, with large elements of socialism mixed in with the Christianity and imperialism. The interpretation is nevertheless still one of
the strangest ever produced by a serious critic and, in its emphasis on
Shakespeare's message as revealing that England has a greater and more
inclusive destiny than Hitler's Germany, one of the most potentially
dangerous.

In this sad renunciation of any pretensions to criticism (in the books all
of Knight's brilliantly suggestive method is gone, leaving in its place
only surface prose meanings and a tissue of quotes expected to seem
contemporary), as in John Middleton Murry's comparable craziness after
his conversion in 1925, Miss Spurgeon perhaps has her revenge. The
same qualities of imagination in Knight and Murry that enabled them to
carry some of her material so much farther are the qualities that produced
Knight's two travesties on criticism and Murry's literary metabiology.
She was never capable of the former, but she would never have produced
the latter. Let Caroline Spurgeon survive as an example of scholarship

at its best, creative enough to discover a mine of wealth for criticism, not quite creative enough to mine it herself. Let her also survive, in contrast to Lane Cooper at one extreme and Knight and Murry at the other, as a warning to scholars and critics. They would do well to keep one foot on the ground; not both, not neither.

CHAPTER 9

R. P. BLACKMUR

and the Expense of Criticism

WITH A critic like Richard P. Blackmur, who tends to use on each work the special techniques it seems to call for and who at one time or another has used almost every type of criticism discussed in this book, the difficulty of placing any single way of operating as his "method" is obvious. What he has is not so much a unique method as a unique habit of mind, a capacity for painstaking investigation that is essential for contemporary criticism, and that might properly be isolated as his major contribution to the brew. In the chapter "Examples of Wallace Stevens" in *The Double Agent*, Blackmur remarks that to read Pound's verse one needs to know "classical and historical references," to read Eliot one needs familiarity with "the ideas and beliefs and systems of feeling" to which he alludes, but that to read Wallace Stevens "you need only the dictionary." What this says of Blackmur himself, quite literally, is that he learns history to read Pound, studies theology to read Eliot, and sits down with a dictionary to read Stevens.

Words are particularly important to Blackmur. No other living critic would be apt to call the dictionary "that palace of saltatory heuristics," but at the same time no other living critic would be apt to write the tribute to words in the Melville chapter of *The Expense of Greatness*. Blackmur writes:

> Words, and their intimate arrangements, must be the ultimate as well as the immediate source of every effect in the written or spoken arts. Words bring meaning to birth and themselves contained the meaning as an imminent possibility before the pangs of junction. To the individual artist the use of words is an adventure in discovery; the imagination is heuristic among the words it manipulates. . . . Yet the adventure into the reality of words has a technique after the fact in the sense that we can distinguish its successful versions from those that failed, can measure provisionally the kinds and intensities of reality secured and attempted, and can even roughly guess at the conditions of convention and belief necessary for its emergence.

Melville is an excellent example for such an assay. We have only to relate the conception of the reality of language just adumbrated to the notion of the putative statement to see whence the strength of the latter comes; and we have only to relate the conception of language to its modifying context of conventions in order to understand the successes and at least excuse the many shortcomings and over-leapings of Melville's attempts at the paramount and indefeasible reality that great words show. For Melville habitually used words greatly.

As a logical consequence of this emphasis, a good part of Blackmur's research is verbal. His study of Cummings, for example, announces the intention of studying Cummings's language as a clue to "the quality of the meaning his use of these words permits." He then goes on to compile a list of Cummings's principal recurrent words, notes that "flower" is the favorite, counts the appearances of "flower" and notes their wide variety of contexts, and makes the discovery that "flower" is, or was, Cummings's god-word. From this and other linguistic analysis he defines the nature of Cummings's poetry, discusses and evaluates it.

Blackmur's analysis of Wallace Stevens, in *The Double Agent*, begins by listing some of his rare or "precious" words: fubbed, girandoles, curlicues, catarrhs, gobbet, diaphanes, clopping, minuscule, pipping, panicles, carked, ructive, rapey, cantilene, buffo, fiscs, phylactery, princox, and funest. He next goes openly to the dictionary and looks them up ("Funest" means "sad or calamitous or mournful and is derived from a French word meaning fatal, melancholy, baneful, and has to do with death and funerals"). He then reads the words in the context of the poem, and emerges with both an excellent exegesis of the poem and a theory of the nature of Stevens's art. With Hart Crane, also in *The Double Agent*, he goes again to the dictionary for help in the reading of an obscure parenthetical passage about the doings of "let sphinxes from the ripe borage" of death. Although he fails to find a satisfactory meaning (he concludes sadly: "But something very near the contrary may have been intended; or both"), he does emerge with a theory of Crane's defective syntax and undelimited vocabulary that explains his failure with the passage as well as Crane's larger failure.

In *The Expense of Greatness* Blackmur continues the same verbal research. The chapter on Emily Dickinson announces that her genius will be found "in the words she used and in the way she put them together"; continues, after quoting a passage: "Let us provisionally inquire what it is in the words that makes poetry of the statement," and then goes on to elaborate linguistic analysis. He counts the number of times she uses "phosphor" and their contexts; traces the sources of her vocabulary (chivalric romance, Shakespeare, Scott, the Bible, the Hymnal, etc.); analyses the sources of the figures in a specific passage (sewing and clothing, law, precious stones, the Civil War, sea-borne commerce, geography, transcendental theology, etc.); and finally traces the various usages of two of her favorite words, "plush" and "purple" (revealing in connection with the latter, incidentally, one of his rare gaps, an apparent ignorance of the Roman sense of "purple" as "noble," like the Russian "red"). In a review of Laura Riding's *Collected Poems* in the same book, to make a casual point, he notes a few of her obsessive negatives (unreproach, unharshed, unloving, unsmooth, unlove, undeath, unlife, undazzle, unmade, unthought, unlive, unrebellion, unbeautifuls, unzoological, unstrange, unwild, unprecious, unbull, unhurriedness, unenthusiasm), remarks that some pages contain as many as fifteen forms of the verbal negative, and concludes: "Miss Riding is the not star of the un no not never nowhere."

It may be argued from these examples that every critic does at least some of the same research, looking up unfamiliar words in the dictionary, checking frequency of usage and contexts, and so forth, and that Blackmur has simply made the process visible, working the procedure into the fabric of his criticism rather than concealing it. To a very slight extent this is true, but of the degree Blackmur has done it, it is not at all true. Things would be better for criticism if it were. Blackmur is almost unique in his assumption that no demand for knowledge the poet makes on the serious reader (that is, the critic) is unreasonable, and that if he doesn't have the information he had better go out and get it. In *The Double Agent* he speaks of things "no amount of outside work can illumine," but they are not many, and he constantly uses words like "responsibility" and "expense" (the "expense of martyrdom," the "expense of greatness"), emphasizing cost and effort. In the ironically titled "A Feather-Bed for Critics" he suggests ways the writer can "secure the conditions of maximum responsibility for his own work" and defines the *labor* of criticism in the imagery of physical work (just as he called a previous piece "The Critic's Job of Work"):

. . . the writer must reflect that he is performing *the most arduous critical act of which he is capable*. He is endeavouring, so to speak, to keep himself in a steady startled state: as if one were about to be haunted: as if one were never to get used to, and hence never to let down, one's powers of vision, one's resources of feeling, and had yet, in such suspense, to judge, to decide—and so to express—the actuality of the job in hand. It is in this sense that the composition of a great poem is a labour of unrelenting criticism, and the full reading of it only less so; and it is in this sense, too, that the critical act is what is called a "creative" act, and whether by poet, critic, or serious reader, since there is an alteration, a stretching, of the sensibility as the act is done. The cost of criticism is, if I may borrow and restrict a little a phrase I have used before, the expense of greatness; as its earnings are in the sense of conviction pervading the job done.

In our day most critics assume that their sensibility and already acquired learning are adequate, and while they are willing to give the poem hard reading, they do not think themselves reasonably required by the poem to give anything else hard reading. The best way to appreciate the value, and uniqueness, of Blackmur's "homework" is to compare his discussion of a few works requiring knowledge with those of other critics. In linguistic analysis, of course, no one can touch him, and innumerable articles had been done on Cummings, for example, without anyone's taking the trouble to check his vocabulary. But compare Blackmur's discussion of Ezra Pound's *A Draft of Thirty Cantos* in *The Double Agent* with that of Allen Tate in *Reactionary Essays on Poetry and Ideas*. Both appeared as reviews of the *Cantos*, the former in the *Hound & Horn*, the latter in the *Nation*.

Tate's piece begins on a theme of ignorance and unconcern. His first sentence, after a quotation, is:

> One is not certain who Messire Laurentius was; one is not very certain that it makes no difference. Yet one takes comfort in the vast range of Mr. Pound's obscure learning, which no one man could be expected to know much about. In his great work one is continually uncertain, as to space, time, history.

Tate then goes on to reveal "the secret of his form," which turns out to be "conversation," the *Cantos* are just a lot of rambling talk, *"and that is what the poems are about"* (Mr. Tate's italics). Having given away his nugget, he goes on to discuss the first Canto, and as a gloss on "the place aforesaid by Circe" writes: "whatever place it may be." And finally, having performed a feat of non-study, Tate concludes with a manifesto for study: "And the thirty *Cantos* are enough to occupy a loving and ceaseless study—say a canto a year for thirty years, all thirty to be read every few weeks just for the tone." It would be hard for the critical function to abdicate further.

Blackmur's review is precisely the opposite. He begins with the statement that the poetry in the *Cantos* is a mask, what Pound calls a *persona*, and goes into the etymology of the Latin word *persona*. Then for twelve pages he studies Pound's two principal finished works, "Hugh Selwyn Mauberly" and "Homage to Sextus Propertius," as clues to the *Cantos*. He analyzes the first poem at some length, among other things translating a Capaneus line Pound quoted in the Greek and explaining references; and he makes his own list of the passages from Propertius Pound used in the second, in the order in which he used them, and compares Pound's translation with the Latin text and with H. E. Butler's literal translation in the Loeb Library in some detail. Then for another twelve pages Blackmur summarizes the principal themes of all thirty *Cantos*. In the course of this, he remarks:

> The reader has the choice either of reading all the Cantos as if they were similarly straightforward and self-explanatory, or of going behind the verses to the same material, or as much as he can discover of it, that Mr. Pound himself used. . . . But an active mind will not always stop short at the uncertain, however persuasive, when the ascertainable is at hand.

Meaning that, in explaining the references to the Malatesta family in the *Cantos*, Blackmur refers to four books on them he has apparently read, three in Italian and one of these unpublished. Finally, at the end of this exhaustive analysis, he interprets and evaluates the poems.

It would be hard to find a better illustration of the strength of Blackmur's method, compared with the ignorance, shallowness, and generally slipshod quality of most contemporary criticism. If the comparison seems unfair to Tate, it is only that he has been singled out; the same contrast could be made with almost anyone. One might compare Blackmur's chapter "The Later Poetry of W. B. Yeats" in *The Expense of Greatness* with C. M. Bowra's sensitive and perceptive chapter on Yeats in *The Heritage of Symbolism*. Each of them analyzes "The Second Coming," but Blackmur's study of the mystical system behind it, from *A Vision* and other writings, compared with Bowra's ignorance of the system and lack of concern with it, gives the former a dimension of understanding that the latter lacks. Or we could compare Blackmur's chapter on T. E. Lawrence in *The Expense of Greatness* with any of the reviews of *Seven Pillars of Wisdom*, say Mark Van Doren's in the *Nation*, reprinted in *The Private Reader*. (This at least is a fair example, since Van Doren's critical precepts insist that the critic know nothing and say as little as possible.) All Van Doren says is that Lawrence is "intolerably, impossibly complex" and that some day he may be explained. Blackmur sets out calmly to explain him, in the course of his explanation studying the *Letters* carefully and going down to the Congressional Library in Washington to read the only copy of *The Mint*, Lawrence's other book, allowed in this country. Using the *Letters* and *The Mint* as clues, he does the job of finding a meaning (if not the meaning) in *The Seven Pillars of Wisdom* that Van Doren shrugged off.

Sometimes, by accident, Blackmur defines the contrast himself. In his discussion of Eliot's "Ash Wednesday" in *The Double Agent*, he reproaches "so intelligent a critic as Mr. Edmund Wilson" (one of Blackmur's weaknesses has always been an excess of charity to his colleagues) for criticizing the poem in ignorance of its Christian significance, and thus misreading it fundamentally as a revelation of weakness rather than of strength. Blackmur explains the religious meaning of the holiday Ash Wednesday, the doctrine of Christian abnegation and humility, the Christian teachings behind the Dante passage Eliot quotes, and so forth. All are essential to an understanding of the poem. Blackmur either knew them or went and found out about them. Wilson didn't know them and didn't care. For his pains, Blackmur achieved the only recompense the critic can receive, a valid reading, "the sense of conviction pervading the job done," rather than Wilson's ignorant misreading or another. It is the recompense he receives generally for his hard work, and it is well worth the cost. Critics like Tate, Bowra (only in this case, however), Van Doren, and Wilson might well ponder the fable of the Ant and the Grasshopper.

2

Like T. S. Eliot, R. P. Blackmur has as yet written no books of criticism, merely a number of articles and reviews. Twelve of these were collected in *The Double Agent* in 1935, another thirteen in *The Expense of Greatness* in 1940, and at least another dozen important pieces have appeared since, so that we may soon be fortunate enough to have another book. For a number of years Blackmur has been working on a critical biography of Henry Adams, fragments of which have appeared in magazines, and at one time a study of Henry James was announced. (His other publications are three volumes of verse and several fugitive pamphlets.) Until a new collection, the Adams, or the James is published, his first volume, *The Double Agent*, is probably the best example of his work to examine in detail.

The book's keynote is set in the subtitle, *Essays in Craft and Elucidation*. Blackmur is probably the subtlest and most distinguished close reader in American criticism (in writing a gloss on a poem he need bow only to William Empson in England), and much of the book is simply brilliant elucidation of texts. The studies of Cummings's language, Pound's *Cantos*, Stevens, and Hart Crane already referred to include first-rate exegeses of a number of difficult poems, as do the studies of Marianne Moore and several others. Perhaps the best concentrated example is the second section of the essay "New Thresholds, New Anatomies," subtitled "Notes on a Text of Hart Crane." The whole section is an elaborate exegesis, alive to every possibility of ambiguity, of a four-line stanza from "The Wine Menagerie" and a total of seven lines from "Lachrymæ Christi." A typical example is Blackmur's gloss on Crane's line: "Thy Nazarene and tinder eyes" in "Lachrymæ Christi":

(Note, from the title, that we are here again concerned with tears as the vehicle-image of insight, and that, in the end, Christ is identified with Dionysius.) Nazarene, the epithet for Christ, is here used as an adjective of quality in conjunction with the noun tinder also used as an adjective; an arrangement which will seem baffling only to those who underestimate the seriousness with which Crane remodelled words. The first three lines of the poem read:

> *Whitely, while benzine*
> *Rinsings from the moon*
> *Dissolve all but the windows of the mills.*

Benzine is a fluid, cleansing and solvent, has a characteristic tang and smart to it, and is here associated with the light of the moon, which, through the word "rinsings," is itself modified by it. It is, I think, the carried-over influence of benzine which gives startling aptness to Nazarene. It is, if I am correct for any reader but myself, an example of syllabic interpenetration or internal punning as habitually practiced in the later prose of Joyce. The influence of one word on the other reminds us that Christ the Saviour cleanses and solves and has, too, the quality of light. "Tinder" is a simpler instance of how Crane could at once isolate a word and bind it in, impregnating it with new meaning. Tinder is used to kindle fire, powder, and light; a word incipient and bristling with the action proper to its being. The association is completed when it is remembered that tinder is very nearly a homonym for tender and, *in this setting*, puns upon it.

One of the techniques on which Blackmur's exegeses rely is a preliminary classifying, almost an indexing, of the complex material with which he intends to deal, and this classifying then has an independent value of its own. This is true of his "exhibition of the principal subject-matters in summary form" of Pound's *Cantos*, and it is even more true of his essay in *The Double Agent* on James's Prefaces, written for the *Hound & Horn* and published as an introduction to the Prefaces when they were issued as *The Art of the Novel*. Here he makes what he calls "a kind of eclectic index or provisional glossary," listing and paraphrasing all the unlocalized major themes, listing and paraphrasing all the important subjects discussed and telling where they may be found, and then doing the same for all the minor subjects. What he ends with is a twenty-page critical index of James on the art of the novel, invaluable alike to the beginner as a way into the Prefaces, and to the specialist as the essential groundwork for any use he might make of the Prefaces. More than the other varieties of Blackmur's "homework," his indexing stands up as a critical contribution apart from his own use of it.

Blackmur is a poet, about two thirds of *The Double Agent* deals with poetry, and it is not surprising that when he is not discussing specific works he should be dealing with general matters of poetic technique. (It is worth noting that Blackmur rarely writes textual or linguistic analysis of prose texts or discusses general problems of prose technique— his essays on prose works deal chiefly either with general problems of the artist's consciousness, like the studies of T. E. Lawrence and Melville in *The Expense of Greatness*, or with ideas, particularly moral ideas, like the later Dostoyevsky and Adams material.) Blackmur has never written a formal poetics, however, and his discussion of poetic technique always arises out of specific problems: the discussion of rhyme accompanying the analysis of Marianne Moore's off-rhymes and buried rhymes, the discussion of tropes and imagery in terms of a comparison of Stevens with Pound and Eliot in the Stevens piece, the discussion of poetic form in the Lawrence chapter, and scattered references to rhythm and meter. (Blackmur has never devoted very much attention to metrics, which he regards as the most superficial category of poetic technique.)

The comparison of Stevens's tropes with those of other poets brings up another of the principal techniques in *The Double Agent*, the comparison of poems and poets. Blackmur makes his point about the nature of Pound's translation of Propertius, not by talking about it abstractly, but by comparing it point for point with the Latin text and a literal translation. He shows by comparison with Pound and Eliot that Stevens's imagination is neither visual, like Pound's, nor dramatic, like Eliot's, but what he calls rhetorical, and that classification is then the essential basis of his essay. In the essay on Lawrence he illustrates what he calls Lawrence's "hysteria" by opposing it to a passage from Eliot illustrating "controlled hysteria," and in the chapter on Crane he illustrates a defect of Crane's sensibility by training on him a barrage of quotations from Dante, Shakespeare, Baudelaire, Yeats, and Stevens. Blackmur has never carried the comparative method to the point Eliot has, where it seems sometimes to take the focus off the work under discussion and carry it outward in an endless spiral of ramifying examples, and all his comparisons, used economically and sometimes discussed at great length, tend to work efficiently for him.

The Double Agent makes little overt use of either of the two main founts of insight in contemporary criticism, psychoanalysis and Marxism, although there is a good deal of buried influence. This results from one of the essential assumptions of Blackmur's method, derived from the early Eliot and best expressed in Blackmur's 1928 *Hound & Horn* study of Eliot, that criticism must deal centrally with literature *as* literature, not as anything else. Even where Blackmur overtly uses psychology, as in his discussion of the "preconscious" in "A Critic's Job of Work" or of Lawrence's hysterical neurosis, it is always *literary* psychology. He is insistent that he is not diagnosing Lawrence as a clinical example, but that "the reality in his verse, and in his later prose . . . is predominantly of the hysterical order." On sociological criticism Blackmur's most significant statement in *The Double Agent* is in a chapter entitled "The Dangers of Authorship," a 1934 review of Malcolm Cowley's *Exile's Return* and T. S. Eliot's *After Strange Gods*. After announcing "With Mr. Cowley's politics I am, I think, pretty much in accord," he writes:

> In making a political choice, and in ordering your mind so as to make that choice of genuine consequence, it does not follow that if you are a writer your new politics will directly influence the substance you write of. Nor, if you are a critic, does it follow that you have uncovered political exigency as a prime standard. The writer, the artist of any kind, is, so far as he has any will in the matter, an independent mirror of the processes of life which happen to absorb him; he creates by showing, by representing; and his only weapons for change are the irony of the intelligence that can be brought to bear on the contemptible and the stupid, and the second irony of a second point of view, implicit in his work, but alien to that of his subject matter. . . . It may so happen that an artist's political convictions are fundamental to his work, when they will appear in it more likely with a tacit than a hortatory strength, as a radical qualification of the bloodstream; and it may happen not. The artist must always reserve the right to exhibit what he sees and feels of the human predicament, and the only thing we may require of him is that he does not exhibit what he neither sees nor feels but only thinks, for political or other reasons.

His conclusion is that Cowley and Eliot have shown us ways to "improve our stature as citizens," but the final aim must be adding "to the stature of our independence as artists." In repudiating sociological criticism in the form of "political" criticism—that is, on its worst terms—Blackmur seems to be aware of his unfairness, and he keeps protesting that these social criteria are valid when defined soundly by men like Cowley, but that they always seem to be misapplied and belied by men like Granville Hicks and Horace Gregory. (One sign of a bad conscience here might be a rather amusing slip. He writes: "If *Piers Plowman* dealt with the class struggle, *The Canterbury Tales* did not." Actually, of course, *The Canterbury Tales* deals more patently with the class struggle than the great majority of literary works, from the decay of feudalism between Knight and Squire in the Prologue to the sharp class alignments in most of the tales. As Kenneth Burke has noted about a similarly poor example in Wyndham Lewis, first pointed out by Stephen Spender, the discontinuity of a poor example, with all the world of examples to choose from

—in Blackmur's case something like "Kubla Khan" would have been pretty safe—is always significant.)

Irony is the only weapon for change Blackmur will grant, and his own use of irony in *The Double Agent* is extensive. At one extreme it turns into a kind of humor (like the statement that a charge "has point but pierces nothing"); at the other it is vast skeptical reservation. In the last chapter of the book, "A Critic's Job of Work," Blackmur equates irony with the free mind. He writes:

> Fortunately, there exist archetypes of unindoctrinated thinking. Let us incline our minds like reflectors to catch the light of the early Plato and the whole Montaigne. Is not the inexhaustible stimulus and fertility of the Dialogues and the Essays due as much as anything to the absence of positive doctrine? Is it not that the early Plato always holds conflicting ideas in shifting balance, presenting them in contest and evolution, with victory only the last shift? Is it not that Montaigne is always making room for another idea, and implying always a third for provisional, adjudicating irony? Are not the forms of both men themselves ironic, betraying in its most intimate recesses the duplicity of every thought, pointing it out, so to speak, in the act of self-incrimination, and showing it not paled on a pin but in the buff life? . . . Such an approach, such an attempt at vivid questing, borrowed and no doubt adulterated by our own needs, is the only rational approach to the multiplication of doctrine and arrogant technologies which fills out the body of critical thinking.

With lesser thinkers and lesser artists, and in the defective works of the greater, Blackmur adds: "we have in reading, in criticising, to supply the scepticism and the irony." One of the ways he himself supplies this irony in *The Double Agent* is through an extreme tentativeness. Here are some samples:

> To apply this dichotomy to Crane is not difficult if it is done tentatively, without requiring that it be too fruitful, and without requiring that it be final at all.
> The analogue should not be pushed, as its virtue is in its incongruity and as afterthought.
> These phrases of distinction are subject to correction and elaboration. . . .

An approach as tentative and inconclusive as this makes great demands on the reader, far more than criticism generally makes, and Blackmur is very conscious of his reader. He expects him either to have a mind

trained for poetry or to turn his attention deliberately on craft, to "look
and read *as if* he had a trained mind." The aim of criticism, he admits,
is appreciation, but he adds, in a fine Jamesian sentence: "But appreciation, even, can take measures to be certain of its grounds, and to be
full should betray the constant apprehension of an end which is the
necessary consequence, the proper rounding off, of just those grounds."
The two functions of criticism as Blackmur defines them are "to promote
intimacy with particulars," and to judge the standard of achievement;
that is, to analyze and to evaluate. For the first he insists that criticism
must always lead the reader *to* the work, and he writes and quotes fragments always with the idea that his analysis will turn his reader to the
details of the poem, rather than substitute for it. For the second, however,
he insists that the reader read with his mind, not his eye, that he experience form as well as content, that he like poetry *as* poetry, that he
bring to it either wide knowledge or a capacity for taking pains. In
short, the reader Blackmur sketches out for himself is something very
close to the ideal reader of poetry, another poet or a critic like Blackmur
himself. He must recognize, of course, that there are too few of these
to constitute even his small public, but at least he can refuse to compromise for the others.

It is in the mind of this hypothetical reader that the book achieves
unity, despite its nature as a collection of occasional essays and reviews.
Besides the major pieces, the studies of Cummings, Pound, Stevens,
Crane, D. H. Lawrence, Marianne Moore, Eliot's post-conversion
writing, James's Prefaces, and contemporary literary criticism, there are
three minor pieces: the joint review of Cowley and Eliot, a review of
Granville Hicks's *The Great Tradition*, and a review of some books on
Samuel Butler, all three from *Hound & Horn*. If the major pieces make
Blackmur's point positively, the reviews make it negatively, by showing
what he would *not* have in his unity: the extra-literary criteria of Eliot's
Christianity and Cowley's radicalism, the tendentious distortion of Hicks,
the passionless quality and dogmatism of Butler. The positive unity is
in the ambiguity of the title, *The Double Agent*, nowhere brought to
earth in the book, but gradually coming meaningful in the reader's mind.
Poetry is a double agent (content and form, the raw material of life and
the shaping imagination), criticism is a double agent (analysis and appreciation, intimacy with particulars and evaluation of achievement),
and poetry and criticism together are a double agent (keyed in the
subtitle—craft and elucidation). The double agent is in fact any pair of
critical terms—form and content, structure and texture, writer and
reader, static and dynamic, tradition and revolt, expression and communication—and out of their interaction arises a third thing, the poem,
the essay, or, in this case, Blackmur's book. It is the final ambiguity of

the title that its dichotomy should conceal a third term that Blackmur later faced explicitly, converting all his duos into trios.

3

Since Blackmur has no formal method, but rather an amalgam of qualities and emphases, his work can only be given a private, rather than a historical, genealogy—that is, the men he derives from can be noted. This is a complicated matter, since after G. Wilson Knight, Blackmur is probably the most eclectic living literary critic. Knight has drawn on and acknowledged almost every contemporary British critic, from Murry and Read to Miss Spurgeon and Miss Bodkin, in addition to a few Americans. In the same fashion Blackmur has used almost every important modern critic in both England and America, although with considerably more resistance, discounting, and modification.

Any genealogy for Blackmur's approach must begin from the precedents he gives for Eliot's technical criticism in his *Hound & Horn* study of Eliot. He points out there that in concentrating solely on "the facts in the work under consideration as they are relevant to literature as such," Eliot is "practically alone not only today but in the past. A fragment of Arnold, a little Coleridge, a little Dryden, and now and then Dr. Johnson; and of these perhaps only Dryden's interest was serene and whole." This is, of course, not true; but it is interesting that at the age of twenty-three, thinking of his own criticism as deriving from Eliot's, Blackmur should have made the list. Some time between 1928 and 1930, when he called him "the most dignified, the most disciplined, and, I should have supposed, the most humanistic of American masters," Blackmur must have discovered the importance of Henry James and his critical Prefaces. These essays supremely fulfilled his requirements for technical criticism, and in his study of the Prefaces he refers to them as "the most sustained and I think the most eloquent and original piece of literary criticism in existence," the only comparable work being other James essays. James's criticism has probably been the major single determinant of Blackmur's: in metaphorical approach, in the application of sensibility, in insistence on the high value of art, even in style (as in the sentence quoted above about the grounds of appreciation, or almost any sentence chosen at random from Blackmur's work). Only in subject-matter did Blackmur depart markedly from James, in turning his analysis chiefly on poetry rather than prose, and on the work of others rather than his own, so that Blackmur's criticism might be considered the application of James's method to other areas.

With, of course, additions. The first and probably the most important is the influence of T. S. Eliot. Note a Blackmur sentence: "What is most striking, in every instance, about this emotion is the fact that, in so far as it exists at all, it is Mr. Cummings' emotion, so that our best knowledge of it must be, finally, our best guess." The distinction, which is that between the poem's emotion and the poet's emotion, is almost certainly Eliot's emotion-feeling distinction, but the style is also Eliot's critical style: that is, an extension of James's style at once more parenthetical and hesitant, and syntactically simpler, so that it gives an impression (sometimes misleading) of great complexity and subtlety of thought forced into the simplicity of precise expression.

Blackmur has used many of Eliot's distinctions and concepts, been somewhat influenced by his style, placed himself in the direct line of Eliot's technical criticism, and even in the last few years followed its shift to a moral emphasis ("moral judgements on literature on grounds that are altogether literary" was Blackmur's description of the process in 1928). He has been obsessed with Eliot's phrase: "the boredom, the horror, and the glory" beneath both beauty and ugliness, quoting it at least four times to my count. From the *Hound & Horn* study in 1928, when he praised "the disciplined (and thus limited) fertility of his ideas," to a contribution to *Partisan Review* in 1944, commenting on Eliot's "Notes toward a Definition of Culture," when he announced his assent to most of the beliefs Eliot expresses in the essay, combined with sharp disagreement with their unexpressed implications, based on "supernatural revelation institutionalized in a particular church," Blackmur's attitude toward Eliot has been remarkably consistent. It has been to recognize their many agreements as well as their basic disagreement, to use what he could and reject the rest.

Another influence Blackmur has absorbed and disagreed with fundamentally is that of Professor Irving Babbitt. His article "The Discipline of Humanism," in *The Critique of Humanism,* a symposium edited by C. Hartley Grattan in 1930, is a sharp attack on Babbitt and the neo-humanists for "their arrogance, their blindness, and their censorious ignorance," finding almost nothing to praise. A much fairer account of his attitude, though, is the article "Humanism and Symbolic Imagination: Notes on Re-reading Irving Babbitt" in the *Southern Review* for Autumn 1941. Announcing his theme as "the deep exorcism of the effort of understanding," Blackmur defines the great limitation of Babbitt, his skimming of "the exemplary" off life while ignoring "the chthonic," and places it as part of a general "decay of Christian imagination."

Blackmur's formula, however, is no longer simple rejection, but acceptance with amplification and modification: "we must be concerned to enrich rather than destroy." The chthonic must be put back, the totality of the Christian imagination must be restored, but this time secularized as "the symbolic imagination" of art, Blackmur's key term in the last few years. Thus Blackmur's full reaction to Babbitt is humanism *plus* symbolic imagination, and it is in terms of this formulation, even long before making it, that he used him: taking Babbitt's "moral" concepts—discipline, proportion, moderation—making them æsthetic criteria of literary form rather than ethical criteria of literary content, and adding to them the extra dimension of the chthonic. Blackmur's association with Harvard, although he never went there, has been close and influential, as befits a sometime resident of Cambridge and editor of the *Hound & Horn*, and Babbitt was a good part of that influence. Of all the critics influenced by Babbitt, however, perhaps only Blackmur and Francis Fergusson avoided both easy acceptance and easy rejection and fitted the man's contribution to their own needs.

The influence of James, Eliot, and Babbitt on Blackmur (as well as of Santayana, whose doctrine of "essence" seems to have influenced him greatly) has been largely one of attitude and approach; technically, he has drawn most on quite another type of critic, the other major contemporary practitioners of the craft, I. A. Richards, William Empson, and Kenneth Burke. Blackmur has derived a good deal from Richards, ("No literary critic can escape his influence," he writes) and seems to respect him greatly, but he has sharp reservations about Richards's scientism. In *The Double Agent*, in the chapter on Marianne Moore (written at a time when the Richards influence was most marked), he tosses one general problem to Richards, "who alone has the equipment (among critics) and the will to determine," and remarks in another place that Richards's *Mencius on the Mind* is "fascinating but engulfing," whereas *The Meaning of Meaning* presents the opposite perspective, the ascetic poverty of a few hundred words allowed verbal omniscience.

In his summary evaluation of Richards in "A Critic's Job of Work" Blackmur defines Richards as "an admirable critic," "whose love and knowledge of poetry are incontestable," but reproaches him with being the victim of the endless expansion of the theoretic phase of practical literary problems and with seeking, in the last analysis, to transform literary criticism into the science of linguistics. After agreeing that these functions are important, he adds:

> But I want this criticism, engaged in this task, constantly to be confronted with examples of poetry, and I want it so for the very practical purpose of assisting in pretty immediate appreciation of the use, meaning, and value of the language in that particular poetry. I want it to assist in doing for me what it actually assists Mr. Richards in doing, whatever that is, when he is reading poetry for its own sake.

The heart of Blackmur's quarrel with Richards, actually, is his remark in "Language as Gesture" in *Accent*, Summer 1943 (and one can presume the emphasis on the first word): "Poetry is the meaning of meaning."

With William Empson, Richards's disciple, Blackmur is much more at home, since Empson does precisely what Blackmur called for: turns Richards's theoretic structure constantly on poetic texts. Blackmur does not seem to have been much influenced by Empson's later contribution, the categorical criticism represented by his book on "pastoral," but Empson's early work, *Seven Types of Ambiguity*, influenced him greatly. His Stevens and Crane essays in *The Double Agent* are particularly Empsonian explorations of ambiguity, the almost endless ramification of the implications of poetic vocabulary and imagery, and he seems to feel with Empson that ambiguity is the focal point of poetic effectiveness, *providing* that it is formalized and limited. In the "Language as Gesture" essay he suggests (crediting Empson) that a Shakespeare word spelled one way in the first quarto, another way in the second quarto and first folio, and a third way in the later folios, in any spelling carries all three suggested meanings as well as a fourth (thus, with Empson, tossing most Shakespeare textual scholarship onto an old pin-point). In his essay in the Yeats Memorial Number of the *Southern Review* Blackmur indulges in an extensive Empsonian pursuit of the meanings of the word "profane" as used by Yeats in "Under Ben Bulben," at the same time announcing that he prefers Philip Wheelwright's term "plurisignation" to Empson's "ambiguity" and using it himself.

Alone of serious contemporary critics, Blackmur seems to have been little affected by Coleridge and the *Biographia*, but he reserves his greatest respect for the closest thing we have to Coleridge, Kenneth Burke, and has several times announced his enlistment under Burke's banner. In *The Double Agent*, where he quotes him several times approvingly on Marianne Moore, the attitude is appreciative but still largely resistant, and in "A Critic's Job of Work" he classes him with C. S. Peirce "for the buoyancy and sheer remarkableness of his speculations," adding that in both cases "one is enlivened by them without any *necessary* reference to their truth." However, Blackmur complains, just as Richards uses literature as a springboard for a philosophy of value, Burke uses it as a springboard for a philosophy of moral possibility. He also suggests as the weakness of Burke's method that it "could be applied with equal fruitfulness either to Shakespeare, Dashiell Hammett, or Marie Corelli." (I may be misreading the tone here, since no judgment is made; it is equally the method's great strength, and Burke has since gleefully admitted the charge.) His final judgment in the essay is that Burke's method does not exhaust the whole of literature any more than Richards's, but that proper reductions by users of Burke make it extremely pertinent and fruitful.

In *The Expense of Greatness* Blackmur continues this moving toward

Burke, using general concepts and approaches like the idea of implicit form, specialized terms like "secular conversion," and even direct quotes of remarks. In the *Southern Review* for Autumn 1939, in a study of Adams, Blackmur pays Burke almost the highest compliment he could muster, classing him as an ironist with his beloved Montaigne. He writes:

> Add candor, add sophistication (to the imagination), and in so far as your mixture is justly proportioned, you will have an imagination free enough, *disponible* enough, and with labor informed enough, to react directly and continuously upon society in motion, no matter what the velocity or what the bearing. The type is rare. It is always ahead of its generation; and indeed, regardless how far back you go for your example, ahead of any generation. The Montaigne of An Apology for Raimond Sebond is one example; André Gide may turn out another; and in our own country, barring those occasions when partisan zeal overtakes him, there is possibly Kenneth Burke.

Finally, in "Language as Gesture," a 1942 Mesures Lecture at Princeton, based almost entirely on a Burkian view and quoting him frequently, Blackmur attempted to define the relationship of his criticism to Burke's. In treating language as gesture, he writes, we shall have made

> an imaginative equivalent for Kenneth Burke's more nearly intellectual thesis, which I share, that the language of poetry may be regarded as symbolic action. The difference between Mr. Burke and myself is that where he is predominantly concerned with setting up methods for analyzing the actions as they are expressed in the symbol, I choose to emphasize the created or dead-end symbol. He explores the puzzle of the language in the process of becoming symbolic. I try to show in a series of varied and progressive examples how the symbol invests the actions in language with poetic actuality. Mr. Burke legislates; I would judge; the executive is between us.

Blackmur has also drawn explicitly on a number of other critics, among them Yvor Winters and John Crowe Ransom. Blackmur has written a tribute to Winters in *Poetry*, November 1940, reprinted in *The Expense of Greatness*, at once appreciative of Winters's moral insight, "intimacy with the matter-and-form of poetry and imaginative prose," and other virtues; and sharply critical of the absurd formulations, comparisons, and judgments he gets through the operation of "a kind of mechanical inadvertence." From Winters, Blackmur has chiefly derived the concept of the fallacy of expressive form, "the dogma that once material becomes words it is its own best form," and has used it consistently through both books, centering his criticism of D. H. Lawrence's poetry on it, using it to demolish writers like Thomas Wolfe and Carl Sandburg, as well as bigger game.

From Ransom, Blackmur has taken not much more than the term "structure-texture," and used it only tentatively. At the same time not only Ransom but the whole Southern school, particularly Allen Tate and Cleanth Brooks, have been influenced by Blackmur, all quote and acknowledge him, and Ransom introduces him in the Preface to *The New Criticism* as the perfect type of the "new critic," at once thoroughly eclectic and completely original, and praises him in reviews and articles in the highest terms. As a matter of fact, the eclectic Blackmur has in his turn influenced almost all contemporary critics, particularly the younger ones, and even with Burke the flow of suggestion runs both ways.

4

In so far as R. P. Blackmur's isolatable critical method is the taking of pains, of various sorts and in every sense of the word, a few other contemporary critical techniques that apply hard labor are worth examining for comparison (although the majority of them are so inferior to his as to be hardly comparable). Most of these fall under the heading of scholarship and are considered in another chapter, but a few are private enough, or eccentric enough, to warrant consideration here. As one might guess from the word "eccentric," foremost among them is the criticism of Ezra Pound. Pound's concept of criticism is extremely modest; it is simply the man at his bookshelf telling a friend what to read, but Pound as the man at the bookshelf is willing to go to great labor with his literary advice. In *Make It New* he defines five types of criticism:

1. Criticism by discussion, extending from mere yatter, logic-chopping, and description of tendencies up to the clearly defined record of procedures and an attempt to formulate more or less general principles.

2. Criticism by translation.

3. Criticism by exercise in the style of a given period.

4. Criticism via music, meaning definitely the setting of a poet's words. . . . This is the most intense form of criticism save:

5. Criticism in new composition.

For example the criticism of Seneca in Mr. Eliot's Agon is infinitely more alive, more vigorous than in his essay on Seneca.

Of these five types, only the first is traditional criticism, and the other four types, all of which Pound has attempted, tend to be not actually a substitute for critical discussion, or superior to it, so much as a pains-taking supplement to it, however suggestive they may seem.[1]

Thus in his first book, *The Spirit of Romance*, as a prelude to exegesis and appreciative analysis, Pound first made fresh translations of a good deal of the material, from Dante to *The Cid*. In the same book he uses his favorite variety of "criticism in new composition," parody, in a merciless parody of Whitman's flatulence as an illustration of his faults. In *A B C of Reading*, Pound explains that he was unable to translate Catullus and Villon and consequently set them to music; and he has also set Guido Cavalcanti and Sordello. Another laborious type of criticism Pound uses, although it is not in his list, is criticism by anthologizing, and in *A B C of Reading* he devotes half the book to a "corrective" anthology of poetry (chiefly distinguished for its rescue of Mark Alexander Boyd's great sonnet) to illustrate his critical points; and his "Study in French Poets," first printed in *Instigations* and reprinted and brought up to date in *Make It New*, relies chiefly on anthologizing them. Pound, who once called himself "an instrument (i.e. a philologist) of the utmost refine-ment," is patently a frustrated scholar (as Hitler was a frustrated artist, perhaps), and the work he does in a critical article sometimes closely resembles traditional scholarship. We may take his "Cavalcanti" essay in *Make It New* as typical: it includes an enormously detailed textual study of one poem, a survey of its background and sources, several translations, elaborate textual emendation, and so on. With the addition of his musical settings and a parody or two, it would represent all of Pound's industrious method, and would be, as much of Pound's early work has been, a demonstration of how slipshod and off-the-cuff most contemporary criticism is, and how thorough a study can be produced by the application of knowledge and hard work. (The fact that Pound seems to be substantially wrong on Cavalcanti, despite all his labor, would actually be irrelevant here. No method can guarantee "correct-ness.")

Another critical method involving homework was Randolph Bourne's. He believed, Van Wyck Brooks tells us in his Introduction to *History of a Literary Radical*, that the book review should be "an independent enquiry with a central idea of its own," rather than simply a discussion of the book, and many of his best pieces follow that practice.[2] Thus his

---

[1] I am reminded by a learned friend that Thackeray's parody of Scott in "Rebecca and Rowena" and Debussy's verbatim setting of Maeterlinck's *Pelleas et Mélisande* are respectively the best criticisms of Scott and Maeterlinck with which he is familiar. I would suggest that in both cases this might be due to the absence of more adequate treatment by conventional criticism, which my friend is unconsciously remedying in his own mind as he reads the parody or hears the music.

[2] This was not, of course, a new theory with Bourne, but merely a revival, in new form, of one of the crazes of nineteenth-century reviewing. Carlyle does it frequently, and his "Burns" is the classic example: a review that takes off from Lockhart's *Life of*

review of Meredith Nicholson's *The Valley of Democracy*, printed in *History of a Literary Radical* as "A Mirror of the Middle West," becomes his own survey of the Middle Western mind and the state of America, and the discussion of Cardinal Newman in the book becomes an essay on his own religious views and beliefs. In the same fashion his review of Mary Fels's *Joseph Fels* in the *New Republic* in 1917 is the opportunity for a discussion of Henry George and his theories, his review of Upton Sinclair's *King Coal* in the *New Republic* for the same year becomes an æsthetic for sociologic fiction, and his review of Hugo Münsterberg's *War in America* becomes a discussion of the social implications of Professor Jacques Loeb's discovery of tropisms. In these, particularly the Sinclair review, he somewhat resembles the Russian critic Dobrolyubov (see above, Caudwell chapter), for whom a book was simply the springboard for a political essay, except that Bourne was always equally aware of the book as an important object in its own right. Ideally, granting an unlimited amount of time, Bourne's theory implies that to review a life of Napoleon, say, the reviewer would do his own research on Napoleon's life and then confront the book with it. As a literal program it is not very practical; as a theoretical counterweight to ill-informed and half-baked reviewing it is invaluable.

In an essay "The Critical Method of R. P. Blackmur," in *Poetry* for November 1938, Delmore Schwartz writes:

> One would guess, merely guess, that whether or not he studied at Harvard, the textual and philological approach to Chaucer and earlier poets by leading teachers at that school may have suggested a good deal to Blackmur. At any rate, his method is original in the extreme to which he has extended it; and it is, in fact, instructive to analyze Wallace Stevens as if he were a Scotch Chaucerian of the 15th century.

Whether or not Blackmur took over the Harvard scholarly technique for criticism (and the connection still seems a little remote), it has been adopted for the criticism of contemporary literature by a number of the younger Harvard literature professors, among them F. O. Matthiessen, Theodore Spencer, and Harry Levin. Spencer and Levin took advantage of the manuscript of an earlier version of Joyce's *Portrait of the Artist as a Young Man* in the Harvard College Library (since edited by Spencer and published as *Stephen Hero*) to make detailed technical comparative

---

Robert Burns to write Carlyle's own life and critical study of the poet, ignoring Lockhart after the first few pages. Thackeray has satirized the absurdity of the method in a passage in *Pendennis*, and unquestionably it was responsible for a good deal of idiocy. Nevertheless, it was also responsible for a number of excellent studies (not the least of them several by Marx and Engels), and in Bourne's variant would seem to combine the ideal of "independent inquiry" with genuine criticism of the book under discussion.

studies of the two versions; the former publishing his results in an essay in the *Sou hern Review*, the latter using his in his oddly academic study *James Joyce*.

Matthiessen has also utilized the resources of the Harvard Library, going over the hundred and fifty thousand words of Henry James's then unpublished working notebooks (presented to the library by James's nephew, and since published, finally, in an edition by Matthiessen and Kenneth B. Murdock) as an important source for his study *Henry James: The Major Phase*. He has also used the resources of his own labors (and those of a group of his students who did "most of the spade work") in a detailed comparative study of James's rewriting of *The Portrait of a Lady*. James's revisions of the three early novels for the New York Edition of his works had previously been examined haphazardly by critics, and the revisions of *Roderick Hudson* were the subject of a scholarly article by Hélène Harvitt in the *Publications of the Modern Language Association* for March 1924 (the point of which was that James had spoiled the book!), but Matthiessen's comparison is as systematic and industrious as the best scholarship and as imaginative as the best criticism. It is printed as a supplement, "The Painter's Sponge and Varnish Bottle," to *Henry James: The Major Phase*, and deductions from it, as to precisely what James wanted of his novels in his final period, are an essential part of the book's thesis. It would be hard to find a better example than this of effective criticism utilizing the hard work of scholarship for its own ends.

Another critic who has relied on homework that misses being scholarship through informality is G. Wilson Knight. Almost all of Knight's Shakespeare criticism has relied on one of the most elaborate research projects ever indulged in by a critic. It is the polarization of the whole of Shakespeare's work in two columns (although certainly never written down in that fashion), one of which could be headed "tempest" and the other "music." Thus all winter associations are tempest and all summer associations music, all sea monsters (Caliban) tempest and all winged things (Ariel) music, villains are tempest forces and heroes are music forces, words like "deaf'd" and "clamours" are tempest words, characters like Hamlet and Ophelia are musically out of tune, and even animals are either tempest beasts or music beasts. The process culminates in *The Shakespearian Tempest*, where Knight takes a stab at finding the same polarity in myth, legend, and authors from Melville to Eliot. Silly as it tends to sound in outline, the process is critically successful, and by reading all of Knight's books (or at least all of his Shakespeare books) as one vast compilation entitled Tempest vs. Music, the reader obtains a great number of genuine insights.

H. L. Mencken in his critical days often went to incredible lengths of research to make a point. In *A Book of Prefaces*, for example, he mentions the fact that Conrad first editions fetched high prices during the author's lifetime, and authenticates it with a footnote compilation of prices in booksellers' catalogues for sixteen books in three different years. Or, in discussing the attack of Comstockery on Dreiser's *The Genius*, he studies the seventy-five lewd passages found by the Comstock Society, notes the thirty-one profane passages they turned up (ranging from three "damns" to one "God Almighty"), and then proceeds to turn up eleven more profane passages they missed, including one "God strike her dead!" Supplementing this, he prints a table showing the results of a canvass of public libraries in twenty-five cities regarding the number of Dreiser books represented on their shelves. Another of Mencken's research projects is giving writers like Irvin S. Cobb or President Harding a much more careful reading than they generally get or warrant, examining their style word by word and idiocy by idiocy (the same sort of thing that George Orwell does with English boys' weeklies and comic postcards, or, on a higher level, that Kenneth Burke does with newspaper editorials and Congressional speeches).

Malcolm Cowley, who has inherited something of Mencken's function as a cultural historian, although he works in a much more literate area, is also addicted to using the same sort of eccentric research in criticism. *Exile's Return* will stop to tabulate the characters of the various little magazines or quote someone's listing of the eccentricities of contemporary writers, and in a review Cowley is apt to list the wartime jobs of poets or make a critical point about Bernard DeVoto by going into DeVoto's frustrated literary and social career at Harvard, or interrupt a review of a book about the German occupation of France to tell the story of the death of Saint-Pol-Roux, or set the tone for reviewing a Koestler book by telling ironic anecdotes about refugees. Cowley's source is generally a little mysterious, but the material is always authentic and in his criticism functional. At the same time he has written formal cultural history not only usable as a background for his own criticism but available to others: the "Literary Calendar 1911–1930," giving all the major literary events (as well as the best-sellers as ironic counterpoint) for each year, printed as an appendix to *After the Genteel Tradition*; *Exile's Return* itself, an informal history of writers and writing in the twenties, with its projected succeeding volumes; and the articles with which he has inundated the *New Republic* and other magazines: "How American Writers Earned Their Livings 1940–46," "The Magazine Business 1910–1946," "American Books Overseas," "American Literature in Wartime," and others. All this apparatus was excellent for getting the critical feel of a period, but until the last few years (when he has published a number of first-rate articles) Cowley was apparently so busy accumulating it as to allow him little time for using it critically.

A number of other critical research projects might be mentioned briefly: Edmund Wilson's plot summaries and exegeses are, or should properly be, a labor preparatory to criticism, as are fuller and more formal exegeses like Stuart Gilbert's *James Joyce's Ulysses* and the rest of the work interpreting Joyce; I. A. Richards's experiment with poetry-readers reported in *Practical Criticism* (discussed below, in the chapter on Richards) is among the most productive researches in criticism in our time; and such surveys as Frederick J. Hoffman's *Freudianism and the Literary Mind* and Henri Peyre's *Writers and Their Critics*, if not quite scholarship and certainly not criticism, are a type of research that serves criticism. At one end of the scale there is a man like Blackmur, tabulating Cummings's use of the word "flower," and then, by making as much from the results as may legitimately be made, more or less removing the fruits of his labor from the public domain. At the other extreme there are writers like Peyre (or scholars like Caroline Spurgeon) amassing a great deal of valuable material and then proving flatly incapable of extending it to critical conclusions. We tend to admire the first type, but the second type suggests a job for us to do and simplifies the doing of it.

5

Blackmur's personal qualifications for the sort of work he does, in so far as they can be deduced from his criticism or gleaned from the very parsimonious scraps of information he furnishes magazines for contributors' notes, are substantial. He has apparently never attended college, for what reason I do not know, although my own guess would be that he simply felt the chances of education to be better outside an institution of higher learning (Kenneth Burke never finished college). In any case, he is remarkably learned. He has enough of a working understanding of architecture, sculpture, painting, dance, acting, and music to use them in his criticism, as his elaborate discussion of their varieties of gesture in "Language as Gesture" shows. He has admitted unfamiliarity with German, but apparently knows Greek, Latin, Italian, and French with some fluency. He is given to scientific metaphors in his criticism, ranging from a Fabre caterpillar to the theoretical concepts of field physics, and he either had or acquired for his study of Henry Adams enough of a usable knowledge of physics not only to follow Adams in his analogies from thermodynamics but to suggest that had Adams known the new physics, quanta and indeterminacy, he never would have bothered trying to use the science to symbolize unity and law. Also probably for his Adams study he has acquired a substantial acquaintance with history (at a lecture at Bennington College on Brooks Adams in 1946, he quoted a vast medley of historical writers from Thucydides and Vico to Acton and Toynbee) as well as politics and economics.

For the past few years Blackmur has been in residence at Princeton, first as a staff member of the Institute for Advanced Study, then as a lecturer in the Creative Arts Program under Allen Tate, now as a Resident Fellow in Creative Writing. With the advantage of not having attended a college, he seems to be seriously interested in liberal education. I have had the privilege of seeing an unpublished report he wrote for Princeton: "Two Practical Experiments in the Direction of Common Knowledge: with a Preface," suggesting two new types of course as experiments in integration, which seems to me one of the most brilliant and persuasive examples of educational theory written. In it Blackmur treats liberal education as he would treat a problem in literary criticism, turning on it what he would call "the symbolic imagination," and his proposed integrative courses are "dramatistic" along the lines of Kenneth Burke's current critical framework, with fields of learning themselves brought into conflict and made to act out thematic plots and subplots.

Blackmur is, of course, as a vital adjunct to his criticism, a working poet, the author of three volumes of verse, *From Jordan's Delight* in 1937, *The Second World* in 1942, and *The Good European* in 1947. It is not in order here to discuss his verse, except to note, in connection with his criticism, that it tends to be earnest, moral, frequently ironic, somewhat metaphysical, traditional in form, and slightly eclectic (so that although it is clearly individual in style, influences like Yeats, Eliot, and Tate are discernible). The sparsity of his poetic output (*The Second World* contains only nine poems, for five years' work) seems to be a reflection, not of any thinness of inspiration or ability, but of the same pattern of conscientiousness and perfectionism that has kept the book on Adams announced for at least a decade and not yet forthcoming.

Since the publication of *The Expense of Greatness* in 1940, Blackmur has published at least a dozen major articles and a number of reviews, or more than enough for a third book (which ought properly to be called *The Symbolic Imagination*). Three of them have dealt with Henry Adams and are either fragments of the Adams book or by-products. One, "Henry and Brooks Adams: Parallels to Two Generations," in the *Southern Review*, Autumn 1939, is a study of the relationship between the brothers; another, "Henry Adams: Three Late Moments," in the *Kenyon Review*, Winter 1940, is a picture of the late Adams as a type of American imagination; and the third, "The Pedagogue of Sensibility," in *Chimera*, Summer 1944, is a study in the development of Adams toward *The Education* and *Mont-Saint-Michel and Chartres*.

Eight of Blackmur's recent pieces are definite studies of texts: "Between Myth and Philosophy: Fragments of W. B. Yeats" in the *Southern Review*, Yeats Issue, Winter 1942; "The Sacred Fount," an interpretation of one of James's most misunderstood works, in the *Kenyon Review*, Autumn 1942; "A Rage of Goodness: The Idiot of Dostoyevsky" in *Accent*, Autumn 1942; "Crime and Punishment: A Study of Dostoyevsky's

Novel" in *Chimera*, Winter 1943; "An Attraction Blooded," a review of
two of Wallace Stevens's books, in *Partisan Review*, May–June 1943;
"In the Country of the Blue," a study of James's treatment of the relationship of the artist to society for the James number of the *Kenyon
Review*, Autumn 1943; "An Adjunct to the Muse's Diadem: A Note
on E. P.," a revaluation of Pound's poetry, in *Poetry*, September 1946;
and "The Jew in Search of a Son," a study of *Ulysses*, in the *Virginia
Quarterly Review*, Winter 1948. All of these are similar to earlier critical
pieces on texts: the Yeats piece is close reading of a few poems; the essay
on *The Sacred Fount* interprets it against a background of James's ghost
stories; the study of *The Idiot* reflects such homework as an etymological
exploration of the word "idiot" and a careful study of Dostoyevsky's
eight different plans for the book; the *Crime and Punishment* essay is
largely a moral exploration; the Stevens review is a pursuit of Stevens's
metaphoric meanings; the James piece makes elaborate comparison with
the treatment of the artist in Mann, Joyce, and Gide; the Pound survey
polarizes Pound's work on a scale from Propertius and prose to Arnaut
Daniel and music; and the Joyce essay reads the book in terms of religious
allegory and symbolism.

Blackmur's remaining five major pieces have been something fairly
new for him, general literary discussions developing themes untouched
or largely unstressed in his work before. The essays are: "Chaos is Come
Again" in the *Southern Review*, Spring 1941; "Humanism and Symbolic
Imagination: Notes on Re-reading Irving Babbitt" in the *Southern Review*, Autumn 1941; "Language as Gesture" in *Accent*, Summer 1943;
"The Economy of the American Writer: Preliminary Notes" in the
Sewanee Review, Spring 1945; and "Notes on Four Categories in Criticism" in the *Sewanee Review*, Autumn 1946. The new æsthetic they develop will be discussed below in summing up Blackmur's views, but here
it might be noted that although written on a wide variety of subjects—
"Chaos" is a discussion of an absurd symposium on American culture
held by the American Philosophic Society, "Humanism" on Babbitt,
"Gesture" a lecture at Princeton, "Economy" a survey, using census
figures and periodical circulation figures, of the trade of authorship in
this country, and "Categories" an attempt to classify literary technique—
they are all essays on the same thing, the value of art.

A number of Blackmur's recent reviews—of Horace Gregory's poetry,
of Delmore Schwartz's *Genesis: Book One*, of a group of books by and on
Melville and James, of Simmons's *Leo Tolstoy*—have been persuasive
brief exercises in the same affirmations. Another, of an omnibus group of
poets in the *Kenyon Review*, is remarkable for one of Blackmur's rare
lapses in perception: a complete inability to appreciate Robert Lowell's
poetry. Others represent Blackmur's attempts to explain and evaluate the
work of his critical colleagues and have shown rather unhappily that

Blackmur is weakest as a critic of criticism: they range from excessive kindliness to writers of the type of Mortimer Adler to utter abasement before Yvor Winters's tissue of bluster (even to the point of still being taken in, in 1947, by Winters's "fallacy of expressive form"). In only one of these has Blackmur written a first-rate piece, his brilliant and comic dissection of the Calder-Warren edition of Coleridge's *Ancient Mariner*, in the *Nation*, March 15, 1947. After demolishing the appearance and price of the book, the illustrations, and the mortuary of dead scholarship in the first half of Warren's essay, Blackmur goes on to praise and interpret Warren's excellent independent work in the rest of the essay. (Not even the peculiar statement that "Mr. Warren is . . . perhaps the best novelist we have" can vitiate an excellent review.)

Despite the shifting emphasis, there has been a remarkable continuity in Blackmur's work. His first important critical piece, the Eliot study in 1928, sets the two principal themes of his later work: criticism by hard labor and the high importance of art. For Eliot's references to the tarot in *The Waste Land* (Eliot had never seen a pack) Blackmur uses four authorities on the tarot, and for the poem's anthropological background he not only studies *From Ritual to Romance*, but supplements it with other anthropological information, like G. Elliot Smith on gold. At the same time the piece is a tribute to the value of literature and particularly to the value of the words that constitute it, "the precision and the indefinable suggestive qualities of words."

Blackmur has always been an occasional writer, apparently willing to write an essay on demand (note that his Hardy and Yeats pieces were written for the Hardy and Yeats issues of the *Southern Review*, his James piece for the James issue of the *Kenyon Review*, his first essay on humanism for a symposium, and a number of other articles in response to specific occasions or editorial demands). At the same time he has taken advantage of each occasional piece to pursue his own preoccupations and to write his own poem, whatever the assigned subject. *Partisan Review*, for example, polled him in two symposia, answering Seven Questions on American Writing in 1939, and commenting on an Eliot article in 1944. He took advantage of the former opportunity to sketch out his æsthetic, and of the latter, five years later, as though continuing the essay, to explore its social and theological implications. In Grattan's symposium against the humanists Blackmur demolishes them with the affirmation of his two familiar principles: that "Great knowledge, obtained by great labor, of the particular subject is necessary," and the presence of "insight, imagination and discipline" in any true art and criticism.

For an occasional writer, Blackmur has allowed himself to engage in surprisingly little polemic, and that little concerned never with the man but always with the principle involved. He has apparently a great distaste for the kind of needling of personality, or the mating combat of male elks, that passes for literary controversy with us. When Blackmur reviewed Robert Frost in the *Nation* in 1936 and Bernard De Voto, as an embattled Frostite, promptly called him a fool, so far as I know Blackmur did not reply; nor has he, to my knowledge, ever replied either to such moderate attacks on his work as that of Howard Mumford Jones in the *Saturday Review of Literature* in 1941 or such stupid and intemperate attacks as those of Alfred Kazin in *On Native Grounds* and Harry Levin in the *New Republic*, December 30, 1940. On the other hand, to Granville Hicks's statement in *The Great Tradition:* "And the criticism of such men as . . . R. P. Blackmur resembles the impassioned quibbling of devotees of some game," Blackmur did make a kind of rejoinder. He reviewed the book in *Hound & Horn* (reprinted in *The Double Agent* as "Heresy within Heresy"), achieving a beautiful and utter demolition, *on the central issue of Marxism versus Hicks's application of it*, and then quoted at the end of the review, without comment and with a wonderful irony, the book's statement about himself. Announcing that he regarded Marxism "revised by a clearer dialectic manipulating enormously augmented data" as a sound economics (just as he had previously announced his substantial accord with Malcolm Cowley's radical politics), Blackmur proceeded to explore the poverty of Hicks's readings of American literature in terms of it, in the course of the review managing to write the sharpest criticism of the weakness of most Marxist criticism with which I am familiar. As the obverse, he proceeded as always to affirm his own values: "the independent mind," pluralism, skepticism, and the imaginative understanding of man.

Blackmur's basic metaphor for criticism might be expressed as the image of the stage magician sawing a woman in half. During the performance one has the illusion that she is cut up, but afterwards she springs up whole and untouched to take a bow. Blackmur writes: "Analysis, in these uses, does not cut deep, it does not cut at all; it merely distinguishes particulars; and the particulars must be re-seen in their proper focus before the labor benefits." In another place, making the metaphor clearer:

> What is that but to make an *ex post facto* dissection, not that we may embalm the itemised mortal remains, but that we may intellectually understand the movement of parts and the relation between them in the living body we appreciate. Such dissection is imaginative, an act of the eye and mind alone, and but articulates our knowledge without once scratching the flesh of its object.

The poetry itself, he insists, is never really touched with the scalpel, and it is interesting to note that the same metaphor for criticism, dissection that does not really dissect, was used by A. C. Bradley in his Introduction to *Shakespearian Tragedy*. In keeping with this sense of the dissection as something visual rather than physical, Blackmur's typical imagery for criticism is not cutting but light. Criticism is "elucidation," "Let us incline our minds like reflectors to catch the light," the poetic object is "revealed or elucidated," a word is "illuminating," a passage "lucid," and so on. As Blackmur's criticism becomes increasingly dramatistic, more and more the imagery suggests footlights or spotlights illuminating the drama performed by the work.

Blackmur has written one essay formally on criticism, "A Critic's Job of Work" in *The Double Agent*, and has scattered innumerable dicta on criticism all through his work. These unite, irrespective of the date, to make a reasoned critical æsthetic, centering in the metaphor of imaginary dissection, the metaphor of lighting, and the central concepts of imagination, craft, irony, responsibility and expense. Blackmur has defined criticism as "the formal discourse of an amateur," has insisted that "any rational approach is valid to literature and may properly be called critical which fastens at any point upon the work itself," but has also warned: "we are ramified entirely in the criticism of critics, and end, each of us, where we began—in kissing, without zest, our favourite cow." He adds:

> Some critics make a new work of art; some are psychologists; some mystics; some politicians and reformers; a few philosophers and a few literary critics altogether. It is possible to write about art from all these attitudes, but only the last two produce anything properly called criticism; criticism, that is without a vitiating bias away from the subject in hand. The bastard kinds of criticism can have only a morphological and statistical relation to literature: as the chemistry of ivory to a game of chess.

Sometimes Blackmur is very humble about the critical function: "We can detach certain notions which we call basic—though we may mean only that they are detachable—as clues to better reading"; or:

> There remains the common labour of literary criticism: the collection of facts about literary works, and comment on the management, the craft or technique, of those works; and this labour, in so far as it leaves the reader in the works themselves, is the only one in itself worth doing.

But in his formula for "the good critic" it is easy to see not only the difficulty and rarity of the task done well, but its high value and essential importance to even the greatest art. He writes:

> A good critic keeps his criticism from becoming either instinctive or vicarious, and the labour of his understanding is always specific,

like the art which he examines; and he knows that the sum of his best work comes only to the pedagogy of elucidation and appreciation. He observes facts and delights in discriminations. The object remains, and should remain, itself, only made more available and seen in a clearer light. The imagination of Dante is for us only equal to what we can know of it at a given time.

Blackmur has always insisted on the tremendous importance of art, but the new emphasis on this theme in his recent work gives him almost a secular religion of art, like Joyce's or Henry James's. Besides Blackmur, only James would be apt to write "in craft, all values lie," and mean it on two levels; not only that craft expresses them but that craft *is* them. Despite his "loss of access to a supernatural order," Blackmur still assumes the radical imperfectibility of man, but its application turns out to be essentially artistic, typified by the curious statement he made on an Invitation to Learning program on *The Education of Henry Adams* in 1941. To a characteristically superficial remark of Mark Van Doren's about Adams as a "failure," Blackmur replied: "I think a great part of the failure was merely the failure that goes with making any very great effort of the imagination."

Along with this has come a new attitude, almost mystic, toward art. The familiar pathetic fallacy of a book's "saying" or "doing" something becomes, in Blackmur's hands, almost literal, so that quite apart from Dostoyevsky, who was saving him for another book, Raskolnikov *happens* to meet Marmeladov in a tavern and brings him and his family into *Crime and Punishment*, or Raskolnikov would have invented Porfiry "had he not turned up of his own accord." A work really seems to attain a life and will of its own, and Blackmur is apt to say of meanings, in a shorthand metaphor teetering on the edge of animism: "neither Yeats nor his poem may have intended to apply all of them."

This is accompanied by a new mysticism of the "triple," a further development of *The Double Agent's* constant "doubles" ("my point about Mr. Damon's work is typical and double," "The advantage of the technical approach is I think double," etc.). The "triples" first turned up obsessively in the Dostoyevsky pieces. The essay on *The Idiot* announces on the first page: "Thus we have a double, perhaps a triple, drama in the finished book," and concludes with a discussion of the work "at all three levels of meaning—the intellectual, the narrative, and the imaginative." The essay on *Crime and Punishment* announces in the opening paragraph that the novel has three impacts, a "triple significance," and that the reader must rebuild them analytically, to which project the rest of the essay is devoted. The Wallace Stevens review, noting Stevens's triad, the three phases of the "supreme fiction," even the three-lined stanzas, makes Blackmur's new preoccupation explicit. He writes:

A triad makes a trinity, and a trinity, to a certain kind of poetic imagination, is the only tolerable form of unity. I think the deep skills of imagination, by which insights, ideas, and acts get into poetry, thrive best when some single, pressing theme or notion is triplicated. It is not a matter of understanding, but of movement and of identification and of access of being. The doublet is never enough, unless it breeds. War and peace need a third phase, as liquid and ice need vapor to fill out and judge the concept of water, as God the Father and God the Son need the Holy Ghost, or hell and heaven need purgatory, or act and place need time. The doublet needs what it makes. This is a habit of the creative mind.

This triad is basically, as Blackmur notes, the Christian Trinity, but it is equally the essentially dramatic dialectic, whether Greek, Hegelian, or Marxist (and it may even be, as Edmund Wilson suggests of the Marxist dialectic generally, originally based on the male genitalia).

The key words for the new emphasis, as has been suggested above, are "imagination" and "symbolic imagination"; and "intellect" is reduced to a minor role. Yeats's unity is an "imaginative" unity, produced out of "great imaginative generalizing power"; "imagination—and I mean the artist's imagination"—is superior to fears and temptations; "It is imagination, not intellect, that is the charity of the understanding," the intellect that sins and the imagination that redeems; "the movements of the intellect are accidental and intermittent," whereas the imagination "is the will of things and continuous." Blackmur insists that the artist creates moral value "out of the actual and by means of imagination"; that "imagination, in the end, is the sole persuader"; that "A frankly provisional, avowedly conventional imagination is the only superrational authority we can muster"; that "science must *implement* the *policy* of the *imagination*," and so forth. (These quotations are lifted from widely different essays.)

The point of Blackmur's mature criticism of Babbitt and the humanists is that their errors arise out of "the decay of Christian imagination, the voiding of religious imagination of any description," that the only contemporary substitute for this is "the symbolic imagination," which is the only expression of "grace" and is itself our form of "grace," so that a satisfactory humanism would include its stated elements *and* the symbolic imagination. The emphasis of Blackmur's proposed courses for Princeton is entirely on producing in the student "an act of imaginative integration"; the emphasis of his Bennington lecture on Brooks Adams is on Adams's maturing from the rigidity of absolute historical law to "a more imaginative power of generalizing history." In Blackmur's "Notes on Four Categories in Criticism," a recent piece, the fourth and highest category, far beyond the other categories that were earlier preoccupations (the formal, the linguistic, and the ulterior or determined), is "the symbolic imagination"; and the ultimately "real," which shines through "the actual," is "the symbol":

> What writing drags into being and holds there while the writing lasts may be called the experience of the actual; what writing creates—what goes on after the writing has stopped—may sometimes be called symbol. It is symbol when it stands, not for what has been said or stated, but for what has not been said and could not be said, for what has been delivered by the writing into what seems an autonomous world of its own. Symbol is the most exact possible meaning, almost tautologically exact, for what stirred the words to move *and* what the moving words made. Symbol stands for nothing previously known, but for what is "here" made known and what is about to be made known. If symbol stands for anything else than itself continuing, it stands for that within me the reader which enables me to recognize it and to illuminate it with my own experience at the same moment that what it means illuminates further corridors in my sense of myself.

It is in terms of the implications of this lofty evaluation of art and the symbolic imagination, almost a mystic religion, that we can perhaps best summarize and evaluate Blackmur's work. Pointed one way, it is precious, snobbish, out-of-the-world; in general, dilettantish. It is easy enough to find evidence for a general charge of dilettantism in Blackmur's work. He *is* snobbish enough to announce that our mass consumption culture has succeeded in producing an art without standards, that America suffers from never having had "a dominant class in our society which has set a high value on the æsthetic mode of understanding or expressing human life," and that "the democratization of the audience, if continued unchanged, will make the artist's true interest either intolerable, incomprehensible, or unavailably remote." He *is* precious enough to discuss a Yeats symbol as "an enantiosis" and "an enantiodromia," as though he were writing for an audience familiar with the classical tropes. His tentativeness and scrupulousness sometimes become the most maddening sort of backing-and-filling, as where he writes: "This essay proposes to approach Herman Melville altogether gingerly and from behind the safe bulwark of his assured position—whatever that is—in American literature—whatever *that* may be." His specialization and discrimination are sometimes a kind of candy-box picking-and-choosing ("the *early* Plato," "The Critical *Prefaces* of Henry James," "The *Shorter* Poems of Thomas Hardy," "The *Later* Poetry of W. B. Yeats"— my italics), and sometimes, as in the last named, his focus is so exclusive you can hardly see it with the naked eye. His opening announces: "The later poetry of William Butler Yeats is certainly great enough in its kind, and varied enough within its kind, to warrant a special approach, deliberately not the only approach, and deliberately not a complete approach."

Blackmur's weakness for the refined sometimes inhibits his appreciation of the not-so-refined, as where he finds Melville oracular and flatulent, ruined by the Gothic novel, and implies that he prefers the dramatistic James; or praises John Wheelwright's poetry in a review to the dispraise of William Carlos Williams's on the issue of form; or, in writing like James, falls to imitating, not the strength and subtlety of James's style, but the mincing, gingerbread aspects it has when it fails, and the reader of those Blackmur sentences has to hack his way with a machete through the appositional clauses and the single words set off by commas. Sometimes instead of analyzing poetry, Blackmur fusses with it and rewrites it, changing the order of the stanzas in a Dickinson poem (he has the grace to admit "one feels like writing the poem oneself—the basest of all critical temptations"), or toying with other titles Dostoyevsky might have given *The Idiot*. And, finally, for the ultimate feature of dilettantism, there is the fact that he has done so much reviewing and occasional writing, and written no books.

And yet, overshadowing each of these frivolous aspects, there is an opposing habit or trait showing Blackmur's essential seriousness. To balance the snobbishness there is his eloquent insistence on the social responsibility of the artist in such pieces as "A Feather-Bed for Critics," and the ultimate social function assigned to art and criticism implicit in his doctrine of dealing with reactionary social formulas "not by pulling down the shades, but by the deep exorcism of the effort of understanding." Weighed against the preciousness there is the naked humility of the statement answering a *Partisan Review* symposium: "I believe that it is due to my own defects—of style and sensibility and scope—that my audience is so limited; I have no personal justification for complaint." There is the additional humility, in the Princeton proposals, of the idea that "common knowledge must be held variously, even doubtfully, as a process of discovery"; in the Bennington lecture, of the ideal as "a composed balance of eccentricities"; in the general doctrine of "imaginative scepticism and dramatic irony." He writes in "A Critic's Job of Work:"

we ought scrupulously to risk the use of any concept that seems propitious or helpful in getting over gaps. Only the use should be consciously provisional, speculative, and dramatic. The end-virtue of humility comes only after a long train of humiliations; and the chief labour of humbling is the constant, resourceful restoration of ignorance.

Outweighing all the tentativeness and finickiness is the one certainty: of the high and absolute value of art and the human imagination. The same essay affirms:

> The arts serve purposes beyond themselves; the purposes of what they dramatise or represent at that remove from the flux which gives them order and meaning and value; and to deny these purposes is like asserting that the function of a handsaw is to hang above a bench and that to cut wood is to belittle it.

Against the specialization sometimes becoming overspecialization, we may put the fact that, with Empson, Blackmur is the sharpest and closest reader of poetry we have, and that a similar lack of specialization has kept their respective masters, Richards and Burke, so preoccupied with the ramifications of their theories that they have never been able to devote a comparable portion of their time to applying them to poetic texts. To weigh against the overrefinement, we may note an increasing tendency in Blackmur to confront and appreciate the flatly unrefined, the sordidness of Dostoyevsky and the coarseness of Yeats balancing the endless good taste of writers like Adams and James. We might also note here, in terms of refinement, the way Blackmur's irony increasingly shades into humor in the recent work. Compare an early forced academic joke with a later development to broad and informal comedy:

> Mr. Munson does not here cry Mahabharata, nor even Mahabra-cadabra; he is perforce restrained, since he is dealing with critics, to the less stringent vocables, Babbitt! More! and a final ghostly Arnold! Arnold! . . . with perhaps as a prevalent echo of equivalence the faint "susurrus of his subjective hosannah." (1930)

> But Mr. Kidder is on a different track; he puts philosophy at a discount only by inadvertence—because he does not happen to tackle it; and you have the feeling in reading him that if only someone had reminded him of it in his early days—when his education was formed—he would have used it all through his paper. (1941)

> [of Calder illustrations to *The Rime of the Ancient Mariner*] you see only their heads, which look like radiator-cap sculpture in 1934, or late exiles returning. The Albatross is in a hurry to be a sitting duck, and succeeds. (1947)

Writing poetry may have given Blackmur a tendency to rewrite poetry instead of criticizing it, but it has also given him an almost unerring taste (with minor exceptions, in my view, noted above) so that a 1937 review of nine poets will unerringly single out for praise Aiken and Stevens, from a jungle of Housman, Masters, Sandburg, Prokosch, and others, and single out only their best work. It has also given him the ability, as well as the courage, to note the parts in the work of writers like Yeats and Dostoyevsky that are "ad-libbing," letting the "pen run where it would in the hope of something turning up." Finally, for the charge that he has written no books, it can only be said that in a more important sense both his books, organized around the unity of the ideas and practices here discussed, are as clearly integrated and large-scale work as any other major volumes of criticism.

In the final judgment, Blackmur is as far from critical dilettantism as anyone can get. He writes in "A Critic's Job of Work:"

> My own approach, such as it is, and if it can be named, does not tell the whole story either; the reader is conscientiously left with the poem with the real work yet to do; and I wish to advance it—as indeed I have been advancing it *seriatim*—only in connection with the reduced and compensated approaches I have laid out; and I expect, too, that if my approach is used at all it will require its own reduction as well as its compensations.

If that is the standard by which he asks to be judged, and it is a good, if modest, one, we can only say that as much of the whole story as can be told, or as much of the real work as can be done, by a critic combining wide learning, hard labor, imaginative brilliance, and humble honesty, Blackmur has done. That statement seems to call for neither reduction nor compensation.

CHAPTER 10

WILLIAM EMPSON

and Categorical Criticism

THE SIMPLEST way to define the progress of William Empson's criticism is to say that it has moved from a primary concern with what John Crowe Ransom calls "texture" to a primary concern with what Ransom calls "structure." This formulation might not be agreeable to Ransom, whose chief charge in a discussion of Empson's work in *The New Criticism* is overconcern with texture, but Ransom only discussed Empson's first book, *Seven Types of Ambiguity*, and the development came with the second, *Some Versions of Pastoral*. With the new book Empson moved into a basically structural area, the implications of the category "pastoral," and although it is much less showy and less discussed than his work with ambiguity and the ramifications of meaning, I would isolate it, at least for our purposes here, as his chief contribution to modern criticism.

The appearance of *Seven Types of Ambiguity* in 1930, by an unknown young man in his twenties, was a major critical event, despite the small number of copies printed. The book dared to treat what had always been regarded as a deficiency of poetry, imprecision of meaning, as poetry's chief virtue; it announced that ambiguities could be classified into seven types and proceeded so to classify them (although its title constituted an ironic eighth, and its classification suggested innumerable others); and still worse, it read poetry in a way and at a length no one had ever read it before. Actually, of course, in finding ambiguity the core of poetic significance, Empson was not stating a new doctrine. As far back as the third or fourth century B.C., the unknown Demetrius wrote in *On Style:* "As wild beasts gather their limbs together for an attack, so language also should gather itself as it were into a coil to acquire force." From Demetrius' "coiled language" to Empson's "any consequence of language, however slight, that adds some nuance to the direct statement" is not very far, the difference lying principally in Empson's determination to explore the types and variety of coil. He writes:

Thus a word may have several distinct meanings; several meanings connected with one another; several meanings which need one another to complete their meaning; or several meanings which unite together so that the word means one relation or one process. This is a scale which might be followed continuously. "Ambiguity" itself means an indecision as to what you mean, an intention to mean several things, a probability that one or other or both of two things has been meant, and the fact that a statement has several meanings.

For Empson, ambiguity is a form of dramatic irony, at one extreme encompassing the fullness of tragedy, at the other simply the inadequacy of bad craft. "These methods," he admits, "may be used to convict a poet of holding muddled opinions rather than to praise the complexity of the order of his mind," and he announces the criteria for distinguishing between good and bad ambiguities:

> In so far as an ambiguity sustains intricacy, delicacy, or compression of thought, or is an opportunism devoted to saying quickly what the reader already understands, it is to be respected. . . . It is not to be respected in so far as it is due to weakness or thinness of thought, obscures the matter in hand unnecessarily . . . or, when the interest of the passage is not focussed upon it, so that it is merely an opportunism in the handling of the material, if the reader will not easily understand the ideas which are being shuffled, and will be given an impression of incoherence.

Nevertheless, Empson sees ambiguity collecting precisely at the points of greatest poetic effectiveness, and finds it breeding a quality he calls "tension," which we might phrase as the poetic impact itself. He writes:

> Most of the ambiguities I have considered here seem to me beautiful; I consider, then, that I have shown by example, in showing the nature of the ambiguity, the nature of the forces which are adequate to hold it together. . . . I wish only, then, to say here that such vaguely imagined "forces" are essential to the totality of a poem, and that they cannot be discussed in terms of ambiguity, because they are complementary to it. But by discussing ambiguity, a great deal may be made clear about them. In particular, if there is contradiction, it must imply tension; the more prominent the contradiction, the greater the tension; in some way other than by the contradiction, the tension must be conveyed, and must be sustained.
> An ambiguity, then, is not satisfying in itself, nor is it, considered as a device on its own, a thing to be attempted; it must in each case arise from, and be justified by, the peculiar requirements of the situation. On the other hand, it is a thing which the more interesting and valuable situations are more likely to justify.

The "seven types" themselves are more or less arbitrary. Empson writes: "My seven types, so far as they are not merely a convenient framework, are intended as stages of advancing logical disorder." Although he nowhere remarks on it, they move not only from simplicity to complexity, but in addition generally from lesser to greater poetic richness. The types are almost meaningless apart from their context of discussion, and Empson nowhere lists them formally, but to give some idea of the sequence I shall attempt to abstract Empson's definitions (a paraphrase differing somewhat from this may be found in John Crowe Ransom's *The New Criticism* pp. 119, 120):

1. When a word, a syntax or a grammatical structure, while making only one statement, is effective in several ways at once.

2. When two or more meanings all add to the single meaning of the author.

3. When two ideas, which are connected only by being both relevant in the context, can be given in one word simultaneously.

4. When two or more meanings of a statement do not agree among themselves, but combine to make clear a more complicated state of mind in the author.

5. When the author is discovering his idea in the act of writing, or not holding it all in his mind at once, so that, for instance, there is a simile which applies to nothing exactly, but lies half-way between two things when the author is moving from one thing to the other.

6. When a statement says nothing, by tautology, by contradiction, or by irrelevant statements, if any; so that the reader is forced to invent statements of his own and they are liable to conflict with one another.

7. When the two meanings of the word, the two values of the ambiguity, are the two opposite meanings defined by the context, so that the total effect is to show a fundamental division in the writer's mind.

Empson is indebted to I. A. Richards, his teacher at Cambridge, for the two basic assumptions behind *Seven Types of Ambiguity:* that poetry is substantially, if not entirely, a matter of communicated meanings; and that its meanings are as open to analysis as any other aspect of human experience, or, as Empson phrases it, "the reasons that make a line of verse likely to give pleasure, I believe, are like the reasons for anything else; one can reason about them." (In essence, of course, this is a phrasing of Dewey's "continuity" principle.) If the assumptions of *Seven Types of Ambiguity* are largely from Richards, its applications are most complete for Shakespeare. Shakespeare is the supreme ambiguist, not so much from the confusion of his ideas and the muddle of his text, as some scholars believe, as simply from the power and complexity of his mind and art. Empson reads a line of Shakespeare quite literally against a potential background of every other line he wrote, noting "how much work the reader of Shakespeare is prepared to do for him, how one is helped by the rest of his work to put a great deal into any part of it." At the same time he also reads the line with the whole corpus of biographical and historical information and literary reference suspended in his mind. Here is a typical, and much quoted, example, interpreting the figure in the sonnet line "Bare ruined choirs, where late the sweet birds sang":

> the comparison is sound, because ruined monastery choirs are places in which to sing, because they involve sitting in a row, because they are made of wood, are carved into knots and so forth, because they used to be surrounded by a sheltering building crystallised out of the likeness of a forest, and coloured with stained glass and painting like flowers and leaves, because they are now abandoned by all but the grey walls coloured like the skies of winter, because the cold and Narcissistic charm suggested by choir-boys suits well with Shakespeare's feeling for the object of the Sonnets, and for various sociological and historical reasons ("for oh, the hobbyhorse is forgot," and the Puritans have cut down the Maypoles), which it would be hard now to trace out in their proportions; these reasons, and many more relating the simile to its place in the Sonnet, must all combine to give the line its beauty, and there is a sort of ambiguity in not knowing which of them to hold most clearly in mind.

The relation of Empson's method to traditional Shakespeare scholarship has been touched on above (in the chapter on Caroline Spurgeon), but a further exploration of it here is in order. In discussing his second type of ambiguity, two meanings both meant by the author (that is, the serious pun), Empson suddenly confesses that he got most of his complicated and particularly Empsonian readings of Shakespeare in the chapter out of the Arden text, that they are the traditional readings of scholarship. He got them, however, by an odd method: when a scholar said "either . . . or," attempting to replace another scholar's reading with his own, Empson generally said "both . . . and," finding both or all the disputed meanings legitimately implied in the text. His assumptions about most of the odd Shakespeare words that scholarship has assumed are misprints and found it necessary to amend include three possible theories: that Shakespeare so corrected and revised his manuscripts (despite Heminge and Condell) that the printer couldn't read them; or that he deliberately wrote a meaningless word that fell between several meaningful words, as Joyce does in *Finnegans Wake*, to make the reader think of them all; or that he actually never blotted, and simply put down the approximate word rather than stop and lose his thought, perhaps hoping to have a chance to fix it some time.

In contrast to these assumptions, or any other "working notion of what this unique mind must have been like when in action," traditional Shakespeare scholarship, Empson claims, simply rejects everything unclear as a misprint. Thus it reduces plurality of meaning and ambiguity to one simple meaning, thinning out Shakespeare; or it works back to Shakespeare's original draft, what he wrote first, on paper or in his head, and then modified as too simple and obvious; or it proceeds "to hack out of the quarry a small poem of one's own." That is, Empson believes that in one way or another Shakespeare's poetic cruces are serious puns and ambiguities, and that in one way or another scholarship has been engaged in canceling them out.[1] (The only suggestion that can be made to any reader who finds these ideas far-fetched or absurd is that he read Empson's argument, with its detailed analysis of a half-dozen very persuasive illustrations.)

The Shakespeare analysis is probably the showiest thing in the book, but perhaps the most valuable ultimately is a single remark foreshadowing Empson's later categorical method. Analyzing a double sestina of Sidney's, he remarks that the six end words, each of them repeated thirteen times in the poem, are "the bones of the situation"; "it is at these words only that Klaius and Strephon pause in their cries; these words circumscribe their world." What Empson implies is that the sestina *form* itself, instead of being a mechanical and difficult fixed form into which the poet fits his content (as in Ransom's poetics), is actually the heart of the content, that the *form is* the attitude being expressed toward death. "This form has no direction or momentum; it beats, however rich its orchestration, with a wailing and immovable monotony, for ever upon

[1] A typical expression of the scholar's attitude of petulant bewilderment in the face of conscious poetic ambiguity can be found in Robert Bridges's notes to his edition of his friend Hopkins's poetry. Bridges writes:

Here, then, is another source of the poet's obscurity; that in aiming at condensation he neglects the need that there is for care in the placing of words that are grammatically ambiguous. English swarms with words that have one identical form for substantive, adjective, and verb; and such a word should never be so placed as to allow of any doubt as to what part of speech it is used for; because such ambiguity or momentary uncertainty destroys the force of the sentence. Now our author not only neglects this essential propriety but he would seem even to welcome and seek artistic effect in the consequent confusions and he will sometimes so arrange such words that a reader looking for a verb may find that he has two or three ambiguous monosyllables from which to select, and must be in doubt as to which promises best to give any meaning that he can welcome; and then, after his choice is made, he may be left with some homeless monosyllables still on his hands. Nor is our author apparently sensitive to the irrelevant suggestions that our numerous homophones cause; and he will provoke further ambiguities or obscurities by straining the meaning of these unfortunate words.

the same doors in vain." One step farther, and Empson would propose calling a "sestina" any poem, written in any form, that treats tragedy with stoic acceptance or unresolved mournfulness (as opposed, say, to the elegy, where the mournfulness is resolved). Which is precisely what his next book was to do with "pastoral."

Seven Types of Ambiguity has a number of other things of value. Most obvious, page after page contains certainly the most elaborate and probably the finest close reading of poetry ever put down, the fantastic, wonderful, and almost endless spinning out of implications and linguistic possibilities. There is not space for any quotation long enough to do justice to it, but the paragraph above on "bare ruined choirs" can suggest the proportionately more elaborate treatments of a whole line, a stanza, or a poem. These readings depend not only on taking up the charge "ambiguous" and flaunting it as a banner, transformed into a praiseworthy feature, but on accepting things generally rejected all along the line. If there is a single secret to Empson, it is this conversion of the negative into the positive, the trick of "Okay, so it is. All the better." Empson folds Shakespeare's particular wickedness, the pun or quibble, to his bosom; it is a focus of meaning, not a distraction. He loves a misprint; it is intelligent and illuminating because it suggests buried meanings. He is perfectly willing to accept the charge of Shakespeare's homosexuality, and goes off immediately into its possible relation to his taste for puns, "a feminine pleasure in yielding to the mesmerism of language." He will confront frankly the shocking sensual imagery of metaphysical religious poetry—Crashaw's tribute to the chastity of St. Teresa in the buried imagery of copulation, or his image of Christ's wound as a bloody teat, at which "The Mother then must suck the Son"—it furnishes fine examples of the seventh type of ambiguity.

Empson even accepts, for Socratic purposes, all the charges that can be made against his method. At one point he says "the practice of looking for it [ambiguity] rapidly leads to hallucinations, as you can train yourself always to hear a clock ticking," and in another place:

A literary conundrum is tedious, and these meanings are only worth detaching in so far as they are dissolved into the single mood of the poem. Many people would say that they cannot all be dissolved, that an evidently delicate and slender Sonnet ought not to take so much explaining, whatever its wealth of reference and feeling, that Shakespeare, if all this is true, wrote without properly clarifying his mind.

(Which intelligent and reasonable hypothetical criticism he then answers in a progression of "One might protest . . . One might apologize . . . Or it may boldly be said. . . .") The other major charge, that analysis mars beauty (cf. Blackmur's facing of the same thing in the metaphor of the woman sawed in half), Empson admits even more bluntly:

> Critics, as "barking dogs," on this view, are of two sorts; those who merely relieve themselves against the flower of beauty, and those, less continent, who afterwards scratch it up. I myself, I must confess, aspire to the second of these classes; unexplained beauty arouses an irritation in me, a sense that this would be a good place to scratch . . . while it may be true that the roots of beauty ought not to be violated, it seems to me very arrogant of the appreciative critic to think that he could do this, if he chose, by a little scratching.

Empson has distinguished himself frankly from the "appreciative" critic as the "analytic" critic, and he sometimes writes as though he were actually the second sort of dog, blind to appreciation and the indefinables of poetry, as where he boasts of having converted something "magical" through analysis into something "sensible." Nevertheless, Empson has stated the assumptions of his method more explicitly than almost any other critic, and these assumptions point ultimately only at appreciation, but appreciation *through* understanding. He writes:

> In claiming so much for analysis I shall seem to be aligning myself with the "scientific" mode of literary criticism, with "psychological" explanations of everything, and columns of a reader's sensitivity-coefficients. There is coming into existence a sort of party-system among critics; those critics will soon be considered mere shufflers who are not either only interested in Truth or only interested in Beauty; and Goodness, the third member of that indissoluble trinity, has somehow got attached only to truth, so that æsthetes are expected to profess a playful indifference to the principles on which they in fact (one is to assume) order their own lives.

At the same time he is equally explicit about the tentativeness and the ultimate reservations implicit in his own method:

> In wishing to apply verbal analysis to poetry the position of the critic is like that of the scientist wishing to apply determinism to the world. It may not be valid everywhere; though it be valid everywhere it may not explain everything; but in so far as he is to do any work he must assume it is valid where he is working, and will explain what he is trying to explain.

Only the reader of *Seven Types of Ambiguity* can know how enormously valid the concept seems to be, and how much it explains.

Empson's second book, *Some Versions of Pastoral* (published in this country as *English Pastoral Poetry* in 1938) appeared in England in 1935.

Since it will be discussed below in some detail, we need only note here that it continued all the features of *Seven Types*, going even farther in close reading of ambiguity, while adding a number of further developments and emphases. The new book concentrated on a category, the "pastoral," that Empson abstracted from its stylistic features as a form and converted into a mode, a complicated ironic attitude, found in literature of the widest disparity. Empson thus demolished the worn critical counters "form" and "content," even as used artificially for purposes of analysis, by a critical approach which refused to admit the two as separate entities, treating the thing traditionally called form *as* content and vice versa. His approach was, unofficially, a Gestalt one to the totality of the poem as a whole, and his term "pastoral," used as an organic and dynamic concept, extended and amplified "ambiguity" to the point where it was a critical mechanism for treating the whole work rather than coiled high spots.

Since writing *Some Versions of Pastoral*, Empson has been rather mysteriously occupied and almost nothing by or about him has appeared, at least in America.[2] In 1937 he did some reviews in the *Criterion*, including one of Richards, and engaged in a bitter literary polemic in the pages of *Poetry* (Chicago) with Geoffrey Grigson, the editor of *New Verse*. Grigson wrote a London Letter criticizing the deadness of English literary activity at the time, Empson wrote a London Letter in reply criticizing the deadness of Grigson's perception of literature, Grigson countered with a torrent of invective at Empson, and Empson concluded the polemic with general abuse of Grigson. It was not much of a contribution to criticism. After it, some time in 1937, Empson went to China to teach (he had been in Japan in 1933) and remained in the East for two years. When the war began in 1939, he returned to England, stopping off in the United States for a short time.

All along Empson had been experimenting in his own poetry with the ironic extension of formal categories similar to what he did with "pastoral," and his first volume of poetry had included two "serious" uses of the villanelle form, more or less successful. In the *Criterion* for May 1937 he published a completely successful "Villanelle," later entitled "Missing Dates," in which the rigid and monotonous nature of the form, as in Sidney's sestina, merged with the philosophic view expressed. Now in America, Empson continued the same technique in criticism. In a review

[2] About 1936 Empson and George Garrett published a shilling pamphlet entitled *Shakespeare Survey*. I was unable to see a copy until after this chapter was in type, and can only note here that the pamphlet contains two brilliant essays by Empson, "The Best Policy," a study of *Othello* in terms of the shifting ambiguities of the word "honest," and "Timon's Dog," an exploration of the dog imagery in *Timon of Athens* as a criticism-by-example of Miss Spurgeon's oversimplifications; as well as a rather unfortunate *jeu d'esprit* by Garrett, "That Four-Flusher Prospero," demonstrating that Prospero is the villain of *The Tempest*.

of Cleanth Brooks's *Modern Poetry and the Tradition* that appeared in *Poetry*, December 1939, he attempted to turn almost the most hackneyed terms of all, Propaganda poetry, Sentimental poetry, and Uplift poetry, into valid categorical distinctions, suggesting features of structure and function supplementing attitude.

At Yale in January 1940 Empson delivered a lecture on "The Use of Basic English for Criticism," developing a new aspect of Richards's critical method. He amplified it in a radio talk, "Basic English and Wordsworth," printed in the *Kenyon Review*, Autumn 1940. Here he suggested Basic English, on which he had been working with Ogden and Richards (he has done Basic translations for Ogden's series), as a technique for the criticism of poetry. Admitting that poetry couldn't be written in Basic, since one of the things poetry requires is complex verbs, Empson proposed that it be read with the help of Basic. (Richards had previously made a similar proposal for prose in *Interpretation in Teaching*.) The reader translates the poem into Basic, thus more or less destroying it in paraphrase. In the course of this effort to translate complicated words into one clear meaning, however, the reader "takes the cover off," sees "why the Basic copy is wrong," and discovers the complex group of ideas behind what appear to be simple feelings. Empson illustrates the scheme with an example from Wordsworth, as first written and as Wordsworth later rewrote it, with a paraphrase into Basic and an analysis. The analysis is extremely undistinguished, for Empson, the points are rather pat, and he seems to be proposing the use of Basic as a mechanical device for doing what the critic's mind, without mechanical devices, automatically does in reading. Empson does not succeed in demonstrating any more need for Basic in the criticism of poetry than for Aramaic or Catalan, since a translation of the poem into those, or any language, would do the job just as well.

During the war years Empson worked in the Chinese section of the BBC and completely disappeared from print, at least in America. In 1946 and 1947 several reviews of his appeared in the *Nation*, done before he went back to China to teach. The first review was of Paul H. Kocher's *Christopher Marlowe* and did not do much more than oppose Kocher's rather pretty view of Marlowe with the reality of "the man ripe for fascism" (a phrase of Radek's, first used of Céline, that Empson has always been rather fond of), and propose as "the primary fact about Marlowe's work" the observation that the climactic horror scenes in his plays are dramatic punishments for Marlowe's own sins, atheism and homosexuality. The second review, of the American edition of Kafka's *Metamorphosis*, was even thinner and did little but reproach the ridiculous Preface and illustrations as "wrong-headed," announce that the story was "like a punch on the jaw" (an American would say "in the jaw"), and count Kafka's inconsistencies and boners in it. A third, of Dylan Thomas's

Selected Writings, discussed Thomas's poetry in vague terms and explored the meanings of one line at some length. A fourth noted in a
paragraph that Robert Graves's poetry is both well written and slight.
The *Nation* reviews confirm a conjecture that almost any reader would
make from the books, that the brief periodical review is not the likeliest
medium for Empson, who seems always to need space in which to turn
around.[3]

2

The statement to begin an analysis of *Some Versions of Pastoral* with is
Empson's surprising announcement in the first chapter that the book is
sociology. He says of his aim: "Probably the cases I take are the surprising rather than the normal ones, and once started on an example I
follow it without regard to the unity of the book. Certainly it is not a
solid piece of sociology; for that matter many of the important social
feelings do not find their way into literature." "Social feelings" is the
important phrase here, for the book is actually devoted to observing,
from a relativistic historical view, the way attitudes find expression in
varieties of the ironic form-content complex he calls "pastoral." It is a

[3] Late in 1947 Empson's long-awaited revision of *Seven Types of Ambiguity* appeared and, unhappily, turned out to be rather disappointing. Many things of value
were added, particularly a Preface to the new edition explaining the intentions with
which the book was written and defending it in detail against criticisms it had received. A "few bits of analysis" regarded as trivial or distracting were cut out, as
were "jokes which now seem to me tedious"; sources were given for quotations, con-
nections were filled in, a summary of chapters and an index were added, errors were
corrected, and a number of footnotes explaining or extending the argument were
added. All of these gains are somewhat outweighed, however, by the bulk of the corrections, which consist of rather scornful footnotes quibbling with what he had to say
in the book or expressing his current, more conservative, view: "it was stupid of me,"
"a folly on my part," "the reason for the clumsiness here," "I now think this example
a mare's nest," "I seem to have missed the point," and so forth. Empson remarks:
"I was surprised that there was so little of the book I should prefer to change," and
it is true that the only serious changes of position seem to be a narrowing of the
concept of ambiguity, from that which "adds some nuance to the direct statement of
prose" to that which "gives room for alternative reactions to the same piece of language," and a greater inclination to believe that a Shakespearian ambiguity may in
fact be a misprint. The thing chiefly disturbing is the new tone of professorial conservatism, the apologies of an author grown seventeen years older for his earlier
wildness and flippancy. (In the Preface, Empson quotes Max Beerbohm's remark
about revising one of his early works, how "he tried to remember how angry he
would have been when he wrote it if an elderly pedant had made corrections, and how
certain he would have been that the man was wrong," but the joke has too much bite
to be very funny.) In some respect the revised edition of *Seven Types of Ambiguity*
is a real improvement on the old one: it is much improved stylistically and much
clearer (this may be Empson's Basic training), it is better-informed, it is much more
dialectic, and it may even be generally sounder. But there is no question that something very important has been lost.

quest, in Kenneth Burke's phrase, for "the permanent forms that underlie changing historical emphases." This permanent form, the pastoral, is at once a philosophy, a social attitude or feeling, an ironic ambiguity, a propaganda subject, and a stylistic device, and in fact it must be all those things together or it is nothing. The key word for pastoral is "simple." Empson defines it in one place as "simple people expressing strong feelings in learned and fashionable language," in another as "the praise of simplicity," in a third as "putting the complex into the simple." He defines the paradoxical essence of pastoral as "the refined thing must be judged by the fundamental thing, strength must be learnt in weakness and sociability in isolation, the best manners are learnt in simple life," and in another place writes: "If you choose an important member of a class the result is heroic; if you choose an unimportant one it is pastoral."

Essentially, Empson's pastoral category is the artificial cult of simplicity, the literary equivalent of Marie Antoinette and her ladies-in-waiting cavorting on the greensward dressed as milkmaids. He must have reached it through a process of abstraction, noting that the rustic background, the sheep, and the greenery of poetry traditionally called pastoral are merely superficial trappings, and that what all the examples of the form have in common basically is an attitude. From this it is only one step to noting that other examples of literature far from the pastoral are ways of expressing this attitude too, some of them simply forms characteristic of other days, including our own, and lumping them in with pastoral too. A pastoral poem is then not a poem about shepherds, but a poem that *acts* like the old pastorals about shepherds. The seven chapters of the book (what is Empson's passion for the mystic number, incidentally?) are simply seven versions of pastoral poetry. The first, and most shocking to the reader full of conventional notions, is on proletarian literature, and uses the incongruity of its concept of the fictional proletarian as a glorified pastoral swain to define the irony of the category. The other six versions of pastoral are only slightly less shocking: the subplot in double-plot drama; a Shakespeare sonnet discussing aristocracy; Marvell's "The Garden"; *Paradise Lost*; *The Beggar's Opera*; and *Alice in Wonderland* ("The Child as Swain"). Moving more or less chronologically through English literature, after the first chapter, the book shows the changes rung on the pastoral idea through the centuries: constituting a lower-level repetition of the heroic story in drama; permitting an ironic reversal in Shakespeare's sonnets; used to resolve contradictions in Marvell; turned theological ("the innocence of man and nature") in Milton; urbanized in Gay; and used as regression to pre-sexuality in Lewis Carroll.

This is, of course, a social progression, and Empson draws heavily on sociology, chiefly of the Marxist variety, to elucidate the social origins and function of each variety. The chief exercise in this analysis is the chapter on "Proletarian Literature," which at the same time repudiates most of the so-called proletarian literature Empson has seen, and outlines some valid concepts for proletarian literature, both of a variety functioning in capitalist culture and a variety that might flower in a socialist culture. At the same time he "class-angles" a number of works, from the *Æneid* as a "political puff" for Augustus (quoting Pope) and the "bourgeois ideology" of Gray's "Elegy" (a wonderful section) to the class basis of fairy tales, border ballads, and the work of Louis-Ferdinand Céline. In fact, Empson uses class analysis all through the book, noting that ironical humor is a device for reconciling one to being ruled, that a play includes heroic plot and pastoral subplot to show "a proper and beautiful relation between rich and poor," that parody operates as a social catharsis, relieving audiences of their impulse to oppose more seriously (it is thus a device for disarming criticism, both social and artistic, rather than for criticizing), and so forth.

Marx is mentioned only once in the book, in connection with the statement that references to money in *The Beggar's Opera* are at least as scornful of it as those in *Timon*, which he "analysed with so much pleasure." Nevertheless, the book is implicitly Marxist throughout, something that only Kenneth Burke seems to have perceived, noting that "the Marxist emphasis has given a new dimension to his work," and estimating: "One will look long among the writings of most self-professed 'Marxist' critics before he finds such profoundly Marxist analysis of literature as this." (It is amusing to note that Alick West, the only Marxist critic who seems to have paid any attention to Empson's work, quotes with approval the factors of social change he finds behind "bare ruined choirs" and ignores all the other factors.)

Some Versions of Pastoral also goes much farther in the use of Freud and psychoanalysis than *Seven Types of Ambiguity*. Here the focal chapter is the one on *Alice in Wonderland*, and it is probably the most completely successful brief Freudian analysis of literature yet written. Empson points out that critics seem to have avoided serious analysis of *Alice* from a fear that it would inevitably involve psychoanalysis and that the results would be "improper," but that Dodgson himself was apparently aware of the book's meanings, and once told an actress playing the part of the Queen of Hearts that her role was a symbol of "uncontrolled animal passion" seen through the sexless eyes of a child. Empson writes: "The books are so frankly about growing up that there is no great discovery in translating them into Freudian terms; it seems only the proper exegesis of a classic even where it would be a shock to the author. . . . I shall use psychoanalysis where it seems relevant." Which he proceeds to do, showing the books as a regressive, even neurotic variant of the pastoral pattern, the "*child*-become-judge," the child envied because it is sexless (since Dodgson equated the development of sex and death). Two small samples of Empson's lengthy analysis will show how he operates:

> To make the dream-story from which *Wonderland* was elaborated seem Freudian one has only to tell it. A fall through a deep hole into the secrets of Mother Earth produces a new enclosed soul wondering who it is, what will be its position in the world, and how it can get out. It is in a long low hall, part of the palace of the Queen of Hearts (a neat touch), from which it can only get out to the fresh air and the fountains through a hole frighteningly too small. Strange changes, caused by the way it is nourished there, happen to it in this place, but always when it is big it cannot get out and when it is small it is not allowed to; for one thing, being a little girl, it has no key. The nightmare theme of the birth-trauma, that she grows too big for the room and is almost crushed by it, is not only used here but repeated more painfully after she seems to have got out; the rabbit sends her sternly into its house and some food there makes her grow again. In Dodgson's own drawing of Alice when cramped into the room with one foot up the chimney, kicking out the hateful thing that tries to come down (she takes away its pencil when it is a juror), she is much more obviously in the fœtus position than in Tenniel's. . . .
>
> The symbolic completeness of Alice's experience is I think important. She runs the whole gamut; she is a father in getting down the hole, a fœtus at the bottom, and can only be born by becoming a mother and producing her own amniotic fluid. Whether his mind played the trick of putting this into the story or not he has the feelings that would correspond to it. A desire to include all sexuality in the girl child, the least obviously sexed of human creatures, the one that keeps its sex in the safest place, was an important part of their fascination for him. He is partly imagining himself as the girl child (with these comforting characteristics) partly as its father (these together make *it* a father) partly as its lover—so it might be a mother—but then of course it is clever and detached enough to do everything for itself.

In addition to this chapter, psychoanalytic insights are scattered all through the book. Empson discusses Ernest Jones's psychoanalytic reading of *Hamlet* as a reading in terms of a double plot, and he takes over Jones's term "decomposition"—the splitting of one character into several, each representing one aspect of him—and extends it as a general literary concept apart from Œdipal repression. He analyzes the related homosexual-pugnacity imagery in Shakespeare and Marlowe, the suggestions of sodomy and incest with which Dryden imbues normal love in his plays, and so on. In *Seven Types of Ambiguity* Empson revealed an extensive acquaintance with Freud, but did not do very much more with it than move in on terms like "transference" and "condensation" to describe literary processes. In *Some Versions of Pastoral* there are only two direct references to Freud, one in discussing his theory of the group mind and the other in connection with the relation between death and sex in the punning Elizabethan use of "die," but the whole book is much more informed with Freudian insights. As in the case of his Marxist insights, this has not been recognized by the orthodox, and, for example, Hoffman's *Freudianism and the Literary Mind*, an extensive catalogue of the literary use of Freud, does not even mention Empson.

In addition to Marx and Freud, Empson makes use of the two other great nineteenth century determiners of the modern mind, Darwin and Frazer. He has a remarkable analysis of the Darwinism implicit in *Alice*, finding that the book dramatizes the principle that ontogeny recapitulates phylogeny as well as makes a number of oblique comments on the moral and political implications of natural selection. *The Golden Bough*, like Freud, is an informing influence throughout. Empson identifies the worker of proletarian literature as a mythical cult figure, the sacrificial hero as dying god, and contrasts him with the Oriental sacrificial type in Frazer, better adapted to socialism, the sincere man at one with nature. *Some Versions of Pastoral* also seems very much influenced by the Cambridge group of anthropological classical scholars (not an unreasonable influence on a sometime Cambridge fellow), although the only one of their books specifically discussed is F. M. Cornford's *From Religion to Philosophy*. In addition to the organizing basis of his criticism, which is psychology, sociology, anthropology, and linguistics, Empson draws on a tremendous fund of relatively abstruse knowledge, in fields ranging from atomic physics to philosophy and theology, for metaphors and examples.

The book is not focused on Shakespeare as markedly as the previous one, but Shakespeare remains the field of greatest success for Empson's method. He notes ambiguities and suggests that Shakespeare deliberately refused to decide between the possible meanings; explores the double plot in *Troilus and Cressida* and *I Henry IV*; analyzes a Shakespeare sonnet at great length; and finally turns the plays and sonnets on each other for their mutual illumination. The analysis of Sonnet 94, "They that haue powre to hurt, and will doe none," is probably the showpiece of the book, Empson's most impressive display of line-by-line close reading. He announces ironically in his opening paragraph that the sonnet yields "4,096 possible movements of thought, with other possibilities," and that he can only consider the few possible meanings that seem important. He then proceeds to read the sonnet in greater detail than a short lyric has probably ever been read before, paraphrasing its attitudes, exploring its relation to ideas as disparate as Christianity and Machiavellianism, conjecturing the social status of W. H., translating the possibilities of all the focal words, and finally concludes on a startling paraphrase of its complex irony:

"I am praising to you the contemptible things you admire, you little plotter; this is how the others try to betray you through flattery; yet it is your little generosity, though it show only as lewdness, which will betray you; for it is wise to be cold, both because you are too inflammable and because I have been so much hurt by you who are heartless; yet I can the better forgive you through that argument from our common isolation; I must praise to you your very faults, especially your selfishness, because you can only now be safe by cultivating them further; yet this is the most dangerous of necessities; people are greedy for your fall as for that of any of the great; indeed no one can rise above common life, as you have done so fully, without in the same degree sinking below it; you have made this advice real to me, because I cannot despise it for your sake; I am only sure that you are valuable and in danger."

Naturally this is not the sort of thing to appeal to Shakespeare scholars any more than his evaluation of their work in *Seven Types*, and Empson's relations with scholarship in general are not of the best. The new Variorum edition of the *Sonnets* treats his comments more or less as eccentricities, and Cleanth Brooks, in his study of Empson's criticism in *Accent*, Summer 1944, in the course of noting an Empson "howler," reports that Geoffrey Tillotson has called attention to several other of his scholarly slips and misquotations. Leavis, too, has noted that he misquotes and mispunctuates. Anyone who wants to can find lacunæ in Empson—mine would be his apparent ignorance of the fact that Elizabethan drama was spoken much faster on their stage than our own, not much slower—but they are all too trivial to be worth bothering about. Empson sometimes errs as he runs, but in a larger sense his work is faultless scholarship, textual and historical, of a high order. Oddly enough, he does have a great respect for textual scholarship, but as a kind of sublimely inaccurate poetry, which is probably more offensive to the scholars than outright rejection of their work. One of the most brilliant and ingenious chapters of *Some Versions of Pastoral*, called "Milton and Bentley," gets at *Paradise Lost* through the incredible textual emendations and readings in the editions of Dr. Bentley and his opponent Zachary Pearce, using them to focus significance without understanding it, precisely the way Henry James might use a well-meaning and uncomprehending narrator.

Much of the book is simply Empson's continued pursuit of the ramifications of ambiguity, although he tries to avoid the word. Typical of his approach here is finding a note in the Oxford edition of Marvell bringing out "a crucial double meaning" in a couplet of "The Garden," and noting that the same ambiguity (called "a double meaning" or "a doubt") runs through almost every other phrase in the poem. Sometimes these ambiguities transcend the poem and the author and get right at the heart of social expression in words, like Empson's gloss on the Victorian term "delicate": "the profound sentences implied by the combination of meanings in this word are (a) 'you cannot get a woman to be refined unless you make her ill' and more darkly (b) 'she is desirable because corpselike.' "

Frequently, like Blackmur, Empson gets his subtleties of meaning not by flash of intuition but as a result of hard labor, as where he lists every use of the word "green" in Marvell and the context of associated ideas before going on to explore the ambiguities of greenness. At other times he is apt to give a cluster of meanings without their sources, and the reader rarely knows precisely how much of an Empsonian meaning was objectively accepted at the time and how much is Empson's insight at present. At their best, however, these merge, and the Empsonian insight hits on the ancient forgotten meaning or is so persuasive that one assumes it must be inevitably the objective meaning for any time. A typical example is Empson's explanation of the Elizabethan custom of having madmen at a wedding:

> The antimasque at a great wedding, considered as subhuman, stood for the insanity of disorder to show marriage as necessary, considered as the mob, ritually mocked the couple (for being or for not being faithful, innocent, etc.) both to appease those who might otherwise mock and to show that the marriage was too strong to be hurt by mockery.

Here, in little, is a summary of all of Empson's method in *Some Versions of Pastoral:* the social and psychological knowledge and insight; the anthropological emphasis on ritual as the hub; the cutting on the bias across scholarship, rather than either accepting or rejecting it; the insistent sense of ambiguity, complexity, different meanings on different levels, and endless ramification; the rationalist conviction of the explicability of anything; the close reading and hard work; the accumulation of lore; the constant tendency to generalize from formal device to form-content category; and the ultimate brilliance and rightness of the insight. The Elizabethan groom would probably not have been able to explain so well why his wedding included madmen, but one feels inevitably that he would have agreed with the explanation. (True, an opponent of the method might answer, but the only one at the wedding apt to verbalize it for him would have been the madman.)

3

The tradition of categorical criticism from which Empson's later work derives is not an ancient one, and more or less stems from eighteenth-century English literature (although there are suggestions of it earlier, in Jonson, Dryden's concept of "heroic" drama, and others). Empson himself notes its origins as applied to the term "pastoral," which may even have given him the clue for the book, when he remarks in the chapter on *The Beggar's Opera* that Swift first suggested to Gay that he write a Newgate pastoral. Empson's reference is ambiguous and leaves the implication that Gay may have thought he had done so, but the actual story, as reported by Pope in *Spence's Anecdotes*, shows otherwise:

> Dr. Swift had been observing once to Mr. Gay, what an odd pretty sort of thing a Newgate Pastoral might make. Gay was inclined to try at such a thing for some time, but afterwards thought it would be better to write a comedy on the same plan. This was what gave rise to the Beggar's Opera. He began on it, and when he first mentioned it to Swift, the Doctor did not much like the project.

Swift was thus able to make the first step of abstraction, to see that a literal pastoral could be laid in Newgate, but Gay made the second step, perhaps unconsciously from the suggestion, writing a Newgate comedy that was essentially "pastoral," while Swift proved unable to follow him. The final step of verbalizing as "pastoral" a work expressing pastoral attitudes in another form was not made until Hazlitt's *Lectures on the English Poets* in 1818. He writes:

> We have few good pastorals in the language. Our manners are not Arcadian; our climate is not an eternal spring; our age is not the age of gold. We have no pastoral-writers equal to Theocritus, nor any landscapes like those of Claude Lorraine. The best parts of Spenser's Shepherd's Calendar are two fables, Mother Hubbard's Tale, and the Oak and the Briar; which last is as splendid a piece of oratory as any to be found in the records of the eloquence of the British senate! Browne, who came after Spenser, and Withers, have left some pleasing allegorical poems of this kind. Pope's are as full of senseless finery and trite affectation, as if a peer of the realm were to sit for his picture with a crook and cocked hat on, smiling with an insipid air of no-meaning, between nature and fashion. Sir Philip Sidney's Arcadia is a lasting monument of perverted power; where an image of extreme beauty, as that of "the shepherd boy piping as though he should never be old," peeps out once in a hundred folio pages, amidst heaps of intricate sophistry and scholastic quaintness.

It is not at all like Nicholas Poussin's picture, in which he represents some shepherds wandering out in a morning of the spring, and coming to a tomb with this inscription—"I also was an Arcadian." Perhaps the best pastoral in the language is that prose-poem, Walton's Complete Angler. That well-known work has a beauty and romantic interest equal to its simplicity, and arising out of it. In the description of a fishing-tackle, you perceive the piety and humanity of the author's mind. . . . He gives the feeling of the open air; we walk with him along the dusty road-side, or repose on the banks of the river under a shady tree; and in watching for the finny prey, imbibe what he beautifully calls "the patience and simplicity of poor honest fishermen."

This is something very close to Empson's use of pastoral, and the form has already largely been abstracted to an attitude. It remained for Georg Brandes, writing *Main Currents of Nineteenth-Century Literature* in Denmark in the 1870's, to make the final step to Empson's usage and identify George Sand's noble proletarians as essentially pastoral conceptions (although without directly using the term).

A much more widespread category than pastoral is the term "Gothic," which also began in the eighteenth century, with Alexander Pope. He wrote of Shakespeare: "With all his faults and with all the irregularity of his drama, one may look upon his works, in comparison of those that are more finished and regular, as upon an ancient, majestic piece of Gothic architecture, compared with a neat, modern building." Bishop Hurd and Warburton continued this categorical, abstracted use of "Gothic," and Dr. Johnson extended the degree of its application to Shakespeare, talking of his "Gothick fairy mythology," for example. "Gothic" was used as a literary term all through the eighteenth and nineteenth centuries, gradually shifting from pejorative to neutral to appreciative. For the past half-century German scholars and critics have proliferated it and similar terms wildly. The Viennese art-historian Alois Riegl at the end of the last century began the movement (which we think of now as Spenglerian) by calling everything "Late Roman" or Romanesque that resembled late Roman art stylistically, whatever its form or period, and in the first decade of this century Wilhelm Worringer continued Riegl's ideas, although he chose to specialize in the category "Gothic." Since then other scholars, like Karlinger, Weisbach, and Wölfflin, have extended the categories until they include in addition classical, Renaissance, baroque, and rococo; and recent German criticism has found versions of baroque in seventeenth-century English poets as disparate as Donne, Milton, and Dryden, versions of rococo in eighteenth-century English poets, etc.

A much sounder German critical use of categories, a good deal closer to Empson's method, is referred to by Walter Pater in *Appreciation*. He notes that *Romeo and Juliet* combines three poetic forms—the sonnet, the aubade, and the epithalamium—within a grander one, the play itself, "which it is the merit of German criticism to have detected." Whatever German criticism Pater may be referring to, has apparently done a thoroughly Empsonian job of abstracting the essential nature and attitude of sonnet, aubade, and epithalamium from their superficial formal characteristics, and used them categorically for modes or motifs in a drama.

Probably the most ambitious of all categorical criticism has been the work of Ferdinand Brunetière, the French critic and literary historian. From his book on the evolution of genres in 1890 at least through his study of Balzac in 1906, all his work is devoted to one giant, perhaps monstrous effort: to write a literary equivalent of Darwin's *Origin of Species*, in which literary forms develop from simple to complex, propagate, branch out and mutate, ripen to perfection, and die, while young and crude forms, better adapted, survive and supplant them. In his hands literary form becomes an organism evolving mystically independent of the writer, in fact determining his fate, since the value of an artist largely depends on his luck in living at a time when a mature form and language are available to him.

Done by a lesser man, this literary Darwinism would have resulted in idiocy; modified by Brunetière's monumental learning, refined sensibility and good taste, and the recognition that in the last analysis his generalization is metaphoric rather than scientific, it resulted in remarkably good criticism. When Brunetière defines "classic," for example, as that type of literature which occurs when the language, the form, and the nation's literary independence coincide in a stage of ripeness, and insists that a work may be "classic" and nevertheless poor and unoriginal, he is engaged in a categorical criticism almost the opposite of Empson's. Where Empson creates a category by abstracting from historically conditioned forms an essential and fixed attitude, Brunetière defines his category as an ultimate form developing only at certain essential and fixed historical conditions. Both are historical and dynamic views, but Brunetière's is a characteristically nineteenth-century teleological evolutionism, with the category a solid organism changing its shape as it develops more and more efficient appurtenances; Empson's a typical twentieth-century view, the teleology gone, in which the category changes by a protean and rather aimless shape-shifting. Only Empson's can wholly satisfy the modern mind, but we can wholeheartedly admire, while rejecting, Brunetière's lovely and ordered vista.

Except for Empson and the little work derived from his, almost all contemporary categorical criticism has been the use of the category to evade analysis—that is, "pigeonholing." At its worst, this is the easy formulation of reviewing, the mechanical and meaningless use of such terms as "romantic," "classic," "realist," "naturalist," and "symbolist." At its best, or at least its most respectable, it is an odd tradition in otherwise valuable literary history which we might call the Lofty Chapter Heading. This seems to have begun with Brandes's *Main Currents in Nineteenth-Century Literature*. Brandes resorted to it in Volume V, the section of the book dealing with the group he was least equipped to handle, the English writers of the first half of the nineteenth century. His chapter titles make a number of arbitrary categorical distinctions, "Naturalistic Romanticism," "Oriental Romanticism," "Historical Naturalism," "Republican Humanism," "Radical Naturalism," "Comic and Tragic Realism," and so on, and the chapters attempt with only partial success to imbue them with content.

Parrington picked up the vice, along with more useful features of Brandes, for his *Main Currents in American Thought*, and some of *his* chapter headings, like "Agrarian Liberal," "Free-Soil Liberal," "Puritan Liberal," "Transcendental Critic," "Transcendental Economist," "Transcendental Minister," run to similar categorical arbitrariness. The great inheritor of this tradition in recent years has been Harry Slochower. His first book, *Three Ways of Modern Man*, reasonably enough posed three categories: Feudal Socialism, Bourgeois Liberalism, and Socialist Humanism. By his latest book, *No Voice is Wholly Lost . . .*. the tendency has proliferated wildly with such relatively pointless categorical headings as Bohemian Freedom, Cosmic Exile, Secular Crucifixion, Æsthetic Redemption, Aristocratic Transcendence, Democratic Transcendence, Faustian Fascism, Spiritual Judaism, and Bohemian Ichschmerz!

Finally, there remains Empson's method in other hands. Apparently before reading *Some Versions of Pastoral*, Kenneth Burke sketched out for *Attitudes toward History*, a similar extension of poetic categories—among them epic, tragedy, comedy, humor, elegy, satire, burlesque, and didactic—and he remarks in the book that Empson's "pastoral" would seem "to fall on the bias across our categories of humor and elegy, with important ingredients of the heroic." In the same section he makes the fascinating suggestion in a footnote that *Lycidas* is not about Edward King at all, but about Milton. He writes:

> "Lycidas" was written in 1637. Milton travelled in 1638 and 1639. And for the next twenty years thereafter, with the exception of an occasional sonnet, he devoted all his energies to his polemic prose.
>
> These dates, coupled with the contents of the poem, would justify us in contending that "Lycidas" was the symbolic dying of his poetic self. It was followed by a period of transition (the "random

casting" of travel). And then he focused upon the work of his "left hand." During this prose period, except for the occasional sonnet, he hid "that talent which is death to hide."

Ever since his schooldays, however, he had planned to write a poem vast in scope. The idea never left him. During the greatest intensity of his pamphleteering, he continued looking for a suitable theme (at one time deciding upon the fall of Adam). And in "Lycidas" he testifies that he is holding his dead self in abeyance, and that it will rise again. For after the funeral solemnities of his catalogue of flowers, he adds a coda:

> *"Weep no more, woeful shepherds, weep no more*
> *For Lycidas, your sorrow, is not dead,*
> *Sunk though he be beneath the watery floor;*
> *So sinks the day-star in the ocean bed,*
> *And yet anon repairs his drooping head,*
> *And tricks his beams, and with new-spangled ore*
> *Flames in the forehead of the morning sky:*
> *So Lycidas . . ."*

So the poet remained, for all his dying; and at the Restoration, after the political interregnum of Cromwell, he would be reborn. "Paradise Lost" is the fulfilment of his contract, though he returns to the poetic matrix as one of the "blind mouths" he tells about in "Lycidas."

Whether in response to this suggestion, anticipating it, or having himself suggested it to Burke, Professor Leonard Brown of Syracuse University spent some time in the thirties doing an unpublished study of *Lycidas* and three other great English pastoral elegies, Shelley's *Adonais*, Tennyson's *In Memoriam*, and Arnold's "Thyrsis." He made the remarkable discovery that in each case the elegy seemed to discuss the symbolic death of the poet in the guise of the friend, and in the promise of rebirth to announce the poet's own artistic rebirth on another level. Abstracting "elegy" as Empson had "pastoral," [4] Brown made it into a category the essence of which was the symbolic death and eventual rebirth of an artist's transition, so it could justly be applied to works in such disparate forms as Mann's *Magic Mountain* and Shakespeare's *Tempest*. It is regrettable that Professor Brown has never chosen to publish this work on the elegy, the only detailed reconstruction of categorical criticism I know to rival Empson's work with "pastoral." It might very well have heralded

---

[4] Brown's "elegy," as a death-and-rebirth rite, in fact, would seem to be closer to the origin and essence of the form from which they both derive, the Babylonian pastoral elegy (typified by the weeping for Tammuz), than would Empson's "pastoral," which, however complex, remains an attitude, and slights the redemptive ritual involved.

and provoked a number of similar Empsonian studies by critics, re-furbishing and making useful again in terms of "essence" and new significance such worn poetic categories as "epic," "ode," "epithala-mium."

4

One of the problems raised by the seeming novelty of Empson's criticism is its relation to other criticism and critics. The closest relation, of course, is to I. A. Richards, who was Empson's teacher at Magdalene College, Cambridge, and who inspired *Seven Types of Ambiguity*, if not all of Empson's work. "A brilliant pupil is presumptive evidence of the brilliant teacher," Ransom writes, "and Richards' fame would be secure if he had done nothing but inspire Empson." Empson has stated his indebtedness at least twice, once in *Seven Types of Ambiguity*, where the prefatory note reads in part: "Mr. I. A. Richards, then my supervisor for the first part of the English Tripos, told me to write this essay, and various things to put in it; my indebtedness to him is as great as such a thing ever should be"; and once in *Some Versions of Pastoral*, where he writes at the be-ginning of the "Marvell's Garden" chapter: "I was set to work on the poem by Dr. Richards' recent discussion of a philosophical argument in Mencius." In both books, he quotes extensively from Richard's work.

In a larger sense, all his writing has been specifically inspired by Rich-ards, in that it is the application of Richards's theories about the nature of meaning and poetic interpretation, and the key concepts of Empson's two books, "ambiguity" and "pastoral," are both implicit in *The Meaning of Meaning*. His basic approach is the continuity principle discussed above, derived through Richards, that poetic experience is human experience like any other and can be comparably studied. From Richards, Empson also derives the rationalism that makes him believe that anything is ultimately analyzable, and the naturalism that makes him prefer some-thing "sensible" to something "magical." In addition, he is indebted to Richards for the physiological emphasis that leads him to discuss prose and verse rhythms in terms of pulse rate in *Seven Types*; for the concern with the reception part of the communicative process that results in his concluding his discussion of *The Beggar's Opera* with a number of complex and ironic hypothetical audience reactions; for his concern with Basic English; for his interest in the Orient (which seems to have been inspired by Richards's Oriental studies, teaching in China, and book on Mencius); and even for the somewhat pedagogic tone, dogma in words of one syllable, into which he slips occasionally ("The idea that pushing in more facts *about the view* makes the lines more interesting is simply an error").

It is not, however, entirely a one-way process. Empson has had a substantial effect on Richards. Richard Eberhart, who studied under

Richards at Cambridge along with Empson, writes in an article on "Empson's Poetry" in *Accent*, Summer 1944:

> The pupil of I. A. Richards inflamed the imagination of his master: Richards understood instantly Empson's value. Although the chief indebtedness in the association of the two Magdalene men since 1927 has been that of Empson to Richards . . . the master exploited the fineness of mind of the pupil, wise to see in Empson's beginning criticism a nice adjunct to and a different end from his own.

Richards wrote a note on Empson inserted in the Spring 1940 issue of *Furioso*, as a program note for Empson's Yale lecture, in which he gives an account of the genesis of *Seven Types*. Discounting for Richards's modesty, it seems nevertheless to suggest far more independence in Empson's plan for the book than his own prefatory note suggests. Richards writes:

> William Empson made his name first with *Seven Types of Ambiguity*, a book which came into being more or less in the following fashion. He had been a mathematician at Cambridge and switched over for his last year to English. As he was at Magdalene, this made me his Director of Studies. He seemed to have read more English Literature than I had, and to have read it more recently and better, so our roles were soon in some danger of becoming reversed. At about his third visit he brought up the games of interpretation which Laura Riding and Robert Graves had been playing with the unpunctuated form of "The expense of spirit in a waste of shame." Taking the sonnet as a conjurer takes his hat, he produced an endless swarm of lively rabbits from it and ended by "You could do that with any poetry, couldn't you?" This was a Godsend to a Director of Studies, so I said, "You'd better go off and do it, hadn't you?" A week later he said he was still slapping away at it on his typewriter. Would I mind if he just went on with that? Not a bit. The following week there he was with a thick wad of very illegible typescript under his arm—the central 30,000 words or so of the book. I can't think of any literary criticism written since which seems likely to have as persistent and as distinctive an influence. If you read much of it at once, you will think you are sickening for "flu"; but read a little *with care* and your reading habits may be altered—for the better, I believe.

The rest of Richards's note discusses Empson's poetry, defining it as "pregnant conversation fitted miraculously into the most insistent formal patterns" and "metaphysical in the root sense." He admits that at one time it "lost itself in over-compressed conceits and turned into a guessing

game," but claims that now "it seems to be back again at railhead working on the track." To make a point about the awareness of the chthonic
in Empson's poetry, Richards gives us one more piece of invaluable
information, his remembrance of Empson's statement "that there are
things in Alice that would give Freud the creeps." It is a curious thing
that Richards seems actually to think more of Empson's poetry than of
his criticism, although this is not to suggest that the poetry does not
warrant a very high estimate. Eberhart reports that Richards, "who may
be excused the bias of a learned teacher upon a learned pupil," thinks
Empson is the best poet of all his contemporaries. Confirming this,
Richards nowhere in his books does more than mention Empson's criticism or quote briefly from it, to my knowledge, but several times goes
out of his way to praise the poetry in very high terms. In *Coleridge on
Imagination* he lists him in two places with Yeats, Auden, Eliot, Hopkins,
and Lawrence. In *How to Read a Page*, he quotes a quatrain from Empson's "Courage means running," from *The Gathering Storm*, with the
remark: "A modern poet—with far more to say than most and, as the
author of *Seven Types of Ambiguity*, with more knowledge of what and
how things may be said—puts every writer's problem with a rare and
lovely candor in these lines . . ." and then furnishes a two-page gloss.
Curiously, even Hugh R. Walpole, a disciple of Richards, refers to
Empson in his book *Semantics*, not as a critic, but in a list of modern
poets who are "fine and rich personalities" (although he uses a passage
from *Seven Types* as a reading exercise in his appendix).

Empson's other chief indebtedness for his method, as Richards suggests
in his anecdote of its genesis, is to Laura Riding and Robert Graves. The
prefatory note to *Seven Types* acknowledging Richards adds: "And I
derive the method I am using from Miss Laura Riding's and Mr. Robert
Graves' analysis of a Shakespeare Sonnet

The expense of spirit in a waste of shame,

in *A Survey of Modernist Poetry*." The reference is to an elaborate discussion of Sonnet 129, in connection with a poem of Cummings's. Miss
Riding and Graves make the point that Shakespeare's spelling and
punctuation in the quarto text are as conscious and meaningful as Cummings's, and that the editors who have modernized and repunctuated the
sonnet texts have reduced all their ambiguous or "interwoven" meanings
and possibilities to one. Their analysis of the poem is unquestionably a
beautiful job, worthy of starting Empson off, but the rest of the book,
even for 1927, does not come up to it. The authors aim at glorifying and
defending Eliot, Cummings, Miss Sitwell, and Miss Stein as triumphs of
"modernism," and they go to elaborate lengths to make their point,
including such Herculean labors as rewriting Cummings's poetry in
traditional forms and defining Miss Stein's linguistic method in philo-

sophic terms. Their taste is arbitrary and uncertain, however: they despise Stevens and Dr. Williams as spurious "modernists," and praise Marianne Moore but classify her work as "matter-of-fact prose demonstrations." They misread Eliot blatantly, getting the usual undergraduate paraphrase of *The Waste Land* as modern sordidity versus Elizabethan romance, and missing many of the references and the ironic twist that gives "Burbank with a Baedeker: Bleistein with a Cigar" its point (that the Venetians in their glamorous prime were a mercantile civilization very like the Jews). In general the authors make it clear that what they don't know, which is plenty, they don't care to know ("Here again we leave pedigrees to more reference-proud critics than ourselves," "Is this . . . or . . . ? We confess we do not care," etc.). Empson clearly skimmed off the best of them.

Cleanth Brooks has claimed, in his study of Empson's criticism, that we may "push the method back further still," to Yeats's "Empsonian" analysis of Burns's "The white moon is setting" and Coleridge's reading of a stanza from *Venus and Adonis*. This is somewhat exaggerating the importance of the Yeats's comment, which is rather an insistence upon unanalyzability than an analysis, Empsonian or other. Yeats writes in "The Symbolism of Poetry" (1900):

> There are no lines with more melancholy beauty than these by Burns—
>
> > *The white moon is setting behind the white wave,*
> > *And Time is setting with me, O!*
>
> and these lines are perfectly symbolical. Take from them the whiteness of the moon and of the wave, whose relation to the setting of Time is too subtle for the intellect, and you take from them their beauty. But, when all are together, moon and wave and whiteness and setting Time and the last melancholy cry, they evoke an emotion which cannot be evoked by any other arrangement of colours and sounds and forms.

The Coleridge analysis, however, *is* rather Empsonian and might very well be regarded as an ancestor of his method. Coleridge discusses the stanza:

> > *Full gently now she takes him by the hand,*
> > *A lily prison'd in a gaol of snow,*
> > *Or ivory in an alabaster band;*
> > *So white a friend engirts so white a foe—*

as an example of Fancy, as opposed to the couplet from the poem

> > *Look! how a bright star shooteth from the sky*
> > *So glides he in the night from Venus' eye,*

which he analyses as an example of Imagination. In both, Coleridge attempts to define a few of the many meanings and possibilities that make the two types of image memorable. (His readings are available in *Literary Remains*, and are amplified and discussed by Richards in *Coleridge on Imagination*.)

Empson's relation to several American critics is worth noting. The oddest is that with Kenneth Burke. In none of his writing with which I am familiar has Empson ever mentioned either Burke or any of his books. Nevertheless, either he has read Burke and absorbed his influence without mentioning him, or the coincidence of their minds is remarkable. The basic conception of *Some Versions of Pastoral* seems almost an exercise in the application of one of Burke's shrewdest insights, "perspective by incongruity"; Empson is constantly dabbling with the sort of pun ("foil-soil" in the chapter on "Double Plots" is the clearest example) that Burke has made characteristically his own; and in general Empson's criticism has a very Burkian cast that cannot be pinned down at any specific point.

Burke, on the other hand, refers frequently and approvingly to Empson. In *Attitudes toward History* he classes *Some Versions of Pastoral*, along with Richards's *Principles of Literary Criticism* and Miss Spurgeon's *Shakespeare's Imagery*, as "the most important contributions to literary criticism in contemporary England," and discusses its views and significance for several pages. In the Appendix to *The Philosophy of Literary Form* he prints his two appreciative reviews of *Some Versions*, the first of the English edition in *Poetry*, the second in the *New Republic* when the American edition appeared. Both praise the book highly, define its limitations as suggestive rather than schematic, better at marginalia than sustained exposition, and conclude with Burke's aligning himself with Empson's emphasis on basic literary likeness rather than difference. Finally, in *A Grammar of Motives*, Burke makes rather glancing use, in both cases credited, of Empson's "pastoral" and "ambiguity" concepts. In summary, the relationship might be formulated: either indebtedness of Empson to Burke or great coincidence with him; appreciative reception and some utilization by Burke.

Empson's principal effect has been on two other American critics, John Crowe Ransom and Cleanth Brooks. Ransom has written on him at more length than anyone else, giving him the last section, thirty pages, of the Richards chapter of *The New Criticism*. It is highly enthusiastic, Ransom writing in one place, of *Seven Types*: "I believe it is the most imaginative account of readings ever printed, and Empson the closest and most resourceful reader that poetry has yet publicly had;" and in another: "Writings as acute and at the same time as patient and consecutive as this have not existed in English criticism, I think, before Richards and Empson." Ransom's reservations are that Empson seems chiefly interested in the "cognitive content" rather than the emotions of poetry, that we fear his readings a little as overreadings, that he has too much imagination (which is better, Ransom says, than having too little), and that his criticism to date has been tangential; that is, that he has emphasized texture rather than structure. Nevertheless, Ransom concludes:

> It does not seem impossible that we should obtain close studies of the structure-texture relations that poets have actually found serviceable in the past. The best endowed critic in the world for this purpose might very well be, I should think, Mr. William Empson, the student of ambiguity. His studies up to date have been very valuable diversions, a little to the side of the great critical problems. But he probably has an unequalled genius for evaluating the intangible sort of thing we call poetic "situation." We have other valuable critics too, but their studies are not of anything so capital as this.

Ransom's reservations can be understood, and largely discounted, I believe, in terms of the fact that although his book was published in 1941, the Empson section refers only to *Seven Types of Ambiguity* and must have been written before the appearance of *Some Versions of Pastoral*, in which Empson very definitely turned (if my understanding of the terms is correct) to problems of what Ransom calls structure and structure-texture relations, as well as to somewhat more restrained readings.

At the same time, in his account of Empson, Ransom remarks that Empson "has not finished with the topic" of ambiguity, and that he provokes the reader to make his own classification of ambiguities. All through the piece Ransom is stimulated into doing precisely that, emerging with a "restrictive or predicative" variety, a "suspended or temporary" variety, and a "total theoretical ambiguity of metaphoric usage" —that is, Types 8, 9, and 10. (By way of ironic comment on this, Empson's only reference to Ransom, as far as I know, has been a rather slighting discussion, in his piece on Cleanth Brooks, of a poem of Ransom's about a little girl whose pet hen died.)

Empson's relation with Cleanth Brooks has been at least two-way. The Brooks-Warren textbook, *Understanding Poetry*, makes frequent reference to Empson. Brooks's first book of criticism, *Modern Poetry and the Tradition*, published in 1939, acknowledges in the Preface "borrowing" from Empson (as well as from Eliot, Tate, Yeats, Ransom, Blackmur, Richards, and others), and in the text quotes at length his "brilliant" work on the Elizabethan subplot and on *The Beggar's Opera*, and mentions his work on *Paradise Lost*. When the book appeared, Empson reviewed it in *Poetry*, December 1939, and although returning the compliment by calling Brooks's book "brilliant," spent most of his space announcing disagreements: unlike Brooks, he would not exclude propaganda from literature, he would not exclude science, and he would quarrel similarly with most of the book's general position as well as with many of its specific judgments. In 1944, when Brooks wrote his *Accent* study of Empson's criticism, which although mildly critical of Empson's scholarly slips, rationalism, and "subjectivity" (the last of which is discussed below) was generally very enthusiastic, he ended on the tribute:

> In a time in which the study of literature threatens to turn into sociology and in which the death of the humanities is prophesied openly, it is impossible to overestimate the significance of the kind of criticism of which Empson remains the most brilliant exponent. He is certainly not the old-fashioned man of letters who charmingly bows us into his snug study with a quotation from Lamb and afterwards bows us out with a quotation from Hazlitt. But he is certainly not, on the other hand, merely the bright young man with a bag full of psychological gadgets. He is one of our ablest critics and one of our soundest, and his work is fraught with revolutionary consequences for the teaching of all literature and for the future of literary history.

Since the latter thirties Brooks has used Empson's concepts in reviews (in one case he discussed Robert Frost's *Collected Poems* as an example of "pastoral"). In his most recent book, *The Well Wrought Urn*, he draws on Empson throughout, centering his new tradition of the paradox on "ambiguity," while at the same time quarreling at length with Empson's social reading of the gems and flowers blushing unseen in Gray's *Elegy*, as forcing a political reading out of context (an objection he had hinted at as early as 1938, in *Understanding Poetry*, where Empson's reading of the stanza is printed, followed by the loaded student assignment: "Criticize Empson's analysis in relation to the entire poem"). Empson then reviewed *this* book in the *Sewanee Review*, Autumn 1947, announcing his disagreements, defending himself on Gray's *Elegy*, and opposing his own reading of Keats's "Ode on a Grecian Urn" to Brooks's; Brooks replied in the same issue; and where the controversy will finally end no one knows.

Empson's influence on Blackmur and Maud Bodkin's reference to him have been noted above, and his relation to the *Scrutiny* group will be discussed below. For the rest, Empson has been widely influential but has received little critical discussion. Herbert Read has praised his "brilliant analysis" of ambiguity. Allen Tate has referred to him briefly, as has Robert Penn Warren. Arthur Mizener has drawn on Empson's insights for at least a decade without ever understanding them very well —or so his review of *English Pastoral Poetry* in *Partisan Review*, December 1937, would argue, which praised Empson in the highest terms and announced that "nearly everything from *The Magic Mountain* to *To*

Have and Have Not is pastoral in Mr. Empson's sense." Randall Jarrell
has done a brilliant Empsonian analysis, "Texts from Housman" in the
Kenyon Review, Summer 1939, but has never discussed Empson's work,
so far as I know. Robert Lowell has praised Empson as one of the five
best living English poets (the others are Thomas, Auden, MacNeice,
and Graves), and Thomas himself has addressed an ironic tribute to him
as a poet, his half-villanelle "Request to Leda," subtitled "Homage to
Wm Empson." William York Tindall, in *Forces in Modern British Literature*, praises Empson's poetry, but has little to say of his criticism, other
than that it amounts to the old *explication de textes* method and that it is
as unattractively written as Richards's.

Herbert Muller in *Science and Criticism* lists him in a group of modern
critics unmatched "for subtle, acute analysis" and makes one or two other
references to him, but does not discuss his criticism. As has been noted
above, the Shakespeare scholars and critics have engaged in almost a
conspiracy of silence to play down his work, as have, to a lesser extent,
the writers on metaphysical poetry, an area in which Empson has done
some of his most brilliant investigation. The two sharpest attacks on his
work with which I am familiar come, characteristically enough, in Henri
Peyre's *Writers and Their Critics*, where he is described in one place,
along with Richards, as bringing forth "infinitesimal mice," and in
another as "temporarily seducing" adolescents; and in *On Native
Grounds*, by Peyre's favorite critic, Alfred Kazin, where he is discussed
abusively, along with Blackmur and Burke, as a "field scientist of
metaphor," writing "self-fascinated puzzles." (It is remarkable how
accurately Peyre and Kazin, whose perceptions are ordinarily so stum-
bling, have singled out the best contemporary critics for special attack.)

Geoffrey Grigson's description of Empson as "a typically inert theorizer and poetical *pasticheur*," writing "quarter-man stuff so unreadably
trivial that it is not worth insulting or attacking," in his controversy with
Empson in *Poetry*, may be put down simply to the bad-tempered necessity
of polemic and does not necessarily represent a measured opinion of his
criticism. Finally, Philip Wheelwright's proposal of the semantic term
"plurisignation" as a clearer term for Empson's "ambiguity" in his
article "On the Semantics of Poetry" in the *Kenyon Review*, Summer
1940, and Margaret Schlauch's use of an Empson ambiguity as a class
exercise in the appendix to *The Gift of Tongues*, may represent the
beginning of a scholarly rapprochement with Empson that could eventually even spread to the Shakespeare variora.

5

One general problem remains to be touched on in connection with Empson's criticism: the problem of the nature and implications of close read-

ing. Traditionally, close reading has been the prerogative of the writer studying craft or of the teacher teaching it. In the first case, the really detailed study was rare, and might be the result of a writer's investigating his own craft, like James in the Prefaces (and, in recent times, Hart Crane and Tate on their own poetry), or of a friend's, as in Balzac's remarkable "Study of M. Beyle" (in which he gets around to technical criticism and suggested improvements on *The Charterhouse of Parma* only after a fifty-five-page blow-by-blow summary of the plot), or simply of an extremely analytic mind, the sort of thing we see in Coleridge's Shakespeare studies. In the case of the teacher's close reading, we have had everything from the great classics of scholarship to Joseph Warren Beach, in *The Outlook for American Prose* particularly, reading contemporary literature with the grammarian's little eye, and rewriting, in a "corrected" form, passages from authors like John Dewey as though they were freshman themes. (Beach might better have spent the time going through his own books rewriting for style, taking out phrases like "equine excrementa" and "in a family way," and changing "Lester Jeeter" to "Jeeter Lester" throughout.)

One of the features of modern criticism, however, is precisely this close technical reading, not as an aspect of learning or teaching craft, but as a general method of critical analysis. Richards introduced it into modern criticism, as he did so many other things, but because of preoccupation with other matters has himself produced only a few examples of really detailed reading. The same thing, with different preoccupations, is true of Kenneth Burke, and it has remained for Empson and Blackmur to base a bulk of detailed close reading on their principles. The Southern group centering on Ransom has written innumerable manifestoes insisting not only that the close technical reading of texts is an important function of criticism, but that it is the *only* legitimate function of criticism. However, Ransom and Tate have done relatively little of it themselves, being, like Richards and Burke, preoccupied with general critical problems, some of them remote from literature; and Cleanth Brooks and Robert Penn Warren have only begun to produce a body of detailed studies from the group's principles, and some of that not really very detailed. This may explain the admiration of the Southern group for Empson and Blackmur; without writing any manifestoes, they sat down and did the work.

A school of critics successfully specializing in the close reading of texts is the Cambridge group around *Scrutiny* in England, little known in America, to which Empson has been somewhat related (the "Marvell's Garden" chapter of *Some Versions* first appeared in *Scrutiny*). In F. R. Leavis's *New Bearings in English Poetry*, *Revaluation*, and *For Continuity*, in Q. D. Leavis's *Fiction and the Reading Public*, in L. C. Knights's *Drama and Society in the Age of Jonson* and *Explorations*, in the anthology *Determinations*, and in *Scrutiny* itself (as well as in its predecessor *The*

Calendar of Modern Letters, which ran from 1925 to 1927 and from which Leavis culled the anthology *Toward Standards of Criticism*), some of the sharpest close reading of our time is combined with a social emphasis of real value. F. R. Leavis, one of the editors of *Scrutiny* and more or less the leader of the group, has turned out a good deal of very usable criticism, at its best when technical and exegetical, particularly of the moderns in *New Bearings;* somewhat vitiated at other times by the characteristic flaws of sociological criticism: the tendency to beat writers with terms like "escape" and "evasion," a kind of Brooksian truncation of socially unsatisfactory writers like Yeats and Henry James, an eighteenth-century rationalism that uses "ritual" exclusively as a term of abuse, and an excessively pedagogic, proselytizing-for-poetry style. In *Revaluation*, which appeared serially in *Scrutiny* as a series of re-estimates, F. R. Leavis set out to revise the history of English poetry to emphasize metaphysical "wit" (what Burke would call "perspective by incongruity") as the tradition, an attempt in which Eliot had informally preceded him (although he opposed Eliot's Dryden-up, Pope-down, with Pope-up, Dryden-down) and in which Cleanth Brooks was to follow him (and solve the problem by tossing both Pope and Dryden out of the tradition).

Q. D. Leavis, the magazine's specialist in fiction, in her *Fiction and the Reading Public*, has written an invaluable socio-literary study of the decline of popular taste in England since 1600, using a method she aptly describes as "anthropological." Both Leavises, although somewhat indebted to Marxism for their social approach, have attacked the Marxists sharply over the past decade. L. C. Knights, another *Scrutiny* editor and perhaps the most brilliant textual analyst of the group, has on the other hand attempted an explicit application of Marxist concepts to literature in *Drama and Society in the Age of Jonson*. In conception the book is a brilliant idea, and sounds like the sort of thing Caudwell would perhaps have lived to do: research into "the relation between economic activities and general culture" by exploring the economic and social conditions of Elizabethan and Jacobean England in detail, and then studying the drama against their patterns. In practice the book fails for a number of reasons. First, Knights does not actually apply Marxist theories (although his book quotes everyone from Marx and Engels to T. A. Jackson and Ralph Fox) so much as Tawney's simpler economic determinism. Second, his book is completely invertebrate, breaking sharply in the middle into two books: one a good socio-economic summary, the other a body of excellent analytic literary criticism, with no relation between the two. Third, and probably the basic factor underlying the other faults, although Knights quotes with approval Marx's doctrine that "the social being [of men] determines their consciousness," he fails to understand what Marx meant, missing the subtlety of the process. His conception is ludicrously oversimple: the social being of men determines their opinions and attitudes. Thus he deals not with the deeper reflections of society in the dramatic structure and conflicts of the plays, but with what the characters *say* about society, about money, about acquisition; with the social character of their *comments*, not of their *natures*. What Knights ends with is an anthology of speeches that "embody the thought and opinion of the time," "reflect some important aspects of the social scene," or furnish "illustration of the life of the period."

Knights's second book, *Explorations*, a collection of essays "mainly on the literature of the seventeenth century," is a much sounder job of socio-literary integration. In it he does invaluable work in insisting on the essentially Gestalt conception of the reader's total complex emotional response as the starting-place of criticism rather than any of the traditional critical abstractions like "character" and "plot." He emphasizes the importance of the work itself as the unit to be investigated, the necessity of beginning all discussion from technique, and the futility of exploring the relationship of the artist to his society (which he still regards as an essential subject for criticism) from any approach but through his artistic style and sensibility. Despite the excellence of these critical principles, the book is sometimes disappointing: Knights inherits F. R. Leavis's "escape" concept (Hamlet, he tell us, is regressive and an escapist, and Hamlet's appeal to us is because we are regressive too), as well as Leavis's inability fully to appreciate writers like Yeats and James, and he adds some failings of his own, particularly a refusal to push any specific line of investigation very far lest it distort the totality of the work. Nevertheless, at his best, when genuine social analysis results from the detailed textual study of a specific poetic sensibility, as in his essay on George Herbert, Knights produces criticism little inferior to the finest we have.

The *Scrutiny* group derives ultimately from Richards as well as Eliot and along the way is greatly indebted to Empson. F. R. Leavis has pursued ambiguities doggedly, acknowledging Empson and suggesting that his work "should be looked up," and at the conclusion to *New Bearings in English Poetry* finds Empson's "remarkable" poems and those of Ronald Bottrall the only "new bearings" worth discussion since Eliot and Pound. Knights has also used Empson, particularly his work on Herbert, has chased ambiguities (he prefers to avoid the word and calls them "sliding constructions" or "keeping two things in mind simultaneously"), and in general has benefited a good deal from the example of Empson's type of reading. At the same time he has criticized the method strongly from his Gestalt position, claiming that Empson obtains his extensive meanings by focusing upon a part of the poem and considering its possibilities in isolation, forgetting the poem as a totality in which most of these possibilities are necessarily canceled out. This is a serious and partially valid charge, but in the last analysis it seems to be the use of the "organismal" concept to restrict meanings rather than to show the organization and interrelationship of the greatest possible depth and complexity of meaning. (Leavis has made substantially the same charge against both Empson and Richards in *Education & the University*.)

At the same time a contemporary critical school has arisen that makes its principal tenet the stubborn refusal to read. The manifesto for this group was Max Eastman's *The Literary Mind* in 1931, which attacked all literature as "loose talk" ("the vague, uncertain and contradictory deliverances of humane letters") and boasted proudly of Eastman's failure as a reader (Joyce spent months working the names of five hundred rivers into the "Anna Livia Plurabelle" section of *Finnegans Wake*, Eastman chortled, and Max Eastman was only able to find three and a half!). In general the book made it clear that Eastman's only problem was a dislike of poetry and an inability or refusal to read it intelligently, elevated into a critical method. Other works along the same line have been: in England, John Sparrow's *Sense and Poetry* and F. L. Lucas's *The Decline and Fall of the Romantic Ideal*, both of them elaborate ways of saying that any poetry Sparrow or Lucas does not understand cannot really mean anything; and in America, Mark Van Doren's *Private Reader*, a manifesto for reading as superficially as possible, thus representing "the private reader," and J. Donald Adams's *The Shape of Books to Come*, a triumph of critical incapacity so complete that it makes Max Eastman seem literate by comparison. But the group hardly warrants even this much discussion.

One of the essential factors underlying Empson's criticism is his poetry, published in *Poems*, 1935, and *The Gathering Storm*, 1940. It is serious and important poetry, even if one does not value it as highly as Richards does, and it is very like his criticism: ironic and frequently broadly humorous, obsessed with form, and metaphysical in every sense of the word, from Richards's "root" sense to the popular connotation of "quirky." It relates to the criticism not only in its categorical use of form, as in the villanelles discussed above, in its structural emphasis on the individual line, and in its insistent puns and ambiguities; but particularly in the prose notes with which Empson rounds it out, explaining in a "Note on Notes" in *The Gathering Storm*: "many people (like myself) prefer to read poetry mixed with prose; it gives you more to go by; the conventions of poetry have been getting far off from normal life, so that to have a prose bridge makes reading poetry seem more natural." The notes are extensive Empsonian criticism, partially glosses on the poems, partially extensions of them, partially equivalents to them. He speaks modestly of his "incompetence in writing" and explains that the poems have "a sort of puzzle interest," with the notes "like answers to a crossword puzzle," but actually Empson is overrating his own obscurity. Particularly in the second volume, which includes a number of fairly political poems on Chinese subjects, translations that appear to be from the Japanese, a cruel parody of Auden, and poems with titles like "Reflection from Anita Loos," his work is not nearly so difficult as a good deal of much inferior modern verse.

An odd charge against Empson, which must be faced in attempting to summarize his value, is the charge sometimes made that his criticism is impressionist, that he reacts to a poem by writing a new poem having only a stimulus-response relation to the original. The humorous aspect of the charge is that Empson, in *Some Versions of Pastoral*, quotes a reviewer of his earlier book as charging him with objectivism, with "treating poems as phenomena not as things judged by a mind," while Cleanth Brooks, in his study of Empson, charges him with subjectivism, with insisting on the fact "that the system of classification of ambiguities is psychological: the categories shift as we change readers or as the reader becomes a better reader; they do not describe fixed properties of the poem (that is, of the poem 'properly' read by an ideal reader)." Obviously, the anonymous reviewer's charge is true, in that Empson certainly does treat poems as phenomena having an existence independent of the judging mind (that is, he is a philosophic materialist). Brooks's charge is equally true: Empson's criteria *are* relativistic and subjectivistic, in that he deals with the poem as a man writing and a man reading, the action of real people in a real world, rather than the bloodless and indefinable Platonic abstractions of Brooks's "fixed properties," "proper reading," and "ideal reader." In other words, Empson is an objectivist or phenomenalist in philosophy, a subjectivist or relativist in criticism, taking man as the measure in both cases. This makes Empson an impressionist only in the sense that his materialism will admit no Leninist absolute objective truth, that a poem for him is what *he* gets; not at all, in the sense of formal impressionist criticism as practiced by Anatole France or Jules Lemaître, that he wants to get away from the poem into his own poetic personality.

This brings us directly to the basic question about Empson's method: what limiting factor prevents it from proliferating endlessly, so that eventually the totality of man's culture becomes a gloss on any given line or word? Empson sometimes does have a tendency to push too hard, to find ambiguities everywhere, to broaden the definition of "pastoral" until any work is "pastoral," to pile on meanings until one breaks the poem's back. Where and on what basis to draw the boundary? Brooks suggests, brilliantly, that it is the criterion Coleridge calls "good sense," expounded and defended by Richards in his chapter of that name in *Coleridge on Imagination*. Richards writes:

Good Sense has sometimes a rather sinister sound as a critical watchword. It is a banner under which every kind of stupidity and every kind of prejudice willingly fight. Even Coleridge, who is so often an exemplar of Good Sense in criticism, is not incapable, in his lesser hours, of using its colours to advance and excuse objections based on careless, inattentive, unresponsive, and unresourceful reading.

And yet, Richards continues, it is the only criterion for the application of theory we have: "There is no measuring-rod virtue in any theory. We must use them as we use a microscope—not as we use a centrifuge or a sieve. They cannot choose for us, but we cannot choose without them; and our life is choice."

In the last analysis, any critical method or concept, including Empson's "ambiguity" and "pastoral," is an extension of the man, a *tool*, and the man must use and guide it. By this test the man behind Empson's theories, Empson himself, is as sound as any critic we have, and, barring a few aberrations, his use of them is at once brilliantly and almost limitlessly fertile, and yet limited by deep concern for the poem itself and essential "good sense." It is hard to say what he will do next. One can hope it will not be permanent and full-time application to Basic English, which seems to be a limiting factor of another and, in his case, less valuable sort: the organization of an economy of critical scarcity rather than one of abundance. As Brooks suggests, *Some Versions of Pastoral* "implies at least a dozen further books." We have no right to demand that they be as much better than his second book as that was than his first, or as the first was than the great body of what passes for criticism among us. And yet, with no right to demand it, the evidence gives us every reason to expect it. It is the final ambiguity of Empson that his work becomes progressively less ambiguous for us, and the triumph of his categorical method that he himself successfully evades each category we set for him.

CHAPTER 11

I. A. RICHARDS

and the Criticism of Interpretation

It is only with the greatest trepidation that one tackles Ivor Armstrong Richards at all. His learning in almost every area of knowledge is so tremendous, his significance so great in half a dozen fields besides criticism, and the brilliance and subtlety of at least his earlier books so overpowering, that any hit-and-run treatment of him in a few thousand words is bound to be laughably superficial. *The Meaning of Meaning* alone, with its problems of "phonetic," "hypostatic," and "ultraquistic" subterfuges, and its "irritants," "degenerates," "mendicants," and "nomads," should serve to discourage the offhand commentator. Nevertheless, no treatment of modern criticism is possible without discussing Richards, since in the most literal sense Richards created it. What we have been calling modern criticism began in 1924, with the publication of *Principles of Literary Criticism*. In it Richards writes of æsthetic experiences:

> I shall be at pains to show that they are closely similar to many other experiences, that they differ chiefly in the connections between their constituents, and that they are only a further development, a finer organisation of ordinary experiences, and not in the least a new and different kind of thing. When we look at a picture, or read a poem, or listen to music, we are not doing something quite unlike what we were doing on our way to the Gallery or when we dressed in the morning. The fashion in which the experience is caused in us is different, and as a rule the experience is more complex and, if we are successful, more unified. But our activity is not of a fundamentally different kind.

More specifically of poetry he writes:

> The world of poetry has in no sense any different reality from the rest of the world and it has no special laws and no otherworldly peculiarities. It is made up of experiences of exactly the same kinds as those that come to us in other ways. Every poem however is a strictly limited piece of experience, a piece which breaks up more or less easily if alien elements intrude. It is more highly and more

delicately organised than ordinary experiences of the street or of the hillside; it is fragile. Further it is communicable.

With those two key words, "experiences" and "communicable," Richards made over literary criticism. In terms of them Richards wrote his celebrated definition of a poem in the book, the only one I know that fails to collapse on application:

> This, although it may seem odd and complicated, is by far the most convenient, in fact it is the only workable way of defining a poem; namely, as a class of experiences which do not differ in any character more than a certain amount, varying for each character, from a standard experience. We may take as this standard experience the relevant experience of the poet when contemplating the completed composition.

All of Richards's work has been devoted to exploring the communication of these experiences to the reader; specifically, to what the reader gets: that is, the poem-audience relationship rather than the poet-poem relationship. At one time he called this area "sign interpretation," later "rhetoric"; recently he seems to have returned to calling it "interpretation." With a remarkable consistency each of his books has filled in some area in the study of interpretation, and the thread running through all his writing is the dual aim of understanding how communication works and making it work better.

Richards's first book, *The Foundations of Æsthetics*, written in collaboration with C. K. Ogden, a psychologist, and James Wood, an authority on art, was published in 1922. In fewer than a hundred pages the authors survey the whole body of æsthetics in pursuit of the nature of "beauty" and, after considering all the principal definitions offered, emerge with their own: that beauty is that which is conducive to synæsthetic equilibrium. In finding beauty an experience or state in the audience rather than a mysterious "thing" in the work of art itself, Richards introduced what was to be the central concern of all his work, and in pursuing it through comparison of multiple definitions and analyses of terms, Richards introduced what was to be his principal method.

The next year Richards and Ogden published their monumental work, *The Meaning of Meaning*. As *The Foundations of Æsthetics* had pursued "beauty" through multiple definitions, *The Meaning of Meaning* pursued "meaning" itself. Ogden and Richards were after no less than a theory of the nature of signs and their interpretation, a science of linguistic communication that could then be turned on art. Their chief tool was eclectic psychology, drawing on almost every modern school; their chief technique was multiple definitions; and they emerged with what they called the science of symbolism, which later in other hands came to be called modern semantics. The authors developed a terminology for discussing signs and sign-interpretation in terms of "symbols" and "referents," discussed the relation of mental processes to interpretation and outlined canons of reasoning, explored the nature of "definition" and "meaning," tested the procedure on æsthetic conceptions of beauty (repeating some of their earlier work) and on examples of philosophic thought, and finally turned the whole framework on poetry. This required a distinction between the "symbolic" meaning of science (what used to be called "prose") and the "emotive" or "evocative" meaning of poetry (more or less an extension of Mill's "denotation" and "connotation").

As Ogden and Richards saw *The Meaning of Meaning*, it was the essential keystone for thought in any area, and all their books were deliberately conceived as supplements and extensions of it. In prefaces to later editions of the book they explained the relationship their other books bore to it. Richards's *Principles of Literary Criticism* (1924), "endeavors to provide for the emotive function of language the same critical foundation as is here attempted for the symbolic." *Science and Poetry* (1926), "discusses the place and future of literature in our civilization" (that is, fills out the relationship between symbolic and emotive functions). *Practical Criticism* (1929), is "an educational application of Chapter X," the chapter on symbol situations, including failures and confusions of interpretation. *Mencius on the Mind* (1932) "examines the difficulties which beset the translator and explores the technique of multiple definition," which *Basic Rules of Reason* (1933) "further elucidates." *Coleridge on Imagination* (1935) "offers a new estimate of Coleridge's theory in the light of a more adequate evaluation of emotive language." The reader can similarly fill out the places of Richards's later books: *The Philosophy of Rhetoric* (1936) explores "misunderstanding and its remedies," as does *Basic in Teaching: East and West* (1935) and, in another area, *Nations and Peace* (1947). *Interpretation in Teaching* (1938), like *Practical Criticism*, is "an educational application of Chapter X," this time applied to prose; *How to Read a Page* and Richards's edition of Plato's *Republic* (both 1942) explore multiple definition in Basic on a text from Plato, and so on.

Ogden's books classify in the same fashion. *The Meaning of Psychology* (1926), abbreviated as *The A B C of Psychology* (1929), furnishes "a general introduction to the psychological problems of language study." *Basic English* (1930) is "the investigation of the general principles of notation with its bearing on the problem of a universal scientific language, and the analytical task of discovering a grammar by means of which translation from one symbol-system to another could be controlled." Ogden's edition of *Bentham's Theory of Fictions* (1932) "has focussed attention on a neglected contribution to the subject" (of signs and sign-interpretation) as has *Jeremy Bentham* (also 1932). *Opposition* (1932) "is an analysis of an aspect of definition which is of particular importance for linguistic simplification." In the same fashion, I imagine, Ogden's earlier books, including *The Problem of the Continuation School* (1914) with R. H. Best, *Fecundity versus Civilisation* (1916) with Adelyne More, and *Colour Harmony* (1926) with James Wood, could be identified as preliminary explorations of the problem by anyone familiar with them.

At the same time Richards's books did a great deal more in connection with specifically literary investigation than illustrate aspects of a theory of sign-interpretation. His first independent work, *Principles of Literary Criticism*, as has been noted above, founded modern literary criticism and is still, after more than two decades, an important and continually influential critical text. In his account of the book in *Books That Changed Our Minds* David Daiches describes it as pioneering the application of psychology to form, and Kenneth Burke has accorded it the highest praise for the same reason. It is generally considered Richards's most important and most basic work, in theoretical and philosophic terms (although in the methodological terms of our present inquiry it must be slighted in favor of *Practical Criticism*). Besides defining poetry experientially and insisting on its basic discussability, Richards attempted in the book to develop criticism as an "applied science," with the dual function of analyzing both the interpretative and the evaluative experiences. At the same time he took on the task, beyond science, of establishing evaluative standards, announcing: "To set up as a critic is to set up as a judge of values," and defining the qualifications of a "good" critic as three:

"He must be an adept at experiencing, without eccentricities, the state of mind relevant to the work of art he is judging. Secondly, he must be able to distinguish experiences from one another as regards their less superficial features. Thirdly, he must be a sound judge of values."

These criteria all point toward a scientific objectivity, but with equal force they point toward purely personal qualifications, the mysterious subjective matter we call "taste." Illustrating his own qualifications here as well as his objective method, Richards attaches as an appendix to the book a brief reading of several of Eliot's poems. If superficial, it is nevertheless extremely keen, sensitive, and informed (he catches more references in the Burbank-Bleistein poem, for example, than critics were noticing two decades later). Nevertheless, *Principles of Literary Criticism* has a number of flaws. One of the most valuable things in the book is its insistence that "stimuli are only received if they serve some need of the organism" (that is, in terms of literary application, that a writer uses references and quotes only where they express him), but Richards proceeds to violate his own principle foolishly, with the dictum that psychoanalytic criticism cannot get at the significance of "Kubla Khan," since its "actual causation" is *Paradise Lost* and other of Coleridge's reading—a fine and quite uncharacteristic example of begging the question. At the same time Richards misreads another of Coleridge's poems, "The Ancient Mariner," finding its "moral" an "intrusion" rather than the heart of the poem's expiatory ritual. Finally, the book's fantastic neurological chart on page 116, picturing the way in which the imagery of a line of poetry is experienced by the mind, creates comic effects wholly at variance with Richards's aims and unfair to his general seriousness and might better have been dispensed with.

Richards's next book, *Science and Poetry*, a collection of seven brief essays, continues the discussion of all these problems. In it Richards develops the concept of "pseudo-questions" and "pseudo-statements" for the emotive utterances of poetry, and introduces the rather childish concept, later exploited tirelessly by Marxist criticism, of "modes of escape" open to the poet, ways of "dodging difficulties." At the same time Richards continues his specific discussions of poetry, devoting the last chapter to criticizing Hardy, De la Mare, Yeats, and Lawrence. These as usual are sensitive and perceptive accounts, despite a vast underrating of Yeats, for which Richards apologized in a footnote in the second edition in 1935 (he also canceled out the earlier statement that Eliot had "effected a complete severance between his poetry and all beliefs," and added an appendix explaining what he meant by "belief").

Practical Criticism, Richards's next book, was planned as a companion volume to the *Principles*, a display of the failures of poetic interpretation that the *Principles* aimed at correcting. It will be discussed at some length below.

The next two critical books, *Mencius on the Mind* and *Coleridge on Imagination*, are extended developments of specific problems. *Mencius*, subtitled *Experiments in Multiple Definition*, explores Mencius' psychological ideas, Chinese modes of meaning, and the Chinese language and the problem of translating from it into English, as a series of related problems in plural interpretation. Richards begins on the first page with twelve alternative readings for two lines from Mencius, goes on to explore the nature of plural readings and the culturally produced characteristics of Chinese language in general, tests his theories on a passage by Herbert Read, and concludes with a formula for multiple definition, illustrated by classified tables of multiple readings of "beauty," "knowledge," "truth," and "order."

In *Coleridge on Imagination* Richards attempts what is essentially another exploration in multiple definition, this time into the meaning of "imagination," taking off from Coleridge's concept. He defines his aim as sifting Coleridge's speculations down to hypotheses still useful, his hope as "their development into a co-operative technique of inquiry that may become entitled to be named a science," and his general method as analysis and experiment rather than evaluation (which had now become for him either "suasion" or a ritual of "communion"). The distinguishing characteristic of twentieth-century criticism, as Richards sees it in the book, is inability to read, and a return to Coleridge on this point at least would be welcome. At the same time he continues to explore the sources of misreadings in stock responses, in taking emotive for symbolic utterances, and so on, but with implicitly pejorative terms like "pseudo-statements" now discarded.

The *Coleridge* is the last of Richards's pentad of major critical books. *The Philosophy of Rhetoric*, published in 1936, is greatly disappointing: a series of Bryn Mawr lectures in the style of a popularization. Richards now calls his field "rhetoric," "the study of misunderstanding and its remedies," or "how words work"; proposes a theory of verbal relativity that if pushed far enough would make all criticism impossible; and repudiates all his earlier neurological psychology. The chief, if not the only contribution in the book is the discussion of metaphor, an extensive analysis developing two new terms, "tenor" and "vehicle." For the most part, though, the book was the first public sign (coming after two books in the Psyche Miniatures series devoted to Basic) that Richards's interest had formally shifted from communication on the highest possible level, the criticism of poetry, to communication on a safely low mass level, Basic English.

Interpretation in Teaching, two years later, was evidence that Basic had not succeeded in robbing Richards of all his critical concerns, but, arising out of his Cambridge course in Practical Criticism and conceived as a supplement to the earlier book, it was clearly a last flurry. In the sense of Richards's preface, the book is a fuller development of *The Philosophy of Rhetoric*, in that it attempts to revive and refurbish the ancient trivium of Rhetoric, Grammar, and Logic, and much of it is written in the new non-rationalist tone: "We must accept our fundamental facts as unexplained"; the trivium is to be considered "*as arts* not as sciences"; reading is full of "unformulatable imponderables." Essentially, however, the book is in the earlier tradition, with a constant emphasis on "experiment." Richards obtained his data for the book by using the same experimental "protocol" method with a class that he used for *Practical Criticism*, although this time working with expository prose. He notes corrections and improvements in the method that were suggested empirically and discusses some of the larger implications, possibilities, and dangers of the method he had not had the data for discussing in the earlier book. At the same time Richards recognizes for the first time that to deal fully with weaknesses of interpretation he must go off into what he calls "characterology," and does so for a chapter, adding the dimension of socially produced real human differences to his previous accidental or eccentric hypothetical readers.

The book's single great weakness is a new faith, of almost panacea proportions, in education as a way of solving larger difficulties, and his suggestions tend to be as out of proportion as the Adler proposal (for clearing up the world's problems by the establishment of "a chair of curative pedagogy") so mercilessly mocked by Christopher Caudwell. After a discussion of the general inability to read and interpret in our society, Richards writes: "The obvious recommendation . . . is that the professional journals should reserve sections—perhaps under special editorship—for such communications from teachers, and encourage, in correspondence columns, a critical discussion of them."

Meanwhile, his preoccupation with Basic had been increasing all through the thirties. In 1920 Ogden and Richards had hit upon the idea of Basic English as a result of their researches for *The Meaning of Meaning*, when they discovered that certain key words tended to appear again and again in their definitions, and realized that a small number of basic words would permit the expression of any thought. Developing this idea, Ogden worked for ten years, and in 1929 published the first Basic word-list in *Psyche*, followed by other works outlining the language and its techniques. In 1933 Richards wrote *Basic Rules of Reason*, in Basic, to illustrate the ability of the language to clarify a complex matter, in this case logic. In 1935 he published a much more ambitious little book, *Basic in Teaching: East and West*, which announces the modern cultural crisis, the general failure in communication, including Richards's experience of it in a particularly extreme form in China, and devotes the rest of the book to arguing for the use of Basic English as the remedy and defending the language against attackers. Of the book the most charitable thing that can be said is that the problem Richards poses, something very like a breakdown of our civilization, is not of the same order as the one he solves, which is better reading in the schools. Since 1938 all his books have been principally devoted to Basic, and since 1939 he has worked in America, where the need is perhaps greatest. In 1942 he published an abridged edition of *The Republic of Plato*, largely in Basic, and as "footnotes" to it, *How to Read a Page*. The latter, ostensibly a critical work, is actually another plug for Basic as the solution to the educational problem, and it opposes its "hundred great words" to the Hundred Great Books program of Mortimer Adler and Scott Buchanan. Stylistically, it is as popularly written as *The Philosophy of Rhetoric*, but it manages nevertheless to be maddeningly obscure, because of Richards's use of seven varieties of specialized small-letter quotation marks on words. In this book, as in *Basic Rules of Reason* and *Basic in Teaching*, problems of multiple definition or translation are into Basic, proposed as a general cure-all; and at the end, when the book has turned into rather simplified Platonic philosophy, Richards concludes with a final plea for education, Basic, and reason. In 1943 Richards published a much less ambitious and more straightforward job of proselytizing, *Basic English and Its Uses,* and since then he has continued the campaign in *The Pocket Book of Basic English,* consisting almost entirely of visual education symbols, and an introduction to the *Pocket Roget's Thesaurus.* In 1947 Richards reached a kind of apogee with the publication of *Nations and Peace.* Again written almost entirely in Basic (Richards used 365 of the words on the Basic list and about 25 others) and illustrated with simple pictures, it is no less than a proposal to eliminate war by world government and Basic English working in conjunction.

Richards has written few periodical pieces, but they have consistently moved along the same path as his books. His article on Hopkins's "Windhover" in the *Dial,* as early as September 1926, which F. R. Leavis called "the first intelligent critique of Hopkins," is an extension of the discussion of specific poetic texts in *Science and Poetry.* Identifying Hopkins as "the most obscure of English verse writers," it analyzes the poem at some length, with references to other of Hopkins's more difficult lyrics, as an illustration of the technique of interpretation applied to particularly obscure or knotted poetry. "Passage to Forster," in the *Forum,* December 1927, is a comparable discussion, this time on prose texts, with Richards turning his analysis on the complicated relation between Forster's views, themes, audience-appeal, and fictional techniques. "Fifteen Lines of Landor," in the *Criterion,* April 1933, reports another experiment in practical criticism, but points the problem more specifically toward educational inadequacies, thus serving as a bridge between *Practical Criticism* and *Interpretation in Teaching.*

"The Interaction of Words," a Mesures Lecture read at Princeton in 1941 and published in *The Language of Poetry,* edited by Allen Tate, in 1942, is the last specifically poetic criticism of Richards's with which I am familiar. It is chiefly an elaborate comparative reading of an elegy by Dryden and one by Donne, to the detriment of the former, and in his detailed exposure of the weaknesses of the Dryden poem in contrast with the subtleties and ambiguities of Donne's, Richards reveals all the old magic, even if his conclusion is somehow that we must therefore all become "Platonic Aristotelians." Two recent communications in *Partisan Review,* the first (July–August 1943) commenting on the Failure of Nerve controversy, and the second (Summer 1944) on an essay of Eliot's on culture, are far from poetic texts, the former somehow mediating, with the aid of an extended forced metaphor, between supernatural religion and naturalistic science, the latter an all-out tribute to education, as no less than "the pursuit of intellectual and moral order," and thus our salvation.

In terms of this bewildering output over almost a quarter of a century, it might be interesting to raise the question of Richards's profession or field. In *The Foundations of Æsthetics* he set up as an æsthetician, and in

The Meaning of Meaning as an epistemologist and what he calls alternately a "symbologist" and a "semanticist." He has always been a psychologist, and calling himself a "centrist," has drawn enthusiastically and impartially on physiological and neurological psychology, behaviorism, Pavlov's conditioned-reflex psychology, psychoanalysis, Gestalt, and snips and snatches from almost every other psychological theorizer or experimenter, as well as on his own empirical observations. In recent years he has attacked educational psychology (and presumably psychology in general) for "jargon" and "the disease of abstractionism," and from the evidence in *How to Read a Page*, is perhaps ready to restore his psychology, as a branch, to the somewhat battered trunk of philosophy from which Williams James originally plucked it. In addition, Richards has always been a teacher, something of a Sinologist, logician, educational theorist, and linguist, and, until a decade ago, was incidentally the greatest and most important of practicing professional literary critics. Perhaps more than any man since Bacon, Richards has taken all knowledge as his province, and his field is the entire mind of man.

2

The achievement of *Practical Criticism* is such that it can hardly be canceled out by any subsequent defections. It was the beginning of objective criticism, the first organized attempt to stop theorizing about what people get when they read a poem and to find out. Its ultimate aim is no less lofty a one than the general improvement of reading, and as a consequence the general improvement of literary appreciation. Richards writes:

> That the one and only goal of all critical endeavours, of all interpretation, appreciation, exhortation, praise or abuse, is improvement in communication may seem an exaggeration. But in practice it is so. The whole apparatus of critical rules and principles is a means to the attainment of finer, more precise, more discriminating communication. There is, it is true, a valuation side to criticism. When we have solved, completely, the communication problem, when we have got, perfectly, the experience, *the mental condition* relevant to the poem, we have still to judge it, still to decide upon its worth. But the latter question nearly always settles itself; or rather, our own inmost nature and the nature of the world in which we live decide it for us. Our prime endeavour must be to get the relevant mental condition and then see what happens.

The more limited aims of the book, as Richards phrases them in the first paragraph of his introduction, are three:

First, to introduce a new kind of documentation to those who are interested in the contemporary state of culture whether as critics, as philosophers, as teachers, as psychologists, or merely as curious persons. Secondly, to provide a new technique for those who wish to discover for themselves what they think and feel about poetry (and cognate matters) and why they should like or dislike it. Thirdly, to prepare the way for educational methods more efficient than those we use now in developing discrimination and the power to understand what we hear and read.

The first purpose has of course widespread implications for both poetry and criticism. Of the second, Richards writes:

My second aim is more ambitious and requires more explanation. It forms part of a general attempt to modify our procedure in certain forms of discussion. There are subjects—mathematics, physics, and the descriptive sciences supply some of them—which can be discussed in terms of verifiable facts and precise hypotheses. There are other subjects—the concrete affairs of commerce, law, organisation and police work—which can be handled by rules of thumb and generally accepted conventions. But in between is the vast *corpus* of problems, assumptions, adumbrations, fictions, prejudices, tenets; the sphere of random beliefs and hopeful guesses; the whole world, in brief, of abstract opinion and disputation about matters of feeling. To this world belongs everything about which civilised man cares most. I need only instance ethics, metaphysics, morals, religion, æsthetics, and the discussions surrounding liberty, nationality, justice, love, truth, faith and knowledge to make this plain. As a subject-matter for discussion, poetry is a central and typical denizen of this world. It is so both by its own nature and by the type of discussion with which it is traditionally associated. It serves, therefore, as an eminently suitable *bait* for anyone who wishes to trap the current opinions and responses in this middle field for the purpose of examining and comparing them, and with a view to advancing our knowledge of what may be called the natural history of human opinions and feelings.

What Richards aspired to, in other words, was no less than advancing the territory of science, with its objective data experimentally obtained, into the field of poetry and analogous realms of disputation. And in reporting this "piece of field-work in comparative ideology," Richards hoped to suggest improved pedagogical techniques that would accomplish his third aim. In addition, Richards found his work had implications in still a fourth direction, the development of a critique of the popular, which he presents ironically, despite its essentially serious implications, writing: "A strange light, incidentally, is thrown upon the sources of popularity for poetry. Indeed I am not without fears that my efforts may prove of assistance to young poets (and others) desiring to increase their sales. A set of formulæ for 'nationwide appeal' seems to be a just possible outcome."

What Richards did is itself absurdly simple. Over a period of years he issued printed sheets of poems, with their authors not given and some slight attempt made to disguise their periods by modernized spelling, to his students at Cambridge. The poems ranged from Shakespeare to Ella Wheeler Wilcox, and were distributed in mixed groups of four. The students, most of them undergraduates reading English for an honours degree, were asked to read the poems carefully at their leisure, as often as they wished to, and comment on them. Richards defined a reading as any number of perusals at one session, and asked the students to record the number of readings with their comments. Since some students listed a dozen or more readings, and hardly any gave fewer than four readings to any poem, the poems were obviously read frequently and carefully. At the end of a week Richards collected their comments, which he calls "protocols," and discussed them, with the poems, in class. There was no compulsion to return protocols, and the sixty per cent who did so must have been particularly interested. Precautions were taken to ensure anonymity, and Richards was particularly careful in his remarks not to influence the group for or against any of the poems, or to give them any hints other than that the poems tended to be a mixed lot.

Practical Criticism, subtitled *A Study of Literary Judgment*, presents some of this material, given organization and significance. The first section of the book is Introductory, explaining the experiment and discussing its various problems. The second, the longest in the book, gives samplings of the protocols on thirteen poems, with the poems, divided into a chapter for each poem and roughly subdivided according to the reaction displayed. The third section analyzes the principal general problems raised by the protocols. The fourth section consists of summary and recommendations, and four appendices are added: one of further notes, one tabulating the relative popularity of the thirteen poems, one giving their authorship (so that the reader, who has been testing himself in the same fashion, is finally let in on the secret), and the last printing the poems as originally set before the students. The thirteen poems discussed in the book range from several generally considered meritous, like Donne's "Holy Sonnet VII" ("At the round earths imagin'd corners, blow") and Hopkins's "Spring and Fall: to a young child," to work by Philip James Bailey, J. D. C. Pellew, Wilfred Rowland Childe, and a man known as "Woodbine Willie."

Richards's procedure in the book is to print the poem, print and analyze reactions to it, and then generalize. His own brilliant readings of the poems come through chiefly by suggestion and incidentally. To make a basic distinction in his protocol material, he uses the term "statement" for utterances chiefly interesting for what they *say*, "expression" for utterances chiefly interesting for what they reflect of the mental operations of the writers. Richards also assures the reader that the protocols are untampered with, with even the spelling and punctuation left unchanged in significant places (even the handwriting, Richards says, is meaningful, but he has no way to reproduce it), and that none of them is manufactured (a reasonable suspicion in view of the utter incredibility of some of the comments). He also insists that he has selected his protocol material as objectively and fairly as possible, with the reservation that he has somewhat slighted the proportion of noncommittal material.

What the protocols reveal, by and large, is probably the most shocking picture, exhaustively documented, of the general reading of poetry ever presented. Perhaps the most frightening single thing Richards got was evidence that his students (and, presumably, all but a few particularly qualified readers and poets) lean absolutely on the authority of the writer's name, and their sense of its rank in the pantheon, as a crutch. Without an author's name, they proved in almost every case unable to guess the author, and when they guessed, guessed wrong and then proceeded to make an automatic evaluation consistent with that wrong guess. As a general rule, their honest opinions, with no authority to lean on, more or less reversed all the accepted judgments of poetic value. Lest this fact serve to discredit the accepted judgments, the idiocy of their remarks and their plain inability to read or notice the simplest and most patent physical fact in a poem make it clear that the fault is theirs.

Richards summarizes the chief difficulties the protocols reveal, and the best way to give some sense of his material is probably to paraphrase his summary, and then to show some typical protocols displaying some of the faults. He found ten principal difficulties:

A. Inability to make out the plain sense of poetry, to construe its paraphrasable prose meaning.
B. Difficulties in the sensuous apprehension of form.
C. Difficulties with visual imagery.
D. Mnemonic irrelevances, chiefly personal reminiscences or erratic associations.
E. Stock responses called into action by the poem.
F. Sentimentality.
G. Inhibition, its obverse.
H. Doctrinal adhesions.
I. Technical presuppositions.
J. General critical preconceptions.

First, a few sample protocols and fragments on the Donne sonnet, perhaps the most distinguished poem in the batch. One reader called it a stanza, failing to recognize it as a sonnet, and another, carried away by his stock response to its subject-matter, identified it as hymn meter, writing:

> Mouthfuls of words. Has no appeal whatsoever. Make a good hymn—in fact, that's the way the metre goes.
> Too religious for one who doesn't believe in repenting that way.

One reader couldn't do a thing with it:

> I confess immediately that I can't make out what all the shouting is about. The poem is completely confusing. The numerous pronouns and adverbs mix up the thought, if indeed there is one definite thought throughout.

One reader finds "round earth's imagined corners" "a pretty conceit," and another writes patronizingly:

> It is difficult to share the poet's attitude, because although he is evidently sincere, his technique is bad. The lines do, however, in spite of this express the simple faith of a very simple man.

One student goes into a bit of autobiography:

> Having tried unsuccessfully to write sonnets myself, I have a perhaps abnormal admiration for sonnet-writers. Had this not been so, I think I would in the end have said that this sonnet was bad.

"The rhymes are not perfect," writes one. "It slows down and stumbles toward the end," writes another. "I felt that the writer had aimed at a high mark, but that the arrow had fallen short," writes a third. A scansion enthusiast gets in his comment:

> The passage seems to be a rotten sonnet written in a very temperamental kind of iambic pentameter. Not even by cruel forcing and beating the table with my fingers can I find the customary five iambic feet to a verse; the feet are frequently not iambic, and there are sometimes four, and even six accented syllables to the verse. In structure the passage sounds like the first labors of a school boy. Particularly displeasing are verses 5, 6, and 7. Yet the idea seems really worth while.

To which another opposes the view: "I should never bother about the sense; the sound is enough for me." "There are no pictures in it," one student writes by way of criticism, and another gives it the final dismissal:

The first point about this sonnet, which seems most obvious is that it could have been written quite, if not more, effectively in prose.

The Donne poem received 30 favorable protocols, 42 unfavorable ones, and 28 noncommittal ones. By contrast we might look at the poem that received the greatest number of favorable protocols (54) and the fewest unfavorable ones (31, the remaining 15 being noncommittal), J. D. C. Pellew's "The Temple," from *Parentalia and Other Poems*, which begins:

> *Between the erect and solemn trees*
> *I will go down upon my knees;*
> *I shall not find this day*
> *So meet a place to pray,*

and continues for five similar stanzas. Some readers simply ignored the poem and engaged in religious disputation, like this one:

I don't like to hear people boast about praying. Alfred de Vigny held that to pray is cowardly, and while I don't go as far as this, I do think that it is rude to cram religious ecstasies down the throat of a sceptical age.

Another critic produced a fine example of mnemonic irrelevance:

When I first read the third verse, a vivid picture came into my mind of a forward breaking away with the ball, from a loose scrum and "with never a swerve" making straight for the line.

Most of the readers, however, liked the poem. Here are some typical comments giving some characteristic reasons for the preference:

The thoughts behind this approach perfection; the expression of the sentiment is as exquisite as the sentiments themselves. . . . I find my thoughts expressed in this.

I think this is a very fine poem indeed. I like the metre, and I like the atmosphere of the whole thing. It gives at once a grand picture of the forest, and the devotional feeling with which the author was imbued by the sight which he depicts. It is a fine communication of a fine feeling.

The rhythm seems to match the march of the thought perfectly.

An atmosphere of peace, and deep reverence, which transports the reader into another world, more pure and white than this.

The poet has succeeded in universalizing his desire to worship. . . . A very lovely poem.

This is the gem of the four pieces. It creates the solemn peaceful reverent atmosphere of a pine wood for us. We recollect how often similar thoughts, occasioned by the reverent calm of the trees, have arisen in us, as we stand awed by their grandeur and majesty. It is calm and beautifully euphonious in sound.

The really terrifying thing about *Practical Criticism* is the realization that the protocol-writers are not typical readers of poetry, but particularly superior readers: prospective teachers, writers, even poets, reading under almost ideal conditions (granting the limitations of having no authority to rely on, no clues from a body of work, and no hint of what Richards calls the poem's "provenance"). Richards writes sadly:

> From such comparisons as I have been able to make with proto-cols supplied by audiences of other types, I see no reason whatever to think that a higher standard of critical discernment can easily be found under our present cultural conditions. Doubtless, could the Royal Society of Literature or the Academic Committee of the English Association be impounded for purposes of experiment we might expect greater uniformity in the comments or at least in their style, and a more wary approach as regards some of the dangers of the test. But with regard to equally essential matters occasions for surprise might still occur.

And in his summary at the end of the book he adds, of the protocol-writers:

> With few exceptions they are products of the most expensive kind of education. I would like to repeat, with emphasis, that there is no reason whatever to suppose that higher capacity for reading poetry will be manifested by any similar group anywhere in the world. Sons and daughters of other Universities who are tempted to think otherwise may be invited to bring experimental evidence collected under the same conditions. But no experienced teacher will be sur-prised by any of the protocols; no teacher, at least, who has re-frained from turning his pupils into sounding-boards that reflect his own opinions. And, candidly, how many of us are convinced, with reason, that we would have made a better showing ourselves under these conditions?

Richards's experiment in *Practical Criticism* was admittedly a first groping toward a laboratory technique, very fragmentary and easily subject to criticism. In the book itself he notes a number of things he might have done and neglected to do: projects like studying variations of judgment in individual readers (what he called "characterology"), and tracing correlations between approval of one type of poem and disapproval of another. He remarks that some of his individual variations may simply be due to fatigue, and suggests that four short poems may be too many for a week's reading, "absurd though this suggestion will seem to those godlike lords of the syllabus-world, who think that the whole of English Literature can be perused with profit in about a year!" In *Interpretation in Teaching* Richards proposes further extensions of the method, including interviews with the protocol-writers, studies of crossings-out in their manuscripts to get at their thought-processes, and so on. A number of other possibilities for corrections and extensions readily come to mind; in terms of characterology: correlations with background and earlier education, with experience in reading poetry, with length of the protocol, with general character traits; in terms of scientific experiment: numerical gradings, comparison with protocols from control groups who are told the names of the authors; as well as further extensions in giving the poems false authors, rewriting them for various effects, antiquing or modernizing them, and an almost limit-less vista of experimental possibilities. Somewhat different results, finally, might have come from simply asking the students to write only on poems they liked.

Perhaps the book's most serious deficiency is one Richards recognizes and attempts to defend: its psychological superficiality. He writes:

> I am anxious to meet as far as may be the objection that may be brought by some psychologists, and these the best, that the proto-cols do not supply enough evidence for us really to be able to make out the motives of the writers and that therefore the whole investi-gation is superficial. But the *beginning* of every research ought to be superficial, and to find something to investigate that is accessible and detachable is one of the chief difficulties of psychology. I believe the chief merit of the experiment here made is that it gives us this. Had I wished to plumb the depths of these writers' Unconscious, where I am quite willing to agree the real motives of their likings and dislikings would be found, I should have devised something like a branch of psychoanalytic technique for the purpose. But it was clear that little progress would be made if we attempted to drag too deep a plough. However, even as it is, enough strange material is turned up.

Even granting the justice of Richards's explanation, it can only be re-gretted that a deeper plow could not have been dragged, since at least it would have dispersed some of the easy optimism from his final sug-gestions for educational reform.

Almost the only thing in the book that allows the reader to keep his sanity and some sense of hope for the future of poetry is the steady counterpoint of Richards's own brilliant and sensitive readings. These are almost never stated directly, but are generally implied by pointing up statements and suggestions in the protocols, so that a valid reading finally emerges by a kind of dialectic process. Richards is fully aware of this dramatistic structure of the book, writing: "I shall proceed poem by poem, allowing the internal drama latent in every clash of opinion, of taste or temperament to guide the arrangement." In a few cases, to clear up points no protocol-writer handles, Richards furnishes samples of his own reading, and they always come like beams of light through the the thick fog. A rare example is his gloss on the line from one of the poems, "O frail steel tissues of the sun":

> "Tissue," to begin with the noun, has a double sense; firstly, "cloth of steel" in extension from "cloth of gold" or "cloth of silver," the cold, metallic, inorganic quality of the fabric being perhaps important; secondly, "thin, soft, semi-transparent" as with tissue-paper. "Steel" is also present as a sense-metaphor of Aristotle's second kind, when the transference is from *species* to *genus*, steel a particular kind of strong material being used to stand for any material strong enough to hold together, as it appears, the immensity of the cloud-structure. The colour suggestion of "steel" is also relevant. "Frail" echoes the semi-transparency of "tissue," the diaphanousness, and the impending dissolution too. "Of the sun" it may be added runs parallel to "of the silk worm," *i.e.*, produced by the sun.

The tremendous value of *Practical Criticism* lies almost wholly in its data on how poetry is actually read by supposedly qualified people, counterpointed by Richards's own readings and amplified and generalized by him. He more or less recognizes the inadequacy of his recommendations at the end of the book, or in fact of any recommendations. The book proposes improvement through education: further experimentation in the universities, the teaching of interpretation as a subject, and even a Chair of Significs ludicrously close to Adler's Chair of Curative Pedagogy. Yet *quis custodiet ipsos custodes*—who will teach the teachers? As Richards recognizes, his protocol-writers are *precisely* the teachers of poetry in the next generation, and it is unlikely that they will be fundamentally altered by his course, this book, or the whole corpus of his books. Constant evidence from life makes it clear that the general inability to experience works of art intelligently and critically extends to the professionals in the field and others presumably qualified.

On the matter of reliance on authority and "rank" alone, Henri Peyre furnishes some amusing anecdotes in *Writers and Their Critics*. He tells as typical the story of a Paris concert given by Liszt in 1837, consisting of a Beethoven trio and one by Pixis, at which the composers' names were inadvertently interchanged on the programs. The audience, consisting

of cultivated and musical people, noisily applauded the Pixis and listened
to the Beethoven indifferently or worse. Liszt commented:

> When the Beethoven trio was played in the place originally as-
> signed to Pixis, it was found so uninspired, mediocre and tedious
> that there were some who left the hall, declaring that the presump-
> tion of M. Pixis in presenting his work before an audience that had
> just listened to one of Beethoven's masterpieces was downright
> impertinent.

Liszt added that the Pixis work was not only mediocre, but very different
from the Beethoven in style.

In the last analysis, all that a work like *Practical Criticism* can do by
way of remedying the situation it presents is to create a clearing of
intelligent and sensitive reading in the jungle of general incompetence.
Where the larger hope lies is that this reading is to some extent collective,
a truth produced out of the meeting of many errors, and we can presume
that Richards's readings are not only presented through the vehicle of
the protocols, but to some extent inspired, directed, and elucidated by
them; a technique similar to the truth-by-accretion technique of his
other work. Obviously, there is no "correct" reading of a poem, but
there are good ones and bad ones, and good ones tend to arise out of the
interplay of many bad ones. Here it is clear that the great contribution
of *Practical Criticism*, and Richards's work in general, to modern literary
criticism, is chiefly one of method and methodology rather than principles
or suggestions for reform. By creating some approximation of experimental conditions, he achieves for the first time an objective account of
how poetry is actually read, and focuses criticism on its least adequately
handled area, poetic communication or interpretation, the poem-reader
relationship. By creating some approximation of a collective condition,
he achieves a technique for improving that reading and that relationship.

3

In a fragmentary and intuitive fashion, as in the case of so many other
modern techniques, literary criticism has always been concerned with the
reader's or audience's part in the communicative process of art. Plato
and Aristotle both generalized about audience-reaction in their opposed
psychosocial doctrines of art as harmful-stimulation-of-the-emotions and
art as helpful-purgation-of-the-emotions, but neither attempted to study
specific audience reactions to specific works. Longinus, in *On the Sublime*,
clearly developed in the use of language the distinction that Mill was
later to name as "denotation" and "connotation," when he wrote (W.
Rhys Roberts's translation): "Further you will be aware of the fact
that an image has one purpose with the orators and another with the

poets, and that the design of the poetical image is enthralment; of the rhetorical, vivid description." This distinction is basic to any study of the audience's experience of art, but Longinus never followed it farther. He did, however, later in the same work, suggest a number of techniques for producing audience effects, of which his discussion of the effect of changing grammatical "person" is typical. After quoting a Herodotus line announcing the hero's doings in the direct address of the second person rather than the third, Longinus writes:

> Do you observe, my friend, how he leads you in imagination through the region and makes you *see* what you hear? All such cases of direct personal address place the hearer on the very scene of action. So it is when you seem to be speaking, not to all and sundry, but to a single individual.
> But Tydeides—thou wouldst not have known him, for whom that hero fought. (*Iliad*, V, 85.)
> You will make your hearer more excited and more attentive, and full of active participation, if you keep him on the alert by words addressed to himself.

Probably the first formal recognition of the need for psychological study of the audience came in the eighteenth century, culminating in Edmund Burke's essay "On the Sublime and Beautiful." In the words of John Morley:

> It was a vigorous enlargement of the principle, which Addison had not long before timidly illustrated, that critics of art seek its principles in the wrong place, so long as they limit their search to poems, pictures, engravings, statues, and buildings, instead of first arranging the sentiments and faculties in man to which art makes it appeal. Addison's treatment was slight, and merely literary; Burke dealt boldly with his subject on the base of the most scientific psychology that was then within his reach. To approach it on the psychological side at all, was to make a distinct and remarkable advance in the method of the inquiry which he had taken in hand.

In pursuing art into the area of the audience, Burke was logically putting into practice the view, growing all through the eighteenth century, that criticism would profit from less conjecture and more data. As Johnson wrote in the *Rambler*, "It is the task of criticism to establish principles; to improve opinion into knowledge." In the next century Coleridge in *Biographia Literaria*, almost echoing Johnson (he said the end of criticism was to establish "the principles of writing"), added a further scientific feature, experimentation. Noting a point Richards was to display at length in *Practical Criticism*, the wide variance and essential inconsistency of audience reaction to poetry (in this case, Wordsworth's *Lyrical Ballads*), Coleridge writes:

> That this conjecture is not wide from the mark, I am induced to believe from the noticeable fact, which I can state on my own knowledge, that the same general censure has been grounded by almost every different person on some different poem. Among those, whose candour and judgment I estimate highly, I distinctly remember six who expressed their objections to the same purport, at the same time admitting, that several of the poems had given them great pleasure; and, strange as it might seem, the composition which one cited as execrable, another quoted as his favourite. I am indeed convinced in my own mind, that could the same experiment have been tried with these volumes, as was made in the well known story of the picture, the result would have been the same; the parts which had been covered by black spots on the one day, would be found equally *albo lapide notatæ* on the succeeding.

At about the time Coleridge was furnishing the theoretical base that would develop into objective reader-experimentation, De Quincey produced a number of introspective, intuitive, studies of reader-reaction, of which "On the Knocking at the Gate in Macbeth" is the best-known example, which would later flower into psychoanalytic researches in the same area. On the knocking at the gate, De Quincey began with the problem of the inexplicable disproportion of the reactions it aroused in him (precisely the problem with which Ernest Jones began his researches into *Hamlet* a century later). De Quincey writes:

> From my boyish days I had always felt a great perplexity on one point in Macbeth. It was this: the knocking at the gate, which succeeds to the murder of Duncan, produced to my feelings an effect for which I never could account. The effect was, that it reflected back upon the murder a peculiar awfulness and a depth of solemnity; yet, however obstinately I endeavored with my understanding to comprehend this, for many years I never could see *why* it should produce such an effect.

After which, by following along an introspective inquiry, he emerges with an answer. (The fact that it is not *the* answer, and that much more satisfying ones have since been produced, does not at all invalidate De Quincey's methodological achievement.)

Through the nineteenth century the Coleridge tradition developed into a general experimental testing in areas previously regarded as sacred to conjecture. Galton's test of the efficacy of prayer (which Richards has several times referred to approvingly) is a typical, if somewhat comic, example. Galton decided, reasonably enough, that more prayers are made on behalf of the lives of sovereigns and the children of clergymen than for other people, and he checked statistics on their comparative lengths of life. (He found that they tended to be shorter than average, but not enough to warrant the assumption that prayer is clearly harmful.)

The views of what is known on the Continent as "the English æsthetic," the physiological æsthetics of Herbert Spencer and Grant Allen, in which the experience of beauty is based in a bodily reaction, developed in Germany into a substantial school of experimental æstheticians. Its founder, Gustav Fechner, began by experimentally testing Adolf Zeising's hypothesis that the divisions of "the golden section" (in which the smaller unit is to the larger as the larger is to the sum) are innately pleasing. His experiments confirming this hypothesis, reported in *Experimental Æsthetics*, introduced the experimental method with its quantitative emphasis and in general created a laboratory approach for studying audience reaction. Von Helmholtz, in *Sensations of Tone*, grounded the æsthetics of music solidly in physics and physiology, but the attempts of investigators like E. W. Brücke, Ewald Hering, and later men to do the same for the pleasurable effects of colors and their combinations have so far not had the same success. (Although it can be presumed that ultimately we shall inevitably have a physics of color harmony, as satisfactory in terms of great pictures as our physics of musical sound is in terms of great musical composition.) Fechner's disciple Wilhelm Wundt, in his *Physiological Psychology*, has sketched out the chief lines of future development for experimental æsthetics. Despite such slipshod misuse as the current talk of "visceral" reactions to pictures and the "empathy" craze, in its direction (probably as taken over by the gestaltists) presumably lies what hope we have for both a body of scientific data on audience reactions and the only genuinely objective æsthetic we are ever likely to get.

To a lesser extent a similar movement developed in France. In 1888 Émile Hennequin published *La Critique scientifique*, founding the science of "esthopsychology." Defining literature as "a collection of written signs intended to produce non-active emotions," Hennequin developed a fantastic battery of terms and systems of classification from the physical sciences for handling the work both as an expression of the author and in terms of its effect on the reader. His purposes and methods were valid, if somewhat premature, but the results he obtained in applying the structure to literature in two volumes of *Études de critique scientifique* the two following years were not very successful. Hennequin's work is clearly in the tradition of much of Richards's, and it has had a great effect on such psychoanalytic critics as Charles Baudouin. It seems even to have influenced so unlikely a prospect for scientific criticism as Remy de Gourmont, who, despite all the pure æstheticism of his theories, has drawn heavily on both physics and physiology, and at one time planned to write a book called *The World of Words*, "to determine whether words have really a meaning—that is to say, a constant value," which sounds as though it would have been something very similar to *The Meaning of Meaning*, at least in intention.

A number of contemporary critics besides Richards have picked up one or the other aspects of this tradition: either attempting experimental laboratory forms of criticism, or studying the communicative process and reader-reactions by means of other techniques. Maud Bodkin's experiments with reader-introspection and accounts of her own introspective reactions, as well as Dr. Wertham's experiments with writer-introspection, have been discussed above (chapter on Miss Bodkin). Probably the most fantastic laboratory experiment yet done with literature was performed by a Columbia psychologist named Frederick Lyman Wells and written up in the *Archives of Psychology* for August 1907 as "A Statistical Study of Literary Merit." Professor Wells collected ten graduate students in English at Columbia and asked them to grade ten American writers— Bryant, Cooper, Emerson, Hawthorne, Holmes, Irving, Longfellow, Lowell, Poe, Thoreau—for ten qualities: charm, clearness, euphony, finish, force, imagination, originality, proportion, sympathy, wholesomeness. According to the gradings, he computed American literary rankings, which turned out to be: Hawthorne in first place, followed in order by Poe, Emerson, Lowell, Longfellow, Irving, Bryant, Thoreau, Holmes, and Cooper.

Without equaling Wells's egregiousness, Teachers' College at Columbia has continued a tradition of literary experiment and measurement. Among many works produced, a few examples might be mentioned. In 1922, before the appearance of *Practical Criticism*, Allan Abbott and M. R. Trabue published a monograph on *A Measure of Ability to Judge Poetry*. Their experiment, which was particularly ingenious, consisted in giving the subjects each poem along with three rewrites of it: one sentimentalized, one made markedly prosy, and one made technically faulty; then tabulating their preferences, which resulted in a fairly dismal picture. Mortimer Adler, for his doctoral thesis, did a similar experiment using music that had been worsened in ingenious ways for him by a professional musician. And Helene Hartley, in 1930, published the record of still another experiment along similar lines, in a monograph entitled *Tests on the Interpretative Reading of Poetry for Teachers of English*.

Levin L. Schücking's *The Sociology of Literary Taste*, which first appeared in German in 1931 and was published in English in 1944, is an attempt at another sort of scientific approach. Actually the book, which is extremely short, is little more than a brief literary history generalizing about the shift in the status of the artist and the criteria of art and taste in modern times. It does, however, manage to suggest some of the lines of investigation that would make an actual sociology of literary taste possible: detailed study of changes in newspapers and periodicals; "inquiry into the views of particular social groups and professions"; examination of statistics on the sales of books, including figures on reprintings of earlier literature; surveys of lending libraries, book clubs, reading groups. Unscientifically, Schücking has already made such a study or series of studies in his imagination, and he announces what they "would show." Actually his book is no more than a useful, rather skimpy sketch for a proposed science. Some of his intuitions and conjectures are extremely shrewd, but Schücking has neither compilations of data nor experimental records to back him up. If any concrete work has been done in the area since, I am not familiar with it. (Without the trappings of scientific sociology, Mrs. Leavis has done a much superior study of literary taste, heavily dependent on Richards, in *Fiction and the Reading Public.*)

Another contemporary attempt to study the communicative aspects of literature scientifically lies in the vast field of semantics (a science more or less founded in its modern form by Richards and Ogden), particularly in the ambitious efforts of the logical positivists, a group Ransom, Tate, and Wheelwright have insisted are carrying Richards's early ideas to their implicit conclusions, although Richards has never concurred. The logical positivists, under the leadership of Rudolf Carnap and Charles W. Morris, in the course of creating a new *International Encyclopædia of Unified Science* serially (endeavoring, as Richards notes, "to reduce logic to the fundamental grammar of a perfect language"), have developed "semantics" into the larger field of "semiotic," the comprehensive science of all signs and sign-interpretations. The nature and implications of this science in general are irrelevant to our purposes here, and in any case I am hardly competent to discuss them, but in the course of their efforts to take over and remodel all of man's knowledge, the new encyclopedists have inevitably come up against poetry. Arthur Mizener has suggested, neatly and rather unfairly, that the implications of Morris's discussion of "the æsthetic sign" in *Foundations of the Theory of Signs* is the treatment of poetry as "a mild form of insanity." In two later essays, however, "Æsthetics and the Theory of Signs" in the *Journal of Unified Science,* VIII, 1–3, and "Science, Art, and Technology" in the *Kenyon Review,* Autumn 1939, Morris has attempted to find a corner in which poetry may legitimately exist. Morris's claim is that æsthetic discourse is a primary form of discourse, chiefly involving the syntactical function of language, and principally devoted to "the vivid presentation of value." Moreover, "since the work of art is an icon and not a statement, æsthetic discourse is not restricted to signs whose truth is confirmable"; that is, it can only be studied in terms of internal consistency, not denotation. This position does not seem to be altered in his later book, *Signs, Lan-*

guage, and Behavior, and Carnap seems never to have revised the position he took in 1934, in *Philosophy and Logical Syntax*, that lyric verse is analogous to laughter, a form of emotional expression. Since the logical positivists have so far left specific examples of æsthetic discourse largely unstudied, we can only wait patiently to see the critical implications of this kindly view. The general semanticists under Korzybski, on the other hand, seem largely to have ignored poetry in their system, although Korzybski remarks in one place in *Science and Sanity* that it may "convey more of lasting values than a whole volume of scientific analysis."

Objectifying poetry still further, we would get to literal machinery, and this too is in existence. A number of critics, Ezra Pound among them, have made rather mysterious references to a machine invented by Abbé Rousselot for measuring the duration of spoken sounds. Whether or not this is the "kymograph," an instrument for the same purpose used in the Phonetics Laboratory at University College, London, I do not know. In any case, I am familiar with no published work based on the Rousselot machine, whereas E. A. Sonnenschein, a classics professor, published *What Is Rhythm* in 1925 on the strength of conclusions derived from the kymograph, including an appendix giving quantitative results he had achieved in experimental syllable-measurement, working in conjunction with professional phoneticists. Professor Sonnenschein's theories are empirically derived from these results. He gives, as the basis for an objective science of metrics, the definition: "Rhythm is that property of a sequence of events in time which produces on the mind of the observer the impression of proportion between the durations of the several events or groups of events of which the sequence is composed." Richards has reasonably enough criticized Sonnenschein's definition, in the appendix to *Practical Criticism*, for treating these elements as though they were *things* in the verse, rather than *actions* in the man reading the verse or speaking it for the kymograph; for recognizing that they are psychological rather than physical phenomena, but not treating them as psychological *enough*, as inextricably tied to poetic meaning. Despite this easy temptation to treat anything recordable on a machine as though it were consequently objective and wholly measurable, the potentiality of the kymograph and similar machinery for the study of prosody, as applied in both writing and reading poetry, seems very substantial.[1]

One last technique for studying reader-reaction that deserves mention, since it is at the other pole from the kymograph, is George Orwell's

[1] On another level, radio is also pioneering in the machine measurement of audience-reaction with such inventions as A. C. Nielsen's "Audimeter," Horace Schwerin's "Reactocaster," the Stanton-Lazarsfeld "Program Analyzer," and the Ernest Walker "Gag Meter." Any reader who can bear to learn about these devices for recording, computing, and evaluating the precise reactions of radio listeners to their æsthetic experiences is referred to Thomas Whiteside's article on the subject of Hooper ratings and allied phenomena in the *New Republic*, May 5, 1947.

ingenious subjective conjecturing about popular culture. In two pieces in *Dickens, Dali & Others*, "Boys' Weeklies" and "The Art of Donald McGill," Orwell develops a technique of pure conjecture for studying the social effects of, respectively, trashy magazines for adolescents and comic postcards. The method almost directly reverses Richards: both are interested in the effects of a work on the reader; Richards consequently goes to the reader, Orwell to the work. In "Boys' Weeklies" Orwell begins by discussing the contents of the small news-agent's shop in any big English town, noting: "Probably the contents of these shops is the best available indication of what the mass of the English people really feels and thinks." He then focuses on the boys' twopenny weeklies, the "penny dreadfuls," giving their history, circulation, and influence, and discussing their contents at length, with liberal quotation. By careful study of the correspondence columns, advertisements, and the contents proper of the magazines, Orwell makes some extremely shrewd conjectures about the readers, their lives and minds, and what the magazines *do* for them, what impulses and needs they satisfy to warrant their popularity. He finds a whole world of fantasy-identification, and explores its social and political implications in detail. The piece is actually a carefully documented, informed, and extremely valuable psychosocial study of a type of commercial literature from the point of view of the reader. "The Art of Donald McGill" is a similar, although less ambitious study of comic postcards, in which Orwell tabulates their subjects and omissions, and then studies the social attitudes and reflections of social reality behind them. It is hard to say from these two excellent pieces whether the same critical technique would work with more reputable art and literature, but there is no question of its worth in Orwell's chosen lowbrow area.

4

Richards seems to have paid little attention to earlier workers in the experimental and audience-study traditions he inherited, and his investigations, even where they substantially repeat earlier studies, seem to have been unconcerned with precedents, evolved by the logic of his own work's development. Richards's specific and conscious indebtedness is to a handful of earlier thinkers, most of them relatively eccentric philosophers and philosophic literary men. The most important of these is Samuel Taylor Coleridge. The influence of Coleridge on Richards is a remarkable example of the meeting of minds across a century. It is so pervasive, so complicated, and in some cases so subtle a relationship that it can only be skimmed here, but in any case there exists an excellent textbook on the subject, Richards's own *Coleridge on Imagination*. The development of Richards's books reads like the record of a love affair.

His earliest work, *The Foundations of Æsthetics*, makes no more mention of Coleridge than quoting his "mystical" view of beauty rather scornfully, and in *The Meaning of Meaning* Coleridge is only the author of a rather high-flown statement about art. In *Principles*, after a number of mentions of Coleridge's poetry, the reader is suddenly startled to find a reference to "the Fourteenth Chapter of *Biographia Literaria*, that lumber-room of neglected wisdom which contains more hints towards a theory of poetry than all the rest ever written upon the subject"; and throughout the rest of the book Richards picks up "invaluable hints," "luminous hints," and so on from the *Biographia*, particularly the concept of imagination, which is "Coleridge's greatest contribution to critical theory" and to which "it is hard to add anything." At the same time Richards insists on his reservations. He writes:

> As critics Lamb or Coleridge are very far from normal; none the less they are of extraordinary fertility in suggestion. Their responses are often erratic even when of most revelatory character. In such cases we do not take them as standards to which we endeavour to approximate, we do not attempt to see eye to eye with them. Instead we use them as means by which to make quite different approaches ourselves to the works which they have characteristically but eccentrically interpreted.

An increasing respect for Coleridge (which eventually succeeded in repealing most of the last quotation), along with increasing use of him, developed through Richards's subsequent books. *Basic Rules of Reason* begins and ends with Coleridge quotations. By *Coleridge on Imagination*, his full-length study, Richards's estimate had risen to the point of seeing Coleridge as almost the founder of semasiology, a genius so vast that if his thoughts on poetry, interpretation, language, and the mind could be "disentangled," extended, and translated into modern terminology, and his metaphysics "reinterpreted," a large part of Richards's and our difficulty would be solved. In the later books Coleridge is quoted with almost the authority of an Aristotle. Ransom has claimed, in *The New Criticism*, that Coleridge as his "chief mentor" assimilated Richards, "as the Chinese are said to assimilate their conquerors," rather than the other way around, converting him from positivism to a belief in the cognitive function of poetry, and so on. It would perhaps be more accurate to say that as Richards moved away from his earlier strict positivism, he found that Coleridge increasingly spoke for him.

After Coleridge, perhaps the greatest single source of Richards's ideas is Jeremy Bentham. This may be the influence of Ogden, who has written one general book on Bentham and has edited his theory of fictions, but again it is more likely that Richards was personally drawn to Bentham both for his pioneering linguistic analysis and because Utilitarianism is so close to Richards's own psychological theory of value, as Richards himself points out in the *Principles*. In *Coleridge on Imagination* Richards calls himself a "Benthamite" and makes an ingenious attempt, following John Stuart Mill's "Essay on Coleridge," to reconcile the two philosophies. He reinterprets Coleridge's idealism from the viewpoint of Bentham's materialism, attempting to find, as Mill suggested, "some natural want or requirement of human nature which the doctrine in question is fitted to satisfy." Richards quotes Mill:

> Whoever could master the principles and combine the methods of both would possess the entire English philosophy of his age. Coleridge used to say that everyone is born either a Platonist or an Aristotelian: it may similarly be affirmed that every Englishman of the present day is by implication either a Benthamite or a Coleridgean; holds views of human affairs which can only be proved true on the principles either of Bentham or of Coleridge.

Richards adds:

> What Mill says is still true—though we might change the labels again and say, "is either a Materialist or an Idealist." It may be argued that these two opposite-seeming types of outlook are complementary to one another: that, in the history of thought they have been dependent upon one another so that the death of one would lead by inanition to the death of the other; that as expiration is only one phase in breathing so the two philosophies in their endless antagonism are a necessary conjoint self-critical process. But, since to hold neither is to have no view to offer, opposition requires a temporary choice between them. I write then as a Materialist trying to interpret before you the utterances of an extreme Idealist and you, whatever you be by birth or training, Aristotelian or Platonist, Benthamite or Coleridgean, Materialist or Idealist, have to reinterpret my remarks again in your turn.

Two other thinkers, who although little referred to since *The Meaning of Meaning*, have substantially marked Richards, are the neglected American philosopher Charles Sanders Peirce and the anthropologist Bronislaw Malinowski. In *The Meaning of Meaning* the authors note on the first page that Peirce might have solved the problem of meaning in advance of their work had he not been prevented by "penury," and in an appendix they summarize the fantastic and wonderful account of signs he did achieve, with its division into ten principal classes of signs: (1) Qualisigns; (2) Iconic Sinsigns; (3) Iconic Legisigns; (4) Vestiges or Rhematic Indexical Sinsigns; (5) Proper Names, or Rhematic Indexical Legisigns; (6) Rhematic Symbols; (7) Dicent Sinsigns (as a portrait with a legend);

(8) Dicent Indexical Legisigns; (9) Propositions, or Dicent Symbols; (10) Arguments; as well as miscellaneous Semes, Phemes, and Delomes. Without the death-defying terminology, Richards has taken over a good deal of the thinking behind these classifications (as have the logical positivists, along with some of the terms themselves), and in *Basic Rules of Reason* he identifies Peirce as a "very great authority."

Also in *The Meaning of Meaning* the authors quote from Malinowski's work on verbal magic among the Trobrianders, and print as a Supplement to the book a brief essay by Malinowski on "The Problem of Meaning in Primitive Languages," with the explanation:

> To Dr. Malinowski the authors owe a very special debt. His return to England as their work was passing through the press enabled them to enjoy the advantage of his many years of reflection as a field-worker in Ethnology on the peculiarly difficult border-lands of linguistics and psychology. His unique combination of practical experience with a thorough grasp of theoretical principles renders his agreement on so many of the more heterodox conclusions here reached particularly encouraging. The contribution from his pen dealing with the study of primitive languages, which appears as a Supplement, will, the writers feel sure, be of value not only to ethnologists but to all who take a living interest in words and their ways.

The Malinowski essay itself is a tremendously significant document, and one of the concepts it introduced, "phatic communion" (for that aspect of language which signifies nothing but cements relationship between speaker and hearer), has had widespread influence. Richards's view, in *Coleridge on Imagination*, of critical evaluation as largely "social communion" is merely a rephrasing of the Malinowski concept.

Richards's relationship to John Dewey constitutes a real problem. So far as I know, he quotes him only once, fleetingly, in *The Meaning of Meaning*, mentions him scornfully in *Basic in Teaching*, and has never given any evidence of familiarity with Dewey's work. (If he is unfamiliar with Dewey, it would be merely another melancholy evidence of the tendency in even the most widely read English critics—Caudwell is another example—to slight significant American thought.) On the other hand, Ogden was quoting seriously from Dewey as early as 1926, in *The Meaning of Psychology*, and it is extremely doubtful, particularly with Richards's years in America and his great philosophic interest, and Dewey's Gifford lectureship in Edinburgh, that Richards could have missed contact with Dewey's thought completely. In any case, as noted above, Richards's basic contribution in *Principles*, the view that revolutionized criticism and began its modern movement, that the æsthetic experience is like any other human experience, is a restatement of a view with which Dewey has become identified. As early as 1903, in *Studies in Logical Theory*, Dewey had invaded the realm of intellectual activity, including the æsthetic, with the essential scientific principle of "continuity," writing:

> This point of view knows no fixed distinction between the empirical values of unreflective life and the most abstract process of rational thought. It knows no fixed gulf between the highest flight of theory and control of the details of practical construction and behavior. It passes, according to the occasion and opportunity of the moment, from the attitude of loving and struggling and doing to that of thinking and the reverse. Its contents or material shift their values back and forth from technological or utilitarian to esthetic, ethic or affectional. . . . The fundamental assumption is *continuity* in and of experience.

(Dewey claimed, in *Logic: The Theory of Inquiry*, in 1938, that Peirce had preceded him in calling attention "to the principle of the continuum of inquiry," but it would take a more intrepid explorer of Peirce's writings than myself to find the spot. Richards may very well, however, have found it in Peirce and thus short-circuited the Dewey influence.)

The principal influence on Richards (making for a relationship of particular complexity because it is difficult to know in any instance which way the influence is going) is that of his collaborator, Charles Kay Ogden. Ogden is, or was, a psychologist of great influence and versatility, relatively unknown in this country, and, like Richards, one of the great encyclopedic minds. His own psychology, in *The Meaning of Psychology* (and its abbreviation, *The A B C of Psychology*) is "centrist," a tremendous eclectic synthesis of the most fruitful modern theories and data. Much of Ogden's work has been synthetic and introductory in this fashion. He has been the editor of the distinguished International Library of Psychology, Philosophy and Scientific Method, which has made available some of the best books by all schools in these fields and others, including important works of literary criticism. At the same time he has edited the History of Civilization series, *Psyche, An Annual Review of General and Applied Psychology*, and the Psyche Miniatures, a series of cheap (they used to be 2/6) and valuable little books similar to the larger ones in the International Library; a series that in its early years specialized in medicine and in recent years has specialized in books relating to Basic English. In all four of these media, with imagination and impartiality, Ogden has given a forum to almost every serious modern scientific or near-scientific view. Meanwhile he has written almost a dozen books of his own or in collaboration, including a brief history of the world, with E. H. Carter, for the Nelson Classics series, and has maintained an active interest in literature, particularly in James

Joyce (Ogden wrote the preface to a section of *Finnegans Wake* published as *Tales Told of Shem and Shaun,* and translated the *Anna Livia Plurabelle* section into Basic in *transition*). He was founder and editor of the *Cambridge Magazine,* which Richards calls "in its day the most exciting weekly in England," and Richards also reports, in *Basic English and Its Uses,* that Ogden is "an active man of affairs with more varied dealings than anyone but himself ever knows," as well as "a connoisseur of wide range" and "a wit—justly celebrated for the extravagance, the absurdity, and the mordancy of his flashes." It is no wonder that when this paragon turned his learning and varied talents on the new edition of the *Encyclopædia Britannica* in 1925, in a review for the *Saturday Review of Literature,* he was able to tear it apart page by page.

At the same time, while engaged in all these activities from 1920 on, he has given his *chief* energies to Basic English. From 1920, when he and Richards first realized the possibilities of a limited-vocabulary English in the course of writing their definitions for *The Meaning of Meaning,* to 1929, when Ogden published his first Basic word-list in *Psyche,* he worked out the theoretical structure of the language and selected its vocabulary. In 1930, in *Basic English,* he published the full system, making a few alterations in his first word-list. During the thirties he edited the *Basic Dictionary,* and, through his Orthological Institute in London, issued series of classics translated into Basic, ranging from the Bible to *Black Beauty,* and various works propagandizing for, popularizing, and extending Basic: *Brighter Basic, Basic for Business, A Basic Astronomy,* etc. In most of this Richards has been his co-worker, although Richards gives Ogden sole credit in *How to Read a Page* for posing the problem, doing the researches, and inventing the language. In all their collaborations, over a quarter of a century, from *The Foundations of Æsthetics* to the latest Basic work, there is no way to tell which ideas, emphases, or parts of the material derive from which of them. It can be presumed, with no actual evidence, that Ogden influenced Richards toward psychology, Bentham, and Basic; and that Richards influenced Ogden toward literature, Coleridge, and Basic in teaching. The only concrete conclusion one can make in a study of Richards, however, is that Richards's contribution to criticism would be different, although it is impossible to say where, and probably less, although it is impossible to say how much, had he and Ogden never met.

The problem of the men Richards has influenced is a good deal easier. In the field of literary criticism he has influenced everyone. Richards's role in inaugurating modern criticism has already been discussed above. One of the first men in this country to give him a sympathetic reading and come under his influence was, reasonably enough, the poet Conrad Aiken, who had made the same basic revolutionary statement *Principles* made in his own *Scepticisms* five years before, in 1919; and who, with a comparable audience, influence, and documentation, would undoubtedly himself have begun the modern critical movement. In *Scepticisms*, subtitled *Notes on Contemporary Poetry* and consisting of a series of periodical pieces, mostly on specific poets, Aiken wrote of Freud's work (with which, unlike most, he was thoroughly and early familiar): "It started with the admirable predicate that after all poetry is a perfectly human product, and that therefore it must play a specific part in the human animal's functional needs." Later in the book, even more completely: "Shall we never learn that there is nothing mysterious or supernatural about poetry; that it is a natural, organic product, with discoverable functions, clearly open to analysis? It would be a pity if our critics and poets were to leave this to the scientists instead of doing it themselves." When Richards's *Principles* appeared, in 1924, Aiken reviewed it enthusiastically and with a rare sense of its importance. This apparently so impressed Richards that when the second edition appeared in 1926 with two new appendices, the first of these, On Value, was a debate with "a friendly reviewer, Mr. Conrad Aiken," which amounts to almost the only notice Richards has ever taken of any of his critical colleagues in America.

The influence of Richards on his pupil and chief disciple, William Empson, and on R. P. Blackmur, has already been discussed above (in the chapters devoted to their work). His other major effect has been on Kenneth Burke. Richards, along with his principal sources, Bentham, Peirce, and Coleridge, has exercised an enormous influence on Burke, but since the *Principles* it has been in large part an influence to go and do differently. In his first book, *Counter-Statement*, Burke attacks Richards's nominalist rejection of Platonic archetypes without mentioning him by name. His next book, *Permanence and Change*, acknowledges its particular indebtedness to *The Meaning of Meaning*, quotes *Mencius on the Mind* to corroborate a point of his own, takes elaborate issue with Richards's concept of "pseudo-statements" in *Science and Poetry* (quoting *Principles* against it), and in general uses Richards as a jumping-off point for his own observations. In *Attitudes toward History* Burke similarly attacks Richards's *Philosophy of Rhetoric* for slighting the "substance" and social function of words, again quoting Richards's early work against him. In *The Philosophy of Literary Form* and *A Grammar of Motives* he takes off similarly from a number of Richards's insights, and in "The Five Master Terms" he criticizes *How to Read a Page* sharply for lacking any sort of "hub."

The book that chiefly influenced Burke, which he quotes from continually and has several times identified as one of the two or three most fertile modern works on literature, is *Principles of Literary Criticism*. From it he derived a number of his concepts, particularly the concept of the incipient action inherent in attitudes. In general, Burke's chief criticism of Richards is his tendency to slight the "symbolic" and "realistic" elements in language and art, the qualities that Burke calls "dream" and "chart" in his dream-prayer-chart triad, while particularly emphasizing the "prayer" or communicative elements. In practice this has led to an effective division of labor, in that Burke himself has tended particularly to emphasize the realistic and symbolic elements, especially the latter; so that the men who are (to my mind at least) the two foremost contemporary literary critics have respectively specialized in art-as-communication and art-as-expression and, between the two of them, have pretty well licked the platter clean.

One more critic influenced by Richards, largely unknown in this country, warrants discussion. He is George H. W. Rylands, a Cambridge fellow like Empson, who published *Words and Poetry*, an expansion of his fellowship dissertation, in 1928. The influence of Richards is very marked, although he is directly referred to only once, as banning the word "beautiful" from criticism, and Rylands is presumably another of his students. *Words and Poetry* is a study of poetic diction as an aspect of style, the first part exploring the general nature of poetic diction, the second part studying Shakespeare's usages in some detail. The general assumptions are Richards's, even to the imagery of "employing the microscope" on poetry, and criticism as "pulling the toy to pieces," and the method tends to be pre-Empsonian, the limited exploration of ambiguities. The book is unusually stimulating and suggestive and anticipates a number of later techniques, among them Blackmur's cataloguing of word usage, Spurgeon's tracing of imagery, and Burke's exploration of cognate musicality. As a finished performance, however, it is fragmentary and disappointing, not really comparable to Empson's or Richards's own work. It is a valuable demonstration, however, that Richards's critical framework, focused on a text, will pay off in any chosen area of investigation; and turned on Shakespeare in particular will invariably produce material that conventional scholarship has failed to unearth.

In England almost no contemporary critic has written without being touched by Richards at some point, and a few of these influences besides Empson and Rylands might be noted. T. S. Eliot, in general disagreement with Richards, has, among other things, more or less accepted his view of the irrelevance of "belief" to poetry and has a long note to "Dante" in *Selected Essays*, expressing qualified assent to that view and qualified dissent to the concept of "pseudo-statements" in *Science and Poetry*. In *The Use of Poetry and the Use of Criticism*, he devotes a chapter, "The Modern Mind," largely to quarreling with Richards's view of poetry as a type of spiritual exercise, while generally conceding his great

value, chiefly as an investigator of "systematised misunderstanding."
Herbert Read, while also, from his very different romantic position,
quarreling with the values Richards finds in poetry, has adopted many
of his specific concepts and insights. F. R. Leavis, like the whole *Scrutiny*
group, has been shaped to a great extent by Richards's work and in his
earlier books quotes, uses, and praises him continually, expressing almost
no disagreement. His review of *Coleridge on Imagination* in *Scrutiny*,
March 1935, is, however, a bitter attack on Richards for social and
political evasion in his criticism, and since then Leavis has been somewhat emancipated.[2] L. C. Knights, who never climbed out so far on the
limb, has felt no necessity to climb back and continues quietly quoting
and using Richards without any fundamental commitment to his values.
Stephen Spender confesses in the Introduction to his *The Destructive
Element* that it was inspired (as well as titled) by a Richards's footnote
on Eliot, and the book picks up Richards again and again in its central
discussion of the relation between poetry and belief. Elsie Elizabeth
Phare, who began her *The Poetry of Gerard Manley Hopkins* while a
student at Cambridge, in it acknowledges Richards's "help and encouragement," and quotes both Empson and Richards extensively.

By two young English critics now resident in America, David Daiches
and Eric Bentley, both very much indebted to the early Richards, he has
been repaid with, respectively, Daiches's enthusiastic account of his
significance and influence in *Books That Changed Our Minds*, and Bentley's
cruel and intemperate attack in the *Rocky Mountain Review*, Winter 1944.
Aside from Bentley's petulance, the sharpest attack Richards has received came from the brilliant English Marxist critic, Alick West. West
devotes a chapter of *Crisis and Criticism* to proving that Richards's work
is vitiated by its attempt to isolate poetry from social action and that his
own reading is inhibited by "the worst kind of stock response," social
conservatism. (It is interesting to note, however, that younger Marxist
critics, following Caudwell's example, are calling for a rapprochement
with Richards. A young poet, Hubert Nicholson, writing to *Our Time*,
May 1944, to attack the idiocies of F. J. Klingender, proposed that
Marxists would do well to pay more attention to Richards's work on
the nature and values of the art-experience, and a number of the contributors to the *Modern Quarterly* would seem to be following his advice.)
Almost the only contemporary British critic of prominence, in fact, who
seems largely unaffected by Richards's work is the passionately eclectic
G. Wilson Knight, who mentions him only once, fleetingly, to my

---

[2] In *Education & the University* (1943), after warning against Empson's "extremely
mixed and uneven book," *Seven Types of Ambiguity*, he identifies Richards's work as
"another mixed provision of the stimulating and the aberrant that the student will
inevitably come across and could with profit be helped to make some critical use of."

knowledge. (Richards once identified Knight as an example of the building of elaborate theories on treacherous terms, which may be the explanation.)

Richards's influence on American critics besides Burke, Blackmur, and
Aiken has been fully as pervasive. In *The Achievement of T. S. Eliot*
F. O. Matthiessen acknowledges a special obligation to Richards (along
with Edmund Wilson!) for "stimulus and challenge during the past
several years," and the book is informed with Richards's insights
throughout, particularly from *Practical Criticism*, which Matthiessen
calls his "most matured discussion of poetry and belief." *American Renaissance* continues and extends Matthiessen's general use of it and the
other books. All of the Southern group have been greatly affected by
Richards's work: Cleanth Brooks relies on it throughout *Modern Poetry
and the Tradition* and even more heavily in *The Well Wrought Urn*;
Warren uses him in his Coleridge study and elsewhere; and Ransom and
Tate, who have written on Richards most fully (Ransom in an essay in
The World's Body and a long section of *The New Criticism*, Tate in two
essays in *Reason in Madness*), have been in general agreement on strongly
attacking his early positivist bias (Tate using terms like "cheat") while
enthusiastically accepting many of his methods and conclusions.

Herbert Muller's *Modern Fiction* is in great part the application, thinly,
of some of Richards's ideas in *The Meaning of Meaning* and the *Principles*,
although he too boggles at "pseudo-statements" (of all the critics who
have used Richards, including the later Richards, only Cleanth Brooks
and F. R. Leavis seem to have been able to take it down without gagging). Muller's *Science and Criticism* makes a somewhat more restrained
use of Richards, if still substantial, and praises him patronizingly in
general, while specifically charging him with too narrow psychology,
neglect for the social context of poetry, and "loss in sharpness and
suggestiveness" in the later work. In *Matthew Arnold*, Lionel Trilling
makes use of Richards as he makes use of almost every aspect of modern
criticism, very gingerly, so stating the concept of "pseudo-statements,"
for example, that it is impossible to say whether he accepts it or not,
and in *E. M. Forster* he quotes some of Richards's statements on Forster
almost as noncommittally. Mark Schorer has made substantial and perceptive use of Richards, particularly of *Science and Poetry* and *Coleridge*,
in his *William Blake*. The list could be extended indefinitely. Of the
principal American critics, only Yvor Winters, like Knight abroad, seems
to have been almost entirely unaffected by his work.

The general pattern that emerges is of Richards marking almost
every serious critic working in our time; yet with almost none of them,
except for confessed disciples like Empson, expressing any sort of un-
qualified agreement with him, and with most of them attacking him

bitterly on specific or general issues. At one end of the scale, Richards in the popular mind is a "nut" (he mentions in *The Philosophy of Rhetoric* getting a substantial and as yet endless fan-mail from unmistakable lunatics on *The Meaning of Meaning*); at the other end of the scale, to our best critics, he is somehow the source of great insight and remarkable error. It seems unlikely that Richards can be as fruitful as he has been and still be as wrong as they think. The men who have taken over his terms and techniques with the conviction that at the same time they can repudiate his ideas about literature are the victims of a fallacy: his terms and techniques *are* his ideas about literature. No rotten apple-tree could bear fruit as sound as this one has seemingly borne.

A few aspects of Richards's work still remain to be discussed. One of the most unpredictable of them is his great interest in the Orient. He was Visiting Professor at Tsing Hua University in Peking, China, during 1929 and 1930, teaching Basic English, studying Chinese thought, and working on his book on Mencius. He was in Peking again in 1937, and between those dates seems to have been responsible for getting Empson to teach in the Orient. Richards has been greatly interested in Chinese thought, however, particularly that of Confucius, from the beginning. Eliot notes in *The Use of Poetry and the Use of Criticism* that Confucius has succeeded in making strange bedfellows. He writes:

> In passing, it is worthy of remark that Mr. Richards shares his interest in Chinese philosophy with Mr. Ezra Pound and with the late Irving Babbitt. An investigation of an interest common to three apparently quite different thinkers would, I believe, repay the labour. It seems to indicate, at least, a deracination from the Christian tradition. The thought of these three men seems to me to have an interesting similarity.

Richards's first book, *The Foundations of Æsthetics*, begins and ends with quotations from the *Chung Yung*, the Doctrine of Equilibrium and Harmony, which are in fact the summation of the authors' theories and the point of the book. In his subsequent books Richards has quoted Confucius, Mencius, Chuang Tzu, and others regularly, and in *Mencius on the Mind*, naturally, tackled Chinese thought at full length, including a forty-four-page Appendix of it in the original characters. Some idea of how important Chinese thought seems to him can be had from the fact that one of his Communications in *Partisan Review*, a letter of a page and a half, is prefaced with an epigraph from Chuang Tzu, probably the only letter to an American magazine ever so prefaced. Without delving into the reasons for Richards's attachment, one might note offhand that the characteristic moderation and balance of Chinese thought might very reasonably have an attraction for a thinker devoted to reconciling (as Richards has at one time or another admitted to doing): Aristotle and Plato, Bentham and Coleridge, materialism and idealism, realism and nominalism, anti-positivism and positivism, naturalism and supernaturalism.

It is this devotion to reconciling dialectic opposites, to the concept exemplified by *Practical Criticism* whereby truth emerges out of opposing errors, that has made Richards's characteristic method what he has at various times called multiple definition, multiple translation, and multiple interpretation (and which we would call "plural meaning"). Each of his books operates as a kind of symposium, in which many opposing views are allowed to play out their drama. *The Foundations of Æsthetics* centers on a classified and interpreted listing of every serious definition of "beauty" ever made. *The Meaning of Meaning* substantially repeats the tabulated form of his classification and does the same sort of job on the word "meaning," as well as creating every key term by multiple definition, English-to-English translation. *Principles of Literary Criticism* relies heavily on compiling other people's definitions of the matters Richards is discussing and out of them dredging his own, as in his famous definition of a "poem." *Practical Criticism*, as has been noted above, is a completely dialectic or dramatistic symposium. *Mencius on the Mind* gives multiple interpretations to passages all the way from Mencius to Herbert Read, as well as compiling multiple readings for terms like "beauty," "knowledge," "truth," and "order." *Coleridge on Imagination* does the same thing for "imagination."

All Richards's books involving Basic center in multiple distinctions or definitions of key words in Basic. Not only is *Interpretation in Teaching*, like *Practical Criticism*, a symposium of protocols, but in it Richards himself furnishes multiple translations of apparently simple sentences. One can see the same phenomenon in an even more striking form in Richards's obsessive use of epigraphs (somewhat exaggerated in the *Partisan Review* letter). *The Meaning of Meaning* begins with eleven on the page facing page 1, and each chapter opens with two or three more. Almost every chapter in every book Richards has written begins with from one to three new epigraphs. The result of this is to make Richards's work, incidentally, almost an anthology of the best of man's thought. When one realizes that this is precisely what Ogden has labored to do systematically, for at least modern thought, in his synthetic psychology, in the International Library of Psychology, Philosophy and Scientific Method, in the History of Civilization series, in *Psyche*, in the Psyche Miniatures, in the Basic Library, and others, one gets a sense of how tremendous the joint resources are that are now being funneled through the relatively narrow neck of Basic. The credo of Richards and Ogden has always been: from the play of opposing thought, truth will emerge. This is a good deal more generally satisfactory than the current: from the play of opposing thought truth will emerge if it can be easily translated into 850 great words.

This leads us directly into the problem, for Richards as a literary critic, of his preoccupation with Basic English. To put it bluntly, there seems to be no way of reconciling the two, and to the extent that he continues working with Basic he renounces criticism and abdicates his position as our foremost living critic. The concept of Basic in Criticism, as noted above in the Empson chapter, seems to be at its best superfluous and at its worst a fraud, and even in the hands of Richards and Empson it has produced no critical insights particularly worth having. Empson reluctantly admits that poetry cannot be written in Basic because poetry needs complex verbs. By the same token we might say that criticism too needs complex verbs. Art is a dialectic *action*, as everyone from Aristotle to Richards has known, and equally criticism is a dialectic *action*, as everyone from Aristotle to Richards has known, and as Richards in particular has devoted all his works to establishing. Actions are verbs and take verbs to describe them. Basic, on the other hand, is the language of nouns, the language of *states* or *stasis*, in which nouns carry all the meaning and verbs are skimped as much as possible. (The seeds of this self-defeating emphasis, we can see now, were present as early as *The Foundation of Æsthetics* when, after presenting their definition of beauty all along in terms of experiences, a synæsthetic equilibrium of opposed implicit *actions*, Ogden and Richards conclude with it as conducive to a *state* of synæsthetic equilibrium.) As this new emphasis develops in Basic, it is accompanied by a shift from Aristotle to Plato, from the real action to the ideal state; and along with it, reasonably, from Aristotle's valuation of poetry to Plato's. To what extent Richards has recognized any of this it is impossible to say. He has, however, taken at least one concrete step to solve the conflict. For almost a decade, except for one or two brief aberrations, he has given up the writing of literary criticism.

What Richards is left with is the teaching function, once peripheral to his work and now central. Once it was poetry that would "save us"; now it is education, "the greatest of human efforts." Where *Practical Criticism* aimed a glancing blow at the teaching profession, furnishing things to make its members "ponder" (in one sense, it was even the professor's long pent-up "practical" joke on his students), *Interpretation in Teaching* is a contribution to "the library of pedagogics." One type of writing is missing from that "library," Richards writes:

> The literature namely which would describe plainly and candidly actual procedures followed by teachers in correcting or discussing

the compositions of their pupils, and detail the explanation they venture to give of their corrections. The technical journals of the teaching profession compare extremely badly with those of dentistry in this respect. They bulge with repetitive discussions of principles, but where can we find case-histories detailing the treatment recommended for a given confused paragraph? The dentist is ready to tell his *confrères* how he rights a rotting tooth. The teacher seems as yet oddly unwilling to confess in equal detail how he criticizes a bad essay. To do so is of course to invite comment that may be disconcerting, but the man of faith will not flinch from that. The literature that would result if studies of interesting confusions and misunderstandings became as regular features in the professional literature as descriptions of procedures are in the dental journals would soon revolutionize practice. We should begin to profit, as dentists have long been profiting, from one another's mistakes.

From the Richards who set out bravely "to make a general revival of poetry possible" to the Richards comparing "interesting" ways to fix a rotting tooth is indeed a come-down. Some sense of the shift in scale that has followed inevitably from the shift in focus comes in seeing Richards contributing (1940) to educational monographs on *Reading and Pupil Development*, or competing with Mortimer Adler and the idiocy of "A Hundred Great Books" and *How to Read a Book* (which recommended his work with the reservation that he didn't show "how to read a *whole* book") by furnishing the counter-idiocy of "A Hundred Great Words" and *How to Read a Page* (which "suggests that their [the Adler group's] recommendations may not go to the root of the problem").

Richards is a man of tremendous, almost unequaled breadth of learning. Not only is he thoroughly familiar with the dozen fields mentioned above that he has staked out as his own, but he has invaded almost every other area of knowledge. To make a minor point, he is apt not only to quote theoretical physics with authority, but to quote Lenin's *Materialism and Empirio-Criticism* against it with equal authority. At the same time the very breadth of his knowledge has resulted in an inability to hold to a consistent point of view at any given time. A relativism with the idea that every point of view is somewhat right results inevitably in the corollary that no point of view can be entirely right. Richards has always had a curiously dilettantish irresponsibility toward ideas (an aspect of the same irresponsibility that could footnote *The Meaning of Meaning* with "darky anecdotes" in questionable taste). This is social irresponsibility in a larger sense, not touched or redeemed by the more limited extreme social responsibility, even dedication, of bringing culture and world government and peace to the world by devoting one's life to education and Basic English. In this larger sense, even the most responsible panacea is irresponsible in that it fundamentally scorns a world too large and complex to be cured by any one panacea.

Poetry, although it was to "save us," was never that sort of panacea for Richards. It included all the complexity and contradiction of the world, and the critic's function was, through love and effort, to increase the general ability to experience it at its fullest, not to simplify it or translate it down. Richards was always, even at his most scientific, the supreme example of the man saved by personal qualifications from the rigidities of his own method (a typically English phenomenon of which Maud Bodkin and Caudwell are lesser examples). The ultimate result of all the machinery of *The Meaning of Meaning*, as noted above, was to be a restoration of the conditions "under which a general revival of poetry would be possible." By making poetry more "efficient," by furthering its enjoyment "at many levels," *Principles* aimed at a *better* poetry, *better* experienced. As requirements of the critic, along with "a capacity for dispassionate psychological analysis," *Science and Poetry* insists on "a *passionate* knowledge of poetry." When *Furioso* (Spring 1940) printed a 1938 letter from Richards to his former pupil Richard Eberhart about Eberhart's poem "A Meditation," it was straight constructive technical criticism, the sort of thing one poet might write to another, full of a "passionate" knowledge of and concern for poetry. The outstanding impression a reader gets from the Princeton lecture on "The Interaction of Words" (Richards's last textual criticism of a poem, so far as I know) is how terribly important and wonderful Donne's "First Anniversary" is to Richards.

The men who have criticized Richards most sharply (with rare exceptions) have always ended with a tribute to his personal qualifications and sensitivity to poetry. "An admirable critic whose love and knowledge of poetry are incontestable," Blackmur writes. "His great intellectual powers, his learning, his devotion to poetry—a devotion somewhat frustrated but as marked fifteen years ago as now—are qualities of an intellectual honesty rare in any age," Tate writes. "The main tendency of his thought was to bring art into vital relation with other major interests, and thereby to make for more freedom and fullness of life," Herbert Muller concludes. "Mr. Richards has done as much as any man in our time to stimulate a clear and honest interest in poetry," Arthur Mizener writes, in the course of a particularly sharp attack (*Southern Review*, Autumn 1939) and concludes: "Mr. Richards at his best is incomparable." Just as there has been general utilization of his criticism and general quarreling with his ideas, so has there been general praise for the man himself. His character, intelligence, sensibility, and humor, it is agreed, have saved his criticism from every danger it has faced.

We can only hope that they will save it now from the latest and most pernicious danger, renunciation in favor of saving the world by panacea. If they fail, and if Richards never returns to the criticism of literature, we shall still have, in his early books, work to rank with the finest of our time, as well as a whole dazzling body of work stemming out of it. Those are in no danger.

CHAPTER 12

KENNETH BURKE

and the Criticism of Symbolic Action

IF, AS Kenneth Burke has sometimes insisted, a book is the indefinite expansion of one sentence, then a critical method is only the securing of material to document that sentence. Actually, Burke has a number of sentences—that is, a number of methods—in each of his books, but if he had to stand or fall by one sentence it would probably be: Literature is symbolic action. To use his own stress-shifting technique, his earlier work emphasized it as *symbolic* action, his later work as symbolic *action*. With a kind of limitless fertility Burke has done everything in criticism's bag of tricks, including several things he put there, but the choice is either to let him represent every aspect of modern criticism, in which case he has written your book for you, or else to restrict him arbitrarily to that critical area, symbolic expression, in which he has particularly specialized, with the additional factor that it is something no one else covers adequately. In his essay "The Problem of the Intrinsic," reprinted as an appendix to *A Grammar of Motives*, Burke is incautious enough to write: "I began by speaking of the three fields: Grammar, Rhetoric, and Symbolic. It is perhaps only in the third of these categories that modern criticism has something vitally new to offer the student of literature." This is not true (even hedged by the word "vitally"), as his own work demonstrates, but it does point at the tremendous shock of novelty in Burke's studies of symbolic action, so that anyone reading him for the first time has the sudden sense of a newly discovered country in his own backyard.

Burke's first book of criticism, *Counter-Statement*, published in 1931, set up most of the principles and procedures he later developed, termed "counter" because they were then (as always) a minority view. The book is a collection of essays, some of them revised periodical pieces, dealing with general literary problems, including the political program implicit in his æsthetic, and with specific writers: Flaubert, Pater, de Gourmont, Mann, and Gide. The concept of symbolic action is as yet undeveloped, but Burke makes constant glancing suggestions of it: Gide's concern with homosexuality made him a political liberal by training "his sense of divergence," Gourmont's "paper" transgressions resulted from his leprosy and seclusion, the biographer "symbolizes" his own problems in choosing to write of Napoleon, and so on. Some of the techniques later developed for studying symbolic action are also suggested, particularly the contextual associations of imagery, as when he notes the malevolent contexts of the word "future" in Shakespeare, in contrast to its confident use in Browning, and the power of "demon" in Keats, opposed to its innocuousness in Tennyson.

The book's chief concern, however, is with rhetoric, and its dichotomous terms are concerned with demarcating rhetoric from grammar: "pamphleteering" versus "inquiry," "declamatory" versus "realistic," "the psychology of form" versus "the psychology of information," with no third term for "symbolic." In fact, Burke's insistence in the book that art is not experience, but *something added* to experience, puts the emphasis in opposition to the concept of symbolic action, but then in a modification, attacking the concept of vulgar economic causation, he presents the germ of the later view. He writes:

> In one sense, art or ideas do "reflect" a situation, since they are a way of dealing with a situation. When a man solves a problem, however, we should hardly say that his solution is "caused" by the problem to be solved. The problem may limit somewhat the *nature* of his solution, but the problem can remain unsolved forever unless he *adds* the solution. Similarly, the particular ways of feeling and seeing which the thinker or the artist develops to cope with a situation, the vocabulary they bring into prominence, the special kinds of intellectual and emotional adjustment which their works make possible by the discovery of appropriate symbols for encompassing the situation, the kinds of action they stimulate by their attitudes towards the situation, are not "caused" by the situation which they are designed to handle.

Here, minus the military metaphor, is the whole concept of works of art as "strategies" for encompassing situations; that is, symbolic action. Besides its great importance for developing the concept of rhetoric in art and its hints of the later symbolic, *Counter-Statement* is chiefly interesting for the passion of its concern with art. "The Status of Art" is an elaborate *Apologie for Poetrie* against subtler detractors than Sidney or Shelley had to cope with; "Thomas Mann and André Gide" is an exercise in scrupulosity that spends ten pages erecting an ethical distinction between them and then demolishes it as oversimple; "Program," "Lexicon Rhetoricæ," and "Applications of the Terminology" are an ironic triptych the parts of which, respectively, set the aims of the good life as Burke sees them, define the concepts that underlie the program, and apply them to problems of art.

Burke's next critical book, *Permanence and Change*, subtitled *An Anat-*

omy of Purpose, appeared in 1935. It is the least "literary" of his books, although precisely how it would classify is hard to say: as social psychology, social history, philosophy, moral possibility, "secular conversion," or what. Its central concern is, as with Burke's latest book, "purpose" (that is, "motives," the situations underlying "attitudes" and "strategies"). The book's three sections are: "On Interpretation," a survey of "criticism" in areas of life rather than art; "Perspective by Incongruity," an exploration of the metaphoric nature of strategies and systems of meaning; and "The Basis of Simplification," Burke's own sketch for a critical frame that would clarify and resolve the confusions he has discussed earlier. Thus, it is a book about society and social communication, but its key metaphor (what Burke would later call its "representative anecdote") is Man as Artist, and it treats social problems in terms of poetic and critical techniques (characteristically, its topic sentence is "All living things are critics"—a greater democratization of criticism than Burke's namesake Edmund ever planned—and its last section states: "all men are poets"). Fittingly, most of what Burke has to say about symbolic action in the book comes in the "Perspective by Incongruity" section. He notes that felling a noble tree (a theme that has always particularly interested him) may be a symbolic parricide; that Darwin's intense attacks of vertigo, like Joyce's blindness, would seem to be the symbolic self-punishment for the "impiety" of his work; that acts from mountain-climbing and bull-fighting to empire-building contain substantial symbolic ingredients; that McDougall's integration-dissociation psychology, analogically related to the structure of the British Empire, is actually a projection of it, and would be particularly curative for British patients. Despite these frequent symbolic readings, the concept of works of art as strategies has not yet coalesced, and the book tends to use the term "strategy" simply to mean a trick, so that rationalizing one's motives as diplomatically as possible is "strategic."

The central concept of *Permanence and Change* is the concept of perspective by incongruity, or metaphor, the seeing of one thing in terms of something that, to a greater or lesser extent, it is not. Burke writes:

> Indeed, as the documents of science pile up, are we not coming to see that whole works of scientific research, even entire schools, are hardly more than the patient repetition, in all its ramifications, of a fertile metaphor? Thus we have, at different eras in history, considered man as the son of God, as an animal, as a political and economic brick, as a machine, each such metaphor, and a hundred others, serving as the cue for an unending line of data and generalizations.

"Perspective by incongruity," as Burke defines it, is a method he first noted in Nietzsche and his pupil Spengler, the switching of a term from its natural context to another where it is revealing although impious, like speaking of Arabian Puritanism, or Eliot's phrase "decadent athleticism," or Veblen's term "trained incapacity." As Burke extends its application in the book, it eventually comes to include even concepts like "rebirth," the principal symbolic action in his later work:

> Once a set of new meanings is firmly established, we can often note in art another kind of regression: the artist is suddenly prompted to review the memories of his youth because they combine at once the qualities of strangeness and intimacy. Probably every man has these periods of rebirth, a new angle of vision whereby so much that he had forgot suddenly becomes useful or relevant, hence grows vivid again in his memory. Rebirth and perspective by incongruity are thus seen to be synonymous, a process of conversion, though such words as conversion and rebirth are usually reserved for only the most spectacular of such reorientations, the religious.

One of Burke's own characteristic perspectives by incongruity in the book, later developed into a major source of insight or irony, is etymology, going back to the root meanings of words for a fresh or "reborn" slant, as where he notes that "theory" means "vision of God," that "caricature" comes from a root meaning to "overload," that "property" and "propriety" "are not etymologically so close by mere accident."

Permanence and Change contains a good deal of general literary discussion, but its specific literary references tend to be incidental, used as examples or analogies, and not discussed in any detail. Burke refers glancingly to the Nietzschean symbol of the mountain in *The Magic Mountain*; some of Shakespeare's techniques of stylistic ingratiation; the planned incongruity of Hemingway's descriptions of violence in terms of Jane Austen delicacies; the inadequate exorcism of their private monsters in the work of Nietzsche and Swift; the "abyss-motif" in Eliot, Milton, and Hart Crane; Lawrence's "ethical universe-building." The only work of imaginative literature quoted from in the book and discussed at any length, curiously enough, is Edwin Seaver's sociological novel *The Company*, and no line of poetry is anywhere quoted.

Burke's next book, *Attitudes toward History* in 1937, is his most significant work in terms of symbolic action and will be discussed below at some length. *The Philosophy of Literary Form*, subtitled *Studies in Symbolic Action*, appeared in 1941 and might be considered almost a supplement of practical applications of the concepts in *Attitudes*. Except for the long title essay, the book is a collection of articles and reviews done in the preceding decade. The essays are united by their common concern with "speculation on the nature of linguistic, or symbolic, or literary action—and in a search for more precise ways of locating or defining such action," or, more generally, Burke's purpose is "to identify the substance of a particular literary act by a theory of literary action in general." In the course of this, Burke is centrally occupied with what he calls "strategies," related to the "attitudes" of his previous book (note the progress of his key metaphor from Man as Declaimer in *Counter-Statement*, to Man as Artist in *Permanence and Change*, Man as Gesturer in *Attitudes toward History*, and Man as Warrior in *The Philosophy of Literary Form*). The first page of the book begins by distinguishing between "strategies" and "situations":

> So I should propose an initial working distinction between "strategies" and "situations," whereby we think of poetry (I here use the term to include any work of critical or imaginative cast) as the adopting of various strategies for the encompassing of situations. These strategies size up the situations, name their structure and outstanding ingredients, and name them in a way that contains an attitude towards them.
>
> This point of view does not, by any means, vow us to personal or historical subjectivism. The situations are real; the strategies for handling them have public content; and in so far as situations overlap from individual to individual, or from one historical period to another, the strategies possess universal relevance.

In "Literature as Equipment for Living," an essay attempting to define a sociological criticism, Burke proposes the classification of sophisticated works of art in terms of the basic strategies he finds in proverbs: "strategies for selecting enemies and allies, for socializing losses, for warding off evil eye, for purification, propitiation, and desanctification, consolation and vengeance, admonition and exhortation, implicit commands or instructions of one sort or another."

These and other strategies are the basic symbolic actions of art. Burke defines the symbolic act as "the dancing of an attitude" and carefully distinguishes it from what we think of as the "real" act:[1]

> Still, there is a difference, and a radical difference, between building a house and writing a poem about building a house—and a poem about having children by marriage is not the same thing as having children by marriage. There are practical acts, and there are symbolic acts (nor is the distinction, clear enough in its extremes, to be dropped simply because there is a borderline area wherein many practical acts take on a symbolic ingredient, as one may buy a certain commodity not merely to use it, but also because its possession testifies to his enrollment in a certain stratum of society).

[1] Allen Tate has a wonderful reference in *Reactionary Essays* to a man who discovers oil under his land and, instead of digging, writes a poem saying: "O Oil, make me thy conduit!"

Burke classifies symbolic action on three levels: the bodily or biological, from insomnia to the over-all sensory experience of a poem (like the sense of drought in reading "The Ancient Mariner"); the personal or familistic, chiefly relations to parents and other "familiar" persons; and the abstract, as in symbolic enrollment or re-enrollment built around rebirth. As a way of getting around resistance to a term as dubious as "symbolic" (and, more seriously, of advancing toward a useful methodological criterion), Burke proposes the substitution of the ultra-respectable word "statistical," in the sense that the "statistical" inspection of a body of images or a body of works will reveal a trend of symbolic significance, whereas any isolated image or work might seem purely "practical." Thus a statistical study of associations and clusters will show the structure of motivation operating. Later in the same essay Burke lists a number of his "rules of thumb," techniques for studying poetic strategies that he uses throughout the book. They include isolating the basic "dramatic alignment" and obtaining its supplementary "equations" inductively from the work; charting associative clusters and structural relations; noting "critical points" or "watershed moments," especially beginnings, endings, peripeties, discontinuities, weaknesses of motivation, and particular strengths of dramatic organization; noting the imagery of "agon" or rebirth; and then, in all these classifications, introducing the "differentia" that gives each symbolic act in literature its unique character.

The chief new terms Burke produces in *The Philosophy of Literary Form* are the concepts of the "Power family" (used throughout, but only so named in the book's Introduction), whereby powers in all areas are related so that any one can do symbolic service for any other; and the naming of the three ingredients in art as: "dream," the symbolic factors; "prayer," the rhetorical factors; and "chart," the factors of realistic sizing up (which would probably coincide with "grammatical"). In terms of the "Power family," Burke is able to translate rapidly and efficiently from literary to non-literary areas and back again in terms of symbolic action, so that, as he says, "one may marry or rape by politics, wage war in argument, be mentally superior by the insignia of social privilege, bind or loose by knowledge, show one's muscle or enhance one's stature by financial income, etc." In terms of the dream-prayer-chart division, Burke is able to achieve a balance of symbolic, rhetorical, and grammatical emphasis in treating any given work (whereas before, in *Counter-Statement* and *Permanence and Change*, he had leaned particularly toward the rhetorical, and in *Attitudes* toward the symbolic).

At the same time Burke develops purely grammatical techniques of analysis (that is, not concerned particularly with either how the device affects the reader or how it expresses the poet, but simply with what it is and how it operates), as in his study "On Musicality in Verse," which explores subtle, almost unnoticeable phonetic effects in poetry, involving such things as cognate variation, augmentation, diminution, and chiasmus. The piece that Burke considers the "most complete" example of analysis focused on a single work in the book, "The Rhetoric of Hitler's Battle," is a balanced chart-dream-prayer analysis of *Mein Kampf:* showing in purely grammatical terms to what extent it reflected realities in Germany and the world situation, in symbolic terms to what extent it was Hitler's great evil poem, and in rhetorical terms to what extent and through what devices it captured the German people, thus ironically converting Hitler's already completed symbolic act of world domination into something that just missed being the real thing. Burke explores the relationship between these emphases, showing the way, for example, that a symbolic factor in Hitler, like the Jew as scapegoat, enters the work as a formal structure, produces a comparable symbolic action in the reader, and thus operates rhetorically to "convert." In thus emphasizing an understanding of the precise nature of Hitler's "snake-oil," valuable pragmatically in coping with it and native variants, Burke ends with the problem returned constructively from the symbolic to the real world.

Most of his studies, however, deal with a "purer" literature. In this book the literary discussion is central rather than peripheral as in *Permanence and Change*. He analyzes Coleridge, particularly "The Ancient Mariner," at great length, as dramatic ritual of major importance; discusses the *Eumenides* of Æschylus in detail to illustrate the sort of full poetic meaning he would oppose to "semantic" meaning; studies Iago's rhetoric as a caricature of the dramatist's art, and Antony's rhetoric as a triumph of it; explores two contemporary novels, Robert Penn Warren's *Night Rider* and John Steinbeck's *The Grapes of Wrath*, to demonstrate the analytic techniques he has listed as "rules of thumb"; and analyzes authors from Homer and Lucretius to Flaubert and Lewis Carroll in the course of exploring other critical problems. In the book's Appendix he includes reviews that demonstrate his critical practice on contemporary fiction, poetry, drama, and even paintings.

Burke's latest book, *A Grammar of Motives*, published in 1945, is the first volume of a gigantic trilogy, planned to include *A Rhetoric of Motives* and *A Symbolic of Motives*, which will be called something like *On Human Relations*. The aim of the whole series is no less than the comprehensive exploration of human motives and the forms of thought and expression built around them, and its ultimate object, expressed in the epigraph: "*Ad bellum purificandum*," is to eliminate the whole world of conflict that can be eliminated through understanding. The method or key metaphor for the study is "drama" or "dramatism," and the basic terms of analysis are the dramatistic pentad: Act, Scene, Agent, Agency, and Purpose. The *Grammar*, which Burke confesses in the Introduction grew from a prolegomena of a few hundred words to nearly 200,000, is a consideration of the purely internal relationship of these five terms, "their possibilities of transformation, their range of permutations and combinations," as reflected in statements about human motives, chiefly as expressed in "theological, metaphysical and juridical doctrines." The *Rhetoric* is to deal with the audience-effect aspect of utterances, drawing its material chiefly from "parliamentary and diplomatic devices, editorial bias, sales methods and incidents of social sparring"; and the *Symbolic* with the psychological-expression aspects, drawing its material principally from "the forms and methods of art."

It is not relevant to our topic here, nor within my competence, to discuss Burke's treatment of all the major philosophic views man has evolved, except to note that his aim is not to debunk or defend them, but to characterize or "place" them, to show which key terms they feature while slighting the others. "It is not my purpose at this late date merely to summarize and report on past philosophies," he writes. "Rather, I am trying to show how certain key terms might be used to 'call the plays' in any and all philosophies." This "placing" requires what Burke calls a "representative anecdote," a key metaphor, and he opens the book with the representative anecdote of the Creation (that is, God as Creator) and concludes it with political Constitutions (that is, Man as Constitutor), while the entire book is framed around Drama as the representative anecdote (Man as Acter or Actor—a great improvement at least in generality over such earlier metaphors as Man as Warrior). He notes that "modern war" would make an unwieldy anecdote, "since it is more of a *confusion* than a *form*," and that the characteristic scientific terminology that uses Man as Laboratory Animal as its representative anecdote is inevitably "reductive." In selecting Drama as his representative anecdote, Burke acquires a terminology and framework with which he can discuss anything from the closet-drama of a man tying his shoelace to the big-spectacle drama of Genesis.

Undismayed by the whole corpus of organized philosophic thought, Burke draws his analytic material from his usual widespread and informal sources, including the familiar introspective memories of his own behavior (he remembers first reading Santayana and dreaming "of a tourist life in white flannels along the Mediterranean"), and conjectures about his unconscious processes (in looking for "terms" that "grandly converge," he notes that he may have been inspired by thinking of "terminals" and "Grand Central"). He quotes, as usual, the revealing remarks, questions, even dreams, of his children, to illuminate the philosophers' problems; and leans heavily on his old etymological trick of casting light on a term by going back to its root meaning; noting, for example, that "investing" means that "one *clothes oneself* in the severe promises of future yield, *donning* the idealizations of what one would like to be, *dressing up* in the symbols of lien and bond."

For a book devoted to "placing" philosophies, the *Grammar* manages to spend a surprising amount of space on literature. It begins and ends on Ibsen (Burke has noted that beginnings and endings are particularly significant), illustrating the scene-act ratio in the opening pages with Ibsen's *An Enemy of the People* and concluding with an analysis of *Peer Gynt* to illustrate "essence." In the course of the book he draws on examples from Pope and Wordsworth to Caldwell, Hemingway, and Richard Wright, and studies the *Phædrus* at length to demonstrate dialectic transcendence.

After the publication of *The Philosophy of Literary Form* Ransom had suggested his doubts that the dramatistic method could handle lyric poetry. Picking up the challenge, Burke analyzes Shelley's "Ode to the West Wind" and Wordsworth's "Composed upon Westminster Bridge" as examples of incipient or arrested "action" in the text of the book, and includes three appendices illustrating the method in practice on various lyric forms: "The Problem of the Intrinsic," a general discussion of the dramatistic method in analyzing lyrics, in contrast to the disguised and unformulated dramatism of the neo-Aristotelian school; "Motives and Motifs in the Poetry of Marianne Moore," the method applied to a body of lyric poetry; and "Symbolic Action in a Poem by Keats," a remarkable tour de force following the development of the action in the "Ode on a Grecian Urn," which, like the essay on *Mein Kampf* in the previous book, is probably the best illustration of the detailed application of Burke's method in its totality.

A Grammar of Motives makes occasional rhetorical and symbolic readings, which Burke was apparently unable to resist, giving a substantial foretaste of what the *Rhetoric* and *Symbolic* will be like. By way of rhetorical meanings Burke notes that there are constant rhetorical motives behind the manipulations of the grammar (as where one deflects attention from an evil in society, the scene-act "ratio" or principle of determination, by situating it as a factor in people, the act-agent ratio); that "whatever speculation and investigation may precede Marxist assertions, there is the pressure to make them serviceable as a Rhetorical inducement to action on the part of people who have slight interest in speculation and investigation *per se*"; that legislatures adopt the "Hamletic" strategy of endless investigations to avoid embarrassing decisions; that "political platforms are best analyzed on the rhetorical level, as they are quite careless grammatically." By way of hints of the *Symbolic*, Burke notes: that "purely philosophic theories of power" may be inspired "by personal problems of potency"; that Henry Adams's *Education* is a rebirth ritual, and *Murder in the Cathedral* a purification ritual; that

Arnold's "Sohrab and Rustum" (for obvious reasons in the son of Thomas Arnold) reverses the Jack the Giant Killer pattern of fantasy and has the son slain in combat by the father; that Hume's questioning of "ancestry" in attacking causality and Bentham's "neutral" or "sterilized" vocabulary are significantly "bachelors'" theories; that pragmatism, instrumentalism, operationalism, and similar philosophies featuring "agency" all point at a fixation on the mother, whereas "purpose" philosophies point at the erotic woman of maturity; that the turn from verse to prose in a writer's work may be a similar development from the "maternal" or "familial" to the "erotic" or adult. One brief section of the book, the last part of the chapter on "Scene," consists of "a few observations" on rhetorical and symbolic meanings in regard to Stoic and Epicurean philosophies, inserted "to illustrate how the other levels impinge upon the Grammatical," and suggesting for the later books a bewildering and wonderful array of possibilities in similar analysis.

Burke's uncollected periodical and symposium pieces have more or less followed the development of his books. The articles prior to 1941 not collected in *The Philosophy of Literary Form*, with the exception of the essay on "Surrealism" in *New Directions 1940*, tend to repeat other work, and the "Surrealism" essay seems largely a foretaste of "placing" material that will probably be handled in the *Symbolic*. The reviews not collected tend to be on other critics, from Tate and Ransom to Mary Colum, and only two of them are still significant: one the review of Spender's *Forward from Liberalism* in the *New Republic*, 1937, because on the basis of Spender's "non-collective" Communism Burke predicted his later disillusionment; and the other the review of two studies of Coleridge, in the *New Republic*, 1939, because it is one of the rare examples of Burke's use of his symbolic-action readings for "debunking," when he disparages the Kafka and Kierkegaard fads because they represent "the stage of masturbatory adolescence" and "quarrels with the father," which is "trivial" compared to the complexity of Coleridge's symbolic action.

Burke's pieces written since the *Philosophy* include three articles that did not find a place in the *Grammar*: "The Character of our Culture" in the *Southern Review*, Spring 1941, a comment on a symposium held by the American Philosophical Society (Blackmur commented in the same issue), with Burke chiefly interested in showing the symposium's avoidance of the "monetary"; "On Motivation in Yeats," in the *Southern Review*, Winter 1942, a preliminary exercise in the dramatistic analysis of lyric poetry; and "The Tactics of Motivation," in *Chimera*, Spring and Summer 1943, a work-out of the whole pentad in commenting on the manifesto for naturalism of the Failure of Nerve series in *Partisan Review*. His recent reviews have dealt briefly with contemporary criticism in reviews of books by Alfred Kazin and Eric Bentley, as well as Ransom,

Tate, Warren, and others, and with a number of historical, linguistic, and philosophic works where he has been content to add levels of meaning to the book (finding more symbolic interpretations for Marguerite Young's *Angel in the Forest*, adding a rhetorical level to Cassirer's magical and semantic levels in *The Myth of the State*). One of Burke's briefer reviews, in the *New Republic* in 1943, of Downes's and Siegmeister's *Treasury of American Song*, reveals an unbecoming ignorance of the material (Burke's only display of that occupational disease of reviewers, so far as I know). In addition, in "Kinds of Criticism" in *Poetry*, August 1946, and "Ideology and Myth" in *Accent*, Summer 1947, Burke has published what seem to be fragments of the *Rhetoric*.

2

In *Attitudes toward History*, 1937, despite the title, literature is central, (whereas in *Permanence and Change* it is peripheral and illustrative). The book is a study of literary attitudes as symbolic action or ritual, and the "history" of the title only points up the concern with grounding literature in society and showing the interrelationships of its attitudes to "the curve of history," politics, and economics. The book's basic division of attitudes is into those of "acceptance" and "rejection" (Schopenhauer's *Bejahung und Verneinung*), and—growing out of them, combining the best features of both—acceptance-rejection, which Burke calls "the comic." "Frames of Acceptance" are orthodoxies and include philosophies like those of William James, Whitman, and Emerson; literary forms like epic, tragedy, comedy, and lyric; and ritual structures in general centering in incest-awe and symbolic castration. "Frames of Rejection" are heresies, the emphasis shifting against the symbols of authority, and include philosophies from Machiavelli to Marx and Nietzsche; literary forms like the elegy, satire, burlesque and the grotesque; and ritual structures in general centering on symbolic parricide. The comic frame is an attitude of ambivalence "neither wholly euphemistic nor wholly debunking." Burke writes:

> A comic frame of motives avoids these difficulties, showing us how an act can "dialectically" contain both transcendental and material ingredients, both imagination and bureaucratic embodiments, both "service" and "spoils." But it also makes us sensitive to the point at which one of these ingredients becomes hypertrophied, with the corresponding atrophy of the other. A well-balanced ecology requires the symbiosis of the two.

The name "comic" has confused many readers, principally through confusion with "comedy." As a matter of fact, the name was probably chosen as Burke's ironic observation that being an accepter-rejecter in a world of ravening accepters and ravening rejecters is a pretty funny thing to be. He admits in the book to choosing "comic" when he might just as well have chosen "humanistic" because it "sounds better" to him (exploring his subconscious to find that it is principally a way of saying his own name, Kenneth, and a preoccupation with death by choking or gagging). Whatever the source of the term, the attitude it represents is basic to Burke's values, and the book concludes with a plea for the framing of comic vocabularies. It seems to connote not only "ironic," "humanistic," and "sceptical," but all the implications of truth emergent out of an *agon* in "dialectic" and "dramatistic."

The basic concept of the book, underlying all three frames or attitudes, is the concept of "symbolic action," that act "which a man does because he is interested in doing it exactly as he does do it." These symbolic acts, as Burke sees them, center in initiation, change of identity, rebirth, purification, and other related magical ceremonies. He writes:

> Our basic principle is our contention that all symbolism can be treated as the ritualistic naming and changing of identity (whereby a man fits himself for a role in accordance with established coordinates or for a change of role in accordance with new coordinates which necessity has forced upon him). The nearest to a schematic statement that we might come is this:
>
> In general, these rituals of change or "purification" center about three kinds of imagery: purification by ice, by fire, or by decay. "Ice" tends to emphasize castration and frigidity. . . . Purification by fire, "trial by fire," probably suggests "incest-awe." . . . Redemption by decay is symbolized in all variants of the sprouting seed, which arises in green newness out of filth and rot. . . . We may also note the two symbols of perspective, the mountain and the pit (sometimes merged in symbols of bridges, crossing, travel, flying). The mountain contains incestuous ingredients (the mountain as the mother, with frigidity as symbolic punishment for the offense). So also does the pit (ambivalence of womb and "cloaque," the latter aspect tending to draw in also ingredients of "purification by decay").

Thus each work of art tends to be a ritual of death and rebirth with identity changed, organized in relation to accepting or rejecting a key symbol of authority. In terms of these rituals Burke analyzes innumerable works of literature, of which his scattered interpretations of Thomas Mann's symbolic actions (which have interested him greatly in all his writings) probably add up to the clearest picture. Burke reads *The Magic Mountain* as a rebirth ritual in which Hans Castorp is prepared for "resocializing" in the war at the end by his seven years on the maternal mountain, for which he is punished by symbolic castration, death, and rebirth in a new existence in the snow scene—the whole a ritual in which Mann himself is reborn from pacifist liberal to supporter of the German cause in the first World War. *Death in Venice* and *Mario and the Magician* are scapegoat rituals for Mann as artist, in the first of which the erotic criminality of the artist, represented by Aschenbach, is punished by death; in the second of which Mann dissociates the artist into two: the bad artist, Cippola, erotic and criminal (as well as Fascist symbol) is punished by death; and the good artist, the narrator, freed of criminality by Cippola's expiatory death, goes off "liberated." The *Joseph* books are rebirth in the pit, as *The Magic Mountain* was rebirth on the mountain. In them Joseph, an endlessly recurring identity, carries Mann to a broader collectivity than the earlier German nationalism, as, purged of the criminality of the artist, he takes on a larger criminality, the bisexuality of the prophetic "nourisher," of which he is finally in turn purged.

Burke sums up the nature of literary ritual for the writer in general:

> The change of identity (whereby he is at once the same man and a new man) gives him a greater complexity of coordinates. He "sees around the corner." He is "prophetic," endowed with "perspective." We need not here concern ourselves with the accuracy of his perspective; we need only note its existence. It makes him either "wiser" or "more foolish" than he was—in any case, it forms the basis upon which the ramifications of his work are based. Thus, in Mann's novels, Joseph is not equipped to be a "prophet" until he has been reborn in the pit.
>
> Rebirth is a process of socialization, since it is a ritual whereby the poet fits himself to accept necessities suggested to him by the problems of the forensic. It will also, as regression, involve concern with the "womb-heaven" of the embryo, and with the "first revolution" that took place when the embryo developed to the point where its "shelter" became "confinement." Hence, when you examine this ritual, you find such symbols as the "pit" a symbolic return-to, and return-from, the womb.
>
> This involves "incest-awe," since the adult can return to the mother not as a sexually inexperienced infant, but as a lover. It involves homosexuality (actual or symbolic) since it involves an affront to the bipolar relationships of mother and father, and since a shift in allegiance to the symbols of authority equals the symbolic slaying of a parent. It involves castration symbolism, connotations of the "neuter," by way of punishment for the symbolic offense. The "neuter" may also take on connotations of the "androgynous," because of the change in identity effected by the ritual.

Just as the individual rituals of specific works are symbolic actions, so
are the poetic forms themselves: thus tragedy is a formalized ritual of
expiation, humor is a ritual for reducing the burden of the situation,
satire a ritual for "projecting" one's vice onto a scapegoat and killing it
off. The writer also expresses himself symbolically in the choice of
subject (as *Counter-Statement* noted about the biographer of Napoleon
writing of his own Napoleonism): he expresses his "deep-lying sympathy" in the passages he quotes from other writers, even when attacking
them; he writes "what is necessary to sustain him." The most rational-
seeming activities have symbolic ingredients, as Burke notes in regard to
the "bachelor" philosophies of Hume and Bentham, or the elements of
ritual purification and castration in Pasteur's campaign for medical
sterilization. Even the most corrupt or evasive hack production contains
these same symbolic ingredients, which tell the truth despite its author.
Burke writes, in a variant of Blake's criterion for asserting that Milton
was "of the Devil's party":

> A writer may *profess* allegiance to a certain cause, for instance,
> but you find on going over his work that the *enemies* of this cause are
> portrayed with greater vividness than its advocates. Here is his
> "truth" about his professions of belief.

And in another place:

> By charting clusters, we get our clues as to the important in-
> gredients subsumed in "symbolic mergers." We reveal, beneath
> an author's "official front," the level at which a lie is impossible.
> If a man's virtuous characters are dull, and his wicked characters
> are done vigorously, his *art* has voted for the wicked ones, regard-
> less of his "official front." If a man talks of *glory* but employs the
> imagery of *desolation*, his *true subject* is desolation.

The mention of "cues" and "clusters" brings up the question of
Burke's techniques for discovering and exploring symbolic action in a
writer's work. He summarizes:

> We get cues as to his "non-realistic" or "symbolic" meaning in
> two ways. By examining the internal organization, noting what
> follows what, we disclose the content of a symbol in disclosing its
> *function*. . . . We can check such disclosures by "metaphorical
> analysis," as we note the tenor of the imagery which the author
> employs. . . . And we can interpret the symbolic content of one
> book by comparing it with kindred symbols in other books.

The most obvious cue or clue is imagery or symbols, particularly in
associated "clusters" of images, of which the mention of any one tends
inevitably to call up others (the sort of thing Caroline Spurgeon found

in Shakespeare and around which Armstrong later built his method), or in a developmental "curve." There are many other points of particular significance. One is the title of the work (Burke has noted, for example, that in Huysmans's transition from naturalism to Catholicism, all the titles of his naturalistic work are nouns, all the titles of his Catholic work are nouns, and all the titles of his transitional work are prepositions or prepositional). Beginning and endings are particularly strategic, "the first setting the tone for the reception of one's message, the second clinching the thesis for a final parting" (and we might note that Burke's own beginnings and endings, perhaps more consciously than most, are not only "strategic" but always particularly eloquent). Breaks in continuity in a writer's work are always significant: either formal breaks, as when *Murder in the Cathedral* shifts from verse to prose; or logical breaks, as when a Wyndham Lewis metaphor is insistently inadequate; or discontinuities in subject-matter. Even puns and sound-relationships are of symbolic significance, so that the name "Desdemona," sounding like "death" and "moan," foretells her fate. In the section on "Cues" in the book Burke has a long discussion of the symbolic mimesis of sounds, based on Sir Richard Paget's work in *Human Speech* and admittedly tentative, in which he suggests symbolic possibilities of "dancing" acceptance in the repetition of the "m" sound and its cognates, rejection in the "p" sound and its cognates, choking from the "k" sound, etc. Finally, history itself is an important clue to symbolic meaning, as Burke demonstrates by tracing the historical transformations of the symbolic action in his poetic forms, and the historical "curve" behind Shakespeare's shifts in imagery.

The core of the book is the last third, the "Dictionary of Pivotal Terms." Burke explains why he has put it at the end of the book rather than at the beginning, remarking that the alphabetical convention of a dictionary is specious, since the definition of the words in "a" requires a prior knowledge of all the words to "z," and consequently he is defining his terms only after they have been displayed in action. He writes:

> In our own case, we have found it advisable to pursue a catch-as-catch-can policy, introducing our terms where there is an opportunity to disclose at the same time something of their function. We hope to make apparent first their general slant or drift, and to sharpen their explicitness as we proceed (showing their function by introducing them into various contexts). Formal definitions should thus be relegated to a final summary, where each term can draw upon the reader's knowledge of *all* the terms.

Burke has frequently used a dictionary of terms to sum up what each of his books has to say, since he believes that his views *are* the terms, and this Dictionary continues the tradition of the Lexicon Rhetoricæ in

Counter-Statement and the list of concepts on page 337 of *Permanence and Change*. In this case the Dictionary is a formalized alphabetical listing of the thirty-three key concepts of the book and Burke's work up to 1937. Some of them are principally the basic devices of symbolic action, like Alienation, Bridging Device, Casuistic Stretching, Communion, Identity, Rituals of Rebirth, Secular Prayer, Transcendence; some of them are principally the basic techniques of his criticism, like Clusters, Cues, Discounting, Essence, Imagery, Lexicological; some are principally social phenomena, like Good Life, which expresses his social program, and Problem of Evil; some, like Perspective by Incongruity, are at a high enough level of generality to cover all three categories, being at once symbolic actions in the work, devices for criticizing the work, and social phenomena. There is no way to summarize or paraphrase these pivotal terms in less space than they take up, and the only way to get a sense of their tremendous value and fruitfulness is to read them in the context of the book. It may be possible, however, to show how inter-related they are in operation by quoting a conveniently short one, on "Sect":

> Those who, faced with the danger of being "driven into a corner," counter by forming a new collectivity. Their cooperation gives them a new positive campaign base, from which they may sally forth to steal the recognized symbols of authority from their opponents. A sect is always threatened with defensive, negativistic, "splintering" tendencies so long as the ingredient of rejection is uppermost.
>
> Troeltsch has pointed out the part that the spread of literacy has played in sectarianism. Sectarianism is "colony thinking." It attains full expression when the group of like-minded forms some material cooperative enterprise that gives the bureaucratic equivalents of its Utopia. The spread of literacy, however, led to a subtler kind of colony, usually lacking material body: the "colonies of the mind." By his preferences in reading, one "recruits his band," and they may be scattered across all the earth and through all periods of history.
>
> The nineteenth century was particularly prolific in sectarian colonies, of both the material and spiritual sorts. There were the colonies of special scientific disciplines. And here and there a lonely man, off by himself, shaped his identity by membership in one or another of such vaguely corporate units.

Although the richest of these terms are abstract enough to include collective social as well as individual literary behavior, the examples are consistently literary. Managing to include both the classic and the contemporary (sometimes, the sublime and the ridiculous), Burke illustrates Alienation with examples from Shakespeare and an Albert Bein play,

Cues with Shakespeare and Cummings, Identity with Shakespeare and Mann's *Joseph* novels, Imagery with Shakespeare and Aragon's *Bells of Basle*, etc.

The central concern of *Attitudes toward History* is with charting attitudes and framing "a comic vocabulary of motives"—that is, with public materials, literary or forensic—and characteristically its chief theoretical reliance is on such authorities on the forensic as Bentham, Marx, Peirce, Veblen, and Malinowski. At the same time, as Burke has made clear, "no statement about motives can ever be anything other than symbolic action" itself, and he has sketched out in the book the ways his system and terminology express himself. In addition to tracing "comic" as a way of saying, among other things, "Kenneth," he finds that one of his other principal terms, "bureaucratization," is a way of saying "Burke" or "burking" the issue, and he suggests that his preference for "p" terms, "poetry," "piety," "petition," "propriety," "possession," "prayer," and "perspective," is a survival of his earlier period "as an æsthete, to whom poetry was synonymous with rejection." Under "Cues" in the book, Burke devotes ten pages to an elaborate introspection into some of the underlying motives revealed in his own work. He pursues his "apparently neutral" title for one section, "The Curve of History," through an early story, "The Book of Yul" in *The White Oxen*, and other writings, finding that the word "curve" has extremely complex associations for him, so that his title is actually "The Mountain-Woman-Church of History," with features of guilt, death, and eroticism smuggled in.

Burke finds that "bureaucratization of the imaginative" is a way of saying that things "die" and are "reborn"; that "perspective by incongruity," in its concern with "neutralization," involves symbolic castration and is consequently a fitting rebirth transition between the first section of *Permanence and Change*, its keynote "the fish, under water," and the third section, a heaven of the secularization of religious terms. He then investigates the "arbitrary" names he gave characters in the stories in *The White Oxen* and finds that they have a "tonal logic"; that his character named Treep, whose role was to cut down a tree, was precisely named "tree-rejection," and when, become gigantic, he is re-named Arjk, the name still fits. Burke explains:

> Looking at these syllables, we speculated: the "r" is the growl of his pugnacity. The "j" is his new *genius* as *gigantic*, as is the "ah" of "a," in contrast with the "ee" of his name before "rebirth." And the "k" is the initial of our given name. Thus, "a-r-j-k" means: "Kenneth, formerly a little man, made big and pugnacious."

He then finds that the same principles are involved in the nicknames he has given his children (so that his third daughter, nicknamed "Jake,"

has all of "Arjk" but the growl), in his poems, and in the key terms of
his conceptual vocabulary. He concludes with the reservation that the
same symbolic expressions could be found in other fashions:

> Of course such matters "radiate" in many directions. We could
> have begun with Treep's felling of the tree, for instance, and de-
> veloped a line of thought from this ritualistic murder, relating it to
> subsequent symbolizations of rape and redemption in the same
> story. . . .
>
> We could, in other words, have considered critical concepts as
> symbols, looking for the ways in which the later pattern of ideas
> parallels the pattern of plot in these early fantasies. Hence, we
> should regret it if the reader carried away the impression that the
> organization of character by the fitting together of verbalizations
> involves "tonal puns" alone.

Burke has used introspection into his own motivations and past experience in all his books since *Counter-Statement:* in *Permanence and
Change*, noting his "great resentment as a child upon learning that lions
were cats, whereas to me they were purely and simply the biggest dogs";
in *The Philosophy of Literary Form*, recalling that the name of a character
in an early story he wrote underlies an arbitrary obscene word he made up
for a hypothetical illustration; in *A Grammar of Motives*, exploring the
adolescent images a reading of Santayana called up and the probable
line of association behind his term "grandly converge." To a certain
extent this is a critical trick, even a cheat, since by admitting the most
tenuous meanings, sometimes of an extremely unattractive nature, about
his own writing, Burke can then go on to find similar things in the work
of other writers with the technique to some extent justified. Actually, of
course, nothing is proved (which Burke would be the first to admit,
since he is trying to "suggest" meanings, not "prove" them), and in the
long run these introspective revelations will probably turn out to be
the more valuable as insights into the mind and working methods of an
utterly scrupulous and supersubtle artist and critic than they will be as
grounds for methodological generalization. In the discussion of his own
underlying motivations Burke writes:

> Perhaps we are here making "admissions" that we should make
> men hire expensive detectives to find out. Our only way of defense
> is to say *"tu quoque."* We hold that, insofar as any man's writings
> contain sincerity of organization, being something more than mere
> disjunct psittacism, we can disclose analogous processes at work.
> We'll even accept an offer to disclose them, if any one cares to come
> forward with the proud claim that his work is psittacism pure and
> unadulterated. A man can, on the surface, maintain any insincerity

he prefers. But in the depths of his imagery, he cannot lie. When being sufficiently *engrossed* in a subject to give it organized expression, the poet or philosopher must embody his variants of such basic psychological processes. He could not do otherwise unless he had a *different kind of body* from other men. So, if any enlightened philosopher or critic cares to challenge us, contending that his own work is free of puns, we are willing, for a consideration, to go on a search for "cues."

So far as I know, no one has ever taken him up on this offer. In thus losing the positive proof of demonstration on a skeptic, we probably get the equally impressive negative proof of the unanswerable conviction the book carries; that many have scoffed, but none remained to pay.

3

Despite the novelty and shock-value of Burke's methods, the study of literature as symbolic action has quite a respectable ancestry. Plato's concern with the ill effects of poetry in *The Republic* is in large part a concern with symbolic action in the audience. Socrates says (Jowett translation): "If you consider, I said, that when in misfortune we feel a natural hunger and desire to relieve our sorrow by weeping and lamentation, and that this feeling which is kept under control in our own calamities is satisfied and delighted by the poets . . ." Aristotle, however, is the true father of symbolic action, as of so many things. In his emphasis on *action*, his insistence in *The Poetics* (Lane Cooper translation) that "happiness and misery are not states of being, but forms of activity," that being good is *acting* good, he laid the groundwork for our reading "pity" and "terror" not as audience states but as audience symbolic actions, responding to the symbolic action in tragedy. Coleridge, whose own poems, particularly "The Ancient Mariner" and "Kubla Khan," are so complete a text of symbolic action, halted on the verge of the concept, perhaps from a kind of "resistance," although he had independently discovered its principal theoretical basis, the concept of non-conscious mental areas. In his *Lectures on Shakespeare* he notes that Shakespeare's titles and opening scenes are particularly significant, as Burke would, but decides that they are significant in terms of conscious artistry. Ruskin continued the tradition with a very Burkian analysis of the symbolic action implicit in the etymological meanings (some of them perhaps dubious) of the names of Shakespeare's characters (I have taken the liberty of printing the Greek transliterated):

Of Shakespeare's names I will afterwards speak at more length; they are curiously—often barbarously—mixed out of various traditions and languages. Three of the clearest in meaning have been

already noticed. Desdemona—"*dusdaimonia*," *miserable fortune*—is
also plain enough. Othello is, I believe, "the careful"; all the ca-
lamity of the tragedy arising from the single flaw and error in his
magnificently collected strength. Ophelia, "serviceableness," the
true, lost wife of Hamlet, is marked as having a Greek name by
that of her brother, Laertes; and its signification is once exquisitely
alluded to in that brother's last word of her, where her gentle preciousness is opposed to the uselessness of the churlish clergy:—"A
ministering angel shall my sister be, when thou liest howling."
Hamlet is, I believe, connected in some way with "homely," the
entire event of the tragedy turning on betrayal of home duty.
Hermione (*herma*), "pillar-like" . . . ; Titania (*titēnē*), "the
queen"; Benedick and Beatrice, "blessed and blessing"; Valentine
and Proteus "enduring or strong" (valens), and "changeful." Iago
and Iachimo have evidently the same root—probably the Spanish
Iago, Jacob, "the supplanter."

In so far as the general assumptions behind the analysis of symbolic
action in art are basic psychological generalities, many of them have
been anticipated by shrewd students of human nature in the past. To
mention a few at random, Goethe noted, according to Eckermann, that
the talents of women seem to cease with marriage and children, raising
the possibility that their works of art are some form of what we would
now call "sublimated" (or symbolic) sexuality or maternal impulse.
Around the turn of the century Ferdinand Brunetière insisted in his
essay on "The Philosophy of Molière" that Tartufe "is an act as much
as a work: a work of combat, as we would now say, and an act of declared
hostility"; and Bernard Shaw noted in *The Quintessence of Ibsenism* that a
writer's use of scriptural quotation tends to signalize bad conscience at
those reinforced points (and is thus symbolic denial through overasser-
tion). Since Freud, of course, these conceptions have become psychoanalytic commonplaces, and analysts deal constantly with problems of
symbolic action. Erich Fromm, for example, has developed a concept
of religious or political doctrines as symbolic expressions of the character
structure and personality traits of their creators, and as satisfying similar
psychic needs in the character structure of those won over to them.
    In a similar fashion a number of Burke's key concepts have been
anticipated by other writers. Tolstoy, for example, in *What Is Art?*
clearly anticipates the condition of psychological dispossession Burke
describes under "alienation": "In regard to religion the upper circles
of the Middle Ages found themselves in the position educated Romans
were in before Christianity arose, that is, they no longer believed in the
religion of the masses but had no beliefs to put in place of the worn-out
Church doctrine, which for them had lost its meaning"; and also the

Burkian concept of "being driven into a corner": "The Church doctrine is so coherent a system that it cannot be altered or corrected without destroying it altogether." Irving Babbitt, in *Rousseau and Romanticism*, precedes Burke in noting how psychic alienation results in movements of negativism, Satanism, Byronism; and in the same book also approximates the Burkian special sense of "communion." Even I. A. Richards, whose interests are so completely turned on the communicative function of language and so little on the expressive, at least once pushed his own concept of the actions implicit in attitudes to its logical conclusion in symbolic action. In *Coleridge on Imagination* (under a Burkian ægis, that is) he writes:

> The saner and greater mythologies are not fancies; they are the utterance of the whole soul of man and, as such, inexhaustible to meditation. They are no amusement or diversion to be sought as a relaxation and an escape from the hard realities of life. They are these hard realities in projection, their symbolic recognition, co-ordination and acceptance. Through such mythologies our will is collected, our powers unified, our growth controlled. Through them the infinitely divergent strayings of our being are brought into "balance or reconciliation." The "opposite and discordant qualities" of things in them acquire a form; and such integrity as we possess as "civilized" men is our inheritance through them.

Finally, D. H. Lawrence's famous remark: "One sheds one's sicknesses in books," only expresses what many artists throughout history have recognized as the symbolic action in their own work.

The men Burke is most indebted to, however, are not the forerunners of symbolic action, with the exception of Coleridge, but a group of relatively eccentric philosophers and philosophic writers (very similar to Richards's group) who tend to resemble him in a curious fashion. One of them is Jeremy Bentham. It is hard to read Hazlitt's account of Bentham in *The Spirit of the Age* without thinking of Burke seen from an antagonistic point of view, even to the "barbarous philosophical jargon" that "is not mere verbiage, but has a great deal of acuteness and meaning in it, which you would be glad to pick out if you could." Like Richards, Burke sees Bentham as the founder of the serious study of language, and in *Permanence and Change* he classes him with Darwin in having become "thousands of selves." He has little faith in Bentham's project for a "neutral" speech and metaphor that would eliminate "poetry" and "rhetoric" (or in the doctrines that have succeeded it in semantics), seeing the project as essentially a vast castration-symbolism; as he sees Bentham's antireligious utilitarianism as essentially a secularized religious pattern, a variant of the Golden Rule. At the same time he finds

Bentham's analysis of speech and classification of its types in *Table of the Springs of Action* an invaluable exploration of these matters, eminently usable once its bias in favor of "neutrality" is discarded; while in Bentham's utilitarian analysis of "interests" and "motives" constituting the "springs" of human action lie the roots of Burke's lifelong attempt to "place" motives, again with the invidious connotations eliminated. In *Attitudes*, announcing: "The best of Bentham, Marx and Veblen is high comedy," he credits Bentham with having developed "debunking" to the point where "epigons" have had to do nothing but cash in on his genius for a century, and in *The Philosophy of Literary Form* he makes it clear that the "epigons" he is talking about are men like Thurman Arnold and Stuart Chase. In *A Grammar of Motives*, while using Bentham a number of times, he adds to his debunking of Bentham's debunking (that it is a "bachelor's" castration symbol) a new symbolic explanation gleefully picked up from Bentham himself (that it is rooted in his childhood, in an abnormally intense fear of ghosts, which became the "fictions" in language that he feared as an adult).

Coleridge is perhaps the man of all the group whom Burke most resembles, and one cannot read Coleridge's writings, particularly the *Biographia*, without being struck by the resemblances: in ideas, methods, even eccentricities. As a study in symbolic action, Coleridge and his work have fascinated Burke, and the core of the long title essay of *The Philosophy of Literary Form* is the analysis of "The Ancient Mariner," just as Coleridge's high degree of consciousness in the subtleties of sound makes him the logical choice for a text on delicate musicality in verse, and his extreme linguistic preoccupation generally makes him perhaps the most frequently quoted writer in Burke's books. Burke has classed Coleridge "among the greatest critics of world literature," and he regards his emphasis as directly opposed to Bentham's debunking, in that it is "tragic" or "dignifying," treating material interests as a limited aspect of "higher" interests. In "The Philosophy of Literary Form" Burke mentions being at work on a monograph entitled "The Particular Strategy of Samuel Taylor Coleridge," which has never appeared (it may have turned into his course on Coleridge during the 1938 summer session at the University of Chicago). He notes the problems and rewards involved:

> At present I am attempting such a "symbolic" analysis of Coleridge's writings. His highly complex mind makes the job of charting difficult. . . .
> However, there are two advantages about the case of Coleridge that make the job worth trying. In the first place, there is the fact that he left so full a record, and that he employed the same imagery in his poems, literary criticism, political and religious tracts, letters,

lectures, and introspective jottings. Thus we have objective bridges for getting from one area to another; these images "pontificate" among his various interests, and so provide us with a maximum opportunity to work out a psychology by objective citation, by "scissor work." . . .

The second advantage in the case of Coleridge is that, along with his highly complex mind (perhaps one of the most complex that has left us a full record) you have an easily observable *simplification*. I refer to the burden of his drug addiction. . . .

Coleridge is not only Burke's favorite subject; he is a kind of banner for him. Thus in his essay on "Surrealism" he puts Coleridge forward as the father of surrealism and the writer of "the great Surrealist masterpiece" ("Kubla Khan"), and then proposes Coleridge's distinction between "imagination" and "fancy" as basic to an analysis of the movement. In the *New Republic* review mentioned above he insists that the current Kierkegaard-Kafka fad should properly be a Coleridge fad. In "The Problem of the Intrinsic" he takes up the charge made by the neo-Aristotelian critics that their opponents are too "Coleridgean," Platonic, or deductive about poetry, converts it into a banner, and shows that precisely at the point where the neo-Aristotelians are making the most critical sense and producing the most valuable readings, they are being most "Coleridgean."

A third thinker on whom Burke has based a good deal of his work is Thorstein Veblen, the only American of the three, and consequently the only one he does not share as a source with Richards. The Veblen influence, however, seems to be more or less wearing off. In *Permanence and Change* Burke relies heavily on Veblen's concept of "trained incapacity," taking it as a basic "perspective by incongruity" or metaphor, and extending its reference until it becomes a major social, psychological and literary phenomenon somewhat similar to what the gestaltists speak of as a "bad *Gestalt*." Unlike almost everyone else but the economists, Burke does not find *The Theory of the Leisure Class* Veblen's "greatest contribution to our thinking," but *The Theory of Business Enterprise*, seeing it as our finest analysis of the "metaphysics" of capitalism. *Permanence and Change* also makes a good deal of some of Veblen's other ideas, particularly his device for avoiding the Manichean dualism implicit in his view of institutions, by postulating opposed "instincts," predatory and altruistic. In *Attitudes toward History* Burke does little with Veblen, except to note that at his best, like Bentham and Marx, he is "high comedy;" and to develop Veblen's "planned incapacity" into his own term "planned incongruity." In *The Philosophy of Literary Form*, although Veblen is quoted frequently, it is almost always as a social thinker; not, as he was originally for Burke, a metaphoric critic of our whole culture. In *A Grammar of Motives* he is not referred to at all (although it can be presumed that both later volumes will have places for him).

Less heavily Burke has drawn on a number of other philosophers and philosophic thinkers, among them two—John Stuart Mill and Charles S. Peirce—who also resemble him somewhat (Blackmur has pointed out the latter resemblance, meaning for "the buoyancy and sheer remarkableness of his speculations," not, one hopes, for his terminology). Burke is one of the few contemporary critics who have made use of A. O. Lovejoy's *Great Chain of Being*; and among more traditional philosophers, he has regularly utilized James, Dewey, Bergson, and a number of other moderns (before the *Grammar*, in which, of course, he surveyed the bulk of philosophy). The general pattern of Burke's philosophic indebtedness, however, is rarely more than the adoption of a basic concept or two, combined with widespread "discounting" or outright attack, and until the emergence of Aristotle as his major influence in the latest book, no philosopher was ever recognizably his master.

Burke's effect on contemporary criticism is, at least in America, fully as pervasive as that of Richards. In addition to R. P. Blackmur (whose relationship to him has been noted above) the men whose work is most closely related to his in this country are Malcolm Cowley, Francis Fergusson, and Harry Slochower. Cowley has not so far published a volume of criticism, but his forthcoming book on American literature, from fragments that have appeared in periodicals, seems to be a major piece of work. In magazine pieces over the past two decades he has utilized many of Burke's concepts, terms, and insights, turning them to his own uses, popularizing them somewhat, and applying them to writers untapped by Burke. His introductory studies of Hemingway and Faulkner for the Viking Portable Library, in particular, are first-rate studies in symbolic action, and almost the first serious examination either writer has received.

Like Cowley, Francis Fergusson is now engaged in writing his first book of criticism after many years of periodical writing. Unlike Cowley, he has been affected by Burke only recently, and then more or less on his own terms. The title "drama critic" has been badly debased until it now means a semi-literate reviewer of plays for a newspaper, but for two decades Fergusson has been a drama critic in the proper sense, a critic of both dramatic literature and performance, and probably the best in America. His criticism has three principal strands. The first is a sharp æsthetic morality, a concept of art as disinterested, digested, measured, disciplined, and final, derived in part from the modern classicist, neo-humanist, and traditionalist critics—Maritain, Benda, Fernandez, Babbitt, Eliot—and in part from the classics and writers like Dante, with which concept he has relentlessly punctured the windy and immature, from Eugene O'Neill to Selden Rodman. (This has not kept him, incidentally, although he is generally scornful of the moderns as "spirit-maiming" or "demoralizing," from valuing highly some very unclassical writers like D. H. Lawrence.) At the same time he has applied the comparative technical standard of the rounded and complete Greek ritual drama, as interpreted by Aristotle and best exemplified by Sophocles' *Œdipus the King*, to the study of the serious modern drama, from Ibsen and Chekhov to Lorca and Cocteau.

The third strand is his use of dramatism and the pattern of the Sophoclean ritual drama as a way of reading non-dramatic literature; which he stated in *Hound & Horn*, as early as July–September 1933, in a review of Boleslavsky's *Acting: the First Six Lessons*, when he proposed the method as a way of reading lyric poetry; and illustrated in the *Hound & Horn* James number the next year with a reading of "The Drama in *The Golden Bowl*." It is this third strand which has principally served to unite Fergusson and Burke, and as Burke's method developed into "dramatism" and the "pentad," Fergusson took advantage of many of its conceptual formulations, particularly its *"poiema-pathema-mathema"* formulation, which he converted into "purpose-passion-perception," the three essential stages of the ritual drama, and made the cornerstone of his own work. Fergusson's review of Burke's *Grammar*, the ablest one to appear, announced in terms of high praise their wide area of agreement as well as their limited areas of disagreement (chiefly his objection to Burke's "rationalistic" slighting of medieval realism and "abstractionist" retreat from the earlier concrete "ritual drama as hub"). Fergusson's forthcoming book (some of which I have had the opportunity of reading in manuscript, and one chapter of which has so far appeared in the *Kenyon Review*, Spring 1947), a study of post-Shakespearian drama as partial developments of "purpose," "passion," or "perception" rather than the Sophoclean ritual whole, gives evidence of being an important literary event.

The man whose books make the most explicit use of Burke is Harry Slochower. Slochower's combination of Marx, Freud, and Gestalt is similar to Burke's socio-psychological integration, although Slochower draws much more heavily on Marxism and on a German philosophic tradition. Some time before the publication of his first book in English, *Three Ways of Modern Man* in 1937 (I have not read his first book, *Richard Dehmel*, written in German), Slochower discovered Burke's terminology, and found it, as did Cowley, Fergusson, and others, an efficient and consistent critical frame for expressing his own ideas. The book appeared with an appreciative Foreword by Burke, and displays a number of Burkian terms, concepts, insights, direct quotes, and even Burke's characteristic quotation marks. At the same time its central emphasis, on novels as expressing formal philosophic "ideologies" (Slochower's three bins are Feudal Socialism, Bourgeois Liberalism, and Socialist Humanism, but in the course of the work they get phrased as Monist, Dualist, Dialectic, even Father, Son, Holy Ghost), is very unlike Burke's personalist "symbolic action" emphasis. Slochower's second book, *Thomas Mann's Joseph Story* (1938) is more like Burke's own work, the lengthy analysis of a single complex work of art in a number of levels, translated into a number of vocabularies, but again with Slochower's distinctive collective-ideology emphasis. His third and most ambitious book, *No Voice is Wholly Lost . . .* (1945) is an attempt to survey almost the whole mass of contemporary literature instead of exploring a few texts in detail. The book is full of brilliant insights, but Slochower has too much ground to cover to be able to integrate them, the treatment of contemporary Americans is frequently weak (hacks like Steinbeck are classed with Malraux and Mann, windy bores like Wolfe are treated as comparable to Kafka and Rilke, and major writers like Hemingway and Faulkner tend to be slighted), and the book as a whole is disappointing. Its extension and application of Burke's terms in what by now has become a very different perspective is an excellent job, however, and in general Slochower is informed, perceptive, and methodologically equipped enough to make his importance certain any time he chooses to desert the survey-course type of book and settle down to do what he has shown he can do best, dig into a major book at length.

One of the oddest and most amusing applications Burke has had was by Yvor Winters, surely the last convert anyone would have predicted. Winters's first book, *Primitivism and Decadence*, appeared in 1937 with the introductory Note, in his characteristic churlish tone:

> I have wherever possible employed the terminology of Kenneth Burke, and have acknowledged it, in order to avoid the unnecessary multiplication of terms; my own analysis of rhetorical devices began, however, about as early as his own, and was dropped for a time while his continued, because it did not seem especially fruitful. My own analysis was resumed when I discovered the key to the ethical significance of rhetoric and the possibility of creating an æsthetic on such an analysis; my quarrel with Mr. Burke, which will appear fully in this volume, is precisely that he has failed to do this.

Winters went on in the book to make desultory use of a number of Burke's terms from *Counter-Statement*, particularly one that seems to have charmed him: "qualitative progression," for a type of poetic structure; but the attempt to use a set of terms while quarreling violently with the ideas for which they are shorthand formulas was obviously foredoomed, and after the first book Winters gave it up and created an ethically weighted vocabulary of his own.

In crediting Burke while quarreling with him, Winters was being more generous than a number of other critics, Edmund Wilson and Philip Rahv among them, who have repeatedly drawn on Burke's concepts and insights without credit. (One of the Rahv cases is particularly amusing, in that it appeared in a review in the December 1937 issue of *Partisan Review*, on the page following the only formal notice the magazine has ever taken of Burke's work, Sidney Hook's venomous attack.) Several young poets and critics in England, among them Francis Scarfe and Christopher Hill, are either familiar with Burke's work or have independently worked out many of his symbolic-action concepts. In America almost every critic has been influenced by him. Ransom, Tate, Brooks, and Warren have all drawn on Burke somewhat and praised him highly, while generally disagreeing with him; and Burke has in turn drawn on their insights, praised them, and, in the case of Ransom in particular, engaged in elaborate and endless literary polemic with him. Warren's study of "The Ancient Mariner" uses a good deal of Burke's work on the poem as well as the general structure of his method, while quarreling strongly with his "personal" emphasis on Coleridge's drug-addiction and marital troubles. (Burke's review of the book, in *Poetry*, April 1947, replies in kind, praising Warren's reading as having "exceptional merit" and then going on to oppose its central contention with Burke's own detailed reading, even more explicitly "personal" than before in its emphasis, and sweeping over the whole body of Coleridge's other writings for correlations.)

Randall Jarrell has written at least one first-rate Burkian analysis, "Changes of Attitude and Rhetoric in Auden's Poetry," in the *Southern Review*, Autumn 1941, announcing in the opening paragraph: "I have borrowed several terms from an extremely good book—Kenneth Burke's *Attitudes toward History*—and I should like to make acknowledgements for them," and then going on to apply the terms brilliantly in exploring Auden's symbolic and rhetorical action. Delmore Schwartz and a number of other young poets have utilized Burke in their criticism, and Muriel Rukeyser has used his concepts in her poetry, acknowledging material from *Attitudes* in *A Turning Wind*. Herbert Muller relies even more heavily on Burke's concepts and insights in his *Modern Fiction* and *Science and Criticism* than he does on those of Richards, and identifies Burke as "perhaps the most acute critic in America today." Some idea of the spread of Burke's influence in America can be had from noting the wide variety of critics who have at one time or another acknowledged some degree of indebtedness to him. In addition to the ones discussed above, the list would include: Philip Wheelwright, Newton Arvin, Arthur Mizener, Lionel Trilling, David Daiches, John L. Sweeney, Joseph Warren Beach, Ralph Ellison, Morton Dauwen Zabel, and innumerable others.

The criticism Burke's work has received makes almost as melancholy a record as that of Richards's, and like Richards he has been most enthusiastically attacked by some of the men he has influenced most profoundly. At the low end of the scale, of course, he has received the honor reserved for only the best contemporary critics, attack by Henri Peyre, Alfred Kazin, J. Donald Adams, and company. The bitterest of all these was the above-mentioned review by Sidney Hook in *Partisan Review*, which dismissed him as an apologist for Stalin and a "weak man of minor talent." (Burke's reply, in the January 1938 issue, confined itself chiefly to quoting the section of his book Hook had distorted, and Hook's counter-reply in the same issue, which continued to misconstrue Burke's term "bureaucratization" as pejorative, made it clear that the distortion was fundamental.) At the other end of the scale Burke has received a number of sympathetic studies: by Gorham B. Munson in *Destinations*, a series of studies of prominent writers of the twenties (1928); by Austin Warren in the *Sewanee Review* (Spring and Summer 1933); by Henry Bamford Parkes in *The Pragmatic Test*, which treats him as a major modern thinker along with men like James, Dewey, Nietzsche, Bergson, and Eliot; and by Howard Nemerov in "The Agon of Will as Idea: a note on the terms of Kenneth Burke," in *Furioso* (Spring 1947), which, recognizing "the impertinence of trying to compass into this brief note the vast complexities and ironies of Burke's writing," instead ingeniously added some of Nemerov's own to them. Somewhere between these two extremes no reviewer has ever quite succeeded in coping with more than one aspect of a Burke book, depending on whether the reviewer (according to the whims of editors) was a semanticist or a linguist, a social psychologist, a philosopher, a critic, a sociologist, or a plain bewildered reviewer.

4

The reason reviewers and editors have had such trouble fastening on Burke's field is that he has no field, unless it be Burkology. In recent years it has become fashionable to say that he is not actually a literary critic, but a semanticist, social psychologist, or philosopher. A much more accurate statement would be that he is not *only* a literary critic, but a literary critic *plus* those things and others. In his article "The Tactics of Motivation" Burke suggests the general problem of synthesis on a higher level than any single field could handle. He writes:

> But if one offered a synthesis of the fields covered by the various disciplines, which of the disciplines could possibly be competent to evaluate it? Where each specialty gets its worth precisely by moving towards diversity, how could any specialty possibly deal with a

project that offered a *unification* among the diversities? Or, otherwise put: if one were to write on the *interrelatedness* among ten
specialties, one would be discussing something that lay outside the
jurisdiction of them all.

The lifelong aim of Burke's criticism has been precisely this synthesis,
the unification of every discipline and body of knowledge that could
throw light on literature into one consistent critical frame. Opposing
every pious or conventional view that would exclude one critical tool or
another as "improper," Burke has insisted: "The main ideal of criticism,
as I conceive it, is to use all that is there to use." In another place, defending the use of biographical information on a poet, he writes: "we
should use whatever knowledge is available," and explains:

> I grant that such speculations interfere with the symmetry of
> criticism as a game. (Criticism as a game is best to watch, I guess,
> when one confines himself to the single unit, and reports on its
> movements like a radio commentator broadcasting the blow-by-
> blow description of a prizefight.) But linguistic analysis has opened
> up new possibilities in the correlating of producer and product—
> and these concerns have such important bearing upon matters of
> culture and conduct in general that no sheer conventions or ideals
> of criticism should be allowed to interfere with their development.

What modern criticism seems to resemble most is pre-Baconian
science, as described by Taine in his *History of English Literature:*

> So long as it [science] limited its effort to the satisfying an idle
> curiosity, opening out speculative vistas, establishing a sort of
> opera in speculative minds, it could launch out any moment into
> metaphysical abstractions and distinctions: it was enough for it to
> skim over experience; it soon quitted it, and came all at once upon
> great words, quiddities, the principle of individuation, final causes.
> Half proofs sufficed science; at bottom it did not care to establish a
> truth, but to get an opinion. . . .

Like Bacon, Burke has set out to do no less than to integrate all man's
knowledge into one workable critical frame. In the course of that, he
has set out to turn psychology on literature, has discovered that he would
first have to synthesize one consistent psychology from the warring
schools, has done it; then discovered the same need to integrate sociologies; then work both together as a social psychology; then add
linguistics and semantics to the formula; still later add philosophies and
theologies; finally, to turn the whole tremendous mass on a poem. His
aim, as stated in the conclusion to *Permanence and Change,* has been "to
show an integral relationship existing among a great variety of cultural
manifestations which are often considered in isolation." The showiest

part of Burke's work has been in the vitally necessary task of integrating Marx and Freud, or what he calls "economics" (I would prefer "sociology") and psychology. Thus he offers "a theory of the psychological processes that go with the economic ones," or proposes to unite Marx and Freud on the basic concept of "the symbols of authority," or treats Machiavelli, Hobbes, Voltaire, Bentham, Marx, and Veblen as "great formulators of economic psychoanalysis."

Burke has drawn heavily on Marxism in all his books while at the same time criticizing its mechanical simplifications in *Counter-Statement*, noting its covert "god-function" in *Attitudes*, and so forth; and all his analyses tend to have a sociological dimension, although they are rarely only that (one or two of the shorter articles in *The Philosophy of Literary Form* are exceptions). At the same time Marx himself is one of Burke's heroes, a great "dramatist" or "impresario" in "Twelve Propositions"; the great poet and rhetorician who made *The Communist Manifesto* "a masterpiece" in *A Grammar of Motives*. Burke has also drawn enthusiastically on a wide variety of other social views, from the historical tragic opera of Spengler to the philosophic social psychology of George Herbert Mead.

Similarly, his psychology is integrative and mediative, what Richards would call "centrist" and which Burke has distinguished as "a *phenomenological* science of psychology, rather than the tenuousness of the purely introspective or the impoverishment of the purely behavioristic." Its chief source is psychoanalysis, although a psychoanalysis socialized somewhat along the lines of the revisionist Freudians, since "the coordinates of individual psychology invariably place a wrong emphasis upon symbolic acts." Burke has used a tremendous amount of Freudian theory and terminology in his work since *Counter-Statement*, which canonized as permanent parts of a critical vocabulary concepts like "compensation," "transference," and "adjustment." He has written two lengthy evaluations of psychoanalysis, one in *Permanence and Change* under "Secular Conversions," and one, "Freud—and the Analysis of Poetry," in *The Philosophy of Literary Form*, reprinted from the *American Journal of Sociology*. The first attempts to "place" psychoanalytic therapy as a type of "conversion downward by misnomer," the second is a specifically literary application, attempting to suggest "how far the literary critic should go along with Freud and what extra-Freudian material he would have to add." Burke concludes that dream mechanisms like "condensation" and "displacement" are the basic mechanisms of poetry, key terms in poetic analysis, and that psychoanalysis is an approach of great value and subtlety to "poem as dream." Beyond that,

I should say that, for the explicit purposes of literary criticism, we should require more emphasis than the Freudian structure gives (1)

to the proportional strategy as against the essentializing one, (2) to matriarchal symbolizations as against the Freudian patriarchal bias, (3) to poem as prayer and chart, as against simply the poem as dream.

Burke's discussions of psychoanalysis deal not only with the theories of Freud, but also with those of the chief dissenters: Jung, Adler, Mc-Dougall, Rivers, Stekel, and Rank (he quarrels particularly with the last two, preferring Freud's free-association dream readings before Stekel's arbitrary "dream book" symbology was imposed on it, and rejecting Rank's oversimple application of the concept of the "death wish" to art in favor of a fuller "death-and-rebirth" concept). At the same time he sees Freud as he sees Marx, a titanic figure, a great tragic poet who "deserves the eternal respect of mankind because of the profound imaginativeness and methodical skill" by which he brought us face to face with the chthonic and the "cloacal" underlying apparently transcendent concerns.

Next to psychoanalysis Burke's greatest psychological indebtedness has been to the gestaltists, although he tends to see their work as a more usable extension of the experimentation of behaviorists like Watson and Pavlov rather than as a sharp break with the behavioral tradition; and it is in keeping with this that he seems to be more familiar with the laboratory work of men like Köhler and Koffka than with the theoretical work of Wertheimer. Some of Burke's most effective exercises in psychological integration have been translating back and forth among behavioral, Gestalt, and Freudian vocabularies to establish their essential agreement at key points. As much as it can be identified, Burke's own psychology seems to be a Gestalt framework with extensive Freudian additions. At the same time he has drawn on almost every other psychology, and has made particular use of Jaensch's *Eidetic Imagery*, Kretschmer's *Physique and Character*, and the laboratory work of Sherrington with animals and Piaget with children. From the frequency with which he has quoted it, Piaget's study *Language and Thought of the Child* seems to be particularly important to him (this conjecture is borne out in his review in the *New Republic* of Mrs. Colum's *From These Roots*, where he reproaches her specifically with ignoring Gestalt, Bentham and his successors, Piaget, and critics like Richards and Empson—a distinguished assortment.)

Burke has been much more critical of the theoreticians of language, although here too he has found it possible to integrate a number of disparate schools. The theory he has accepted most uncritically is the gesture-origin theory of speech of Sir Richard Paget, which he transforms into a gesture-essence theory.[2] Burke first used it in *Attitudes*

[2] This translation of theories about "origin" into theories about "essence" has become one of the major tactics in Burke's recent work. In "Ideology and Myth" in

toward History, exploring some significant consonant-sounds in writings, including his own, with the reservation that "most of our vocabulary has come from the accretions of *social* layers that carry us far from biological mimetics." Under attack by Margaret Schlauch and other philologists for holding a theory that is essentially that of the Platonic archetypes and in any case doesn't seem to fit the evidence, Burke defended Paget's theory in "The Philosophy of Literary Form" as not philology but "poetics," philology being the field studying *"the ways in which, if Paget's theory were 100 per cent correct, such linguistic mimesis as he is discussing would become obscured by historical accretions."* This is ingenious, and it may very well be true, but unfortunately Burke has himself discredited precisely this sort of escape-clause argument in *Counter-Statement:*

> Let us further note the "heads I win, tails you lose" mechanism which the psychoanalysts have at their disposal. Having defined the nature of a man's psychosis, they can fit any act into the scheme. For if the act follows the same pattern as the psychosis, they can explain it as consistent—but if it does not follow this pattern, they can account for it as "sublimated" or "compensatory." With such *vaticinium post eventum* (such explanation by epicycles) at their command, there is no reason why they should ever be at a loss for explanations in keeping with their tenets.

Modern semantics has had short shrift from Burke. His long essay "Semantic and Poetic Meaning" in *The Philosophy of Literary Form* is an eloquent exploration of the barrenness of the semantic ideal of a "neutral" vocabulary. His own ideal, like theirs, is the "purification of war," but he would achieve it, not through a wild-goose chase after "terms that avoid ambiguity," but by seeking "terms that clearly reveal the strategic spots at which ambiguities necessarily arise." Where the semantic ideal would "eliminate," Burke would "rechannelize," and the most eloquent sentence in *A Grammar of Motives* (which was written all through the war years) is the statement:

> And so human thought may be directed towards "the purification of war," not perhaps in the hope that war can be eliminated from any

---

Accent, Summer 1947, he points out that the savage, having no way to express concepts of "substance," "essence," or logical priority in general, expresses them in terms of temporal priority, as myths of "origin." For a number of years, apparently, Burke has been treating aspects of nineteenth-century evolutionary thinking like Paget's theory of the origins of speech in gesture, Freud's theory of the origin of the Œdipus complex in the slaying of the primal father, the Cambridge theory of the ritual origin of drama, as higher types of this savage myth-making, and translating them back into statements about the gesture-*nature* of speech, the ritual-*nature* of drama, etc. The process is discussed at some length under "The Temporizing of Essence" in the *Grammar*, pp. 330–40.

organism that, like man, has the motives of combat in his very essence, but in the sense that war can be refined to the point where it would be much more peaceful than the conditions we would now call peace.

Nevertheless, while quarreling somewhat with Korzybski and his followers (for nominalism, a "reductive" frame, falling into their own "two-valued orientation" pit, and so on) and Carnap and Morris (for their barren positivist ideal), Burke manages to use a number of concepts and insights from both semantic schools; as distinguished from Ogden and Richards, whom he uses pretty much without attack, and such popularizers as Thurman Arnold and Stuart Chase, whom he attacks without using (although he has credited Arnold with one "serviceable" insight, the distinction between "political government" and "business government").

Into his integration of sociologies, psychologies, linguistics, semantics, and some physical and biological science, Burke has recently added philosophies and theologies. Characteristically, his imagery in *A Grammar of Motives* is of "bargaining with" the philosophers, as where he writes: "It is an important spot to haggle over, however, if you are going to haggle at all. For once you let this point go by unquestioned, you give Kant some important advantages." Burke must have lost his shirt in the deal, because his integrative frame now draws heavily on Aquinas, Augustine, and great numbers of the saints; philosophers from Plato and Aristotle to Nietzsche, Bergson, and Santayana; and he himself has a philosophy or metaphysic, of "substance," which is chiefly defined in terms of the positivism it opposes. Burke even has a curious kind of theology, not of "gods" but of "god-terms," since "gods" are only "names for motives or combinations of motives" common to a group, and every man has the right to worship God "in his own metaphor." Burke's gods are metaphors, terms, or even words (it is amusing and typical that his reference to "the good book" should be to the dictionary). In "The Tactics of Motivation," he speaks of animals transcending the animal dimension at times "just as complex dialectical operations, developing imagery to conceive beyond imagery, may enable men slightly to transcend the human dimension." In an older theology this would have been to the third realm, the angelic or the divine; it is characteristic of Burke to make it to the "dialectic" or "poetic." (For the record, it might be noted that Burke's angels, in an early story in *The White Oxen*, spend their time in heaven singing their own compositions.)

The most complete integration of all these strains Burke has so far achieved is his concept of "dramatism." In a sense, it follows from all his previous work and all the previous methods he has absorbed. In "The

Five Master Terms" in *View*, Series III, No. 2, he writes: " 'Dramatism' is certainly no invention of ours. We lay claim only to have looked at the matter a bit more quizzically than usual, until the meditation yielded some results. Instead of saying, 'Life is a drama and the world is its theatre,' then hurrying on, we tried to ponder this metaphor long and hard." It has developed out of his constant antinomian dichotomies in *Counter-Statement*, out of the concept of attitudes as incipient "actions" in *Permanence and Change*, most particularly out of the dialectic that runs through all of Burke's work from the first as a basic principle. Burke sometimes equates all of these ("that 'attitudinal action' which we have called the dramatistic, but which might also be called the dialectical"), but actually they are a deepening and a progression, from dichotomy to attitudinal-action to dialectic to dramatism. To some extent it is the idealist dialectic of Coleridge and Hegel; to a much greater extent it is Marx's historical materialist dialectic; it is even the rationalist dialectic of "that great modern dialectician, Sigmund Freud" (although Burke has elsewhere protested that Freud "is not dialectical enough"). With Marx and Freud, Burke gets beyond dialectic into dramatism, noting that "for all the talk of 'mechanism' in the Freudian psychology, we may see its underlying dramatistic nature," and proposing a union of Marx and Freud in terms of "an over-all theory of drama," since "Freud gives us the material of the closet drama, and Marx the material of the problem play, the one worked out in terms of personal conflicts, the other in terms of public conflicts." More than any of these, of course, it is the dialectic of Plato's Socrates, *"the act of definition* in his conversation," as inherited by Aristotle.

Philosophically Burke's "dramatism" is derived most completely from Aristotle, and the Aristotelian realism of scholastic thinkers like Aquinas, in their philosophy of "action." [3] In literary terms he seems to have been chiefly influenced by Henry James's Prefaces. As early as his Yeats article in the *Southern Review*, Winter 1942, Burke wrote: "It is a dramatists's concept, the sort of concern we read much of in Henry James's prefaces, where he is offering us an analysis of the novelist's motives in terms of the dramatist's exigencies." In "Motives and Motifs in the Poetry of Marianne Moore," in *Accent*, Spring 1942, one of his earliest uses of the terms "act," "scene," and "agent," he explains them as "the three terms central to the philosophy of drama embodied in Henry James's

[3] It may be relevant here to mention a remarkable and characteristically scholastic book, Scott Buchanan's *Poetry and Mathematics* (1929), which may have influenced Burke toward dramatism, and certainly, if he read it, suggested his listing of such "reductive" metaphors for man as "Man is a machine," "Man is an animal," etc. Buchanan's book is a treatment of imaginative literature in terms of the metaphors of mathematics, and eventually a treatment of mathematics and science themselves as contemporary expressions of the pattern of Greek tragic drama.

prefaces." In "The Tactics of Motivation," *Chimera*, Summer 1943, he amplifies these references:

> Henry James's prefaces as a whole, however, exemplify a much wider use of "dramatistic" co-ordinates than this. Many of his notes deal with the relation between agent and scene (in the sense of the relation between a given work and the situation under which he wrote it). Many others deal with the author's mind as the source of the work, relations between agent and act. And many deal with the purely internal relationships prevailing among act, scene, and agent in a given novel. But throughout the prefaces, he consciously and systematically considers the novel in dramatistic terms.

As a full dramatistic perspective this is an insistence on *"ritual drama as the Ur-form, the hub,"* and all of Burke's earlier frameworks fit into it (even Paget, whose "theory of 'gesture speech' obviously makes a perfect fit with this perspective"). "Human affairs being dramatic, the discussion of human affairs becomes dramatic criticism." This ritual drama is the *agon*, with competing protagonist and antagonist, and it must be complete, "take us into-and-out-of," not incomplete, taking us into and seeking "to leave us there" (what Francis Fergusson has called, describing Wagner, "the luxury of running down a steep place into the sea"). It must be the full rhythm of "purpose to passion to perception," or "poiema, pathema, mathema," which Burke describes in "The Tactics of Motivation": "Out of the agent's action there grows a corresponding passion, and from the sufferance of this passion there arises a knowledge of his act, a knowledge that also to a degree transcends his act."

The individual ritual of "symbolic action" is thus clearly based on the pattern of ancient collective ritual, is in fact modern society's substitute for it (so that, for example, hypersexuality would be a private "erotic dance" to replace the lost tribal erotic dance). Consequently a good deal of Burke's dramatism relies on anthropology and ethnology. "He begins by considering the poet as a medicine man, and the poem as the medicine," Ransom has written, adding that he is "wonderfully keen at sniffing out ritualistic vestiges—taboo, fetish, name-calling, and so on." Burke has made a great deal of the pattern of the sacrificial king, from concluding *The Philosophy of Literary Form* with a long burlesque treating the democratic President as sacrificial king to proposing it as a ritual pattern that would have added another dimension to Bentley's study of figures like Nietzsche and D. H. Lawrence in *A Century of Hero Worship*. Burke has been greatly concerned in general with the behavior of primitive groups, drawing equally on the sweeping formulations of theorists like Frazer and the concrete and scientific reporting of modern field workers like Malinowski. He has called *The Golden Bough* "comic," his highest term of praise, since, "by showing us the rites of magical purification in primitive peoples," it "gives us the necessary cues for the detection of similar processes in even the most practical and non-priestly of contemporary acts." To my knowledge, Burke has never directly referred to the Cambridge school of classical scholars who have applied Frazer to the detection of the patterns of ancient dramatic ritual underlying Greek art and thought (Gilbert Murray, Jane Harrison, F. M. Cornford, A. B. Cook, etc.), and he seems never to have read them. Nevertheless, particularly in the *Grammar*, in his perception of "tribal patterns" behind philosophic notions, the "*agon*" behind the "dialectic," the property concepts behind the Greek "*Moira*," the "Dionysian dramas that underlay the patterns of Greek thought," he is clearly following in their line; and his appreciative review of Lord Raglan's *The Hero* (a somewhat diluted but more ambitious assertion of the same theory) and his willingness to call his work "folk criticism" suggest either some acquaintance with their work or a striking pattern of identical thinking.

The matter of Burke's terminology in general requires some consideration. In his proliferation of terms Burke is in the tradition of Bentham, Peirce, and Veblen, and their credo was stated ironically by Peirce in a letter to William James (and quoted by Burke, who calls it "these uncomfortable rigors"):

> It is an indispensable requisite of science that it should have a recognized technical vocabulary, composed of words so unattractive that loose thinkers are not tempted to use them; and a recognized and legitimate way of making up new words freely when a new conception is introduced; and that it is vital for science that he who introduces a new conception should be held to have a *duty* imposed upon him to invent a sufficiently disagreeable series of words to express it. I wish you to reflect seriously upon the moral aspect of terminology.

Burke has not, however, like Peirce, made up new words as a matter of principle, but rather, like Veblen, restored and redefined old ones wherever possible. (Chinese lawmakers, Richards informs us, recommend "that those who introduce new terms or make unauthorized distinctions should be put to death.") In this use of old words in a new precise sense, there is a loss as well as a gain. Joubert, who insisted on the employment of the common words of everyday speech even for such subjects as metaphysics, noted the gain: people are shown "what they do really think" in their own terms, the writer gives a greater impression of having assimilated "life and its concerns." Coleridge, who made up a great many words, like "intensify," which have since become current, noted the loss:

In such [scientific] discourse the instructor has no other alternative than either to use old words with new meanings (the plan adopted by Darwin in his Zoönomia;) or to introduce new terms, after the example of Linnæus, and the framers of the present chemical nomenclature. The latter mode is evidently preferable, were it only that the former demands a twofold exertion of thought in one and the same act. For the reader, or hearer, is required not only to learn and bear in mind the new definition; but to unlearn, and keep out of his view, the old and habitual meaning; a far more difficult and perplexing task, and for which the mere semblance of eschewing pedantry seems to me an inadequate compensation.

He conceded, however, that where "it is in our power to recall an unappropriate term that had without sufficient reason become obsolete, it is doubtless a less evil to restore than to coin anew." Burke thus gains a number of real values from his use of common terms in a transformed, unfamiliar, or obsolete sense; but the fact that his "comic" does not mean what people think of as comic, and his "prayer" does not mean what people think of as prayer, is undoubtedly responsible for some confusion in his readers, and probably contributes to the numerical limitation of his audience.

On the other hand, Burke's terms have been moving toward greater and greater clarity, each developing out of the set before, and the current dramatistic pentad—act, scene, agent, agency, purpose—would probably come closest to satisfying Joubert as being the language of common speech. Burke writes:

It must be our purpose ever to perfect our terminology—for in an adequate terminology there are adequate exhortations and admonitions. And basic to the structure of a terminology is the need for an essential complexity or pliancy—not merely complexity got by the accumulation of terms, but complexity *at the start*. . . .

A curious device of this development in Burke's work is the nursing along, in each book, of the metaphor that eventually burgeoned as "dramatism." Thus *Counter-Statement* defines form as "the psychology of the audience," and concludes on the development of dramatic form as "representative anecdote." *Permanence and Change*, in its conclusion, suggests that the "ultimate metaphor" for discussing the universe and man's relations to it would be "poetic or dramatic man." *Attitudes toward History* speaks of the inventor's "drama," Burke's own historical "drama," and argues in a footnote:

In brief, we contend that "perspective by incongruity" makes for a *dramatic* vocabulary, with weighting counter-weighting, in contrast with the liberal ideal of a *neutral* naming in the characterization of processes. . . .

The neutral ideal prompts one to forget that terms are *characters*, that an essay is an *attenuated play*. . . .

The element of dramatic *personality* in essayistic *ideas* cannot be intelligently discerned until we recognize that names (for either dramatic characters or essayistic concepts) are shorthand designations for certain fields and methods of action.

By 1941, when *The Philosophy of Literary Form* was published, Burke's dramatist metaphor had developed the two basic terms of the pentad, and he trots out the act-scene terminology on the first page of the Foreword and continues it through the title essay, discussing symbolic action in terms of "agons" and, in a footnote, explaining all five terms of the pentad and what his next work will do with them. At the same time the essay "Semantic and Poetic Meaning" distinguishes the poetic ideal as going "through" drama rather than around it, and the eleventh proposition of Burke's "Twelve Propositions on the Relation between Economics and Psychology" is flatly: "Human relations should be analyzed with respect to the leads discovered by a study of drama," while the development of this proposition announces Freud and Marx as "impresarios."

The only other terminological metaphor that Burke has carried through from his earliest books is the ironic use of the terminology of business and finance for markedly non-financial matters, a device he shares with Thoreau. He speaks of "investment," "socialization of losses," "cashing in on," "discounting," "mergers," as though matters of art and ideas were important enough to get on ledgers. "Once the comic proviso is added," he notes, "the whole terminology of capitalism is found remarkable for its clear simplification of social processes." In "Character of Our Culture" in the *Southern Review*, Spring 1941, Burke calls his attitude "speculative," with the melancholy note:

> I use the word "speculative" with full awareness of its monetary pun, for in calling myself here a "speculator" I fully believe that I am exemplifying a social value that has been affected by the monetary motivation—though I must speak, alas! as one who has not had the advantage of much original field work in this subject, one whose knowledge of it is at best second-hand, indeed, one who has money much more on his mind than in his purse.

Burke's dramatist pentad is an attempt to find a set of terms so basic and so all-embracing that they can handle any area of discourse. As such, it is the successor of a long line of triads, tetrads, pentads, etc. The most obvious relationship, to which Burke himself calls attention in the book, is to Aristotle's Four Causes—formal, material, efficient, and final—which Burke equates respectively with act, scene, agent, and purpose, with agency also included under "final." Burke also equates his pentad with Aristotle's six elements of tragedy, plot as act, character as agent, thought as purpose, melody and diction as agency, and spectacle as scene. After Aristotle, Ben Jonson had a more or less Aristotelian triad in *Discoveries*—poem, poesy, poet—which would probably correspond to Burke's agency, act, and agent. Lessing's bodies-actions dichotomy in the *Laocoön* is a very close approximation of scene-act, and Lessing later fills out the other terms. Emerson's triad of cause-operation-effect in "The Poet," which he translates poetically as Jove-Pluto-Neptune, Father-Spirit-Son, and Knower-Doer-Sayer, would probably be the equivalents of purpose, act, and either scene or agent. Santayana, in *Interpretations of Poetry and Religion*, in describing the way in which nature, an "engine" under paganism, becomes "a temporary stage, built for the exigencies of a human drama" under Christianity, clearly has a dramatist set of terms that includes at least act and scene. Finally, Ernest Fenollosa, in his essay on "The Chinese Written Character as a Medium for Poetry," has an agent-act-object triad very close to Burke's pentad.

One major aspect of Burke's work has been somewhat slighted in the discussion above: his treatment of "rhetoric," the poem-audience relationship, which has been arbitrarily assigned as Richards's territory. Actually Burke has been concerned with rhetorical action almost as much as with symbolic action in his work, and in *Counter-Statement* and *Permanence and Change* much more. In "The Philosophy of Literary Form," he proposes a relationship between the poet-poem and the poem-audience ratios that involves rhetoric with a kind of symbolic action in the audience. He writes:

Many of the things that a poet's work does for *him* are not things that the same work does for *us* (i.e., there is a difference in act between the poem as being-written and the poem as being-read). Some of them are, some of them are not. . . .

But my position is this: That if we try to discover what the poem is doing for the poet, we may discover a set of generalizations as to what poems do for everybody. With these in mind, we have cues for analyzing the sort of *eventfulness* that the poem contains. And in analyzing this eventfulness, we shall make basic discoveries about the *structure* of the work itself. . . .

And I contend that the kind of observation about structure is more relevant when you approach the work as the *functioning* of a structure. . . . And I contend that some such description of the "symbolic

act" as I am here proposing is best adapted for the disclosure of a
poem's function.

A poem is thus designed to "do something" for the poet and his readers,
and the poet's manipulation of this symbolic action in the reader is
rhetoric, or what is more generally called "communication" as distinguished from "expression." Burke also identifies it with "prayer" in
his dream-prayer-chart triad, or "the choice of gesture" to embody the
poet's attitude "for the inducement of corresponding attitudes." The
poem is thus a symbolic act of the poet, but "surviving as a structure
or object, it enables us as readers to re-enact it," so that reading too is
the enactment of symbolic "rites."

Burke has two elaborate studies of rhetoric in *The Philosophy of Literary
Form*, "Antony in Behalf of the Play," a long monologue by Antony to
the audience explaining Shakespeare's mechanisms as they focus in his
oration over Cæsar's body, and "Trial Translation (from Twelfth
Night)," a less ambitious but similar explanation by the Duke. Burke
has called these studies of the "reader-writer relationship," but more
properly they are studies of the reader-poem relationship, since they
work from the text rather than from Shakespeare. His fuller study,
"The Rhetoric of Hitler's 'Battle,' " is more accurately a study of the
reader-writer relationship, since it covers Hitler's symbolic expression
in the book, the audience's symbolic action in reading it, and the rhetorical relation between the two. It unites the private and public, the
introspective (conjectural in this case) psychology best designed for
getting at the author's symbolic expression, and the behavioral psychology best designed for getting at what is rhetorically communicated.

Counter-Statement attempts to develop the concept of rhetoric, first
through a distinction between "clinical" and "songful" handling, then
between "realistic" and "declamatory," "observation" and "ritual,"
"information" and "ceremony"; finally fixing on the distinction (later
"chart" versus "prayer") between "the psychology of information"
and "the psychology of form." "Form," which *Counter-Statement* defines as
"the psychology of the audience" and "the creation of an appetite in the
mind of the auditor, and the adequate satisfying of that appetite," or
"the arousing and fulfillment of desires," is thus equivalent to "rhetoric," which is no more than "effective literature." By his next book,
Permanence and Change, Burke was calling this phenomenon "stylistic
ingratiation," to leave room in the term "form" for structure symbolically as well as rhetorically determined.

Edmund Wilson quotes H. L. Mencken as saying that he even enjoys
the prospectuses put out by bond houses, because everything written
is an attempt to express the aspirations of some human being. Burke's
concepts of "symbolic action" and "rhetoric" result in a similar embrac-

ing of trash of every description (although we can doubt that he "enjoys" it as Mencken does), which frequently illustrates the mechanisms of more significant works in a fashion easier to follow. For purposes of analysis or illustration Burke draws as readily on a popular movie, a radio quiz program, a *Herald Tribune* news item about the National Association of Manufacturers, or a Carter Glass speech on gold as on Sophocles or Shakespeare. Those things are a kind of poetry too, full of symbolic and rhetorical ingredients, and if they are bad poetry, it is a bad poetry of vital significance in our lives. In immersing himself in this cheap "forensic" material as much as he does (we can presume that *A Rhetoric of Motives* will consist largely of it), Burke is himself a kind of sacrificial king, bored to death that the tribe's crops may grow.

5

Finally, a brief look at Burke's own situation, strategies, attitudes, motives, symbolic actions, purposes, is in order. One factor of great importance is his non-critical writing, of which he has been moderately prolific. He has published two works of fiction, *The White Oxen*, a collection of short stories, in 1924, and *Towards a Better Life*, a novel written as "a Series of Epistles, or Declamations," in 1932. Both works are subtle, ambiguous, fairly obscure, stylized, and highly eloquent: the former progressing from fairly realistic stories to stories bewilderingly symbolic and rhetorical, as a kind of "counter-statement" at a time "when rhetoric is so universally despised"; the latter a gesture of return "to more formalized modes of writing," "from the impromptu to the studied," its concern with plot "peripheral," its central concern with what Burke calls the Six Pivotals: "lamentation, rejoicing, beseechment, admonition, sayings, invective." Both books have been little read or recognized, although they have clearly influenced such writers as Robert M. Coates and Nathanael West, have been praised by William Carlos Williams and attacked as "duller than Thackeray" by Yvor Winters, and *Towards a Better Life* at least seems to me one of the important works of fiction in our time. In relation to his criticism, the only ground for discussing them here, they echo many of the ideas, demonstrate many of the theories in practice, function as the same imaginative "placing" of human motives from a different angle; and while they were written chiefly as rhetorical action, they have given his later criticism endless material for identifying symbolic action.

Wilde, I believe, somewhere remarks that he got his education in public, as a reviewer, and Burke has used his reviewing in a similar fashion. As a comparison of the articles in *The Philosophy of Literary Form* with the reviews printed as an Appendix reveals, the subject of this year's review becomes the subject of next year's references, and by going far afield from imaginative literature in his reviews, he has consistently broadened the horizons of his work. At the same time Burke gets critical ideas directly from problems that arise out of his reviewing ("It was in the attempt to review two books of this sort that we first found ourselves confronting what we consider the typical properties of constitutions"); and in some cases he even writes his reviews in whole or part into his later text. Burke has also written music criticism, including a stint as music critic for the *Nation*, and occasional art criticism, so that his work, particularly *Counter-Statement*, is larded with authoritative musical and plastic references and analogies (although it must be admitted that his art references, unlike his music references, tend to be to rather literary, rarely abstract or modern, works). Burke has also done a great deal of translating from the German, including some of Mann's short stories, and works by Spengler, Schnitzler, von Hoffmannsthal, Emil Ludwig, and others, which then too became grist for his critical mill. Finally, he has published a number of poems, most of them free in form, rhetorical, and emphasizing irony and social protest, which have never been collected in book form.

Burke's social ideas, as expressed most directly in his poetry and in a more complex fashion in his criticism, form a complicated and ambiguous pattern. The chief element is an outspoken dislike for technology and our machine civilization, with its cults of "efficiency," "the higher standard of living," and so on; with a remarkable consistency all of his works from the earliest to the latest have constituted a "counter-statement" to the technological ideal, opposing it with "negativism," "opposition," "interference"; in short: "the æsthetic would seek to discourage the most stimulating values of the practical, would seek—by wit, by fancy, by anathema, by versatility—to throw into confusion the code which underlies commercial enterprise, industrial competition, the 'heroism' of economic warfare; would seek to endanger the basic props of industry." This is from the "Program" in *Counter-Statement*, Burke's early manifesto for æstheticism, but the same themes continue in the Conclusion to *Permanence and Change*, formalized as a poetic communism; and in the section on "Good Life" in *Attitudes toward History*, stated more positively in terms of ideals of active participation and ecological balance. In *The Philosophy of Literary Form* they become more bitter, with references to "our despicable economic structure" making us do "despicable things"; and more pessimistic, with Burke seeing "a dismal political season" in store for us, the only hope temporarily "a campaign base for personal integrity, a kind of beneath-which-not," which is actually Eliot's last-ditch ideal, to "keep something alive." By *A Grammar of Motives*, the social view becomes at once less bitter and less pessimistic. Burke is still antagonistic to our cult of the "gadget," "the higher standard of living," [4] the "fantastic hardships" that men undergo to have technological "conveniences," but the industrial system and the money motive are now "poignant" rather than "despicable," and he finds an ironic hope:

> At a time when the liars, the stupid, and the greedy seem too greatly in control of a society's policies, philosophies of materialistic reduction may bring us much solace in reminding us that *the very nature of the materials* out of which a civilization is constructed, or in which it is grounded, will not permit such *perfection* of lies, stupidity, and greed to prevail as some men might cause to prevail if they could have their way.

His conclusion is the proposal of "a kind of 'Neo-Stoic resignation,'" since "For better or worse, men are set to complete the development of technology."

There are two strains in this attitude, which after a time separated. One is an objection to machinery, technology, industrialization per se, in any society, with Burke opposing to them a "maximum of physicality," less button-pressing, less mobility and more action, biological adaptation and "metabiology," and a larger ecological efficiency opposed to the limited "efficiency" of technology. This is the most "reactionary" (in the pure sense of the word) strain in Burke, an agrarian, backward-looking ideal that he shares with Thoreau, the Jeffersonians and Populists, and less savory groups, and which has led Henry Bamford Parkes to write, with a certain accuracy: "he would like to have lived in Confucian China." At its most extreme this is even a dislike of science itself, and there is some truth in a reviewer's charge that Burke, like the old ladies of the anti-vivisection societies, tends to see laboratory scientists as "sadistic rat-torturers." At the other extreme he is prepared to find some good in technology, even defending it against an archæologist named Kidder in his article "Character of Our Culture," finding such real, if negative values as its lessening the ravages of crop failure, pestilence, and other natural disasters. Somewhere in the middle he himself lives ("His life itself is a design," William Carlos Williams wrote in the *Dial*), combining the simple, immobile, and agrarian life with the technology necessary to get him, by car, train, and subway, to the New York Public Library.

The other strain in Burke's social attitude is his objection, not to industrialization per se, but to the specific features of the capitalistic

---

[4] By 1947, in an article on "The American Way" in the December *Touchstone*, Burke was describing the whole of American culture as derived from the generalizing principle of "the higher standard of living," used in a non-pejorative sense, with American philosophic and æsthetic concepts either expressions of it or reactions to it.

system. In *Permanence and Change* he embraces Communism (largely of an out-of-the-world variety), proposing a dialectical materialism altered into a "dialectical biologism," and a "poetic" and "stylistic" life achieved through and beyond the Communist society. He argues that Communism is "the only coherent and organized movement making for the subjection of the technological genius to human ends," and that it polarizes such valuable c-words (or "Kenneth-words") as co-operation, communication, communion, collectivism, and communicant. In *Attitudes toward History* he finds collectivism inevitable as the next stage in his curve of history, but presents his collectivist communism with "comic correctives," and the section on the "Good Life" made it clear that his social ideal is actually much more Confucian (if not more confused). Although he still refers approvingly to such orthodox Communist equipment as "dialectical materialism," his later works have veered away from calling his agrarian and decentralized Jeffersonian social ideal "Communism." Fordism is apparently to his mind still Fordism, whether of the American or the Soviet variety.

Burke's ideas on poetry and criticism are inextricably tied up with his ideas on life (he defines art, for example, as "biological adaptation," thus the "good life") and are frequently on a high enough level of abstraction to be both at once. On criticism his keynote is the topic sentence of *Permanence and Chance:* "All living things are critics," with the example of the trout, becoming a critic after his jaw is ripped, learning "a nicer discrimination between food and bait." His critic, like Matthew Arnold's, is, in the last analysis, a critic of life; and his job: "to present as many counter-influences as possible," "to integrate technical criticism with social criticism," "to look a gift horse in the mouth." Where the "poet" hypnotizes, it is "the function of criticism to supply the sharp sound that awakens us"; and "whatever poetry may be, criticism had best be comic."

This view is not, however, contemptuous of poetry. The theme that "poetry" (whether as a written lyric, a world-view, or a way of life) is very close to the central value of our existence runs through all of Burke's writing; it is "equipment for living," it "comforts," "protects," and "arms" us. At the same time he insists on the importance of the poetic sensibility, what Blackmur calls "the symbolic imagination," as the ultimate feature of criticism, writing:

> The objection arises when philosophers of science are loath to grant that this very capacity of science demands a compensatory counterpart, variously named "intuition," "imagination," "vision," "revelation," etc. For though one could scientifically break a work of art into many ingredients, and by test arrive at some extremely subtle and perfectly just discriminations about these ingredients, it

is when confronting the *synthesis* of the ingredients that the scientific method becomes inadequate.

The other essential ingredient in Burke's scheme is the element in irony, humor, "the comic." He defines humor as the "humanization" that "enables us to accept our dilemmas"; irony as the "humility" that comes from "a sense of fundamental kinship with the enemy"; the comic as a "charitable" attitude containing the paradox of acceptance-rejection, give and take. Essentially all these are aspects of the same thing: an attitude of scrupulosity, reservation, "getting off before the end of the line," counterstating, corrective discounting, "rolling with the punch." Burke's good life would not only be good; it would be comic, ironic, perhaps even funny. In any case it would certainly be undignified. Burke writes in an early essay:

> Dignity? Yes, there seems to be a thirst for personal dignity. There is a trace of the hysterical, the devious, in this need of dignity. Dignity belongs to the conquered; one leaves the room with dignity when he has been routed; the victor can romp. Dignity is a subjective adjustment. It is objectively unpliant; it is unbiological, a dignified man could not run from a lion. One meets facts objectively without dignity. One sacrifices his authority, first asking what mean task the outside thing demands of him. Dignity is Ptolemaic, indignity is Copernican. The development of man in Europe, some one has said, has been a loss of personal dignity in proportion to his mastery of nature.

Finally, there is the matter of Burke's critical writing itself. He has always had a relatively small audience, although it has been a regularly increasing one, and the sale of *A Grammar of Motives* was substantial enough to constitute, finally, a kind of public recognition and success, the sort that artists of unyielding integrity (Martha Graham comes to mind as another example) tend to achieve late in life, after a generation of popular "sell-outs" have had their brief fames and blown away. The chief reason, in my experience, given for resistance or inability to read him is the charge of "obscurity" or "jargon." Not referring to himself, Burke answered the "obscurity" charge in *Counter-Statement*, writing: "There are some forms of excellence (such as complexity, subtlety, remote inquiry, stylistic rigor) which may limit a book's public as surely as though it were a work on higher mathematics." Actually Burke's writing itself is very clear and very straightforward, the obscurity being entirely a matter of the concepts and terms. Even John Crowe Ransom, who has sometimes been his severest critic, has granted him a prose of "literary distinction." The charge of "jargon" is somewhat more accurate. Although Burke has frequently kidded the German philosophic style (he notes that Kant, Fichte, Schelling, and Hegel "write like the shifting of cars in a freight yard"), he is at the same time somewhat drawn to it, defends its "cumbersome nomenclature" as "a form of poetry," and in such terms as "Neo-Malthusian Principle," "Bureaucratization of the Imaginative," and "Perspective by Incongruity" comes very close to its characteristic jargon.

A number of his stylistic habits and devices have been known to irritate readers. The trick of stress-shifting, the distinction between "knowledge of the *Good*" and "*knowledge* of the Good," although a meaningful and effective dialectic device, tends to be used enough in the late work to be irritating. The distinction between "what are years?" and "what all are years?" is a barbarism, pure and simple. Less justifiable reader annoyance is sometimes felt at two of his most characteristic and most brilliantly effective devices: his use of words in a special sense by putting them in quotation marks, and his footnotes. The quotation marks ("And the childless priest could be named a 'father' because he had 'spiritual' progeny, the 'children' of the church") are a way of emphasizing, pointing up double meanings, marking off a special sense. The footnotes rise in an arc from a few in *Counter-Statement*, more in *Permanence and Change*, and most in *Attitudes toward History;* and then fall off, with fewer in *The Philosophy of Literary Form* and almost none in *A Grammar of Motives*. At their height, in *Attitudes*, where the footnotes bulk almost as large as the text, they serve as a wonderful counterpoint melody: the specific against the general, the peripheral against the central, the random against the planned, the suggestive against the explored (Burke has thrown off in footnotes enough suggestions regarding things he has never had a chance to investigate to keep a flotilla of critics busy for a lifetime). Nevertheless, the constant footnotes carrying along another story occasionally get the reader feeling a little schizoid, and there is no doubt that at their apogee they represented some similar unreconciled dissociation in Burke, which he seems to have reconciled since. Finally, Burke's style sometimes tends to be unnecessarily repetitious, as when he restates a thing three times, using a slightly different figure each time, rather than stating it fully once and for all; he splits infinitives without qualm; and he mixes metaphors wickedly (Margaret Schlauch, who pointed some out in a review, noted that the issue is not a grammarian's purism, but that Burke tends to blunt the usefulness of his metaphors by mixing them, as in his "frames" that "melt," "struggle," and "contend").

On the other hand, one of the most ingratiating features of Burke's style is his constant reliance on the joke and the pun, even the elaborate burlesque, to make serious points. His jokes, when they are successful, are wonderful, a wry and ironic humor that always bites; but the pun has an even more important and serious function in his work. Like the ancient Egyptians, who used to fill their sacred rituals with puns to increase their magic effectiveness, Burke puts into his puns the heart of what he has to say. Like Shakespeare's, Burke's puns are lightning metaphors, Empsonian ambiguities, perspectives by incongruity, reinforced by his passionate interest in etymology and awareness of linguistic significance on a great number of levels, including the psychoanalytic.

Another feature of Burke's writing, which has markedly increased in the recent books, is a concern with the scatological. Burke is insistent on the need for "making peace with," alternately, "the soil" and "the fæces." He has identified Freud's work as "an interpretative sculpting of excrement"; Stoicism as "the transcendence of offal"; Eliot's *"Merdes" in the Cathedral*, an "ecclesia super cloacam." One section of *A Grammar of Motives* explains his concept of the "Demonic Trinity," the interrelationship of the erotic, urinary, and excremental, and he has increasingly tended to translate back and forth among all three and related motifs like the mystical vision and the monetary. Burke's scatalogical concern unquestionably represents a serious and profound attempt, like Freud's, to confront the "cloacal" underlying our "transcendent" activities, but at times the flippancy of his presentation makes it seem merely another "counter" or antinomian expression; to try a Burkian pun (encouraged by his "latent patent, covert overt"), we might say that he has received so little of the world's "increment" that he has been forced to devote himself to its "excrement."[5]

The final question about Burke's work is what it all adds up to. If it has seemingly had a lack of focus, gone after a bewildering number of quarries in no apparent sequence, it has had the compensatory virtue of endless fertility, suggestiveness, an inexhaustible throwing off of sparks. This view would seem to be borne out by the readiness with which Burke seems reducible to aphorisms: the "Flowerishes" printed in the *Rocky Mountain Review*, Winter 1943; the facility with which brief excerpts from the *Grammar* stood alone in a publisher's brochure called "The Burke Sampler" and *Accent*, Autumn 1945; the "memorability" of isolated lines from his work: America as a country in which death "is in exceptionally bad repute," "Thou shalt not commit adulteration," the right of each man "to worship God in his own metaphor," "Die as a mangled wasp dies," "The man did good for the oppressed? Then he made them oppressors," and so on.

And yet, valuable as this quality is, it is more likely that Burke's work

5 It has been suggested to me that Burke's critical preoccupation with the cheap forensic material of the movies, the radio, and the newspapers may not represent the sacrificial boredom to which I attribute it so much as another aspect of this fascinated scatological concern.

is intensely organized and that with the conclusion of his current trilogy a total pattern will emerge to embrace all his previous work. It will be probably the most all-embracing critical system ever built up for turning on a single poem, and we can expect a period of unequaled critical fruitfulness as Burke and his followers turn it on poem after poem in succession. What would not one give, for example, for a full-length study by Burke of such a work of endless fertility as *Moby Dick*, never satisfactorily explored? (He has, incidentally, in several places mentioned making notes on it.) To raise the obvious objection immediately, suppose the poem or work collapses flat under the tremendous weight of the critical system? Our faith here must lie in Burke's genuine humility, the ironic humor that keeps him always backing away from his own machinery. In *Towards a Better Life* his hero aphorizes: "Watch the mind as you would eye a mean dog";[6] and in the sobering conclusion of *Permanence and Change* Burke reminds us "that men build their cultures by huddling together, nervously loquacious, at the edge of an abyss."

In "A Critic's Job of Work" R. P. Blackmur charges that Burke's method "could be applied with equal fruitfulness to Shakespeare, Dashiell Hammett, or Marie Corelli." In *The Philosophy of Literary Form* Burke admits the charge (after he "got through wincing"), adding: "You can't properly put Marie Corelli and Shakespeare apart until you have first put them together. First genus, then differentia. The strategy in common is the genus. The *range* or *scale* or *spectrum* of particularizations is the differentia." What we can expect with the completion of Burke's system is the detailed studies of "differentiæ," what Burke elsewhere calls "the miracle of evaluation," built on the present somewhat indiscriminate lumping by genus. From the brief samples of it Burke occasionally vouchsafes us, we can be sure that it will be literary criticism almost unequaled for power, lucidity, depth, and brilliance of perception. In the ultimately unclassifiable man who once had a protagonist remark: "One is not quite at rest when he has accounted for so much nobility by trivial mechanisms," all we can be sure of beyond that is that it will be a literary criticism constituting a passionate avowal of the ultimate and transcendent importance of the creative act.

[6] As Burke would be the first to point out, this terrifying relationship of "mind" to "*mean dog*" was probably inspired by a tonal pun.

CONCLUSION:

ATTEMPTS AT AN INTEGRATION

I. The Ideal Critic

IF WE could, hypothetically, construct an ideal modern literary critic out of plastics and light metals, his method would be a synthesis of every practical technique or procedure used by his flesh-and-blood colleagues. From all the rival approaches he would borrow as much as could be used in a synthesis without distorting the whole, he would balance one bias or excess or overspecialization against another so that both canceled out, and he was left with only neutral elements adaptable to his own purposes. From Edmund Wilson he would take the function of translation or interpretation, of explaining the work's paraphrasable content, and augment it with the greater concern for poetic and formal values found, say, in the early interpretive criticism of Ezra Pound. From Yvor Winters he would borrow the emphasis on evaluation and comparative judgment, as well as Winters's refusal to be intimidated by conventional opinions in his judgments, rather than the judgments themselves. He could use T. S. Eliot's passionate concern with grounding literature in a tradition although his tradition would probably look more like V. F. Parrington's, and he could also use Eliot's functional relationship between poetry and criticism. From Van Wyck Brooks our ideal critic would take the biographical method of the early books, and the general concern with the cultural climate of a writer. Constance Rourke would contribute her emphasis on the folk background of a work, as well as her insistence that this tradition tends to be one of form rather than content, and abstract rather than realistic. Maud Bodkin's psychoanalytic method would go into the synthesis, augmented by theories and procedures from Gestalt, revisionist Freudian, and other psychologies; as would Christopher Caudwell's Marxist method, modified by Plekhanov's historical relativism, Alick West's detailed concern with specific texts, and many insights from other sociologies.

Our ideal critic would adopt Caroline Spurgeon's conscientious scholarship, going to John Livingston Lowes's lengths and extending the results with the imaginative rashness of G. Wilson Knight; as well as Armstrong's preoccupation with the image cluster as a unit of special poetic significance. From R. P. Blackmur he would take the technique of hard

395

work and research, the preoccupation with language and diction, and the insistence on the high importance of art and the symbolic imagination. William Empson would furnish his exploration of categories and ambiguities, his close and ingenious textual reading, and his general concern with the significance of literary forms. From I. A. Richards our ideal critic would borrow the concern with communication, techniques of interpretation, and the experimental method; from Kenneth Burke, the concern with symbolic action, techniques of integration within a framework of dramatism, and the introspective method. Other critics would furnish still other elements to the synthesis: Jane Harrison's ritual anthropology and Margaret Schlauch's linguistics; Herbert Read's sympathetic attention to every new current of thought and every youthful artist; the balanced concern with the totality of the work of the *Scrutiny* group; F. O. Matthiessen's subtle correlations between the sociological and the æsthetic; Francis Fergusson's use of the ritual drama and William Troy's use of the ritual myth; the focus on poetic structure of John Crowe Ransom, Allen Tate, Cleanth Brooks, and Robert Penn Warren; and much else from others. Finally, the ideal critic would be a neo-Aristotelian, scrupulously inducing from poetic practice, as well as a neo-Coleridgean, frankly deducing from philosophic concepts.

At the same time our ideal critic would discard from all these critics those features of their practice that seemed to him irrelevant, worthless, or private to them, stripping from the neutral and objective method their special obsessions, preoccupations, and weaknesses. He would have no use for Wilson's superficiality or dealings in second-hand ideas or impatience with form. He would not want Winters's obsessive morality, nor his semantically meaningless dogmatism with no basis for judgment given, nor his bad temper, nor his high percentage of error. In adopting Eliot's concern with tradition, he would husk it of its religious and political bias, and in adopting Eliot's organic continuity between the poetic and critical function, he would maintain criticism's independence and integrity. Rejecting Brooks's *a priori* assumptions and contempt for imaginative literature, the ideal critic would not use his biographical method as a Procrustean bed for writers, or as an excuse for escaping from the work to the personality, or as a way of dispensing sweetness and light at a literary tea. In taking over Miss Rourke's method, he would steer clear of both the "folksy" and the "*volkisch*," and would operate from a far wider learning than hers. Miss Bodkin's mystic and religious emphasis would be discarded (along with Jung's Nazi racialism and blood-and-soil irrationalism, which she avoided); as would Caudwell's bias against psychoanalysis, guilt about poetry, class debunking, absolutism, and preference for generalities rather than texts. Both Freud and Marx would be used with as sharp a sense as theirs, and a sharper sense than their followers', of the limitations of their approaches applied to literature. Our ideal critic would operate from the same sharp awareness of the limits of scholarship, the area where it must shade over into criticism to be fulfilled, and he would adopt neither Miss Spurgeon's timidity about following through on conclusions nor her personal mysticism. He would probably find not very much to reject in Blackmur, Empson, Richards, and Burke, but could probably get along without the traces of preciousness in the first, the occasional overelaboration of the second, the blind alley of Basic English in the third, and the anachronistic resistance to progress in the fourth. From the other critics he drew on he would make similar scrapings, and in most cases would probably find more to scrape away than to keep. Even Aristotle and Coleridge would not be entirely to his purpose.

This ideal integration of all of modern critical method into one super-method could not be on the analogy of stew, with everything thrown at random into the pot, but would have to be on the analogy of construction, with the structure built up according to an orderly plan on some foundation or around some skeleton framework. What, then, would that foundation, framework, or basis be? The most enthusiastic candidate for the job is Marxism, whose spokesmen have regularly insisted that dialectical materialism is an integrative frame able to encompass and use the newest advances in all fields of knowledge, and in fact must do so to function. This was undoubtedly true of Marx and Engels, who drew enthusiastically on immense accumulations of knowledge in every area, and adapted to new developments so elastically that Engels remarked: "With each epoch-making discovery in the department of natural science, materialism has been obliged to change its form." It is also to a large extent true of Caudwell, who insists in the Introduction to *Illusion and Reality*: "But physics, anthropology, history, biology, philosophy and psychology are also products of society, and therefore a sound sociology would enable the art critic to employ criteria drawn from these fields without falling into eclecticism or confusing art with psychology or politics." Later Marxists, however, with the exception of a few isolated figures like Caudwell, have lacked the elasticity and scrupulousness of Marx and Engels, as well as their learning and brilliance, so that Marxism in practice has hardly made good its claim as an all-embracing integrative system. Most contemporary Marxist thinkers, in fact, would toss the greater part of our ideal critical method out the window immediately as "decadent" frippery.

Few other individual methods or disciplines are even formulated so as to embrace other approaches, and where they are sciences or near-sciences, like psychology and anthropology, or clearly demarcated fields, like scholarship or biography, they obviously could not invade other territories without automatically losing their special character. Clearly, the basis for an ideal critical integration would have to be a literary or philosophic concept (it should be obvious from the foregoing that when Marxism sets itself up as a giant integrative frame, it is not in its aspect as a sociology but in its aspect as a philosophic *Weltanschauung*). Without aspiring to solve the problem offhand, we might note a few possible bases for such a synthesis. One would be the concept of Organicism, the organic unity of the human personality, Richards's continuity of experience, in terms of which all these critical approaches could be unified as dealing with related aspects of human behavior: man as poet, man as reader, the family man, the social man, man communicating, and so on. Another, avoiding the nominalism inherent in the first, would be Social Activity, organizing the various approaches as relational aspects with different groups, inherent in the work of art. Others would include: Burke's metaphor of Dramatism, with its pentad of act, scene, agent, agency, and purpose, treating the other approaches as emphases on one term or another, conflicting and co-operating like characters in a play; Empson's concept of Ambiguity extended, with all other approaches as further ambiguities of meaning in the words of the poem; or even Blackmur's doctrine of Hard Work, equated with Burke's Use All There Is to Use, as simply the rather disorganized organizing principle of investigating every possible line of significance.

In our ideal critic we would assume not only the use of all the fruitful methods of modern criticism on some organizing base, but necessarily all the abilities and special aptitudes behind them, a fearful assumption of personal capacity, as well as the requisite learning in all these areas, and the requisite flexibility of focus. Our ideal critic would not only have to *do* more than any actual critic, he would have to *know* more, *range* farther, and *be* more (as well as *write* better, certainly). The classification of critics in this book has been largely by method; noting other possible classifications that cut across this one on the bias should suggest how much else is involved. Thus classification by focus would have: Blackmur the specialist in words, Miss Spurgeon in images, Empson in forms, Burke in the totality of a man's work, and so forth. Classification by learning would have: Eliot the man knowing literature temporarily out of fashion, Caudwell the man knowing modern science, Brooks the man knowing minor writers of the period, Miss Bodkin knowing the classics, and so on. Classification by attribute (which has been necessarily assumed as underlying the method) would have: Empson the keen reader, Burke the intelligence shooting sparks, Richards the patient teacher, Blackmur and Miss Spurgeon (in different senses) the painstaking workers. (It might be pointed out here that Blackmur's hard work, which has been treated throughout as a method, is much more definitely a personal attribute. It has been classified as a method only because it seems both essential and transmissible: any critic can and must do hard work, in the sense in which he cannot or need not at all set himself to becoming an intelligence shooting sparks.)

The last problem that our ideal critic would have to face, and the most overwhelming of all, is that each of the methods developed by modern critics is only in a first preliminary stage of exploration, and at one time or another all of their originators have had to recognize that they have only scratched the surface and will hardly be able to do more in their lifetimes. Each method is capable of almost limitless extension and ramification, and our harried ideal critic would have not only to use them all, but to proliferate each of them enormously, solving the problems and adjusting to the perspectives confronting each method in isolation (which have been suggested in the individual chapters and need no recapitulation here). He would have to do it all himself, too. Each of our modern critics needs disciples, a school to carry on, apply, and extend his work; but the difficulty is that in so far as the disciples are themselves brilliant and creative (and the problem if they are not is obvious), they inevitably tend to go off in their own directions—as in the case of Richards's star pupil, Empson—and in turn to need disciples of their own. Blackmur, Fergusson, Slochower, and Cowley are all to some extent applying Burke's method to other literary problems and texts, but at the same time they are in business for themselves, and they will be efficient disciples in inverse proportion to how original, creative, and ultimately valuable to criticism they are. Only in the world inhabited by our ideal critic do people use a method with exactly the same aims and in exactly the same fashion as its originator. In the real world of criticism there is probably nothing we would want less.

To sum up, our ideal critic would extend his whole integrated method just as far as its individual component methods are capable of extension in isolation. He would, in short, do everything possible with a work of literature. For a brief lyric, as can be imagined, this would result in a tome of several volumes; for a more elaborate work, a long poem, play, or novel, it would obviously be a life study. Our ideal critic, however, has an infinity of time, and we might take advantage of his patience to note at random some of the things he would do with a poem, without attempting to assign any temporal or hierarchical priorities. He would tell what the poem is about, that is, translate its paraphrasable content as far as possible (considering the economy inherent in the work of art, this in itself should bulk much larger than the work). He would relate it to its sources and analogues in earlier literature, place it fully in a tradition, and compare it at length with contemporary and earlier works both within and outside of the tradition. He would analyze it exhaustively in terms of any available biographical information about its author: his mind, life, and personality; his family, amatory, and marital relations;

his occupation, his childhood, his social relations, his physical appearance and habits. He would find its folk sources and analogues, and investigate the author's dependence on his native folk tradition, the poem's surface texture of folk speech and characteristics, and its deeper polarization in the patterns of timeless primitive ritual. He would interpret it psychologically as an expression of the author's deepest wishes and fears, in terms of complexes, repressions, sublimations, and compensations, as an expression of the archetypal patterns of collective experience, as an expression of behavioral, neurological, and endocrinological phenomena, and as an expression of the socially conditioned patterns of the author's personality and character structure; he would relate it to comparable manifestations in primitives, psychotics, children, and even animals; he would explore its organization in terms of clusters of imagery related in unconscious associations, in terms of structure functioning as psychological ritual, and in terms of the Gestalt configurations of its totality and their relation to other configurations.

He would interpret the poem socially as a complex and interacting reflection of the poet's social class, status, and occupation; analyze it in terms of the productive relations of his time and nation and their related climate of ideas, and the climate of ideas transcending those productive relations and going backward or forward to others; and he would discuss the social and political attitudes the poem advocates, states, or implies. He would turn all the vast resources of literary scholarship on it, or utilize all that had already been done, and follow the conclusions through with a quite unscholarly courage and imagination. He would explore at the greatest length possible its diction and the relevant ambiguous possibilities of meaning and relations in the significant words; its images and symbols and all their relevant suggestions; its formal pattern or patterns and their function and effects; its formal or informal sound-devices, rhythmic structure, and other musical effects; and its larger patterns of movement and organization; as well as the interrelationships of all the foregoing. He would study all the things outside the poem to which it makes reference and interpret it in their light. He would explore and categorize the key attitude that arises out of the interrelationship of the poem's content and form, note the implications of that category, and discuss the poem comparatively with contemporary and earlier literary expressions of the same category in different terms. Our ideal critic would investigate the whole problem of what the poem communicates, how, and to whom, using every available source of information to find out what it was meant to communicate; and then every technique, from introspection to the most objective laboratory testing, to find out what it actually does communicate, to differing individuals and groups at different times and under different circumstances. He would investigate the whole problem of symbolic action in the poem, what it does sym-

bolically for the poet, what it does symbolically for the reader, what the
relationship is between these two actions, and how it functions within
the larger symbolic structure of the total development of the author's
writing, or even larger symbolic movements, like a literary age. He
would discuss a vast number of other problems involved in the poem,
far too many to be even listed, from ultimate philosophic and ethical
questions like the beliefs and ideas reflected by the poem and the values
it affirms, and their relation to beliefs and values (or their absence) in
the reader and the cultural context; to such minutiæ as the poem's title
and any unusual features of typography, spelling, or punctuation. He
would place the poem in the development of the author's writing from
every angle (for which purpose, naturally, he would be familiar with
everything else the author wrote), confront the problem of the circumstances under which it arose, and discuss the unique features of its style
and its unique reflections of a mind and personality. Finally, on the basis
of all this analysis, our ideal critic would subjectively evaluate the poem
and its parts æsthetically in relation to aim, scope and validity of aim,
and degree of accomplishment, place its value in terms of comparable
works by the same poet and others, estimate its present and future significance and popularity, assign praise or blame, and, if he cared to, advise
the reader or writer or both about it. If he were so inclined, he could go
on and discuss his data and opinions in relation to the data and opinions
of other critics, ideal or not. He would then wipe his brow, take a deep
breath, and tackle another poem.

II. The Actual Critic

OUR ideal critic is of course nonsense, although perhaps useful nonsense
as a Platonic archetype. Let us demolish him and return to the real
world and the practical human possibilities of the individual. A substantial and quite impressive amount of integration is possible in the work
of one rounded man using a number of methods and disciplines. At one
time or another Kenneth Burke has done almost everything in the reper-
toire of modern criticism, and generally a number of things in conjunction. This has been only less true of Richards, Empson, and Blackmur;
they have not synthesized quite so much, and they have tended, particularly Blackmur, to do only one thing at a time, whichever the work under
discussion seemed particularly to call for. These are our best critics, and
their individual and shifting integrations tend to be enormously successful. Their formula for avoiding the endless labors of theoretical total
integration is: pursuing none of their techniques to the end of the line,
but merely far enough to suggest the further possibilities; and stressing
at any given time only those approaches that seem most fruitful for the
specific work under discussion, slighting or ignoring others temporarily

402   THE ARMED VISION

less fruitful, which would then have their place in dealing with a different type of work. Even within these limitations our best critics never seem to have enough time or space to go as far as they would like, and the demand on their learning is formidable. In the future we can expect that the burden of having a working command of every field of man's knowledge applicable to literary criticism will grow increasingly difficult to bear, and eventually simply become impossible.[1] With the tremendous growth of the social sciences in particular, sooner or later knowing enough of any one of them to turn it fruitfully on literature will demand a life study, leaving no time for anything else except some acquaintance with the corpus of literature itself. The Baconian critic, taking all knowledge for his province, is our most impressive figure, but the days of the Baconian critic in an age of more and more complete specialization seem inevitably numbered.

We must, then, consider the specialist critic, the man using one highly developed method. The ones we have had are individually less impressive than the Baconians, and we tend to feel that their very specialization makes them lopsided, inevitably distorters of literature. For the most part, they are either extremely limited figures able to do only one thing well, like Edmund Wilson's paraphrases or Van Wyck Brooks's biographies; or else they are specialists in some extra-literary field: Miss Bodkin's psychoanalysis, Caudwell's Marxism, or Miss Rourke's folk material. These critics with a single developed method are most fruitful either when specializing in literature that their method is best equipped to handle, as the Cambridge school does in Greek literature, so close to its ritual origins; or when specializing in those aspects of any work of literature which their points of view can best elucidate, as psychoanalytic and Marxist critics do (or should do).

Both these types of critical specialization need something else to make them fruitful. That something must be some form of plural, co-operative, or collective criticism—Eliot's hope, expressed as far back as "Experiment in Criticism" in the *Bookman*, November 1929, for "the collaboration of critics of various special training, and perhaps the pooling and sorting of their contributions by men who will be neither specialists nor amateurs." This collaborative criticism we might call the Symposium, a word that, whatever heavy-handed use it has had in the past, still carries some pleasant associations from its root meaning, a convivial drinking-party. We have had a number of published examples of the critical symposium, some of them fairly successful, some less so. They include: scholarly and reference works done by specialists, like *A Companion to*

[1] Thomas Young, an English physician, optical physicist, physiologist, Egyptologist, etc., who died in 1829, is supposed to have been the last man who knew everything scientific there was to know. No one since has come forward to dispute the honor.

Shakespeare Studies; symposia on special topics, like *Humanism in America* and its answer, *The Critique of Humanism, Books That Changed Our Minds,* and *The Mind in Chains;* symposia on a country or a period, like *American Writers on American Literature, After the Genteel Tradition,* and *The Great Tudors;* symposia on a writer, sometimes memorial, like *A Garland for John Donne, Herbert Read: an introduction to his work,* and *Scattering Branches: Tributes to the Memory of W. B. Yeats;* or special issues of one of the literary magazines devoted to a writer, like the *Hound & Horn* James number, the *Southern Review* Yeats number, the *Kenyon Review* Hopkins numbers, the *Quarterly Review of Literature* Valéry number, and the *Harvard Wake* Cummings number; or even periodical symposia devoted to a single work, like the *transition* series on *Finnegans Wake,* published as *Our Exagmination etc.,* or a topic, like the *Chimera* Myth and Detective Fiction numbers, or problems of varying scope, like the several issues of *Focus.* In addition, we have had a number of false symposia or anthologies compiled after the fact, assemblages of work written at different times for different purposes, like *The Question of Henry James, The Kafka Problem,* the Critics Group *Ibsen,* and others.

The chief fault with all of these, particularly the false symposia, is that they are not specialized enough: the choice of critics tends to be haphazard and overlapping, with many methods and points of view not represented at all. In some cases the fault lies in attempting to cover too much ground, so that the contributors never meet on the same subject at all, losing the chief value of the symposium, which is not in the differences of subject-matter, but in the differences of approach to the same subject-matter. A wholly successful critical symposium would have to consist in the planned and organized co-operation of specialists, with the lines of their specialties rigidly drawn on the basis of method rather than subject. (Even the *Hound & Horn* Henry James issue, one of the best of the symposia so far, assigns most of its contributors a reserve safe from poaching, "The Early Novels," "The Critical Prefaces," and so on, and in only a few cases is the specialization purely one of method, like Francis Fergusson's study of "Drama in *The Golden Bowl.*") At the same time such a symposium would of necessity encourage an increasing division of labor, men more and more clearly demarcating just what they are doing in criticism, and doing that one thing and nothing else. It would thus tend to make modern critics even more partial, limited, specialized, and fragmentary, but they would gain in depth and assurance by way of compensation, and the whole critical job would have the virtues of scope and completeness that the modern critic can rarely get except at the cost of superficiality.

What possibilities are there in practice for such a symposium criticism? First, of course, there are the literary quarterlies, in their special numbers on a man or a topic. Even granting that the planning and organization were ideal, their handicap is that they are rarely in complete control: they cannot get any critic or type of critic they want for any project and perforce have to make do with what they can get; they lack the power to impose rigid limits of subject or method on professional critics, who tend to spread out automatically, or the money to make it worth the critic's while to remain within imposed limits; their information as to just who is capable of doing what is always haphazard; they are restricted to the amount of detailed critical study their readers will put up with; and frequently they are forced to build a symposium around work already written for other purposes and fill in the cracks as best they can, sometimes in the office. A new magazine, calling itself the *Critic* or the *Symposium*, devoted to a detailed collective study of a man or a book or a poem in each issue, acquiring and training a body of specialist critics capable of doing the things it wanted done, and gaining the prestige to get independent critics to bend their work to its purposes and readers to like it, could solve some of these problems; others would still remain.[2]

Next there are the universities, which have the money and prestige for such a project and are accustomed to procedures of specialization almost identical, in scholarship of all sorts. Whether they would be likely to indulge it in so dubious an activity as criticism, either in the form of a magazine, a series of books, or even the organization of their own literature studies in such a fashion is another thing. One of the most encouraging signs is the recent publication by the press of Princeton University of several series of papers on literature and the humanities, including *The Intent of the Artist*, *The Intent of the Critic*, and *The Language of Poetry*, each of them a small excellent symposium by four or five specialized authorities. Another is the sponsorship, by the English Institute, of precisely such a symposium or experiment in co-operative criticism as is here described. A seminar was held at Columbia University during a week in September 1941, under the direction of Norman Holmes Pearson of Yale. Four critics spoke for an hour each on the same poem, each on a different day. The critics chosen were Horace Gregory, Lionel Trilling, Cleanth Brooks, and Frederick Pottle (a fifth critic invited, Morton Dauwen Zabel, was not able to be present). The poem chosen was Wordsworth's "Ode on Intimations of Immortality." The audience numbered almost a hundred. I was not present at the affair, but from Donald Stauffer's account of it in "Cooperative Criticism: A Letter from the Critical Front" in the *Kenyon Review*, Winter 1942, I would guess that its relative failure lay chiefly in its narrowness of range. An

---

[2] The closest thing to this ideal in existence is probably the English critical magazine *Scrutiny*, which certainly has both the body of co-operating talents and the requisite prestige. Its scope is too limited ever to give the complete picture, however, and its celebrated "scrutinies," or co-operative surveys, have tended to be on cultural or educational problems rather than on writers or literary works.

even more encouraging long-range sign is the existence of a few teachers in universities throughout the country (among them Professor Leonard Brown of Syracuse University, under whom I studied) whose advanced literature classes study by the symposium method, with each student tackling the work over a long period from a different viewpoint and method, and the whole organized and assembled by the teacher. Besides the quarterlies and the universities, no likely area for the critical symposium to flourish in comes to mind. A good many oral critical symposia go on over the radio and in various forums, but the nature of impromptu speaking and the demands of a mass audience tend to confine them to inevitable triviality (as a reading of the published programs of one of the best of them, Invitation to Learning, makes unhappily clear).

One of the greatest hopes for collective criticism by symposium is that it would be equipped to unravel works so complex that they have not yet been successfully dealt with by any individual critic. *Moby Dick* is the obvious example here. When Matthiessen remarked in the introduction to *American Renaissance:* "I have not yet seen in print an adequately detailed scrutiny . . . of *Moby Dick*," he was understating badly; we have not yet had any reading that made much sense beyond the most superficial and one-dimensional. To perhaps a lesser extent this is true of every great work of literature; all readings are inadequate, and we only satisfy ourselves by an act of impromptu collective criticism, by suspending several in our mind at once. Even where we are satisfied with our reading of the work, the addition of other meanings gives it greater depth and richness. When the old-fashioned Shakespeare professor tells his class that Hamlet's line to Polonius about Ophelia: "Let her not walke i' th' Sunne," does not carry any weight unless it is seen as a complicated pun, with at least the four suggestions of the sun as a source of madness, corruption and decay, the King and his court, and the son (Hamlet), added to its explicit meaning of pregnancy by spontaneous generation, he is not suddenly enlisted in the cause of Empsonian ambiguity, but merely recognizing that no one meaning, however reasonable, quite explains the line's sense of significance and ominousness.

In so far as great works, or key spots in any work, or the bulk of serious modern literature as a special product of the divided modern mind, all have many levels of meaning, we must have a many-leveled criticism to deal with them. Essentially this means that where the work is worth the trouble, the critic going into it with any vocabulary will emerge with a meaning paraphrasable in that vocabulary. Increasingly this has been generally recognized in recent times. Charles Baudouin, in *Psychoanalysis and Æsthetics*, speaks of it as "multiple parallelism" and compares it with the polyglot Bible. Richards calls it "multiple definition" or "multiple interpretation," and it is actually (as noted above in the chapter on Richards) the subject of all his work. Burke calls it "multiple causation" and speaks of "a set of widening circles, ranging from the uniquely particularized, through placement in terms of broad cultural developments, to absolute concepts of relationship or ground." Erich Fromm is working from a similar concept in things like his palimpsest reading of Kafka in psychoanalytic, social, and religious terms, as is Harry Slochower in his psychoanalytic, social and philosophic readings of Mann and other writers. William Troy is after the same thing in his mythic, psychoanalytic, and social readings of a number of authors, as well as in his campaign to revive the medieval "four levels of meaning" or something analogous; and on a smaller scale Jack Lindsay operates similarly in his Marxist, psychoanalytic, and anthropological readings. F. C. Prescott's "multiple significance," Herbert Muller's "multiple meaning and multivalence," Donald A. Stauffer's "multiplex meanings," and Raymond Preston's "co-operative reading" all approximate it; Empson's "ambiguity" points at it, and Philip Wheelwright's "plurisignation" and Austin Warren's "concurrent multivalence" come even closer. All criticism of *Finnegans Wake* has been automatically pluralistic from the first.

Whatever this type of criticism is called, plural or multiple or many-leveled, it is clearly becoming increasingly essential. We might if we wish call it "continuum criticism" and leave a place for all possible levels of meaning on a continuum from the most completely individual, subjective, and personal (the unconscious) to the most completely social, objective, and impersonal (the historical). The addition of Jung's "racial unconscious" would bring the two ends of our continuum together in a circle. Thus we could take, say, Eliot's symbol of the Waste Land in the poem of that name, a symbol of great depth and complexity, and read it at any level we cared to insert a vocabulary: at the most intimate level, to the Freudian, it would be castration and impotence; at a more conscious level, to a post-Freudian psychology, perhaps the fear of artistic sterility; on the daily-life level, in the biographical terms of Van Wyck Brooks, the symbol of Eliot's preconversion state; on a more social level, to a critic like Parrington, the empty life of the artist or the frustration of the upper class; to Eliot himself, the irreligion of the times; in broadly historical terms, to the Marxist, the decay of capitalism; in Jungian terms, the archetypal ritual of rebirth. Similarly, the symbol of Mynheer Peeperkorn in Mann's *Magic Mountain* would range from the Œdipal father, through the forceful rival personality, to the power of agrarian capital or the Corn God; Hitler's concept of German unity in *Mein Kampf* would range from the Œdipal mother, through "in unity there is strength," to such events in history as the absorption of Austria and Czechoslovakia, and so forth. In the symbol or work of depth there are as many meanings as critics can find levels or vocabularies with which to explore; name it, in other words, and you can **have it.**

There is another advantage to this sort of multiple-level or plural-meaning criticism. Thinking about the fact that Italian criticism contemporary with it completely ignored the Commedia dell' Arte, and that Elizabethan criticism for a long time completely ignored Shakespeare and the Elizabethan drama, the critic sometimes gets the nightmare idea that we in our time may similarly be ignoring works and whole art forms that will ultimately prove to be of greater significance than anything with which we deal. By sampling the movies, the detective story, the radio, and the comic book, the likely fields for this great ignored art form in our time, the critic generally manages to assuage his fears. Nevertheless, the nightmare itself is significant. What is actually disturbing his peace of mind is the tremendous responsibility the individual critic carries. He is, alone and on the authority of his own knowledge, taste, and intelligence, the sole guardian of art and its magic portals. A collective or symposium criticism would have the virtue not only of establishing a multiplicity of readings and meanings, but also of giving them all a hearing, and in the last analysis of establishing some true and valid ones. It would be not only plural, but in a very real sense dialectic or dramatistic. From the interplay of many minds, even many errors, truth arises, as our wise men have known since Plato's dialogues. This synthesis of critical method is not simple multiplicity or plurality or anarchy, but a genuine dialectic contest or *agon*. From it, too, truth will arise. We may get it within the individual critic, in an integrated method, or outside the individual critic, in the group symposium, but in some form or other we must get it. And "we" here stands for the whole world, for where "truth" is at issue, we are all of necessity critics.

A SELECTED BIBLIOGRAPHY
OF MODERN CRITICISM SINCE 1912

ABBOTT, CHARLES D. *Poets at Work*. New York, 1948.
AIKEN, CONRAD. *Skepticisms*. New York, 1919.
ALLEN, WALTER. "A Note on Franz Kafka," in *Focus One*. London, 1945.
"A Note on André Malraux," in *Focus Two*. London, 1946.
"Graham Greene," in *Writers of To-day*. London, 1946.
"Henry Green," in *Little Reviews Anthology 1946*. London, 1946.
ARMSTRONG, EDWARD A. *Shakespeare's Imagination*. London, 1946.
ARVIN, NEWTON. *Hawthorne*. Boston, 1929.
Whitman. New York, 1938.
AUDEN, W. H. "John Skelton," in *The Great Tudors*. London, 1935.
"Psychology and Art To-day," in *The Arts To-day*. London, 1935.
Introduction to *The Oxford Book of Light Verse*. Oxford, 1938.
"The Sea and the Mirror," in *The Collected Poetry of W. H. Auden*.
New York, 1945.
"The People *v.* The Late Mr. William Butler Yeats," in *Partisan Reader*. New York, 1946.
BAUDOUIN, CHARLES. *Psychoanalysis and Æsthetics*. New York, 1924.
Contemporary Studies. New York, 1925.
BENTLEY, ERIC. *A Century of Hero-Worship*. New York, 1944.
The Playwright as Thinker. New York, 1946.
Bernard Shaw. Norfolk (Conn.), 1947.
BLACKMUR, R. P. *The Double Agent*. New York, 1935.
The Expense of Greatness. New York, 1940.
"Humanism and Symbolic Imagination," in the *Southern Review,* Autumn 1941.
"Language as Gesture," in *Accent*, Summer 1943.
"Notes on Four Categories in Criticism," in the *Sewanee Review,* Autumn 1946.
BODKIN, MAUD. *Archetypal Patterns in Poetry*. Oxford, 1934.
The Quest for Salvation in an Ancient and a Modern Play. Oxford, 1941.
"The Philosophic Novel," in the *Wind and the Rain*, Autumn 1942.
BOURNE, RANDOLPH. *Untimely Papers*. New York, 1919.
The History of a Literary Radical. New York, 1920.
BOWRA, C. M. *Greek Lyric Poetry*. Oxford, 1936.
The Heritage of Symbolism. London, 1943.

Sophoclean Tragedy. Oxford, 1944.

From Vergil to Milton. New York, 1946.

BROOKS, CLEANTH. *Modern Poetry and the Tradition.* Chapel Hill, 1939.

    The Well Wrought Urn. New York, 1947.

BROOKS, VAN WYCK. *John Addington Symonds.* New York, 1914.

    The World of H. G. Wells. New York, 1915.

    The Ordeal of Mark Twain. New York, 1920.

    The Pilgrimage of Henry James. New York, 1925.

    Three Essays on America. New York, 1934.

BUCHANAN, SCOTT. *Poetry and Mathematics.* New York, 1929.

BURGUM, EDWIN BERRY. *The Novel and the World's Dilemma.* New York, 1947.

BURKE, KENNETH. *Counter-Statement.* New York, 1931.

    Permanence and Change. New York, 1935.

    Attitudes toward History. 2 vol. New York, 1937.

    The Philosophy of Literary Form. Baton Rouge, 1941.

    A Grammar of Motives. New York, 1945.

CALVERTON, V. F. *The New Ground of Criticism.* Seattle, 1930.

    The Liberation of American Literature. New York, 1932.

CAMPBELL, JOSEPH, and HENRY MORTON ROBINSON. *A Skeleton Key to Finnegans Wake.* New York, 1944.

CARPENTER, RHYS. *Folk Tale, Fiction and Saga in the Homeric Epics.* Los Angeles, 1946.

CAUDWELL, CHRISTOPHER. *Illusion and Reality.* London, 1937.

    Studies in a Dying Culture. London, 1938.

    The Crisis in Physics. London, 1939.

CORNFORD, F. M. *From Religion to Philosophy.* London, 1912.

    The Origin of Attic Comedy. London, 1914.

COWLEY, MALCOLM. *Exile's Return.* New York, 1934.

    Introduction to *The Portable Hemingway.* New York, 1944.

    Introduction to *The Portable Faulkner.* New York, 1946.

DAICHES, DAVID. *Literature and Society.* London, 1938.

    The Novel and the Modern World. Chicago, 1939.

    Poetry and the Modern World. Chicago, 1940.

    Virginia Woolf. Norfolk (Conn.), 1942.

    Robert Louis Stevenson. Norfolk (Conn.), 1947.

DAMON, S. FOSTER. *William Blake.* Boston, 1924.

DAVIS, ROBERT GORHAM. "Art and Anxiety," in *Partisan Review*, Summer 1945.

DAY LEWIS, C. *A Hope for Poetry.* Third edition, revised. Oxford, 1936.

    "Revolution in Writing," in *A Time to Dance.* New York, 1936.

    The Poetic Image. London, 1947.

    (ed.). *The Mind in Chains.* London, 1937.

DUPEE, F. W. (ed.). *The Question of Henry James.* New York, 1945.

ELIOT, T. S. *Selected Essays.* New York, 1932.

    John Dryden. New York, 1932.

    The Use of Poetry and the Use of Criticism. London, 1933.

After Strange Gods. London, 1934.

Essays Ancient and Modern. New York, 1936.

ELLISON, RALPH. "Richard Wright's Blues," in the *Antioch Review*, Summer 1945.

EMPSON, WILLIAM. *Seven Types of Ambiguity.* London, 1930.

Some Versions of Pastoral. London, 1935.

and GEORGE GARRETT. *Shakespeare Survey.* London, n.d.

"Basic English and Wordsworth," in the *Kenyon Review*, Autumn 1940.

"Thy Darling in an Urn," in the *Sewanee Review*, Autumn 1947.

FARRELL, JAMES T. *A Note on Literary Criticism.* New York, 1936.

The League of Frightened Philistines. New York, 1945.

Literature and Morality. New York, 1947.

FARRINGTON, BENJAMIN. *Science and Politics in the Ancient World.* New York, 1940.

Greek Science. New York, 1944.

FERGUSSON, FRANCIS. "T. S. Eliot," in *The American Caravan.* New York, 1927.

"Eugene O'Neill," in *Hound & Horn*, January 1930.

"D. H. Lawrence's Sensibility," in *Hound & Horn*, April–June 1933.

"James' Idea of Dramatic Form," in the *Kenyon Review*, Autumn 1943.

"Action as Passion," in the *Kenyon Review*, Spring 1947.

FERNANDEZ, RAMON. *Messages.* New York, 1927.

FLORES, ANGEL (ed.). *Henrik Ibsen.* New York, 1937.

Literature and Marxism. New York, 1938.

The Kafka Problem. New York, 1946.

FOWLIE, WALLACE. *Clowns and Angels.* New York, 1943.

Rimbaud. New York, 1946.

Jacob's Night. New York, 1947.

FOX, RALPH. *The Novel and the People.* New York, 1937.

Ralph Fox: A Writer in Arms. New York, 1937.

FRANK, WALDO. *Salvos.* New York, 1924.

In the American Jungle. New York, 1936.

FREEMAN, JOSEPH, JOSHUA KUNITZ, and LOUIS LOZOWICK. *Voices of October.* New York, 1930.

FREUD, SIGMUND. *Leonardo da Vinci.* New York, 1910.

Delusion and Dream. New York, 1917.

"Dostoevski and Parricide," in *Partisan Review*, Fall 1945.

GIDE, ANDRÉ. *Dostoevsky.* New York, 1926.

Imaginary Interviews. New York, 1944.

GILBERT, STUART. *James Joyce's* Ulysses. New York, 1931.

GORKY, MAXIM. *On Guard for the Soviet Union.* New York, 1933.

Culture and the People. New York, 1939.

Reminiscences. New York, 1946.

and others. *Problems of Soviet Literature.* New York, n.d.

GOURMONT, REMY DE. *Decadence.* New York. 1921.

GRANVILLE-BARKER, HARLEY, and G. B. HARRISON. *A Companion to Shake-speare Studies*. Cambridge, 1934.

GREGORY, HORACE. *Pilgrim of the Apocalypse*. New York, 1933.
    The Shield of Achilles. New York, 1944.

GRIB, V. *Balzac*. New York, 1937.

HARRISON, JANE ELLEN. *Themis*. Cambridge, 1912.
    Ancient Art and Ritual. New York, 1913.

HENDERSON, PHILIP. *Literature and a Changing Civilisation*. London, 1935.
    The Novel Today. London, 1936.

HICKS, GRANVILLE. *The Great Tradition*. New York, 1935.
    John Reed. New York, 1936.
    Figures of Transition. New York, 1939.

HOFFMAN, FREDERICK T. *Freudianism and the Literary Mind*. Baton Rouge, 1945.

HORTON, PHILIP. *Hart Crane*. New York, 1937.

HOTSON, J. LESLIE. *The Death of Christopher Marlowe*. London, 1925.
    Shakespeare versus Shallow. London, 1931.

HULME, T. E. *Speculations*. London, 1924.
    Notes on Language and Style. Seattle, 1929.

JACKSON, T. A. *Charles Dickens*. New York, 1938.

JAMES, HENRY. *Notes on Novelists*. New York, 1914.
    Notes and Reviews. Cambridge (Mass.), 1921.
    The Art of the Novel. New York, 1934.

JARRELL, RANDALL. "Changes of Attitude and Rhetoric in Auden's Poetry," in the *Southern Review*, Autumn 1941.

JONES, ERNEST. *Essays in Applied Psychoanalysis*. London, 1923.

JOSEPHSON, MATTHEW. *Portrait of the Artist as American*. New York, 1930.
    Stendhal. New York, 1946.

KASHKEEN, J. "Ernest Hemingway," in *International Literature*, No. 5, 1935.

KENYON CRITICS, THE. *Gerard Manley Hopkins*. Norfolk (Conn.), 1945.

KLINGENDER, F. D. *Marxism and Modern Art*. New York, 1945.

KNIGHT, G. WILSON. *The Wheel of Fire*. Oxford, 1930.
    The Imperial Theme. Oxford, 1931.
    The Shakespearian Tempest. Oxford, 1932.
    The Burning Oracle. Oxford, 1939.
    The Starlit Dome. Oxford, 1941.

KNIGHTS, L. C. *Drama and Society in the Age of Jonson*. London, 1937.
    Explorations. London, 1946.

KRUTCH, JOSEPH WOOD. *Edgar Allan Poe*. New York, 1926.
    Samuel Johnson. New York, 1944.

KUBIE, LAWRENCE S. "The Literature of Horror," in the *Saturday Review of Literature*, October 20 and November 24, 1934.

LAFORGUE, RENÉ. *The Defeat of Baudelaire*. London, 1932.

LANGER, SUSANNE K. *Philosophy in a New Key*. Cambridge (Mass.), 1942.

LAWRENCE, D. H. *Studies in Classic American Literature*. New York, 1924.
    Phœnix. New York, 1936.

LEAVIS, F. R. *New Bearings in English Poetry*. London, 1932.
    For Continuity. Cambridge, 1933.

    Revaluation. London, 1936.

    (ed.). *Toward Standards of Criticism*. London, 1933.

    (ed.). *Determinations*. London, 1934.

LEAVIS, Q. D. *Fiction and the Reading Public*. London, 1939.

LEHMANN, JOHN. *New Writing in England*. New York, 1939.

LENIN, V. I. "Party Organization and Party Literature," in *Dialectics 5*, 1938.

    "Five Essays on Leo Tolstoy," in *Dialectics 6*, 1938.

LEVIN, HARRY. *James Joyce*. Norfolk (Conn.), 1941.

    "Toward Stendhal," in *Pharos*, Winter 1945.

LEWIS, WYNDHAM. *The Lion and the Fox*. London, n.d.

    Time and Western Man. New York, 1928.

    The Diabolical Principle and the Dithyrambic Spectator. London, 1931.

    Men without Art. London, 1934.

LIFSCHITZ, MIKHAIL. *The Philosophy of Art of Karl Marx*. New York, 1938.

LINDSAY, JACK. *John Bunyan: Maker of Myths*. London, 1937.

    The Anatomy of Spirit. London, 1937.

LOVEJOY, ARTHUR O. *The Revolt against Dualism*. New York, 1930.

    The Great Chain of Being. Cambridge (Mass.), 1936.

LOWES, JOHN LIVINGSTON. *Convention and Revolt in Poetry*. Boston, 1919.

    The Road to Xanadu. Boston, 1927.

    Of Reading Books. Boston, 1929.

    Geoffrey Chaucer. Boston, 1934.

    Essays in Appreciation. Boston, 1936.

MACNEICE, LOUIS. *Modern Poetry*. Oxford, 1938.

    The Poetry of W. B. Yeats. Oxford, 1941.

MACY, JOHN. *The Spirit of American Literature*. New York, 1913.

    The Critical Game. New York, 1922.

MANN, THOMAS. *Past Masters*. New York, 1933.

    Essays of Three Decades. New York, 1947.

MARX, KARL, and FREDERICK ENGELS. *Literature and Art*. New York, 1947.

MATTHIESSEN, F. O. *Sarah Orne Jewett*. Boston, 1929.

    Translation: An Elizabethan Art. Cambridge (Mass.), 1931.

    The Achievement of T. S. Eliot. New York, 1935.

    American Renaissance. New York, 1941.

    Henry James: The Major Phase. New York, 1944.

MEHRING, FRANZ. *The Lessing Legend*. New York, 1938.

MIRSKY, D. S. *A History of Russian Literature*. New York, 1927.

    The Intelligentsia of Great Britain. New York, 1935.

MORTON, A. L. *Language of Men*. London, 1945.

MULLER, HERBERT J. *Modern Fiction*. New York, 1937.

    Science and Criticism. New Haven, 1943.

    Thomas Wolfe. Norfolk (Conn.), 1947.

MUMFORD, LEWIS. *The Golden Day*. New York, 1926.

    Herman Melville. New York, 1929.

MURRAY, GILBERT. "Excursus on the Ritual Forms Preserved in Greek Tragedy," in *Themis*. Cambridge, 1912.

    Euripides and His Age. New York, 1913.

The Rise of the Greek Epic. Third edition, revised. London, 1924.

The Classical Tradition in Poetry. Oxford, 1927.

Greek Studies. Oxford, 1946.

MURRY, JOHN MIDDLETON. *Fyodor Dostoevsky*. New York, 1916.

Aspects of Literature. New York, 1920.

The Problem of Style. Oxford, 1922.

Keats and Shakespeare. Oxford, 1925.

Shakespeare. New York, 1936.

NABOKOV, VLADIMIR. *Nikolai Gogol*. Norfolk (Conn.), 1944.

OGDEN, C. K., and I. A. RICHARDS. *The Meaning of Meaning*. New York, 1923.

OGDEN, C. K., I. A. RICHARDS, and JAMES WOOD. *The Foundations of Æsthetics*. New York, 1925.

OLSON, CHARLES. *Call Me Ishmael*. New York, 1947.

ORWELL, GEORGE. *Inside the Whale*. London, 1940.

Dickens, Dali, & Others. New York, 1946.

"Politics and the English Language," in *Modern British Writing*. New York, 1947.

PARKES, HENRY BAMFORD. *The Pragmatic Test*. San Francisco, 1941.

PARRINGTON, VERNON L. *Main Currents in American Thought*. New York, 1930.

PHARE, ELSIE ELIZABETH. *The Poetry of Gerard Manley Hopkins*. Cambridge, 1933.

PLEKHANOV, GEORGE V. *Art and Society*. New York, 1936.

"Historical Materialism and the Arts," in *Dialectics* 3 and 4, 1937.

POUND, EZRA. *The Spirit of Romance*. New York, n.d.

A B C of Reading. London, 1934.

Make It New. New Haven, 1935.

Polite Essays. Norfolk (Conn.), n.d.

Culture. Norfolk (Conn.), 1938.

PRAZ, MARIO. *The Romantic Agony*. Oxford, 1933.

PRESCOTT, F. C. *Poetry and Dreams*. Boston, 1919.

The Poetic Mind. New York, 1922.

RAGLAN, LORD. *Jocasta's Crime*. New York, n.d.

The Hero. New York, 1937.

Death and Rebirth. London, 1946.

RAJAN, B. (ed.). *T. S. Eliot: a Study of His Writings by Several Hands*. London, 1947.

RANK, OTTO. *The Myth of the Birth of the Hero*. New York, 1914.

Art and the Artist. New York, 1932.

RANSOM, JOHN CROWE. *God without Thunder*. New York, 1930.

The World's Body. New York, 1938.

The New Criticism. Norfolk (Conn.), 1941.

READ, HERBERT. *Reason and Romanticism*. London, 1926.

Wordsworth. New York, 1931.

Collected Essays in Literary Criticism. London, 1938.

Poetry and Anarchism. New York, 1939.

A Coat of Many Colors. London, 1945.

RICHARDS, I. A. *Principles of Literary Criticism.* New York, 1924.

Science and Poetry. London, 1926.

Practical Criticism. New York, 1929.

Mencius on the Mind. New York, 1932.

Coleridge on Imagination. New York, 1935.

RIDING, LAURA, and ROBERT GRAVES. *A Survey of Modernist Poetry.* London, 1927.

ROSENFELD, PAUL. *Port of New York.* New York, 1924.

Men Seen. New York, 1925.

ROSENZWEIG, SAUL. "The Ghost of Henry James," in *Partisan Review,* Fall 1944.

ROURKE, CONSTANCE. *Trumpets of Jubilee.* New York, 1927.

Troupers of the Gold Coast. New York, 1928.

American Humor. New York, 1931.

Charles Sheeler. New York, 1938.

The Roots of American Culture. New York, 1942.

RYLANDS, GEORGE H. W. *Words and Poetry.* New York, 1928.

SACHS, WULF. *Psychoanalysis; Its Meaning and Practical Applications.* London, 1934.

SCARFE, FRANCIS. *Auden and After.* London, 1942.

SCHLAUCH, MARGARET. *Chaucer's Constance and Accused Queens.* New York, 1927.

Romance in Iceland. Princeton, 1934.

"The Language of James Joyce," in *Science and Society,* Fall 1939.

The Gift of Tongues. New York, 1942.

SCHORER, MARK. *William Blake.* New York, 1946.

SCHÜCKING, LEVIN L. *The Sociology of Literary Taste.* London, 1944.

SIMON, HENRY W. *The Reading of Shakespeare in American Schools and Colleges.* New York, 1932.

SLOCHOWER, HARRY. *Three Ways of Modern Man.* New York, 1937.

Thomas Mann's Joseph Story. New York, 1938.

No Voice is Wholly Lost . . . New York, 1945.

SMIRNOV, A. A. *Shakespeare.* New York, 1936.

SMITH, BERNARD. *Forces in American Criticism.* New York, 1939.

SONNENSCHEIN, E. A. *What is Rhythm?* Oxford, 1925.

SPENCER, THEODORE. *Death and Elizabethan Tragedy.* Cambridge (Mass.), 1936.

Shakespeare and the Nature of Man. New York, 1942.

(ed.). *A Garland for John Donne.* Cambridge (Mass.), 1931.

SPENDER, STEPHEN. *The Destructive Element.* London, 1935.

Poetry since 1939. London, 1946.

SPURGEON, CAROLINE. *Mysticism in English Literature.* Cambridge, 1913.

Keats' Shakespeare. Oxford, 1928.

Shakespeare's Imagery. Cambridge, 1935.

STAUFFER, DONALD A. *The Nature of Poetry.* New York, 1946.

(ed.). *The Intent of the Critic.* Princeton, 1941.

STRACHEY, JOHN. *The Coming Struggle for Power*. New York, 1933.
    Literature and Dialectical Materialism. New York, 1934.
TATE, ALLEN. *Reactionary Essays on Poetry and Ideas*. New York, 1936.
    Reason in Madness. New York, 1941.
    (ed.). *The Language of Poetry*. Princeton, 1942.
THOMSON, GEORGE. *Æschylus and Athens*. London, 1941.
    Marxism and Poetry. New York, 1946.
TINDALL, WILLIAM YORK. *Forces in Modern British Literature*. New York, 1947.
TRILLING, LIONEL. *Matthew Arnold*. New York, 1939.
    "The Legacy of Sigmund Freud: Literary and Æsthetic," in the *Kenyon Review*, Spring 1940.
    E. M. Forster. Norfolk (Conn.), 1943.
    "A Note on Art and Neurosis," in *Partisan Review*, Winter 1945.
TROTSKY, LEON. *Literature and Revolution*. New York, 1925.
    "Novelist and Politician," in the *Atlantic Monthly*, October 1935.
TROY, WILLIAM. "The D. H. Lawrence Myth," in *Partisan Review*, January 1938.
    "Thomas Mann: Myth and Reason," in *Partisan Review*, June and July, 1938.
    "On Rereading Balzac," in the *Kenyon Review*, Summer 1940.
    "Stendhal: In Quest of Henri Beyle," in *Partisan Review*, January–February 1942.
    "Scott Fitzgerald: The Authority of Failure," in *Accent*, Autumn 1945.
VALÉRY, PAUL. *Variety*. New York, 1927.
    Variety: Second Series. New York, 1938.
WARREN, ROBERT PENN. "A Poem of Pure Imagination," in *The Rime of the Ancient Mariner*. New York, 1946.
WERTHAM, FREDERICK. *Dark Legend*. New York, 1941.
    "An Unconscious Determinant in *Native Son*," in the *Journal of Criminal Psychopathology*, July 1944.
WEST, ALICK. *Crisis and Criticism*. London, 1937.
WESTON, JESSIE L. *From Ritual to Romance*. Cambridge, 1920.
WHIPPLE, T. K. *Spokesmen*. New York, 1928.
    Study Out the Land. Berkeley, 1943.
WILSON, EDMUND. *Axel's Castle*. New York, 1931.
    The Triple Thinkers. New York, 1938.
    To the Finland Station. New York, 1940.
    The Boys in the Back Room. San Francisco, 1941.
    The Wound and the Bow. Boston, 1941.
WINTERS, YVOR. *Primitivism and Decadence*. New York, 1937.
    Maule's Curse. Norfolk (Conn.), 1938.
    "The Sixteenth Century Lyric in England," in *Poetry: A Magazine of Verse*, February, March, April 1939.
    The Anatomy of Nonsense. Norfolk (Conn.), 1943.
    Edwin Arlington Robinson. Norfolk (Conn.), 1946.

WITCUTT, W. P. *Blake: A Psychological Study*. London, 1946.
YEATS, W. B. *Essays*. London, 1924.
  The Autobiography of William Butler Yeats. New York, 1938.
  A Vision. New York, 1938.
ZABEL, MORTON DAUWEN (ed.). *Literary Opinion in America*. New York, 1937.
  "The Thinking of the Body: Yeats in the Autobiographies," in the *Southern Review*, Winter 1941.
  "Graham Greene," in the *Nation*, July 3, 1943.
  "Willa Cather," in the *Nation*, June 14, 1947.
  Introduction to *The Portable Conrad*. New York, 1947.

INDEX

i

A NOTE ON THE TYPE
IN WHICH THIS BOOK IS SET

This book is set in Monotype Bell, a copy of the English Monotype face of the same name. The Englishman John Bell (1745–1831) was responsible for the original cutting of this design. The vocations of Bell were many—among a few might be mentioned bookseller, printer, publisher, type-founder and journalist. His types were considerably influenced by the delicacy and beauty of the French copper-plate engravers. Monotype Bell might also be classified as a delicate and refined rendering of Scotch Roman.

Composed, printed, and bound by Kingsport Press, Inc., Kingsport, Tenn.